AFRICAN HISTORICAL DICTIONARIES
Edited by Jon Woronoff

1. *Cameroon*, by Victor T. LeVine and Roger P. Nye. 1974
2. *The Congo (Brazzaville)*, by Virginia Thompson and Richard Adloff. 1974
3. *Swaziland*, by John J. Grotpeter. 1975
4. *The Gambia*, by Harry A. Gailey. 1975
5. *Botswana*, by Richard P. Stevens. 1975
6. *Somalia*, by Margaret F. Castagno. 1975
7. *Dahomey*, by Samuel Decalo. 1975
8. *Burundi*, by Warren Weinstein. 1976
9. *Togo*, by Samuel Decalo. 1976
10. *Lesotho*, by Gordon Haliburton. 1977
11. *Mali*, by Pascal James Imperato. 1977
12. *Sierra Leone*, by Cyril Patrick Foray. 1977
13. *Chad*, by Samuel Decalo. 1977
14. *Upper Volta*, by Daniel Miles McFarland. 1978
15. *Tanzania*, by Laura S. Kurtz. 1978
16. *Guinea*, by Thomas O'Toole. 1978
17. *Sudan*, by John Voll. 1978
18. *Rhodesia/Zimbabwe*, by R. Kent Rasmussen. 1979.
19. *Zambia*, by John J. Grotpeter. 1979.
20. *Niger*, by Samuel Decalo. 1979.

Historical Dictionary
of
ZAMBIA

by

John J. Grotpeter

African Historical Dictionaries, No. 19

The Scarecrow Press, Inc.
Metuchen, N.J. & London
1979

Library of Congress Cataloging in Publication Data

Grotpeter, John J
  Historical dictionary of Zambia.

  (African historical dictionaries ; no. 19)
  Bibliography: p.
  1. Zambia--History--Dictionaries. I. Title.
II. Series.
DT963.5.G7   968.9'4'003   79-342
ISBN 0-8108-1207-X

To the people of Zambia, may this volume be of service.

To my wife Peggy, and my daughters, Jenny and Becky, who have tolerated my absence while writing and have made my non-writing hours so delightful.

EDITOR'S FOREWORD

Not all that long ago, the country known as Zambia was called
Northern Rhodesia. Unlike its neighbor Southern Rhodesia (which
may ultimately be called Zimbabwe), it managed to attain independence peacefully toward the end of the slow wave of emancipation
that worked its way south. Thanks to rather well organized political
parties and trade unions, recognized leaders and a smaller, less
rabid settler community, the new state could be established in 1964.
A year later, it faced a major continuing crisis when Ian Smith
made the Unilateral Declaration of Independence in Southern Rhodesia.

Thus, Zambia became one of the "front line" states looking
out over settler dominated southern Africa, and in some ways it was
on more of a tightrope than the others. Although it has probably
been more hurt economically for upholding African rights, it has
made less noise about its hardship. For, Zambia is not one of the
African socialist or radical regimes whose policies are adapted to
this sort of confrontation. Since Zambia is still on good terms with
the West politically, and there is a considerable degree of free enterprise in its economy and because it hopes for as peaceful a solution as possible to all problems and prefers economic progress over
political activism, it has developed spectacular but exceedingly difficult goals. This insistence on a humanist and gradualist approach
to many matters, although it does not appeal to all, has, however,
won President Kaunda his worldwide reputation and kept Zambia going
relatively smoothly.

We are pleased to be publishing this volume about the same
time as our Rhodesia/Zimbabwe dictionary since the two are largely
companion pieces. Many of the same historical patterns, ethnic
groups and even geographical features are common to both, and in-

deed many Zimbabwe leaders have sought refuge in Zambia. In the past both "Rhodesias" were temporarily united and in the future the relations should also be particularly close unless, by choosing sharply divergent policies on both sides of the border, they become that much more hostile.

Dr. John J. Grotpeter, who also wrote the Swaziland dictionary, is the author of this excellent study on Zambia. He is Director of the Liberal Arts Division of the St. Louis College of Pharmacy where he is also Professor of Political Science. He has published several other books dealing with politics and history in Central and Southern Africa. This Dictionary is extraordinarily comprehensive, covering a very broad range of topics and fields of endeavor: economics, politics, sociology and others. It covers Zambian history all the way from the Broken Hill Man to today's leaders. And in many ways it serves as a "who's who" not only of major and minor figures but also of ethnic and linguistic groups, political parties, trade unions, religious entities, and even state or private corporations, as well as covering places and events. The bibliography is quite broad and doubly useful since it is clearly broken down by subject matter. The dictionary should thus become a major research tool for Zambians and anyone interested in Zambia.

Jon Woronoff
Series Editor

CONTENTS

ACKNOWLEDGMENTS

No work of this nature could have been written without my drawing extensively on the works of countless researchers and scholars whose accumulated years in Zambia would add up to centuries. I cannot overestimate the value of this material, especially by authors such as Mutumba Mainga, Henry Meebelo, Andrew Roberts, Richard Hall, Robert Rotberg, and David Mulford.

At a different level, but equally important to me, I must thank two of my students, Connie Urbanski and Laurie Gaskell, for the diligent application of their skills, primarily typing, to the successful completion of this manuscript. However, any errors of omission or commission which may be found in this work are my own responsibility.

A final word of appreciation is owed to the Dean of the St. Louis College of Pharmacy, Byron A. Barnes, for his encouragement and his willingness to allow occasional use of the College's facilities for completion of this endeavor.

John J. Grotpeter

ABBREVIATIONS AND ACRONYMS

AMU	African Mineworker's Union
ANC	African National Congress
ARC	African Representative Council
BSAC	British South Africa Company
CAP	Central Africa Party
DC	District Commissioner
DO	District Officer
DPP	Democratic People's Party
EDP	Emergency Development Plan
FNDP	First National Development Plan
INDECO	Industrial Development Corporation
LC	Legislative Council
LME	London Metal Exchange
LMS	London Missionary Society
MASA	Mines African Staff Association
MINDECO	Mining Development Corporation
MLSA	Mines Local Staff Association
MUZ	Mineworkers' Union of Zambia
NPP	National Progress Party
NRAC	Northern Rhodesia African Congress
PAFMECA	Pan-African Freedom Movement for East and Central Africa
PAFMECSA	Pan-African Freedom Movement for East, Central, and Southern Africa
PDC	People's Democratic Congress
PMS	Paris Missionary Society
RTUC	Reformed Trade Union Congress
SNA	Secretary of Native Affairs
TUC	Trade Union Congress

UDI	Unilateral Declaration of Independence
UFP	United Federal Party
UMCB	United Missions in the Copperbelt
UMU	United Mineworkers' Union
UNIP	United National Independence Party
UP	United Party
UPP	United Progressive Party
UTUC	United Trade Union Congress
WENELA	Witwatersrand Native Labour Association
ZANC	Zambia African National Congress
ZANDU	Zambia African National Democratic Union
ZCTU	Zambia Congress of Trade Unions
ZEMA	Zambia Expatriate Miners' Association
ZIS	Zambia Information Services
ZIMCO	Zambia Industrial and Mining Corporation
ZMU	Zambia Mineworkers' Union
ZYS	Zambia Youth Service

CHRONOLOGY

30,000 B.C.   Rhodesian man lives in area.

50 B.C.   Iron Age begins in Zambia.

A.D. 650-900   Prime period of the southern Zambian trading civilization, Ingombe Ilede.

1100   Tonga settle in Zambia.

1500-1800   Major migrations into Zambia, primarily from the Congo.

1514   Portuguese first enter Zambia.

1798   Dr. deLacerda, Portuguese Governor of Sena, travels in Northern Rhodesia and dies near Kazembe's capital, close to Lake Mweru.

1802   Traders Pedro Baptista and Amaro Jose, leave Angola and visit Kazembe during a journey across Africa to Mocambique.

1832   Major Monteiro and Captain Gamitto visit Kazembe.

1835   The Ngoni, under Zwangendaba, cross the Zambezi and move north.

1851   David Livingstone meets Sebituane, Chief of the Makololo, on the Chobe River near the Zambezi.

1853   Livingstone revisits Barotseland at the outset of his great trans-African expedition.

1855   Livingstone "discovers" the Victoria Falls (Nov. 16) during his crossing of Africa from Luanda on the west coast to Quelimane on the east.

1872   First English traders arrive at the court of Sipopa of Barotseland.

1873   Death of Livingstone at Chitambo's Village (May 1).

1877   London Missionary Society begins work in Central Africa.

1878   Lewanika becomes king of the Lozi.

1886   Rev. François Coillard of the Paris Evangelical Mission Society is received in Barotseland by King Lewanika and sets up a permanent mission station and, in 1887, a school.

1889   Lewanika makes first request (Jan.) for British protection over Barotseland.
Ware concession signed by Lewanika (June). Later bought by Rhodes.
Royal Charter granted to British South Africa Company. Received by Cecil Rhodes.

1890   Lochner-Lewanika Treaty signed in Barotseland (June 27).
Various treaties concluded by Alfred Sharpe in Kazembe and Luangwa areas.

1891   Anglo-Portuguese Treaty (June 11) under which Portugal abandons claim to belt of land across Africa.

1895   Opening of Mwenzo Mission by Free Church of Scotland.
BSAC territories formally named Rhodesia by proclamation (May 3).

1896   Forbes appointed first Deputy Administrator of North-Eastern Rhodesia (July).

1897   Coryndon arrives in Barotseland as British Resident (Oct.).

1898   Lawley and Lewanika meet at Victoria Falls and sign a treaty giving the BSAC exclusive mineral rights (June 25).
Mpezeni's Ngonis defeated in North-Eastern Rhodesia by British force.
Last slave cargo stopped at Chipata.

1899   North-Western Rhodesia Order-in-Council (Nov. 20).
BSAC Deputy Administrator moves from Blantyre to Fort Jameson (Chipata).

1900   Lewanika treaty renegotiated.
North-Eastern Rhodesia Order-in-Council (Jan. 29).

1902   Death of Cecil Rhodes (March 26).
Mining starts at Broken Hill in Northern Rhodesia.
Collier discovers Bwana Mkubwa and Roan Antelope mines.

1904   Railway reaches Victoria Falls (April 25).   Opened on
            June 19.   Bridge opened (Sept. 12).

1905   King Victor Emmanuel of Italy sets frontier between
            BSAC territory and Portuguese Angola.

1906   Railway from the south reaches Broken Hill (Kabwe).
            Broken Hill copper mine discovered at Kabwe.

1907   Seat of administration of N. W. Rhodesia moved from
            Kalomo to Livingstone.
            Codrington appointed Administrator of N. W. Rhodesia,
            Wallace of N. E. Rhodesia.

1909   Wallace becomes Administrator of N. W. Rhodesia.
            Railway reaches Congo border (Nov.).

1910   Moffat Thompson discovers Nkana copper source.

1911   Northern Rhodesia Order-in-Council (May 4) unites
            N. W. and N. E. Rhodesia as Northern Rhodesia.
            Wallace becomes Administrator of the whole terri-
            tory.

1912   First copper concentrator erected in Northern Rhodesia
            at Bwana Mkubwa.
            Founding of Mwenzo Welfare Association by Donald
            Siwale, David Kaunda and others.

1917   Advisory Council of five elected members set up in
            Northern Rhodesia.

1921   Fossil of Rhodesian man discovered at Kabwe.
            Sir Drummond Chaplin named Administrator of North-
            ern Rhodesia.

1922   Start of major development of Northern Rhodesian
            Copperbelt.

1923   Agreement between BSAC and British Government
            (Sept. 29) on future administration of Northern Rho-
            desia.
            Discovery of large oxide ore-body at Nchanga.

1924   End of BSAC rule and establishment of N. R. Protec-
            torate under British Colonial Rule.
            Sir Herbert Stanley becomes first Governor (April 1).
            Birth of Kenneth Kaunda, April 28.

1926   Anglo-American Corporation of South Africa establishes
            itself in Broken Hill.

1927   Roan Antelope Mining Company formed.

Sir John Maxwell becomes Governor of Northern
Rhodesia.

1929   Hilton Young Report on closer association of East
            African territories published (Jan. 24).

1930   Boom in Copperbelt construction work, terminated at
            the end of the year by limitation of output due to
            fall in world prices.
            First suggestion by colonial officials that Northern
            and Southern Rhodesia unite in Federation.

1931   Price of copper drops rapidly due to world depres-
            sion.

1932   Sir Ronald Storrs named Governor of Northern
            Rhodesia.

1933   Copper slump ending.
            Work at Mufulira copper mine begins.

1934   Sir Hubert Young becomes Governor of Northern
            Rhodesia.

1935   First African strike on the Copperbelt.
            Capital of Northern Rhodesia transferred from Living-
            stone to Lusaka.

1936   Resolution by Southern Rhodesia Parliament in favor
            of amalgamation with Northern Rhodesia followed by
            conference at Victoria Falls demanding amalgama-
            tion.

1938   Sir John Maybin becomes Governor of Northern
            Rhodesia.

1939   Establishment of Munali, at Lusaka, as secondary
            school for Africans.
            Bledisloe Report on closer association between the
            Rhodesias and Nyasaland published (March 21).

1939-1945   World War II causes a boom in copper prices.

1940   Second Copperbelt African strike.

1941   Sir John Waddington named Governor of Northern
            Rhodesia.

1944   Central African Council set up (Oct. 18).

1946   Federation of African Welfare Societies established.
            Colonial government forms African Representative
            Council.

1947   Sir Gilbert Rennie becomes Governor of Northern
            Rhodesia.

1948   Publication of Dalgleish Report on "The Place of
            Africans in Industry. "
            Appointment of first two African members of N. R.
            Legislative Council.
            N. R. African Congress formed out of Federation of
            Welfare Societies.
            First African mineworkers union organized.
            Change in Northern Rhodesia Legislative Council in-
            cludes two African members elected by the African
            Representative Council and two European members
            for African interests nominated by Government.

1949   Victoria Falls Conference on Federation between
            Southern Rhodesia and unofficial representatives of
            Northern Rhodesia (Feb.).

1950   Agreement between Northern Rhodesia Government
            and BSAC for the transfer of the mineral rights to
            the Government in 1986 and for payment of 20 per-
            cent of the company's revenue from mineral rights
            to the Government in the intervening period.
            Compulsory education for Africans begins.

1951   Harry Nkumbula elected President of N. R. African
            Congress, re-named African National Congress.
            Kaunda appointed Northern Provincial Organizing Sec-
            retary of Congress.
            Official conference in London on Federation.   Report
            published on June 14.
            Victoria Falls conference on Federation between rep-
            resentatives of the United Kingdom, Southern Rho-
            desia, Northern Rhodesia and Nyasaland Govern-
            ments (Sept.).

1952   Further conferences in London on Federation and pub-
            lication of draft scheme.

1953   Queen Elizabeth II signs Order-in-Council establish-
            ing Federation (Aug.).
            Federation endorsed by legislatures of all three ter-
            ritories and by United Kingdom Parliament.
            Federation begins operation, October 23.   Lord
            Llewellin becomes first Governor-General.
            First Federal general election (Dec.).
            Sir Godfrey Huggins becomes Prime Minister.

1954   ANC boycott of butcheries in Lusaka and other towns
            (Jan.).
            Sir Arthur Benson named Governor of Northern
            Rhodesia.

Sir Gilbert Rennie appointed Federal High Commissioner in London.

1955   Kaunda and Nkumbula sentenced to three months' imprisonment (Jan.).

1956   N. R. Government declares State of Emergency on Copperbelt (Sept.).
Welensky succeeds Huggins (Lord Malvern) as Federal Prime Minister (Oct.).
Kariba hydroelectric scheme begins.

1957   Congress boycott of beer halls (July).
Disturbances in northern provinces (Aug.).
Earl of Dalhousie sworn in as second Governor-General of the Federation (Oct. 8).

1958   Publication of the "Benson Constitution" (March).
Copperbelt Mine strike (Sept.)
ANC emergency conference: Kaunda and others "split" from Nkumbula. ZANC formed (Oct.).
Second General election in Federation (Nov. 12).
United Church of Zambia organized.

1959   Zambia African National Congress banned in Northern Rhodesia (March 12).
First multiracial elections held in Northern Rhodesia (March).
First Session of Second Federal Parliament opened (April 7).
Sir Evelyn Hone appointed N. R. Governor (April).
Kariba Dam Wall completed (June 22).
Kaunda sentenced to nine months' imprisonment (June).
Mainza Chona leads United National Independence Party (UNIP) (Sept.).

1960   Kaunda elected President of UNIP (Jan.).
Monckton Commission created by British government to study Federation problems (April).
UNIP declared an "unlawful" society (May).
Federal Review Conference in London (Dec.).

1961   London Conference on N. R. Constitution (Jan.).
Macleod announces "15-15-15" constitutional proposals (June).
UNIP Conference at Mulungushi. "Cha-cha-cha" starts (July).

1962   Maudling announces modified constitutional plan (Feb.).
General Election produces deadlock (Oct.).
Publication of Kaunda's Zambia Shall Be Free.

UNIP and ANC form Coalition Government (Dec.).

1963   Tension rises between Lumpa Church members and
              non-Lumpa in Northern Province (Jan.).
              Victoria Falls Conference to dismantle Federation
              (June).
              New Constitution for N. R. announced (Sept.).
              Federation officially dissolved, December 31.

1964   UNIP wins General Election: Kaunda appointed
              Prime Minister (Jan.).
              London Conference on Zambian Independence (May).
              Lumpa "War." (July.)
              Kaunda proclaimed President-elect of Zambia (Aug.).
              End of BSAC royalties (Oct.).
              Birth of the Republic of Zambia (Oct. 24).

1965   Rhodesia unilaterally declares independence from
              Great Britain (Nov. 11).

1966   First National Development Plan (FNDP) goes into
              effect.

1967   Lusaka International Airport completed.

1968   Kenneth Kaunda re-elected as president, announces
              philosophy of Zambian Humanism.   Mulungushi
              Declaration introduces major economic reforms
              (April 19).

1969   Kwacha becomes official unit of currency (Jan.).
              University of Zambia graduates its first class.
              Lusaka Manifesto accepted.

1970   Lusaka is host of third Nonaligned Nations Summit
              Conference.

1971   Kariba North power station construction begins.

1972   Second National Development Plan put into effect
              (Jan.).
              One-Party participatory democracy officially created
              (Dec. 13).
              First stage of Kafue Dam and Hydroelectric Scheme
              completed.

1973   President Kaunda approves new Constitution after
              passage by Parliament (Aug.).
              Kaunda elected President of Zambia in first elec-
              tions of Second Zambian Republic (Dec.).

1974   Tan-Zam Railway reaches Zambia's border (April 7).
              World copper prices begin a lengthy plummet after
              reaching a record high.

1975 Zambia arrests fifty Zimbabwe political activists over the murder of Herbert Chitepo, one of the Zimbabwe leaders in Zambia (March).

Tan-Zam Railway reaches Copperbelt (March).

Times of Zambia and privately-owned land are nationalized (June).

1976 University of Zambia closed (Feb.-May) after student disturbances.

President Kaunda allows Zimbabwe nationalists to use Zambia for a base of operations against the Smith Government of Rhodesia (May).

1977 Kaunda places army on full alert and announces that Zambia is "in state of war" with white-ruled Rhodesia (May).

Rhodesian planes attack across the border in Feira District (Sept.).

Government plans major economic cutbacks and a "Back to the Land" campaign as copper prices continue at extremely low level (Nov.).

1978 Daniel Lisulo replaces Mainza Chona as Prime Minister. Chona becomes secretary-general of UNIP (June).

Rhodesian troops invade deep into Zambia, attacking Zimbabwe guerrilla bases.

Kaunda reelected President (Dec.).

INTRODUCTION

The Republic of Zambia was officially born on October 24, 1964, when the British flag was lowered and the multi-colored (green, red, black and orange) flag of Zambia was raised. The people of Zambia, however, have roots in the territory that are traceable in some cases to ancestors who were there thirteen centuries before. Others are more recent immigrants, but even they have traceable roots that go back about three centuries.

Bordering a huge neighbor such as Zaire makes Zambia appear smaller than it actually is. Its area of 290,586 square miles compares, for example, to a combined total of about 307,000 square miles for the United Kingdom and France. It is about one thousand square miles short of the combined areas of the American states of Texas and West Virginia, but its population of about four million in 1969 was roughly equal to that of the state of Maryland that year, which gave Zambia a population density of only thirteen people per square mile. By the late 1970's its population appears to be approaching the level of five million people.

The peculiar shape of Zambia is owed, of course, to the colonial process that carved Africa into many pieces, one of which became known as Northern Rhodesia. The British South Africa Company acquired rights throughout the territory starting in late 1889. One of its agents was unsuccessful in securing the signature of a tribal leader named Msiri, or the copper-rich area of Katanga (now Shaba) would be part of Zambia today. Instead it became King Leopold's territory as part of the Congo and now cuts deeply into Zambia, creating a distinctive "waist." The shape has been aptly compared to that of a butterfly heading north. At its widest point Zambia is about 725 miles east to west; a north to south trip (crossing the Katanga Pedicle) would cover about 650 miles.

The climate of Zambia could be compared to that of southern California but with more rainfall. In the coolest season the night-time temperature rarely dips below 40 degrees Fahrenheit, while the hottest season will not normally have daytime temperatures above the 90's. Forty-five to fifty inches of rainfall would be close to an annual median. All of these figures are subject to variation, of course, as certain parts of the country are somewhat colder than others, and rainfall likewise varies.

1

Zambia

The topography of Zambia is gently undulating, with pla-
teaus (elevation about 3500 to 4500 feet) broken by occasional hills.
In eastern Zambia, however, the Muchingo Mountains jut upwards
to six thousand feet in some places; then a huge escarpment is
created as the eastern side of the mountains plunge to a point in
the Luangwa River valley about three thousand feet below. Several
important lakes are found either along or within the borders of
Zambia. Lake Mweru and Lake Tanganyika, both along its northern
border, are part of the East Africa Rift system, and their waters
are shared with Zaire and Tanzania. Lake Bangweulu and its adjacent swamps are a little farther south but still in northeastern
Zambia. Along Zambia's southern border is the man-made Lake
Kariba, part of a hydroelectric system on the Zambezi River that
is shared with Zimbabwe (Rhodesia).

There are four major rivers in Zambia. The largest,
from which the country derived its name, is the Zambezi. It
starts in the northwestern part of the country on a southern route,
picking up tributaries along the way, then turns east and serves as
the southern border of the country en route to the Indian Ocean.
Its major tributary is the Kafue, which begins in north central
Zambia and heads generally southwest before hooking back to the
east and eventually joining the Zambezi in south-central Zambia.
The Luangwa River begins in northeastern Zambia and flows southwesterly before merging with the Zambezi River in southeastern
Zambia. The Luapula River is not a part of the Zambezi system,
developing just east of the Katanga Pedicle near Lake Bangweulu.
It ultimately forms the Zambia-Zaire border as it flows north into
Lake Mweru.

The people of Zambia are almost all within the Bantu-
language family. Most of them have origins in either Luba or
Lunda kingdoms slightly to the north in Zaire; but some have East
African roots, and one group, the Ngoni, migrated from South
Africa in the nineteenth century. Remains of the Broken Hill man
(or Rhodesian man) were found at Kabwe in 1921 and indicate that
the land was inhabited thirty thousand years ago. However, proof
of a much more sophisticated society that traded with the peoples
on Africa's east coast locates the Ingombe Ilede civilization in
southern Zambia between the seventh and tenth centuries A.D.
The ancestors of most of today's Zambians arrived in the country
by 1800.

Figures about the number of "tribes" and "languages"
found in a country are almost meaningless unless definitional
ground rules are first explained in detail. It is generally agreed,
however, that there are more than seventy "tribes" in Zambia, and
one source calculates thirty different dialects. Only the Tonga and
the Bemba peoples constitute close to 10 percent of the population
each, while there are about nine groups in the 2.5--6 percent range.
Bemba-speakers account for about a third of the population, Tonga-
and Nyanja-speakers combine to account for another third. English is the language that links people from distant parts of the

country.   Zambia also has fairly small populations of Asians,
Eurafricans, and Europeans, some of whom are now Zambian citizens.

Zambia's political history must be separated into regions,
as sections of the country had their own individual histories, only
occasionally linked with other sections.   The history of the western
part of the country particularly revolves around that of the Aluyana
or Lozi nation, which eventually came to dominate much of that
area.   Southern Zambian history has been influenced heavily by the
Tonga, although their lack of a centralized kingdom reduced their
power considerably.   Southeastern Zambia was first controlled by
the Chewa people who entered from the east (Malawi today), but
the Ngoni became nineteenth-century conquerors in that area.
Many groups were important in the history of northeastern Zambia,
but ultimately the Bemba came to dominate much of that region.
The western portion of the northeast was under the influence of
the Lunda, however.

Europeans first touched parts of Zambia in the early sixteenth century, but few non-Africans spent much time within the
present borders until the early nineteenth century when Portuguese
entered from the southeast and, a little later, Arab traders entered
from the northeast.   The object at this point was purely trade,
primarily for slaves and ivory.   Some of the stronger African
chiefdoms, especially among the Bisa, Bemba, and Lunda, became
major partners in this trade, often prospering at the expense of
their neighbors.   The Swahili (Arabs) set up some villages for
trading purposes, but only in a few instances did they establish
permanent settlements.   The Portuguese, coming up the Zambezi
River from Mozambique, were interested in little more than trade.

Missionaries did not arrive until the middle of the nineteenth century, with Dr. David Livingstone being the first of this
new breed of Europeans.   His activities and writings encouraged
others to follow his path.   Thus Revs. Arnot and Coillard entered
southern and western Zambia, while the Livingstonia Mission of
the Free Church of Scotland and the White Fathers (Catholic) entered northern and eastern Zambia.   They met with varying degrees of success initially, but ultimately mission posts and schools
were established on opposite ends of the country.

The coming of colonial rule to Zambia was the result of
the efforts of Cecil Rhodes, the South African mining magnate.
He persuaded the British Government to grant a charter to his
British South Africa Company (BSAC) in October, 1889.   The
Company immediately sought to acquire signatures from African
leaders throughout the country.   With the slave trade creating a
great deal of insecurity among some northeastern peoples, the
BSAC was successful in winning concessions from several of the
more insecure chiefs.   Company posts in this area led to a decline
in both the slave trade and the inter-African fighting associated
with it.   In southwestern Zambia there was a similar insecurity,

as King Lewanika of the Lozi sought British protection against the Matabele. Thus he signed documents in which he unwittingly opened the door to extravagant BSAC claims to the western half of Zambia. The inaccuracy of the claims was not of concern to unscrupulous seekers of fortune. When the railroad from South Africa crossed the Zambezi in 1905, the interior of Zambia became fair game for any Europeans seeking land for farms or, preferably, the discovery of precious minerals. While initial discoveries hinting at the country's copper resources were made about this time, development of the Copperbelt was still about two decades away.

The BSAC controlled Zambia administratively until 1924 when the British Colonial Office officially took over. With the opening of several major copper mines during the 1920's, European interest in "Northern Rhodesia" began to grow. Increasing numbers of Europeans entered the territory to gain their fortune. The interests of the Africans were secondary. For two decades the Europeans had been taxing the Africans in order to force them to work at European enterprises in order to pay the tax. Now a new effort to promote European interests began. Southern Rhodesia had attained self-rule in 1923. It was now proposed that the two Rhodesias be amalgamated under one rule. The Africans north of the Zambezi opposed this from the beginning, recognizing the oppressed state of their fellow Africans to the south. The British Government was also reluctant to move in this direction, proclaiming that its duty was to promote African interests in Northern Rhodesia. The all-European Legislative Council of Northern Rhodesia supported amalgamation, and its subsequent variations, incorporation and federation.

Finally in 1953 the Central African Federation of the Rhodesias and Nyasaland was born. Its leading forces would be Godfrey Huggins and Roy Welensky. The Federation would last just months past its tenth birthday, for African nationalists had decided that they could tolerate European rule no longer. Harry Nkumbula and Kenneth Kaunda had begun their political efforts prior to the coming of the Federation, but failed to prevent its birth. They now set about to ensure its quick demise. The African National Congress was the first major nationalist organization to have nationwide effect, but Nkumbula's leadership did not please many of the younger activists. Thus men like Kaunda, Simon Kapwepwe, and Reuben Kamanga broke away and formed a new group in 1958. It was soon banned by the Government, however, and the United National Independence Party (UNIP) arose with the same leadership. UNIP soon demonstrated national strength, and by March, 1961, it was obvious that it would be only a matter of time before the Federation would break up and Zambia would be free.

Independence for Zambia came on October 24, 1964. Kenneth Kaunda became its President, and UNIP its ruling party. The fourteen years since then have not been easy for the country. When white-ruled Southern Rhodesia unilaterally declared its independence from Great Britain in 1965, Zambia found it necessary to cut off all links with the territory that had been its most important trading partner and the principal outlet for Zambia's copper exports. The Tan-Zam Railway neared completion in 1974 and promised a safe outlet for the copper, but that same year world copper prices reached a peak and then began to plummet to new lows. The Zambian economy was hard hit.

Meanwhile the Government of Zambia functioned with the Independence Constitution until 1972 when it was announced that a new Constitution would take effect the next year, and that henceforth Zambia would be a one-party participatory democracy. In December, 1978, elections were held again. Despite some economic difficulties in the country, President Kaunda was reelected.

THE DICTIONARY

ABERCORN. Renamed Mbala (q. v.) since Zambian independence, the town is about 30 miles southeast of the southeastern edge of Lake Tanganyika. It is on a major road into Tanzania, about twenty-five miles from the border, in the extreme northeastern part of Zambia. It was first created as a government post in 1893. (The President of the British South Africa Company was also Duke of Abercorn.) Hugh Marshall was sent as the Magistrate and Collector for the Tanganyika District, and Abercorn was to be its administrative center. Marshall had about six Sikhs and a few Nyasaland Tonga to aid him as a police force. The post was near the village of Zombe, chief of the Lungu. Marshall built there an impregnable stockade of ten feet high poles. Refugees from the slave trade and its raids came there for protection. In September, 1914, it was attacked by the Germans but was held when reinforcements came. At the end of World War I, the local German commander, Von Lettow, surrendered to General Edwards at Abercorn on November 18, 1918. Abercorn eventually became a major town. In 1969 it had a population of 5200.

ABERCORN NATIVE WELFARE ASSOCIATION. Founded in 1932 with Franklin Temba as its first chairman, it was one of only two welfare associations in the Northern Province before World War II. It had some significance as a body in which anti-colonial issues could be raised and discussed. It took its complaints to the District Commissioner at Abercorn. Its jurisdiction was limited to the township of Abercorn itself by the government, and never faced problems as serious as those of its sister organizations on the Copperbelt.

ABOLITION OF SLAVERY PROCLAMATION OF 1906. This rule was imposed upon Barotseland by the British South Africa Company on July 16, 1906. On that date Resident Magistrate Frank Worthington of the BSAC forced the Ngambela to read it aloud to a crowd of several thousand gathered in Lealui. As a result, the Lozi ruling class could no longer require workers to assist the indunas and headmen to build their homes or cultivate their fields. However, it thereby "freed" Africans to work for Europeans in order to pay the hut tax to the Company.

ACTION GROUP. A sub-group of the African National Congress that began organizing and recruiting in October, 1953. It was

7

supported by Kenneth Kaunda and Simon Kapwepwe, who saw it
as a disciplined and non-violent way to oppose the color bar,
especially in business. Its members were younger and more
radical than the ANC leader, Harry Nkumbula, and he saw in
its vigor and enthusiasm a potential threat to his leadership.
The ANC National Executive Council finally tightened its control
over it by absorbing the Action Group's funds.

ADMINISTRATION OF NATIVE PROCLAMATION NO. 8 OF 1916.
A rule promulgated by the British South Africa Company Administration during World War I to enable chiefs and headmen to
recruit labor for the war effort. In redefining the powers and
duties of the chiefs and the obligations of the commoners to provide "reasonable" requests for free labor, it restored some
power to the chiefs that had been diminished for twenty years.

ADVISORY COUNCIL. In response to protests from the new settlers
in Northern Rhodesia, the British South Africa Company finally
granted the settlers the right to form an elected Advisory Council in 1918. Composed of five settlers, it had no legislative
power but merely afforded the settlers a place to have their
voices heard. Voting was by white, male, British subjects, at
least twenty-one years old, with incomes or property of £150.
Four members were to represent North-Western Rhodesia and
one for the North-East. Sir Lawrence Wallace, Administrator
of Northern Rhodesia, had suggested such an Advisory Council
as early as 1914. This council was terminated in 1925 when
the British Government took over the direct administration of
Northern Rhodesia.

AFRICAN AFFAIRS BOARD. A feature of the governing Constitution
of the Central African Federation, it was a standing committee
of the Federal Assembly, designed to serve as a safeguard for
African interests. It had the power to examine and even veto
bills which appeared to discriminate against Africans. The
veto, however, could be overridden by the Governor General or,
if necessary, by the British Parliament. This Board consisted
of a nominated chairman, the three white members appointed to
uphold African interests, and three of the African members. In
the first constitutional discussions the African Affairs Board was
to have been much stronger, thus hopefully to reassure the Africans that the Federation would protect them. Subsequent constitutional talks reduced its power progressively, however, so that
its final form was as outlined above. The demise of the Board
came in late 1957 when it objected to two constitutional changes
passed by the Assembly and the British House of Commons overruled the Board. Its chairman, Sir John Moffat, resigned, and
the Board was considered to be dead.

AFRICAN DEMOCRATIC SOCIALISM. The officially stated guiding
ideology of the Zambian Government at the time of independence,
it was heavy on economic goals. It promised the attempt to
raise the standard of living, to provide a more equitable distri-

bution of wealth, to humanize labor conditions, and to increase
social services such as health and educational programs.   In
1967 this phrase was dropped and replaced by the new ideology,
Zambian Humanism (q. v.).

AFRICAN LAKES COMPANY (originally the Livingstone Central Africa Trading Company).   A European commercial agency founded
by James Stevenson and John and Frederick Moir in 1878.   Glasgow businessmen were trying to support Scottish missionary activity in Nyasaland so the Company was designed both to supply
the missions and to oppose the slavery trade by opening other
trade with the natives.   Its initial business was in Nyasaland,
but the ivory and rubber trade forced it to build the Stevenson
Road (q. v.) through Northeast Rhodesia.   Around the turn of the
century the company (to be reorganized as the African Lakes
Corporation in 1893) had trading stations on Lakes Tanganyika
and Mweru and along the Luangwa and Kafue Rivers.   The company was hindered by many battles with the Arab slave traders.
Ultimately Cecil Rhodes acquired a large share in the financially pressed company.   His British South Africa Company acquired
4310 square miles of land in the Abercorn area near Lake Tanganyika from the African Lakes Corporation.

AFRICAN METHODIST EPISCOPAL CHURCH (AME).   A church
founded in America by a black preacher, Richard Allen, in 1816.
It was his answer to the color bar in the orthodox American
Methodist Church.   It became important to Zambia when a Suto
evangelist, Willie J. Mokalapa (q. v.), founder of the Ethiopian
Church of Barotseland (q. v.), joined the AME.   In 1897 he in-
corporated his church into the AME and eventually became the
Presiding Elder of the African Methodist Episcopal Church in
Barotseland.   The Church provided an alternative to the white
missionaries.

AFRICAN MINEWORKERS UNION.   Officially the Northern Rhodesia
African Mineworkers Trade Union, it was founded in 1947 with
the assistance of a representative of the British Labour Party,
then in power in England.   Lawrence Katilungu (q. v.) became
its first chairman.   In 1949 he became its President and the
union also gained official recognition by the mining companies
that year.   It gained considerable authority and prestige in the
next several years and was recognized as one of the two strongest unions in the country.   In 1956 it had a bitter struggle for
survival against the Mines African Staff Association (q. v.), a
group with strong company backing.   This resulted in a series
of eighteen "rolling strikes. "   Though each was brief, copper
and lead production was disrupted by them.   Katilungu was replaced as President by John Chisata in December, 1960.   It was
renamed the Zambia Mineworkers Union (q. v.) in January, 1965.

AFRICAN NATIONAL CONGRESS (of Zambia).   The Term "African
National Congress" (ANC) has been used by a number of African
political groups, notably in South Africa, but also in both

Northern and Southern Rhodesia. It was first founded in July
1948 as the Northern Rhodesia African Congress (q. v.) by
Godwin M. Lewanika (q. v.) and was merely the new name for
the Federation of African Societies (q. v.). During the controversy over federation with Southern Rhodesia the membership
surged. Harry Nkumbula (q. v.) became its President in August
1951, and immediately renamed it the African National Congress. This group, led by Nkumbula and Kenneth Kaunda was
to be the leading force of Northern Rhodesian nationalism for
many years. Kaunda's election as Secretary-General resulted
in an organizational drive that allowed ANC to function in most
of the country. It bitterly opposed federation and it boycotted
shops where Africans were discriminated against when being
served (see HATCH SYSTEM). Both its main leaders were
imprisoned in 1955 for possessing prohibited literature. In
1957 they visited London and began to receive help from the
British Labour Party. Both leaders pressed for constitutional
reform and independence for Northern Rhodesia, but they split
over the issue of supporting the British-imposed constitution in
December, 1958. Kaunda formed his own party. Other officers, notably Mainza Chona and Titus Mukupo, also broke with
Nkumbula who ran for a seat in the new Legislative Council
and won.
     ANC's biggest difficulties seemed to be the lack of or-
ganizational ability of Nkumbula, and its willingness to compromise with white settler groups on some issues (in contrast with
Kaunda's more militant stand). In 1959 and 1960 it lost much
support to Kaunda's UNIP; nevertheless it retained a degree of
viability throughout the 1960's, winning parliamentary seats,
notably in the Southern Province, but also getting many votes
(and some seats) in the Central and Western Provinces. Its
greatest support has been among the Tonga-speaking people,
especially in the Southern Province. For a period of nine
months in 1961 and 1962, while Nkumbula served a short jail
sentence, the party's acting presidents were Lawrence Katilungu
and (after his accidental death) Edward M. Liso.
     The 1962 Constitution resulted in elections that year
which produced the necessity for an alliance between ANC and
UNIP in order to have a black majority in the Legislative
Council. This sharing of power lasted only until the pre-independence election of 1964, won decisively by UNIP. In the
1968 general election ANC won 23 seats (to UNIP's 105), receiving about 25 percent of the total votes cast. The existence
of the ANC continued (under Nkumbula's leadership) until the
one-party state was officially created by President Kaunda, December 13, 1972. ANC members sat in the Legislative Assembly until it was dissolved in October, 1973.

AFRICAN NATIONAL FREEDOM MOVEMENT. A small political
     organization founded in May, 1959, by Barry Banda, Dauti
     Yamba, and Paskale Sokota. They announced a "non-violent
     campaign for self-government. " In June they merged with the
     United African Congress to form the United National Freedom
     Party (q. v.).

AFRICAN NATIONAL INDEPENDENCE PARTY. A party founded
at the end of May, 1959, by Paul Kalichini, the ex-Deputy
President of the Zambian African National Congress (ZANC),
and Frank Chitambala, also a ZANC activist. In August, 1959,
it merged with the United National Freedom Party and formed
the present ruling party, the United National Independence
Party (UNIP).

AFRICAN REPRESENTATIVE COUNCIL (ARC). An advisory body
of Africans set up by the British in 1946 to allow the Africans
a territory-wide voice in government. Although most of its
proposals were ignored, it was a place where ideas could be
formally exchanged, not just with the British but also between
the younger intellectuals and the chiefs. It supplemented the
prior existing Urban Advisory Councils and Provincial Councils.
There were twenty-nine members of the ARC, all but four of
them chosen by and from the five Provincial Councils. The
Western Province was allotted ten members and the Southern
Province had three. The others had four each. The remaining four members were chosen by the Barotse King from
among his councillors. It was presided over by the Secretary
for Native Affairs. In 1948 the ARC was authorized to select
two of its members to be appointed as "nominated unofficials"
on the Northern Rhodesia Legislative Council. The ARC lasted
until 1960, when the Northern Rhodesia Government, under the
Federation, voted to abolish it.

AKUFUNA (or AKAFUNA), TATILA. King ("Litunga") of the
Barotse from his installation in September, 1884, until he fled
his land in July, 1885. A son of Imbua (q.v.), he was selected to take on this position after rebels successfully forced
Lubosi (later called Lewanika) to flee the country. The leader of this revolt was Mataa (q.v.), who was to become his
Ngambela. Akufuna was young, however, and a weak ruler.
His relations with his people were poor. Even Mataa came to
despise him. Groups loyal to Lubosi plotted to replace Akufuna in March, 1885, but by July, Akufuna fled to Sesheke, as
Mataa and others were bringing Sikufele to replace him. This
never occurred, as Lubosi returned to his former position.

AKWANDI (or MAKWANDI). The followers of the early Lozi leader, Mwanambinya (q.v.). The name for this fairly large group
derives from a Luyana word meaning "fish." The Akwandi
were great fishermen and consumed much fish.

ALUYANA (or A-LUYI or LUYI). A people, probably related to
the Lunda in northwestern Zambia, who moved south and conquered the early inhabitants of what is now Bulozi or Barotseland. The name means "foreigners." This invasion probably
occurred prior to the mid-eighteenth century. In the mid-
nineteenth century the Aluyana were conquered from the south
by the Makololo, who renamed them Lozi (q.v.).

AMALGAMATION. A term used actively in Central Africa for over two decades, it meant the absorption of Northern Rhodesia (and Nyasaland) into Southern Rhodesia. It preceded the use of such words as partnership and federation. It was first used in this context around 1920. Both the Ormsby-Gore Commission of 1925 and the Hilton Young Commission of 1928 looked into its feasibility. In 1933 members of the Legislative Council voted to suggest that amalgamation would have favorable economic results for all. The Bledisloe Commission of 1938 found that the Africans, chiefs and commoners alike, abhorred the possibility of amalgamation, mostly because of Southern Rhodesia's record of race relations.

AMALONGWE. An important group of commoners among the Namwanga. Like the bakabilo among the Bemba, they have as a body the power to appoint chiefs and to carry out the rituals concerning installing and burying chiefs. Although chiefly authority rests with themselves, as the guardians of tradition, they are also subordinate and subject to the chiefs.

AMBO. A small tribe in southeastern Zambia near Mozambique, it is an offshoot from the Lala (q. v.). They represent almost one per cent of Zambia's population. They are noted for wood carvings in the form of household objects.

AMERY, LEOPOLD S. Great Britain's Colonial Secretary from November, 1924, and also Secretary of State for Dominion Affairs from July, 1925, until leaving both posts in June, 1929. He was in favor of some kind of close union between Britain's East and Central African territories. In 1927 he persuaded the British government to state that this would be desirable. Instead of immediate action, however, his success only resulted in the appointment of the Hilton Young Commission (q. v.) to investigate and report.

ANATAMBUMU. A council of Lozi women existing prior to the Makololo invasion. The word means "Mothers of the King." Only the brightest girls were chosen for this honor, and they were allowed to play a part in the running of government affairs. They were under the supervision of the Makoshi (q. v.), the Queen Mother.

ANGLO-AMERICAN CORPORATION OF SOUTH AFRICA, LTD. A multipurpose company engaged in commerce, investment, finance, manufacturing, and mining, it was established by Sir Ernest Oppenheimer in 1917. In 1926 he made plans to start a branch in Northern Rhodesia with its headquarters at Broken Hill, and it was incorporated two years later. It quickly became one of the two dominant mining companies in the country. This dominance in the economy was to grow as the country's economy was geared to the copper industry. After independence the Minister of Commerce and Industry said that no companies controlled from South Africa could operate in Zambia.

The company quickly reincorporated its Zambian firm as the
Anglo-American Corporation of Zambia, Ltd. (ZAMANGLO).
It has also made great strides in staffing its company with
young Zambians. The establishment of the Metal Marketing
Company of Zambia (q.v.) in 1968 has given the Government
influence in pricing and marketing copper. In 1970 the Government acquired a 51 percent interest in the ownership of all the
operating mines, including those of Anglo-American, which had
been renamed the Nchanga Consolidated Mines Ltd. (q.v.).
Its Zambian subsidiary, usually called ZAMANGLO, moved its
operations to Bermuda where it created a new subsidiary,
Zambia Copper Investments Limited, which now holds all of
ZAMANGLO's mining assets that have not been nationalized.
The individual mining companies that had been controlled by
the Anglo-American group, namely those at Bancroft, Nchanga,
and Rhokana, were first amalgamated into Bancroft Mines
Limited, which then changed its name to Nchanga Consolidated
Copper Mines Ltd.

ANGLO-GERMAN CONCORDAT OF 1890. An agreement which set
the Caprivi Strip (q.v.) as German territory, allowing the Germans access to navigation on the Zambezi River. It also drew
the line between the south end of Lake Tanganyika and the north
end of Lake Malawi. However the 210-mile border with Tanganyika was formally approved by Germany and Great Britain
in 1901.

ANGLO-PORTUGUESE AGREEMENTS OF 1891 AND 1893. These
agreements between the British and Portuguese Governments
resulted in a provisional boundary along the Zambezi and Kabombo Rivers, dividing the two spheres of influence. This also had the result of dividing the area considered by the Barotse
King to be part of his nation. Protests to the British High
Commissioner by the Barotse Litunga, Lewanika, were to no
avail. These agreements were finally altered as a result of a
decision in 1905 by a commission led by King Victor Emmanuel of Italy (q.v.).

ANGOLA. Independent since November, 1975, this former Portuguese colonial territory is the neighbor immediately west of
Zambia. For centuries people have migrated east across the
present border, especially those moving east within the great
Lunda empire. Within the last several centuries the Lozi
(Barotse) established hegemony over a large region of western
Zambia, including over the people in the border region. These
people included the Luchazi, the Chokwe and the Mbunda. The
establishment of a Northern Rhodesian-Angolan border occurred
in stages. The first of these were the Anglo-Portuguese Agreements of 1891 and 1893 (q.v.) which set a provisional boundary
along the Zambezi and Kabombo Rivers. Ultimately the final
border was set as a result of an arbitration decison by King
Victor Emmanuel of Italy (q.v.) in 1905. This was needed
because Lewanika, the Lozi King, was greatly disturbed by the

construction of Portuguese forts in "his" territory. The final
border was moved somewhat west of the prior agreements, dividing the disputed area evenly, along the twenty-second parallel. The Zambia-Angola Border did not become a problem
again until the advent of the anti-Portuguese warfare in the
early 1960's by African nationalists, some of whom used Zambian territory as a staging area for troops. This invited re-
taliation by the Portuguese rulers of Angola, who controlled a
major outlet for Zambian copper exports, the Benguela railway,
which runs through Zaire and Angola to the port of Lobito.
Problems with Angola continued even after its independence in
November, 1975. Zambia was not quick to support Dr. Neto,
the winner among the warring Angolan nationalists, and guerrilla activity kept the Benguela line unusable for crucial periods
of time, seriously hurting Zambian trade.

ANGONI. A word found often in early colonial era writings to refer to members of the Ngoni (q.v.) group of people.

ARABS. Traders who have been bringing the East African and Indian Ocean trade into Central Africa for many centuries. They
traded beads, cloth and shells for gold, copper, and ivory.
Later guns were brought in, and slaves were taken out. A
Portuguese explorer described the Arab trade in Zimbabwe in
1514, but other sources indicate the trade was going on among
the Nsengas of Zambia even earlier. Arab traders were recorded later in both southern and western Zambia. Often the
Arabs were referred to as either Balungwana (q.v.) or Swahili
(q.v.). From 1750 to 1820, dissention among the coastal Arab
communities slowed the trade considerably. However, Arab
trade in the final two-thirds of the nineteenth century hit its
peak. Slaves, ivory, and salt were among the products sought
from Zambia. The peoples most influenced by the trade were
the Bemba (and their northeastern neighbors) and the Lunda of
Kazembe along the Luapula River. Arab settlements dotted
the interior countryside, controlling the trade. In 1872 they
even helped a refugee Lunda prince overthrow the then Kazembe. Among the most significant Arab leaders or traders
involved in Zambia were Mlozi, Tippu Tip, Kumba Kumba,
and Abdullah ibn Suliman (qq.v.). Many of the Arabs had
much African blood in them. Few were "pure" Arabs. Only
the extension of British control over North Eastern Rhodesia
around the beginning of the 20th century diminished the influence of the Arabs. British intervention had been motivated
earlier by the desire to control the slave trade reported by
Dr. Livingstone and others.

ARNOT, FREDERICK STANLEY (1858-1914). A missionary who
came to Barotseland representing the Plymouth Brethren (q.v.),
a lay body that had seceded from the Anglican Church. He
was their first missionary to southern Africa. He was a great
admirer of Dr. Livingstone, a fellow Scot. He entered Barotseland in 1882 through the intercession of George Westbeech

(q. v.) and met the King (Litunga), Lubosi. He was warmly
received and stayed at Lealui, the Lozi capital, for eighteen
months. Lubosi permitted Arnot to open a small school for
royal and noble children. Arnot claims in his books that he
was an advisor to Lubosi and persuaded him to make an alliance with Khama of the Bamangwato rather than with Lobengula
of the Ndebele. Arnot left Barotseland in 1884 having achieved
no successful conversions and pursued his goals in Angola and,
especially, Katanga. He passed through Lealui again in 1910
and visited with Lubosi, who was known as Lewanika by this
time.

ASIANS. Amost all of the Zambian residents described as Asian
     are from the Gujarat Province in western India or descended
     from immigrants from there. There are over eleven thousand
     of them in Zambia. About three-quarters of them are Hindu.
     Over 86 percent of the families are in commerce, mostly in
     large cities, especially Ndola, Kitwe, and Lusaka. Most of
     them came in the late 1940's, some from Rhodesia, others
     (including the first Asians in Northern Rhodesia), entered at
     Fort Jameson (now Chipata) from Nyasaland (Malawi). The
     Mulungushi Declaration (q. v.) of 1968 had a major impact on
     the Indians in Zambia, as its economic reforms were designed
     to eliminate the non-citizen from the Zambian economy. Most
     of the Asians in Zambia had not heeded earlier suggestions
     and had not taken out Zambian citizenship. Only 298 of the
     eleven thousand Asians became citizens between 1965 and 1971.
     The Government granted very few of the citizenship requests
     received after the reforms took effect. Thus many of them
     lost their businesses, especially in rural areas, or were
     forced out of business by regulations which favored citizens.
     Some left the country, but even then the Government placed a
     strict limit on the amount of money emigrants could take out
     of Zambia. In recent years there has been an influx of Chi-
     nese into Zambia in conjunction with the building of the Tan-
     Zam Railway. They are not expected to be permanent resi-
     dents.

ASKARI. An African serving in a police capacity, especially dur-
     ing colonial times. Men enrolled in the armed forces during
     World War II were also called askaris. Some considered this
     demeaning to the soldiers.

AUSHI see USHI

AWEMBA. A word used by many early colonial administrators
     when designating those people we refer to now as Bemba. The
     name carried over to the "Awemba District, " one of the first
     administrative districts to be delineated by the British South
     Africa Company. It had Lake Bangweulu as its border in the
     southwest, and the middle section of the Chambezi River al-
     most dissected it diagonally from southwest to northeast.

AWEMBA WAR. A term used by the British to describe their
last battles against Bemba groups. In early 1899 a contingent
led by Charles McKinnon and Robert Young defeated Ponde
(q. v.), who claimed to be the new Mwamba, at his new village.
Shortly after, in April, 1899, a force led by H. T. Harrington
and Andrew Laws required a day long battle before capturing
the stockaded village of Mporokoso (q. v.). The village defenders were led by Arabs under Nasaro bin Suliman. This
marked the end of Bemba resistance to the establishment of
white rule in the Northern Province.

AYRSHIRE FARM. A site southwest of Lusaka, near the Kafue
flats, where a group of rock engravings are found. The metal
tools (axes and hoes) depicted are fairly modern, thus the engravings are of comparatively recent origin.

                              - B -

BA -. A standard Bantu language prefix that denotes more than one
person when it is added to a root word that identifies a group
of ethnically related people. Thus some will refer to the
Baila, Barotse, and Batwa tribes or peoples, for example.
For convenience in this book, all such groups will be found
under the letter of the alphabet that immediately follows this
prefix.

BABENYE. The personal relics of Bemba chiefs, for example,
spears, tools and bows. Possession of the relics belonging to
his predecessor is essential to a chief's legitimacy. They are
closely guarded in special huts and are not available to outsiders.

BAFILOLO. Plural of Cilolo (q. v.).

BAKABILO (or BAKEBILO). These hereditary priest-councillors
among the Bemba play very important ritual roles. Although
these commoners are ineligible for the chiefdomship, they are
important both in a chief's installation and, for some of them,
his burial. They usually trace their family descent to the first
coming of the Bemba to their land. In addition to legitimatizing
the chief through a series of rituals, each of the approximately forty bakabilo has his own village near the capital.
During times of interregnum, they serve as regents and guide
the government. Once the new chief receives the babenye
(q. v.) from the bakabilo, they are subordinate to him, but as
non-removable hereditary leaders, they continue to act as
something of a constitutional check on the chief. Their neu-
trality (as commoners) gives them special respect from con-
testants to the chiefdomships. A group of six senior bakabilo
are the most important in dealing with crucial issues. They
are referred to as bashilubemba (q. v.).

BAKAFULA. A name surviving into fairly recent times that was
applied to some of the "little people" who once inhabited many
parts of Zambia. While it may refer to pygmies, it more
likely was applied to the Bushmen (q.v.).

BAKALUNDA. Commoners who fill certain ritual roles among the
eastern Lunda. Their special duties involve both installing
chiefs and burying them. While subordinate to the chief, they
are also his legitimatizers. See BAKABILO for a parallel
among the Bemba.

BALDWIN, REV. ARTHUR. Along with the Rev. and Mrs. H.
Buckenham, Rev. Baldwin attempted to serve among the Ila
for the Baila-Batonga Mission of the Primitive Methodist
Church (q.v.). They reached the Zambezi River at Kazungula
in 1889, but were stopped by the Lozi who resented the white
men aiding their traditional opponents. In 1891, after the intercession of Rev. Coillard of the Paris Mission, they were
allowed to come to the Lozi capital, where they stayed for two
years at the Sefula Mission station. Finally in June, 1893,
they were allowed to proceed to the country of the Ila. In December of that year they set up a Methodist Mission at Nkala
on the Nkala River, a tributary of the Kafue River. Baldwin's
journal tells us much concerning the dominance of the Lozi
over their neighbors in the 1891-93 period.

BALOVALE DISTRICT. Now called the Zambezi District, it is located in the North-Western Province of the country, along the
upper sections of the Zambezi River. Its population in 1969
was over 61,000, most of whom are either of the Lunda or
Luvale peoples. The district became part of a controversy in
the late 1930's when it was still administered as part of Barotseland, despite its non-Lozi population. There were serious
resentments and complaints by the residents, and in 1938 the
Government appointed a commission to investigate the question.
The commission was led by Sir Philip MacDonell. It made its
report in 1939, but the Government did not act on it until July,
1941. At that time it removed almost all of the district from
the control of the Barotse King and transferred it to the Kaonde-
Lunda Province (later called the Western Province).

BALUNGWANA (or BANGWANA). A name meaning "outsiders"
which was applied to many of the Arab traders by Zambians,
regardless of their ethnic heritage. See also ARABS and
SWAHILI.

BANCROFT MINE. Only about ten miles from the border with
Zaire and ten miles north of Nchanga, this important mine is
part of the Anglo-American Corporation group. Construction
work began on it in 1953, but copper production did not begin
until January, 1957. It temporarily ceased production early in
1958, but reopened in April, 1959. It was named after Dr.
Bancroft, for many years the consulting geologist to Anglo-

American. The city of Bancroft (population of about 40,000) has had its name changed to Chililabombwe.

BANDA, BARRY. One of the founders of the African National Freedom Movement (q.v.) in May, 1969. He was just a young clerk, but had been active in Nkumbula's African National Congress. In June he merged his group with the United African Congress to form the United National Freedom Party, of which he became Secretary-General.

BANDA, BETTY. The maiden name of Betty Kaunda (q.v.), wife of President Kenneth Kaunda.

BANDA, DR. HASTINGS KAMUZU. The first President of Malawi, Zambia's southeastern neighbor. His leadership of the Nyasaland African Congress led Britain to break up the Central African Federation by giving his country independence. This announcement was further stimulus for Zambian nationalists to fight for the same, especially since Banda and Kaunda had worked together on several anti-Federation efforts. Dr. Banda was born May 14, 1906, in northern Nyasaland (Malawi). He received higher education in the United States, including a medical degree from Meharry Medical College. He practiced in England for many years and Ghana for five years. He returned home triumphantly on July 6, 1958, to lead his people toward freedom.

BANDA, HAYDEN DINGISWAYO. An Ngoni from the Eastern Province, a bookkeeper by profession, this militant UNIP member was appointed its Director of Youth in 1961. He was instructed by Kaunda to improve its organization and effectiveness. He held the post for eight years. A hardworking political activist with experience in ANC, ZANC, and UNIP since 1954, he was very popular among young members of UNIP. He was imprisoned in both 1960 and 1961 for his militancy. During that time he was also UNIP's Provincial Chairman for the Copperbelt. A close associate of Kenneth Kaunda for many years, he served in a variety of high government posts. In the first Government he was Minister of Housing and Social Development. Several months later (January 22, 1965) he became Minister of Transport and Works. Two years later he became Minister of Co-operatives, Youth, and Development. In 1969 he became Minister of the Western Province (soon renamed the Copperbelt Province) and later the Southern Province. In October, 1970, he returned to be Minister of Power, Transport, and Works. He was briefly suspended for misappropriation of government funds and, after being reinstated, served briefly until being dismissed from the cabinet in June, 1971. He rejoined the Cabinet as Minister of Labour and Social Services on December 10, 1973.

BANK OF ZAMBIA. A state-owned bank, set up by the Government in August, 1964, with power to regulate credit in the

country. It was created in order to serve as a counterweight
to the foreign owned "giants, " Barclays Bank and Standard
Bank. In fact there was a requirement that the commercial
banks keep fixed percentages of their deposits as balances at
the Bank of Zambia. It issues the national currency and controls foreign exchange.

BANTU BOTATWE GROUP. One of the subgroups formed within
UNIP in the late 1960's stressing sectional interests and demands. It united UNIP leaders in the Southern Province and
parts of the Central Province. The term, meaning "three
peoples, " also refers to the Ila-Tonga-Lenje group of peoples
who have a language and traditions of their own, and somewhat
different from most Zambian peoples. They formed the basis
for this modern political faction.

BANTU LANGUAGES. One of the several major linguistic families
in Africa. With the exception of a few Khoisan-speakers (notably among the small community of Bushmen) almost all the
people of Zambia speak one of the Bantu languages. Swahili
is a mixture of Bantu and some Arabic.

BANTUNGWA. The priest-councillors among the Bisa people.
They are very much like the bakabilo (q.v.) among the Bemba.

BAOBOB TREE. The giant baobob tree can be found in a number
of areas in Zambia, especially in the lower and hotter parts.
Some of them have a trunk circumference as large as sixty-
five feet. Some are as old as two thousand years. Their
huge, gnarled branches are easily recognizable. From its
fruit comes cream of tartar and fibers for cloth. Its seeds
produce an oil for cooking. Ropes and cloth are made from
its bark, and its wood can be used for canoes. Some people
have even hollowed out homes in its trunks.

BAPTISTA, PEDRO JOÃO. An African from Angola who, with a
traveling companion, Amara José, was sent by the Portuguese
from Luanda, Angola across the continent to Tete, Mozambique. The trip took nine years from their start in 1802.
They returned then through the territory of Chief Kazembe and
Mwato Yamvo. They were jailed for four years by Kazembe
and were released only after negotiations with traders from
Mozambique. His diary mentions a war between the Lunda and
the Bisa over the Katanga trade, and also refers to Africans
mining copper.

BARK CLOTH. Bark, especially from the baobob tree, was a
traditional source of cloth for clothing, especially among the
people in the northeastern part of the country.

BAROTSE ANTI-SECESSION SOCIETY (or MOVEMENT). An organization founded in November, 1960, by Nalumino Mundia
(q.v.), and other reform-minded Lozi living outside Barotseland.

Its goal was to attract Lozi support against the Litunga's desire to separate Barotseland from the rest of Northern Rhodesia. Some of its organizers had been members of the Barotse National Association (q. v.). Mundia was to become a
major organizer for UNIP in Barotseland before forming his
own party, the United Party, several years later.

BAROTSE NATIONAL ASSOCIATION (or SOCIETY). A group
started by Lozi along the line of rail circa 1954 to advocate
reform in the Barotse Native Government. Among its leaders
were Godwin Mbikusita and, later Sekeli Konoso, a Lusaka
businessman. A faction hostile to the Litunga and led by
Konoso demanded that Akabeswa Imasiku resign as Ngambela.
The trial of Konoso (q. v.) in 1957 for defaming the Litunga
resulted in a protest demonstration and more arrests.

BAROTSE NATIONAL COUNCIL. Sometimes referred to as the
Barotseland Parliament, this Council served as the traditional
advisory body to the Lozi (Barotse) Litunga (King). It did not
have regular meetings, sometimes gathering once or twice a
year, but usually met primarily to discuss really important
matters such as new treaties or the selection of a new king.
Its membership was about thirty, half of them councillors living at the capital, Lealui, and half representing the five District councils. More often meetings were held by smaller
groups, such as the Saa (q. v.), Sikalo (q. v.) or the Katengo
(q. v.). The leader or prime minister of the National Council
was called the Ngambela (q. v.).
      In 1963 the British Government re-formed the National
Council by creating twenty-five elected seats, elections to be
held in July. UNIP nominated candidates for each of the
seats. Independents opposed them for eighteen of the seats,
but UNIP won them all. In mid-1965, the Zambian Government introduced the Local Government Bill which abolished the
National Council, replacing it with five district councils. None
of these new councillors could be appointed by the Litunga.
The Bill was signed by President Kaunda in October and the
Council was abolished in November, 1965. See also MULONG-
WANJI.

BAROTSE NATIONAL SCHOOL. Founded in 1906, it was for many
years the best school in Northern Rhodesia, as well as the
only one not run and financed by a mission society. It was
sanctioned by the British South Africa Company and had the
strong support of King Lewanika. Important in its curriculum
at its initiation was the teaching of English and "useful technical knowledge. " It was financed from part of Lewanika's income from the hut tax. Its student body included many sons
of ranking Lozi leaders. As a result of its success, the missions were forced to improve their schools in Barotseland.
Decades later, Lozi held most of the jobs open to indigenous
Northern Rhodesians.

BAROTSE NATIVE AUTHORITY ORDINANCE OF 1936. A special
ordinance for Barotseland passed by the Government of
Northern Rhodesia with the approval of the Barotse Litunga
and Kuta. The Native Authorities Ordinance of 1936 (q. v.)
did not apply to Barotseland because of its special status.
The main differences are provisions that recognized the special status of the Litunga as Barotse King and the necessity
of the Government to consult with him.

BAROTSE NATIVE COURTS ORDINANCE OF 1936. As in the previous entry, this was a special ordinance involving judicial
procedure in Barotseland which differed from that authorized
elsewhere by the Government of the Northern Rhodesian Protectorate. Among the differences was that Administrative officers of the Government could only intervene in criminal cases
in Barotseland. Also, in certain cases, Government action
was only permissible after receiving a recommendation from
the Litunga.

BAROTSE NATIVE POLICE. A force put together at the beginning
of the twentieth century and first commanded by Colonel Colin
Harding. It was to be a native force for keeping the peace,
which it did, for example, by patrolling the Barotse border
and by suppressing disturbances among the Ila. The police
were primarily Ngoni and Lozi. Upon union of the North-East
and North-West in 1911, the Barotse Native Police became
part of the Northern Rhodesia Police.

BAROTSE PATRIOTS. A short-lived political group formed in the
early 1960's to urge governmental reform in Barotseland. The
group wanted also a commission of inquiry to investigate recent unrest "before it becomes too late. " This commission
was ultimately led by Sir Charles Hartwell.

BAROTSE PROVINCE. From independence (October 24, 1964) until October, 1969, when the Barotseland Agreement, 1964 (q. v.)
was disavowed by the Government, the area known historically
as Barotseland was called the Barotse Province. The name
was changed to Western Province in October, 1969. (The previous Western Province was renamed Copperbelt Province.)
With the name change there was also a loss of special privileges.

BAROTSE TREATY OF 1890 see LOCHNER CONCESSION

BAROTSELAND. An area in the southwestern part of the Republic
of Zambia. Today it is referred to as the Western Province
and was formerly (from 1964 to 1969) the Barotse Province.
It is adjacent to Angola, Zambia's western neighbor, the border between them only being finalized in 1905. The king or
Litunga of the Barotse (also known as Lozi) maintains his capital at Lealui, four hundred miles west of the "line of rail, "
and substantially isolated from the rest of the country. While

parts of this Lozi homeland include part of the Kalahari desert and forest land, much of it is comprised of the rich allu-
vial Flood Plain (called Bulozi "proper" or Ngulu) along the
upper Zambezi. Other areas, especially to the north and east,
were conquered by 18th- and 19th-century Lozi kings. British
protection was first brought to the area as a result of the
Lochner Concession (q. v.), a treaty between the Barotse Litunga and the British South Africa Company. As Northern
Rhodesia sought independence from England in the late 1950's
and early 1960's, the Barotse Native Government sought independent statehood. A petition to the British Government in
September, 1961, specifically sought this. The British opposed subdividing the future Zambia. Ultimately the Barotseland Agreement, 1964 (q. v.) between Kenneth Kaunda and the
Litunga acknowledged the traditional Barotse rights within an
independent Zambia. The agreement was cancelled by a Zambian law in 1969.

BAROTSELAND AGREEMENT, 1964. An agreement signed in London on May 18, 1964, by Kenneth Kaunda and the Litunga of
Barotseland. It was approved for the British Crown by Duncan Sandys. The Litunga assumed that this agreement gave
Barotseland a permanent part of the new Zambia but with all
traditional privileges maintained. Kaunda saw it as a way of
getting the Lozi to accept the new constitution through an act
that could be changed later. Indeed, a law passed in October,
1969, cancelled the agreement and made Barotseland just
another Province.

BAROTSELAND NATIONAL PARTY   see   SICABA ("NATIONAL")
PARTY

BAROTSELAND/NORTH-WESTERN RHODESIA ORDER IN COUNCIL
OF 1899 see ORDER IN COUNCIL OF 1899

BASHILUBEMBA.   The six senior bakabilo (q. v.) among the Bemba. Of the six (Chimba, Chitikafula, Kapukuma, Katenda,
Munuca, and Nkolemambwe), each has an important role during the rituals of installing and burying the Chitimukulu of the
Bemba. In addition, the Chimba also acts as regent during
the long period of burial rites and calls himself a chief.

BASUNGU.   A name applied to the Europeans by the Bemba.

BATOKA GORGE.   An area below Victoria Falls near the city of
Livingstone. It was noted for its exposed walls of basaltic
lava.

BATOKA PLATEAU.   A highlands area in southern Zambia, east
of Livingstone and north of Lake Kariba. A healthy area,
free of many disease-bearing insects, it was an area desired
by invaders. The local Toka (q. v.) especially had to defend
against the Makololo of Chief Sibitwane in the nineteenth

century. The Toka lost, and the Makololo dominated the area
for some years, raiding among the Toka as far east as the
confluence of the Kafue and Zambezi Rivers. The plateau
dwellers were isolated from most trade routes that ran up the
Zambezi valley.

BAXTER, ERNEST CHARLES. Acting Administrator of North-
Western Rhodesia for a very brief period in November and
December, 1906.

"BAYETE." A royal salute among the Ngoni and other groups
classified broadly as Nguni, such as the Swazi. Roughly
translated as "Hail" but usable in many contexts, the salute
is given on festive occasions to a variety of important leaders,
including important political figures.

BAZIMBA. A chiefly clan found among the Lungu and Tabwa
peoples, it is often called "the Leopard Clan." A matrilineal
clan, its first chiefs came from the western shores of Lake
Tanganyika in the late eighteenth century to settle north and
west of the Bemba. The main group settled in Itabwa under
a chief called Nsama (q. v.). This was the beginning of the
Tabwa chiefdom of Nsama. Dr. Livingstone described Nsama
III Chipili as "the Napoleon of these countries."

BEAUFORT, SIR LEICESTER PAUL. Acting Administrator of
North-Eastern Rhodesia for the last six months of 1905 and
again from January, 1909, until May, 1911.

BECHUANALAND EXPLORATION COMPANY. A subsidiary of the
British South Africa Company which, in 1902, sent William
Collier into what is now called the Copperbelt. He discovered
ore deposits at spots which he named Bwana Mkubwa and Roan
Antelope as well as at Chambishi. All were to become im-
portant sources of Zambia's copper.

BEIRA. An Indian Ocean port city in Mozambique that has become
an increasingly important trading port for Zambia since 1965.
It is reached via the Great East Road from Lusaka to Salima
in Malawi and from there south by rail to Beira.

BELL, JOHN. An administrator for the British South Africa Company, he was Collector for the Chambeshi District near the
end of the nineteenth century. Although involved mostly with
the Bemba, he is remembered for using his police to put
down African resistance to forced labor in 1896 by the Namwanga people of Headman Ilendela (q. v.). He burned the village
when the Africans resisted and one African was killed by a
gunshot.

BEMBA (or AWEMBA, WEMBA, BABEMBA). One of the largest
and perhaps most influential of the ethnic subdivisions of Zambia. Though only about 9 percent (about 350,000) of Zambia

are Bemba, over a third of the population speaks chiBemba
(or ciBemba) as their native tongue.   This is due to the
spread of Bemban political control in the last half of the nineteenth century.   ChiBemba has also become virtually the lingua
franca of the Copperbelt, due in part to the high percentage of
chiBemba speakers working there.   In contemporary Zambia,
Bemba influence has been very strong in the ruling party,
UNIP.

There is a very large body of literature on the Bemba;
the best works to appear recently are by Andrew D. Roberts.
What follows is obviously a superficial and select review of
the facts.

The dominant group of Bemba appear to have arrived in
Zambia early in the eighteenth century, settling ultimately in
the north-central part of the eastern half of Zambia.   They
seem to have been Luba from the great Luba-Lunda empire
that stretched across the savannah belt of Africa, virtually
from coast to coast.   At that time a group calling themselves
Bemba, under a chief called Mulopwe, already lived there.
The new arrivals may have adopted the name.   Bemba legend
says that the immigrants from Luba or Kola (q.v.) included
sons and a daughter of a man named Mukulumpe (q.v.).   They
were all members of the Crocodile Clan (bena ng'andu, q.v.),
which has become the royal clan of the Bemba.   They established a settlement on the Kalungu River and created a leader
to be called the Chitimukulu (q.v.).   The name means "Chiti
the great" and was assigned because its first holder was
named Chiti.   This chieftainship has remained for the most
part the senior one among Bemba.   As many as twenty other
chieftainships have been established among the Bemba, some
of the most senior being: Mwamba, Nkula, and Nkolemfumu
(qq.v.), all of which must be filled by bena ng'andu.   It is a
clan that observes matrilineal descent.   Whereas each of the
chiefdoms is somewhat autonomous, all owe some allegiance
to the Chitimukulu.   Holders of lesser chieftainships may be
"reappointed" or "promoted" to more important ones, including ultimately the position of Chitimukulu.

Early Bemba men saw themselves more as great hunters and warriors than as farmers or herdsmen.   They were
thus not as closely tied to one area of the land.   They also
attacked weaker neighbors, thus absorbing them and their
land (causing the creation of new chiefdoms).   They became
greatly feared.   In the nineteenth century their expansion under
the leadership of two Chitimukulus, Chileshye (q.v.) and Chitapankwa (q.v.), got them heavily involved in the East African
and Indian Ocean trade pattern.   Ivory, copper, and slaves
were the major items.   This expansion was partly at the expense of their southern neighbors, the Bisa (q.v.) who had
been major traders.   Raids on their other neighbors brought
further conflicts, notably with the Ngoni (q.v.).   Many of the
groups thus defeated adopted the Bemba language.   Some internal dissension also occurred as the Mwamba chiefdomship,
better situated geographically to take advantage of East African

trade, rivaled Chitimukulu in power and importance. Bemba
unity depended on a basic understanding between the two leaders.   Often a close blood relationship between them existed,
making agreement easier.
        The coming of the British to central Africa had a great
impact on the Bemba in that it cut out the slave trade, elimi-
nating both the profit and the raids on neighbors.   Missionaries,
notably the Roman Catholic order called the White Fathers, had
a settling effect on the Bembas through conversion and education.   When the copper mines opened, the Bemba flocked to
the Copperbelt.   In part they were driven by the requirement
to pay taxes, but they also had more freedom in that they
lacked strong ties to farmland or herds.   Both on the Copperbelt and in their home provinces the Bemba responded readily
to the appeal of modern political activity.   Bemba like Justin
Chimba and Simon Kapwepwe were very able organizers of
ZANC and UNIP, as the Bemba speakers in the Northern,
Central, Copperbelt, and Luapula Provinces were the political
backbone of the nationalist parties.   In fact, this influence has
required Zambian leaders to be conscious of ethnic balance in
the Government as such jealousies have caused some political
difficulties.

BENA MILENDA.   Commoners among the Lamba people who fill
    certain ritual roles, including both installing chiefs and bury-
    ing them.   They are comparable to the bakaLunda among the
    eastern Lunda and the bakabilo among the Bemba.

BENA MUKULU.   A group of about 40,000 people living north and
    west of Lake Bangweulu in the area near the Chimpili Hills.
    They are members of the bena ng'oma or Drum Clan.   Their
    chiefs hold the title Chungu.   Their location made them vul-
    nerable to attack from both the Lunda of Kazembe and the
    Bemba, especially in the nineteenth century.   They periodical-
    ly came under the control of the latter, and like the Bemba,
    with whom they often intermarried, they are matrilineal.   Cas-
    sava became a staple in their diet and iron-working an impor-
    tant industry which they used in trades.   The White Fathers
    spent much time among them, eventually publishing the history
    of the Mukulu chieftainship of Chungu in 1949.

BENA NG'ANDU.   The "Crocodile Clan," or people of the croco-
    dile, this is the royal clan of the Bemba, from which come
    most Bemba chiefs, and all of the prominent chieftainships.
    Even some headmen in the heart of Bemba country are tradi-
    tionally of this clan, even though far removed from the main
    line.   Perhaps of Lunda descent, the bena ng'andu arrived in
    the vicinity of Lake Bangweulu, probably from the Congo,
    about the seventeenth century.   Some of them, descended from
    chiefs, established a settlement on the Kalungu river where
    they created the principal Bemba chieftainship, Chitimukulu
    (q. v.).   The bena ng'andu are looked upon by the Bemba as
    the founders of their nation and the source of their glory and

pride, although Bemba began to reject the clan in the face of
European intervention at the beginning of the twentieth century.

BENA NG'OMA. A clan (also called the Drum Clan) that migrated
from Luba country perhaps in the seventeenth century to settle
north and west of Lake Bangweulu. Among the chiefs to come
from this clan were those of the Bena Mukulu (q.v.), Chishinga
(q.v.) and Bena Ng'umbo. Although related, they formed no
binding alliances.

BENA NG'ONA. Also called the Mushroom Clan, it is a clan that
migrated from Luba country, perhaps in the seventeenth century, to settle east of the Chambeshi River, due east of Lake Bangweulu. Here the clan became the source of all the principal
chiefs of the Bisa people, their royal clan. Nevertheless the
major Bisa chiefs seem to have retained independence from
one another.

BENGUELA RAILWAY. One of Zambia's outlets to the African
coast, this railway was built in 1931 by a British firm, Tanganyika Concessions, Ltd. (Tanks), a company that also owned
a part of the Congolese mining company, Union Miniere du
Haute-Katanga. The railway goes from Lubumbashi in Zaire
to Luso, Angola to the coast at Lobito, Angola. To reach
Lubumbashi, Zambia Railways connects with a branch of the
Congo-Katanga rail system (BCK). This route to Lobito is
about the same distance from the Copperbelt as the routes
that terminate at either Beira or Maputo (Lourenco Marques).
Nevertheless an agreement with Rhodesian Railways kept Zambian trade off the BCK-Benguela route from 1936 to 1956.
While Zambian imports and exports on this road have increased considerably since 1956 (especially because of Lobito's
location on the Atlantic shipping route), fighting in Angola both
before and after its independence in 1975 has made this means
of travel less reliable. Periodic guerrilla attacks have disrupted its operations.

BENSON, SIR ARTHUR EDWARD TREVOR. Governor of Northern
Rhodesia from 1954 to 1959. Born in England, December 21,
1907, he attended Oxford where he received a Master of Arts
degree. He joined the Colonial Office in the 1930's, and
after service in the War Office he came to Northern Rhodesia
as a district commissioner after World War II. He was also
secretary of the Central African Council and served in major
posts in Uganda and Nigeria before becoming Governor in 1954.
At that point he was given the task of preparing a constitution
which would take the Territory into its next stage of political
development. His job became very difficult as both Africans
and settlers were becoming more militant. While he sometimes came into conflict with Sir Roy Welensky, he was even
more determined to oppose more African self-rule and to destroy, if possible, the African nationalist parties, especially
Kenneth Kaunda's. He arrested many of ZANC's leaders,

blaming a Copperbelt state of emergency on them and comparing them to Chicago racketeers.   He said that the problems
were the result of a few men who threatened others much like
"Murder Incorporated. " Thus he banned ZANC in 1959, claiming that most other Africans favored Federation.   He was responsible for drawing up the "Benson Constitution" (q. v.).

BENSON CONSTITUTION.   A Constitution for Northern Rhodesia
that was drawn up by Sir Arthur Benson (q. v.), the Governor,
and presented to the Legislative Council in March, 1958.   It
went into effect the next year and thus is sometimes called
"the 1959 Constitution. " Benson prepared it after many consultations with white political groups and African members of
the Legislative Council but minimally with African nationalists.
It was a "multi-racial" constitution based in part on the Moffat Resolutions of 1954 (q. v.).   Simply put, a political balance
had to be found so no race predominated and all were protected.   Despite the complicated set of voter qualifications
which provided for a gradual transition to African majority
rule, Kaunda's supporters opposed it as providing too little,
too slow.   Revisions in the plan in a September, 1958, White
Paper favored the European voters over the Africans.   The
Constitution provided for thirty members of the Legislative
Council (twenty-two elected) and ten members of the Executive
Council (six elected, two of them Africans).   Native Authorities
were also given some added powers.   The ANC finally accepted
the Benson Constitution and participated in the 1959 elections.
Kaunda's ZANC boycotted them.   The Benson Constitution was
replaced by a new one in 1962.

BILONDA.   A Lunda leader and warrior, who led an army of his
people in the early eighteenth century.   The army traveled
eastward across the Luapula River, defeating the Shila people
and then moved northwest across the Tanganyika plateau.   Bilonda returned in triumph.   His successor, Kazembe II, further tightened Lunda control of the Luapula valley by 1740.

BISA.   One of the ten largest ethnic subdivisions in Zambia, the
Bisa constitute only about 3 percent of the population.   The
approximately 125,000 Bisa live mostly in the central part of
the eastern half of Zambia.   All Bisa chiefs originated in the
bena ng'ona (q. v.), or Mushroom Clan.   Its descent system is
matrilineal.   The Bisa speak the language of the Bemba, who
subdued them in the mid-nineteenth century.   The Bemba are
now their northern neighbors.
        The eighteenth and early nineteenth centuries saw the
Bisa at a peak of power.   Their land stretched to near the
present border with Malawi where they inhabited land currently belonging to the Yombe.   Likewise land to the north where
Bemba now live was also controlled by the Bisa.   They were
heavily involved in trade, dealing in ivory, slaves, and copper,
as well as cloth they made from their own cotton.   The Bisa
were so large that one group, the Tambo, broke off and moved

north to a less crowded area, eventually losing their Bisa
identity. Between 1760 and 1860 the Bisa, along with their
allies, the Lunda of King Kazembe, dominated Zambia's north-
eastern trade to the coast. Near the end, however the Bisa
chiefs found their land being attacked by the Bemba, Lunda (to
whom they paid tribute), and even the Ngoni to the east and
south. Part of the problem was that the five principal Bisa
chiefs, Matipa (Lubumbu); Kopa (Mwansabamba), Mungulube,
Mukungule, and Chibesakunde, never united. As five separate chiefdoms (and there were other smaller ones) without
binding alliances, they were very vulnerable to more centralized groups, especially the Bemba.

BLEDISLOE COMMISSION. Led by Lord Bledisloe, a former
Governor General of New Zealand, this Commission (appointed
at the end of 1937) spent three months the next year in the
Rhodesias and Nyasaland interviewing people of all races concerning the future government of these areas and possible
amalgamation. Reporting in early 1939, it noted that greater
cooperation between the territories would inevitably develop
but that current differences, in native policies and ratios between the races for example, would not allow amalgamation
for some time. It did suggest that Northern Rhodesia and
Nyasaland could be combined without delay, and that an inter-
territorial council to advise in coordinating future development
for all three could be set up. The war in Europe that same
year prevented implementing the proposals. The council,
called the Central African Council, was formed in 1945.
Some observers note that the Commission was significant because of the attention it paid to African critics of current native policies, the result being a postponement of amalgamation
with Southern Rhodesia.

BOMA. An African word used commonly, especially in Eastern
Zambia, to indicate any colonial administrative headquarters.
It usually included a small settlement, and was often sur-
rounded by a stockade for security.

BOTSWANA. A southern neighbor of Zambia, bordering at a
small map point along the Zambezi River (see Botzam Road).
It has been independent from England since September 30,
1966, under the leadership of Sir Seretse Khama. Prior to
that it was called Bechuanaland. Only the Caprivi Strip separates more of Botswana from southwestern Zambia. Many
peoples traversed this border region, notably the Kololo (or
Makololo) of Sebituane (q.v.) in the mid-nineteenth century.
They had a great impact on the history of various Zambian
peoples, especially the Barotse. Many missionaries also
entered Zambia by this route, some as friends of Tswana
leaders, notably the great Bamangwato leader, Khama the
Great.

BOTZAM ROAD. A three hundred and sixty-five kilometer road

in Botswana from Nata to Kazangula that was opened formally
on January 20, 1977, built largely with American financial aid.
At Kazangula the road ends at a ferry which transports traffic
to the Zambian side of the Zambezi River. It is significant
as a controversial point of contact, as South Africa has maintained that Zambia and Botswana have no common border
point. Southern African freedom fighters could utilize this
route from or to Zambia in addition to its value as a trade
route.

BRELSFORD, WILLIAM VERNON. Author of numerous books on
the peoples of Northern Rhodesia, especially on the Bemba in
whose area he served in the Colonial Service for many years.
He was born in England and educated at Oxford University.
He came to Northern Rhodesia in the Colonial Service in 1930.
In 1937-1938 he established the Rhodes-Livingstone Institute
and Museum. Later he served as Director of Information
first in Northern Rhodesia, and then in the Federation from
1953 to 1960. He was a Southern Rhodesian Member of Parliament from 1962 to 1965.

BRITISH CENTRAL AFRICAN PROTECTORATE (or BRITISH CEN-
TRAL AFRICA). The term used from 1893 to 1907 to denote
the territory to the east of Zambia. It was first declared to
be a Protectorate in 1891 but the official Order in Council
came in 1893. In 1907 it was renamed the Nyasaland Protectorate. After independence in 1964 it became the Commonwealth
of Malawi.

BRITISH COLONIAL OFFICE. On April 1, 1924, administrative
control of Northern Rhodesia was passed to the British Colonial Office from the British South Africa Company. The first
Colonial Governor was Sir Herbert Stanley, a South African.
The change was initiated by settlers who protested a company-
imposed income tax. The coming of formal rule by the Colonial
Office (rather than just supervision of company administration)
brought also a fourteen member legislature composed of five
white settlers and nine Colonial Office men.

BRITISH SOUTH AFRICA COMPANY (BSAC). A company devoted
primarily to exploiting mineral resources north of the Limpopo
River, it was granted a Royal Charter on October 29, 1889,
by Queen Victoria. The petitioners were led by Cecil Rhodes
(q.v.), but included the Dukes of Abercorn and Fife, Lord
Gifford and George Grey among others. Action soon followed
as explorers and company representatives quickly made contacts with African chiefs in the area, mostly limited to what
became the Rhodesias and Nyasaland. Harry Johnston and Albert Sharpe made treaties in 1890 with chiefs in Nyasaland
(soon called British Central Africa) and eastern Northern Rhodesia. Lewanika (q.v.) of the Lozi signed with Frank Lochner
of the Company in 1890 to give the BSAC rights in much of
the western part of the country. Agreements with Africans in

Southern Rhodesia came the same year. In exchange for
Rhodes' promise to pay administrative costs and supervise the
territory, Great Britain had granted the BSAC the right to allocate lands and settle whites in the area as well as giving
the company all mining rights.

The company had little real interest in Northern Rhodesia. It was included only because of the suspicion that
copper existed there and further north in Katanga. The company did little with Northern Rhodesia. A few copper mines
were begun and a railway to Katanga was also installed. A
tax on Africans to help meet administrative costs of the few
bomas (q.v.) forced the Africans to find work on white farms
or mines in one of the Rhodesias or Katanga. The presence
of the administrators also ended some of the inter-tribal warfare and Arab slave trade. Finally resentment of the company
by white settlers pushed it to transfer administrative control
to the British Colonial Office in 1924.

Although the BSAC had its greatest financial interests
in Southern Rhodesia, it continued to receive mineral royalties
from the other areas as well. By its charter its mineral
royalty rights would not be terminated until 1986. It also became involved through investment in many of the mining companies. In the year prior to Zambian independence, Kaunda
and his Government offered to buy out BSAC royalty rights for
$150 million, equal to about six years of normal royalty pay-
ments. The BSAC negotiators hesitated to accept this and
Kaunda reduced the offer to $12 million and forced a settle-
ment. Early the next year, in February, 1965, the company
announced it was terminating its activities in Zambia and selling its real estate to the Government.

BROKEN HILL. A major city in central Zambia along the line of
rail. It is about half way between Lusaka and the Copperbelt.
Since independence it has been renamed Kabwe (q.v.). It is
the site of both the important Broken Hill mine (q.v.) and an
important archeological discovery called the Broken Hill man
(q.v.).

BROKEN HILL MAN (or RHODESIAN MAN). The earliest human
skeletal remains found in South Central Africa were found in
1921 in central Zambia at the present city of Kabwe (formerly
Broken Hill). The human skull was found accidentally during
mining operations. Some anthropologists think it is related
closely to the Neanderthal man found elsewhere in the world
(thus Homo sapiens), while others feel it might be a late example of Homo erectus. The skull had large teeth, a pro-
nounced brow, a low forehead, and a large brain. Broken
Hill man probably lived about 30,000 years ago. The remains
are now in the British Museum of Natural History in London.
A cave at Broken Hill has also yielded stone implements and
bone and ivory tools.

BROKEN HILL MINE. A multi-ore mining operation at Kabwe

(formerly Broken Hill) in central Zambia. The mineral potential was first discovered by Thomas G. Davey (q.v.) in 1902.
The mine was opened in 1906 and is still producing. Its main
products have been lead and zinc, but it also has produced
quantities of silver, cadmium, vanadium, and copper. The
Anglo-American Corporation group controls the mine. The
existence of the lead and zinc was the motivation for extending the line of rail north of the Zambezi to Broken Hill. The
name "Broken Hill" was given by Davey who saw a similarity
in the geological configuration to a mine in Australia by that
name.

THE BROKEN HILL NATIVE WELFARE ASSOCIATION. An Afri-
    can association formed in 1930 by a civil servant, P. J. Sila-
    we, to assist Africans in taking matters of common interest
    before the government. Such matters involved schools, hospi-
    tals, and markets, among others. While independent, the
    Broken Hill Association was similar to other Native Welfare
    Associations found in other communities in Northern Rhodesia
    prior to an elected Legislative Council.

BU-. A Bantu language prefix that frequently indicates "the coun-
    try of ... " when linked to the name of some Bantu people.
    For example, Bulozi is the land of the Lozi.

BUILD A NATION (BAN) CAMPAIGN. A special program begun in
    November, 1961, by the United Federal Party, it was orga-
    nized to win African support for the Central African Federa-
    tion's racial "partnership" principle. It was a well-financed
    campaign clothed in the disguise of non-partisan politics, but
    Africans recognized its origin in Welensky's party (the UFP)
    and the campaign failed. It was stopped after several months.

BUKANA. A specially designed fighting axe used by Mbunda
    tribesmen who fought alongside their Lozi allies during several
    mid-nineteenth-century campaigns, notably against the Luvale
    and Nkoya.

BULOZI (or NGULU). The flood plain of the Zambezi River run-
    ning north to south through Western Zambia, it is considered
    by the Lozi to be the core of their homeland. It is about a
    hundred miles long, and ranges in width between ten and thirty
    miles. It is usually flooded for the first several months of
    the year. It is bordered on east and west by forests and
    higher ground. Additionally the term may be used to refer to
    all of the land belonging to the Lozi.

BULUBA. Also called Kola, it is the area of the Congo from
    which the Bemba reportedly emigrated to northeastern Zambia
    about the end of the seventeenth or early eighteenth centuries.
    Buluba's exact location is unknown but was probably in the Ka-
    tanga region of Zaire (Congo).

BURTON, MRS. LILLIAN. The victim of a violent attack that
provoked much reaction throughout Northern Rhodesia and elsewhere. A white housewife, she was driving her car in Ndola
on May 8, 1960. Her car was stopped, purportedly by an
angry crowd of UNIP supporters whose rally (held in defiance
of a ban) had been broken up by the police. Gasoline was
thrown into the car and ignited. Mrs. Burton saved her two
daughters but, after a week, she died of the burns. Many of
all races were horrified and outraged. Hundreds of UNIP
members were arrested and UNIP was banned on the Copperbelt. Kaunda apologized to the widower, Mr. Robert Burton,
saying that he preached only non-violence but that some hooli-
gans can spoil any good intentions. Some Africans reacted
that too much fuss was being made over one white death by
comparison to centuries of cruelty to black Africans. In later
political campaigns the "Burton murder" was used by some
white politicians to oppose black nationalists.

BUSH, RONALD. Secretary for Native Affairs in Northern Rhodesia in the early 1950's. He succeeded Rowland Hudson in
that position in 1949. Bush was not very sympathetic to the
founders of the African National Congress. He worked toward
getting the African masses to favor the plan for a Federation
in opposition to the ANC.

BUSHMEN. A nomadic people, Khoisan-speaking, who have inhabited much of central and southern Africa. Small in stature and
presumably of different racial stock from most Bantu Africans,
they appear to have lived in many sections of Zambia in the
course of past centuries. Only a few now remain in Zambia,
mostly in the extreme southwestern part.

BUTLER, ROBERT A. Britain's Home Secretary in March, 1962,
when Prime Minister Harold Macmillan appointed him Secretary of State for Central African Affairs. Roy Welensky
favored this, and Africans were suspicious. "RAB" Butler
visited Northern Rhodesia in May, 1962, and pressured Federation officials to accelerate voter registration among Africans.
Ultimately, in December, 1962, it was Butler who agreed in
principle that Nyasaland could secede from the Central African
Federation, confirming that the Federation was dead.

THE BUXTON REPORT OF 1921. The product of a commission
led by Lord Buxton, it was primarily a report to the British
South Africa Company encouraging a referendum in Southern
Rhodesia; it also suggested policy north of the Zambezi. It
recommended establishing a Legislative Council in Northern
Rhodesia, and a survey of settler ideas. It also suggested
that a case could be made by the Africans that much of the
land belonged to them.

BWALWA. A kind of home-brewed beer produced in the Northern
Province of Zambia.

BWANA. A title roughly meaning "boss" given by many Zambians
to white men during the colonial period. The term is also
found in other parts of central and eastern Africa.

BWANA MKUBWA MINE. One of the oldest producing copper
mines in Zambia, it is located within the boundaries of a
modern city, Ndola. Excavation and smelting was done there
by Africans long before Europeans found it. One of the old
excavations was half a mile long and as deep as 160 feet. A
trader, Robert Wright, showed it to William Collier and Jock
Donohoe of the Rhodesia Copper Company in 1902. Actual production by Europeans did not begin until 1913 and has been
sporadic since then. Its reopening in late 1970 has made
Ndola a mining center as well as an administrative capital.
An eminent author, C. M. Doke, states that the Lamba people
had called Robert E. Codrington (q. v.), a representative of the
British South Africa Company, Bwana M'Kubwa. Another writer, A. J. Wills, says the same name was attached to a different administrator, Moffat Jones. The mine was reopened
in 1970 (after being closed for over thirty years) by Nchanga
Consolidated Copper Mines, Ltd., formerly the Anglo-American
Corporation.

BWEMBYA. Predecessor as Chitimukulu to the great Chitapankwa,
he served as principal leader of the Bemba nation for only a
brief period around 1860. He succeeded his brother, Chileshye,
despite speech difficulties and some mental impairment. As it
soon became evident that raids by Ngoni warriors would endanger the nation, the bakabilo (q. v.) agreed that Bwembya
must be replaced. Chitapankwa was given the babenye (q. v.)
and installed as Chitimukulu. Bwembya retired to another village, where he died.
        In the mid-twentieth century another Bwembya rose to
prominence. This man served as Chikwanda IV from 1935 to
1946 when he became Nkula IV. He relinquished this post in
1970 to become the Chitimukulu.

BWILA. Meaning "the land of the Ila," from the Bantu language
form "Bu-ila." The Ila (q. v.) live in central and southern
areas of western Zambia.

BWILE. A very small Bemba-speaking tribal group living on the
eastern edge of Lake Mweru on the northern border of Zambia.
Their economy is based mostly on fishing. In the mid-eighteenth century they had been defeated by the Lunda of Kazembe
further south, along the Luapula River.

- C -

CABINET. The Zambian Cabinet consists of the ministers of a
large and variable number of executive departments plus ministerial heads for each of the eight provinces. Thus, while the

independence constitution limited the Cabinet to fourteen members, it now has regularly about twenty-three ministries. The
titles and tasks of some of them have changed periodically, as
reorganization occurred regularly, notably in 1969. Also the
people holding the posts have shifted frequently to other ministries, almost like musical chairs. Thus executive efficiency
has been retarded. Though the Cabinet consisted of a number
of important advisors to the President at independence, since
1968 it has met less frequently and only debates the more important issues. The power of the President has increased by
comparison to the Cabinet. Early in Zambia's independence
the President was extremely conscious of ethnic balance in the
Cabinet. This has not been considered as important today,
but it also is not ignored. Until February, 1969, there was a
Secretary to the Cabinet. This post was replaced by that of a
Secretary General to the Government, who is in charge of the
Cabinet office. The Cabinet has also been subdivided into different committees. By 1966 it was already broken into sixteen
committees, some standing, while others were ad hoc. Generally speaking the Cabinet has lost some of its significance, in
part because the President has chosen to rely more on certain
close aides than on the Cabinet, which no longer meets weekly.
The President may nominate as ministers individuals who were
not elected to the national assembly, or he may select elected
members. Under the new constitution, decisions of the Cabinet are subordinate to those of the UNIP central committee.

CALO. The Cibemba word for the chiefdom. This is the basic
unit for administration and there are about twenty of them
among the Bemba. Within it the chief dispensed justice, received tribute and commanded military service. Its borders
are frequently natural features such as rivers and streams.
Traditional Bemba chiefdoms do not play a major role in
modern Zambia.

CAMINHO DE FERRO DE BENGUELA (CFB). The formal name
of the Benguela Railway (q.v.).

CAPRICORN AFRICA SOCIETY. A very controversial organization
with branches throughout East and Central Africa (including the
area near the Tropic of Capricorn, thus its name). It ultimately became active in politics in many of the countries. In
Zambia it influenced the formation of the Constitution Party
and the Central Africa Party (qq.v.). It was founded in 1949
by Colonel David Stirling, originally with the idea of supporting an East and Central African Federation. Ultimately Stirling's vision switched to the idea of encouraging a common
citizenship or patriotism that would unite people of all races.
After a couple of years of preparation it produced a Capricorn
contract which called for rights and freedom for all, the end
to all racial discrimination, and the establishment of a qualified right to vote which would give some better qualified individuals (usually Europeans) as many as six votes, while most

Africans would have only one or two. While some Europeans saw this as a moderate organization with realistic goals based on ideals such as the establishment of racial harmony in a true multi-racial society, many Africans saw it as just another attempt to restrict true democracy of a one-man/one-vote type, and a subterfuge to allow Europeans to continue to rule by frequently raising the qualifications. Many Europeans, on the other hand, saw it as being far too liberal in its concessions to the Africans. Despite its widespread organization and such things as a series of interracial conferences at Salima on the shores of Lake Nyasa in 1956, the Capricorn Society never attained many real successes.

CAPRIVI STRIP. A long finger of land reaching across northern Botswana and southern Angola and Zambia, it is currently being governed by the Republic of South Africa under the original League of Nations mandate that took all of South West Africa from the Germans and placed it under South African supervision (but not sovereignty). Germany got the Caprivi Strip as part of the Anglo-German Concordat of 1890 (q.v.), despite Lozi protests to the British that it was a legitimate part of Barotseland and could not be given away. The Germans wanted the land along the Chobe River because it would give them access to the Zambezi River. Decades earlier the land had been under the Makololo rule of Chief Sebituane. In fact Sebituane himself stayed at Linyanti in the present Caprivi Strip. After the Makololo were defeated the Lozi claimed the area, as one of the major Lozi administrative centers was at Sesheke (just across the Zambezi from the Caprivi Strip).

In contemporary times the area has taken on added significance as Africans struggling to free Namibia (South West Africa) from South Africa have set up offices in Lusaka. One group was even called the Caprivi African National Union. Also in 1965 the South Africans set up an Air Force base in the Strip near the Zambian border. Refugees from both Angola and Namibia have used the strip as a two way route to and from Zambia. Finally, a controversy over the exact end point of the Strip has existed, with Botswana claiming the right to a small water border with Zambia at the Strip's tip. A bridge has been proposed where currently a ferry boat links the two countries.

CARDEN, LT. COL. JOHN. Acting administrator of North Western Rhodesia from October, 1907, to February, 1908.

CARLTON HOUSE TERRACE CONFERENCE. Held in January, 1953, in London, this was the final intergovernmental conference which decided upon the constitution for the Central African Federation. All the delegates were Europeans, as the Africans boycotted the meeting. They had previously informed the British of their opposition to the whole idea of a Federation.

CASSAVA. Also called manioc, it is a starchy root that is a
staple crop in some of the poorer agricultural areas of Zambia.
It is a popular part of the diet in the western third of the country and also in the area near the Luapula River and Lake Bangweulu, but it is found to some extent almost everywhere in the
country. It was first brought in to Zambia by Portuguese
traders as the Portuguese had found it in the Western Hemis-
phere. It came into the country from Angola in about the
eighteenth century. It is estimated that about 145,000 metric
tons of the crop is grown annually.

CENTRAL AFRICA. Perhaps too vague a term to define, it was
used by many people in different parts of Africa to mean a
variety of territories or areas. For Zambians, however, the
term could refer either to the area covered by the Central
African Federation (thus Northern and Southern Rhodesia and
Nyasaland), or in a different context to Nyasaland, which had
been known as the British Central African Protectorate from
1893 to 1907.

CENTRAL AFRICA PARTY (CAP). A party formed early in 1959
as a liberal (actually moderate), multi-racial party to compete
in the 1959 territorial elections. Like its predecessor, the
Constitution Party (q.v.), it was inspired in part by the principles of the Capricorn Africa Society (q.v.). Its best known
leader was Garfield Todd, former Prime Minister of Southern
Rhodesia and past leader of the old United Rhodesia Party.
He had split with the United Federal Party, and his URP had
been firmly defeated in June, 1958, elections. The CAP was
formed from the liberal wing of the URP, combined with many
of the members of the merging Constitution Party, notably John
Moffat and Harry Franklin. The party was a moderate party
of whites and blacks who believed in a multi-racial state based
on true partnership. They wanted the principles behind the
Federal Constitution fully supported, therefore bringing Africans eventually to full leadership in the Federation. This approach satisfied neither the African nationalists nor the European supremacists, yet it attracted some support from each
race. It also advocated an immediate end to all racial discrimination. In the 1959 elections Todd and his supporters
failed to win a single seat in Southern Rhodesia. Moffat and
his colleagues were more successful in Northern Rhodesia.
Moffat and Franklin beat UFP candidates in the two European
reserved constituencies, and A. H. Gondwe, an African, won
a 'Special Constituency.'' When Todd resigned from the party
in 1960, the Southern Rhodesian section became even weaker
and less effective. Meanwhile in October 1960, Moffat changed
the name of the Northern Rhodesia section of the CAP to the
Northern Rhodesia Liberal Party (q.v.).

CENTRAL AFRICAN AIRWAYS CORPORATION. The parent company of Central African Airways, the national airline of the
Federation of Rhodesia and Nyasaland. The CAA was created

on June 1, 1946. Its roots go deeper to the Rhodesia and
Nyasaland Airways Ltd. that was formed in 1933 but which
was absorbed into the war effort in 1939 and became known as
the Southern Rhodesian Air Services (SRAS). Despite its name,
it operated essential air services in all three territories. After World War II the CAA was set up, taking over the SRAS
fleet of planes. Capital for new equipment came from all
three territories: 50 percent from Southern Rhodesia, 35 percent from Northern Rhodesia, and 15 percent from Nyasaland.
It provided services between the parts of the Federation and to
and from outside territories. When the Federation was dissolved at the end of 1963 it became an international agency,
but it began to formally break up after Southern Rhodesia's
Unilateral Declaration of Independence in November, 1965. Its
assets were to be divided, with Nyasaland receiving 10 percent
and Zambia and Rhodesia splitting 90 percent equally. Final
dissolution of the CAA Corporation occurred at the end of
1967, several months after Zambia Airways began operations.

CENTRAL AFRICAN COUNCIL. A forerunner of the Central African Federation, it was originally suggested by the Bledisloe
Commission (q.v.). Its formation was announced in 1944 and
held its first meeting in June, 1945. It met twice a year
thereafter until 1953. It consisted of the Governors of Northern
and Southern Rhodesia and Nyasaland and three ordinary members chosen by the government of each territory. In fact the
latter were always leading political figures. It succeeded in
coordinating communications between the territories and solved
some problems concerning migrant labor. It also extended
some Southern Rhodesian services to the other territories.
While the Council was seen by some as a step toward amalgamation, it didn't go far enough to satisfy many settler leaders.
While it was purely an advisory body with no real executive
powers, it concerned itself with a very broad range of common
services and problems, seeking ways to coordinate action. In
this sense it laid the groundwork for many activities of the
later Federation.

CENTRAL AFRICAN FEDERATION. Also called the Federation of
Rhodesia and Nyasaland, it came into being in October, 1953,
as the result of many years of urging by Europeans in Northern
and Southern Rhodesia and Nyasaland who saw many possible
benefits personally from increased levels of co-operation.
Southern Rhodesians especially saw the copper wealth of the
North as an attraction, whereas Europeans in the two Northern
territories saw greater security coming from associating with
the higher percentage of Europeans south of the Zambezi River.
Godfrey Huggins (q.v.) and Roy Welensky (q.v.) were major
moving figures in the establishment of the Federation. The
actual bill passed the British Parliament in May, 1953, and
was approved by Queen Elizabeth I on August 1, 1953. The
Federation was ruled by a Federal Parliament based in Salisbury, Southern Rhodesia and by a Prime Minister. Each of
the three territories also had its own legislature.

The end of the federation was the result of rising movements of African nationalism led by Dr. H. K. Banda in Nyasaland, and Kenneth Kaunda in Northern Rhodesia.   When they
precipitated the failure of the Federal Review Conference of
December, 1960, and Dr. Banda soon got approval to move
Nyasaland toward secession, the end of the Federation came
into signt.   The Federation flag was finally lowered for the
last time at the end of December, 1963.

CENTRAL AFRICAN MAIL.   Newspaper founded originally in 1960
with financial aid from the London Observer, it was first
called the African Mail.   It was at that time the only newspaper in Northern Rhodesia that was oriented toward the Africans and that supported nationalist goals.   As such it had a
strong impact on African public opinion.   The paper changed
its name to the Central African Mail in 1962.   Its editorial
policy was strongly anti-Federation and for "one-man, one-
vote" as well as for independence.   It was a weekly newspaper
in 1965 when the Observer withdrew its support and the Government bought the paper and called it the Zambia Mail.   It is now
the Zambia Daily Mail (q. v.).

CENTRAL AFRICAN PEOPLE'S UNION.   A party that existed during 1962, but mostly just in the mind of its President, Dixon
Konkola (q. v.).   It surfaced early in 1962 when Konkola campaigned for a seat in the Federal Parliament.   The April 27,
1962, election chose two Northern Rhodesia Africans for the
Parliament.   Konkola and Edward Mukelabai actually campaigned
under another party name, the National Republican Party (q. v.).
They received only twenty-two and twenty-five votes, but they
won, as only 1.37 percent of the eligible electorate voted.
The CAPU supported the continued existence of the Federation.
It reportedly received aid from both the United Federal Party
and from Moise Tshombe in Katanga.   Late in 1962 the CAPU
reportedly "merged" with the ANC.

CENTRAL COMMITTEE OF UNIP.   As a result of the 1973 Constitution that made Zambia a one party state, UNIP's Central
Committee is superior to even the Cabinet.   In the early days
of UNIP, however, the Central Committee was simply a party
matter, its permanent executive.   It had the power to call
periodic meetings of the National Council, the Party's chief
policy-making organ.   A 1962 reorganization of the Party gave
it additional powers.   It was to appoint full-time regional organizing secretaries, who were then responsible to it.
       In August, 1967, elections to the Central Committee
caused a major split in the Party, only partly smoothed over
by President Kaunda.   It remained disunited.   This surfaced
again in August, 1969, when Simon Kapwepwe (q. v.) resigned
from the vice-presidency.   While perhaps not related to this,
several hours later Kaunda dissolved the Central Committee
and assumed Party power directly, aided by an interim executive committee, which was not very powerful.   In March, 1970,

the Chuula Commission (q. v.) issued a draft for a new UNIP
constitution.   Its proposals for the Central Committee, however, were rejected.   Instead, new provisions in 1971 called
for a twenty-five member Central Committee consisting of
twenty members elected by the general party conference every
five years, the secretary general, and four nominated members.
Under the party constitution of 1971, however, it was less
powerful than under the 1967 arrangement.   Still it was, however, the party's most important administrative organ.   The
previous party squabbles over ethnic balance were bowed to in
the 1971 changes by suggesting that choices should be based on
both merit and the need to represent all parts of the country.
The constitution called for the outgoing Committee to draw up
an official slate of candidates for approval of the rest of the
party.   Presumably this would avoid the divisive politicking of
the 1967 general conference.   At the May, 1971, conference, a
geographically balanced slate was presented and elected.   Also
it was decided that no Cabinet Minister could be simultaneously
a member of the Central Committee.

The new national constitution creating the Second Zambian Republic in 1973 did not produce major changes in the
Committee, but added significant powers.   With UNIP now the
sole recognized party, its Central Committee reviews the lists
of candidates for office and can disallow some if it chooses.
It is divided into eight subcommittees, roughly equivalent to
Cabinet divisions.   In fact the Committee has more powers
than the Cabinet, whose decisions are subordinate to the Central Committee.   All members of the Committee must be full-
time officials of UNIP.

CENTRAL PROVINCE.   The province that lies basically at Zambia's narrow neck south of the Congo Pedicle and also covers
land to the east and west of this area.   Its districts include
Serenje, Mkushi, Mumbwa, Feira, Kabwe (both Rural and Urban) and Lusaka (also both Rural and Urban).   Its total population in 1969 was nearly three quarters of a million people.
The major ethnic groups in the area are the Lala, Ambo, Soli,
Swako, Lenje, Sala, Ila, Luano, and Nsenga.

CEWA.   Variant of Chewa (q. v.).

"CHA CHA CHA" CAMPAIGN.   The term reportedly made its first
appearance at a speech Kenneth Kaunda gave to a party conference at Mulungushi on July 9, 1961.   It eventually came to
symbolize a campaign of political consciousness and civil disobedience that would result in the British and Northern Rhodesian Governments conceding independence for Zambia.   The
term derived directly from the popular dance of the day.
Kaunda's impassioned speech had the theme that the time to
act was now, but he insisted that all action must be non-
violent.   As he spoke, the phrase "cha cha cha" was heard
repeatedly through the audience.   The interpretation was
varied, but to many it meant that it was time to "face the

music" and everyone was expected to join in the "dance. "
Even Sir Roy Welensky and the Queen will have to learn the
Cha-Cha-Cha, it was said. Despite Kaunda's plea for non-
violence, UNIP youths in some provinces burned schools and
destroyed bridges and roads. But many demonstrations were
peaceful, such as burning bonfires of identification cards or
"passes" (q. v.). Perhaps it was the widespread nature of the
campaign that convinced the British that this unified nationalist
movement could not be ignored.

CHADIZA. A town in the extreme southeast part of the Eastern
province of Zambia, it is near the sites of several good examples of rock art (q. v.), notably that at Sejamanja and at
Mbangombe. The flat plateau country nearby has some kopjes
and outcrops of granite and quartzite. Much game formerly
roamed the area and the area became populated with hunters.

CHAFISI HILL. A site between Chipata and Chadiza in southeastern Zambia where there are some good examples of rock
art, notably outline drawings of "reptiles. "

CHAKULYA, WILSON MOFYA FRANK. A long-time political and
labor activist who ultimately served in the Zambian cabinet
from 1971 to 1973. As early as 1953, when the African National Congress formed a Youth League, its leadership was
given to Chakulya by Kaunda and Nkumbula. After the split
between the two, he eventually joined UNIP. In the area of
labor unions, Chakulya had been active in the Reformed Trade
Union Congress and became an officer of the United Trade
Union Congress after the merger of the opposing Congresses.
Later he served as general secretary of the Zambia Congress
of Trade Unions (q. v.). In 1969 he became the first trade
union officeholder to be elected to Parliament, winning the
Copperbelt seat of Kantanshi. In April, 1971, he was appointed a Cabinet Minister, serving as Minister of the Central
Province until June when he was made the Minister of Labour
and Social Services. He served in that capacity until December 5, 1973, as he was defeated in the general election on
that date. He was then appointed by the Government as managing director of Nchanga Consolidated Copper Mines. In 1976
he entered the diplomatic service as an Ambassador.

CHAMBESHI RIVER (or CHAMBEZI; CHAMBESI). Beginning in the
northeastern corner of Zambia, the river flows in a southwesterly direction, passing through the Bangweulu swamps in a
large number of channels. Some of them find their way to
Lake Bangweulu, but most of them empty into the Luapula
River enroute to Lake Mweru. Among its tributaries are the
Luchindashi and Kalungu Rivers.

CHAMBEZI DISTRICT (or CHAMBESHI). A district created in the
northeastern corner of Zambia by the British South Africa
Company in the late 1890's. It became the location of several

of the Company's early outposts.   It was later renamed the
North Luangwa District of the Northern Province of Northern
Rhodesia.   Today the area is all or part of the Isoka, Chin-
sali, and Lundazi Districts.

CHAMBISHI MINE.   One of the major mines on the Copperbelt that
is owned by the Roan Consolidated Mines Ltd. (q.v.).   It is
located at the small new settlement called Chambishi that was
created in 1965 when the mine was opened.   Its location is
about halfway between Nchanga and Kitwe, with the latter being
near the center of the Copperbelt and Chambishi being to its
north.

CHANGALA.   An early ancestor of the Mambwe paramount Chief
Nsokolo, he probably lived in the eighteenth century.   It is
also the name of a mid-nineteenth century "perpetual son" of
the Bemba Chief Makosa.

CHANGUFU, LEWIS MUTALE.   A Zambian businessman who was
one of the early nationalist activists and remained active in
both UNIP and numerous Cabinet positions until his defeat in
the December, 1973, general elections.   Born in Kasama, October 5, 1927, he attended school in both Kasama and Ndola
before entering the Civil Service.   He entered politics in 1950,
joining the Congress movement.   In 1953, as Congress Branch
Chairman for Lusaka he became active in bringing a successful end to discrimination in some of the butcheries which the
ANC was boycotting.   He lost his Civil Service job in 1954
because of his political activities.   He then became manager
of a printing company.
        In October, 1958, Changufu joined with Kaunda and
others in forming ZANC and was appointed to its executive
committee.   When the Government detained many ZANC activists in 1959, Changufu was arrested and sent to Chadizi for
seven months.   He returned to become UNIP's chief national
trustee and transport officer in January, 1960.
        After a brief period of study in the U.S.A. in 1963 he
returned home and was elected to Parliament from Mansa.
In the January, 1964, Government he was appointed Kaunda's
Parliamentary Secretary.   Later that year he helped put an
end to the Lumpa uprising of Alice Lenshina (q.v.).   At independence he was made Minister of State for Defense and Security, but several months later, in January, 1965, he entered the Cabinet as Minister of Information and Postal Services.   He then changed positions almost annually, serving
successively as Minister of Home Affairs, Labour and Health,
Home Affairs again (1970-72), Transport, and Home Affairs
again.
        He has always been considered to be a firm adminis-
trator, and a man who stood for law and order.   He has also
been a good party organizer and fund raiser, and has been a
trouble shooter for Kaunda.   In December, 1973, he lost his
bid for re-election to Parliament.   It has been suggested that

his support among his fellow Bemba was lost when he failed
to join Simon Kapwepwe in the United Progressive Party.
After his defeat he returned to private business.

CHAPLIN, SIR FRANCIS DRUMMOND PERCY. Administrator of
  Northern Rhodesia from March, 1921 until February, 1924.
  His appointment to this post stirred up major opposition among
  many Northern Rhodesians because he was simultaneously ad-
  ministering Southern Rhodesia. This seemed like a major step
  towards the amalgamation of the two territories that was opposed by so many in the North (as well as in the South) at that
  time.

CHEWA TRIBE (or CEWA). The third largest ethnic group in
  Zambia, comprising close to three hundred thousand people.
  The matrilineal Chewa are Nyanja-speaking and live in Malawi
  as well. Generally they inhabit the Eastern Province of Zambia, but they are of Congo origin, deriving originally from the
  Luba. In turn, the Nsenga are offshoots of the Chewa. They
  both are among those people known to early explorers as Maravi. The Maravi (or Malawi) evidently left the Congo as early
  as the fourteenth or fifteenth centuries. The Chewa around
  Chipata are the result of the expansion of a Chewa chiefdom
  called Undi (q.v.) which was in Mozambique around the seventeenth century. Some of the Chewa chiefs from Undi moved
  westward into Zambia, although many of them remained subordinate to Undi and sent back tribute. One group of Chewa
  under the chieftainship called Mwase moved up the Luangwa
  Valley as early as the eighteenth century. A Chewa Kingdom
  called Mkanda (q.v.) was especially strong and independent
  from Undi as early as the beginning of the nineteenth century.
  It was located in southeastern Zambia but somewhat north of
  Chipata. Despite its prosperity and strength it fell victim to
  the powerful Ngoni under Mpezeni (q.v.) who by 1880 had
  killed Mkanda and taken over his kingdom with the aid of Chikunda (q.v.). Under colonial rule the Chewa were very hard
  hit by their forced removal to African reserves around 1930.
  The new land was not at all sufficient to meet their agricultural needs. Another incident occurred because the British
  drew a boundary line through Chewa land, placing some in
  Nyasaland and some in Northern Rhodesia.

CHIBALE. A Senga Chief in the upper Luangwa valley during the
  1890's. An Arab named Kapandansalu built a stockaded village
  nearby that became a major slave market, buying slaves heavily from the Bemba. Thus the Bemba were disturbed when
  Chibale, who tolerated the Arabs, also allowed the British
  South Africa Company to build a station nearby at Mirongo.
  He hoped that the Company could free his people from the
  Arab dominance, as the Senga had to grow grain and hunt elephants for the Arabs. Chibale told Robert Young (q.v.) of the
  BSAC that Bemba leaders had threatened to cut off his head
  for allowing the Europeans to settle. On September 15, 1897,

the Arabs and some Bemba attacked Chibale's village. Young
arrived with fifteen policemen and forced out the attackers who
then laid siege. On September 21, reinforcements arrived for
the Company forces led by Charles McKinnon and the Arab
forces received a crushing defeat. Many were taken captive,
including Kapandansalu their leader, and hundreds of slaves
were released. The Bemba chiefs, especially Mwamba, were
very disturbed at the Company's success, as this was one of
several battles in which Bemba vulnerability to European forces
was demonstrated.

CHIBANGWA, HENRY. Outspoken leader of the Luanshya Native
    Welfare Association in the early 1930's. The association was
    not granted recognition by the Government, in part because of
    his "subversive activities." Even when brought before J. Mof-
    fat Thomson, the Secretary for Native Affairs, he repeated his
    demands for equal treatment and justice for Africans. He es-
    pecially opposed the pass system (q.v.) that was enforced
    against urban Africans.

CHIBANZA. A major chief of the Kaonde (q.v.) in northwestern
    Zambia during the nineteenth century. He controlled a copper
    mine at Kasanshi where bullets were cast for muzzle-loading
    guns. Nevertheless he was forced to send tribute to the Yeke
    leader, Msiri, in Katanga.

CHIBEMBA. Variant of Cibemba (q.v.).

CHIBESAKUNDA. One of the major chieftainships among the Bisa
    peoples of eastern Zambia. These chiefs belonged to the bena
    ng'ona, or Mushroom Clan, as did many other Bisa chiefs, but
    they were independent of the others and have kept distinct line-
    ages. During the 1870's much of the land of Chibesakunda was
    attacked by Bemba leaders and the Bisa were forced to move
    further east and north. Some lived as far north as the head
    of the Luangwa valley in the mid-1880's. Many years later,
    under the protection of British rule, the Bisa of Chibesakunda
    were allowed to reoccupy their original territory.

CHIBULUMA MINE. One of the smaller mines owned by Roan Con-
    solidated Mines Ltd. on the Copperbelt, it was opened in April,
    1956. It is located south of Chambishi and west of the major
    mining center of Kitwe.

CHIBWA MARSH AND SALT PANS (or CHIBWE). A major source
    of salt in the eastern half of Zambia, it is located along the
    Luitkila River. The salt, which became a major item for
    trade or sale in the area, was produced from the abundant
    supply of rich saline grass in the marsh along the river.
    Bemba and Bisa both used it for salt on occasion, and later
    it was sold to Europeans.

CHIEF JUSTICE. Under the constitution of Zambia's Second

Republic, the Supreme Court is the highest court of the land
and serves as the highest Court of Appeal. The Chief Justice
is appointed by the President, but can be removed only by an
independent Judicial Service Commission. As a result of an
incident in 1969, Zambia's first Chief Justice, James Skinner
(q.v.) resigned. He was replaced by Brian Doyle (q.v.).

CHIFUBWA STREAM. A rock shelter along this stream south of
Solwezi in north-central Zambia houses the most important collection of rock engravings found in Zambia. A mass of engravings are located along the back wall of the shelter. There
are good indications that they are from the Late Stone Age,
possibly dating more than two thousand years B.C. if neighboring carbon-dated findings are a good guide. The most common
motif of the engravings is an inverted V with a vertical bar
through the center, and they may have been painted originally.

CHIKANAMULILO. The senior Namwanga chief who successfully
beat off an attack by Chitapankwa and Makasa IV in 1877 but
who was defeated and put to flight by a subsequent Chitapankwa
(q.v.) raid in 1879. In January, 1891, the defeated chief
ceded his territory and all his peoples' rights to it in a document Alfred Sharpe (q.v.) put together for the African Lakes
Company. The Company paid the chief goods valued at fifty
pound sterling. It is very possible that the chief did not know
the nature of the agreement, but regardless, the property he
ceded was currently in the hands of a powerful Bemba leader
so hardly of use to him (or the British).

CHIKULO, DICKSON MUKWENJE. Formerly a UNIP member of
Parliament before he joined the United Party (q.v.) and became
its national treasurer.

CHIKUNDA. A name given by the Africans to a large and diverse
group of slave traders who ravaged the peoples of southeastern
Zambia and neighboring territories, especially in the last half
of the nineteenth century. The Portuguese Government gave
them titles to land west of Tete in order to control it indirectly. Some of the traders had escaped from the black slave
armies of Portuguese estates further east. Although of diverse
origin (many of them were of mixed race) they developed a
common cultural identity and a language (Nyungwe) that was a
mixture of several African tongues. Two of the most notorious
of this generally brutal breed were known as Kanyemba and
Matakenya. Their bases were usually just outside Zambia's
present borders but they terrorized much of the southeastern
part of the country. Some, however, got as far as the upper
Luapula River, and some Chikunda settled among the Lala,
Lenje, and Lamba. Some Chikunda, such as Matakenya, were
very wealthy and could put as many as twelve thousand armed
slaves into a battle. One group of Chikunda armed with mus-
kets fought alongside a dissident Lozi, Sikabenga, as far west
as Tonga country in 1885. Some Tonga also joined with the

slave trading Chikunda to their mutual advantage. One reason
Joseph Thomson (q.v.) was successful in getting treaties with
various Zambian chiefs and headmen was that they hoped he
could help protect them against the Chikunda. There are about
nine thousand descendants of these Chikunda living in Zambia
today.

CHIKWANDA. The title of one of the major chieftainships among
    the Bemba, it was established around 1830 when the Bemba in-
    vaded Bisa territory in the Chinama area, southeast of the
    Bangweulu swamps. The Bisa moved east, and the Bemba
    took over the Chibwa salt pans, the only source of salt on the
    plateau. The first holder of the title was Chikwanda I Nkum-
    bula, and he built his capital immediately south of the salt
    marsh. He eventually had a conflict over tribute to be paid
    to Chitimukulu, however, and also angered other senior Bemba
    chiefs. He was killed, perhaps in the late 1840's, by Bisa
    whom he had tried to placate after his arguments with the other
    Bemba.
        Chikwanda II Mutale Lwanga was not appointed to the post
    and the Chinama area until about the 1870's, and he too would
    have difficulties with Bisa. He reigned until 1913 and was
    quite successful. In 1898 a visitor reported an army of six
    hundred or more men at his court. Late in his reign, how-
    ever, a high-handed attitude alienated Bisa chiefs in the area,
    notably Nkuka, with whom he had a long dispute. He also ex-
    panded his area into that of the Lala, whom he frequently
    raided, stealing their cattle. In addition he developed his own
    access to the coastal trade. In 1913 he gave up his title and
    became Chitimukulu until his death in 1916.
        Chikwanda III Musungu left the chieftainship in 1935 and
    moved up to Nkula and later Chitimukulu.
        Chikwanda IV Bwembya served from 1935 until 1946 when
    he became Nkula and finally Chitimukulu.
        Chikwanda V Mutale served until 1970 when he became
    Nkula. He was one of the chiefs who followed the nationalist
    leaders in walking out of the Federal Review Conference (q.v.).

CHIKWANDA, ALEXANDER BWALYA. One of the rising political
    leaders of Zambia, he was born in December, 1938, at Kasana
    in the Northern Province. He attended Lund University in
    Sweden, then worked as a clerk at the mines and became ac-
    tive in politics on the Copperbelt. He joined UNIP as a con-
    stituency secretary in 1959 and served in several other posts.
    He won the Kitwe seat in Parliament in 1964. He was given
    several administrative posts in 1969 and 1970, the latter in
    the President's Office. In 1971 he was appointed Minister of
    National Guidance and was switched to Minister of Health in
    1972. In 1973 he was made Minister of Planning and Finance,
    and in 1975 was named Minister of Local Government and
    Housing.

CHILANGA. A major town just south of Lusaka along the line-of-

rail. It is the site of a major Government-sponsored plant
producing cement. The first cement plant was built there in
1951 and it was expanded in 1968.

CHILESHE, SAFELI. One of the moderate African nationalists,
his political career was from the 1940's to the 1960's. He
was a government employee in 1948 when he and another African were flown to London to sit in on talks concerning the
possibility of federation. The talks also included Roy Welensky
and the Northern Rhodesian Governor, Gilbert Rennie. When
he reported to the Federation of Welfare Societies about the
talks, he was denounced for even attending. Nevertheless, a
few years later he was elected to the African Representative
Council. This was in 1953 and followed his actions earlier
that year when he led a peaceful boycott of butcher shops in
Lusaka. Although he had been a founding member of the ANC,
he became one of the founders of the multi-racial Constitution
Party (q. v.) in 1957. He was also one of the Africans who
had been appointed to the Northern Rhodesian Legislative Council. He was denounced by the ANC for selling out the nationalist movement, but he responded by accusing it of using tactics
of intimidation. When the Government banned ZANC in 1959,
Chileshe sympathized with the desire for greater African political participation, but also said that few Africans approve
of gangster methods. In 1964, with independence around the
corner, Chileshe was appointed the first non-European mayor
of Lusaka.

CHILESHYE CHEPELA. An important Bemba Chitimukulu of the
nineteenth century who reigned for over three decades, from
the mid-1820's to about 1860. He was a distant relative of
Chiliamafwa (q. v.) a Chitimukulu, the son of his niece, so
was not normally in the line of succession. Indeed he was
born with a stunted arm and was abandoned by his mother.
Raised by others, he became quite close to Chiliamafwa and,
according to some, was the Chitimukulu's choice to succeed
him. Instead the bakabilo chose Susulu Chinchinta (q. v.), who
turned out to be a poor choice. Sometime around 1826 Chileshye deposed Chinchinta by raiding his capital while the bakabilo put up minimal resistance.
     Chileshye was responsible for the considerable expansion
of the Bemba sphere of influence. He took over a large trade
route through Bisa country from Kazembe (q. v.) of the Lunda,
for example. Chileshye's capital was at Kansansama, on the
northern bank of the Kalungu River. But the revival of the
Bisa in the 1850's and the coming of the Ngoni left the Bemba
with little more territory when he died in 1860 than when he
became Chitimukulu in the 1820's. One important development,
however, was that his accession and long reign switched the
regal line to a new branch of the royal clan.

CHILIAMAFWA. The Bemba Chitimukulu from about 1790 to about
1820. He was the successor of his uncle, Mukuuka (q. v.).

Among his more lasting acts was to appoint his son Kalulu as
the first holder of the Makasa title in the chiefdom of Mpanda
north of Lubemba. This both established a precedent and expanded the influence of the Chitimukulu. It was also the direct result of military action by the Bemba against their
northern neighbors, the Mambwe. In his last years, Chiliamafwa became very friendly with Chileshye Chepela (q. v.), who
would himself become Chitimukulu in less than a decade. He
died about 1820.

CHILILABOMBWE. A northern Copperbelt town and district, extremely near the Congo Pedicle and thus near the border with
Zaire. Prior to independence the town was named Bancroft
(see Bancroft Mine). The population of the district was about
forty-five thousand in 1969, up from thirty-four thousand in
1963. The town itself has about forty thousand people, many
of them miners. A major incident occurred there in August,
1968 led primarily by Lozi miners, many of them active in
the United Party (q. v.). The party was banned soon after the
disturbances.

CHILUFYA. An eighteenth-century leader of the Bemba, little
about his reign is known. His uncle was the great Chiti (q. v.),
and when Chiti's death was followed quickly by that of his brother
Nkole, their nephew Chilufya was chosen their successor. He
was the son of their sister Chilufya Mulenga. Because Chilufya was too young to rule, Chiti's half-brother, Chimba, served
as regent, holding the bows of Chiti and Nkole as symbols which
he eventually gave to the maturing Chilufya. It is thought that
Chilufya was succeeded by Mulenga, who was perhaps a brother.

CHIMBA. A half brother of Chiti (q. v.), the early Bemba leader
and founder, Chimba accompanied him on the great migration
to their new lands. He became keeper of the bows of both
Chiti and Nkole, eventually passing them on to their nephew
Chilufya who became Chitimukulu. Chilufya allowed Chimba to
keep Nkole's bow, and Chimba founded a village a few miles
north of the Kalungu River at Chatindubwi. Among the Bemba,
the current bearer of the Chimba title is also one of the six
senior bakabilo. These men, known as bashilubemba (q. v.)
resolve major issues, notably royal successions. In addition,
Chimba serves as Regent during the long burial ceremonies of
Chitimukulu, as the first Chimba had done.

CHIMBA, JUSTIN MUSONDA. One of the most prominent of the
early nationalist leaders, and ultimately a high ranking official
both in UNIP and in the Government. Born a Bemba in the
Northern Province, he eventually became active in the trade
union movement. In the early 1950's he was the organizing
Secretary and later the President of the Northern Rhodesian
General Workers Trade Union. In 1950 he became a co-
founder of the Anti-Federation Action Committee (q. v.). In
1951 this group joined the African National Congress, supporting

Harry Nkumbula as its leader. While he became a very active ANC member, he continued his union activities as well,
serving in the mid-1950's as a member of the Executive Committee of the African Trade Union Congress. In October,
1958, Chimba was a leader of the walk-out from the ANC conference, in protest of Nkumbula's leadership. He quickly became an activist in ZANC, organizing it in the Eastern Province. In 1959 he was detained by the Government for these
activities and was held in Barotseland. From 1961 to 1964
he served as UNIP's representative in Cairo and Dar es
Salaam. Upon his return for Zambia's Independence in 1964
he was appointed Deputy General Secretary of UNIP (a post he
held until 1969) and Minister of Labour and Mines. In January, 1965, however, he was made Minister of Justice. A
year later he switched to the Ministry of Labour and Social
Development, but in March he moved to the Ministry of Commerce and Industry (and Trade, later). In January, 1969, his
title changed to Minister of Trade, Industry and Mines, but he
became Minister of National Guidance two months later. In
January, 1971, he was appointed Minister of Trade and Industry, but became embroiled in controversy a couple of weeks
later and was dropped from the Government on January 29,
1971. The problem involved charges made by Chimba and
John Chisata that the Government was guilty of both a cover-
up and of tribalism for failing to prosecute certain non-Bemba
political figures. These accusations were investigated by the
Doyle Commission (q. v.) but the lack of firm evidence resulted
in Chimba's dismissal as well. In August, 1971, Chimba
joined Simon Kapwepwe's new United Progressive Party (q. v.),
and also became its Director of Youth. He was detained by
the Government in 1972; however, he filed suit against the
Government for assault ("degrading and humiliating treatment")
by the police and false imprisonment. A high court judge
awarded him K7000 (about $9800 U. S.) damages plus costs in
December, 1972. On September 9, 1977, he announced that
he would rejoin UNIP for the sake of national unity.

CHIMBOLA. A Bemba chieftainship held by bena ngandu whose
lineage is rather remote from the present ruling line. However, it was closely associated with the line of Chandaweyaya,
which held the position of Chitimukulu for several paramount-
cies until Chinchinta was overthrown by Chileshye (q. v.). The
Chimbola title is associated with the lineage that occupied
Iyaya, north of the Kalungu River but south of the Chambeshi
River.

CHIMBWI SHINTA. A Shimwalule (q. v.) of the Bemba in the
1880's and 1890's, he had administered the burial rites for
Chitimukulu Chitapankwa and other important Bemba leaders.
When Chitimukulu Sampa died in 1896 Chimbwa did not want
to relinquish his position, contrary to Bemba tradition where
a Shimwalule administers the rites for only one Chitimukulu.
The Mwamba ordered him to step down in favor of Chimbwi's

nephew. Chimbwi went to the BSAC administrator at the Mirongo Boma. There Robert Young (q. v.) agreed to look into the matter, but the nephew fled, leaving Chimbwi as burial priest.

CHINA, PEOPLE'S REPUBLIC OF. As a result of China's financing and building of the vital Tan-Zam Railway (q. v.), relations between the two countries have become very cordial. Actually relations began at independence when China established a chargé d'affaires in Lusaka, and Zambia announced its recognition of China and support for a U. N. seat. Numerous visits of Zambian ministers to China in 1965 and 1966 culminated in Kaunda's visit in June, 1967, the result of which was China's offer to provide the railway. This included an interest free loan of K286 million to cover the construction of the railway and the purchase of locomotives and rolling stock. Payment over thirty years was to begin in 1973. In order to minimize China's loss of foreign exchange, Zambia ordered the import of K33 million of Chinese goods in 1973. China is also helping to build a road to the Western Province. President Kaunda visited China again in 1974.

CHINCHINTA, SUSULA. Chitimukulu of the Bemba for a relatively few years in the 1820's, perhaps from about 1820 until 1826 or so. Chosen by the bakabilo over several other candidates, he was the third successive Chitimukulu from the lineage of Chandaweyaya. It was not long, however, before it was discovered that he was a bad choice. He was extremely harsh with the people, burning down their granaries if they didn't respond quickly enough to his call to work his fields. (One unsubstantiated report indicates he may also have been a leper.) Many Bemba decided that he had to be replaced. Finally his successor, Chileshye (q. v.), organized an opposition force and even arranged with some bakabilo to put up only token resistance to an attack. Thus Chileshye attacked the capital and Chinchinta fled to the land of the Mambwe chief, Nsokolo, where he soon died.

CHINGOLA. A city and district along the northern part of the Copperbelt, it is considered a twin city to its northern neighbor, Nchanga. Thus you will often see them written as Nchanga-Chingola. The city of Chingola had a huge population increase of 78 percent between 1963 and 1969, bringing the total to ninety-three thousand people. The rest of the district had only an additional ten thousand people. The reason for the increase was the Nchanga Mine, one of the largest open-pit copper mines in the world. The town's golf course is one of the best in southern Africa.

CHINSALI. A thinly populated district as well as a town in the Northern Province, it had a population of only fifty-eight thousand in 1969. At one time this area in the northeastern part of Zambia was part of the Chambeshi District under the BSAC,

and later was called the North Luangwa District after the river that began in the north-central portion of that district and
flowed south through it.   Two important religious figures made
a name in this area.   David Kaunda, father of Zambia's first
President, was the missionary pioneer in the area near the
beginning of this century.   It was in the mid-1950's that Alice
Lenshina (q. v.) began her Lumpa Church near the town of
Chinsali in the west-central part of the district.   It soon
spread to other parts of the district.

CHINSALI AFRICAN WELFARE ASSOCIATION.   One of the many
Welfare Associations (q. v.) which were to play an important
role in embryonic African nationalism in Zambia.   One of its
first major leaders was the Rev. Mr. Paul Mushindo, and two
of its most important young members in the early 1950's were
Kenneth Kaunda and Simon Kapwepwe.   In the 1950's two of its
secretaries were Reuben Mulenga and Samson Mukeya Mununga.
The Chinsali Association was strongly opposed to Federation
because it felt that "partnership" in practice might not turn
out to be what had been promised the Africans.   It was centered in the town of Chinsali.

CHINYAMA.   Reputedly a founder of the Luvale (or Lovale) tribe
of northwestern Zambia, as well as parts of Angola and Zaire.
This occurred around 1600 when a Luba clan called Tubungu
was splitting over the rights to the chieftainship.   Chinyama
and his two brothers disputed their sister's right to the position.   Her husband, Ilunga (q. v.), assumed the royal symbols
and ultimately led a branch of the Lunda.   Chinyama went west
with his clan and settled on the Luena River near the upper
Zambezi River.   By the end of the eighteenth century Chinyama
was a major chieftainship in the area.

CHIPANGO, W.   National Secretary of the United Party (q. v.).
He had been an active member of UNIP prior to that and in
fact was its mayor of Livingstone.

CHIPATA.   A town and district in the Eastern Province of Zambia,
it is located in the southeastern part of Zambia.   The town
(called Fort Jameson (q. v.) prior to independence) had a population of 13,300 in 1969 and is located only five miles from
the Malawi border.   Fort Jameson had been planned in 1898 as
the capital of what was called Northeast Rhodesia.   The Great
East Road (q. v.) runs through the town, which is a stopping
point for tourists visiting the game reserves in the Luangwa
Valley.   The district had a population of 261,000 in 1969, over
9 percent above its figure only six years earlier.

CHIPEKENI.   The site of an important battle between the Bemba
and Ngoni around 1870, it was an Ngoni camp east of the
Kabishya River in northern Zambia.   It was important for two
reasons.   First, the defeat of the Ngoni under Mperembe
(q. v.) forced them to drop plans to subdue the Bemba.   Second,

it was truly a united force of Bemba chiefdoms that beat the
Ngoni, with the Chitimukulu joined by Mwamba, Nkule, Shi-
mumbi and several others in putting together the army.

CHIPENGE.   An Ndembu commoner who united his people (after
their chiefs failed) in the 1880's, enabling them to defeat the
marauding Luvale forces of Kangombe.

CHIRENJI.   A site near the head of the Luangwa valley northeast
of Bemba country that was among the first mission stations in
northern Zambia.   The Livingstonia Mission (q.v.) of the Free
Church of Scotland opened a station there in 1882, but they
closed it in 1888, moving west to Mwenzo in 1894.

CHISAMBA.   One of the larger towns along the line of rail, it is
north of Lusaka, about halfway from there to Kabwe.

CHISATA, JOHN.   The successor to Lawrence Katilungu as president of the powerful African Mineworkers Union in December,
1960.   He had been chairman of the Mufulira branch of the
union and had represented it at the Miners International Federation in Sweden the previous August.   Although a supporter of
UNIP, he warned the party's leaders in July, 1962, that they
should stay out of industrial disputes.   This occurred when
UNIP workers tried to persuade miners to ignore a strike call
because it could have negative effects on the coming election.
Chisata himself became a UNIP candidate in the 1962 election
and won by over eleven thousand votes.   He was then appointed
a parliamentary secretary.   He later served as a Minister of
State, but fell from favor in 1971 when, along with Justin
Chimba (q.v.), he accused the Government of failing to prosecute certain Ministers who were under suspicion for misuse of
funds.   The two charged that people in the government were
showing tribal favoritism through this cover-up.   But they were
discredited when the charges were not substantiated and they
joined Kapwepwe in the United Progressive Party in August,
1971.   On September 9, 1977, they announced that they would
rejoin UNIP for the sake of national unity.

CHISHINGA.   One of Zambia's middle-sized ethnic subdivisions,
consisting of about eighty-five thousand people whose territory
is sandwiched between that of the Lunda and Bemba, north of
Lake Bangweulu.   They appear to have been of Luba origin,
seemingly splitting off from those migrants who later founded
the Bemba nation.   The Chishinga chiefs belong to the bena
ng'oma (q.v.), or Drum Clan, and the people follow a matrilineal descent system.   In the nineteenth century they were
noted as iron-producers.   At the same time, however, they
were subject to paying tribute to the Lunda of Kazembe.
Their territory, a little south and east of Lake Mweru, was
also subject to raids by Arab ivory traders.   However, the
Chishinga chief Mushyota defeated one of them, Kumba Kumba
(q.v.), in 1873.   In the early 1890's, however, a Bemba force

sent by Mwamba III defeated the Chishinga Chief Chama and
took most of his territory.

CHITAMBALA, FRANK. A close associate of Kenneth Kaunda in
politics for over two decades, he had been a militant member
of the ANC in the 1950's. He had been imprisoned in 1958
for involvement in some riots. When released he became the
Acting Provincial Secretary of ANC for the Eastern Province,
working with Reuben Kamanga (q. v.) and later with Kaunda.
In August, 1958, he was responsible for getting the Eastern
Province executive to pass a motion of "no confidence" in
Harry Nkumbula. When Kaunda split to form ZANC, Chitambala also joined it. He was one of the ZANC leaders who was
detained in 1959, being rusticated in the Balovale District of
the North-Western Province where a prosecution against him
failed. Thus released in May, 1959, he cofounded the African
National Independence Party (q. v.) with Paul Kalichini. He attacked Nkumbula for collaborating with the government and selling out the nationalists. A few months later his party merged
with another to form UNIP, and he worked hard to build its
organization. In October, 1959, he was elected its Secretary-
General. He has remained active in it. In his latest move
he was switched in August, 1977, from his Central Committee
post as Chairman of the Rural Development Subcommittee to
become chairman of the Youth and Sport Subcommittee. Meanwhile he has also served in Parliament. In March, 1969, he
was appointed Minister of the North-Western Province, serving
until November, 1969.

CHITAMBO'S VILLAGE. The site of the death of Dr. David Livingstone on May 1, 1873. His African friends who served as
guides and aides buried his heart there but returned his body
to England. Chitambo was a Lala Chief whose village was located, by Livingstone's map, about fifteen miles south of Lake
Bangweulu, on the Lulimala River. It is now called Chipundu.

CHITAPANKWA (or CHITAPANGWA). One of the most dominant of
the Bemba Chitimukulus (q. v.), he reigned for over twenty
years (from the early 1860's to 1883), a period in which there
was a significant expansion of Bemba territory. One authority
on the Bemba indicates that land under Bemba rule doubled or
even tripled during Chitapankwa's reign. He was the nephew
of a previous ruler, Chileshye (q. v.), and the younger brother
of the man who was Mwamba II. When Chileshye died, he was
replaced as Chitimukulu by an elderly and ill man, Bwembya
(q. v.). The bakabilo soon realized their error, and were willing to assist when Chitapankwa produced a plan to replace
Bwembya. Mwamba II declined to switch titles and also supported his younger brother's goal. Thus after a ruse, Chitapankwa obtained the symbols of office (babenye, q. v.) and assumed
the throne. One of his visitors a few years later, in February,
1867, was Dr. David Livingstone. Chitapankwa persuaded him
to stay for several weeks, hoping to get from him as gifts most

of his European-made possessions. The two men developed a good relationship and Livingstone was very impressed, as was the French explorer, Victor Giraud (q.v.) in 1883.

The first major expansion led by Chitapankwa was south across the Chambeshi River in the mid 1860's. There he occupied land belonging to Bisa chiefs, such as the territory called Isunga ruled by Chief Mungulube. He also intervened in a succession dispute in the Bemba chiefdom called Ichinga (q.v.), ultimately sending his own daughter as a regent. Once things were settled there, he sent a brother, the noted Sampa (q.v.) to replace her, but this didn't work out and the two brothers almost came to blows, thus Sampa was replaced by a sister's son.

While Chitapankwa was solidifying and extending Bemba power to the south and east, his brother, Mwamba II Chileshye was doing the same to the southwest, notably at the expense of the Lungu. This led to a conflict with Munshimbwe, a Lungu chief. Chitapankwa became involved when he killed the son of the Lungu chief. Munshimbwe then called on the powerful Ngoni leader Mperembe (q.v.) to fight the Bemba. While Ngoni did join him, Mperembe either did not fight then or brought only a small force. Munshimbwe was killed in this battle on the Kafubu River, perhaps in 1867.

The major battle against the Ngoni and Mperembe came in about 1870 when, after a series of Ngoni raids from territories bordering the Bemba (in one of which a sister of Chitapankwa was killed and a niece captured), Chitapankwa formed an alliance and army of at least eight Bemba chiefs. The result was an attack on the Ngoni village at Chipekeni (q.v.) and a major defeat for the Ngoni and Mperembe, who now gave up their plans to take over Bemba territory.

Next the Bemba turned to the northeast and Chitapankwa raided and conquered such peoples as the Mambwe under Mpande and Nsokolo, and the Namwanga under Chikanamulilo. The latter turned back a Bemba attack by Chitapankwa and Makasa IV in 1877, but a couple of years later the Bemba were more successful. Likewise the Lungu led by Zombe repelled a Chitapankwa attack in 1872, but were crushingly defeated by him in 1882 or 1883. The Tabwa were also conquered during this period, but by Chitapankwa's brother, Mwamba II. Both of these great Bemba leaders died of the smallpox in 1883, a year when an epidemic of it swept through parts of northeastern Zambia. His brother Sampa (q.v.) replaced Chitapankwa, who died in October, 1883.

CHITEMENE (or CHITIMENE; CITIMENE). A system of agriculture, based on the slash-and-burn approach, that has been used for centuries in Zambia and still is quite common today. During the dry season, essentially June to November, the men clear the woodland to prepare the area for a crop (usually millet). They cut many of the small trees and branches from larger ones. These are stacked across the clearing and, late in the dry season, burned. Seed is then spread through this

bed of ash after early rains soften the earth. With the ash as
fertilizer, the crops are ready the following April or May and
stored for use through the next year. A problem intrinsic to
this system is that before many years, all land close to a
village has been stripped of trees and the families must move.
It is years before the area can be so used again. Villages
based on this system are not large, by necessity. Around the
beginning of the twentieth century, however, the British found
a new settlement pattern called mitanda (q.v.) which was allied
to the chitemene system and which created extremely small
garden villages. This worked against the colonial attempt to
place more power in the chiefs, aside from the fact that the
British thought the chitemene system was a very wasteful form
of cultivation. Thus they banned both chitemene and mitanda
in 1906. One government report indicated that this would make
collection of the hut tax easier also. The large villages that
were created as a result of the ban caused disastrous social,
political, economic and health problems. Strong resistance
grew up among the people of North-Eastern Rhodesia, and in
1909 the British allowed chitemene to be practiced again.
Even today the Zambian government encourages more modern
agricultural methods but it is reluctant to prohibit the chitimene
system that is still used widely.

CHITENGE. An item of female clothing in contemporary Zambia,
it is a piece of material wrapped around the body to form a
long skirt. Long skirts were adopted when the missionaries
first arrived, but many Zambians seem to prefer to see wom-
en continue to wear them rather than above-the-knee skirts.
Zambian women are also discouraged from wearing long pants
or shorts.

CHITI. According to the Bemba legend of their origin, Chiti was
the first of the leaders of these people. He lived in a place
called Luba or Kola, somewhere west of the Luapula River.
His father was Mukulumpe, and his mother, said to have been
of divine origin, was Mumbi Mukasa. His brothers Katongo
and Nkole, and his sister, Chilufya Mulenga (qq.v.) are
also important to the Bemba legend. The young men had built
a tower which fell down, causing great loss of life. The father was very angry, blinded Katongo and banished Chiti and
Nkole. Although he invited them back later, it was only to
punish them, so Chiti led many others in a great eastern migration. The entourage crossed the Luapula River and eventually went around the northern part of Lake Bangweulu, proceeding east to the Chambeshi River which they crossed. Periodically small groups broke off, one of which purportedly became
the bena ng'ona (q.v.), the royal clan of the Bisa. In the
Luangwa valley they encountered the Senga people and Chiti
was attracted to the wife of a Senga chief, Mwase. When
Mwase returned from hunting to find the other two in a roman-
tic situation he attacked Chiti. In the battle Chiti was wounded
by a poisoned arrow and soon died. He was buried by Nkole

in a grove of trees called Mwalule (q. v.) or Milemba, north
of the Senga country. Nkole also soon died and a nephew,
Chilufya (q. v.), became the first of the line of Bemba paramount chiefs to take the title Chitimukulu (literally "Chiti the
Great"). While this story is important to the Bemba, historians find it difficult to verify its accuracy. Regardless, they
project that such events, if they occurred, probably took place
in the late seventeenth century.

CHITIMUKULU (or CITIMUKULU; KITIMUKULU). The title of the
senior or paramount chief of the Bemba people, it literally
means "Chiti the Great" and derives from the Bemba founder,
Chiti (q. v.). The title was first assumed, according to legend,
by Chiti's nephew Chilufya (q. v.) and his successors, perhaps
around the year 1700. The title and position continues down
to the present day. All the Chitimukulus, as well as the
holders of lesser chieftainships among the Bemba, are members of the royal Crocodile clan, the bena ng'andu (q. v.).
Though the major chiefs are all related through this clan,
their ties are looser than might be anticipated, and the Chitimukulu does not possess real control over them unless the individual Chitimukulu is strong enough to establish this control
through force or by influencing appointments of close relatives
to the other chieftainships. The potential successors to the
ruling Chitimukulu are in fact these other Bemba chiefs, some
of whom have held three or four of the lesser chieftaincies
before being selected as Chitimukulu.
     Each chief rules his own territory or calo (q. v.). The
calo of the Chitimukulu is Lubemba (q. v.). Its first capital
was established along the Kalungu River, east of the current
city of Kasama. The Chitimukulu is considered to be something
of a divine king, with supernatural control over his land and
people. His powers traditionally were extensive. He was assisted by a group of councillors, the bakabilo (q. v.). (To
understand better the history of the Chitimukulu, see especially
the entries for the following noted holders of the title: Chilufya,
Mukuuka, Chiliamafwa, Chileshye, Chitapankwa, Sampa, and
Ponde.)

CHIVUNGA, JONATHAN KALUNGA. A labor leader who has since
become a top rank ambassador after serving in a variety of
ministerial positions. Born in 1924 in the Eastern Province,
he worked for eight years in the civil service and business before becoming full-time Provincial Secretary of the Western
Province for the African National Congress from 1956 to 1958.
He became President of the Union of Shop Assistants in 1959.
In 1958 he had switched from the ANC to ZANC and then continued in its successor, UNIP. In 1960 he protested Lawrence
Katilungu's leadership of the Trade Union Congress and formed
the Reformed Trade Union Congress (q. v.), of which he be-
came President. He ran for Parliament in 1964 and became
M. P. for Kitwe South. From 1964 until 1970 he served in the
Government as Minister of State for six different ministries.

In November, 1970, he was appointed Ambassador to the People's Republic of China, and in 1974 was transferred to France.

CHOBE RIVER. Also known as the Kwando River (or the Mashi or Linyanti River), it flows in a southeastern direction through parts of Angola until it touches Zambia. It then serves as the Zambian-Angolan border for 138 miles until it dips into the Caprivi Strip, south of Zambia. It then turns east and becomes the southern border of the Caprivi Strip until it joins the Zambezi River just west of Kazungula. The Makololo people (q.v.) chose to live in the unhealthy, swampy area north of the Chobe in the mid-nineteenth century (despite urgings from Dr. Livingstone to move) because they saw the Chobe River as the best defensive barrier they could find against the Matabele of Chief Mzilikazi.

CHOKWE. One of the smaller ethnic subdivisions of Zambia, the Chokwe are part of the Lunda-Luvale language sub-group that lives in northwestern Zambia. This matrilineal group had been dominated by the Lozi but broke away. They came in from Angola to the west, with whose people they continued to trade. Among other things they acquired were guns from Portuguese slave-traders. They are skilled artisans who are especially admired for their woodcraft and pottery. Today they number about twenty-seven thousand people.

CHOMA. A town along the line of rail in south-central Zambia near Lake Kariba. It is also one of the districts in the Southern Province. The district had a population of eighty-six thousand in the 1969 census, and the town's population was a little over eleven thousand.

Choma is also the name of a station of the British South Africa Company that was opened in the early 1890's about halfway between Lakes Tanganyika and Mweru.

CHONA, MARK CHUUNYU. One of the most influential and trusted advisors of President Kaunda, he was born June 6, 1934, at Monze in the Southern Province. His father was Chief Chona, and his brother Mainza Chona is Secretary General of UNIP. His education has been truly international, including a B.A. in History and Economics at Salisbury University. He also studied at Cambridge University and in both Canada and Washington. This was all in the early 1960's, between some minor government posts. He joined Kaunda's staff in October, 1964. On April 1, 1965, he became Permanent Secretary for Foreign Affairs, a post he held three years. In 1968 he returned to work in the President's Office, serving principally as an international representative and trouble-shooter, but also involved with domestic political matters.

CHONA, MATHIAS MAINZA. The first President of UNIP, Mainza Chona was chosen Secretary General of UNIP in June, 1978. Born January 21, 1930, at Monze, he is the son of a

Tonga chief. He completed Munali Secondary School and
worked as a clerk-interpreter at the High Court in Livingstone
for four years until 1955. He then went to England on a
scholarship and studied law at Gray's Inn, London, ultimately
becoming in 1958 Zambia's first African barrister.

Prevented by color-bar obstacles from opening a practice
in his own country, Chona entered politics in 1959. Since
ZANC had been banned, Chona joined ANC, hoping to make it
more progressive. Two years earlier in London he had tried
to persuade Kenneth Kaunda to challenge Harry Nkumbula for
party leadership because of Nkumbula's conservative approach
to political advancement for the Africans. Within the ANC
Chona challenged Nkumbula himself. Aided by a dissident
ANC wing led by Titus Mukupo (q.v.) who had instituted a
party split in June, 1959, Chona was elected President of one
faction of the ANC on September 13, 1959. A decision by the
Registrar of Societies a month later, however, went against
the Chona-Mukupo faction and recognized Nkumbula's faction
as the legitimate ANC. Meanwhile Chona's speeches on national issues had begun to attract a large following, and he
was quickly welcomed into the United National Independence
Party (q.v.) that had been formed in September by the merger
of two splinter parties. He was elected the President of UNIP
in October as soon as his faction joined, but he made it clear
that he was only holding the post until Kaunda was released
from detention. This occurred in early January, 1960, and at
a party conference on January 31, Kaunda became President
and Chona Vice President. Meanwhile Chona had left the country for a meeting in Tunis a week earlier and stayed away for
over a year because the Northern Rhodesian Government had
a "sedition" charge out against him. This didn't prevent him
from working for UNIP in London and serving as a UNIP dele-
gate to the Federal Review Conference there in December,
1960. When the charge was dropped he returned home in February, 1961, and became UNIP's National Secretary. Serving
in this post for eight years, he made it into a very well-
organized party. Also in 1961 he became editor of the party
paper, The Voice of UNIP.

He was elected to Parliament in January, 1964, and became the first Zambian to become Minister of Justice. In
September, however, he was switched to Minister of Home Affairs. On January 1, 1967, he was appointed Minister of
Presidential Affairs, the first of numerous changes in the next
ten years. From then on he has worked closely with President Kaunda, taking on whatever jobs most needed doing. In
September, 1967, he became Minister without Portfolio which
only gave official title to his varied tasks. In the next several
years he served briefly as Minister for the Central Province,
Minister of Provincial and Local Government and Ambassador
to the United States. He became Vice-President of Zambia on
November 1, 1970, a post he held until August, 1973, when he
became Zambia's Prime Minister under the new Constitution.

The Chona Commission (q.v.) which he headed had made

many of the recommendations ultimately implemented in the new Constitution. During the years 1972 through 1974 he made numerous trips abroad on behalf of his country, visiting four continents. While Vice President he also served as Minister of Development and Planning and National Guidance. He kept these same ministerial tasks while Prime Minister from August, 1973 to May, 1975. In May, 1975, he resigned as Prime Minister because of ill health. From May, 1975, until July, 1977, he was Minister of Legal Affairs and Attorney General. In July, 1977 he was reappointed Prime Minister, but was chosen UNIP's Secretary General in June, 1978. A staunch supporter of Kaunda, he appears to many to be the logical successor if an emergency should arise.

CHONA COMMISSION. The popular name for the National Commission on the Establishment of a One-Party Participatory Democracy in Zambia. It was established by President Kenneth Kaunda in February, 1972. Vice-President Mainza Chona (q.v.) was appointed its chairman. The twenty-one members represented a wide spectrum of the country's institutional elites (business, army, churches, chiefs, public service, and UNIP). Even leaders of the African National Congress were invited to be members, but they declined. Since the decision had been made already to establish a one-party system, this advisory commission was established to sound out the country's views on the structure of the new constitution. Open hearings were held throughout the country for over four months, with testimony being taken in both written and oral form. An impressive report filled with recommendations for the form of Zambia's Second Republic was presented to Kaunda on October 15, 1972. The new Constitution was supposedly based on this report but with modifications, sometimes extensive. The Commission's major suggestions concerned the supremacy (even monopoly of power) to be held by UNIP. In these recommendations it was influenced somewhat by the nearby model in Tanzania. While these were generally accepted by the Government and included in the new Constitution, the Commission was overruled when it proposed limiting some presidential powers through curtailing his veto power and limiting his tenure in office. Numerous other reforms were also not implemented immediately, such as strengthening the national assembly, encouraging electoral competition, and the reform of UNIP.

CHRISTIAN COUNCIL. An ecumenical body representing over twenty churches, missions, and Christian organizations. It was formed in 1944 to replace the General Missionary Conference of Northern Rhodesia (q.v.).

CHUNGA, ELIJAH HERBERT. A civil servant who with Ernest A. Muwamba (q.v.) was one of the co-founders of the Ndola Native Welfare Association in 1930.

CHUNGU. The name of leaders of a minor Lungu chiefdom. This chiefdom gained importance because of its proximity to the

Bemba. In 1889 the reigning Chungu signed a "treaty" with
Harry Johnston, who was attempting to secure territory for
Cecil Rhodes. Chungu's land was on the northeastern border
of Mporokoso's. Chungu II managed to defeat a Bemba-Swahili
army in the 1890's, and Mporokoso made an alliance with him.
Chungu is also the name of a Bena Mukulu chieftainship that
was more active in the early part of the nineteenth century.

CHURCH OF CENTRAL AFRICA, PRESBYTERIAN (CCAP). The
name adopted in 1924 by the Central African branch of the
Free Church of Scotland (q. v.).

CHUULA COMMISSION. A Commission appointed in September,
1969, to examine UNIP's constitution with the hope of recom-
mending changes which would remedy the intense sectional competition then in evidence within the party. Mr. Fitzpatrick
(Frank) Chuula, the Attorney General, was appointed its chairman. Its instructions allowed it also to look into the relationship between the party and the government and the question of
party discipline. The Commission held hearings and wrote a
report which it gave President Kaunda in March, 1970, but the
report was not made public until September 23, 1970. The
report included a complete draft for a new UNIP constitution.
Contrary to its goal, the report produced an immediate split
in the party, as some of its proposals infuriated an element of
Northern Province militants who had been party activists for
many years. Its most important recommendations (and also
the most controversial ones) attempted to limit the intense
competition for central committee posts and the sectional nature of that competition. But its suggestion that provincial
equality (two members each) exist on the central committee
was a major cause of discord. Most of its proposals concerning the central committee were substantially changed by the
Party's national council that met in November, 1970 (see Central Committee of UNIP). The Commission Report also recommended the abolition of the posts of President and Vice-President of the Party. UNIP's Secretary-General would also be
the party's nominee for the presidential elections.

CiBEMBA (or ChiBEMBA). A Bantu language spoken by eighteen
tribal groups in Zambia, comprising over a third of the population. Its speakers include two of the largest groups, the
Bemba and the Lunda of the Luapula, both of whom also use
an archaic form of it, ciLuba, in the praises of their chiefs.
It is also the lingua franca of the Copperbelt, and is one of
the official languages of the country.

CILOLO (pl. , bafilolo). A Bemba elder who is appointed by the
chief to be headman of one of the sections of the Chief's capital village. He is responsible for maintaining law and order
in that section. He may also be called on by the chief to give
advice and counsel, especially on judicial matters. He also
helps to organize tribute labor for the capital and to allocate

land for cultivation. As the power of Bemba chiefs began to
diminish around the turn of the century, some bafilolo broke
away to form their own villages.

CiNYANJA. The third most widely spoken of the languages of
Zambia, it is used primarily by the Chewa (q. v.) who brought
it to Zambia, and the Nsenga, Ngoni, Kunda, and Chikunda.
Together they number about 16 percent of the population. Thus
it was chosen to be one of the country's official languages.
All its speakers originated in eastern Zambia.

CITEMENE. Variant form of Chitimene (q. v.).

CiTONGA. One of the official languages of Zambia, ciTonga is
spoken by eight ethnic groups which comprise over 17 percent
of the population, thus ranking it second behind ciBemba for
widespread use. Its speakers are primarily from southern
Zambia. The largest group of them, about two-thirds, are the
Tonga themselves.

CLAN. A subdivision of a tribe, it is a family group that has a
common ancestor. The ancestor may have been real or mythi-
cal. Clan membership can be very important as some take
precedence over others. Where territorial chieftainships dominate an area, only the ruling clan continues to have major significance. Clan membership much affects the rituals and customs of the people. See also BENA NG'ANDU; BENA NG'OMA;
and BENA NG'ONA.

CLARK, J. DESMOND. The father of archeological research in
Zambia, he became Curator of the Museum attached to the
Rhodes-Livingstone Institute in 1938 and remained there until
he retired as Director of the Rhodes-Livingstone Museum on
May 1, 1961. He was born in 1916 and received degrees from
Christ's College of Cambridge University. Dr. Clark later became Professor of Anthropology at the University of California
at Berkeley. He is the author of numerous books and articles
on the early history of Africa, especially the south-central
part.

COAL. After copper, one of the most important minerals found in
Zambia. The Southern Province has very large reserves.
Large-scale coal mining became a high priority of the First
National Development Plan, with the goal being to make Zambia
self-sufficient as soon as possible to eliminate dependence on
imports from Rhodesia. Large-scale production at the Maamba
mine, begun in late 1968, allowed Zambia to cease its imports
from Rhodesia in mid-1970.

CODRINGTON, ROBERT EDWARD. One of the earliest of Zambia's European Administrators, he was born in England in 1867
and educated at Marlborough College. He came to southern
Africa and became a sergeant in the Bechuanaland Border Police

He later saw action in Matabeleland and then joined the Foreign
Office in Nyasaland. When the British South Africa Company
took over North-Eastern Rhodesia he was hired by it. In July,
1898, he became Deputy Administrator of that territory, and
served as Administrator from August, 1900, to April, 1907.
At that point he switched to the other half of Zambia, serving
as Administrator of North-Western Rhodesia until his death in
December, 1908. As Administrator of the eastern half of the
country, he laid the foundation for the country's public service.
His preference was to hire young, middle-class, university-edu-
cated men fresh from England. He set up a regular, graded
Civil Service, dismissing unsuitable men quickly. He was also
something of an autocrat as Administrator, seldom compromis-
ing his beliefs. When white craftsmen protested that Africans
were working in the construction of government buildings at
Broken Hill, Codrington overruled all opponents. In 1907 he
had brought skilled African workers to North-Western Rhodesia
from Fort Jameson. This precipitated the controversy, but
Codrington stood firm.

   As Administrator in the northeast, Codrington was responsible for completing the BSAC control over the area, and
at one point sent an armed force to pressure the Lunda leader
Kazembe into submitting. Also he proved to be sympathetic to
Bishop Dupont and the White Fathers, supporting them in setting up missions among the Bemba. While working later among
the Lozi he instituted the practice of referring to the Lozi King
as only "Paramount Chief. " The demotion was symbolic but
typical as Codrington insisted that all Africans should take off
their hats to white men, whom they should always treat with
respect.

COILLARD, FRANCOIS. After Dr. Livingstone, perhaps the most
   influential European missionary to live in the boundaries of today's Zambia. Rev. Coillard was born in France in 1834 and
   decided as a youth to join the Paris Missionary Society (q.v.).
   He and his wife, the former Christina Mackintosh, arrived at
   their first assignment, which was in Basutoland, in 1858. In
   1877 they led a large party that included their niece and four
   Sotho evangelists to open a new mission station among Lobengula's Ndebele. When they reached this area in Southern Rhodesia
   they were not allowed to stay and moved west to the territory
   of Chief Khama's Bamangwato. Since they knew the Sotho language, Khama (q.v.) encouraged them to travel north to the
   Lozi who had adopted the same language when it was forced on
   them by the Makololo. Khama even interceded with the Lozi
   King for Coillard and his party. They then reached the Zambezi in July, 1878, and received permission to cross the river
   to Sesheke. There they had to wait while further messages
   proceeded between Sesheke and Lealui, where the subject of
   the missionaries' presence was debated in the Kuta. Finally
   the answer came that they could not come further north now
   but would be accepted at a later date. In addition it appears
   the party was mistaken to be traders.

Coillard was enthused about the prospect and returned to
Europe to raise money to finance a Barotseland mission. He
returned to the upper Zambezi in 1884. Now with the aid of a
respected trader, George Westbeech (q.v.), along with the
recommendation from Chief Khama, Coillard and his party entered Barotseland. Although delayed by a civil war in which
King Lewanika was temporarily deposed, the party arrived in
the capital, Lealui, in early 1885. They remained only briefly, however, returning in April, 1886, after Lewanika had been
reinstated. The Lozi King welcomed them and provided a mission site twenty miles away at Sefula where a school was
opened in March, 1887. This was the first of many mission
locations of the PMS in Barotseland. Coillard remained there
until 1896 when he took a two-year break by returning to Paris.
There his famous book Sur le Haut Zambezi (On the Threshold
of Central Africa) was published in 1898. It came from his
letters, notes from his journals, and articles he had written
for missionary publications. He returned to Barotseland in
1898, where he died in 1904. His wife had died in October,
1891, and was buried at Sefula.

The historic importance of Coillard does not rest in his religious conversions, as he was only marginally successful.
Even King Lewanika, his close friend who was so cooperative
and encouraged his youths to study at the schools, refused to
abandon polygamy in order to be converted. Coillard's importance was based on Lewanika's confidence in him as an advisor
in dealings with Europeans and as one who could help the Lozi
acquire the protection of the Queen of England, as Chief Khama
had done in 1885. Thus the missionary handled correspondence
on this subject for the King. When Harry Ware (q.v.) arrived
in June, 1889 and proposed a mining concession, Coillard in-
duced the King to sign as a first step toward British protection.
Coillard later denied that he had proposed the signing, and he
also handled the Lochner Concession (q.v.) the next year in an
ambiguous fashion. His pro-British (and thus British South
Africa Company) stand reflected a desire to more quickly
"civilize" the Lozi, while at the same time he feigned neutral-
ity in order to rebut the accusation of some Lozi that he was
encouraging the King to give away their country to the Europeans. As a result of his work, the Lozi leaders thought that
the treaty with Lochner was actually a treaty of protection with
Queen Victoria.

COLLECTORS. A term used by the British South Africa Company
in the early days of its rule to designate many of its administrative officers north of the Zambezi River. But the Company
was inconsistent and sometimes used the term Native Commissioners. Later it preferred to call them District Commissioners. They were called Collectors because one of their prime
duties was to serve as collectors of revenue, especially in
North-Eastern Rhodesia where they had certain taxes to collect
from the Africans.

COLLIER, WILLIAM. One of the early mineral prospectors in
    Zambia, he was sent into Lamba country in 1902 by the Bechu-
    analand Exploration Company. Near Ndola's village he found
    a deposit of ore which he claimed for the company and named
    "Bwana Mkubwa. " With the aid of a local guide he traveled a
    little northwest and found a rich lode of copper ore, and named
    the area after a Roan Antelope he had just shot in the vicinity.
    Several days later he also found the Chambeshi deposit. The
    Bechuanaland Exploration Company was linked to the Rhodesia
    Copper Company, itself a subsidiary of the British South Africa
    Company.

COLOUR BAR. A term applied to a whole series of harassments
    and discriminatory policies, both official and unofficial, to
    which the Africans were subjected. While racial discrimination
    in employment was perhaps the most serious aspect, other pat-
    terns may have been met more frequently, especially in urban
    areas. These would include, for example, separate entrances
    to banks and post offices, poor "native coaches" on trains, ac-
    cess forbidden to cafes for Africans, and long shopping lines
    at the "pigeon-holes" (see HATCH SYSTEM) where Africans
    were served, often with abusive language.

COLOURED. A term referring to people of mixed racial back-
    ground, usually meaning that one of the direct ancestors was
    African, and one European. It is a term rarely used in Zam-
    bia today, stemming mostly from South Africans who introduced
    it. The term Eurafrican (q.v.) is generally preferred. Most
    of these people are to be found in urban areas such as Lusaka,
    Chipata, and Ndola.

COMMISSION FOR TECHNICAL EDUCATION AND VOCATIONAL
    TRAINING. A parastatal organization created by the Zambian
    Government to encourage the improvement of technical educa-
    tion so that Zambianization could proceed more quickly.

COMMITTEE OF THIRTY. A group of many of the best "thinkers"
    among UNIP's members who were organized in April, 1962, by
    Sikota Wina for the purpose of drawing up a UNIP platform for
    presentation to the voters. They drew up specific policies on
    such subjects as economics, health, agriculture, prisons, the
    judiciary, education, local government, and foreign trade and
    commerce. This April conference, also called the "Easter
    School of Political Policies" produced a sixty-page election
    brochure called UNIP Policy.

CONCESSION OF 1906. A letter dated January 23, 1906, signed
    by King Lewanika of the Lozi which reiterated the facts of
    earlier concessions to the British South Africa Company in
    1900 and 1904. The letter reasserted that the King had given
    the Company the right "to dispose of land to settlers" (exclud-
    ing the heartland of the Lozi) as it saw fit, and to retain any
    money received. The Lozi complained in 1911 to L. A.

Wallace, the Administrator, that this concession only granted
plowing rights, as it was basic to all Lozi tradition that the
King never could grant perpetual alienation of its national land.
While they were accurate, the Europeans were not convinced.

CONCESSION OF 1909. A concession agreed upon by King Lewanika of the Lozi and his Ngambela at meetings held at Lealui on
August 6 and 9, 1909. L. A. Wallace, Acting Administrator
of the area was also present. Many doubts as to true Lozi
agreement to this exist because they appear to have given something to the BSAC in exchange for "nothing." The agreement
seemingly granted rights to the Company to use or dispose of
large areas of land within Barotseland in exchange for returning to Barotseland the territory west of Upper Zambezi but
east of Angola. This area had in fact already reverted to
Barotseland as a result of the 1905 boundary decision of the
King of Italy, so the Lozi had nothing at all to gain. Thus
many suspect that it was never a truly granted concession.
This was argued by the King and advisors in 1911 when they
reminded Wallace that Lozi tradition did not allow the King to
grant perpetual alienation of the national land, only temporary
use rights. The Lozi did not win.

CONFEDERATE PARTY. A very conservative, Federal-level party
that also contested the territorial elections, it appeared in
1953 as a party opposed to the Federation. It campaigned for
partitioning Northern Rhodesia into black and white segments,
with the white parts (the Copperbelt and the line-of-rail) being
merged with Southern Rhodesia. The party was composed of
several disparate elements: Afrikaners who had belonged to
the Southern Rhodesia Democratic Party; members of an old
S. R. Liberal Party that had been renamed the Rhodesia Party;
some elements of the S. R. Labour Party who opposed racial
partnership; several former Indian Army officers; and a small
number of dissident S. R. United Party members, notably J. R.
Dendy-Young. The Northern Rhodesians who participated actively and ran for election as Confederates included John Gaunt
(q. v.) and Guillaume Van Eeden (q. v.). One source calls Van
Eeden the founder of the Confederate Party. In the January,
1954, Federal elections, the Federal Party overwhelmed the
Confederate Party which, despite winning one-third of the votes
cast in Southern Rhodesia, only won one seat in the Parliament.
Dendy-Young was the winner and became the acknowledged party
leader. In the election the Confederates had campaigned for
separate development within the Federation, with "special native representation" in the Territorial legislatures. In the
Territorial elections, none of the sixteen Confederate candidates won in Southern Rhodesia, but two Confederates (John
Gaunt being one of them) won as Independent candidates in
Northern Rhodesia. By mid-1954 the party had vanished as an
organization. However, a number of Confederates found their
way into the Dominion Party (q. v.) that formed in February,
1956. This included Gaunt and, in 1958, Van Eeden. In 1960

the name Confederate Party was revived in Southern Rhodesia
by Stanley Gurland for his white supremacist organization.

CONGO (KINSHASA) see ZAIRE REPUBLIC

CONGO PEDICLE (or ZAIRE PEDICLE; KATANGA PEDICLE). The
copper-rich region of southern Zaire that lies adjacent to Zambia's Copperbelt and which dips deeply into the heart of central
Zambia. One major road cuts across this area (part of the
old Katanga Province--now the Shaba Province of Zaire) from
the Zambian Copperbelt to Zambia's Luapula Province. Zambia maintains Zaire's forty-three mile portion of this important
road. The area became part of the Belgian Congo as the result of expeditions of men working for King Leopold in 1891.
As a result of an argument, one of these men killed the powerful King Msiri, whose followers then did not resist. A treaty
between King Leopold and the British in 1894 agreed that this
land would now be part of the Congo. The same treaty clari-
fied other parts of the border.

CONGRESS CIRCULAR. A successor of the Congress News (q. v.),
it was published by the African National Congress monthly from
1955 until at least 1958. During most of this time Kenneth
Kaunda was its editor and responsible for much of its content,
which was anti-Federation and which encouraged the Africans
to political action.

CONGRESS NEWS. A mimeographed monthly publication of the
African National Congress that was started in October,
1953, by Kenneth Kaunda, Titus Mukopo and Wittington Sikalumbi. As a result of its publication in October and
November, the police arrested (but did not imprison) Kaunda
and Harry Nkumbula. Kaunda's name began to be widely
known as a result. The publication was not resumed until
January, 1955, under the title Official Gazette. Kaunda, its
editor, was imprisoned after the first issue, which was not as
large as the original issues of the Congress News. A second
issue of the Gazette was produced by Dixon Konkola.

CONSTITUTION AMENDMENT BILL 1957. A law passed by the
Federal Parliament of the Central African Federation on July
31, 1957. Despite objections by the African Affairs Board, it
was debated and approved by the British House of Commons.
It was objectionable to the Africans because it increased the
membership of the Federal Assembly from thirty-five to fifty-
nine, but only increased the African representation from nine
to fifteen. Thus there would be a slightly smaller proportion
of African representation in the new Assembly. In addition
since the six new African members would be chosen by an
electorate dominated by Europeans, they would be more likely
to be concerned with European interests than African ones.

CONSTITUTION PARTY. A multi-racial party founded in Lusaka

in October, 1957, by moderate to liberal Europeans such as
Dr. Alexander Scott, a Federal M. P.; David Stirling; Harry
Franklin; and several Africans, including Lawrence Katilungu
and S. H. Chileshe. It hoped to deal "a death blow to the
doctrine of racial hatred and malice." Its convention unanimously approved a motion by Chileshe calling for legislation to
"abolish the monster of social and economic discrimination."
There was also an attempt to find a common ground for cooperation with the African National Congress. The party did
not limit its activities to Northern Rhodesia. In the June,
1958, general elections in Southern Rhodesia it did not run
candidates but suggested that its supporters should vote for
the most liberal candidates available. By the time the March,
1959, elections for Northern Rhodesia's Legislative Council
came around, the Constitution Party had given way to the better
organized branch of the Central African Party (q. v.) led by
John Moffat (q. v.) in Northern Rhodesia. Many of its members
found a home there, and also later in the Northern Rhodesia
Liberal Party (q. v.).

COOPERATIVES. There has been a major drive by the Govern-
    ment of Zambia since the mid-1960's to develop farming coop-
    eratives. In April, 1965, President Kaunda issued his Chifuba
    declaration on cooperatives, which the government followed up
    in 1966 with a massive expansion of them. The purpose of
    these farming cooperatives was to foster a feeling of mutual
    self-help (a goal of Zambian Humanism) as much as it was to
    boost agricultural production. The Government created a sys-
    tem of subsidies for lands cleared for cash crops by a regis-
    tered cooperative. Groups clearing fifty or more acres would
    qualify for a Government grant to buy a tractor. The response
    in the country was immediate and actually overwhelmed the
    marketing and transportation system of the country. Some
    changes had to be instituted in 1967 and 1968.

COPPER. The mainstay of Zambia's economy today and amounting
    to about 95 percent of Zambia's exports, copper has provided
    the economic base for the development of the country. Zam-
    bia's copper ore reserves are extremely rich, accounting for
    about one-fifth of the world's known reserves. While the coun-
    try is consistently either third or fourth in the world produc-
    tion of copper, it exports more than either Russia or the United
    States, two of the larger producers. Production of copper in
    Zambia is over a thousand years old and perhaps much older.
    Copper products have been found in the diggings at Ingombe
    Ilede, a civilization dating back to about A. D. 650. Copper
    was certainly a part of the long distance trade that involved
    many Zambian peoples in the nineteenth century. The Lunda
    of Chief Kazembe were especially good suppliers of copper for
    this trade. Europeans entered Zambia in search of copper
    about the beginning of the twentieth century. William Collier
    (q. v.) named his discovery in 1902 after a Roan Antelope he
    killed nearby, and today the town of Luanshya is located there,

alongside the mine named after the antelope. Within a decade
most of the major claims were staked, but little was done to
produce the copper. The 1920's was a growth period for Zambian copper. Not only were major new deposits in the copperbelt found, but international financing became interested. Both
the Anglo-American Corporation (now Nchanga Consolidated
Copper Mines, Ltd.) and the Rhodesian Selection Trust Ltd.
(now Roan Consolidated Mines Ltd.) formally became incorporated in Northern Rhodesia in 1928. While the worldwide depression affected copper production in the early 1930's, the
production soon resumed and by the 1940's Zambian mines
reached the top levels of world production. While both open
pit and underground mining exist in Zambia, about 75 percent
is underground. The demand for miners has proven to be a
major boon to the employment of Zambians, as about forty-
five thousand Zambians work in the copper mines. Associated
industries and the economic spin-off provide employment for
many thousands more. Zambia is now mining regularly over
seven hundred thousand metric tons of copper every year. The
four biggest mines are the Roan Antelope Mine at Luanshya,
the Mufulira Mine, the Nchanga Mine at Chingola, and the
Nkana Mine at Kitwe. As a result of the nationalization of the
mines under the Mulungushi Declaration of 1968, the Zambian
Government collects 51 percent of the profits as taxes.

COPPER CROSSES. A form of currency found in Zambia and in
the neighboring Shaba area of Zaire, these crossed iron bars
were cast in ingots and kept to a fairly standard weight. The
earliest ones found would indicate that they were used in trade
as long as one thousand years ago. The heaviest ones found
at Ingombe Ilede (q.v.) weighed about five thousand grams.
Those found in the old Katanga (Shaba) area of Zaire are sometimes called the Katanga Cross.

COPPERBELT. The economic heartland of Zambia, the mining
area known as the Copperbelt (as distinguished from the larger
Copperbelt Province, q.v.) is about ninety miles long and
thirty miles wide. It has made Zambia the world's third
largest producer of copper. It regularly produces over seven
hundred thousand metric tons of copper, and some estimates
calculate that the supply could last into the 1990's or even the
twenty-first century. There are eight major urban centers on
the Copperbelt, including five of the country's six largest
cities. Eighteen percent of all Zambians live on the Copperbelt, which is served by both major railroads and highways.
It is adjacent to the western border of the Shaba (Katanga)
Province of Zaire, sometimes referred to as the Congo Pedicle (q.v.).

COPPERBELT PROVINCE. Formerly called the Western Province
until 1969 when it was renamed. (Simultaneously Barotseland
was renamed the Western Province.) It naturally includes the
area that is tremendously rich in copper, plus a large area to

its west and south.   The Province is divided into eight districts, the Ndola (Rural) District and seven urban ones: Chililabombwe, Chingola, Kalulushi, Kitwe, Mufulira, Luanshya,
and Ndola (Urban).   The total population of the Province in
1969 was 816,000.   The Province grew in population by 50
percent between 1963 and 1969.

COPPERBELT SHOP ASSISTANTS UNION.   The first African union
   to form in Zambia, it was founded in 1948, thus predating the
   African Mineworkers Union by one year.   The British Labour
   Party Government had sent labor advisors to Northern Rhodesia
   to assist the Africans in organizing.

COPPERBELT STRIKE OF 1935 see STRIKES OF 1935 AND 1940

CORYNDON, SIR ROBERT THORNE.   An Administrator of Barotseland in the early twentieth century, he was born in South Africa in 1870 and educated partly in England.   Cecil Rhodes hired
   him as one of the original twelve members of the Pioneer
   Column which occupied Mashonaland.   He also served for a
   year as Rhodes' private secretary.   In 1897 he was appointed
   Resident (Commissioner) of Barotseland, chosen by the British
   South Africa Company but approved by the British High Commissioner to South Africa.   When he arrived in the Lozi capital of Lealui in October, 1897 with one assistant and five
   troopers, he did not impress King Lewanika as truly representing the kind of British protective force the King had been
   awaiting.   Eventually his skill as a hunter and his charm and
   diplomacy won the respect of the Lozi, however, and with the
   aid of Arthur Lawley, the Lewanika Concession of 1900 (q. v.)
   was successfully negotiated (in June, 1898).   This confirmed
   British power in Western Zambia.
       In September, 1900, he was appointed Administrator of
   North-Western Rhodesia, a post he held until April, 1907.
   Much of his influence among the Lozi rested on his claim to
   be the representative of the Queen of England.   In obtaining
   concessions he appeared to imply that the alternative was that
   the Lozi would be conquered, either by other Africans or, perhaps, by the British.   Coryndon then served as Resident Commissioner of Swaziland from 1907 to 1916, and later in Basutoland.   He also served as Governor of Uganda and, later, of
   Kenya.   He died in 1925.

COTTON CLOTH.   Although not much cotton is grown in Zambia in
   comparison to other products, some cotton is produced every
   year.   It has been known in Zambia for a thousand years,
   however, as graves at Ingombe Ilede (q. v.) along with other
   archaeological digging has proven conclusively that cotton cloth
   was produced and worn there.   Much more recently, in the
   nineteenth century, the Bisa were known as excellent weavers
   of cotton cloth, an item they traded.   It was a rare commodity,
   generally, and thus was more valued for its prestige than for
   its intrinsic value.

COURT OF APPEAL. Also referred to as the Supreme Court, it
is the highest court in the land and is the country's final ap-
pellate body. It is higher than the High Court, although the
Chief Justice presides over both. Below them both are Magis-
trates' Courts and local courts. The Chief Justice and other
judges of both the Court of Appeal and the High Court are appointed by the President.

COUSINS, C. E. (Ted). A former civil servant from the Luangwa
area, he was a member of the African National Congress and
one of its successful candidates in the 1962 election for the
Northern Rhodesian Legislature. This became crucial when
UNIP and the ANC decided on creating a coalition to rule the
Legislative Council, as part of the constitutional rules required
two of the Cabinet posts to be held by Europeans. Although
the ANC had only seven of the twenty-one seats in the coalition
group, it had the only two Europeans, Cousins and Frank
Stubbs (q. v.). Thus it could demand half of the six ministerial posts, and got them. Cousins was named Minister of Land
and Natural Resources. After a series of disagreements with
Harry Nkumbula of the ANC over party leadership, Cousins
resigned or was expelled (or both) from ANC late in November,
1963. He quickly joined UNIP and became its candidate for
one of the ten reserved roll (European) seats in the January,
1964, election. He narrowly lost to a candidate of the National
Progress Party (the former UFP).

CROCODILE CLAN. The royal clan of the Bemba, also called the
bena ng'andu (q. v.).

CROWN COLONY. A term applied to Northern Rhodesia when in
1924 it came officially under the authority of the British Government and ceased to be under the administration of the
British South Africa Company.

CROWN LANDS AND NATIVE RESERVES (TANGANYIKA DISTRICT)
ORDER-IN-COUNCIL, 1929. The result of the work of the
three Reserves Commissions (q. v.), this 1929 Order in Council
created native reserves and Crown lands in the Tanganyika District, and gave the Africans a four year time limit in which to
move to the reserves. The Government rationalized this act
by claiming that the addition of European farms to the district
would provide local jobs for Africans as well as training so
they could some day manage their own farms. The Africans
strongly opposed the Order-in-Council, which gave about five
million acres (out of about thirteen million) to a European population of forty-three, including eleven women and eight government officials. The 106,000 Africans shared the remaining
acreage.

CUNNINGHAM, COLIN. A European politician and Lusaka lawyer
who was especially active during the period of the Central
African Federation. At one point he was very close to

Kenneth Kaunda, even meeting him when Kaunda was released
from jail. Later, however, he formed the Federal Fighting
Fund (FFF), sometimes called the Federal Fighting Force,
which pledged strong support of Roy Welensky and the Federa-
tion. It favored establishing a Federal Police force to combat
"Communism" and all those who opposed Federation. Later
Cunningham was a leader of the extremist Rhodesian Republican
Party (q. v.).

- D -

DALGLEISH COMMISSION. A Government-appointed commission
chaired by Andrew Dalgleish. It met in 1948 to inquire into
the advancement of Africans in industry (primarily on the
mines) into jobs being performed by Europeans. It concluded
that Africans could not be held back indefinitely. While Europeans should not be fired, as vacancies occurred Africans
should be trained and given the jobs, otherwise problems
might soon occur. The Commission's recommendations were
ignored by both the British and Northern Rhodesian Governments. Of course the European union rejected it. Dalgleish
was a prominent member of the British Trade Union Council.

DALY, CAPTAIN HENRY LAWRENCE. Acting Administrator of
North-Eastern Rhodesia (eastern half of present day Zambia)
from June, 1897, to July, 1898.

DAMBO. An open patch of swampy ground found at the upper end
of drainage systems throughout Zambia. Although the soil is
black, it is not usually fertile. Its main value is to provide
grazing during the dry season, as it is often inundated in the
rainy season. It is estimated that dambos cover about 5 percent of Zambia's territory. They constitute a regular water
supply for many rural settlements.

DAMBWA. An archaeological site near the city of Livingstone on
Zambia's southern border, it contained much evidence of Early
Iron Age inhabitants of Zambia. The artifacts are from the
first millenium A. D. , some dated specifically at A. D. 620.
Copper wire found there demonstrates that the inhabitants
traded with Africans to the north near the Kafue River. Skele-
tal remains indicate that intermarriage between Bushmen and
Negro types took place.

DAR ES SALAAM. The major seaport and present capital of Tanzania, Zambia's neighbor to the northeast. Of great economic
importance have been the lines of commercial communication
between Zambia and "Dar" provided by the Great North Road
which has brought petroleum imports to Zambia and taken out
copper exports. This has lessened in importance since the
Tan-Zam Railway (q. v.) was finished in 1976, also linking Dar
with Zambia.

DAVEY, THOMAS G. An Australian mining engineer for the
British South Africa Company who discovered in 1902 the mineral deposit that became the Broken Hill mine (q. v.). He and
a guide were looking for some old workings when they became
lost. They stumbled upon it by accident. He named the area
Broken Hill after a similar geological configuration he had
known in Australia.

DAVIS, SIR EDMUND. A noted financier and mining tycoon whose
companies were ultimately consolidated as the Rhodesia Copper
Company. One of his early ventures, the Northern Copper
Company in 1899 discovered the copper deposits in the Hook of
the Kafue River that became the Sable Antelope and Silver King
Mines. Although they did not reach expectations and eventually
closed, they were the first commercial copper holdings by
Europeans in Zambia. Davis also sent out a fellow Australian,
T. G. Davey (q. v.) who discovered the deposit that became
the Broken Hill mine (q. v.). Davis also developed the Wankie
Colliery in Southern Rhodesia. In the mid-1920's he was already in his seventies but was still active in the buying and
selling of mining properties.

DE LACERDA, DR. FRANCISCO JOSE MARIA. One of the first
European explorers to attempt a coast to coast trip across
Africa, he was a former Court Astronomer in Lisbon as well
as a mathematician. He was from Brazil where he had been
an explorer as well as an administrator. It was his goal to
open up central Africa to trade by traveling from Tete in Mozambique to Angola via the Lunda capital ruled by Mwata Yamvo. Instead his expedition of almost 460 people (four hundred
were porters) only got as far as the Lunda leader Kazembe on
the Luapula River. Along the way he had much trouble with
his porters and many fled. His journal provides interesting
data on the people and the land. After leaving Tete in July,
1798, the expedition reached Mwata Kazembe in October. But
de Lacerda soon died of a fever. His chaplain, Father Pinto
(q. v.) took over as leader and returned to Tete in November,
1799. De Lacerda's bones were lost in a battle with the Bisa.

DEMOCRATIC PEOPLE'S PARTY (DPP). A short-lived party
formed in March, 1972, by Foustino Lombe and other former
members of the United Progressive Party that had been banned
the month before. It was organized as a protest against President Kaunda's announcement that Zambia was going to become
a one-party democracy.

DEPUTY CHIEFS. A Native Administration ordinance of 1960 provided for the appointment of deputy chiefs to take over the administrative duties of infirm, aged, or otherwise incompetent
chiefs. The position was open to members of the chiefly families who then competed in an election. In some cases, notably
in one among the Yombe, this opened the way to partisan politics and a supporter of UNIP won.

DEVELOPMENT BANK OF ZAMBIA. Founded in Lusaka in 1974
with 60 percent Government funding, it was instituted with the
goal of encouraging Zambian-owned business. This would be
done through both loans and special services such as consulting and research assistance.

DEVONSHIRE AGREEMENT OF 1923. The actual agreement between the British Colonial Office and the British South Africa
Company that turned over administration and control of lands
of Northern Rhodesia to the Colonial Office. It also allowed
the BSAC to retain mineral rights and its freehold estates. It
was formally signed on October 1, 1923. It was named after
the ninth Duke of Devonshire, Colonial Secretary from 1922 to
1924.

DIRECT RULE. The form of administration used by the British
South Africa Company, which used the chiefs merely as instruments of European rulers. The change to British Colonial Office rule in 1924 brought a gradual shift to indirect rule (q. v.).

DISTRICT. A term used under British South Africa Company administration to designate the main subdivisions of North-Eastern
Rhodesia. Nine of these "districts" were established for administrative and tax collecting purposes. In charge was a District Commissioner (D. C.), and Native Commissioners. In
the 1930's, under Colonial Office rule, districts were replaced
by provinces, which were soon reorganized so as to total seven
in the whole Territory. Today there are eight provinces, each
of which is separated into a number of "districts." There are
over forty districts today, some primarily rural, others urban.
The rural districts were usually set up on a tribal base where
possible.

DISTRICT COMMISSIONER (D. C.). Under the British South Africa
Company, administrators of the major subdivisions of the territory were usually called District Commissioners. Under them
were Native Commissioners. The D. C. was also usually a
magistrate. The early D. C. had to travel extensively, learning languages and customs and taking a census. Later, under
the Colonial Office and until the birth of Zambian government,
the District Commissioners were the chief administrators in
the district, which now were subdivisions of the provinces.

DISTRICT GOVERNOR. In January, 1969, President Kaunda added
a layer of administration by placing district governors as administrative chiefs of the country's districts, supplanting the
district secretaries (q. v.). Politicians, not civil servants,
were appointed to the position of governor. They thus became
the senior party representatives in the districts.

DISTRICT SECRETARY. Under the Zambian Government, district
secretaries took over the duties of the old district commissioners as the major administrators of the districts, at least

several of which exist in each province. As such these individuals were the top civil servant representatives of the President in the district. Duties included responsibility in the area
of economic development. District secretaries found their positions undercut in 1967 when the Government gave the position
of chairman of the district development committee to UNIP
party politicians, demoting the civil servants to being secretaries for the committees. Their positions were lowered further when the Government decided in 1969 to appoint District
Governors (q. v.) to administer the districts. These were political (not "merit") appointees. The secretaries, still func-
tioning, now as local ombudsmen, sometimes clash with the
politically-oriented Governors.

DOBO-DOBO. The name for fourth-class carriages found on trains
in the old Northern Rhodesia. The vast majority of Africans
had to travel in them. Both furniture and toilet facilities were
minimal, making the ride uncomfortable and the air unpleasant.

DOMINION PARTY see FEDERAL DOMINION PARTY

DONGWE RIVER. One of the major tributaries of the Kabompo
River, which is itself one of the first tributaries of the Zambezi. Rising near the city of Kasempa, the Dongwe flows from
east to west until it joins the Kabompo in the northwestern part
of Zambia.

DOYLE, HON. BRIAN ANDRE. Chief Justice of Zambia since
1969 and Chairman of the Doyle Commission (q. v.) in 1971.
He was born in Burma in 1911 and educated in Dublin. He is
the holder of B.A. and LL. B. degrees. He served in various
legal posts throughout the Commonwealth from 1937 until he
became Attorney General of Northern Rhodesia in 1956. From
1959 to 1965 he was both Attorney General and Minister of
Legal Affairs.

DOYLE COMMISSION. Chaired by Chief Justice B. A. Doyle (q. v.),
the Commission was impaneled to investigate charges by Government Minister, Justin Chimba (q. v.), that civil service appointments by some Government officials were being made on
a tribal basis and that the Government had shown tribal bias
in criminal prosecutions. The Commission held hearings in
1971 and its report was critical of several Ministers, notably
concerning their financial integrity. President Kaunda dismissed the Ministers who the report criticized, and the original complainant, Chimba.

DRAPER, CHARLES RICHARD EARDLEY. A District Commissioner in North-Eastern Rhodesia in 1919 when a series of incidents involving adherents of the Watch Tower Movement caught
his attention and ultimately resulted in his use of a police force
against them. In one incident he arrested 138 Watch Tower
Africans in the vicinity of Fife. Some see the incidents as

early examples of anti-colonial activity. Others praised Draper's restraint for avoiding a bloody conflict.

DUPONT, BISHOP JOSEPH. A Roman Catholic missionary of the order called the White Fathers, Rev. Dupont came south from East Africa in 1890 to begin a settlement along the Stevenson Road at Mambwe. From there he planned to move further south to convert the Bemba. He was personally involved in two notable (and successful) attempts to set up missions among the Bemba, both of which laid the groundwork for British authorities as well. The first was the result of the White Fathers' attempts in 1894 and 1895 to set up a mission near Makasa's (q. v.) village at Mipini, despite Chitimukulu Sampa's (q. v.) edict prohibiting white men from Bemba country. Makasa vacillated, granting permission and then withdrawing it in the face of Sampa's threat to attack Makasa. Sampa had also seemed to encourage it at one point but again withdrew permission. Finally in July, 1895, Dupont visited Makasa again and, defying instructions to leave the village, forced Makasa to call Sampa's bluff. When Sampa did not attack, Makasa willingly allowed a mission to be started at Kayambi, near Mipini. Twice later Sampa invited Dupont to visit his capital, but was turned down. In 1897 Dupont was named Bishop of the "Nyassa" region. The other successful mission came as a result of a request by another Bemba chief, Mwamba (q. v.), to visit his village in 1898. Dupont arrived on October 11 to find Mwamba mentally alert but not far from death. Mwamba hoped the Bishop could heal him or, if Mwamba died, succeed him so other Bemba leaders would not invade his capital and kill his followers. Dupont built a chapel nearby, provided morphine as a pain-killer, and helped Mwamba until his death on October 23. From his mission along the Milungu stream, Dupont then accepted the authority of Mwamba, presumably to serve as regent at minimum. In his successful effort to maintain local order, however, Dupont began acting more as a chief, knowing that eventually the British would send a force and impose their rule. This finally happened when Robert Codrington (q. v.), Administrator of North-Eastern Rhodesia came to settle the matter of succession in May, 1899. The new Mwamba was installed in September.

THE DUTCH REFORMED CHURCH. The principal church of the Afrikaners in South Africa, it instituted missionary work in Nyasaland in 1889 and in North-Eastern Rhodesia (the eastern half of Zambia) near the turn of the century. It never gained a large following except among whites from South Africa, although its missionaries worked among the Nyanja-speaking peoples for many years. Its successor under African control is called the Reformed Church of Zambia.

- E -

EASTERN PROVINCE.   One of the eight provinces of Zambia, it
    stretches along most of the eastern and southeastern borders
    from south of the city of Isoka in the northeast to north of the
    city of Feira in the south.   It consists of three rural districts,
    Lundazi, Chipata, and Petauke.   The provincial capital is in
    Chipata.   The 1969 census showed the district had a population
    slightly over half a million (509, 000).   Over half of these
    (261, 000) live in the Chipata district.   The town of Chipata
    was formerly known as Fort Jameson.   Among the major ethnic
    groups in the province are Chewa, Senga, Ngoni, Nsenga and
    Kunda.   Part of the reason for the narrow shape of the prov-
    ince is that its western border is fixed for a long stretch by
    the Luangwa River.

ECONOMIC SURVEY MISSION ON THE ECONOMIC DEVELOPMENT
    OF ZAMBIA   see   SEERS REPORT

ELWELL, ARCHIBALD H.   An experienced British civil servant
    who was sent to Kitwe on the Copperbelt in 1944 by the Co-
    lonial Office to serve as a social welfare officer.   His sympa-
    thy for African aspirations led to "the Elwell incident."   On
    the request of a leader of the Kitwe African Society, he ad-
    dressed the group in January, 1946.   He suggested that such
    groups interested in the welfare of Africans might consider
    sponsoring welfare centers or even forming political or labor
    organizations.   A well-conducted strike by an African trade
    union could bring benefits.   His brief speech angered mine of-
    ficials and the local district commissioner.   Elwell was soon
    transferred to Livingstone and, a few months later, sent back
    to London.

EMERGENCY DEVELOPMENT PLAN (EDP).   Initiated in March,
    1964, the plan allocated one million pounds for accelerating
    and expanding the educational program at both primary and
    secondary levels.   Education was also seen as the main nation-
    al priority in the Transitional Development Plan (q. v.) with
    which it was merged when the TDP began in January, 1965.

EMRYS-EVANS, PAUL V.   President of the British South Africa
    Company during the period around Zambian independence.   It
    was he who represented the Company during the negotiations
    which resulted in the Company agreeing to give up all of its
    mineral royalty rights in exchange for four million pounds.
    The announcement came just hours before the moment of Zam-
    bian independence.

ENGLISH COMMON LAW.   The basis of jurisprudence in Zambia.
    This is in contrast to the Roman-Dutch law adopted in Southern
    Rhodesia after the pattern in the Republic of South Africa.

ETHIOPIAN CHURCH OF BAROTSELAND.   A church movement

run by Africans in Barotseland immediately before and after
1900. With ties to both the Ethiopian movement in South Africa and the African Methodist Episcopal Church (q. v.), it was
led by a man from Barotseland, Willie Mokalapa (q. v.). (Ethi-
opianism in general is a trend where Africans break away from
European-dominated churches to create their own.) Mokalapa
was a trusted worker for the Paris Mission Society (PMS) in
Barotseland. In 1898 he began to express his displeasure with
the treatment of African churchmen by the missionaries. The
Lozi King, Lewanika, responded favorably to Mokalapa's proposal to begin schools that would teach English and practical
skills to his people. Lewanika did not favor the religious education in the Lozi language taught by the missionaries. Ultimately the Colonial administration and missionaries had to offer what the Lozi wanted. The result was the creation of the
Barotse National School (q. v.) in 1907. Meanwhile Mokalapa's
church grew rapidly as he broke from the PMS, taking with
him large numbers of African followers, including relatives
of Lewanika. The Church and schools prospered until late
1905 when Mokalapa was swindled of 750 pounds of Lewanika's
money in Cape Town where he was supposed to buy some large
equipment such as carriages. The Church declined when Mokalapa failed to return out of humiliation.

EURAFRICAN (or EURO-AFRICAN). A word used to refer to
people of mixed racial origin, one parent predominantly European, and the other predominantly African, and to the descendants of such people. A 1965 estimate suggested that there
were about 2500 Eurafricans in Zambia, but this figure could
be quite deceptive. Another source estimates the figure is
closer to ten thousand. Another word for Eurafrican is
Coloured (q. v.). Politically, they formed the Northern Rhodesian Eurafrican Association (q. v.).

EUROPEAN MINE WORKERS' UNION (EMWU). Formed in 1936,
its goals included the maintenance of racially distinct pay
scales and job restrictions limiting certain skilled and semi-
skilled jobs to Europeans. Recruitment from Europe was encouraged when needed to meet demands. In 1955 the Anglo-
American Corporation accepted the right of the EMWU to veto
any changes in the color bar as applied to jobs, although some
new job categories were opened to Africans that year. An
agreement in November, 1960, indicated that the EMWU acknowledged the inevitable. Its 4700 members voted by a
majority vote to open sixty more job categories to Africans.
It also voted equal pay for the races and promotion patterns
which eliminated race as a factor.

EUROPEANS. A term used to apply to all "white" men, regardless of their continent of origin. Basungu is one of the African words for the same concept. In 1963 there were about
seventy-six thousand Europeans in Zambia. In 1969 the figure
was down to 43,490. Many left after independence, many be-

cause they feared they would lose their privileged life style under African rule. Others have gone because their jobs were Africanized.

EVANS, IFOR. A justice of the Zambian High Court whose decision in July, 1969, to release two Portuguese soldiers who had been arrested for illegal entry into Zambia set off violent demonstrations against the court. Even President Kaunda condemned Evans for his decision. In June of that year Evans had ruled that eight UNIP MP's (including three Ministers) had been invalidly elected the previous December, and had criticized the Commissioner of Police for "deliberate misconduct and mismanagement." Eventually Kaunda apologized for the attacks on the court, but Evans and the other justices, including Chief Justice James Skinner (q.v.) resigned or retired.

EVELYN HONE COLLEGE OF APPLIED ARTS AND SCIENCES. Located in Lusaka, this is the second largest institution of higher education in the country (after the University of Zambia). It offers a wide variety of vocational and trade courses which lead often to immediate employment. It was named after Sir Evelyn Hone (q.v.), the Governor of Northern Rhodesia at the time of independence.

EXECUTIVE COUNCIL. A body created to advise the Governor of Northern Rhodesia on executive matters, it was provided for in the 1924 Order in Council that established British Colonial rule there. It was composed entirely of colonial officials. While the Governor was required to consult with it, he could reject its advice but then had to report his reasons to the Secretary of State for the Colonies. Seldom did he reject their advice. In 1939 the election of non-official members ("Unofficials") was provided for. Changes in 1945 left the Council with five official members to three unofficials. Only officials held Ministerial portfolios. In 1948 the Council was expanded to eleven members. Four of them were Unofficials; one of them was nominated (not elected) and was designated specifically to represent African interests. In 1949 two Unofficials were given portfolios. An Order in Council that went into force on December 31, 1953, reduced the officials to five, but they retained a five to four majority. Constitutional change in 1959 gave the Unofficials (dominated by the ruling party) a majority on the Executive Council and five of the portfolios. However the membership was composed of four officials, four elected unofficials and two Africans both with full ministerial status. The 1964 Constitution replaced the Executive Council with a Cabinet (q.v.).

- F -

FEDERAL DOMINION PARTY (FDP). The principal opposition party in the Federal House, it was formed in 1958 when

Winston Field, leader of the Southern Rhodesia Dominion Party
was elected to the Federal Parliament and joined with G. F.
van Eeden, head of the Northern Rhodesia Commonwealth Party.
The right wing party had support among white farmers in the
Southern Province of Northern Rhodesia and among South African miners on the Copperbelt. One of its principal proposals
was to subdivide the Federation into segregated spheres of influence for Europeans and Africans. Voting rights for Africans would be severely restricted by extreme qualifications.
Near the end of the Federation, there were proposals to merge
the FDP and the Rhodesian Republican Party to force Sir Roy
Welensky's resignation. At the time the FDP had seven
seats. In March, 1962, the Dominion Party in Southern Rhodesia merged with various dissident conservatives to form the
Rhodesian Front.

FEDERAL ELECTORAL BILL. Introduced in the Parliament of the
Central African Federation in September, 1957, it became law
the following January. It was passed despite the objections of
the African Affairs Board. Its provisions included two voting
rolls with separate qualifications. Most of those on the upper
roll were Europeans, while the lower roll was mostly Africans.
The Africans objected to the fact that the eight seats to be
filled by Africans were to be chosen by members of both rolls,
whereas only upper roll voters could fill the remaining forty-
four seats.

FEDERAL FIGHTING FUND (FFF). A drive to collect money in
support of Roy Welensky (q. v.) and the Federation, it was
started by Colin Cunningham (q. v.) in 1960. It was announced
at a meeting held in Kitwe where about a thousand Europeans
contributed to send a delegation to England to make public ap-
pearances in support of the Federation. They also pledged
support of law and order and opposition to Communism. While
Cunningham called the African politicians "dirty agitators,"
Kaunda called the FFF, "Fifteen Fighting Fools. "

FEDERAL PARTY. Formed in 1953 in order to contest the January, 1954, Federal elections, it grew out of the United Central
Africa Association (q. v.). Its most prominent members were
Sir Roy Welensky (q. v.) and Sir Godfrey Huggins (Lord Malvern). Pledged to the concept of "partnership, " it won twenty-
four of the twenty-six contested seats in the Federal Parliament.
In February, 1954, it won ten of the twelve elected seats in
the Northern Rhodesia Legislative Council. Huggins became
Prime Minister but retired in 1956 when Welensky succeeded
him both as Federal Prime Minister and as leader of the
Federal Party. In March, 1958, the Federal Party merged
with the United Rhodesia Party and the two became the United
Federal Party (q. v.).

FEDERAL REVIEW CONFERENCE. Held in London from December 5, 1960, until December 16, it was supposed to review the

constitution of the Central African Federation with the assumption that changes would occur.   The three African nationalists, Kenneth Kaunda, Joshua Nkomo, and H. K. Banda, had planned to boycott it, but finally participated when Britain agreed to schedule conferences for Northern Rhodesia and Nyasaland for mid-December. The three leaders walked out on December 12 along with Northern Rhodesian chiefs, but Kaunda and his delegation returned in time for a final session on December 16. The abortive conference did convince the British of the irreconcilable differences between the nationalists and the federalists.

FEDERATION. A concept suggested by some settlers in the late 1940's who did not like the concept of amalgamation (q.v.).   It was felt by some, such as Stewart Gore-Browne (q.v.) that a federation of the Rhodesias and Nyasaland could bring the benefits of economic interdependence yet also preserve African rights.   Ultimately, of course, the Central African Federation was the result.

FEDERATION OF AFRICAN SOCIETIES OF NORTHERN RHODESIA (or FEDERATION OF WELFARE SOCIETIES). An organization formed on May 18, 1946, it was to change its name in 1948 to the Northern Rhodesian African Congress (q.v.).   The welfare societies of the country had met at Kafue in 1933 with the idea of forming a union of concerned Africans from around the Protectorate.   Officials saw it as subversive and forbade any political activity.   Thus no organization developed until 1946 when Dauti Yamba (q.v.), Godwin Lewanika (q.v.) and representatives of fourteen African societies created this organization.   Yamba became its President.   The Government reacted by forming the African Representative Council, but this act of tokenism did not defuse the budding nationalists.   The fourteen societies included traders' groups and farmers' organizations in addition to six welfare societies.   Under the leadership of Yamba and George Kaluwa (q.v.), the Federation opposed both amalgamation and federation with Southern Rhodesia, attempted to get seats on the African Representative Council, and sought representation at London constitutional talks.   While they lost, the Government was forced to recognize them and deal with them.   A general conference of the organization in July, 1948, passed a number of resolutions but also made its political goals explicit by changing its name to the Northern Rhodesia African Congress.   It was soon to be renamed the African National Congress.

FEDERATION (or CONSTITUTION) ORDER IN COUNCIL. The official act that created the Central African Federation.   It passed the British Parliament in May, 1953, and received the approval of Queen Elizabeth II on August 1, 1953.   Two months later the Federation became a reality.

FEIRA. The least populated district in Zambia, located in the

Central Province, it contains the small settlement also called
Feira.   It is primarily of historic interest, as its location on
the confluence of the Zambezi and Luangwa Rivers gave it
prominence.   A market or fair (after which it was named) was
established there in 1732, and travelers would use it as a link
in their travel into the interior of Central Africa after having
come up the Zambezi River from the Indian Ocean coast.
The Portuguese soldiers considered it a dangerous outpost.

FIELD, WINSTON.   Leader of the Federal Dominion Party (q. v.)
in the Federal Parliament and also a leader of the Rhodesian
Front in Southern Rhodesia.   He became Prime Minister of
Southern Rhodesia as a result of the December, 1962 elections.
He resigned from this position under Cabinet pressure in April,
1964, to be succeeded by Ian Smith.

FIFE.   An outpost and trading station founded in 1894 by the African Lakes Company.   It was situated on the road between Lake
Nyasa and Abercorn, which was one hundred miles northwest
of Fife.   It was named after the Duke of Fife, son-in-law of
the Prince of Wales and a member of the board of directors of
the British South Africa Company.   In 1914, as part of World
War I, a German force moved into Northern Rhodesia and
fired on both Abercorn and Fife, with little effect.

FINANCIAL DEVELOPMENT CORPORATION (FINDECO).   A parastatal body set up in 1971 by the Zambian Government to oversee financial institutions run by the government, such as the
insurance company, the building society, and government shares
in the Commercial Bank of Zambia, Ltd. and the National Commercial Bank, Ltd.   It has also helped finance some African
businessmen and is working on the diversification and development of the rural economy.   FINDECO has successfully financed Zambia's economic reforms, and is currently concen-
trating on the promotion of industries geared to import substi-
tution, the creation of employment, and the earning of foreign
exchange.

FINGER MILLET.   One of the staple foods of Zambia, especially
in the northeastern part.   Because of poor soil, it is usually
grown by farmers who practice chitimene (q. v.), a form of
slash and burn agriculture.   The millet seed is planted in a
bed of ash from burned branches.   Harvested in April and May,
it is stored until used.   It can be ground into a white flour and
made into a kind of dumpling.   Beer can also be made from it.

FIPA.   A people living north of the Bemba in Southwestern Tanzania, east of Lake Tanganyika.   It appears that some Fipa, known
then as 'Sukuma, " lived in what is now Bemba territory around
1800.   A few may still live there.   The Fipa are well known
for their skills as smiths.

FIRST NATIONAL DEVELOPMENT PLAN (FNDP).   Replacing the

Emergency Development Plan in June, 1966, the FNDP was
supposed to provide development projects and guidelines for
four years. Ultimately it was extended to December, 1971,
however. Its original budget of $400 million (U.S.) was also
increased. Among its long range goals was creating 100,000
new jobs, increasing production of goods by 11 percent each
year, and expansion of educational facilities. It also tried to
reorient its economy away from Rhodesia and toward East
Africa. Specific projects included the international airport at
Lusaka, a petroleum pipeline from the Copperbelt to Tanzania,
greatly improved roads, and several hydroelectric projects,
notably the large Kafue Dam. Other projects involved expansion of hospitals and the University of Zambia. Even agricultural projects were included. Its goal of reducing development
inequality among the provinces of Zambia was not really attained.

FIRST ZAMBIAN REPUBLIC. The title now given the Zambian
governmental form from independence on October 24, 1964, until December, 1972. At that time a one-party participatory
democracy was created which is now called the Second Zambian
Republic.

FLAG OF ZAMBIA. Introduced to Zambians in June, 1964, by
President Kaunda, its base color is green, representing the
grassland of the country and its agricultural products. About
one-third of it however is taken up by an orange eagle flying
over a block of three vertical stripes, colored orange, black
and red. The eagle in flight represents Zambian freedom.
The orange stripe symbolizes the country's mineral resources
(heavily copper), the black represents the color of most of the
population, and the red stripe is symbolic of the blood that was
shed for freedom.

FORBES, MAJOR PATRICK WILLIAM. Deputy Administrator of
Northern Rhodesia (but in fact only North-Eastern Rhodesia)
from July, 1895, to June, 1897. He made his reputation with
his employer, the British South Africa Company, by successfully leading the Company's forces in battles against both the
Portuguese and the Ndebele nation, among others, in the early
1890's. Thus in 1895 he was made the principal administrator
of the Company's land north of the Zambezi and west of Nyasaland. His headquarters were actually outside his own territory,
at Zomba. His major task was to extend BSAC influence deep
into the region and try to have much of it explored and mapped.
He also tried to stop the slave trade, and thus set up bomas
(q.v.) in the northeastern part of his territory near Fife and
near the present-day Isoka. He also encouraged Father Dupont
of the White Fathers to establish mission stations among the
Bemba.

FORT JAMESON. Renamed Chipata (q.v.) since Zambian independence, Fort Jameson became an important administrative

town for the British South Africa Company when Robert Codrington, the Deputy Administrator of North-Eastern Rhodesia,
transferred his headquarters there from Blantyre in 1899. It
was then a new outpost, created near the town of the Ngoni
leader, Mpezeni (q.v.), who had only been subdued by force
the previous year. Its location is in the southeastern part of
Zambia, only five miles from the border of Malawi. Within
a year there were twenty brick houses built. As Europeans
settled nearby, Fort Jameson became a small center for trade
and services, kept busy by European planters and officials.
Codrington encouraged colonization, and tobacco for export became a popular crop just before World War I. In the succeeding ten years there was an influx of settlers born in India,
many of them taking over petty trade. Still Fort Jameson
never became large. An estimate in 1960 gave the population
as about four hundred Europeans, three thousand Africans in
employment, and three hundred of "other races," mostly Indians.

FORT JAMESON NGONI. A term frequently used to refer to that
group of Ngoni (q.v.) who were under the leadership of Mpezeni (q.v.) and settled around what is now the city of Chipata
(formerly called Fort Jameson).

FORT ROSEBERY. Known as Mansa (q.v.) since independence,
the town had its beginning as a British South Africa Company
outpost in the 1890's. Alfred Sharpe, a BSAC representative,
chose a site for it along the Luapula River in 1892. He
named it for Lord Rosebery, the current British Foreign Secretary. While it was never built there, maps recorded its
existence on the Luapula for many years. When it was finally
constructed years later, the new site was about thirty miles
east of the Luapula River and about fifty miles west of Lake
Bangweulu. It became the administrative boma for District
Commissioners. As a district center its population grew to
about 5700 by 1969 and it had acquired a small airfield.
Manganese has been mined nearby. During the 1950's and
60's it became a center for ZANC and UNIP political activity.

FOX-PITT, COMMANDER THOMAS S. L. A British colonial officer who served in a variety of posts, one of which was as
provincial commissioner in Barotseland in the late 1940's.
While he retired in the early 1950's, he was significant as an
adviser and confidante to African nationalists. Before he returned to his home in England he joined the African National
Congress. He continued to meet Kaunda and others in England
and to correspond with them at home. The government of the
Central African Federation banned his return there, but Kaunda
reversed that when he took power.

FRANKLIN, HARRY. Specially Nominated Member of the Legislative Council for African Interests, he was especially interested
in the possibilities of a multi-racial society. He was something

of a political moderate, however, and because of his support
of and close friendship with Harry Nkumbula he alienated many
of the more militant Africans.   In 1957 he helped form the
multiracial Constitution Party (q. v.), which merged with the
newly created Central Africa Party (q. v.) in 1959 to contest
the Federation elections.   Franklin and Sir John Moffat became
two of the best CAP candidates in Northern Rhodesia, winning
two of the seats reserved for Europeans, but with overwhelming support from African voters.   Franklin and Moffat also led
the Northern Rhodesia wing of the CAP to an independent status
as the N. R. Liberal Party in 1960.   When the United Federal
Party resigned from the Government after the London Conference of February, 1961, Franklin and two other Liberals took
ministerial posts on the Executive Council.

FREE CHURCH OF SCOTLAND.   One of the numerous churches
    which, inspired by the work of Dr. David Livingstone, came to
    Central Africa.   Much of its work was centered in the present
    day Malawi, notably the Livingstonia Mission.   This mission
    did set up stations in Northern Zambia, opening one at Chiren-
    ji in 1882-83.   While it was closed in 1888, a new station was
    opened at Mwenzo in 1894-95.   Among the Africans influenced
    by missionaries from the Scottish Church was the father of
    Zambia's first President, David Kaunda, himself an evangelist
    for them.   In 1924 its Central African program was renamed
    the Church of Central Africa, Presbyterian.   It later became
    part of the United Church of Zambia (q. v.).

FREEDOM HOUSE.   A building along Freedom Road in Lusaka
    that houses the offices of the ruling party, UNIP.

FWAMBO.   The name of both a town in extreme northeastern Zam-
    bia and of an important Mambwe chief in the same area.
        As a location it became the site of a mission station of
    the London Missionary Society.   It was opened in 1887.
        Fwambo the chief had become the most powerful Mambwe
    chief by the mid-1880's.   His section of the Mambwe, living
    near the Tanganyika border, were famous for mining iron ore,
    and smelting and exporting it.   This was part of the reason
    for their strength.   Fwambo was one of the few chiefs to suc-
    cessfully fight off the Bemba before the arrival of the British.
    Ponde was one of the Bemba leaders whose forces were de-
    feated by Fwambo as late as the mid-1890's.   He also was re-
    luctant to welcome British administrators, notably Hugh Mar-
    shall (q. v.), first Collector of the Tanganyika District.

- G -

GAMITTO, CAPTAIN ANTONIO.   An officer in the Portuguese
    army stationed in Mozambique in 1830 when a caravan of ivory
    came from the Lunda King Kazembe (q. v.) to the post at Tete.
    Gamitto and Major Jose Monteiro were made leaders of an

expedition to Kazembe's capital along the Luapula River. The
trip began in 1831 and cut in a northwest direction through
eastern Zambia, notably through Bisa and Bemba territory before reaching Kazembe. Gamitto's journal tells of the growing
power of the Bemba throughout the region, especially through
military conquest, and also documents the elegance of Kazembe
and his capital. The mission was frustrated in its attempt to
establish trade with the Lunda, however, as the Arabs were
firmly in control of it. After threats on their lives, the two
leaders returned their expedition in 1832 to Tete where Gamitto's negative report discouraged future Portuguese attempts
to establish this trade.

GAUNT, JOHN. A prominent political figure in Northern Rhodesia,
especially during the period of Federation, he was born in England in 1905 and went to Africa in 1925. He farmed in
Northern Rhodesia briefly before entering the Colonial Service.
In 1937 he became a District Commissioner, serving in Mkushi,
Lusaka, Mankoya, and Livingstone. From 1950 to 1953 he
was Director of African Affairs in Lusaka. In 1953 he formed
the segregationist Confederate Party, and eventually merged its
remnants into the new Dominion Party in 1956. He united this
with groups in Southern Rhodesia and called it the Federal
Dominion Party. Winston Field was its head and Gaunt was
the Deputy Leader. Gaunt had been elected to the Northern
Rhodesia Legislative Council in 1954 as an Independent. In
1957 he was expelled from the Dominion Party but was elected
to a Lusaka seat in the Federal legislature in 1958. In 1960
he founded the Rhodesia Reformed Party. When Winston Field
was elected Prime Minister in 1962 with his Rhodesian Front
Party, he chose Gaunt to be his Minister of Mines. Considered
to be an extremist even by some right wing friends, Gaunt was
very antagonistic toward African nationalists, comparing people
like Julius Nyerere and Dr. H. K. Banda to Adolf Hitler. He
claimed to favor the "best" leadership, regardless of race, but
clearly expected little quality to emerge in Africans. At one
point he favored partitioning Northern Rhodesia into African
and European sections. The Copperbelt and line of rail would
be European under that plan.

GENERAL MISSIONARY CONFERENCE OF NORTHERN RHODESIA.
An attempt at some degree of unity and cooperation among the
various mission churches in Zambia, it first met in 1914. It
continued to meet regularly until it was replaced by the Christian Council (q.v.) in 1944. For a while the Roman Catholics
maintained an associate membership, but generally it has been
a Protestant gathering.

GERMAN EAST AFRICA. The name given to Zambia's northeastern
neighbor until the end of World War I when the British took
over and renamed the area Tanganyika. After union with Zanzibar in 1964 it became Tanzania.

GIBBONS, MAJOR A. ST. H. One of the early explorers of the
    western part of Zambia. He first visited and mapped out part
    of the Lozi kingdom in 1895-96. He hoped to determine for
    European prospectors and settlers whether the area could have
    much value for them. He returned with another expedition in
    1898. This one was sponsored by the British South Africa
    Company and the Royal Geographical Society, among others.
    This time its goals included making an ethnographic survey of
    all the Lozi territory, judging the area's economic potential,
    and determining the exact limits of the kingdom of the Lozi.

GIRAUD, VICTOR. A French explorer who took a small expedition
    through Bemba territory and the area around Lake Bangweulu
    in 1883 and 1884. He visited Chitimukulu Chitapankwa, who
    reportedly gave him a "splendid reception."

GLENNIE, A. F. B. Provincial Commissioner and, later, Resi-
    dent Commissioner of Barotseland for eleven years from the
    mid-1940's to the mid-1950's. A tough and sober-minded ad-
    ministrator, he oversaw (and demanded) major reforms in the
    traditional Barotse Government. He especially demanded re-
    form of the Barotse National Council (q. v.) and reinstatement
    of another council, the Katengo (q. v.). His efforts to modernize
    the councils by adding younger and better educated Lozi only
    alienated both the traditionalists and the modernizing elements.

GONDWE, A. H. A member of the Central Africa Party who was
    successfully elected to the Legislative Council in the 1959 elec-
    tions, the only African among the three CAP members elected.
    In February, 1961, he and the other two (Harry Franklin and
    John Moffat) received ministerial posts on the Executive Coun-
    cil when the United Federal Party withdrew from the govern-
    ment. He ran again in the 1962 elections and, though defeated,
    he received more votes than any others in his party--which had
    been renamed the Northern Rhodesia Liberal Party in 1960.

GONDWE, JEREMIAH. One of the evangelists of the Watch Tower
    Movement in the late 1920's and early 1930's. Originally from
    Nyasaland, he preached heavily in the Ndola district. Eventu-
    ally he had to flee to the Congo to avoid arrest, as the govern-
    ment saw political unrest as a possible aftermath of his preaching.

GOODE, RICHARD ALLMOND JEFFREY. Acting Administrator of
    Northern Rhodesia for the British South Africa Company from
    March, 1922, until May, 1923. He returned as Acting Admin-
    istrator from September, 1923, until the British Colonial Office
    took over in February, 1924.

GOOLD-ADAMS, MAJOR H. A British Colonial Office official in
    Bechuanaland who was sent to Barotseland in 1896 in order to
    clarify the boundaries of the domain of the Lozi King Lewanika
    (q. v.). The Major arrived at the capital, Lealui, in October,
    but it took the intervention of the missionary, Adolph Jalla

(q. v.) to convince Lewanika that he was a representative of
Queen Victoria. It was the British hope that Goold-Adams
could provide facts to allow a settlement with the Portuguese
over the Barotseland-Angola border. Since later expeditions
contradicted his report, however, it would eventually take international arbitration to settle the matter.

GORE-BROWNE, COLONEL (SIR) STEWART. One of the most important of the settler-politicians, and certainly the one closest
   to the Africans and their nationalist cause. Born in Great
   Britain, he first came to Northern Rhodesia in 1911 as an officer with a joint Anglo-Belgian commission seeking to set the
   Congo-Northern Rhodesia border. He returned in 1921 and set
   up a farming estate in an isolated part of Bemba country (in
   northern Zambia). There he built a virtual baronial fortress
   for a home. In 1935 he was elected to the Legislative Council,
   and quickly demonstrated an understanding of the rural African.
   He opposed racial segregation and favored cooperation between
   the races in running the country. In 1938 he was picked to
   represent African interests on the Council. In this capacity he
   played an important role in getting Urban Courts and African
   Advisory Councils initiated on the Copperbelt. Speaking ciBemba, he traveled extensively to discuss problems with the Africans. He especially made the point that Europeans should lis-
   ten to the educated Africans, not just the Chiefs. He frequently spoke to African Welfare Societies, and encouraged the
   growth of nationalist groups. He came into conflict with the
   nationalists, however, when he proposed in 1948 that Northern
   Rhodesia could be partitioned into an African-controlled area
   and a European part. He consistently favored African self-
   rule, and thus angered many Europeans who favored amalgamation with Southern Rhodesia; yet he alienated African nationalists when he advocated self-rule for Africans in Northern Rhodesia but within a Central African Federation. He fought hard
   for the Federation, which he saw as a healthy compromise
   which would help both Africans and Europeans. Early in 1961,
   Gore-Browne officially joined UNIP. In April, 1962, he accompanied Kenneth Kaunda to give testimony in New York before the U.N. Commission on Colonialism. In the October,
   1962, elections he ran on the UNIP ticket for a seat in the
   Legislative Council, but he failed to get elected despite heavy
   support from the Africans. Kaunda ordered a state funeral after Gore-Browne's death on August 4, 1967.

GOVERNOR OF NORTHERN RHODESIA. An office created on
   February 20, 1924, shortly before Northern Rhodesia became
   a Protectorate under the jurisdiction of the British Crown (on
   April 1st). Executive power was vested in the Governor who
   was appointed by the Crown on the advice of the British Government. He was directly responsible to the Government in
   London for all matters concerning the government of the Territory. He was assisted by an Executive Council. If he chose
   to reject their advice, which he seldom did, he was required

to explain his reasons to the Secretary of State for the Colonies. As election to the Legislative Council became the norm and Unofficials came to dominate the Executive Council, the Governor was expected to consult the majority party in the Legco before appointing the Executive Council. All subordinate administrators and provincial commissioners were also responsible to the governor. During the period of peak nationalist activity, notably while Sir Arthur Benson (q. v.) was governor, the use of emergency powers and other formidable powers by the governors brought the latter into considerable conflict with the emerging African leaders.

GREAT EAST ROAD. One of the two major roads in Zambia, it starts at Lusaka and travels east for five hundred miles to the town of Salima in Malawi. It crosses into Malawi at Chipata, Zambia. The considerable amount of commercial traffic traveling this road proceeds from Salima, a railhead, to the port of Beira in Mozambique by means of the railway. This route became important for Zambia after the closing of traffic through Rhodesia (Zimbabwe). The Great East Road is now almost fully tarred, due in part to a major loan from the World Bank.

GREAT NORTH ROAD. One of the oldest and most important routes in Central Africa, it has carried traffic for many centuries, crossing Zambia from its northeastern corner south to near Victoria Falls. Travelers south have probably included Bushmen, Hottentots, many Bantu groups, and Arab traders. Boers have traveled north on it en route from South Africa to Kenya and Tanganyika (now Tanzania). The "Cape-to-Cairo" railway dream of the nineteenth century would have followed much of this route. The road, fully tarred with the help of a World Bank loan, goes north from Livingstone to Lusaka and on to Kapiri Mposhi near the northern edge of the Copperbelt. From there it angles northeast to the border, crossing near Tunduma, Tanzania. It then heads east to the port at Dar es Salaam. It has become a crucial commercial link with the world, especially since southern rail traffic through Rhodesia (Zimbabwe) has been eliminated. The Tan-Zam Railway (q. v.) follows a route parallel to the Great North Road. Since the road was only gravel for many years and was very treacherous from November to April due to the rainy season, it became known as the "Hell Run," notably by the truck drivers who had to carry the copper and petroleum along the road in spite of poor conditions.

GREAT UHURU RAILWAY. Same as Tan-Zam Railway (q. v.).

GRIFFITHS, JAMES. British Labour Party Minister who headed the Colonial Office from March, 1950, until October, 1951. He replaced Arthur Creech Jones as Colonial Secretary. Griffiths agreed to the convening of a conference in London in March, 1951, to discuss Central Africa. This conference produced a recommendation for a federal constitution. Griffiths then toured Central Africa and continued to encourage unity, despite finding considerable African opposition. It was he who introduced the soon widely used word "partnership" (q.v.) which he also defined. His party lost its majority and he his post soon after. As an Opposition M.P., however, he served as spokesman for the cause of adequate African influence in the Federation. He feared they would be at the mercy of the settlers.

GROUNDNUTS. One of the common agricultural products, especially in the northeastern part of Zambia. They are not indigenous to Central Africa but entered via trade routes. They were being grown by the Bisa before the end of the eighteenth century and were fairly common among the Bemba by the mid-nineteenth century.

GUJARAT PROVINCE. The province in Western India that is the original home province of the families of almost all the Indians in Zambia.

GWEMBE TONGA. One of the subdivisions of the broader ethnic group called the Tonga (q.v.), they live in the Gwembe Valley (q.v.). Around 1908 they caused considerable difficulty for the British South Africa Company by vigorously protesting and resisting the imposition of taxes. Problems arose again in the late 1950's. The Kariba Dam (q.v.) had been built and the waters of Lake Kariba were rising and flooding their homeland. About twenty-nine thousand people were resettled, six thousand being moved a hundred miles away, to Lusitu. Again major resistance occurred, especially among those bound for Lusitu, and in a clash with police on September 10, 1958, eight people were killed and thirty-four wounded. The Government has trained many Gwembe Tonga as fishermen to use Lake Kariba as the source of a fishing industry.

GWEMBE VALLEY. Now partly inundated by the vast, man-made Lake Kariba (q.v.), it was the traditional home of the Gwembe Tonga. The flat-bottomed valley, hot and inhospitable, started about sixty miles from the Victoria Falls. The Zambezi River poured out of the Batoka Gorge and into the valley where it flowed peacefully. It was the home of enormous herds of elephants, which the Tonga hunted for their tusks. This created a major trading industry with Asian traders on the east coast of Africa. The tusks were traded for numerous imports, including glass beads, sea shells, and porcelain items. The ivory trade was occurring as early as the second century A.D.

GWISHO HOT SPRINGS. An area in south-central Zambia, nine miles from the Kafue River, where Late Stone Age hunter-gatherers similar to the Bushmen (q.v.) lived. The site, near the edge of the Kafue flood plain, where large herds of game can still be found, has been radiocarbon-dated between 2800 and 1700 B.C.

- H -

HAMMARSKJOLD, DAG. Secretary General of the United Nations
    from April, 1953, until his death on September 18, 1961.
    Near the city of Ndola in Northern Rhodesia, his plane crashed
    while he was on a mediation visit to the Congo.

HARDING, COLONEL COLIN. A senior official of the British
    South Africa Company who served in several capacities in
    North-Western Rhodesia (especially Barotseland) in the period
    around the beginning of the twentieth century. His experiences
    are recorded in his several books. He appears to have been
    the only European official to place the interests of the Lozi
    above those of the company, costing him his job in 1906. He
    served as Acting Resident of Barotseland from November,
    1898, to February, 1899. In October, 1900, he served as a
    witness when Lewanika signed an important concession to BSAC.
    Later he implied that the principal company representative,
    Robert Coryndon, had not informed the Lozi of the full details
    of the concession they signed. From the end of 1900 through
    much of 1901 Harding was Acting Administrator of North-
    Western Rhodesia. He also served as the first commander of
    the Barotse Native Police (q.v.) in the first years of the cen-
    tury.

HARRINGTON, H. T. Assistant Collector (administrator) for the
    British South Africa Company in the Luapula-Mweru District
    stationed at Abercorn near the end of the nineteenth century.
    In 1899 he became Collector at Kalungwishi on Lake Mweru.
    In April, 1899, he was called upon by Andrew Law, Collector
    at Abercorn to aid him in attacking the Arab slave traders who
    were functioning out of Chief Mporokoso's (q.v.) stockade.
    Harrington brought nearly a hundred armed men and the Arabs
    were defeated after a day-long battle. The defeat of Mporo-
    koso marked the last attempt by the Bemba to resist the es-
    tablishment of European rule in the Northern Province.

HATCH SYSTEM. One of the widespread discriminatory practices
    found throughout Northern Rhodesia (and other parts of Central
    and Southern Africa). Until the mid-1950's, it was the custom
    that Africans were not permitted to enter the main doors of
    shops but instead were handed their purchases through hatches
    or "pigeon-holes" at the side or back of the buildings. It was
    an unwritten law but was seldom violated. As African national-
    ist consciousness rose, the Hatch System became the focus of
    increasing agitation, especially around 1950 when boycotts of a
    number of businesses engaged in this practice took place in
    many cities. It began in Broken Hill. In 1954 the Northern
    Rhodesian Congress picketed stores in Lusaka, notably butcher
    shops which also sold Africans the poorest meat. Successes
    there resulted in further protests in other cities, many of them
    at least partly successful. Some stores sealed their hatches.
    Further boycotts in April, 1956, in Lusaka (and later elsewhere)

seemed to put an end to the hatch system, especially in the
major cities. The first major step in dismantling the color
bar had been taken.

HEMANS, JAMES. A controversial missionary of the London Missionary Society, he arrived in North-Eastern Rhodesia in 1888.
A black man from the West Indies, he came into conflict with
his white colleagues over his tolerance of native customs that
others considered to be immoral. Hemans also felt that the
advantage of his skin color was not being fully utilized by his
superiors, especially in view of the prejudice of certain Bemba
leaders against white missionaries.

HIGH COURT. A High Court was established in North-Eastern
Rhodesia as a result of an Order in Council of 1900. It was
given full civil and criminal jurisdiction. In 1906 a similar
High Court was established in North-Western Rhodesia. An
Order in Council of 1911 abolished both of them, replacing
them with a High Court of Northern Rhodesia. English Common Law was enforced except where modified or changed by
an Order in Council. Native laws and custom could be considered sometimes when cases involved Africans and the justices saw fit. Treason and murder cases and the like were
reserved for trial by the High Court. Since independence the
High Court has retained most of its authority. It is presided
over by the Chief Justice (q. v.). Constitutional provisions
maintain the independence of the Judiciary, despite the controversy in 1969 involving Justice Ifor Evans (q. v.).

HILTON YOUNG COMMISSION. A commission chaired by Sir Edward Hilton Young that was sent by the British Government in
1928 to investigate the possibility of closer association of the
Central African countries with each other or even with the East
African Territories. Its members included Sir Reginald Mant,
Sir George Schuster and Dr. Joseph Oldham. The testimony
that they took in Nyasaland and Northern Rhodesia was mainly
from the settlers, most of whom favored closer ties with the
South, not with East Africa. Few Africans were heard. Yet
its wide-ranging report stressed concern that African interests
be safeguarded and not subjugated to those of the European
settlers and the South. It was even proposed that some form
of union between Nyasaland and Northern Rhodesia might be attempted, possibly even linking the two with East Africa.

HOLE, HUGH MARSHALL. Acting Administrator for North-Western
Rhodesia for several months in 1903, from July to October.
He was a senior administrator for the British South Africa
Company and as such was more active in the struggle against
Lobengula in Southern Rhodesia. He was the author of The
Making of Rhodesia.

HOLUB, DR. EMIL. Born in Bohemia in the Austro-Hungarian
empire in 1847, the young surgeon went to the Kimberly mines

to practice in 1872. From 1883 to 1887 he and his wife Rosa
and a small party of Europeans traveled through South Central
Africa (recorded in a two volume book). It is said that they
crossed the Zambezi in June, 1886, with the goal of reaching
Cairo on a "Cape-to-Cairo" route. They spent a month or so
at Sesheke with Rev. Coillard (q. v.) in Lozi country, where
fever and other problems cost the Holub Party both human
lives and cattle. With the permission of the Lozi King, Lewanika, plus Toka porters they crossed into the land of the Ila
("Mashukulumbwe") where they were attacked on several occasions. In the Hook of the Kafue area, they lost all valuables
in a raid, along with the life of one of the Europeans. Three
of the Ila also lost their lives in the raid. After crossing the
Kafue they eventually reached comparative safety across the
Zambezi on August 22, 1886. Rev. Coillard sent them some
aid. Holub died in 1902.

HOMO RHODESIENSIS.   Rhodesian man, also called Broken Hill
    man (q. v.).

HONE, SIR EVELYN DENNISON. Born in Salisbury, Southern Rho-
    desia, December 13, 1911, he became a Rhodes scholar and
    received his B. A. degree from Oxford University. He entered
    the Colonial Service in 1935 in Tanganyika, and also served in
    the Seychelles, Palestine, British Honduras, and Aden. He was
    Chief Secretary to the Governor of Northern Rhodesia from
    1957 to 1959, a time when he had many difficulties getting
    Africans registered to vote because of a boycott by ZANC. In
    an unusual pattern of promotion, he became Governor in 1959.
    He quickly began talks with African nationalists. He developed
    an excellent relationship with Kaunda and continued as Governor
    until October, 1964. He returned to England and has served
    in a variety of advisory posts. In 1971 he became Deputy
    Chairman of the Commonwealth Institute.

HOOK OF THE KAFUE. The Kafue River flows in a southwesterly
    direction from the Copperbelt area into west-central Zambia.
    It then flows due south until it turns and flows east again into
    the Kafue Flats and toward the Zambezi. This giant "Hook"
    region was the center of copper mining among the Africans for
    many centuries, perhaps as early as the time of Jesus Christ.
    The British didn't find copper there until almost the end of the
    nineteenth century. This area was under the jurisdiction of the
    Lozi King during the last third or more of the nineteenth cen-
    tury, but colonial rule refused to recognize it. The Ila people
    generally inhabit the area.

HOPKINSON, HENRY (later LORD COLYTON). Conservative Party
    Colonial Secretary (Minister of State for Colonial Affairs) in
    the early 1950's. He toured Central Africa in 1952 to test
    African reaction to the impending Federation. His statements
    infuriated Africans as he blamed extremists for the negative
    responses he received. He also said that 90 percent of the

Africans knew nothing about Federation. He addressed seventy-
eight formal meetings with Africans, in each of which he encouraged acceptance of federation. His great error was his
inability to recognize the legitimacy of the widespread African
rejection of the plan for the Federation. He also told the
House of Commons that it could safely entrust the care and
political advancement of the Africans to the settlers.

HOUSE OF CHIEFS. Although the Zambian Parliament is unicameral, both the 1964 and 1973 Constitutions provide for a
House of Chiefs. It provides a voice at the national level for
Zambia's traditional leaders, many of whom still have a great
deal of local influence. The body now has twenty-seven members (one more than the 1964 Constitution allowed), and it is
basically advisory in nature. The President must submit to it
those bills dealing with tribal matters, seeking its advice. In
1966, however, the Government failed to do this and ignored
the protests of the Chiefs when it passed the Local Courts Bill,
which deprived traditional leaders of their judicial role. The
House normally meets before the Parliament comes together,
so that its reactions can be considered by the legislators. Its
power to affect the passage of laws, however, should not be
exaggerated.

HUDSON, ROWLAND SKEFFINGTON. Secretary for Native Affairs
in the Government of Northern Rhodesia from 1945 to 1949
when he was succeeded by Ronald Bush. Hudson was somewhat sympathetic to the African founders of the Northern Rhodesia African Congress. He even gave the opening speech at
a meeting of the Federation of Welfare Societies in September,
1948. It was at this conference that the group changed its
name and became the NRAC. Eleven years earlier, however,
in a lower administrative capacity, Hudson had opposed such
an organization because it could interfere with the work of the
Chiefs. Hudson began his administrative career in Barotseland and later served in the Lusaka Secretariat. During the
early 1940's he was the labor commissioner and endeavored to
introduce the concept of collective bargaining for Africans into
the mines, at least at the level of "boss boys." He opposed
unionization of the mass of African workers, feeling that they
were "not ready." As Secretary for Native Affairs he recognized the potential leadership of the more advanced Africans,
but he opposed their formation of political parties which, he
said "would be fatal." In a speech before the African Representative Council in 1948 he suggested that Northern Rhodesia
should be based on a "partnership" between Africans and Europeans. The word was later used frequently in regard to federation, but had really been introduced in 1935 by Sir Stewart
Gore-Browne (q.v.).

HUGGINS, GODFREY MARTIN (LORD MALVERN). A Southern
Rhodesian politician, Huggins was the principal moving figure
behind the creation of the Central African Federation and its

first Prime Minister. Born in England in 1883, he was educated as a doctor. He emigrated to Southern Rhodesia in 1911.
After returning from World War I, he entered politics, taking
his first seat in the Southern Rhodesian Parliament in 1924.
As leader of the Reform Party he became the Prime Minister
in 1933 on a segregationist platform. He rejected apartheid
and merger with South Africa, favoring partnership between
the settlers and the more advanced Africans, both eventually
sitting in the same Parliament. Firmly convinced that Federation would solve Central Africa's race problems, he urged
England to accept the plan. When the Federation began he
resigned as Prime Minister of Southern Rhodesia (a post he
held for twenty years) and became Federal Prime Minister and
Minister of Defense. In 1955 he was named Lord Malvern;
and he resigned as Prime Minister on October 3, 1956.

HUMANISM see ZAMBIAN HUMANISM

HUT TAX. First imposed in North-Eastern Rhodesia in 1901, the
    hut tax required every adult African to pay three shillings per
    year for his hut plus payment for a maximum of six additional
    huts inhabited by female relatives or elderly male relatives.
    It was payable in cash or, until 1905, in saleable commodities.
    It was first extended to North-Western Rhodesia in 1904 and
    by 1913 was being collected throughout the Territory. By
    1907 it produced a revenue of £33,000 in North-Western Rho-
    desia. Administrators were even known as Collectors (q. v.)
    The hut tax was considered by many Africans to be the worst
    aspect of rule by the British South Africa Company. Those
    not able to pay were often required to do forced labor (collect-
    ing rubber or building roads, for example). It also resulted
    in a great number of Africans fleeing their land to work on
    the mines, producing some starvation at home. Others went
    to work for settlers or the missions. Many administrators
    used the tax deliberately to encourage an abundance of cheap
    labor in Southern Rhodesia. Imprisonment was the penalty for
    non-payment. Even some of the administrators saw the tax as
    being very unfair and destructive. In 1914 the hut tax was re-
    placed in North-Eastern Rhodesia by a similar tax on plural
    wives. The tax was five shillings a year for a man and his
    first wife, plus five for each of his other wives or concubines.
    This was increased to ten shillings in 1920 but was reduced
    again to seven and a half shillings in 1925. In 1929 the tax
    on plural wives was also dropped.

- I -

ICALO (pl. , Ifyalo). The Bemba word for one of many historically
    important geographical (and political) subdivisions of Bemba
    territory. These units have fixed boundaries, historic names,
    and chiefs with fixed titles. For example, the icalo of Chief
    Mwamba is called Ituna, the icalo of Chief Nkolemfumu is Miti.

Even the Bemba king, Chitimukulu, has his icalo, called Lubemba. He rules Lubemba in addition to being overlord of all
Bemba territory. Each icalo was allotted long ago to a member of the royal clan, usually a close relative of Chitimukulu.
The icalo is also a ritual unit, with each capital containing its
sacred relics (babenye, q. v.).

ICHINGA. The icalo (q. v.) of Chief Nkula, it is a Bemba district
on the eastern end of Bemba country. Bordering Bisa and
Senga country, along the Luvu River, it made a convenient
base for slave-raiding. The modern city of Chinsali is in this
district. In 1883 the French explorer Giraud visited Ichinga
and described the trade patterns, which were extensive. While
the chieftainship is now called Nkula, in earlier centuries it
was named Katongo and, later, Chewe. This Katongo (q. v.)
was a blind brother of the great Bemba founder, Chiti.

ICHITUPA (pl. , Ifitupa). The African Identification Certificate that
pre-independence governments required Africans to carry with
them at all times, much like the "pass system" in South Africa.
In July, 1961, there were mass burnings in several Northern
Rhodesian cities of the ifitupa as symbolic rejection of foreign
rule. Some also burned their Marriage Certificates (imichato).
This was during a period of nationalism referred to as Cha-
cha-cha (q. v.).

IKAWA. The site of one of the first trading posts established by
the British South Africa Company in the Northern Province, it
became the location of the boma of the Collector of the Chambeshi District. Located in the northeastern corner of the country, near Fife, the post was opened there by Major P. W.
Forbes in 1895, but Collector John Bell was its major administrator.

IKELENGE, CHIEF. One of the traditional leaders appointed to attend the Federal Review Conference in London in December,
1960. When the three nationalist leaders of Central Africa
(Kaunda, Nkomo, and Banda) walked out of the meeting, Chief
Ikelenge and the other traditionalists followed.

ILA (or MASHUKULUMBWE). One of the better-known peoples of
Zambia, living in South Central Zambia, the Ila perhaps originated east of Lake Tanganyika and moved southwestward, not
unlike their closely related neighbors, the Tonga. There are
about thirty-five thousand Ila now in Zambia. They also share
with the Tonga a matrilineal descent system but a patrilocal
residence pattern. Most importantly, the Ila and Tonga are
among the few Zambian peoples without a formalized chieftainship nor a strong oral tradition of past leadership. The Ila
are part of the so-called Bantu Botatwe group (q. v.). The
homeland (called Bwila) of the Ila is not large, and is surrounded on three sides by the Kafue River, as it is located in
the huge bend of the river. The authoritative anthropological

studies about the Ila are two volumes by Edwin Smith and Andrew Dale, a missionary and a colonial officer. But one of the first Europeans to mention them was Dr. David Livingstone, who referred to them as the Bashukulompo. The term "Mashukulumbwe" was used for them by the Lozi and Makololo. Presumably it is derived from Lozi words that refer to the unusual hair style of the Ila. Called the isusu, it is a vertical spear of hair, sometimes four feet upward from the head. Dr. Livingstone and other Europeans seemed to avoid Ila territory when possible, as they had a reputation as fine warriors. Around 1860 the Makololo were conquering a great deal of territory in southern Zambia until they were beaten back by the Ila. In 1882, however, the Lozi under their great leader Lewanika (q. v.) had a very successful raid against the Ila, winning many thousands of cattle. A similar Lozi raid, their last against the Ila, was successful in 1888. At that point the Ila went to Lewanika to offer tribute and accept Lozi dominance in their area.

ILA-TONGA PEOPLES. A general term of more linguistic than ethnic validity, it refers to the large group of people, predominantly found in south-central Zambia, who speak similar languages and have some common traditions. The term, "Bantu Botatwe" (q. v.) also refers to these people. The Ila (q. v.) and the Tonga (q. v.) are themselves separate groups. One thing that bound them together in the nineteenth century was the invasion into these areas by the Lozi, whereby they came under similar influences. Once under European dominance, both groups responded to the introduction of cash-crop farming.

ILENDELA. A Namwanga headman in the 1890's whose village near the northeastern corner of Northern Rhodesia was the site of the first popular display of resentment to forced labor. His village was near the boma called Ikawa, where John Bell (q. v.) was administrator. When Bell sent his police to collect laborers to work on the new boma, Ilendela refused and his people fired guns and arrows at the police. They in turn drove off the villagers' goats and sheep to Ikawa. Bell then went to the stockaded village to investigate the incident and Ilendela's people again opened fire. In the exchange of shots, a villager was killed. Bell then burnt down the village. A local missionary, Rev. Alexander Dewar, wrote a critical letter to Collector Bell, urging the administrator to pay compensation. Bell was furious at the meddling of the missionary in administrative affairs.

ILISHUA. A brother of Mboo (q. v.), the first king of the Lozi. Together with his sons Kaputungu and Mulombwe and some followers he left Bulozi (q. v.) to set up his own settlement at Mashi, in the southwestern corner of Zambia.

ILUNGA. A name used by a number of Lunda, an important nation of people whose empire has extended across much of

Central Africa. According to one legend, a Luba hunter
named Chibinda Ilunga married a Luba woman, Lueji, who had
inherited a chieftainship. He took possession of the royal symbols of office and assumed the powers of chieftainship. Lueji's
brothers, who had disputed her office, migrated to other areas.
Soon after, the followers of Lueji and Ilunga called themselves
baLunda. This was early in the seventeenth century. In the
late eighteenth century the Lunda Kazembe on the Luapula
River in Northern Rhodesia was also named Ilunga. During
his long reign the Lunda expanded their influence into Katanga
and as far east as Malawi. The Portuguese-sponsored traveler, Dr. de Lacerda (q.v.), tried to visit him in 1798. The
elderly Ilunga refused to meet the traveler, seeing the Portuguese as business competitors in the area of long distance
trade. Eventually, however, he did meet with Father Pinto
(q.v.), who had taken over the expedition when de Lacerda
died. But Ilunga would not allow the expedition to continue
through his territory to Mwata Yamvo. Instead he demanded
the presents reserved for that great Lunda leader be given to
himself instead.

IMASIKU. Son of the Lozi King Mubukwanu, he escaped with his
father to Lukulu when the Barotse valley was attacked by the
Kololo of Sebituane. King Mubukwanu died of poison, however,
and Imasiku became ruler-in-exile. He was also attacked by
Sebituane's soldiers, however, and fled northeast across the
Kabompo River, east of the Manyinga River. This was in
1838. Imasiku died in this Lukwakwa country as the result of
a local battle with the Mbunda.

IMASIKU, AKABESWA. The Ngambela (Prime Minister) of the
Barotse from 1956 to 1962 to the King Mwanawina III. The
King wanted to appoint him to this position in 1948. Imasiku
was related to him through marriage. He was also chief
councillor at the Mankoya Kuta. Opposition by Commissioner
Glennie led to the appointment of Muheli Walubita instead.
Under pressure from Mwanawina, Walubita resigned in 1956
and a conflict occurred among Lozi leaders when Imasiku was
again nominated. Finally an election was held and, with
Mwanawina counting the votes, Imasiku was declared the winner. Although some charged fraud, Imasiku served as Ngambela for six years.

IMATONGO. A settlement established by the early Lozi leader,
Mwanambinyi (q.v.).

IMBUA. A son of the Lozi King (Litunga), Mulambwa, and a
younger brother of Mubukwanu, he was the candidate of one
faction of Lozi that wanted him to succeed his father. When
the Makololo attacked Barotseland in 1833, Imbua and his followers fled to Nyengo country near the present Angola-Zambian
border. Later Imbua's forces attacked one of his competitors,
Imasiku (q.v.), but was repelled and returned to Nyengo.

Later Imbua and his followers moved to Lukwakwa where he
succeeded Sipopa who had been accepted as King after his followers had defeated the Makololo. Eventually, in September,
1884, Tatila Akufuna (q.v.), a son of Imbua, became King of
the Lozi.

IMPANDE SHELL (or MPANDE). The impande is a small sea
shell that has been traded from the East African coast, especially Beira, since as early as A.D. 650. The shell became
a kind of currency in the slave and ivory trade. Ingombe Ilede
(q.v.) in southern Zambia was the center of this trade. In recent centuries European manufacturers have begun producing them
in porcelain and even celluloid. Some Zambian peoples, notably the Ila and some others influenced by the Baluba saw it as
an emblem of chieftainship. Many men and women might wear
one or two around their neck, but a chief would wear seven or
eight. The Ila also believed that an impande shell must be put
on the graves of their dignitaries to insure their acceptance by God.

IMPI. An Nguni word for army, it is used frequently to depict the
well disciplined units under the Zulu leader, Chaka. It would
also be used to describe the Ndebele (or Matabele) units of
Mzilikazi or Lobengula in Southern Rhodesia, or the military
units of the Ngoni of eastern Zambia and Malawi who, like the
Zulu and the Ndebele, are of Nguni origin.

IMWIKO. A son of King Lewanika of the Barotse, and himself the
King (Litunga) from 1945 to 1948. Upon his father's death in
1916, he was favored for the position by a number of indunas.
Imwiko had been educated in England, and many Lozi felt that
he would stand up to the Administration better. However his
half-brother Litia (later King Yeta III) was chosen instead.
When the very infirm and aged Yeta abdicated in 1945, he
asked that Imwiko succeed him. Imwiko, now sixty years old,
had been appointed Chief of Sesheke in 1916 by Yeta and served
there until 1945 when he became King. As King, however, Imwiko found that the Colonial Administration, represented by Commissioner Glennie (q.v.), was forcing on him a number of
changes in the traditional Barotse government. This attempt at
modernization involved especially reforms of the Kuta (q.v.)
and a revival of the Katengo council (q.v.) with new personnel.
While collaborating with the British on the establishment of a
Development Center, Imwiko stated firmly that Barotseland
would secede from Northern Rhodesia if amalgamation with
Southern Rhodesia should occur. Imwiko died in June, 1948,
presumably of a stroke, although many suspected foul play.
Many indunas were angry at him, and some felt that his brother
and successor, Mwanawina, might have caused him to be poisoned. Likewise some suspected Mwanawina in the mysterious
murder of Imwiko's son, Akashambatwa Imwiko in 1959. Leaders of UNIP used this incident to force the Government to investigate the matter thoroughly, thus getting political gain out
of opposition to Mwanawina.

INDABA. A Bantu word used mostly in the Northern Province of
Zambia to refer to a large gathering of chiefs and commoners,
often called for a specific purpose. Colonial officials made it
a practice to ask that indabas be called so that they could talk
to the Africans.

INDEPENDENCE CONSTITUTION. Written during final negotiations
in London in May, 1964, the constitution went into effect with
independence itself on October 24, 1964. No elections were
held in the interim, and the Constitution specifically named
Kenneth Kaunda as the first President of Zambia. It provided
for a unitary republic with a strong, executive President, modified by some elements of a parliamentary system. While the
National Assembly was to be a unicameral legislature, a House
of Chiefs with consultative influence also was created. A High
Court and the Court of Appeal topped out the judicial structure,
and English Common Law became the basis of jurisprudence.
Regional provinces and districts were also provided for. A
new Constitution providing for a one-party democracy replaced
the Independence Constitution on December 13, 1972.

INDIRECT RULE. A pattern of colonial government instituted by
the British and credited primarily to Lord Lugard who developed the concept while in India and Northern Nigeria. His
book, The Dual Mandate, published in 1922, described the system in which traditional leaders (now called "Native Authorities") and their councils were retained, subject however to occasional orders from the Colonial Administrators. The Native
Authority Ordinance of 1929 attempted to initiate this. Native
Authorities were allowed to make rules and orders to regulate
their districts, subject to veto by the district commissioner.
They were also given limited judicial responsibility. All this
was contrary to the Direct Rule policy of the British South
Africa Company, which ended in 1924. Even after 1929, however, district commissioners were very reluctant to allow their
powers to devolve upon Africans. The system did not work
well until 1936 when the British added Ordinances which set up
native treasuries and acknowledged tribal councillors, and replaced the 1929 Native Courts Ordinance with a new one.
Nevertheless the system never quite lived up to expectations,
especially among the Northern Rhodesian tribes where no centralized chiefs existed, the Tonga for one, and the British had
to appoint Native Authorities. The system was more successful in Barotseland, however.

INDUNA. A word used in various parts of central and southern
Africa to refer to a chief's councillor, often a man who himself is considered to be an administrator at a lower level as
the representative of the chief or king. In Zambia the term
has been used most among the Lozi, although the invading Makololo also used the term. Among the Lozi, the importance of
an induna and the degree of his wealth often depended on the
King. Yet since a number of induna lived at Lealui, the capital,

and were part of the important traditional council, their influence was substantial at different points in Lozi history.

INDUSTRIAL CONCILIATION ACT.   Although there have been several such acts passed in Northern Rhodesia during the colonial period, the one passed by the Parliament of the Federation in 1959 and in operation in 1960 had an important result. By including Africans in the word "employee," it led to the formation of multi-racial trade unions and allowed Africans to have access to conciliation machinery. It also opened the way to multi-racial apprenticeship arrangements.

INDUSTRIAL DEVELOPMENT CORPORATION OF ZAMBIA, LTD. (Indeco). Founded by the Northern Rhodesian Government in 1960, it has become since independence an important part of Zambia's state-run industrial program. It initiates and operates industrial projects and controls about forty (one source says seventy) subsidiaries and companies. It usually controls 51 percent of the stock, an authority given it by the 1968 Mulungushi industrial policy. It also works in partnership with foreign countries, including Italy, Japan and Yugoslavia in companies including a car assembly factory, an oil refinery, a chemical fertilizer plant, a textile mill, Zambian Airways, and construction projects such as the Kafue hydroelectric project. Indeco is itself responsible to its holding company, the Zambia Industrial and Mining Corporation (Zimco). When Indeco was formed in 1960 with a capital of £850,000 it acted as a semi-independent corporation supporting chosen projects being undertaken by private enterprise. In May, 1963, it was given to private control but in August, 1964, it returned to full government ownership and control to serve as its instrument for industrial promotion and development (not just providing financial support). It was to promote Zambian businessmen and projects which the state might get involved in. Much of its early vitality and growth was due to the work of a young Greek Cypriot, Andrew Sardanis (q.v.), but since 1971 it has been run by a Zambian, E. A. Kashita, M.P. Indeco has been reorganized several times, notably in 1969 and 1971. Among Indeco's tasks have been: 1) to help in the Zambianization of industry by promoting Zambians to decision-making positions; 2) to help make Zambia as self-sufficient as possible in key areas such as construction and both food and metal processing; and 3) to foster the development of rural areas of Zambia, which have not always shared in Zambia's riches. It also has taken over trading companies and set up a wholesaling subsidiary.

INGOMBE ILEDE.   The site of an important Iron Age trading community in southern Zambia, thirty-two miles east of the Kariba Dam, near the confluence of the Lusitu river with the Zambezi. The community was accidentally discovered by Government workmen in 1960 while digging the foundation for a water tank. Archaeologists have discovered that the residents were very

active in the East Coast trade. Ivory was an important item,
as the area abounded in elephants, and salt was also plentiful
for trade. Slaves were sold, and the copper mines were also
not far distant. Among the products imported in trade were
sea shells (see impande), glass beads, gold, cloth, and copper
bracelets. The items probably came from as far away as
India. This community was probably occupied from about
A.D. 650 until about 900. While their skills included making
pottery as fine as thinnest-walled china, they also were farmers. Their crops were heavily cereal types, notably sorghum,
but they supplemented them with wild vegetables. They hunted
animals for food. The graves of some, presumably the wealthy, included jewelry of beads, seashells, gold and copper.
Trade routes seem to have shifted south to the area of the
gold mines of Mashonaland about a thousand years ago, because
the site was abandoned then.

INSTITUTE OF SOCIAL RESEARCH. The new name of the famous
Rhodes-Livingstone Institute (q.v.).

INTER-TERRITORIAL CONFERENCE. A frequent series of meetings held between 1941 and 1944 by the Governors of Northern
and Southern Rhodesia and Nyasaland and their representatives.
It was established by the British to further cooperation between
the territories on non-political matters. It even had its own
secretariat. The Conference was used by settlers and some
officials, however, to try to develop closer governmental association, with amalgamation as the goal. The British rejected
amalgamation but in 1944 continued the close association by
replacing the Conference with the Central African Council
(q.v.).

IRON AGE ZAMBIA. In Zambia the Iron Age began only as recently as about the first century A.D. and is considered to have
closed around the beginning of the twentieth century. It is
characterized by the use of iron implements by the Africans,
most of whom were farmers living in small communities.
Among the earliest such sites presently confirmed, most are
found in one of several areas: the Kalambo group near Lake
Tanganyika, the Chondwe group along the Copperbelt, and several groups along and near the southern border of Zambia from
the area near Victoria Falls eastward as far as the environs
of Lusaka. In addition to agricultural production, some of the
Iron Age sites show signs of animal domestication and the
techniques of metallurgy, pottery, and permanent or semi-
permanent building construction. Some of the Iron Age people
also were responsible for some of the Rock paintings found in
Zambia.

ISANGANO NATIONAL PARK. A national park located along the
Chambeshi River due east of Lake Bangweulu in the Northern
Province. It contains both a game reserve and hunting areas,
especially for tourists.

ISHINDE (or SHINDE). A Lunda chieftainship in what is now the
Balovale District, north of the Barotse, near the northwestern
corner of Barotseland. Its founder, Ishinde, was a captain
under the Lunda emperor Mwata Yamvwa in the Congo in the
seventeenth century and was sent out with several other leaders to expand the empire. He traveled westward. Among his
descendants, one had the occasion to meet the adventurous Dr.
Livingstone (who spelled the name Shinte) in 1854. The Doctor
was impressed by the royal court and the Lunda themselves.
Ishinde traded slaves to Portuguese traders for cloth. He had
also acquired guns. This was necessary as Ishinde was not
on good terms with the neighboring Luvale. In 1885 the problem of the aggressive Luvale was coming to a head. In both
1890 and 1891 Ishinde requested aid from Lewanika, leader of
the Lozi. In 1892 the Lozi responded by attacking the Luvale
and put the chief, Ndungu, to flight.

ISOKA. A town and district near the northeastern corner of Zambia. According to the 1969 census the district (located in the
Northern Province) contained seventy-eight thousand people, or
about fifteen per square mile. In the nineteenth century it was
part of the area where trade with East Africa occurred, and
also was the site of battles between the Bemba and the Ngoni.
Eventually the British calmed the area and the village of Fife
became the administrative center for the Isoka District. In
the 1960's many of the inhabitants of the District became supporters of the controversial Lumpa Church (q.v.) of Alice
Lenshina.

ITABWA. The land of the Tabwa people, it is between Lake
Mweru and the southwestern end of Lake Tanganyika. Its location made it a very important crossroads area for trade, especially for trade with the East African coast. The Arab trader Tippu Tip made the first step toward establishing a permanent settlement of coastal traders there in 1870.

ITUNA. The icalo (q.v.) of the important Bemba chief Mwamba.
On the eastern side of the Chambeshi River near the source of
the Kalungu River, it is in the very heart of the Bemba territory. Founded by Chitimukulu Mukuuka (q.v.), it was the first
chieftainship created for a close relative of Chitimukulu. Its
name came from a ciBemba phrase "ni kwituna" used in the
command by Chitimukulu to Mwamba to set up a chieftainship
there. Lubemba, the district of Chitimukulu, lies to its east.
One Mwamba in the nineteenth century refused to accept the
post of Chitimukulu, even though Lubemba was larger than
Ituna, because Ituna also virtually controlled the large neighboring areas of Mporokoso and Munkonge.

IVORY. Along with copper and slaves, the trade in ivory has been
one of the most profitable over the centuries for Zambians.
The society at Ingombe Ilede (q.v.) in southern Zambia traded
much ivory from the huge elephant herds as late as one

thousand years ago. More recently ivory trade with the East
African coast originated more in Bemba country near Lake
Tanganyika in Northern Zambia. The most famous of all the
ivory traders was Tippu Tip (q. v.), who worked this area
heavily in the 1860's. He even gave chiefs credit in goods to
get them to stockpile ivory for him. He might get between
fifteen and thirty loads of ivory from each chief. As the demand for ivory increased dramatically late in the nineteenth
century, the price skyrocketed, more than doubling between
1870 and 1890. The supply of elephants in the Northern Province dwindled as ivory in 1893 soared to as much as $180 per
35 pounds. When ivory became scarce, slaves replaced the
ivory in the East African trade.

IWA. The Iwa people, numbering about thirty thousand today, live
in the northeastern corner of Zambia. Originally migrating
from East Africa, they are part of a broader family of peoples,
all of whom are neighbors today. They speak the Mambwe
language like the Namwanga, from whom they probably split.
Living along the Chambeshi River, just east of the Bemba,
they were periodically affected by Bemba raids. The Iwa chief
Kafwimbi was driven off his lands by the earliest Bemba immigrants sometime in the early eighteenth century. In the nineteenth century the Iwa were known for smelting and working
iron, as were the Mambwe. They also kept large herds of
cattle, but like other East Africans they would not trade them
commercially. The cattle were used for marriage payments,
though. Under pressure from the Bemba, however, they supplied them with both cattle and grain. On the other hand the
Iwa were themselves dominant over the Tambo. When European rule eventually came, the Iwa did not provide any real
resistance. In 1917 and 1918 when the Watch Tower Movement
came into Northern Rhodesia, the Iwa were among the first
converts.

- J -

JALLA, ADOLPHE and LOUIS. Missionaries of the Paris Mission
Society who worked especially in the Lozi area of Northern
Rhodesia from as early as 1887 into the twentieth century.
Both wrote on their experiences at that time, but Adolphe
Jalla's many writings on the Lozi provided Europe with
much new information on Barotseland. Their colleague
was Francois Coillard (q. v.). The Jallas were accompanied
by their wives. Both families had a child die in Northern
Rhodesia of illness. Louis' child died in 1888 and Adolphe's
in 1897. The two Jalla brothers and Coillard each had influence with Lozi King Lewanika and he used them as intermedi-
aries with the British. Likewise the British South Africa Company used them to get its representatives accepted by Lewanika.
Both Frank Lochner (q. v.) and Robert Coryndon (q. v.) relied
on them to persuade Lewanika to deal with them as representatives

of the British government, although they worked for the BSAC.
The Jallas also served as interpreters frequently. It is doubt-
ful that the infamous Lochner Concession (q.v.) of 1890 would
have been accepted by Lewanika had it not been for the advice
of the missionaries, notably Coillard and Adolphe Jalla.

JEHOVAH'S WITNESSES. A name often applied to the Watch Tower
Bible and Tract Society (q.v.), and specifically to its members.

JOHANNESBURG. The center of the mining industry in the Republic of South Africa. Many Africans flocked there from Northern
Rhodesia early in the twentieth century to earn money to pay
their hut tax (q.v.). After the opening of the Copperbelt,
"Jo'burg" lost some of its attraction.

JOHNSTON, HENRY HAMILTON (SIR HARRY). British traveler
and colonial officer who played an important role in the establishment of colonial administration in Zambia and Malawi.
Born in London in 1858 and educated at King's College as a
botanist, he traveled widely in North, West, and East Africa
from 1879 to 1884. He served as a vice-consul in the Niger
River area until 1888. Returning to London he met Cecil
Rhodes in 1889 and the two persuaded Lord Salisbury to act
firmly in Central Africa. In March, 1889, Lord Salisbury
sent Johnston as consul in Mozambique, in order to work out
a settlement that would keep Portugal out of Central Africa.
He had permission to sign treaties with the African chiefs.
Inspired by Rhodes' Cape-to-Cairo dream (Rhodes was at that
same time securing his royal charter for the British South
Africa Company), and financed by two thousand pounds from
Rhodes, Johnston spent the rest of 1889 in parts of present-day
Malawi and eastern Zambia securing twenty-four concessions
from African leaders including chiefs of the Namwanga, Mambwe, and Tabwa. In 1890 he sent Alfred Sharpe on a venture
to get Katanga for Rhodes. While this ultimately failed, other
concessions were signed. All of these treaties helped to define the borders between British and German territory at the
1890 conference between those nations. In May, 1891, the
British declared a protectorate over British Central Africa
(today's Malawi) and made Johnston the Commissioner. He
held this position until the British South Africa Company took
administrative responsibility for the area north of the Zambezi
in June, 1895. In the intervening years Johnston, working out
of Zomba, solidified the British authority in both Malawi and
eastern Zambia. With the aid of Sikh soldiers from India he
cut the slave trade, thanks to ten thousand pounds a year from
Rhodes to pay the Sikhs. He was in the awkward position of
serving two masters: Rhodes and the Foreign Office. Also
as a result of the Lochner Concession of 1890 (q.v.) with King
Lewanika of the Lozi, Johnston was nominally in charge of
North-Western Rhodesia as well. After 1895, Johnston spent
much of the rest of his life writing and traveling. He wrote
a minimum of eleven books on Africa or other parts of the
British Empire. He died in 1929.

JOSE, AMARO. An African who traversed the continent from Angola to Mozambique and back at the beginning of the nineteenth century. His companion, more famous because of the diary he left, was Pedro João Baptista (q. v.). The two are sometimes referred to as the Pombeiros.

- K -

KABOMPO. One of the smallest districts in Zambia in terms of population (only thirty-three thousand in 1969), it is located in the northwestern corner of the North-Western Province and shares part of a border with Angola. The Kabompo River is an important part of the district.

Kabompo is also the name of the town that is the administrative center of the district, and is located on the river bank north of its juncture with the Dongwe River. Kenneth Kaunda, Frank Chitambala and other ZANC activists were held in detention at Kabompo during the 1959 "Emergency. "

KABOMPO RIVER. One of the major tributaries of the Zambezi River, the Kabompo drains a major part of the North-Western Province before joining the Upper Zambezi north of Lukulu. One of its own major tributaries is the Dongwe River. Traditionally the Kabompo River has been the northern border of the Lozi flood plain. During the nineteenth century when a split occurred among the Lozi, one of the groups fled north of the Kabompo and established themselves at Lukwakwa (q. v.).

KABWE. One of the larger municipalities in Zambia, it had a population of about 67, 200 in 1969. That was an increase of 50 percent since 1963. It was called Broken Hill until the name was changed after independence, and is the site of the Broken Hill mine. Kabwe is one of the larger cities along the line of rail, located about halfway between Lusaka and the southern part of the Copperbelt. Its location on the Great North Road and its position as headquarters of Zambia Railways and of a major trucking firm has made it one of Zambia's true transportation hubs. It is also serviced by an airport. Kabwe (Broken Hill) was founded as a British military post. Today it is the capital of the Central Province.

KAFFIR. A derogatory and belittling word used by many Europeans toward Africans, especially during colonial days. A rough English equivalent could be "nigger. "

KAFUE HYDROELECTRIC SCHEME AND DAM. Originally conceived in the 1950's as the major project for supplying the energy needed by Northern Rhodesia, it was by-passed by the leaders of the Central African Federation in favor of a cooperative effort by the two Rhodesias on their border, the Kariba Dam (q. v.). When that was built, however, it was vulnerable to unilateral action by the white rulers of Southern Rhodesia.

Thus the leaders of Zambia devised the project on the Kafue
River as part of the First National Development Plan. This
could enable Zambia to acquire economic independence from
Southern Rhodesia by alleviating the need to import coal from
its Wankie Mine. Not only would it provide energy to supplement the Kariba Dam, but it would also allow for irrigation
projects in Zambia. Thus with considerable assistance from
Yugoslavia, major construction was begun in 1969.

The first stage of the project is at the Kafue Gorge (see
KAFUE RIVER) where a dam controls a six-mile long tunnelled
race to the turbine house. The dam produces 600 megawatts
of energy and will be increased to 900 megawatts after a second stage (based on a storage dam near the head of the Kafue
Flats) is added. The first stage was fully completed in 1972,
but was producing its initial power in 1971. The dam and
power station are about twenty-seven miles southeast of Lusaka.

KAFUE NATIONAL PARK. A huge game reserve with 8650 square
miles of territory, it is located in the western half of Zambia,
generally along the west bank of the Kafue River. It is an
excellent place to see wild game, including rare species like
the aardwolf, the pangolin, and the red lechwe antelope. One
of the camps is located on an island in the Kafue and is noted
for its fine fishing.

KAFUE RIVER. One of the three major tributaries of the Zambezi
River, it rises north of the Copperbelt and soon drifts into a
southwesterly flow. When it is joined by the Lunga River in
the Kafue National Park it heads in a more southerly direction.
Later it hooks back and flows due east until it joins the Zambezi River. On that part of its course it passes through the
Kafue Flats flood plain and then through a gorge before crash-
ing over a series of rapids and waterfalls. The Kafue Basin
involves almost sixty thousand square miles, second in Zambia
only to the Zambezi's. The Kafue Gorge, mentioned above, is
the source of much of the power for the Kafue hydroelectric
scheme and dam. The native Ila people call it Kavuvu ("the
Hippopotamus River").

KAFWIMBI. A major participant in a succession dispute for the
Nsama chieftainship of the Tabwa people. The dispute ultimately resulted in the Bemba making major inroads into Tabwa
territory. The incident began in about 1868 when Nsama III
Chipili died. The next year he was succeeded by a nephew,
Katandula, who became Nsama IV. Kafwimbi was a cousin of
the latter and an unsuccessful challenger for the position.
When Katandula sought to expel Arabs led by Kumba Kumba
(q.v.) from his area, Kafwimbi came to the Arabs' aid by per-
suading the Bemba chief Mwamba to help defeat Katandula.
When the latter was thus killed, Kafwimbi became Nsama V,
although he had to get aid from both Mwamba and Kumba Kumba to defeat two of Katandula's brothers and other relatives.
After this victory it became impossible to get Mwamba's forces

to leave, and Kafwimbi had to give them land in an area called
Isenga. Some years later he was killed in a battle with East
African traders.

KAKENGE. The senior chieftainship among the Luvale people, the
Kakenge dynasty controls an area in northwestern Zambia very
close to the Angolan border and in fact it was once based in
Angola. It began perhaps as early as the sixteenth century
and is presumably of distant Lunda ancestry.

While Kakenge is the senior chief, he is not considered a
King, as the Luvale preferred independent chiefdoms. By the
late eighteenth century Kakenge was actively trading with the
Portuguese in Angola. The Luvale were receiving guns and
cloth and selling slaves. By 1830 they were also trading with
the Lunda of Chief Kazembe on the Luapula River. Around
that same time, however, Kakenge had begun paying tribute
to the Lozi to his south. That connection was to be responsible for problems between the Lozi and the Portuguese at the
beginning of the twentieth century when Portugal tried to get
much of Kakenge's land included within Angola.

KAKUMBI, MATEYKO. A carpentry instructor at the Chitambo
Mission of the Church of Scotland, he was elected the first
treasurer of the Northern Rhodesia African Congress in July,
1948.

KAKUNGU see TAFUNA

KALABO. One of the western-most districts of Zambia, it is in
the Western Province (formerly Barotseland) and has a long
border with Angola. The district contained 106,000 people in
1969. Its administrative center is the town of Kalabo, located
on the southern bank of the Luanginga River, south of the
Liuwa Plain. Some authorities feel that the Lozi kingdom
first began to solidify in the Kalabo area, and certainly it
was the center of the region controlled by Yeta I (q.v.).

KALAMBO FALLS EXCAVATIONS. Not far from the town of
Mbala (formerly Abercorn) is the famous Kalambo Falls on the
Kalambo River (q.v.). Above the falls the river runs through
a small basin where a lake had been. In 1953 the discovery
was made that artifacts in great numbers existed in the several layers of the lake bed as exposed on the steep river banks.
Desmond Clark (q.v.) spent the next ten years studying the
area, excavating it, and examining the wealth of data so revealed. (See his works in the Bibliography.) Some of the
earliest tools found in the sandy beds were hand-axes which
have been radiocarbon-dated to about sixty thousand years ago.
They reveal human settlements and camp sites from that Early
Stone Age era, and it is anticipated that older evidence could
be found below the present water level. The people were hunters and gatherers, and possibly fishermen. At higher levels,
Middle Stone Age findings also have been studied and dated at

about 28,000 B.C. Also Early Iron Age societies in the area
have been radiocarbon-dated in the fourth or fifth centuries
A.D. Perhaps the most remarkable finds, however, relate to
the Early Stone Age findings which give a remarkably clear
picture of the society, thanks in great part to the waterlogged
condition of the site which allowed even wooden objects to be
recovered in a very good state of preservation. Surprising to
the researchers was the evidence found that these people had
both experienced and used fire. Pollen grains were also found,
but unfortunately no bones from this early period were discovered.

KALAMBO RIVER. A small stream in northeastern Zambia that
     forms the boundary between Zambia and Tanzania on its way
     into the southeast corner of Lake Tanganyika. En route from
     a high plateau region to the lake at the bottom of the Rift Val-
     ley, the river flows over a 726-foot waterfall (over twice that
     of Victoria Falls) in spectacular fashion. The Kalambo Falls
     is the twelfth highest in the world.

KALE (or KAHADI). A chief of the Mbwela (q.v.) who brought
     some of his people from the area of the Upper Zambezi valley
     to settle near the Upper Kafue River in the early nineteenth
     century. He later welcomed to the area a party of Luba, one
     of whose chiefs was Kapidi (q.v.), even giving a daughter to
     Kapidi as a wife. Quarrels eventually occurred between the
     groups over the right to wear the emblem of chieftainship, the
     impande shell. War ensued and lasted for three years. At
     one point Kapidi was captured and his head shaven. His people
     ransomed him and he resumed the war. The Luba killed Kale's
     younger brother and were chased across the Kafue River into
     Ila country. Kale was bitten by a rabid dog just before cross-
     ing the Kafue in pursuit and died. The Luba Chiefs settled
     there in Ila country.

KALELA DANCE. A non-traditional dance that grew up among the
     workers on the Copperbelt. Its roots seem to be in the
     Northern Province from which many of the workers came.
     Groups of men (each team consisting of members of the same
     tribe) perform on Sundays and holidays in the townships of the
     Copperbelt. The verses of the songs performed during the
     dance mirror the ethnic diversity of the area, as the teams
     praise their own people and satirize other groups. The verses
     may also be topical, reflecting urban life and problems. Cos-
     tumes may be as formal as Western business suits, or tradi-
     tionally African if the dancers prefer.

KALICHINI, PAUL. One of the earliest leaders of the Zambia
     African National Congress, he was elected its Deputy President
     at its inaugural meeting in Broken Hill in November, 1958.
     Because of these ZANC activities, however, when the Govern-
     ment declared the "Emergency" in March, 1959, he was ar-
     rested and subjected to rustication (q.v.) at Chadiza in eastern

Zambia, near Petauke. He was released from detention in
July and immediately announced the formation of the African
National Independence Party. Actually Frank Chitambala (q. v.)
had laid the party's foundations at the end of May, and the
two men proceeded to be its co-leaders. On August 1, 1959,
they merged their party with another small splinter group
called the United National Freedom Party and the merger created today's ruling party the United National Independence
Party (UNIP). Two things were clear among all the members:
they were waiting for Kaunda's release so he could assume the
presidency, and they did not want to fraternize in any way
with the ANC. In October, 1959, however, Mainza Chona, a
dissident member of the ANC, joined UNIP along with a large
following. A conference was called to elect interim leaders
and Chona defeated Kalichini for the Presidency. Angered by
his defeat, he would not run for any other party post and ultimately retired from active politics.

KALIF PIANO OF KALIMBA. A musical instrument found almost
everywhere in Zambia. It has from eight to thirteen metal
strips of varying lengths attached by one end to a wooden
board or box. The "piano" is played by vibrating the free end
of each strip with one's thumbs.

KALIMANSHILA. War leader and chief councillor to Mwamba III,
a major Bemba chief near the end of the nineteenth century.
Kalimanshila was the principal councillor opposed to accepting
the Europeans, either the British South Africa Company or the
White Fathers' missionaries. He especially opposed the growing influence of Father Dupont (q. v.) who he tried to have sent
away. After Mwamba died in October, 1899, however, most of
Kalimanshila's followers at court chose to accept Rev. Dupont
as a stabilizing force. Thus he also switched sides and made
a dramatic speech in which he pledged support to the Europeans
as protectors against the bena ng'andu (q. v.) who threatened to
raid the mourning village.

KALIMINWA. A Lungu chieftainship northwest of Lubemba, it was
influenced strongly by the Bemba. The chief at the beginning
of the twentieth century was not actually of the Lungu royal
family but owed his position to the fact that a Bemba chief,
Mwamba, had given the chief his daughter Kasonde NaKabwe
for a wife. The majority of the people in the area were
Lungu, but there were also many Bemba. Many Lungu left the
region rather than accept Kaliminwa's rule, but others (members of the royal clan) tried to remove him. A noted member
of the latter group was a man named Tomboshalo (q. v.). He
was even encouraged by the missionaries. The Native Commissioner supported Kaliminwa, however, and the incident was
resolved with Tomboshalo accepting Kaliminwa's rule. A different kind of struggle involving the chieftainship evolved in
the period 1918-1920 when the new young Kaliminwa (son of the
earlier one) withdrew his recognition of the rights of either of

the Bemba chiefs Mwamba or Mporokoso to rule over him.
He said they were of "junior standing." Mporokoso demanded
that the Native Commissioner and the BSAC administration
force Kaliminwa to pay tribute and respect to the Bemba
chiefs. An enquiry was held on July 9, 1920, and after hearing local testimony the Commissioner agreed with Mporokoso
that this Kaliminwa should be dismissed. His reasons were
not very substantial, and seemed to rest in large part upon
his respect for Mporokoso's opinions.

KALOMO. One of the southern-most administrative districts of
Zambia, it borders Rhodesia just west of Lake Kariba. It is
one of the districts in the Southern Province, and its population in 1969 was about seventy-seven thousand. The area has
been populated for at least sixteen hundred years. A few
miles southeast of the town of Kalomo (which is along the line
of rail north of Livingstone and west of Choma) is the fifth
century A.D. Kalundu mound. Excavations at this site have
produced much evidence of Early Iron Age communities, including notable examples of their pottery. Another mound,
Isamu Pati, exists a few miles west of Kalomo. Later pottery dates have been pinpointed in the period from the ninth
to the thirteenth centuries. During the nineteenth century there
was much activity going on near the site of today's town of
Kalomo. The Tonga Chief Siachitema had a village east of the
present town. The Makololo leader Sebituane defeated an Ndebele force near there in about 1840. About a half century
later a Lozi rebel, Sikabenga took refuge with the Tonga Chief.
In 1900 the British South Africa Company made Kalomo the
headquarters for the administration of North-Western Rhodesia.
Robert Coryndon (q.v.) was the administrator there. However,
in 1907 they moved the headquarters south to Livingstone.
Kalomo continued then as a small settlement serving the nearby farming areas.

KALOMO PEOPLE. A term loosely applied to the inhabitants of
southern Zambia from roughly A.D. 300 to 1200 whose civilizations, centered around mounds, have been recently unearthed
and studied by archaeologists and anthropologists. Many of the
mounds are located just a few miles in one direction or another from the present town of Kalomo (q.v.) on the Batoka
plateau. Among the largest mounds are those called Isamu
Pati and Kalundu. The settlements cover a wide area, however, from near Barotseland in the west to the middle Zambezi River in the east. The inhabitants of the small villages
cultivated some grain and other minor crops, and had many of
the normal domesticated animal species such as cattle, sheep,
goats, chickens and dogs. Some of the early Kalomo people
were also hunters and gatherers like the Bushmen they evidently forced out of the area. They also used iron hoes. They
lived in mud and pole huts and maintained bins to store grain,
all of which were built around a central enclosure. Presumably some kind of thorn fence protected them from wild animals
and raiders. They were generally isolated from outside trade.

KALUE, EDWARD. Purportedly the leader of an abortive coup against the Lozi King Yeta III while the King was in England in May, 1938. The well-educated and ambitious second son of Yeta, he had served earlier as his father's private secretary, only to be replaced under the pressure of British officials who saw him to be an "extremist." Proof that Kalue was the instigator of the plot was claimed but never demonstrated, but the Lozi Kuta banished him from the Barotse Province.

KALULU, SOLOMON. A Zambian with one of the longest records of service to both the African political movement and to the Zambian government. He was born in Lusaka on June 18, 1924. He became a headmaster before he abandoned the teaching profession in 1952 in order to enter politics. He was secretary of the African National Congress from 1952 to 1955 and then served as Treasurer-General. He left this post and the ANC after a party conference in 1959 where he had suggested that Harry Nkumbula should be made only honorary Life President since his time would be taken up as a member of the Legislative Council. Kalulu was outvoted and left the party. He was left briefly without a party because ZANC had been banned, but he soon joined a small group called the United National Freedom Party (q.v.) and was named its vice-president general, although he acknowledged that its true leader, Kenneth Kaunda, was in jail. When that party joined another in August, 1959, to create UNIP, Kalulu was an active participant in the merger and soon was chosen its secretary-general. When Kaunda was elected president of UNIP on January 31, 1960, Kalulu was made its national chairman, a post he held until 1969.

In the 1962 general elections, Kalulu lost the Lusaka Rural constituency election to the ANC national chairman, Edward Liso, by about 550 votes out of 2700. After the 1964 elections he was appointed as Minister of Lands and Natural Resources. During his three years in that position he led a successful drive to reestablish a domain for the Red Lechwe antelope that was in danger of extinction. January 1, 1967 he was appointed as Minister of Transport, Power, and Communications. Two years later he was made Minister of the Eastern Province, but in August, 1969, he returned to his post as Minister of Lands and Natural Resources.

With the new Constitution of 1973 placing much more power in UNIP's Central Committee, Kalulu was appointed head of the Social and Cultural subcommittee of the Central Committee in August, 1973, and left the Cabinet. He was still active in that post several years later.

KALULUSHI. A town of about twenty-four thousand people (in 1969) in the Copperbelt of central Zambia. It is also one of the Urban Districts of the Copperbelt Province. It is located due west of Kitwe and is one of the newer Copperbelt towns, built almost completely by the mining companies.

KALUNGU RIVER. A minor tributary of the Chambeshi River, it
is nevertheless very important to the Bemba people. It flows
from west to east in northern Zambia. Its historical importance is tied to the migration of members of the bena ng'andu
(Crocodile Clan) who settled on the Kalungu River and established the chieftainship called Chitimukulu, which was to become the major Bemba chieftainship. The capital, Ngwena
(the word for crocodile), was set up there because they found
a dead crocodile on the riverbank and took this to be a good
sign.

KALUNGWISHI RIVER. A river in the northwestern corner of
northeastern Zambia, it flows into Lake Mweru. In 1893 the
British South Africa Company established a station called Kalungwishi near the point that the river entered the lake. The
location was in the heart of the area where the Bemba, Lunda,
and Arabs competed for supremacy. There is also a good example of rock art on a large boulder near Kundabwika Falls
on the river. There is a panel of red schematic paintings on
it, based on a large, complex grid consisting of horizontal
and vertical lines.

KALUWA, GEORGE W. CHARLES. A storekeeper and farmer in
Mazabuka who had tried to get African nationalist movements
going in the late 1930's. He finally succeeded in May, 1946,
when he, along with men like Dauti Yamba (q.v.), created the
Federation of African Societies of Northern Rhodesia (q.v.).
When it changed its name to the Northern Rhodesia African
Congress (q.v.; a name also used in 1937 by Kaluwa for an
organization in Mazabuka) in 1948, he was chosen its Assistant
Treasurer.

KALYATI, ALBERT. A militant, left-wing member of UNIP who
helped form the Reformed Trade Union Congress (q.v.) in
1960 as a break-away from Lawrence Katilungu's Trade Union
Congress. Kalyati had denounced Katilungu for agreeing to
become a member of the Monckton Commission. When the
United Trades Union Congress was formed by merger in 1961,
Kalyati remained as one of its top leaders.

KAMANGA, REUBEN CHITANDIKA. One of a small core of Zambians who has been active in nationalist politics and the current Zambian Government for about three decades, he served
for three years as Zambia's first Vice-President. Born at
Chitandika near Chipata in the Eastern Province on August 26,
1929, he is the son of a Nyanja-speaking Cewa village headman. He was educated at mission schools before attending the
famous Munali Secondary School (q.v.) at Lusaka. Before entering the nationalist movement he worked first as a clerk,
then in a government office in provincial administration, and
then entered private business. He also worked as a trade union
organizer. In 1950 he worked with Justin Chimba, Simon Zukas, and Mungoni Liso as editors of The Freedom Newsletter

and was a co-founder of the Anti-Federation Action Committee.
In 1951 they all became members of Nkumbula's African National
Congress.
In August, 1956, he was chosen to the ANC National Executive Committee. In part this was a reward for his activi-
ties in organizing a boycott against the color bar in Fort Jameson in his capacity as chairman of the Eastern Province branch
of the ANC. Kamanga was one of the group that split from the
ANC in October, 1958, and was a charter member of ZANC.
At its first general conference on November 8, 1958, he was
elected its deputy treasurer. When the Northern Rhodesia
Government banned ZANC and arrested its leaders the following March, Kamanga was sent under detention to Sesheke.
When Kamanga was released he traveled to Ghana and then
proceeded to Cairo, Egypt, where he opened a party office for
UNIP. In July, 1961 he was elected the party's Deputy Presi-
dent. Although he had a major disagreement with Kenneth
Kaunda over the strongly anti-British tone of a memorandum
Kamanga signed in September, 1961, he was soon back in
everyone's good graces. He remained as UNIP's Eastern
Province Chairman during this whole period.
In 1962 he ran for Parliament from his home area and
won the Petauke South seat (after barely beating the filing dead-
line). In the coalition cabinet that followed, he was named
Minister of Labour and Mines. In Kaunda's January, 1964,
cabinet, Kamanga was named Minister of Transport and Communications. At independence in October he became Zambia's
Vice-President, serving until September 7, 1967. Meanwhile
in August, 1967, at the UNIP triennial general conference at
Mulungushi there had been a bitter intra-party fight for posts
on the Central Committee and other top party posts. Ethnic
divisions were a major part of the split, and Kamanga lost
for reelection as the Party's Deputy President to Simon Kapwepwe. He lost by several hundred votes out of about five
thousand. He then left the post of Vice-President and became
the country's Foreign Minister until January, 1969. It was
during this period that he was also charged with criminal misconduct, a charge labeled a "political maneuver" by Chief Justice Brian Doyle who cleared him on June 1, 1971.
From January 1969 until December 1973 (and the coming
of Zambia's Second Republic), Kamanga served as Minister of
Rural Development. He was elected to UNIP's Central Committee in August, 1973, and became Chairman of its Rural Development Subcommittee. Since 1975, however, he has been
Chairman of its powerful Political, Constitutional, Legal, and
Foreign Affairs Subcommittee.

KAMBULUMBULU. The site of some interesting rock art from the
Late Stone Age, it is located in the Eastern Province in the
Luangwa escarpment northwest of Lundazi. A number of dif-
ferent schematic art motifs are found there, including ladders,
winged objects, circles, and objects looking like long hair pins.
They are done in red.

KAMBWILI. A Bisa chieftainship that was active in nineteenth-century trade with the Bemba and Arab traders. It was also active in the coastal trade with the Portuguese. From them it acquired guns to defeat a Chewa chief in the 1880's.

KANGOMBE. A Luvale chief in the mid 1880's who was spreading his dominance into areas occupied by Lunda, Ndembu, and Lozi, until Chipenge (q.v.), an Ndembu commoner, defeated him. This encouraged the neighboring peoples to challenge the Luvale.

KANONGESHA. An Ndembu chieftainship in northwestern Zambia between the Lungu and upper Zambezi Rivers. Its existence as such is owed to the attempt by Mwata Yamvo (q.v.), a Lunda leader in the seventeenth century, to spread his influence by sending several aides into the neighboring country. One of them, Kanongesha, was able to establish himself among some of the Lukolwe people in that area. The chieftainship he established became involved with some more distant traders to the west, notably the Ovimbundu slave-traders from Angola. The Lukolwe (or Mbwela) among whom the chieftainship was established retained much of their independence from the chief, even retaining their matrilineal descent system, and the unity that was imposed was primarily of a ritual nature.

KANSANSAMA. The capital of an important Bemba Chitimukulu, Chileshye Chepela (q.v.). Located on the northern bank of the Kalungu River, it was also the site of an attack by the Ngoni against the Bemba around 1850. The Bemba retained their capital and the Ngoni moved on.

KANSANSHI. The site of an old copper mine in northern Zambia near the modern Solwezi (q.v.). Africans mined the copper for their own use long before the Europeans found the lode at the very end of the nineteenth century. Decades earlier the Kaonde chief Chibanza had its copper cast into bullets for muzzle-loaders.

KANYANTA. One of the more prominent Bemba leaders of the last century, he had held the title of Nkolemfumu from 1884 until 1899. The Mwamba III Mubanga Chipoya died in October, 1898. After a brief interim during which Rev. Dupont (q.v.) maintained order, Kanyanta succeeded as Mwamba IV in September, 1899. The British Administrator Robert Codrington agreed to this succession (and Rev. Dupont assented) after a meeting of the headmen. When Ponde, the Chitimukulu, died in 1923, a dispute arose over succession, and again Kanyanta was involved, this time in conflict with Nkula II Bwalya. The dispute was resolved in Kanyanta's favor after a lengthy enquiry by the District Commissioner of the Awemba District, H. G. Willis. Kanyanta then served as Chitimukulu until his death in 1943.

KAOMA. The new official name for the district and administrative

center known formerly as Mankoya (q. v.). It is located in the
Western (formerly Barotse) Province. The change occurred in
the early 1970's.

KAONDE (or KAUNDI). One of the seven largest language sub-
groups of Zambia with about 150,000 members (and thus specifically serviced by Radio Zambia, for example), the tribe resides primarily in the Solwezi and Kasempa districts of the
country's North-Western Province. The people are probably of
Luba origin but paid allegiance to a Lunda chief, Musokantanda,
when they entered their present area around the sixteenth or
seventeenth century. The Kaonde have a matrilineal descent
system, but combine it with a virilocal residence pattern.
The Kaonde have never been a highly centralized people, although their early history revolves around a young man, Jipumpu, who rebelled against a major chief (his cousin) named Ka-
wambala. After a series of battles and at least one retreat
into the Congo area, Jipumpu dominated the area and ruled with
the title Kasempa (q. v.). Although the Kasempa chieftainship
became a major one in the region, a number of other Kaonde
chieftainships also emerged, for example, Mushima and Kata-
tola. The Lozi dominated many of these people at different
times in the nineteenth century, especially while the Lozi were
led by King Lewanika. On the other hand, Kasempa once also
defeated a force of Lozi sent by Lewanika. The Kaonde also
were noted for sending slave-raiding parties south of the Kafue
River against the Ila.

KAPANDANSALU. An Arab (q. v.) slave trading chief in the late
nineteenth century whose stockaded village was built in the
upper Zambezi valley near the village of a Senga chief named
Chibale (q. v.). This village became a major slave market,
attracting traders such as the infamous Arab, Mlozi (q. v.).
An army of warriors led by Kapandansalu and several other
local Arab chiefs attacked Chibale's village. The force included many Bemba as well. A warning by Robert Young of
the BSAC did not prevent the force from renewing the attack
a day later. Young's police and Chibale's forces killed twenty-
five of the attackers, and two Arab chiefs, one of them Kapandansalu, were taken prisoner later.

KAPASA. A half-brother of the early Bemba leader Chiti (q. v.).
In the Bemba legend on the migration of their founders, Kapasa
was sent with several aides by Chiti and Nkole to rescue their
sister Chilufya Mulenga from her detention by Mukulumpe. Kapasa succeeded but during their return he seduced the girl.
Kapasa was disowned by Chiti when he discovered that she was
pregnant by Kapasa.

KAPENTA. A small dried fish that is a staple of the Zambian
diet.

KAPIDI. A Luba chief who was involved in a three year war with a Mbwela clan led by Kale (q.v.) in the early nineteenth century. After Kale's death Kapidi settled south of the Kafue River in Ila territory.

KAPIRI MPOSHI. A town along the line of rail about forty miles north of Kabwe, and south of the Copperbelt. Its only real significance is that it lies just a couple of miles south of the junction of the Great North Road (q.v.) and the main North-South road between Lusaka and the Copperbelt.

KAPWEPWE, SIMON MWANZA. Part of the earliest cadre of Zambian nationalist politicians, he served in the nationalist movement, in UNIP, and in the Government until 1971 when he bolted the party. He was born of Bemba parents at Chinsala in the Northern Province on April 12, 1922. His father had been a BSAC policeman and gradually worked his way up to being Head Messenger for the District Commissioner. At the age of twelve, Simon became a very close friend of Kenneth Kaunda. The two met again at the Lubwa Mission School where they qualified as teachers, Kapwepwe qualifying in 1945. His political consciousness and dissatisfaction with the Government were already in evidence at that time. He began teaching elementary school at Kitwe on the Copperbelt, and in 1948 became a founding member of the Northern Rhodesia African Congress (NRAC). He became a member of the Executive, and Secretary of its Kitwe Branch. However in 1949 he and Kaunda returned to Lubwa to start a farm, although Kapwepwe also continued to teach. They stayed active in the Chinsali African Welfare Association which was, in effect, the local branch of the NRAC. In 1950 he resigned from teaching when the Congress acquired for him a four year scholarship to India, where he included journalism in his Bombay studies.

Upon his return to Zambia on January 6, 1955, he found the African National Congress (new name of the NRAC) leaderless with both Harry Nkumbula and Kaunda in jail for possessing "subversive" literature. Kapwepwe assumed the leadership and began improving the ANC's organization as well as its activities. A persuasive orator, he quickly acquired a reputation as a firebrand. When Nkumbula was released, he appointed Kapwepwe Provincial President of the Northern Province Branch of the ANC. In 1956 he was elected party treasurer. It was undoubtedly Kapwepwe's urge toward greater political activism that led to the 1958 split in the ANC that resulted in the formation of the Zambia African National Congress (q.v.). Not only was he one of its founding members and its first treasurer, but according to one account it was he who suggested the word "Zambia" to identify the territory and the party. When the Northern Rhodesia Government incarcerated ZANC's leaders in March, 1959, he was taken to Mongu in Barotseland. He was released in December, 1959, and before leaving Barotseland he immediately began organizing provincial and district organizations for UNIP there. With UNIP now the major nationalist party, Kapwepwe became its treasurer, a

post he held until 1967. In December, 1960, he accompanied
Kaunda to London where they laid the foundation for the final
drive toward independence by their actions at the Federal Review Conference (q.v.). In the 1962 election for the legislature, Kapwepwe opposed Dauti Yamba (q.v.), and a United
Federal Party opponent. He won by a margin of 3840 votes to
Yamba's 87 and UFP's 24. In the subsequent coalition cabinet
with the ANC, Kapwepwe was named Minister of African Agriculture. When UNIP won control of the Parliament in January,
1964, he was made Minister of Home Affairs. In the Cabinet
of September 24, 1964, anticipating independence, he switched
portfolios to become Minister of Foreign Affairs. In this capacity (a post he held for three years), he was a bitterly vocal
critic of British policy, or lack thereof, toward Rhodesia and
its unilateral declaration of independence.

At the August, 1967, general conference of UNIP, Kapwepwe led an ethnic-based alliance in an attempt to sweep Central
Committee and party offices for the Bembas and their allies.
He succeeded, winning the post of deputy party leader from his
old colleague Reuben Kamanga (q.v.). He was also shortly
thereafter raised to Kamanga's former position of Zambia's
Vice-President. In that capacity he became active in economic
affairs, both in budgeting matters and in those involving unrest
on the Copperbelt. Also in 1970 and 1971 he initiated a campaign to preserve traditional Zambian culture, especially by
encouraging the use of Zambian languages in schools.

Kapwepwe's political victories were at the expense of deep
dissension within UNIP, however, as other ethnic groups resented what they saw as a Bemba power play. Kaunda himself
resented this divisiveness caused by an old friend. Knowing
that an effort to oust him from office was under way, Kapwepwe resigned as both Vice-President and deputy party leader on
August 25, 1969. He said that his people (the Bemba) had
been hurt because of his new position. Kaunda urged him to
return, however, so he resumed both posts. He was relieved
as Minister of Development and Finance, a job added in January, 1969, and took on the post of Minister of Culture instead.
In January, 1970, he became Minister of Provincial and Local
Government in addition. When Mainza Chona succeeded him
as Vice-President in October, 1970, Kapwepwe retained his
two Ministerial Portfolios.

A new phase of Kapwepwe's career began in August, 1971.
He resigned from the Government after Kaunda dismissed four
other Bemba-speaking Ministers. Kapwepwe then formed the
United Progressive Party, along with a number of other prominent former members of UNIP. Justin Chimba (q.v.) became
one of his chief aides. When the Government called by-elections on December 21, 1971, to fill the vacated seats, Kapwepwe defied all odds by winning the Mufulira parliamentary seat
for his UPP by 2120 votes to 1810. His was the only success,
however, and the party was banned on February 4, 1972. He
was arrested along with 122 of his followers. He was released
on December 31, 1972, just a day before the new one-party

state came into effect. On February 3, 1973, he was charged
in court for possession of two guns but received a two year
suspended sentence. In January, 1973, Kapwepwe brought a
libel suit against the Times of Zambia and was rewarded
K20,000 when he won the case. He also won K10,000 from
the Daily Mail and K30,000 from the State radio and television
services. These cases stemmed from their reports that Kapwepwe was sending people for military training outside Zambia.
He then returned to farming in northern Zambia, but on September
9, 1977, he announced that he would rejoin UNIP for the sake of national unity. In 1978 he failed to win UNIP's nomination for the
presidency of Zambia.

KARIBA DAMS AND HYDROELECTRIC PROJECTS. The first of
the Kariba power stations was planned and built during the period of the Central African Federation. It was completed in
1960. Built on the south side of the Zambezi River, and thus
under the potential control of the Southern Rhodesian Government, it was nevertheless designed to provide power to both
Northern and Southern Rhodesia. The basis for the hydroelectric scheme was the huge Kariba Dam built across the Zambezi. It is 420 feet high and eighty feet thick, and caused the
creation of Lake Kariba (q.v.), which covers an area of about
two thousand square miles. When the dam was built there
were numerous political problems concerning the moving of
about sixty thousand Valley Tonga (34,000 in Zambia) from
their homelands. Likewise thousands of animals had to be
moved in Operation Noah.
    The South Bank power station (Kariba I) was supplying 70
percent of Zambia's power in 1966, but with its control potentially in the hands of Rhodesian leaders (despite 50 percent
ownership by Zambia), the building of Kariba II on the north
bank was imperative. The need for it was only partly lessened
by the completion of the Kafue hydroelectric project (q.v.) in
1972. Work on Kariba II began in mid-1971. Its goal was to
provide 600 megawatts, as did Kariba I (which was later up-
graded to 705 megawatts). A future third stage could add another 300 megawatts. British contractors working on Kariba
II ran into numerous difficulties and ceased work in February,
1973. A Yugoslavian contractor took over a month later, but
the project's completion date was pushed back to 1976. Now
the North Bank power station is used exclusively by Zambia
and the South Bank by Rhodesia, although joint control of the
total project continues.

KASABA BAY. Located in the Sumbu Game Reserve on the southwestern shore of Lake Tanganyika, Kasaba Bay is an area
noted for its outstanding game fishing. This resort area is
also good for boating and is popular among tourists.

KASAMA. A town of about nine thousand people (in 1969), it is
also the administrative center of the Kasama District in Zambia's Northern Province. The District is in northeastern Zam-

bia and had a population of 108,000 in 1969, ranking it about
tenth among Zambia's districts by population. The town itself
is on the line of rail of the Tan-Zam (Great Uhuru) Railway.
The town was founded in 1898 as a station set up by the British
South Africa Company on the Milima stream. It was a few
miles east of Mwamba's village, and a few miles north of the
site of Kasama today. In 1901 the station was moved south a
little to its present site. At the very end of World War I,
Kasama was mistakenly left undefended by the Northern Rhodesia Police and was attacked by a German force led by General P. E. von Lettow-Vorbeck. During the attack on November
9, 1918, the Germans blew up the Government Offices. The
troops left the town on November 12. (European women and
children had been evacuated from Kasama on November 8 in
anticipation of the attack.)

KASAMA NATIVE WELFARE ASSOCIATION. Sanctioned by the
Northern Rhodesian Government near the end of 1932, this association was limited by a government restriction to Africans
living in Kasama township itself. No political activity was allowed and membership was limited to those who had no allegiance to a local Native Authority. Its chairman was Aaron
Nkata and its secretary was John Mulenga. Despite the restrictions, the association became involved in issues such as educational facilities and the operation of lorries. While its membership was never large and in fact declined as the 1930's drew
to a close, it was nonetheless one of the few such organizations in Northern Rhodesia before WWII.

KASANKA NATIONAL PARK. A small game reserve and national
park just east of the Congo Pedicle in the eastern half of Zambia.

KASEMPA. An administrative center and a district in the North-
Western Province of Zambia. The district's population in 1969
was thirty-three thousand. It is located west of the Lunga
River, near the source of the Dongwe River. The area presumably got its name from the Kaonde chieftainship that ruled
under the title Kasempa. Late in the nineteenth century Kasempa and his Kaonde warriors crossed to the south of the
Kafue River on raids, fighting and capturing slaves among the
Ila. Kasempa had received guns in his trade with Bihe. At one
point he defeated a large army of Lozi sent by Lewanika.

KASHINDA. The village established by Chief Mporokoso after he
left his original chiefdom, Maseba, probably late in the 1870's.
He located it several miles north and east of the Luangwa
River near its bend. The first major mission school of the
London Missionary Society in Zambia was established nearby
and in 1908 became known as Kashinda Mission.

KASOKOLO, REV. MR. HENRY. One of the first two African
members of the Legislative Council, he and Nelson Nalumango
were appointed in 1948. A couple of years later the African

Representative Council replaced them with Dauti Yamba and
Paskale Sokota. He then became an organizer for the African
National Congress. In the 1962 election he unsuccessfully opposed Kenneth Kaunda for a seat in the Legislature, losing by
a margin of 4347 to 229.

KATABA. A town in southwestern Zambia west of the Kafue National Park. It is located at the northern end of the Sawmill
Railway that runs north from Livingstone. The Kataba Valley
was the site of a major nineteenth-century battle when Sebituane, leader of the Kololo, confronted and defeated a large
force of Lozi. This site was nearer the Zambezi River than
the present town.

KATANGA. Now called Shaba, it is the southernmost province of
the Republic of Zaire (formerly the Belgian Congo or, after
independence, the Democratic Republic of the Congo). It is
Zambia's northern neighbor, but the Congo Pedicle (or Katanga
Pedicle) dips down into the heart of Zambia, causing the latter
to have a narrow waist. Geologically Katanga and Zambia have
much in common, notably the large storehouse of ore-bearing
rocks. Copper is a major export item of both areas. There
are also numerous historical and anthropological similarities.
Most of the Africans in Zambia have at least distant ethnic
roots in the Congo, and usually in Katanga. Most of the
groups in northeastern Zambia recognize beginnings among the
Luba people, whose later migrations originated in Katanga.
Several other Zambian peoples originated among the Lunda of
Mwata Yamvo. While they were a little north of Katanga, the
migrations of some, notably Kazembe's Lunda, came through
Katanga en route to their current lands. Also the traders of
the nineteenth century usually crossed back and forth from the
Congo to Northern Rhodesia as if no real borders existed.
Had the agents of Cecil Rhodes been more successful in
the early 1890's or had a Lunda Chief been less dominant, Katanga may also have become part of Rhodes' land rather than
King Leopold's, and Zambia today might include most of Katanga. As it developed, the copper mines of Katanga attracted
many Zambians to jobs prior to the full development of Zambia's Copperbelt.
Katanga became important to Zambia again in the late
years of the Central African Federation. Moise Tshombe's
regime in Katanga impressed Northern Rhodesian Europeans
who felt that an African like Nkumbula or Katilungu might play
a similar role in Northern Rhodesia. Thus Sir Roy Welensky
made several attempts to secure an equivalent to Tshombe.
Covert European financing of certain African parties or leaders, sometimes with financial aid promised from Katanga itself, marked the early 1960's.
Problems in Katanga (now known as Shaba) affected Zambia
again in 1977 when an invasion force of Lunda fighters (based
in Angola since the unsuccessful Katangese secession attempt
of the 1960's) attempted to retake the Shaba Province. Zairian

forces counterattacked and inadvertently bombed Zambian territory. Finally the invaders were beaten back, but a similar
invasion with similar results occurred in 1978.

KATANGA CROSS see COPPER CROSSES

KATANINO. A town along the line of rail at the southern end of
the Copperbelt, south of Ndola.

KATENGO KUTA. This kuta, or council, has had a varied and
disputed history. Under Lozi King Lewanika in the late nineteenth century it had been a secret council called to discuss
vital matters such as plots, executions, and witchcraft cases.
Lord Hailey reports that after Lewanika, however, it became
a more formal institution, composed of minor indunas and even
commoners. Some considered it to be the closest thing the
Lozi had to a representative body within their Government.
Its voice was considered to be closer to the masses than was
that of the Saa Kuta or Sikalo Kuta. It became a council within the larger Mulongwanji (q. v.). When the Katengo met inde-
pendently it discussed national matters and passed suggestions
on to the Saa Kuta (q. v.). Nevertheless it fell into disuse from
the mid-1930's to the mid-1940's. Most of the above is based
on the discussion by Lord Hailey in his Native Administration
in the British African Territories, Part II. Other writers,
however, indicate that the Katengo Council was non-existent
after King Lewanika. All agree however that it was revived
in 1946-47 by the British when the Resident Commissioner of
Barotseland, A. F. B. Glennie, insisted that it be restored as
a representative body that would make advisory recommendations to be sent to the National Council (Mulongwanji). Its members
were elected by secret ballot under a universal male (and in Senanga District also female) suffrage. However, it met only once a
year under the chairmanship of the Ngambela, who could control
matters for the King. The new Katengo was resented by the traditional elite, and its recommendations were generally ignored. Katengo elections in 1963 were won by UNIP candidates.

KATILUNGU, LAWRENCE (1914-1961). Pioneer Zambian trade
union leader, and politician. He was born in January, 1914,
at Chipalo in the Northern Province, and was a cousin of the
Bemba Chief Chitimukulu. He was mission-educated, becoming first a teacher and then a headmaster before starting to
work in the copper mines in 1936 because of the higher wages.
He was one of the leaders of the famous 1940 mine strikes,
and then left the country to work in the Congo for seven years.
He returned to Nkana in 1947 and soon became a senior interpreter. The same year he worked closely with a man sent by
the British Labour Party Government who helped the Africans
form a Copperbelt union. Katilungu was elected its first
chairman and worked for two years to build its membership.
The Government recognized the African Mineworkers Union
(and Katilungu as its President) in 1949. Meanwhile he had

also entered politics as Chairman of the Kitwe Branch of the
Northern Rhodesia African Congress. His political interests
continued for several years, as he was active on the African
National Congress' Supreme Action Council which opposed the
idea of a Central African Federation. In 1952 he went to London with an ANC delegation to protest the coming Federation.
But soon he would devote full time to the union movement for
several years.

After encouraging other Africans to form unions in their
fields of labor, Katilungu formed the Northern Rhodesia Trade
Union Congress (TUC) in 1950 and was elected its President.
For the next decade his leadership of the mineworkers union
was virtually unchallenged. He attended meetings in Britain,
led an orderly and successful strike in 1952, and was involved
in a very controversial and bitter strike in 1955. Some union
members claimed he called off the latter strike before the ob-
jectives were achieved. He made it a point to keep the union
under his own personal control. In 1955, however, he was defeated for TUC President. When he accepted appointment to
the controversial Monckton Commission (q. v.) in 1959, some
unionists finally rebelled. It resulted in some TUC members
resigning to form the Reformed Trade Union Congress (q. v.)
in 1960. They were also protesting his moderate approach to
union activity. In December, 1960, he lost his union power
when the AMU branches deposed him by vote as President of
the mineworkers.

Meanwhile Katilungu had not really abandoned the political
arena. In 1950 he had been chosen to the Urban Advisory
Council and as a member of the African Representative Council. While he remained interested in the ANC, he did not encourage his union members to join in a two day "National
Prayer" work boycott in 1953. He was also criticized by the
ANC in the mid-1950's for drawing people out of the party and
into his union activities. His anger with ANC attempts to un-
dermine his union support led him to support the formation of
the Constitutional Party (q. v.) in 1957. Nevertheless, when
Kaunda and his supporters broke away from the ANC in 1958
to form ZANC, Katilungu stood by Nkumbula. In fact, he ap-
plauded the Government's banning of ZANC in March, 1959.
In the 1959 election he ran for the Copperbelt seat in the Legislature, but lost because of heavy European voting for an
African candidate of the United Federal Party. By mid-1959
Katilungu returned to close friendship with ANC's Nkumbula
and campaigned with him. Sir Roy Welensky and others saw
him increasingly as a moderate leader to be courted by the
Europeans, especially after his acceptance of a position on the
Monckton Commission when most Africans were boycotting it.
In March, 1961, he was elected ANC's Deputy National President, and when Nkumbula was jailed for nine months for drunk-
en driving, Katilungu became its Acting President. He also
filled Nkumbula's seat in the Legislative Council. As leader
of the ANC he received further attention from Roy Welensky
and the UFP. Katilungu was receptive to the attempts by the

Europeans to link him with Moise Tshombe in Katanga (q. v.),
who was in a position as a conservative leader to supply the
ANC with both counsel and financial support in their forthcoming electoral struggles with UNIP. All of this scheming, Katilungu's hard work in organizing the ANC, and the meetings
with Tshombe came to naught when an automobile accident in
November, 1961, claimed the life of Katilungu.

KATONGO. The oldest son of Mukulumpe and brother of Chiti and
Nkole, the founders of the Bembe. One estimate has it that
around 1670 Mukulumpe (his father) deliberately blinded Katongo
out of anger, and that it was this and a similar threat to Chiti
that motivated Chiti and Nkole to lead many followers to new
territory, away from their despotic father. The Bemba legend
says that the father tried to lure Chiti and Nkole back into a
trap, but Katongo warned his brothers by sending a message
on the talking drum.
     Katongo is also the name of one of the titled chiefdoms of
the Bemba. It later changed its name to Chewe and now is
the chiefdom of Nkula at Ichinga. Some sources say that Katongo left his father's village ultimately, following Chiti and
Nkole, but settled on the Luvu River and here began this chieftainship. At least one bearer of the Katongo title has served
as Chitimukulu.

KAUNDA, BETTY. The wife of Zambia's first President, Kenneth
Kaunda, she is the mother of nine children. The daughter of
John and Milika Banda, she was born on November 17, 1928,
and named Mutinkhe after a grandmother. Her father had
worked for the African Lakes Corporation and was transferred
to Chinsali where he met David and Helen Kaunda. The family
moved again, however, and she was seventeen before she was
introduced to the twenty-two-year-old Kenneth Kaunda. The
next year, 1946, she attained an Elementary Teacher's Certificate, but also plans were made for the wedding, which took
place at Mpika on August 24, 1946. The couple's first home
was at Lubwa. The story of the next twenty years is one of
tremendous courage and patience displayed by Mrs. Kaunda as
she kept her growing family alive during long periods of low
political salaries and high expenses, imprisonment of her husband, and long periods of his absence both within Zambia and
abroad. Her first six children were boys. The seventh was
a girl, and twins arrived in 1964. In addition, Mrs. Kaunda
found time in later years to travel abroad with and without her
husband, and to be active in the UNIP Women's Organization.

KAUNDA, DAVID JULIZYA (1878-1932). The father of Kenneth
Kaunda, Zambia's first President, he was a teacher, and ordained minister, and an early advocate of Africans' rights.
Born at Lisali in the Mwambazi district of Tongaland in 1878,
he was named Julizya. He took the name of David only after
being received into the Presbyterian Church later. His father,
Mtepa, was killed in battle when Julizya was a small child.

His mother, NyaChirwa took her four children to live in the
large Ngoni village of Elangeni around 1885, and here he was
raised. He grew up with a deep love of religion, as some
African evangelists, notably William Koyi, were active in the
area. He attended Ekwendi Mission School through Standard III
and then Overtoun Institution where he went through teacher
training. His future wife Helen also studied at Overtoun.
They were married in 1904. About 1905 David Kaunda began
traveling as a part of an Overtoun team, working at evange-
listic and educational efforts. He is still considered to have
been the missionary pioneer in the Chinsali District. Around
this same time he became quite close to men like Donald Siwale (q.v.), Peter Sinkala, Hezekiya Kawosa, and Hanoc Mu-
kunka. This group of comrades often discussed the attitude of
Europeans toward Africans. Their discussions over the next
couple of decades led to the formation of the Mwenzo Welfare
Association (q.v.) by Siwale, Kawosa, and Kaunda. It was
one of Zambia's first African "nationalist" organizations.

The Kaunda family lived at Chinsali until 1913 and moved
to Nkula for two years. David continued as a teacher and missionary. He was tremendously effective everywhere at establishing schools. He traveled extensively among the Bemba and
Bisa peoples, as well as others, establishing numerous schools.
Kenneth Kaunda was born in 1924, twenty years after his
parents' marriage, and was an unexpected addition to the group
of Kaunda siblings. Although David had taught since 1904, he
went back to Overtoun for theology studies from 1927 to 1929
when he was ordained. He died three years later at the age
of fifty-four. He had been conducting religious services and
was returning home to Lubwa when he was struck ill. He died
in his home.

KAUNDA, KENNETH DAVID. The attempt here at a biographical
sketch of Kenneth Kaunda must be recognized as being only a
token effort. Several major biographies exist, notably Richard
Hall's Kaunda--Founder of Zambia and Fergus Macpherson's
Kenneth Kaunda of Zambia. In addition, of course, is Kaunda's
autobiography, Zambia Shall Be Free, and his numerous other
writings. Since Kaunda has been the shaper of modern Zambia,
much of this book involves him in one way or another, and his
name occurs frequently in other entries. Brevity here merely
reflects the massive amount of information elsewhere.

Born on April 28, 1924, at Lubwe near Chinsali in the
Northern Province of Zambia, Kaunda was the eighth child of
a couple married twenty years, Helen and David Kaunda (q.v.).
Both were teachers, and David was also a missionary for the
Livingstone Mission. The Kaunda's were of Malawi origin, but
Kenneth grew up among the Bemba of Zambia. His education
began in Lubwe at the Mission School, and continued when he
went to Munali Secondary School. At Lubwe he became good
friends with a long-time political colleague Simon Kapwepwe
(q.v.). Kaunda returned to Lubwe as a teacher (after a teacher training course at Munali) in 1943. He served as Headmaster

there from 1944 to 1947, and was a scoutmaster and athletic
coach as well. In 1946 he married Betty Banda; together they
would raise nine children. For part of 1947 and 1948 Kaunda
taught in Tanganyika, but he returned in 1948 to teach in Mufulira at the United Missions in the Copperbelt School. He
also worked as a welfare assistant at the Nchanga mine.

Kaunda returned to Lubwe in 1949 to begin a farm with
two old friends, Simon Kapwepwe and John Sokoni. There
they became active in the Chinsali African Welfare Association,
the local branch of the Northern Rhodesia African Congress.
Kaunda was elected its Secretary in 1950. The next year he
became a district organizer as it changed its name to the African National Congress. The following year he was named Organizing Secretary in the Northern Province, and his skills and
boundless energy and dedication led to his being selected as
the ANC Secretary-General in August 1953, second in authority
only to its President, Harry Nkumbula. Two months later he
began editing the Congress News (q. v.). Because of it he was
arrested (but not imprisoned) in November, 1953.

Kaunda's next arrest came on January 6, 1955, when he
was arrested and ultimately sentenced to two months in prison
for possessing banned political literature. At that time he began his austere life style, foregoing both tobacco and alcohol.
He also does not eat meat. In May, 1957, he visited England
as a guest of the Labour Party, staying six months in order to
study the British political system. In May, 1958, he traveled
to Tanganyika and then India, returning in October. Upon his
return Kaunda and many of his ANC colleagues rejected the
"go slow" leadership of Nkumbula and broke away to form the
Zambia African National Congress (q. v.) on October 24, 1958,
at Broken Hill. Kaunda was made President. In December
he attended the first All African People's Conference in Ghana.
A nervous Northern Rhodesia Government banned the party in
March, 1959, and on March 12, at 1:00 a. m. Kaunda was arrested. He was sentenced to nine months' imprisonment, and
was sent to Kabompo in northwestern Zambia. Kaunda was
released on January 9, 1960, and on the last day of January
was elected President of the United National Independence
Party. In April, Black Government, a book that he had written with Colin Morris, was published. 1960 was a very important year for Kaunda's UNIP. He spent it in a vigorous
campaign to get England to renounce the Federation and to allow Zambia to become independent. The first sign of hope
came in December, 1960, when Kaunda and his nationalist colleagues at the Federal Review Conference (q. v.) in London
walked out of the meeting. This precipitated further action on
the part of British leaders that led to the demise of the Central African Federation. The first break was when Great
Britain indicated a willingness to allow Nyasaland to secede.
Zambia would eventually follow. Nevertheless Kaunda and
UNIP bitterly opposed the constitutional proposals being put
forth by the British. Still Kaunda decided that UNIP
should contest the October, 1962, elections. While UNIP would

not win a clear parliamentary majority, it did form a coalition cabinet with the ANC. Kaunda became Minister of Local Government and Social Welfare, and was clearly the dominant African in the Government. Also in October, 1962, his autobiography, Zambia Shall Be Free, was published. He then negotiated a new Constitution for his country and led UNIP to a sweeping election victory in January, 1964, thus becoming Prime Minister. (In the interim, in May, 1963, Kaunda was awarded the Honorary Degree of Doctor of Laws by Fordham University in New York.) The rest of 1964 was spent preparing the country for independence. Only the "holy war" of the Lumpa Church (q.v.) caused a serious distraction for Kaunda and his Cabinet. Finally, on October 24, 1964, Zambia received independence, with Kenneth Kaunda as its first President.

During 1963 Kaunda had also been elected President of the Pan-African Freedom Movement of East, Central and Southern Africa (q.v.). His concern for freedom movements in southern Africa has prompted him to tolerate the existence of their offices in Lusaka, but his close involvement with the Lusaka Manifesto (q.v.) reflects a sincere realism and even a moderate approach toward revolution and change. As a leader of the Front Line States, he has repeatedly sought moderate solutions to the Zimbabwe crisis as long as they seemed feasible. By 1977 he seemed to have despaired of a peaceful solution. Likewise Kaunda's policies towards South Africa have reflected both a sense of realism and a willingness to compromise, not in ultimate goals, necessarily, but in the process of change.

While concerned about international issues, Kaunda's first goal has been the proper development of Zambia. Although stressing the importance of Zambianization (q.v.) as a goal, he has consistently assured the Europeans that he hopes they will remain as part of a multi-racial society in which everyone contributes. Also Kaunda has developed an ideology for his country's development called Zambian Humanism (q.v.). Two of his books deal with the subject: A Humanist in Africa (published in 1966) and Humanism in Zambia and Its Implementation (1967). Government control of the economy and especially of the major industries is essential to his program. But far from being a mere socialist approach to development, Kaunda's Humanism is rooted deeply in both his Christian beliefs and in the traditions of the Zambian people.

President Kaunda has faced numerous challenges as a political leader as well. UNIP unity began to splinter at the party's general conference in 1967 when Kaunda's previous efforts to keep the party leadership balanced ethnically unraveled as the result of an ethnic electoral coalition set up for the party elections. Great political skill was needed, and while Kaunda patched things up for a while, the roots of serious difficulties for UNIP were firmly set. When Simon Kapwepwe created the United Progressive Party in 1971, he took with him many followers from UNIP. Kaunda's banning of the party and arrest of its leadership could not provide the ultimate answer. Finally Kaunda approved the idea of making Zambia

a One-Party Participatory Democracy. A new Constitution
and changes in UNIP's structure have implemented these
changes. Some internal unrest, perhaps caused by a sluggish
economy based on low world copper prices, or perhaps merely expressing disapproval of the one-party state, seems to continue. Elections held in December 1978 resulted in a strong
approval of Kaunda to remain as President, although he had
faced an earlier challenge to retain UNIP's nomination.
    The period since independence has seen Kaunda continue
in his posts of President of Zambia and leader of UNIP.
However he has also retained the post of Minister of Defence
(1964-70, 1973-), and other portfolios briefly. In 1970 he
also served as Chairman of the Organization of African Unity.
He has been Chancellor of the University of Zambia since
1966. Kaunda has also received several more honorary degrees, numerous awards and honors, and has traveled as Head
of State to most of the major countries of the world. He is
considered by many to be one of Africa's most honorable
Statesmen.

KAWAMBWA. The largest district in the Luapula Province as well
    as a town that serves as the administrative center of the dis-
    trict. In 1969 the district's population was 164,000, a slight
    decline since 1963. The district starts on Zambia's northern
    border and extends about halfway down the eastern edge of the
    Congo Pedicle. The Zambian shoreline of Lake Mweru is to-
    tally within the district.

KAWOSA, HEZEKIYA NKONJERA. One of the earliest of Zambian
    nationalists, in 1905 he met with such colleagues as David
    Kaunda and Donald Siwale (q.v.) to discuss this discontent with
    the Europeans. Almost twenty years later these same men
    formed the Mwenzo Welfare Association (q.v.). It failed to
    survive the transfer of both Kawosa and Siwale to jobs else-
    where.

KAYAMBI MISSION. A mission established by the White Fathers
    (q.v.) in Bemba territory, it was started on Kayambi Hill
    near Mipini along the Luchewe River on July 23, 1895. Per-
    mission to begin this work was obtained by Father Joseph Du-
    pont (q.v.) from a Bemba chief, Makasa (q.v.). The Chief
    was not originally willing because he feared reprisals from
    Chitimukulu Sampa who had ordered that Europeans should be
    kept out of Bemba Territory. When it became clear that
    Sampa would not act against them, Father Dupont summoned
    Father Guillé from the Mambwe mission with two hundred
    freed slaves and they built the mission. Sampa and other
    Bemba leaders sent messengers and presents as a sign of
    good will. A school started at the Mission by the priests soon
    attracted many students.

KAZEMBE (or CAZEMBE). The principal chieftainship of the
    Lunda (q.v.) people in the eastern half of Zambia, its territorial

base is on the eastern shore of the Luapula River, adjacent to
the Zaire Republic.   Contrary to part of the Bemba legend of
migration that depicts Kazembe as a half-brother of the Bemba
founder Chiti and as one who broke off from the migration to
dwell along the Luapula, the actual origins go back to the Lunda
empire of Mwata Yamvo in the Katanga (Shaba) area of Zaire.
The origin of the name Kazembe (and the title Mwata that properly precedes it) begins with an expedition sent out by Mwata
Yamvo early in the eighteenth century.   He sent his brother,
Mutanda Yembeyembe (also called Kanyembe Mutanda) as its
leader, assisted by Chinyanta, also of the royal line.   They
were seeking the location of a Lunda man, Lubunda, who had
fled earlier from Mwata Yamvo.   Instead they subdued two
groups of people they encountered, and they also discovered
some excellent sources of salt.   Chinyanta returned to Mwata
Yamvo with leaders of the conquered peoples under instructions
from Mutanda not to mention the salt.   He did, however, and
Mutanda had him killed when he reported back to him.   Hearing this, Mwata Yamvo wished to reward Chinyanta's family
for news of the precious salt and punish his brother.   He thus
appointed Chinyanta's son, Ng'anda Bilonda as the "Kazembe"
and made him leader of the expedition with instructions to kill
Mutanda (who vanished and was not heard from again).   This
expedition had evidently reached at least the Lualaba River.
Now Kazembe I (Ng'anda Bilonda) moved further east of the
Lualaba where he defeated the Sanga chief Mufunga who was
killed in the battle.   After the process of purifying Mufunga's
head, Kazembe I died, and the Lunda returned to Mwata Yamvo who would choose the successor from the two claimants.
He chose Kanyembo, another son of Chinyanta, who became
Kazembe II and who then conquered most of the area between
the Lualaba and the Luapula Rivers.   He then crossed the
Luapula and conquered the area that is today Kazembe's kingdom.   This was about 1740.
    Kazembe III expanded the territory much more and ruled
until about the nineteenth century.   Kazembe IV succeeded and
ruled for about a half century.   Kazembes V through IX all
ruled briefly and in a hectic period in which they lost much of
their territory to the Yeke (q.v.) who had originated in East
Africa and who had even been befriended by the Lunda.
    Kazembe X took over in 1874, but about all that could
still be claimed was the land in the vicinity of the Luapula
valley.   He accepted "protection" from the British (through Sir
Alfred Sharpe, q.v.) in 1890.   He opposed a British force
sent from a distant boma in 1897, repulsing them.   A larger
force came in 1899, however, and he fled to the Johnston
Falls Mission where he acknowledged British rule again.   He
returned to his capital in 1900 and was recognized as chief
when he submitted to the British.   The chieftainship has continued.   In 1957, Kazembe XVI rose to the throne.
    The Kazembe is the senior Chief (or even "King") of the
Lunda based along the Luapula River.   All other peoples whose
lands were conquered accepted his overlordship, while often

retaining their own leaders. The royal line continued to be
recognized, with the Kazembes controlling what might be called
a centralized chiefdom. The Kazembe supervised governors,
many of whom were hereditary rulers from the non-Lunda
peoples. Their main task was to collect tribute and send it to
Kazembe. Basically a conquest state, Kazembe's kingdom retained a great deal of cohesion among the diverse people.
Many of the Lunda adopted the Bemba language of their conquered subjects, but the Lunda language remained as the language of the royal court at the capital. Each Kazembe built
his own capital somewhere near the Mofwe Lagoon until Kazembe X moved it about twenty miles south of the lagoon about
1884. It remains there today on a hill overlooking the swamps.
During the hundred years from the mid-eighteenth to the mid-
nineteenth centuries, the Kingdom of Kazembe dominated the
trade routes and much of the political life from Katanga to at
least Lake Bangweulu and actually much of northeastern Zambia.

KAZEMBE II KANYEMBO MPEMBA. A son of Chinyanta (as was
the first Kazembe, q. v.), he was chosen by Mwata Yamvo to
succeed his brother. He thus returned to the Lualaba River
and subdued most of the Sanga, Lamba, and Lomotwa peoples
to its east. In about 1740 he crossed the Luapula River and
began to conquer the peoples there. He first overcame the
Ushi (q. v.) and then successfully overtook the Bisa near Lake
Bangweulu. He defeated two minor Shila chiefs in the Luapula
Valley, but died about 1760 in the village of one of them,
Katele. This was along the Lunda River, about twelve miles
east of Mofwe Lagoon. He was the first Kazembe to be buried
there. During his reign he continued to send tribute back to
Mwata Yamvo. This took the form of both copper and salt.
Also during his reign he was opposed by a half-brother, Na-
wezi, who wanted to seize power. Nawezi was killed by the
Lunda.

KAZEMBE III LUKWESA ILUNGA. The son of the first Kazembe,
Ng'anda Bilonda, he succeeded his uncle as Kazembe in about
1760 (see KAZEMBE II). He resumed his uncle's pattern of
conquest and subdued chiefdoms among the Chishinga, Tabwa,
Lungu, Shila, and Bisa. By the time he died in about 1804
his rule was acknowledged as far east as the Chambeshi River.
On one trip he and his forces proceeded as far east as the
Ngonde of Lake Malawi before returning to the Luapula River.
Through Mwata Yamvo he was actively engaged in trade with
the Portuguese on Africa's west coast, acquiring guns in return, and through Bisa traders he was involved in trade with
the east coast, exchanging copper and ivory for beads and
cloth. Kazembe was not pleased with having to go through
Bisa middlemen, thus he attempted to make contact directly
with the Portuguese on the Lower Zambezi. He did this
through the intercession of Gonçalo Pereira (q. v.), a Goan
miner and trader with whom he made contact in 1793. This
resulted in a visit to Kazembe's capital by Manuel Pereira in

1796.   Upon his return in 1798 Manuel brought with him two
ambassadors from Kazembe who announced that Kazembe
wished to trade ivory with the Portuguese at Tete and, in turn,
invited the Portuguese to set up a trading post on the Luangwa
River.   This led to an expedition under Dr. Francisco De Lacerda (q.v.), who wished to set up trade through Kazembe that
would stretch to Africa's west coast.   The expedition included
both Pereiras, and Fr. Francisco Pinto (q.v.), who took over
when De Lacerda died shortly after reaching Kazembe's capital.
The negotiations failed, as Kazembe feared that his own trade
with Mwata Yamvo would suffer if he allowed the Portuguese
to head west.   Kazembe III died in 1804 and his son, Kazembe
IV, (q.v.) succeeded him.   Kazembes V and VI were also his
sons.

KAZEMBE IV KELEKA MAYI.   The successor to his father Kazembe III Lukwesa Ilunga (q.v.) in 1805, he ruled for almost
forty-five years, solidifying the territorial gains of Kazembes
II and III.   For about ten years he maintained the trade contacts established with the Portuguese by his father, even exchanging embassies with the Portuguese government at Tete in
1810-11 and again in 1814.   Soon after, however, the trade
stopped, as Portuguese traders became disinterested in Kazembe's ivory because of the financial rewards of the growing
slave trade.   Nevertheless the Portuguese governor at Tete attempted to reopen trade with Kazembe throughout the 1820's.
Kazembe finally responded by sending an ivory caravan in 1830
to Tete.   This resulted in the Portuguese sending an expedition
led by two soldiers, Captain Antonio Gamitto (q.v.) and Major
Jose Monteiro in 1831-32.   With their expedition beset by both
sickness and death, the men also discovered that Kazembe was
not interested in increasing trade.   Although trade did not develop, the expedition resulted in an excellent literary work,
Gamitto's journal, which gives an outstanding description of
Kazembe's capital and his wealth.   Much of this wealth was
short-lived, as Kazembe's power had peaked.   Kazembe IV
was a brutal dictator, feared even by his own people, whereas
his father had been respected as well as feared.   Also the
Bemba, Luba, and Arabs were all beginning to chip away at
Kazembe's trade routes and his subject peoples.   The Portuguese feared that further trade with Kazembe might be unduly
interrupted by other forces.   When Kazembe IV died around
1850 his two immediate successors, his younger brothers, did
not inherit the power Kazembe IV had inherited.   They reigned
briefly, as did Kazembe VII.   Kazembes VII, IX, and X were
sons of Kazembe IV Keleka Mayi, and Kazembes XIII, XIV,
XV, and XVI were all his grandsons.

KAZEMBE X KANYEMBO NTEMENA.   Reigning from 1874 until
his death in 1904, he was the leader of the Lunda who signed
the agreement with Sir Alfred Sharpe in 1890 accepting British
dominance in the area.   He resisted British rule in 1897 and
1899 (see KAZEMBE) but finally submitted in 1900 and was

recognized by the British as the Chief. It was he who established the present Kazembe capital in about 1884, when he returned from seeking Bemba aid against the Yeke (q. v.). It is
on a hill about twenty miles south of the Mofwe Lagoon. In
1893 he finally managed to subdue a force of Lunda rebels and
their Yeke allies with the aid of the Bemba.

KAZUNGULA. A town on the Zambian-Rhodesian border at the
point of the confluence of the Chobe and Zambezi Rivers. In
January and February, 1973, there were a series of landmine
explosions near the town by which many people were killed or
injured. The Rhodesians were assumed to be responsible.
The town has added significance as its location makes it the
only point at which neighboring Botswana touches another
black-ruled state. Thus Botswana has built a major road up
to the opposite river bank and both products and people enter
Zambia at Kazungula.

KELA. A Mambwe chief of the late nineteenth century. An enemy
of Nsokolo, the Mambwe paramount chief, he made a treaty
with the Bemba leader, Chitimukulu Chitapankwa. After the
latter's death, however, Kela was to have considerable difficulties with the Bemba, who were repeatedly beat off after attacking Kela's villages. In 1889 Harry Johnston (q. v.) was
able to make a treaty with Kela for the British South Africa
Company.

KHAMA III (THE GREAT). Chief of the Ngwato (Bamangwato) in
neighboring Botswana from 1875 until his death in 1923. He
came to be a very respected friend of the Lozi ruler Lewanika.
When Khama agreed to the establishment of a British Protectorate in 1885, Lewanika became convinced that this would also
be his own best safeguard against the Ndebele led by Lobengula.
Thus the Lozi ruler signed an agreement with the British South
Africa Company in 1890. Khama also played an important role
in encouraging the missionary François Coillard (q. v.) to go
to Barotseland, where he ultimately became an important advisor to Lewanika, the Lozi King.

KILWA. The Indian Ocean city and trading center (in present day
Tanzania) where many of the East African trade caravans into
Zambia started and/or ended. Both the Bisa and Senga traders traveled to Kilwa frequently with their caravans through
much of the nineteenth century.

KING VICTOR EMMANUEL, KING OF ITALY. A friend of the
Kings of both England and Portugal, he was asked to be the
chairman of an arbitration commission that in 1905 would
settle the question of the precise location of Zambia's western
border with Angola. Although a treaty of 1891 had presumably
set the border, the Lozi King, Lewanika, complained that the
river boundaries chosen had arbitrarily split his land in two
and that the British South Africa Company should see to it that

his territory be restored. The Italian King and his commission found Lewanika's arguments difficult to evaluate (for example, does the paying of tribute acknowledge control?) and
thus resorted to a straight line border that was accepted by
both the British and the Portuguese.

KITAWALA. Another name for the Watch Tower Movement (q. v.)
in both Northern Rhodesia and the Congo. This name was derived from the sound of the English name as the Africans
heard it. Thus a member of the Movement was sometimes
called a Kitawalan.

KITCHEN KAFFIR. A language used by Europeans and Asians to
communicate with the Africans, it was a mingling of different
languages. It is rarely heard now, as the Africans consider
it belittling. Its origins were in South Africa, thus is a hybrid of English, Afrikaans, and Zulu, but it includes many
Bemba words and phrases added to it along the Copperbelt.

KITIMUKULU. Variant of Chitimukulu (q. v.).

KITUTA. The site of a trading station belonging to the African
Lakes Company (q. v.) late in the nineteenth century, it was
located on the southeastern shore of Lake Tanganyika. It was
the beginning point for many trade caravans heading east along
the Stevenson Road to Lake Malawi, and of course much trade
followed the reverse path as well.

KITWE. The second largest city in Zambia, its population of
179,300 in 1969 was topped only by that of Lusaka. In addition, its population had grown by 50 percent in the previous
six years. The largest city on the Copperbelt itself, its history is closely tied to the development of the Nkana copper
mine. It is also the regional administrative and technical center for the whole Nchanga Consolidated Copper Mines Group
(formerly Anglo-American). It also serves as a retail and
service center for the surrounding area, and some manufacturing exists also. It has been a well-planned city with a central
business district, movie houses, good educational facilities,
television and radio stations, and sporting facilities which include a major horse racing track. Water sports have been
made possible by the Mindola Dam. It is difficult to realize
that fifty years ago the area was the middle of a mosquito-
infested swamp.

KITWE AFRICAN SOCIETY. Founded in the early 1940's by such
later political activists as Godwin Mbikusita Lewanika (q. v. ;
its President) and Harry Nkumbula (q. v. ; its Secretary), it was
a typical urban voluntary association. As such it attempted to
find effective ways of furthering the interests of Kitwe's Africans. One of its meetings in January, 1946, was the occasion
of the "Elwell Incident" involving Archibald H. Elwell (q. v.).

KNIFE-EDGE BRIDGE. A short footbridge built by the Zambian
Government in 1969 to provide easier viewing of Victoria Falls
from the Zambian side. The bridge leads to a promontory
that directly faces the Falls.

KOLA see BULUBA

KOLOLO. Variant of Makololo (q. v.).

KONKOLA, DIXON. An important trade union leader of the 1950's
and 1960's who probably set a record for the number of different political parties he either founded or had membership
in. President of the Railway African Worker's Trade Union
(RAWU) in the early 1950's, he favored a continuing link between the African National Congress and the union movement.
This stemmed in part from the fact that he had been an active
organizer for the ANC in Broken Hill in 1952 and 1953. His
position differed from that of Lawrence Katilungu (q. v.), who
he defeated as President of the African Trade Union Congress
in 1955. In January of that same year, with Nkumbula and
Kaunda both in jail, Konkola was Acting Secretary-General of
ANC. In that position he edited the second issue of the party's
paper, then called the Official Gazette. His political activity
continued in 1956 when Konkola organized in Broken Hill a
very effective boycott (although brief) of the grocery stores
owned by non-Africans, a movie house, and a butcher shop.
Nevertheless, in August, 1956, he was replaced as the ANC
Deputy Secretary General by Titus Mukupo. Early in 1957 Konkola talked about forming a Socialist Party, but he was opposed
by the membership of the Trade Union Congress, although his
call for one man/one vote was cheered. Nevertheless he resigned from both the Trade Union Congress and the Railway
African Workers Union in mid-1957, claiming Nkumbula was
working against him.
     When the Zambia African National Congress (q. v.) was
formed in October, 1958, Konkola wanted the Presidency. Instead he was offered the position of Kaunda's Deputy President
but he declined. With ZANC banned in March, 1959, Konkola
established the United African Congress about two months
later. In June, however, the UAC joined with the African
National Freedom Movement to create the United National Freedom Party (q. v.). Konkola as its President-General promised
a non-violent campaign for self-government. By April, 1961,
there were reports that Konkola was trying to form a Republican Party in northeastern Zambia. While a "National Republican Party" (q. v.) briefly made an appearance as a United
Federal Party front organization, Konkola showed up in April
1962 as a successful candidate for one of two Federal seats as
a member of the Central African Peoples Union (q. v.). Finally in June, 1964, he applied for membership (and was accepted)
into the United National Independence Party.

KONOSO, DR. KABELEKA DURTON. A Lozi politician, closely

related to the traditional leaders of Barotseland, who was
named Minister of Justice in January, 1966. He had been active in UNIP and elected to Parliament in January, 1964. In
January, 1967, he was switched to the post of Minister of
Natural Resources and Tourism. In the December, 1968, elections he was defeated along with Arthur Wina and Munu Sipalo,
two other Lozi cabinet ministers, as the ANC received considerable support in Barotse constituencies from the banned
United Party (q. v.).

KONOSO, SEKELI. A Lusaka businessman who was a leading
member of the Barotse National Association (q. v.), which
started in communities along the line of rail in the mid-1950's,
and which was antagonistic to the Lozi King. He was especially furious over the appointment of Akabeswa Imasiku (q. v.) as
Ngambela. His attempt to address the Lealui Kuta in 1956
was thwarted so he returned to Lusaka. In October, 1956,
Mwanawina (the Lozi King) charged Konoso with passing out
pamphlets while in Barotseland which defamed and insulted the
Lozi King. Thus Konoso appeared before the Lealui Kuta in
January, 1957, accompanied by thousands of chanting supporters. Nevertheless the Kuta found him guilty and he was sentenced to three years in solitary confinement (which the Federal High Court reduced to six months at hard labor). This
produced further demonstrations by his supporters and more
arrests. As a result, the Northern Rhodesian Government
appointed the Rawlins Commission (q. v.) to recommend changes
in the Barotse Native Government, but its recommendations
were superficial and did not satisfy Konoso or his supporters.
Ironically, a few years later Konoso became reconciled with
the Lealui leaders.

KOPA. A Bisa chieftainship formerly called Mwanasabamba, the
chiefs are from the bena ng'ona (q. v.), or Mushroom Clan,
from which the other major Bisa chiefs also derive. Their
common ancestor is Mukulumpe. In the last half of the nineteenth century there were occasional conflicts with Bemba who
intruded on Kopa's territory. Chikwanda II came into conflict
with Kopa I, Mwanasabamba Mwape Yumba, and both Kopa II
Londe and Katepela (later Kopa III) had dealings with Mwamba
III. The British administrators opened up a major controversy around 1930 when they tried to implement the principle of
Indirect Rule. They wished to work with one Bisa leader as
'Superior Native Authority, " whereas in fact the Bisa had retained almost total autonomy, even those belonging to the same
clan. Thus there was considerable resentment when they chose
Chief Kopa as the Supreme Native Authority. After hearing the
complaints of other Bisa chiefs they reconsidered the situation
but decided finally to leave Kopa as their chosen leader.

KULUHELA. The return trip to the Lozi royal capital after the
annual Zambezi flood, it occurs in July and is now an important ritual ceremony. See also KUOMBOKA.

KUMBA KUMBA. An Arab trader from the East African coast, he
was also the half-brother of the famed Tippu Tip (q. v.). His
real name was Muhammed ibn Masud el-Wardi. Tippu Tip
brought Kumba Kumba on a couple of trading ventures in the
1860's. On one in 1866 he visited the area of Mwamba, a
Bemba chief. While there was no ivory, he left Kumba Kumba
there in charge of fifteen armed men. Tippu Tip returned in
1867 to pick up his brother and the men to return to the coast.
In 1869-70 Tippu Tip made another trip into Central Africa and
revisited the village of Nsama whom he had defeated earlier.
This time he acquired much ivory and left Kumba Kumba at a
stockade by Nsama's village. This was to be an ivory depot.
In 1873 a group of men under Kumba Kumba's leadership were
defeated by the Chishinga chief Mushyota, which encouraged the
Nsama to try to expel the Arab traders. The trader then
sought the aid of Kafwimbi (q. v.), who was a challenger to the
post of Nsama. Kafwimbi went to the Bemba chief Mwamba
for additional support. Mwamba sent seventy men and the combined force beat the Nsama, named Katandula, who died in the
fighting. Kafwimbi then succeeded to the post of Nsama, in
part through some military support from Kumba Kumba. The
latter left for the African east coast a couple of years later
(1876 at the latest).

KUNDA. A Nyanja-speaking people numbering about sixty-three
thousand in 1969, they live in southeastern Zambia. They are
of Congo origin and presumably were part of the Bemba migration. They are related to both the Ushi and the Bisa. They
seem to have split from the Bisa, under whose pressure they
moved east of the Luangwa River in the early nineteenth century. They follow a matrilineal descent system. Having been
overtaken by the Ngoni during the nineteenth century, some of
their customs have also been influenced by the Ngoni.

KUNDABWIKA FALLS. A tourist site on the Kalungwishi River in
the northern part of the Luapula Province near Lake Mweru.
Near the falls is also a large boulder on which a notable piece
of rock art from the Late Stone Age exists. There is a panel
of red schematic paintings and a large grid of horizontal and
vertical lines, with additional painted "ladders. "

KUOMBOKA. An important ceremonial ritual of the Lozi that is
still performed today as a kind of ceremonial pageant. It is
as important to them as the first-fruits ceremonies among
other southern African peoples. The kuomboka commemorates
the practice of the Lozi who lived in the capital at Mongu
which is in the Zambezi flood plain. When the Zambezi had
its annual flood it deposited rich new soil on the plain. Meanwhile it was necessary for the Lozi in Mongu to travel to higher land at Limulunga, the "flood capital. " The king or Litunga
led this procession in his royal barge in about February of
every year. The return trip, also ceremonialized, occurs in
July and is called kulahela.

KUTA. In the broadest sense, the term is the Lozi word for a
council which exercises various governmental functions, especially executive and judicial but also sometimes legislative.
In this sense there have been kutas throughout Barotseland for
centuries, at both national and local levels. Kutas have assisted councillors (indunas) who have held local administrative
posts, for example. At the national (Barotse) level, however,
the word refers to at least five different but oftentimes interrelated councils: the Saa Kuta, the Sikalo Kuta, the Katengo
Kuta, the Situmba sa Mulonga, and the Mulongwanji (qq. v.).
The greatest problem concerning this word, however, is that
both scholarly and "popular" writers will lapse into the use of
the word without clarifying which of the five national kutas is
the one to which reference is being made. If the author is
implying the National Council, the Mulongwanji is the one. If
the King (Litunga) quickly calls together his closest advisors,
however, the kuta in question is the Situmbu sa Mulonga.
Otherwise most authors would refer specifically to the Saa,
Sikalo, or Katengo Kutas or Councils. To add to the confu-
sion, some authors familiar with Sotho tribes used Sesotho
words in place of the word "kuta. " The most frequently used
word was lekhotla, with its variants: kgotla, kotla, and
khotla.

KWACHA. A word meaning either "the dawn is coming" or "the
dawn is here, " it was used by African nationalists as a rally
cry in the period prior to independence (see KWACHA NGWEE).
In addition the word was chosen for the name of the standard
currency of Zambia when the Zambian pound was replaced in
January, 1968. Two kwacha were to be worth one of the old
pounds. The kwacha in turn is divisible into one hundred
ngwee. In December, 1971, the kwacha was pegged to the
American dollar at the rate of one kwacha equal to $1. 40. In
February, 1973, the equivalency became $1. 5556. In Decem-
ber, 1978, one kwacha equaled $1. 30.

KWACHA NGWEE. Two words which were used either separately
or together as nationalist slogans during the several years
before Zambian independence (and likewise used in Malawi).
As a result it was declared a criminal offense by the Government of Northern Rhodesia to shout out the words. "Kwacha"
means either "the dawn is coming" or "the dawn has come, "
depending on inflection. "Ngwee" is an intensifying expletive,
the root of which is derived from a word meaning "light" or
"bright. " The combination of the two, used as a slogan,
meant (in effect) "Cheer up and have faith, for a great new
day is almost here. "

KWANDO RIVER (or QUANDO). Also known as the Mashi River,
Linyanti River or Chobe River (q. v.).

KWANGWA (or MAKWANGWA). A group of about 72,000 people
living in southwestern Zambia, they are Luyana-speaking. The

Kwangwa are related to the Lozi, presumably through a man
named Mange who is said to have been the founder of the
Kwangwa and a brother (or some say nephew) of the Lozi leader, Mboo. The Kwangwa now live east of the Lozi, mainly in
the forest area of the Mongu Lealui District known as "Makan-
da" because of all the lakes there. The Kwangwa are noted
for excellent wood carving.

KYUNGU (or CHUNGU). An Ngonde chief near the north end of
Lake Malawi in what is today the country of Malawi. A number of northeastern Zambian peoples, including the Lambya,
Fungwe, and Yombe sent him tribute although they retained
political independence.

- L -

LABOUR PARTY   see   NORTHERN RHODESIA LABOUR PARTY

LACERDA, DR. FRANCISCO DE   see   DE LACERDA, DR. FRAN-
CISCO

LAKE BANGWEULU. The only one of Zambia's four major lakes
that lies solely within Zambia's boundaries, it encompasses
about a thousand square miles. The Bangweulu swamps to the
southeast of the lake are about twice that size. The Chambeshi River (q.v.) contributes some of its flow to the lake by
way of the swamps. On the other hand, the Luapula River
drains some water from the lake on its path to Lake Mweru.
The lake is a fairly shallow basin, about thirty feet deep, and
is easily traveled by fishing boats. The Bisa, Unga, and even
some Twa people live in the swampy area. The great Bemba
migration went around the northern edge of the lake on the
road to settlement to the northeast. Generally the area around
the lake has seen a great deal of movement of peoples, and it
is still heavily populated.

LAKE KARIBA. Situated on the border with Rhodesia, Lake Kariba is the third largest man-made lake in the world (about two
thousand square miles). It is 175 miles long and 20 miles
wide at its widest point. It was developed in 1959 when the
Zambezi River was dammed in order to supply electrical power
for Northern and Southern Rhodesia (see KARIBA DAM). The
creation of the lake necessitated the relocation of about fifty-
seven thousand residents of the Gwembe Valley (not without
their opposition), and the execution of "Operation Noah" to rescue thousands of animals trapped on islands by the rising water.
While the Lake's purpose was to supply a source of water power, it has also created a fishing industry and a tourist attraction. The seeded lake and the boating centers with housing
accommodations attract people fishing for perch, bream, or
tiger fish. Its proximity to both Lusaka and Livingstone makes
it ideal for tourists.

LAKE MALAWI. Formerly known as Lake Nyasa until Nyasaland
became the new, independent nation of Malawi and the new
rulers changed its name. It is located on the eastern border
of Malawi, in some places as close as thirty miles to Zambia's
eastern border. It was not at all unusual in recent centuries
for Africans, especially those engaged in trade, to travel freely between Lake Malawi and the various major lakes of Zambia
where trading stations were maintained.

LAKE MWERU. A result of one of the furthest branches of the
Great East African Rift system, Lake Mweru is located in the
northwestern corner of the eastern half of Zambia. It forms
a good natural border with Zaire. About two-thirds of the
Lake's approximately fifteen hundred square miles is considered to be within Zambian boundaries. A great deal of fishing, both commercial and subsistence, occurs there. The first
BSAC station was set up on the northeastern corner of the lake
in 1891 at Chiengi. In 1893 the Company added a post at the
mouth of the Kalungwishi River, one of Zambia's few large
rivers that empties into the lake.

LAKE NYASA. Old name for Lake Malawi (q. v.).

LAKE TANGANYIKA. A major East African lake, the southern
edge of which constitutes part of Zambia's northeastern border.
Actually the lake is a border between Zaire and Tanzania; to
its southeast is the Zambia-Tanzania border, and to its southwest is the Zambia-Zaire border. This area was heavily
traveled by traders, especially in the nineteenth century when
Arabs from East Africa were involved along the lake's southern
edge in both ivory and slave trading with the Africans. This
was also an area in which the Bemba were trying to spread
their influence at the expense of smaller groups like the Tabwa,
Mambwe, and Lungu. This same area was the site of many
of Zambia's earliest mission stations as well as some of the
first administrative stations of the British South Africa Company. The excellent modern tourist facilities at Kasaba Bay
(q. v.) exist today on the lake's southwestern edge near the
Sumbu Game Reserve.

LALA. The third largest sub-group of Bemba-speaking people in
Zambia, they number about 140,000. They reside in central
Zambia, south and east of the Congo Pedicle, and west of the
Luangwa River. They are of Luba origin, migrating south
from the Congo. A Portuguese report around 1650 indicates
they were already in their present area. The Ambo and
Swaka peoples are offshoots of the Lala. The traditions of the
Lala indicate that small-statured people were there when they
arrived. The Lala, like many other Zambians, follow a matrilineal descent system. They are justly noted for their artistry,
notably practicing wall painting on their houses. They have
also been noted for the outstanding quality and quantity of their
iron production, which they then used in trade. They had a

very large open mine at Msomani as well as their own smelters. By the late nineteenth century, the nyendwa clan had attained a monopoly of Lala chieftainships. According to the legend of the great Bemba migration, however, the Bemba migrants are said to have encountered the Lala, who requested a
chief to rule them, so the Bemba gave them a man named
Kankomba.

LAMBA. A group of people who speak uwulamba (a language related to that of the Bemba) and who live south and west of the
Congo Pedicle in the Copperbelt. In 1930 it was estimated
that their land covered about twenty-five thousand square miles.
Recent estimates indicate a population of about eighty thousand
Lambas. They are a matrilineal and matrilocal group, primarily agriculturalists historically. Chipimpi and Kawunda are
regarded as their first two chiefs. The Lambas were victims
of the Arab slave trade; their women especially were taken for
their beauty. The Lambas had a serious smallpox epidemic in
1891. They have never been happy with the miners coming
from all over the country to work on the Copperbelt mines.
They feel that parts of their land have been alienated to others.
In 1968-69 they alleged that they were being treated with economic neglect, as their territory tends to be rural and unde-
veloped.

LAMBYA. A very small tribe living in the northeastern corner of
Zambia. Their origins seem connected to peoples in East
Africa, especially the Ngonde at the north end of Lake Malawi
to whom they once paid tribute.

LANCASTER HOUSE CONFERENCE, 1952 see LONDON CON-
FERENCE, 1952

LAND ACQUISITION ACT. A law passed in 1970 that allowed the
Zambian Government to acquire large tracts of land without
compensation if they were abandoned by their foreign owners.

LANGUAGES OF ZAMBIA. There are reputedly hundreds of languages and dialects spoken in Zambia, some of them not yet
even properly studied and differentiated. However, English is
used as the language of convenience in government and business.
There are also seven official African languages, Bemba, Kaonde, Tonga, Lozi, Nyanja, Lunda, and Luvale. Bemba is
spoken by about a third of the Zambians. Nyanja and Tonga
share another third of the population, and the remainder are
spoken by about a third. This overlooks the fact that
many Bemba speakers also speak different dialects. In
addition, Town Bemba (q.v.) is widely spoken on the Copperbelt.

LAVUSHI MANDA NATIONAL PARK. Not one of the larger national parks of Zambia, it is nearly fifty miles from north to
south. It is located in the east-central part of the country,

about fifty miles northeast of Serenje.   Hunting is allowed
there.

LAWLEY, CAPTAIN ARTHUR.   The Administrator of Matabeleland
for the British South Africa Company near the end of the nineteenth century.   He traveled to Victoria Falls in June, 1898 to
conclude the agreement with the Lozi King Lewanika that is
called the Lawley Concession of 1898 (q. v.).   He insisted that
the Lozi King cross to the south bank of the Falls for the ceremony to symbolize the superiority of the Europeans.

LAWLEY CONCESSION OF 1898.   Concluded by Captain Arthur Lawley (q. v.) of the BSAC in June, 1898, it was based on the
groundwork laid by Robert Coryndon (q. v.).   King Lewanika
of the Lozi agreed to it and signed it on the south bank of the
Zambezi River at Victoria Falls.   It differed from the earlier
Lochner Concession (q. v.) in three major ways.   It allowed
the BSAC to grant farm land in Toka and Ila country to approved
white men; it allowed the Company to handle and judge all cases
of disputes between whites or between Africans and whites; and
it cut the annual grant to the King from £2000 to £850.   It
also contained a clause urged by King Lewanika that excluded
the basic Lozi homeland area from Company prospecting or
settlement.   The Lawley Concession was superseded by the
Order in Council of 1899 (q. v.), but served as the essence of
the Lewanika Concession of 1900 (q. v.) that Coryndon finalized
with the King.

LAWS, DR. ROBERT.   An ordained medical missionary from Scotland who was the founder of the Livingstonia (or Overtoun) mission at Kondowe in today's Malawi.   He had first arrived in
Malawi in 1875 with a party of Presbyterian missionaries of
the Free Church of Scotland.   He moved from earlier bases to
set up the mission at Kondowe in 1894.   Its school had a great
influence on many individuals from northeastern Zambia who
studied there, as he taught practical European construction
skills and elementary Western medicine in addition to standard
education and the Bible.   Two of its pupils who had a direct
effect on contemporary Zambia were David and Helen Kaunda,
the parents of Zambia's first President.

LEADERSHIP CODE.   Originally suggested by the Chona Commission (q. v.) in 1972, it was introduced as a regulation in August,
1973.   Its purpose is to impose strict standards of financial
conduct on national leaders in order to set an example for the
nation.   It begins by listing all leadership posts from President
to the civil service, including employees of parastatal boards.
It then states what a leader may earn or own.   For example,
he may not own land larger than 10 hectares on which a dwell-
ing is situated.   Rules prohibiting the reception of gifts or rewards are listed.   All assets must be made public.   Only the
President may grant exemptions to the list of Code requirements.   A panel administers the Code, with penalties provided
for breaking it.   Some amendments to it were added in 1974.

LEALUI. A town built by the Lozi leader Lewanika (at that time called Lubosi) to be the permanent flood plain capital of the Lozi. Construction began in 1878 and some of the work was still being completed in 1884. The town is located in Zambia's Western (Barotse) Province, on the east bank of the Zambezi River. It is situated immediately south of the confluence of the Luanginga River with the Zambezi, in the heart of the flood plain. As a result, it is abandoned for several months every year as the residents move to higher ground at Limulunga (q. v.). With the establishment by the British of Mongu (q. v.) as an administrative center about twenty miles east of Lealui, Mongu became a center of Lozi royal activity that would compete with Lealui. Mongu has the additional advantage of not being very susceptible to the annual Zambezi flood.

LEGISLATIVE ASSEMBLY. The name of the legislature of Northern Rhodesia in the period between the attainment of self-rule in January, 1964 and independence in October, 1964. Prior to that it was called the Legislative Council (q. v.) and after independence it became the National Assembly or, simply, Parliament.

LEGISLATIVE COUNCIL. A standard feature of British colonial rule, the Legislative Council (Legco) in Northern Rhodesia was instituted by the Northern Rhodesia (Legislative Council) Order in Council, 1924, at the time when the British Government formally replaced the British South Africa Company as administrator of the territory. The first Legco consisted of nine official members (the five ex officio members of the Executive Council and four nominated members) plus five elected unofficial members. In 1929 two more elected "Unofficials" were added. An Order in Council in 1938 raised the number of Unofficial members to eight, simultaneously reducing the Officials to eight, by dropping one nominated Official member and replacing him with a nominated Unofficial who was specifically charged with representing "native" interests. With that one new member as an exception, the Legislative Council was totally dominated by settler interests. Most of the members pushed for either a self-rule arrangement such as Southern Rhodesia had, or for some form of amalgamation with Southern Rhodesia.

In 1941 two new seats were added to the Legco, one new elected seat and the restored official seat. A major change occurred in 1945, however, when four new nominated Unofficial seats were added, three of them to represent African interests. While the Unofficials now outnumbered the Officials thirteen to nine, only eight of the thirteen were elected. This meant however that the official majority was ended, and the Governor had to consider the views of the Unofficials when presenting legislative proposals.

During most of the 1940's, the leader of the Unofficials was Roy Welensky (q. v.), and in 1948 he won further changes from the Government. The Legco's term was extended from three years to five, and an elected Speaker replaced the Governor as President of the Legislative Council. Furthermore, there were to be ten elected Unofficials to equal ten Officials, plus four nominated Unofficials, two Africans and two Europeans representing African interests. In 1948 the Legco began to push for the creation of a Central African Federation.

With the coming of the Federation in 1953, the new Legislative Council was to number twenty-six seats, twelve elected Unofficials, eight Officials, four Africans selected from the African Representative Council (q.v.), and two Europeans to represent African interests. As in the past, franchise requirements were such that only a dozen or so Africans could qualify to vote for the elected members.

The Benson Constitution (q.v.) which took effect in 1959 provided for an elected multi-racial Legco. There were to be eight Official seats out of the thirty provided. Of the twenty-two Unofficials, fourteen were elected in such manner that they would undoubtedly be Africans. Two of each race would fill "reserved" seats and the remainder "ordinary" seats. The 1962 Constitution was much more complex in its attempt to balance racial interests. It provided for forty-five elected members, as many as six Officials, and an undetermined number of nominated members to be decided upon later by the British Government. Fifteen of the elected members would be chosen by an "upper roll" of voters, and fifteen by a "lower roll." An additional fifteen would be selected from National constituencies by both rolls. One of these National seats was to be reserved for Asian and Coloured voters, the rest would be paired in seven two-men constituencies, four of which were to be divided into one African seat and one European seat. A complicated formula required National seat candidates to secure certain percentages of votes from both the upper and the lower rolls. This proved impossible in some instances and eight National seats went unfilled. Nevertheless, an African majority now controlled the Legco.

Under the 1964 Constitution that led to Independence, the Legislative Council was renamed the Legislative Assembly. It was expanded to seventy-five members, sixty-five elected by Africans on the main roll, and ten from reserved roll constituencies by European voters.

LENJE. A Tonga-speaking people in central Zambia, there are about 125,000 of them today. They are second in number among Tonga-speakers only to the Tonga themselves. Like the Tonga, they are not centralized around large chieftainships. Of Luba origin, it is possible that they migrated from the Congo as early as the sixteenth century. They claim to have found some groups of Sala and Soli peoples already there, some of whom they absorbed.

LENNOX-BOYD, ALAN. British Conservative Party Member of Parliament who served as Colonial Secretary from 1955 until October, 1959, when he was made a Viscount and resigned his

post. When Harry Nkumbula of the ANC attempted to meet
him while in London in late 1955, Lennox-Boyd refused to see
him. The Secretary then visited Central Africa in January,
1957, and made it clear that he supported the continuation of
the Federation and Roy Welensky's policies. This was despite
the fact that a meeting of the African Representative Council
informed him that the ARC rejected the Federation. He opposed all suggestions for changing it, telling the Africans in
Northern Rhodesia, "It is good for you, and you must accept
it. " In 1958 he assured the traditional leaders of Barotseland
that he would allow no constitutional changes affecting their
area without full consultation with and consent of the Paramount
Chief (King).

LENSHINA, ALICE MULENGA. Founder of the religious sect
called the Lumpa Church (q.v.) or the "Lenshina Movement"
that was especially active in the eastern half of Zambia and
the Copperbelt from its founding in 1953 until its bloody confrontation with the Government in 1964 that led to its being
banned. Alice Lenshina is a Bemba woman who was married
to Peter Mulenga (a co-founder of her church who died in detention in the early 1970's). In 1953 she claimed to receive
a calling as a prophetess from Jesus Christ himself, who met
her near a river and gave her a sign. This occurred, she
claimed, after having died four times, each time "rising
again. " During one of her deaths she claims to have had a
long conversation in Heaven with God who told her to return to
earth and help rid the people of the evils of magic and witchcraft. God also gave her the "true" Bible from which to
preach. Thus in September, 1953, she began the Lumpa
Church at Kasomo, later renamed Sioni (Zion), which is about
seven miles from Chinsali. Membership grew quickly but
exact figures are not known. It has been estimated that there
were 50,000 to 100,000 followers of Lenshina at the peak of
the movement. At first the Church was neither political nor
extreme. It preached a strict morality forbidding drinking,
smoking, dancing, and adultery. Total renunciation of magic
and sorcery was necessary to be saved and reborn. Baptism
by Lenshina would provide protection against sorcery and witchcraft. The only threat the movement posed was to some established churches, especially in northeastern Zambia, as it attracted away many of their members. In the early 1960's,
however, a conflict developed between Lenshina's church and
the major nationalist organization, UNIP. Many of its members were drifting away from the church movement and into
the political arena. Lenshina countered this in 1962 by forbidding her followers to belong to any political movement or
even vote. Robert Kaunda, brother of Zambia's first president
and also a Lumpa "deacon," claims that Welensky's United
Federal Party bribed Lenshina with £8000 in order to help un-
dermine UNIP's support. No formal proof of this has surfaced. Regardless, animosity between the Church and UNIP
quickly developed. From mid-1962 to mid-1963 numerous

Lumpa churches in Northern and Eastern Province villages
were victimized by arson. UNIP organizers saw the Church
as both a political opponent and an enemy of the nation.
Lumpa members sometimes countered UNIP with their own
form of harassment, including accusations of witchcraft
against some individuals.

Finally in 1964, with UNIP now running the Government,
bloody battles broke out. The Lumpa had acquired guns which
they stored in stockaded Lumpa villages. A minor incident led
to the killing of two policemen by Lumpa members on July 24.
Fighting between armed church members and Government
forces seeking to restore order resulted in at least five hundred deaths in a three week period. Some of the Lumpa were
almost suicidal in their fighting tactics, seeing themselves as
"saved" martyrs. In some areas Lumpa fighters killed inno-
cent villagers. The Church was banned by Kenneth Kaunda on
August 3, 1964, and on August 12, Alice Lenshina surrendered
to authorities and asked her followers to return home peacefully. Some fighting continued until mid-October, however, as
one battle then resulted in sixty Lumpa dead. An amnesty was
granted for Lumpa members in 1968, but some remain in Zaire
and Malawi. Lenshina was released from detention in December, 1975, but temporarily restricted to the Lusaka area.
Her church remains permanently banned.

LEOPARD CLAN.   The translation of the name Bazimba (q.v.).

LETTOW-VORBECK, GEN. P. E. VON. A German General who
    led a campaign in East and Central Africa during the closing
    years of World War I. His force of fifteen hundred soldiers
    and the same number of bearers moved into northeastern
    Zambia in October and November, 1918. They came through
    Fife and traveled southwest to Kasama. The Northern Rho-
    desia Police and the King's African Rifles were in pursuit.
    On November 8, the District Commissioner at Kasama, Hec-
    tor Croad, sent all the women and children to Mpika for safe-
    ty. One of the town's few defenders (the Police had been
    sent to defend Abercorn) was told to burn the military supplies
    in storage and mistakenly burned the Government offices as
    well. Thus, contrary to reports that Lettow-Vorbeck burned
    Kasama, he found it burning when he arrived on November 9
    and so on November 12, continued to march his men south to
    the Chambeshi River. On November 13 they began an attack
    on the rubber factory buildings there. By this time the war
    was already over in Europe, but the news did not reach the
    Chambeshi until the 13th. Informed of the German surrender
    in Europe, the general agreed to cease fire. He formally sur-
    rendered to General Edwards of the King's African Rifles at
    Abercorn on November 18.

LEWANIKA (also known as Lubosi). Litunga of Bulozi (King of
    Barotseland), 1878-84 and 1885-1916, he is probably the Lozi
    leader best known to the non-African world. His major goals

throughout his reign were to restore and strengthen the power
of the Lozi Litunga and to help his nation attain physical security and technical progress. In most of this his primary
means was to be the establishment of good relations with the
Europeans and, preferably, a treaty with the British Queen,
Victoria. Unfortunately he signed several treaties, none of
them with Queen Victoria, and only succeeded in transferring
effective control of his land to the British South Africa Company of Cecil Rhodes.

He was born in 1842 in Bulozi, the son of Litia, himself
the son of the noted Lozi King, Mulambwa (q.v.). At the
time of his birth the family was fleeing the Makololo invaders
who were dominating his homeland. Thus the child (not known
as Lewanika until 1885) was named Lubosi, "the escaped one."
About 1856 Litia (q.v.) decided to try conciliation with the
Makololo, and took his family back to their homeland. In
1863 Litia was executed by the Makololo, but Lubosi was
spared. Within two years, however, the Lozi regained their
territory, and their leadership was taken over by Sipopa. He
ruled as Litunga until 1876. A young man, Mwanawina, ruled
for two years until he was forced to abandon the throne and
flee the country. The National Council then selected Lubosi
as Litunga in mid-1878. His strongest backer in the Council
was Silumbu (q.v.), who was then appointed Ngambela (Prime
Minister) by Lubosi.

There had been others in contention with Lubosi, and their
backers would have some success six years later, but for now
Lubosi had the upper hand. His forces caught up with the
sons of Sipopa and killed them. When Mwanawina returned
with a military force in 1879, Lubosi's forces defeated him
also, although Mwanawina himself escaped. On the other
hand, one organizer of the opposition, Mataa (q.v.), remained
in Lubosi's administration.

Meanwhile Lubosi was making contacts with the outside
world. He began to communicate with a neighbor to the south,
Khama III (q.v.) of the Bamangwato. It was Khama whose
treaty with the British encouraged Lubosi to attempt a similar
arrangement, seeing this as a means of protection against Lobengula, leader of the Ndebele. Thus Lubosi became friends
with British traders and travelers, like George Westbeech
(q.v.), and gave encouragement to missionaries such as Frederick Arnot (q.v.) and Rev. François Coillard (q.v.). An important internal reform by Lubosi was the reintroduction of the
old makolo (q.v.) system, which had been in disuse since the
Makololo invasion. He hoped this action would prevent his opponents from mounting a force for a new civil war.

Despite his efforts, a successful uprising occurred in
July, 1884, forcing Lubosi to flee the capital to Mashi. The
rebel leader, Mataa, brought a son of Imbua, Tatila Akufuna
(q.v.), back from Lukwakwa to become Litunga in September,
1884. Mataa became Ngambela, a post he had long coveted.
Akufuna proved to be a very poor choice, however, and opposition to him quickly surfaced, independent of Lubosi. Mataa

was able to defeat one group, but Silumbu gathered a large
army for Lubosi in July, 1885, and Lubosi mobilized a second
one.   A major battle in November, 1885, was won by pro-
Lubosi forces, and both Silumbu and Mataa were killed.
Akufuna had fled months earlier.   Lubosi now chose the praise
name "Lewanika" for his name.   Its literal meaning is "to add
together," but loosely translated comes out, more appropriate-
ly, "conqueror."
   In April 1886, Rev. Coillard returned to Lealui and was
allowed by Lewanika to set up a mission and school.   This
was the beginning of a long and close relationship between the
two, but a relationship which would serve the King poorly.
With Lewanika eager to get protection from Queen Victoria
and Coillard eager to bring other Europeans into the area, the
missionary assisted several Europeans in working out concessions with Lewanika.   An agreement with Harry Ware (q. v.)
in 1889 led quickly to the involvement of the British South
Africa Company.   This was followed in June, 1890 by an agreement with Frank Lochner (q.v.), a representative of Cecil
Rhodes (see LOCHNER CONCESSION).   Subsequently the Lawley Concession of 1898, and the Concessions of 1906 and 1909
(qq. v.) resulted in the loss of most of Barotseland to European
sovereignty, despite protests by the Lozi that they had been
continually deceived by the European negotiators.   Lewanika
also charged that the provisions of the agreements were not
being fulfilled by the BSAC, thus voiding them.   He cited provisions for schools, internal development, financial payments,
and military protection against the Matabele.   Regular appeals
by King Lewanika to England brought no satisfaction and, in
fact, the Order in Council of 1911 (q. v.) provided for the incorporation of Barotseland into a larger unit called Northern
Rhodesia.
   Lewanika died in February, 1916.   He was succeeded by
his eldest son, Litia (q. v.).   Despite the loss of his nation's
sovereignty to the British, Lewanika's efforts won greater
concessions and assurances for his people than any other Central African leader could achieve.   Barotseland was to retain
a degree of autonomy and separate identity even into the
1960's.

LEWANIKA, GODWIN MBIKUSITA   see   GODWIN MBIKUSITA

LEWANIKA CONCESSION OF 1900.   The agreement that affirmed
   British administrative authority in the western half of Zambia,
   it was agreed to by Robert Coryndon (q. v.) and the Lozi King
   Lewanika at Lealui, the Lozi capital.   Its basis was the Lawley Concession of 1898 (q.v.).   The new concession was
   needed for technical reasons, as the Order in Council of 1899
   (q. v.) had superseded the Lawley Concession.   Even this new
   agreement was not official enough, and the Concession of 1906
   (q. v.) was needed to finalize the agreement between the Lozi
   leaders and the BSAC.

LEYA (or BALEA). A small group of Tonga-speaking people numbering eighteen thousand, who live in extreme southern Zambia along the Zambezi River, near the town of Livingstone. Several history books record a nineteenth century conflict between Sekute, a Leya chief, and Sundamo, a chief of the Subiya, in which Sundamo finally resorted to calling on the powerful Makololo leader Sebituane (q. v.) for assistance against the Leya.

LEZA. A word meaning "The Supreme Being" that is found in many of the Bantu languages and dialects in Zambia.

LIBERAL PARTY see NORTHERN RHODESIA LIBERAL PARTY

LIKOLO. Singular form of Makolo (q. v.).

LIKOMBWA. One of the major subdivisions within the Lozi National Council (Mulongwanji), this group sits on the left side of the King. The members of this group are considered to be very close to the King and are expected to attend to his concerns, rather than those of the public. They are expected to support his policies. In addition, they can be assigned special duties relating to the king's household. Senior members are considered to be personal representatives of the King.

LIMA. A Bemba-speaking people, numbering about thirty-six thousand, who live in central Zambia, both along and west of the southern Copperbelt. Its chiefdoms were founded by members of the Nyendwa clan that also founded or controlled almost all of the chiefdoms among the Ambo, Swaka, Soli, and Lala peoples. The Lima were successful in avoiding defeat at the hands of the powerful Yeke chief Msiri in the 1880's.

LIMULUNGA (or LIMALUNGA). The so-called "flood capital" of the Lozi to which the Lozi King retires with great pomp during the Kuomboka (q. v.) ceremony. He stays there from about February until July, the period each year during which the Zambezi overflows and floods the plain on which the regular capital of Lealui is located. Limulunga was built during the 1930's by the Lozi King Yeta III.

LINABI. One of the three basic subdivisions within the Lozi National Council (Mulongwanji), it consists of members of the royal family, princes and prince consorts.

LINE-OF-RAIL. An often used term, its most common meaning is that region along or near the major railway line through Zambia from Livingstone north to the Copperbelt. This area became heavily populated, mostly because the existence of the railway attracted towns, European farms, and business enterprises to that stretch. Thus also it became an attractive area for Africans seeking employment. In fact, of course, the term could be applied to the area adjacent to any railway, but in Zambia the only significant rail line until recently was the aforementioned one.

LINYANTI (or LINYATI). The capital or principal village of the Makololo under Chief Sebituane in the mid-nineteenth century. The town was located in what is today the Caprivi Strip, and was just north of the Chobe (or Linyanti) River. Sebituane maintained his influence throughout most of southern and western Zambia from this location. Dr. David Livingstone met Sebituane at Linyanti in 1851, two weeks before the chief died. Livingstone and his party stayed on for another month after Sebituane's death, and Livingstone's wife gave birth there.

LINYANTI RIVER. Also known as the Kwando or Chobe (q. v.).

LIONDO. The site of a battle between Lozi forces under Mubukwanu and the Makololo under Sebituane in about 1838. It is somewhat north of the Kataba valley. During this battle, lost by the Lozi, two of Mubukwanu's sons, Sibeso and Lutangu (better known later as Sipopa, q. v.) were captured by the Makololo.

LIPALILE, L. MUFANA. Vice-president of the Northern Rhodesian African Congress, 1948; vice-treasurer of the African National Congress of Zambia, 1952; chairman of the Chingola Welfare Society and headmaster of the Chingola school; outspoken foe of the Federation in 1952; in August 1969 tried to persuade Zambian government to drop plans to cancel Barotseland Agreement of 1964 (q. v.).

LISO, EDWARD MUNGONI. An early fighter for African rule in Zambia, he stayed with his cousin, Harry Nkumbula, in the ANC until 1973 when he switched over to join UNIP. In 1950 Liso was a founder of the Anti-Federation Action Committee along with Reuben Kamanga, Justin Chimba, and Simon Zukas. They were publishing the Freedom Newsletter in Ndola. Soon they all joined the ANC. Liso quickly rose to the position of ANC President in the Western Province. In 1956 he was involved in boycotts against Mufulira shopkeepers who discriminated against Africans. He and several other officers of the Western Province were put to trial for these activities, but the court acquitted them, finding that they had sufficient justification. In August 1956 at the ANC annual conference, Liso was chosen Deputy President, replacing Robinson Puta. The next month, however, the police detained Liso and forty-four other leaders of the African Mineworkers Union, one of them for three years. Liso was soon out again, however, and returned to his party activities. In November, 1961 he suddenly became acting President of the ANC when Lawrence Katilungu, serving as President while Nkumbula was in jail, was killed in a road accident. Two months later Nkumbula was released from jail and replaced him.
    Liso ran for the legislature in 1962 in the Lusaka Rural district against UNIP's Solomon Kalulu. Relying in part on support by farmers away from the line of rail, Liso defeated Kalulu by over five hundred votes. In the coalition Cabinet with UNIP, he was appointed Parliamentary Secretary to the Chief Secretary. After independence, in November, 1965,

there was an attempt by some members of the ANC to run
Liso, now the party's Secretary General, for party President
against Nkumbula, but Liso refused to run. He did return to
the National Assembly in subsequent elections, although it took
a court decision at one point to decide that he held the seat for
Namwala. In October, 1970, however, he was expelled from his
seat in the Assembly for the remainder of its term. This resulted
from his failure to substantiate his charge that the Government
paid young women to entertain delegates to the Summit Conference
of Non-Aligned Nations that was held in Lusaka. Despite this,
when the one-party state was instituted in 1973, he was chosen as
a member of UNIP's twenty-five member Central Committee.

LISULO, DANIEL MUCHIWA. Appointed Prime Minister of Zambia in
    June 1978, he has a long record of service to UNIP and the Govern-
    ment. Born December 6, 1930, in Mongu, he was educated at Loy-
    ola College of Madras University and the Law Faculty at Delhi Uni-
    versity, attaining an LL. B. Active in the 1953-1963 independence
    struggle, he has continued to work in UNIP, serving on committees
    and as its Legal Counsel. He has been on the party's Central Com-
    mittee since 1972. Lisulo's business experience includes working
    for the Anglo-American Corporation from 1963-1964, and running
    his own law firm, Lisulo and Co. since 1968. He has been a Di-
    rector of the Bank of Zambia since 1964. In July 1977 he was
    named Minister of Legal Affairs and Attorney General. In June
    1978 he was promoted to Prime Minister by President Kaunda.

LITIA (or LETIA). The name of both the father and the son of
    the noted Lozi King Lewanika (also known as Lubosi). The
    first Litia was the son of King Mulambwa. At the time that
    Lewanika was born in about 1842 Litia was fleeing the Makololo
    invaders. Around 1856 Litia decided to collaborate with the
    invaders, and thus returned to the homeland to join the Mako-
    lolo. In 1863 Sekeletu, the Makololo leader, had Litia killed
    by Mpololo (q.v.) when it was reported that Litia and Sibeso,
    another returned Lozi, were leaders of a plot to overthrow
    Mpololo and put Litia in his place. The orphaned Lubosi (Le-
    wanika) was adopted by Sipopa and survived to become King of
    the Lozi. He was succeeded in that position by his son who
    he had named Litia, but who ruled under the name Yeta III (q.v.).

LITUNGA. The "keeper (or owner) of the earth," this title desig-
    nates the leader of the Lozi people whose position is equiva-
    lent to the European concept of King. The title implies that
    one of his responsibilities entails the preservation of Lozi
    rights to their land and the power to designate its temporary
    use. The Litunga has a very elaborate court, and is very
    much involved in royal rituals, the most famous of which is
    the Kuomboka (q.v.), where the royal capital is moved out of
    the flood plain for a few months every year during the rainy
    season. The kingship of the Lozi stays within the royal fam-
    ily which is of divine ancestry, according to the Lozi. All
    its members are descended from Mbuyu (q.v.), the daughter
    of God. Any member of the royal family may be selected Li-

tunga, but support by the principal indunas (q. v.) is crucial
to his choice, especially when the successor is not obvious
and some competition for the position is evident.   (The indunas
themselves are not of the royal family and thus are ineligible
for the post.)

Once chosen the Litunga is the subject of numerous ceremonies and rituals and is elevated to a place above all the
other royals.   He is installed through a series of purification
rites.   He is soon surrounded by mystery.   He does not appear in public frequently, and speaks to the people only through
someone else.   Even after death he is considered special, as
it is believed that he takes another form and continues to intervene in earthly events, thus becoming even more powerful than
during his lifetime.   He is buried at a site chosen by him,
which is guarded by a Nomboti (q. v.) and a number of families
who set up a village nearby.   After his death his spirit is regularly petitioned for aid.   New kings are only confirmed after
having been presented to and accepted by their predecessors
at the grave sites.

The term "Litunga" was disallowed by a European administrator, Robert Codrington, early in the twentieth century.
He did not want the Lozi leader to have the status of a King,
so he used the term "Paramount Chief."   The Lozi themselves
never ceased using the term, however, and in 1961 the British
Colonial Secretary, Iain Macleod, approved the use of "Litunga."

LIUWA PLAIN NATIONAL PARK.   One of Zambia's medium-sized
national parks (about eleven hundred square miles), it is located in northwestern Zambia in the Liuwa Plain.   It is about
ten miles north of the town of Kalabo at its nearest point, and
likewise about the same distance west of the Upper Zambezi River.

LIVINGSTONE.   Originating in February, 1905, with the completion of the bridge over the Zambezi River, it is now a town
of about fifty thousand people situated just within Zambia at
Victoria Falls along the border with Rhodesia.   It has been
important historically, as it is on the "line of rail" (q. v.)
where it crosses the Zambezi.   When Northern Rhodesia was
officially created in 1911, Livingstone became its administrative capital.   It remained the capital until 1935.   Its location
on the rail line and by the Falls has made it a tourist center
(hindered now by the problems in Zimbabwe/Rhodesia), as
well as a commercial center for the area.   The Livingstone
Museum there is a popular attraction containing memorabilia
of Dr. Livingstone as well as examples of African Art from
the earliest times to the present.   Some industry is located
in the town, producing textiles and clothing, radios, and other
items.   Power, from the Kariba Dam, is plentiful.   Unfortunately much of its economy was based in the past on trade
with the now troubled area south of the Zambezi.   These ties
can no longer exist until African rule comes to Zimbabwe.

In addition to its status as a town, Livingstone is the administrative center of what is called an Urban District of the
Southern Province.

LIVINGSTONE, DR. DAVID. The pioneer missionary in Zambia
as well as other parts of Central and Southern Africa, he has
had an immense amount of literature written about him.
Among the best may be George Seaver's David Livingstone:
His Life and Letters (see the Bibliography for numerous other
sources). His own volumes of course tell his story as well
as any others, and constitute an important source of information about nineteenth century Zambia. With the mass of readily available information elsewhere, this treatment will be
merely a cursory sketch of his career as it relates to Zambia.
    Born in Scotland in 1813, he eventually decided to study
medicine. While pursuing these studies at Anderson's College
in Glasgow, he decided to become a medical missionary to
China. He joined the London Missionary Society, but the Opi-
um War had closed off China, so instead he joined Robert
Moffat at his mission station at Kuruman, South Africa, in
1841. Livingstone soon moved further inland to work in Bechuanaland. He also married Moffat's daughter, Mary. In
1851 the Doctor (he was called Ngaka--"doctor"--by many Africans) crossed the Zambezi with his family and a small expedition. There at Sesheke he met with the great Makololo leader
Sebituane (q. v.). He also began to realize the extent of the
slave-trade, which became a major object of his opposition
throughout his next twenty-two years in Central Africa. He
hoped that by introducing the Christian religion and alternative
forms of commerce he could destroy the slave trade. Later
his work would inspire many other missionaries from a variety
of sects to pursue the same goal in Central Africa.
    After traveling to Cape Town to send his family to England,
Livingstone returned to Zambia in 1853, however he put together an expedition and traveled west into Angola. He soon
retraced his steps with his Makololo guides and porters, however and on November 16, 1855 he was the first European to
see what he named Victoria Falls. He then traveled through
southern Zambia into Mozambique, reaching Quelimane on the
Indian Ocean in May, 1856. He returned to England, where
he received awards, wrote a book and prepared to return to
Central Africa. He returned in 1858, and spent most of the
next five years near Lake Nyasa (Malawi), although he made a
trip with his brother and a botanist to Victoria Falls in 1860.
They went a little further to Linyanti, where the doctor renewed acquaintances with Sekeletu, the son and heir of Sebituane. The party left the Zambezi valley late in 1860 to return
to Lake Nyasa.
    Returning to England in 1864, Livingstone stayed for two
years before arriving back in Zanzibar in 1866. This time
his determination to stop the slave trade was even stronger.
In addition he was seeking more information on the sources of
both the Nile and Congo Rivers. He pursued all of these interests while his body was growing weaker with diseases over
the next seven years. He crossed through Zambia on several
occasions, reaching Lake Mweru and Lake Bangweulu in 1867-
68. His famous meeting with Henry Stanley occurred in 1871.

Rejecting Stanley's appeal to return to England, he went southwest again into both Zambia and the Congo. He died at Chief
Chitambo's village southeast of Lake Bangweulu in Zambia on
May 1, 1873. His body was buried there by his close friends
and guides, who took his heart back to England.

LIVINGSTONE MAIL. Founded in 1906 in the town of Livingstone
by a pharmacist, Leopold Moore (q. v.), it was Northern Rhodesia's only newspaper for many years. As such it was very
important both in shaping opinion and in reflecting the news of
the settlers. It regularly attacked BSAC rule, shouting loyalty
to the British Crown and Empire instead. It has continued as
an English language weekly.

LIVINGSTONE NATIVE WELFARE ASSOCIATION. Founded in 1930
by the residents of Maramba, the main African township or
"location" of Livingstone, it quickly became an articulate fighter for social justice. Many of its founders were civil servants
from Nyasaland, men like Isaac R. Nyirenda, Edward Franklin
Tembo, Samuel K. K. Mwase, its Acting Chairman, J. E. C.
Mattako, its Vice-Chairman, and Gideon M. Mumana, its
Treasurer. When the Government granted it permission to organize, it envisioned a social club, but the founders were already protesting police injustices at a general meeting on July
15, 1930. They argued that race was the basis for mistreat-
ment of many people, and that the courts always favored Europeans over Africans. At a meeting a month earlier several
local chiefs had attended and expressed their bitter resentment
of the Europeans who had taken their land. African grievances
continued to flow from the meetings as the year went on, but
while the Government made no effort to satisfy the complaints,
there was an important result: Africans began forming similar
associations in many other towns throughout the territory.

LIVINGSTONIA CENTRAL AFRICA COMPANY. The original name
of the African Lakes Company (q. v.).

LIVINGSTONIA MISSION. The working name for the series of missions set up in Central Africa by the Free Church of Scotland
(q. v.) to commemorate the work begun by Dr. David Livingstone.

LLEWELLYN, LORD. The first Governor General of the Federation of Rhodesia and Nyasaland, he served from its inception
on September 3, 1953. He was succeeded by the Earl of Dalhousie who was inaugurated on October 8, 1957.

LOANGWENI. The village of the great Ngoni Chief Mpezeni in the
late nineteenth century, it was located near the present Zambian border, southeast of Chipata. After the British defeated
the Ngoni there in 1898 it was renamed Fort Young, and there
is now a national monument there.

LOBENGULA. The son and successor of the great Ndebele (Matabele) leader Mzilikazi, he was elevated to the kingship in 1870.
The next twenty-five years found Lobengula's military forces
continually threatening their neighbors north of the Zambezi
River. The Lozi especially were very fearful of Lobengula.
Although their homeland was seldom endangered, the Lozi influence over the Ila, Tonga, Toka, and other southern peoples
was regularly threatened by Ndebele raids. Nevertheless, at
one point in the early 1880's Lobengula contacted Lewanika,
the Lozi King, with a proposal that the two peoples work together to resist the invading white men. Lewanika rejected
this approach in favor of closer ties with Chief Khama of the
Bamangwato. In 1891-92 Lobengula did send an army (impi)
north toward the Lozi heartland, but problems with Europeans
south of the Zambezi required Lobengula to recall his men before an attack could occur. It was fear of Lobengula that
played a big part in Lewanika's search for British protection
and thus his signing of several ill-advised treaties that ultimately tied him to rule by the British South Africa Company.

LOBITO. The important port town of Angola that is the end point
of the Benguela Railway (q.v.), one of Zambia's more important
sources of international imports and exports.

LOBOLA see MPANGO

LOCAL GOVERNMENT ACT. A law passed by the Zambian Parliament and signed by President Kaunda in October, 1965. Os-
tensibly it was designed to create a fairly uniform pattern of
democratically controlled local authorities throughout Zambia.
One of its greatest practical effects, however, was to abolish
the Barotse National Council and to replace it with five district
councils. It also had the effect of lowering the status of the
Lozi King to "just another chief," as he lost his authority to
appoint councillors and judges, to veto legislation, and to control the Barotse Treasury. Considerable resentment arose
among members of the Lozi traditional elite, and many other
Lozi likewise resented the imposition of central government
controls.

LOCATIONS. A word used throughout most of British-controlled
Africa, especially where there were large communities of
Europeans, it referred to those areas of African residence,
often times of very low caliber, that ringed the central towns
and business areas. The Africans working in the towns or
for the Europeans lived in these "locations."

LOCH, SIR HENRY BROUGHAM. Governor of the Cape Colony
and British High Commissioner in South Africa from 1889 to
1895. A series of letters passed between the Lozi King Lewanika and Loch between 1890 and 1894 in which the King repeatedly requested assurance from Loch that his people would
be under the protection of the British government. He feared

the neighboring Ndebele, and he distrusted the BSAC with whose representative, Frank Lochner (q. v.), he signed an agreement. Loch assured the King that a resident commissioner would soon be appointed (associated with the BSAC, however, it turned out), and that, eventually, the Ndebele would be conquered.

LOCHINVAR NATIONAL PARK. One of the smaller national parks, consisting of about one hundred fifty square miles, it is located in south-central Zambia. It has a small northern border with the Kafue River. It is the site of the important archaeological find of the oldest Tonga settlement known in Zambia, at the top of Sebanzi Hill (q. v.) at Lochinvar Ranch.

LOCHINVAR RANCH. An important archaeological site in south-central Zambia, which is more commonly referred to by the specific geographic location, Sebanzi Hill (q. v.).

LOCHNER, CAPTAIN FRANK ELLIOTT. A former officer of the Bechuanaland Police, he was working for Cecil Rhodes at Kimberley in 1889 when Rhodes sent him as his agent to negotiate a concession from the Lozi King Lewanika (see LOCHNER CONCESSION). He reached Kazungula in December, 1889, and crossed the Zambezi. He met Lewanika at Sesheke in March 1890. Negotiations continued then in other locations in Barotseland until the Lozi leaders signed the document on June 27, 1890. They undoubtedly would not have agreed to it had Lochner not deceived them into thinking that this was a treaty of protection with the British Crown rather than a business transaction with the BSAC.

LOCHNER CONCESSION (also known as Lochner Treaty of 1890 or Barotse Treaty of 1890). One of the most significant documents in Zambia's history, it was signed by King Lewanika of the Lozi and forty of his major advisors along with Frank Lochner (q. v.) of the BSAC on June 27, 1890, at the Lozi capital of Lealui. The agreement is important because it was recognized by other Europeans (albeit incorrectly) that the Lozi King had granted the British control over the entire western half of today's Zambia including the Copperbelt. The controversy over the Concession breaks down into several parts. First, the actual concession granted mineral rights over all the territory of the Barotse nation to the BSAC. This would include all future Lozi land including "subject and dependent territory. " Thus rights could be asserted over any land which one could even weakly tie to the Lozi people. The Europeans added territory to the concession that could not have been included under any stretch of the imagination. Secondly, the Lozi, misled by both Lochner and the translations of Rev. Coillard (q. v.), thought they were signing an agreement with England's Queen Victoria for British protection. The fact that Lochner agreed to a £2000 annual subsidy which King Lewanika could use to buy guns was an important part of the agreement.

The location of a Resident Commissioner in Barotseland would
also provide the "Queen's" presence that Lewanika felt would
give him some security, especially against Lobengula (q. v.) of
the ever-threatening Ndebele. Third, Lewanika understood that
this agreement only amounted to a "loan" of the land to the
Europeans, not a "grant. " Again Coillard's translation (inten-
tionally or not) was partly to blame, and Lewanika and the Lozi
would protest for many years that Lozi tradition could never allow the King to permanently alienate national land. This agreement did not actually give the Company any administrative
rights, only mineral rights over an area estimated by Coillard
at about two hundred thousand square miles. While guaranteeing to protect the Lozi against outside attack, the Company
pledged not to interfere with the relationship between the King
and his subjects. It also promised to build schools and industries in order to help in the "education and civilization of the
native subjects of the King. " The Company failed to fulfill any
of its promises, at least for a time. In some instances it
totally ignored them. The high hopes of the King were totally
frustrated, while the BSAC ultimately reaped great profits.

LOMBE, FOUSTINO. A former member of the United Progressive
Party before it was banned, he founded the short-lived success-
or, the Democratic People's Party (q. v.) in March, 1972.

LONDON CONFERENCE, 1951. A conference held in March, 1951
between pro-Federationists led by Godfrey Huggins (q. v.) and
the British Colonial Office, represented by James Griffiths
(q. v.). The conference produced an agreement that Central
Africa must be more closely tied together, and that a federal
constitution would be desirable. Another result of the meeting
was the calling of the Victoria Falls Conference, September,
1951 (q. v.).

LONDON CONFERENCE, 1952. Held in Lancaster House in London
during April and May, 1952, it brought together representatives
from Northern and Southern Rhodesia and Nyasaland with the
Colonial Secretary. All the African delegates from Nyasaland
and Northern Rhodesia boycotted the meetings, but Joshua
Nkomo and Jasper Savanhu from Southern Rhodesia did take
part. Of course representatives of the settlers eagerly took
part, with Julian Greenfield from Bulawayo and Edgar Whitehead playing prominent roles in addition to Roy Welensky and
Godfrey Huggins. The conference produced a draft document
for a federation, and commissions were appointed to investigate
fiscal, judicial, and Civil Service concerns.

LONDON CONFERENCE, 1953. A meeting in London in January,
1953 which finalized the work of the 1952 London conference and
which agreed upon the constitution for a Federation of the Rhodesias and Nyasaland. Representatives from all three Governments met with British Colonial officials to set in motion the
legal machinery that would allow the Federation to proceed.

LONDON CONFERENCE ON ZAMBIA'S INDEPENDENCE. Beginning on May 2, 1964, this conference was planned merely to formalize the known fact that Zambia would be independent before the end of the year. Zambia's delegation consisted of Kenneth Kaunda, Simon Kapwepwe, Arthur Wina, Elijah Mudenda, Aaron Milner, Jonathan Chivunga, and Hanock Kikombe. The conference took place at Marlborough House in London.

LONDON CONSTITUTIONAL CONFERENCE, 1961. Also called the Lancaster House Conference of 1961, this was hardly a conference at all, in that the representatives of the United Federal Party boycotted the talks. The background for the Conference must include the Federal Review Conference (q. v.) of December, 1960, in which the African delegates walked out. The British Government finally announced that the Review Conference would not be resumed until the conferences for the individual territories occurred. The Northern Rhodesia conference would begin on December 19, 1960, but recess immediately until January 31, 1961. In the interim, Roy Welensky of the UFP (and Federal Prime Minister) tried to get the British Colonial Secretary Iain Macleod, to agree not to give majority rule to the Africans. Macleod would not guarantee this, however, so on January 28, 1961, Welensky, supported by delegates from the Dominion Party, announced that they would boycott the talks. The hope was to delay the Northern Rhodesia talks until after the Federal Review Conference was held, or at least until the Southern Rhodesian talks were completed. Macleod was thus forced to cancel plenary sessions and begin a series of informal talks with the various groups. The African parties, cooperating in a united front, demanded African majority rule based on universal adult suffrage. This was in total conflict with Welensky's ideas. He even tried confidential talks with Prime Minister Harold Macmillan. The boycott succeeded in delaying the conference until after agreement was reached with the Africans from Southern Rhodesia. If Welensky thought that this would force the Northern Rhodesia Africans to give in, it didn't succeed. The Conference was ended in deadlock on February 17. Some of the delegates continued to discuss the situation with Macleod after the Conference was closed. On February 20, Macleod presented his own Macleod Plan to Parliament (see MACLEOD CONSTITUTION).

LONDON MISSIONARY SOCIETY (LMS). One of the earliest of the missionary groups to be active in Zambia, its main concern was in the region immediately south of Lake Tanganyika. The missionaries reached the Lake from Zanzibar in 1878, and while they built a depot there in 1883, it was 1884-85 before they established a mission on the Lake's southern shore at Niamkolo. In 1887 they opened a station at Fwambo near the Mambwe chief of that name. The Society also played a different part in Zambian history, as it was the LMS stations in South Africa at Kuruman and Kolobeng that were the starting points for Dr. David Livingstone's first trips into Zambia.

Today the Society's work is done within the framework of the
United Church of Zambia (q. v.).

LONRHO ZAMBIA LTD.   A jointly owned British and South African
firm formerly known as the London and Rhodesian Mining and
Land Company. It has numerous investments and subsidiaries
in Zambia, with interests that include mining, newspapers,
transportation, breweries, and construction.

LOVALE.   Variant of Luvale (q. v.).

LOWER ROLL   see   UPPER ROLL

LOZI (or ROTSE; BAROTSE).   One of the most prominent of all
the Zambian peoples historically, they actually number only
about 125,000, placing them about tenth in population. Yet
their principal language, Silozi (q. v.)--or just "Lozi"--is one
of the country's official languages. The prominence of the
Lozi stems from several factors. First, they maintained a
strong centralized kingship under their leader, the Litunga
(q. v.). Thus their tradition, ritual, and national unity have
been preserved through the centuries despite one desperate
period in the nineteenth century when the Makololo (q. v.) conquered them and controlled their land. Otherwise the Lozi,
residing in Western Zambia along the Upper Zambezi, have retained a strong sense of national identity.

A second reason for their prominence is that the Lozi,
based in their home area called Bulozi (q. v.) in the Zambezi's
flood plain, moved in all directions to dominate many of their
neighbors militarily. Thus many of the peoples west of the
Kafue River, and a few in southern Zambia as well, have paid
tribute to the Lozi, especially in the nineteenth century.

The third reason for Lozi prominence rests in the fact that
they were the first major group of Zambian peoples, at least
in western Zambia, to be involved with the Europeans who entered the country. Missionaries like Dr. David Livingstone,
Frederick Arnot, Rev. François Coillard and others all wrote
back to Europe about their contacts with the Lozi, as did other
Europeans such as Emil Holub. In addition, Cecil Rhodes secured rights within Lozi territory through concessions secured
by men like Frank Lochner, and Harry Ware. Thus the
British South Africa Company opened up Barotseland (q. v.) to
European influence.

The actual name "Lozi" was given by the invading Makololo people to the Luyi or Luyana people they had conquered
in the nineteenth century. The Luyana appear to have been of
Lunda origin, tracing back to the dynasty of Mwata Yamvo
(q. v.), although Luba origins are also possible. Perhaps Lunda invaders subdued Luba settlers when they arrived. This is
confused even more by the merger of Luba and Lunda empires
centuries ago. Regardless, the Luyana have been in the Bulozi
flood plain for about three hundred years. They either drove
out or absorbed the existing peoples and set up a strong

centralized state along the Zambezi. Cultivation of the flood
plain is essential to their production and way of life. Garden-
ing, fishing, and pasturing are all part of their economy and
thus affect their village settlement patterns and concepts of
land tenure. They are unusual among Zambian peoples in that
they practice bilateral descent and in that they place no importance in clans and lineages, other than that of the royal
family itself.

During the twentieth century the Lozi were very open to
European education, and thus provided many of the African
civil servants working in other parts of the country, notably
along the line-of-rail and in the Copperbelt. There has been
a major struggle for many years by the Lozi to retain separate status for their nation, distinct from either Northern
Rhodesia or, later, Zambia. See also BAROTSELAND.

LUAMBE NATIONAL PARK. One of Zambia's smallest national
parks, it is located between the Luangwa North and Luangwa
South National Parks, except that it is on the east bank of the
Luangwa River, and thus across from the others.

LUANGWA NORTH NATIONAL PARK see LUANGWA VALLEY
GAME RESERVE

LUANGWA RIVER. There are actually two Luangwa Rivers in
Zambia. The lesser of the two is a tributary of the Kalungwishi River in the northwestern sector of the eastern half of
Zambia, southeast of Lake Mweru. Dr. David Livingstone
traveled this Luangwa River Valley in December, 1872.

The better known of the two Luangwa Rivers drains a major part of Zambia on the eastern side of the Muchinga Escarpment, traveling over four hundred miles on a northeast
to southwest path until it joins the Zambezi River at Feira on
Zambia's southern border. The major tributary of the Luangwa is the Lunsemfwa River (q.v.), which joins the Luangwa a
little north of the Zambezi. The Luangwa Valley is hot, hu-
mid, and unhealthy. It is not heavily populated by humans,
as malaria is a major problem there. Also the tsetse fly in-
fects and kills domestic animals. Thus a large central part
of the Luangwa Valley is taken up by the Luangwa Valley Game
Reserve (q.v.). Teak forests also thrive there.

One major incident involving the River occurred in 1968
when the vital Luangwa River bridge on the Great East Road
into the Eastern Province was blown up, presumably by Portuguese infiltrators seeking to avenge Zambia's tolerance of
bases in Zambia which were used by Mozambique guerrillas.

LUANGWA SOUTH NATIONAL PARK see LUANGWA VALLEY
GAME RESERVE

LUANGWA VALLEY GAME RESERVE. One of Zambia's finest attractions and one of the best game parks in Africa, it covers
six thousand square miles, mostly on the western side of the

Luangwa River and east of the Muchinga Mountains. The park
is almost bisected by a narrow waist that divides it into a
Luangwa North National Park and a Luangwa South National
Park. It is heavily populated with animals, including about
twenty-five thousand elephants. Its two fully catered lodges at
Mfuwe and Luamfwa are favorite spots for game watching,
some of which can be done on foot when led by experienced
guides. The Reserve is about a 340-mile drive from Lusaka,
but a nearby airstrip also provides access.

LUANO. One of the smaller ethnic subdivisions of Zambia, the
Luano people number about nine thousand and reside in south
central Zambia, east of Lusaka.

LUANSHYA. One of the urban districts in the Copperbelt Province,
this mining center had a population of ninety-six thousand in
1969. The town is located near the southern end of the Copperbelt, a little over ten miles southwest of Ndola. Luanshya
is one of the older mining centers, its economy based on production at the Roan Antelope mine (q.v.). Production began in
1931. Luanshya also has some manufacturing plants and other
minor industry. The town is adjacent to an important airfield.

LUANSHYA MINE see ROAN ANTELOPE MINE

LUANSHYA NATIVE WELFARE ASSOCIATION. One of the many
Welfare Associations (q.v.) which played an important role in
the growth of African nationalism in Zambia. Its leaders in
its important years of existence, the early 1930's, were northern-
ers: Henry Chibangwa and John Lombe from Mporokoso and
Kenny Rain, a Bemba from Kasama. The Government refused
to grant recognition to this organization because it felt that
these leaders were too radical and "subversive." Yet their
major goals as expressed in their slogans seem very moderate
today. They asked for "Equal rights," "Better treatment,"
and "Justice to the Native People of this colony." The leaders
were particularly opposed to the pass system (q.v.). A visit
to the Secretary of Native Affairs in Livingstone by the leaders
did not accomplish anything, as the passes remained.

LUAPULA PROVINCE. Situated in the eastern half of Zambia,
along the eastern border of the Congo Pedicle (q.v.), the province is divided into three districts: Kawambwa, which includes
Lake Mweru and stretches up to Zambia's northern border;
Mansa, south of Kawambwa along the Luapula River and the
border with Zaire; and Samfya, situated east of Mansa. The
three had a total population of about one-third of a million in
1969, a drop of twenty thousand since 1963. Only the North-
Western Province has fewer people. The western border of
the Province is the Luapula River (q.v.) which separates it
from the Congo Pedicle of Zaire. The most famous inhabitants of the Province are the Lunda of Chief Kazembe, but
other groups in the Province include the Bwila, Shila, Chishinga,
Ushi, and Kabende.

LUAPULA RIVER. One of Zambia's major rivers, it forms the
border between Zaire and Zambia south from Lake Mweru along
the eastern border of Zaire's Congo Pedicle (q. v.). It actually
begins as an extension of the Chambeshi River (q. v.), draining
the swamps and marshes south of Lake Bangweulu. It then
turns westward before heading north toward Lake Mweru where
it empties. At one point it fights its way through large rocks,
rapids, and cataracts until it plunges over Johnston Falls. It
then becomes a broad, deep, and peaceful river on the last
hundred miles of its trip to Lake Mweru. The river is a rich
source of fish, supplying a livelihood for many Zambians. The
river and its vicinity are justly famous as the location of the
great Lunda empire of Kazembe that dominated trade in central
Africa from about 1750 to about 1850.

LUBA (or BALUBA). A major family of Central African peoples
whose original homeland is in southeastern Zaire near Lake
Kisale. A member of the royal lineage, Chibinda Ilunga, married a Lunda princess Lueji (q. v.), and their people, now
called the Lunda, founded many of the important chieftainships
of Zambia, in part through the leadership of Lueji's grandson
Mwata Yamvo (q. v.). Lueji's brother, Chinyama, who disputed her right to the chieftainship, founded the Luvale tribe
(q. v.). One Lozi historian thinks the Luyana (early name for
the Lozi) could also have been part of a Luba migration. It
is also probable that the Bemba in northeastern Zambia (and
many of the related peoples there) are of Luba origin. The
great migration of their leaders (see CHITI) began in a place
sometimes called Luba (or Kola) by the Bemba. The Luba
traditions concerning chieftainship have strongly influenced the
Bemba. The Lenje (q. v.) of south central Zambia also claim
to be of Luba origin. Around 1830 the Congo (Zaire)-based
Luba kingdom began to expand and a Luba army attacked the
Lunda capital of Kazembe (q. v.), but it was driven off.

LUBEMBA. The calo (q. v.) or territory under the direct supervision of the Bemba senior chief, the Chitimukulu. This is
distinct from the rest of Bemba territory which other Bemba
chiefs controlled. Lubemba was larger than the other chiefdoms and was considered the Bemba heartland because of Chitimukulu's senior position. On occasions in the nineteenth century some of the stronger chiefs on the border of Lubemba intruded into the territory when the reigning ruler was weak.

LUBITA, NGOMBALA. A Lozi politician who was active in a number of parties, primarily in the 1960's. Born in 1929 at Lealui, he is a grandson of King Lewanika. He was active first
in the ANC in the 1950's, and then joined UNIP. This caused
him to be arrested and detained in 1959. After his release he
became active in the Barotse Anti-Secession Society (q. v.) in
1960, an organization with some UNIP ties. He resigned in
1962, however, when Munu Sipalo was burned by a "Molotov
cocktail" that some blamed on Bemba members of UNIP. He

then became active in the Sicaba Party (q. v.) and took over as
its president when its previous leaders were about to dissolve
it after its overwhelming defeat in the 1962 elections.   He then
made an attempt to affiliate Sicaba with the ANC in 1963.
This did not work out as planned, and the Sicaba Party was
dissolved in 1963.   During the next year Lubita went on a
lengthy trip into Rhodesia and South Africa on behalf of the
Lozi King, Mwanawina.   The journey was undertaken in part
to secure a better financial arrangement for the Lozi from
Wenelu (q. v.).   Contact was also made with the South African
Government about possible ties with Barotseland, but this failed
to develop.   Ultimately Lubita has returned to membership in
UNIP.

LUBOSI (or LUBOZI; ROBOSI; LOBOSI).   Lozi leader, son of Litia
(q. v.), who would become the Litunga (King) of the Lozi in
1878.   He was later challenged by the rebels but regained the
throne in 1885.   At that point he took the praise name Lewanika (q. v.), which means "conqueror," loosely translated, under
which name he would rule until his death in 1916.

LUBUMBU.   A Bisa chiefdom located northeast of Lake Bangweulu
that was especially strong in the late eighteenth century.   It
evidently once had control over as many lesser chiefdoms as
did the great Bemba leader Chitimukulu.   In the nineteenth
century, however, its leaders were defeated by the Bemba who
were pushing south.   At one point in the eighteenth century the
chiefs at Lubumbu were under the dominance of another Bisa
chiefdom at Chinama, but by the end of that century this had
ceased and Lubumbu itself dominated many other chiefs.   About
this time the sixth Lubumbu chief, Kalenga, moved the capital
of the chiefdom from an island in Lake Bangweulu to a land-
based location called Mwala by the Lukuta River.   In 1831 a
Portuguese expedition led by Antonio Gamitto (q. v.) traveled
through Lubumbu, and he described the political leadership of
the area in his published journal.   About 1840 a new chief of
Lubumbu, Muma, took the title of Matipa (q. v.) when he succeeded Nkalamo as chief.   The latter had put his capital back
on Lake Bangweulu because of the imminent danger of Bemba
attacks.   Matipa reoccupied Mwala on the mainland, but was
attacked by Mwamba I and returned to an island capital.   Bemba raiders killed all the children of Matipa.   When Mwamba I
died late in the 1850's, Matipa again returned to the mainland,
driving the Bemba out of Lubumbu.   However in the 1860's
Mwamba II defeated chiefs subordinate to Matipa, and about
1870 drove Matipa himself back onto an island in Lake Bangweulu.   Then Mwamba installed a Bemba chief over most of
Lubumbu.

LUBWE (or LUBWA).   A town on the western shore of Lake Bangweulu.   One of its greatest claims to fame is that it was the
birthplace of Zambia's first President, Kenneth Kaunda.   He
was educated there at the Mission School and returned there
years later to teach briefly.

LUCHAZI.   One of the many ethnic subdivisions of Zambia, the
Luchazi people number about fifty thousand and live in the
northwestern part of the country, south of the Ndembu.   They
are of the Lunda-Luvale linguistic sub-group, and are very
closely related to other members of that sub-group such as the
Chokwe and Luvale.   All three groups are artistic, and the
Luchazi have demonstrated originality in the carving and color-
ing of their masks.

LUCHINDASHI RIVER.   A small tributary of the Chambeshi River
in northeastern Zambia.   Its historic interest is that an argument between two women near this river resulted in one group,
the bena ng'ona (Mushroom Clan) splitting away from the larger
"Bemba" migration led by Chiti (q. v.).   This group, which established themselves near the river, became the royal clan of
the Bisa people.

LUEJI (or RUEJI).   A Lunda (some sources say Luba) princess of
the Tubungu clan who according to legend lived in the Congo
area during the early seventeenth century.   Her story, widely
told in Central Africa, is that of the beginnings of many of the
peoples in the area.   She had inherited a chieftainship and retained it through the strength of her Luba spouse Ilunga (q. v.).
Their followers, according to the legend, became the Lunda.
One of her brothers, unhappy with the situation, moved west
and founded the Luvale tribe.   A grandson of Lueji inherited
the chieftainship and called himself Mwata Yamvo (q. v.), and
became the center of a large Lunda empire that influenced the
development of many of the Zambian tribes.

LUENA FLATS.   A very wet area in the western part of Zambia,
it is on the east bank of the upper Zambezi River and the
south bank of the Luena River.   This swampy area is more
densely populated than most of the rest of the country.   The
Lozi came to control the region by defeating its previous inhabitants, the Nkoya.   The Luena Flats were probably once
lakebeds covering several hundred square miles.

LUENA RIVER (or LWENA).   A tributary of the Zambezi River,
it rises in west-central Zambia, just west of the Kafue National Park, and flows northwesterly past Kaoma (formerly Mankoya) en route to the Zambezi.   It enters the Zambezi north
of the Lozi capitals of Lealui and Mongu.   The northern Luvale
people are called Luena.

LUFUBU RIVER.   A major river in the northeastern part of Zam-
bia as it takes a winding path flowing northward through the
Sumbu Game Reserve into the southwestern corner of Lake
Tanganyika.   Its location made it a very popular site for vil-
lages in the area, vigorously contested by Arab traders and
Africans (especially the Bemba) in the nineteenth century.
Also the London Missionary Society built a depot at its estuary
in 1883.

LUI RIVER (or LUYI RIVER). A river in Barotseland that joins the Zambezi River south of the town of Senanga. Its confluence with the Zambezi is considered to be the southern limit of Bulozi, the rich Flood Plain inhabited by the Lozi people.

LUKANGA SWAMP. A large basin south and east of the Kafue river in central Zambia, west of the city of Kabwe. It is a permanently flooded area where various types of reeds and aquatic plants are dominant.

LUKULU. A town along the Upper Zambezi River, a little south of its confluence with the Lungwebungu River in northwestern Zambia. It was a site in the nineteenth century of a fortified village built by Luyi (or Lozi) after they had been severely beaten by Makololo forces under Chief Sebituane. The Lozi leader Mubukwanu died there, to be succeeded by Imasiku. The Makololo then isolated the village, forcing the defenders to the brink of starvation. Imasiku managed to escape shortly before Lukulu surrendered to the Makololo who, with this victory in 1838, now controlled Barotseland.

LUKUSUZI NATIONAL PARK. A game reserve in the Eastern Province about twenty-five miles southwest of Lundazi and fifteen miles west of the border with Malawi. It encompasses about one thousand square miles.

LUKWAKWA. An area in northwestern Zambia near Kabompo, north of the Kabompo River but east of the Manyinga River. According to the tradition of the Aluyana (q.v.), later called the Lozi, one group of Aluyana settled here while the rest proceeded south into the area called Bulozi (q.v.). During the civil war over succession following the death of the Lozi King Mulambwa (q.v.), the Makololo under Chief Sebituane invaded Bulozi in 1833. One of the three warring factions, led by Sinyama Sikufele, fled to Lukwakwa. In 1838 Chief Imasiku (q.v.) fled across the Kabompo also. When he was later killed, Sipopa (q.v.) took over the Lukwakwa leadership. When Sipopa later moved south to Bulozi, Imbua (q.v.) moved to Lukwakwa and succeeded Sipopa. The Lukwakwa area continued to be a haven for dissatisfied Lozi for many years. As a result it was a threat to the Bulozi leadership. Thus in late 1889 King Lewanika began a military campaign against it. He took a very large force including many of the top Lozi leaders. The Lukwakwa group was defeated and ultimately accepted the authority of the Bulozi leader.

LUKWESA ILUNGA see KAZEMBE III

LULIMALA RIVER. A very small river flowing north into Lake Bangweulu on the south-central shore of the lake. It is on this river that Chitambo's village was located, the death site of Dr. David Livingstone.

LUMBE RIVER. A minor tributary of the Zambezi River, joining it south of the Zambezi's confluence with the Lui River. It drains part of southwestern Zambia.

LUMPA CHURCH. The religious movement with strong political implications founded in 1953 by Alice Lenshina (q. v.). It remained active at least through the 1960's, despite the problems incurred during its "holy war" against the Government in 1964. The word "Lumpa" is a Bemba word meaning "better than all the rest. "

LUNDA. One of the major ethnic and linguistic subdivisions of Central Africa, the Lunda inhabit large areas in Angola and Zaire as well as Zambia. The Lunda language is one of Zambia's eight official languages, spoken primarily in the northwestern part of the country. There are about a hundred thousand Lunda in northwestern Zambia, and about a quarter of a million Lunda (most Bemba-speakers) in the Luapula Province. Lunda chieftainships began developing in parts of Central Africa about the tenth or eleventh centuries. As they grew, some Lunda moved south into Zambia, primarily in the seventeenth and eighteenth centuries. Among the chieftainships to split away from the Lunda empire are those of the Luvale and Ndembu (qq. v.), who have resided in Zambia for several centuries. Lunda involvement in trade with the Portuguese in Angola also brought that influence into the area. As the Lozi (q. v.) began to dominate western Zambia, some of the Lunda were forced to pay them tribute, but later their independence from the Lozi was reestablished.

The major Lunda ruler to affect Zambia was a Congo-born emperor, Mwata Yamvo (q. v.), whose initiative led to the founding of the kingdom of Kazembe (q. v.) along the Luapula River. The Lunda of Kazembe at one time controlled large areas in the Congo Pedicle (q. v.) and in northeastern Zambia. Many non-Lunda were thus under Kazembe's rule, but he made no attempt to assimilate them (although some became "Lunda" through some act of distinction). Patrilineal descent is practiced among Kazembe's Lunda as it was at Mwata Yamvo's capital. Centralized authority patterns were established by Kazembe, and district governors served Kazembe in their districts, paying tribute to him just as he continued to send tribute to Mwata Yamvo. The Lunda of northwestern Zambia also have some traditions that point to Mwata Yamvo's capital for their origins.

LUNDAZI. A town and district in the Eastern Province. The town of Lundazi is only a few miles from Zambia's eastern border, and is the administrative center of the district. In 1969 the population of the district was 123,000, unchanged in the six years from the previous census. There is an airfield southwest of the town, which is located near some excellent game reserves as well as some hunting areas.

LUNGA RIVER. A major tributary of the Kafue River, it begins
in north-central Zambia near the Zaire border and the town
of Solwezi. It flows due south into the Kafue National Park
where it merges with the Kafue on a southern path.

LUNGU. Living generally north of the Bemba along the southern
part of Lake Tanganyika in northeastern Zambia, the Lungu
people number about a hundred thousand today. They belong
to the Mambwe language group, although some Lungu further
south speak primarily ciBemba. These latter ones are probably of Luba origin, but did not come with the Bemba migration. The southern Lungu observe matrilineal descent like
their Bemba neighbors, but the northern Lungu near the Lake
observe patrilineal descent. It seems that the Northern Lungu
may have had East African origins along with the neighboring
Mambwe. The lakeshore Lungu fish and grow rice and cassava. They trade some of this to the Lungu further south, in
exchange for millet. The Lungu were also noted for wearing
clothes in the nineteenth century that they made from cotton
cloth, unlike most Zambians who were wearing bark cloth
clothes. Cotton cloth also became an item that they traded.

The Paramount Chief of the Lungu bears the title Tafuna
(q.v.), and usually has ruled from his capital at Isoka. Other
chiefs are subordinate to him. Because of international boundaries drawn in the nineteenth century, some Lungu live north
of the border with Tanzania.

The territory of the Lungu on the lakeshore was inevitably
to become the traveling path for African and Arab traders
alike. Thus the Lungu were subject to numerous invasions,
especially by Bemba and Arabs. The Arab influence is still
there today in their clothing style and even boat design. To
escape the slave traders, the Lungu lived in stockaded villages,
but abandoned them for open villages once the British intervened
in the area and stopped most of the bloodshed in the late nineteenth century.

The northern Lungu are ruled by chieftainships dominated
by the bazimba (q.v.), or Leopard Clan. These people were
besieged by the Bemba as much as by the Arab slave traders.
The southern Lungu, however, were often as concerned with
the Lunda of Kazembe, to whom they paid tribute in the nineteenth century. Nevertheless they faced the Bemba in battle
also, such as their battle against the invading Mwamba II
Chileshye in the 1860's. A junior Lungu chief, Chitoshi, lost
his life in this war. Around the same time, the northern Lungu under Chief Tafuna were subject to the domination of the
Ngoni (q.v.) who under Mperembe settled in their territory and required the Lungu to both work and fight for
them. At a battle on the Kafubu River in the mid 1860's,
the Bemba fought the Lungu and the Ngoni, but the battle was
not decisive. A major leader of the Lungu named Zombe (q.v.)
had several battles with the Bemba under Chitapankwa (q.v.).
Zombe was victorious until the Bemba defeated him in a major
confrontation in the early 1880's.

Throughout the nineteenth century the Lungu were noted as iron-producers. Lungu smiths were in great demand, especially among the Bemba. Sometimes Lungu smiths would even settle among the Bemba, paying tribute with hoes and axes. One even built smelting furnaces in Mpanda. Some Lungu kept herds of cattle and other livestock in tsetse-free zones. Only the Mambwe and Iwa among the northeastern peoples shared this pattern with the Lungu.

Perhaps because the Lungu were so frequently attacked by their fellow Africans, they were quick to sign up for European "protection." Harry Johnston (q. v.) found several Lungu chiefs, including Tafuna himself, willing to sign his "treaties." (For a story of conflict between two Lungu leaders, see KALIMINWA and TOMBOSHALO.)

LUNGWEBUNGU RIVER. The first major tributary of the Zambezi River from the west, it rises in Angola and flows southeasterly into the Zambezi. This occurs just south of the Kabompo River's confluence with the Zambezi, and just north of the town of Lukulu. This point of confluence is considered to be the northern edge of the Flood Plain that the Lozi people call Bulozi, their heartland.

LUNSEMFWA RIVER. The major tributary of the Luangwa River, joining it about fifty miles north of the Luangwa's confluence with the Zambezi at Feira. One branch of the Lunsemfwa begins in the Muchinga Mountains and flows southerly, while the other branch moves on a due east course from central Zambia. They merge about twenty-five miles before they join the Luangwa. The Lunsemfwa basin has been estimated to encompass about 16,800 square miles.

LUSAKA. The capital city of Zambia since 1935 (although chosen as such in 1931), it has a population today of over a quarter of a million people. (Lusaka is also the name of one of the districts in Zambia's Central Province. The district, of which the city of Lusaka is also the administrative center, had a population over 350,000 in 1969.) The city of Lusaka is located along the line-of-rail and is on the Great East Road. It also has an international airport. With transportation so accessible, it is the leading industrial, commercial, and financial center of the country in addition to its governmental functions.

The city originated as the site of a railroad siding in 1905, serving the nearby Broken Hill mine at Kabwe. The siding was named after Lusaakas, the headman of a neighboring village. European farms developed in the vicinity, producing maize and beef. A village management board was created in 1913. Real growth only began after it became Northern Rhodesia's capital in 1935. A British planner, Professor Adshead, was responsible for laying out the basic plan for the capital city. Today it has grown to take in numerous local African townships and has sprawled far beyond the original plan. The University of Zambia is located at Lusaka, as is

the copper-domed Mulungushi Conference Center that was completed in 1970. Thirty miles south of Lusaka is the new town
of Kafue, which will serve as Lusaka's heavy industrial area.

LUSAKA AFRICAN WELFARE ASSOCIATION. Founded about 1930
by I. Clements Katongo Muwamba and Henry Mashwa Sangandu,
its first chairman and secretary respectively, it was originally
called the Lusaka Native Welfare Association. As such it protested the unsanitary and degrading manner in which Africans
were compelled to buy meat. It also requested the right to
develop farming plots outside the boundaries of the urban townships. This was refused by the Secretary for Native Affairs.
In 1932 it began a campaign against legislation that discriminated against Africans, especially the "pass" law. The officers even met with the acting-Governor of Northern Rhodesia,
but to no avail. In 1933 the members changed the word "Native" in the association's title to "African." At the same time
they were actively protesting against the proposals by some
settlers that Northern and Southern Rhodesia be amalgamated.
With the attempt by Muwamba to organize a national association of welfare associations late in 1933, the Government intervened and restricted the activities of all welfare associations.
In 1943, however, the Lusaka Association again became active,
meeting frequently and again taking up causes in which it could
fight for African interests generally.

LUSAKA INTERNATIONAL AIRPORT. One of the best airports in
Central Africa, it was completed in 1967. It has a hard-
surfaced runway thirteen thousand feet long which can serve
large jets on international flights, including regular service to
Rome and London.

LUSAKA MANIFESTO. A manifesto on relations with Portugal,
Rhodesia, and South Africa, it was signed by fourteen states
from East and Central Africa in Lusaka on April 16, 1969 at
the East and Central Africa Summit Conference. In September,
1969 it was adopted by the OAU Heads of State and subsequently
approved by the United Nations General Assembly. The document is very moderate in tone, advocating peaceful change to
majority rule unless all such attempts fail. It notes that the
states remaining under European rule all differ in their circumstances, and that African responses to each must also differ. Flexibility is the key to the Africans' approach. But, it
warns, without progress, "patience will be exhausted." The
document also explicitly rejects black as well as white racism.
It notes that the whites in southern Africa have strong ties, as
many of them have made their homes there for generations,
and must be considered Africans regardless of their skin color.
Thus cooperation between all peoples of southern Africa for the
benefit of all is the ultimate goal. This can not be achieved,
however, if the white Africans refuse to recognize the legitimate aspirations of black Africans.

LUSAKA NATIVE WELFARE ASSOCIATION. The early name of
the Lusaka African Welfare Association (q. v.).

LUSENGA PLAIN NATIONAL PARK. A game reserve in the Luapula Province in northern Zambia. It is about twenty-five
miles southeast of the southeastern shore of Lake Mweru. The
reserve encompasses about four hundred and fifty square miles.

LUSITU RIVER. A minor tributary of the Zambezi River that
flows into it just prior to (i. e. , south of) the Kafue River's
confluence with the Zambezi. The river's importance in Zambian history is the fact that the important civilization of Ingombe Ilede (q. v.) was near the confluence of the Lusitu and the
Zambezi. Perhaps one reason for the choice of this site for
the capital was the very large salt deposit found along the
Lusitu there. Dr. Livingstone noticed the importance of salt
in the nineteenth century trade when he passed through. The
Lusitu flows from west to east.

LUTANGU. Later known as Sipopa (q. v.) or as Lutangu Sipopa.

LUVALE (or LOVALE; LUBALE; LUENA). One of the major ethnic subdivisions of northwestern Zambia, the Luvale number
over a hundred thousand people today. The Luvale language is
one of the eight official languages of Zambia. Tradition indicates that Chinyama (or Cinyama), a Lunda prince and brother
of Lueji (q. v.), left his homeland in the Shaba or Katanga area
of Zaire in the early seventeenth century and moved west to
the Luena (or Lwena) River near the Upper Zambezi. There
he subdued the local Luena people and set up a chieftainship.
The senior chieftainship today among the Luvale is that of
Kakenga (q. v.), founded by a man called Chinyama Kakenge.
    The Luvale never established a formal state structure,
and chieftainships regularly subdivided, as formal powers of
the chiefs seem to be limited. Lineages play very important
political and ritual roles for the Luvale, and commoner lineages are traced back as far as seventeen or so generations in
some instances. The Luchazi and Chokwe peoples who live
near the Luvale appear to have split from Luvale chiefs in the
recent past. Clans, lineages, and even the territory of the three
groups overlap. All three also are noted for wood carving
and pottery. Luvale lineages combine matrilineal descent systems with virilocal residence.
    The Luvale have strong traditions as hunters and fishers,
but they also developed an interest in growing cassava, which
was traded to the Lozi for cattle. They also traded pottery
and European cloth and beads to the Lozi. The European products came in trade with Portuguese and Brazilian traders in
Angola with whom they traded as early as the eighteenth century. The Luvale also were engaged in armed conflict with
their neighbors. Dr. Livingstone indicated that the neighboring peoples greatly feared the Luvale. In the late nineteenth
century local Luvale chiefs Kangombe and Ndungu threatened

the Lunda of Chief Ishinde (q. v.). An Ndembu Lunda commoner, Chipenge, stopped Kangombe with an armed force, and Lewanika of the Lozi helped Ishinde defeat Ndungu in 1892. With
this victory the Lozi claimed the right to all Luvale land. The
Luvale claimed that only one local Luvale leader (Ndungu) had
been defeated, thus denying the claim. Nevertheless, the Lozi
claim (supported by the BSAC interests) was allowed until the
late 1930's when the Balovale District (q. v.) was separated by
the British from Barotseland. Meanwhile Mambari slave traders were busy supplying the Portuguese in Angola with porters
who they captured among the Luvale and their neighbors. This
slave traffic continued into the first quarter of the twentieth
century. The 1890's were not good years for the Luvale in
other ways. The beginning of the decade saw a smallpox epidemic hit them hard and locusts caused famine among them in
1895.

LUWINGU. An administrative center and a district in the Northern
Province of Zambia. It is located about forty miles north of
Lake Bangweulu. In 1969 the district had a population of about
seventy-nine thousand, a slight decrease since 1963. An ad-
ministrative center had already been established there by the
British South Africa Company prior to 1903.

LUYANA. A word applied to both a group of people (see ALUYANA)
who later were renamed Lozi or Barotse, and to their language.
A number of neighboring groups speak languages which are said
to be in the Luyana family of languages. The most significant
member of that family is Siluyana, the language of the royal
court in Bulozi (Barotseland). While of scholarly interest, it
is an archaic language now spoken only by a small number of
people. As the common language of the Lozi it has been replaced by Silozi (q. v.).

LUYI see ALUYANA

LWAMBI. The second or southern kingdom of the Lozi as established by Ngombala. Its capital is now at Nalolo (q. v.). Its
influence was never as substantial as that of Namuso, the
northern kingdom, but the problem of establishing the proper
hierarchial and political relationship between the two was one
that was not solved until the nineteenth century when Sipopa
(q. v.) began the tradition of appointing a female relative as
ruler at Nalolo.

LWENA. Another name for the Luvale (q. v.).

LYONS, GEORGE. Resident Magistrate of Barotseland from 1916
until his death in 1924. He was to be very unpopular with the
Lozi King Yeta III, who had a continuing dispute with him
from 1919 until Lyons' death. In fact in December, 1923,
Yeta wrote to Richard Goode, the Acting Administrator, requesting that Lyons be transferred. The problem began when

Lyons advised a group of Africans that the Abolition of Slavery
Proclamation of 1906 freed them from certain traditional obligations to the ruling class. Yeta complained that he was un-
dermining the royal authority without having cleared the matter
first with the King and his Council. Two years later Yeta and
his young but well-educated and articulate Council presented
the British High Commissioner in South Africa with a demand
that all concessions to and agreements with the BSAC be canceled. The Lozi complained that the Company had failed to
fulfill its pledges and obligations. When they were turned
down, Lyons became the center of Yeta's anger. Lyons represented the degree to which traditional authority and prerogatives had been undermined by the BSAC. When Yeta demanded
in 1923 that Lyons be replaced, Lyons was outraged and demanded a personal apology from the King. Yeta refused.
Lyons' sudden death in early 1924 mooted the issue.

LYTTELTON, OLIVER (later, VISCOUNT CHANDOS). A member
of the British Conservative Party who replaced James Griffiths
as Colonial Secretary in October, 1951. The next month he
announced that his government agreed fully with the conclusions
of the Victoria Falls conference held in September and that
federation was desirable and even urgent. He announced that
a meeting would be held the next year to follow up on the idea.
This was then done (see LONDON CONFERENCE, 1952). When
Lyttelton visited the Federation in January, 1954, he refused
to meet with the leading African politicians of either Northern
Rhodesia or Nyasaland. Kaunda and Nkumbula timed the beginning of new commercial boycotts to coincide with his visit
to Lusaka.

- M -

MA- . A common prefix to the name of a people, e.g., Ma-
Lozi or Ma-Subiya. The prefix is usually omitted in regular
usage, however.

MAAMBA MINE. Zambia's major supplier of coal, this source
was discovered at Maamba in the Gwembe Valley in 1966. The
mine began production in 1968 and actually supplies more than
Zambia's needs, thus replacing the Wankie mine in Rhodesia
on which Zambia had been dependent for many years. (A mine
at Nkandabwe (q.v.) already had partly replaced Wankie earlier.)
The Maamba mine is wholly owned by the Zambian Government.

MACDONALD, MALCOLM. British Colonial Secretary for much of
the last half of the 1930's. He opposed any amalgamation of
Nyasaland and the Rhodesias because he felt it would be detri-
mental to the best interests of the Africans. He was afraid
that it would produce situations where the non-African minority
would have its interests furthered in place of those of the
African majority.

MACDONELL, PHILIP JAMES. A judge of the High Court who
served as chairman of the Reserves Commissions (q.v.) of
1924 and 1926. Generally pro-African, he favored developing
the reserves in order to allow Africans to produce economic
crops. This, he felt, would help to stabilize village life by
preventing the exodus of African workers. He was displeased
with the ultimate report of the 1924 Commission, feeling that
too many concessions were made to Europeans and an inadequate amount of land was allowed to the Africans.

MACHILI FOREST STATION. The earliest dated Iron Age site in
Zambia, it is on the eastern border of Barotseland. Radiocarbon-dating of the area indicates a settlement existed there
in the first century A.D. Pottery fragments were found, as
well as indications that the people knew how to work iron.

MACLEOD, IAIN. British Colonial Secretary for two years from
October, 1959. A liberal and pragmatic member of the Conservative Party, he was relatively unexperienced in African
matters when appointed, but soon made his mark on Central
Africa. He decided to find a constitutional formula which
would ensure African political advance and might also be acceptable to the European settlers. His strength was in his
ability to find a middle ground between Africans and Europeans.
While his constitutional proposal (see MACLEOD CONSTITU-
TION) was one that neither side wanted, at the same time
neither side felt it could reject it. When he took office he decided that there must be a series of independence constitutions
throughout the British Empire. Thus Kaunda was pleased by
his approach. He arrived in Lusaka in March, 1960, and
made arrangements to meet with all the participants. This
ultimately lead to both the Federal Review Conference (q.v.)
of December, 1960, and the London Constitutional Conference,
1961 (q.v.). On the other hand, when the Litunga and Ngambela of Barotseland flew to London in April, 1961, demanding
of Macleod the right to secede from Northern Rhodesia, the
Colonial Secretary refused. He did reassure the Lozi King
that his rights and those of his people would continue to be
protected, however. And significantly, he restored the right
to use the title of Litunga, rather than the old, limited term,
"Paramount Chief."

MACLEOD CONSTITUTION. As a result of the deadlock at the
London Constitutional Conference, 1961 (q.v.), British Colonial
Secretary, Iain Macleod, presented his own plan on February
20, 1961. It provided for a forty-five member legislature consisting of fifteen upper roll seats, fifteen lower roll, and fifteen "national" constituencies. The plan also insisted that at
least two Africans and two non-Africans be included among the
six Unofficials on the Executive Council. Kenneth Kaunda and
UNIP protested that Africans would be unable to get the upper
roll support for the "national" seats, but reluctantly accepted
the plan. Roy Welensky and his UFP were very critical of
the plan and immediately sought revisions.

Both sides seemed to accept the thirty single-member constituency seats to be decided by the upper and lower rolls. The problem was the "national" seats and the complex vote percentage system involved in determining electoral winners. Welensky feared that it would allow an African majority to be elected. After a series of threats and pressures, in part involving what might happen in Southern Rhodesia, Welensky got Macleod to modify his plan on June 26, 1961. The changes included requiring four of the seven double member constituencies to have one African and one non-African representative. The fifteenth seat would be for Asians or Coloured. In addition, the percentages would be weighted a little differently to aid European candidates. Finally, by-elections would be called to fill any seats frustrated by lack of proper percentages. This time it was the turn of the African leaders to protest. They predicted violent reaction in the African communities. Indeed strife did begin and continued for several months. In mid-September Macleod and Kaunda agreed to further changes in the plan if the disturbances stopped immediately, which they did. Macleod was replaced by Reginald Maudling in October, 1961, and talks continued. On March 1, 1962 it was announced that a minor change was made in the percentages needed to win the "national" seats. While minor, it broke the stalemate and also returned hope to the Africans that they could win a majority of these crucial seats in the election planned for October, 1962.

The Macleod Constitution was only in force until January, 1964, but it served as a transitional governmental form that allowed the Africans to win control of the Northern Rhodesian Government, thus also signalling the end of the Central African Federation and the inevitable independent status for Zambia.

MACMILLAN, HAROLD. British Conservative Party Prime Minister from January, 1957, until October, 1963. It was under his Government that most of the events occurred that brought about the demise of the Central African Federation and the birth of modern Zambia. He created the Monckton Commission (q. v.); he visited the Federation in 1960 personally, experiencing a huge rally of African nationalists at Ndola that denounced the Federation; and he eventually appointed Home Secretary Robert Butler as Minister with special responsibility for the Federation in hopes of resolving the crisis.

MAIZE. One of the most important crops of Zambia, it was originally brought into the area along the trade routes after being brought from America by the Portuguese. It entered Zambia sometime before the end of the eighteenth century. Production of maize in Zambia has ranged generally between 500,000 and 600,000 metric tons a year, but the country has had to import it in some years to meet national needs. The fertile Tonga plateau astride the Kafue River became known as the country's "Maize Belt. "

MAKASA (or MUKASA). The title of a Bemba chieftainship begun
in the early nineteenth century by the Chitimukulu Chiliamfwa
(q. v.). Holders of the title are always sons of a Chitimukulu,
but not always the current one. The chiefdom governed by the
Makasa is called Mpanda (q. v.), and lies north of Lubemba.
The territory includes villages conquered from both the Namwanga and Mambwe, the inhabitants remaining under Bemba
rule.

Several major sources conflict on the early history of the
chieftainship, but it appears probable that the first bearer of
the title was Kalulu, a son of Chiliamfwa. He evidently
reigned for several decades before being killed in a battle with
the Ngoni of Mpezeni in about 1850 at Chisenga. Kalulu's
brother, Chanso, was evidently the next Makasa, but he too
died in battle with the Ngoni.

Makasa III was Bwalya, a son of the reigning Chitimukulu,
Chileshye. Bwalya ruled not only Mpanda but Chilinda (east
of Lubemba) as well. His duty was to protect it against the
Ngoni. He set up a village at Manga, located between the
Kabishya and Mombo Rivers. The Ngoni attacked it unsuccess-
fully and were even followed in retreat by Makasa III. Later
they returned with additional forces and successfully captured
Manga, driving Makasa III to a village where he took refuge.
In about 1870 he returned with a large force representing many
Bemba chieftainships and defeated the Ngoni at Chipekeni (q. v.),
the former site of Manga. Makasa III later killed Mpande V,
an ally of the Ngoni, in 1871 or early 1872, but Makasa III
Bwalya died soon after.

MAKASA IV CHISANGA CHIPEMBA. The son of Chitapankwa, the
Chitimukulu, he was appointed Makasa IV by his father in 1872
after the death of Makasa III Bwalya (see MAKASA). Father
and son lead their combined forces in various attacks on Namwanga, Lungu, and Mambwe country for about the next decade.
Bordering the Mambwe, Makasa IV took advantage of their
military weakness. He later married the daughter of Mpenza,
a Mambwe chief. One of his greatest military successes was
in defeating the Lungu leader, Zombe (q. v.). After his father's
death in 1883, he looted his father's capital, taking especially
Chitapankwa's cattle. This angered Sampa, the new Chitimukulu, who unsuccessfully attacked him at Chiponde. Makasa
did return the cattle, however, and Sampa and Makasa IV later
fought together in a campaign against the Mambwe. Makasa IV
Chisanga Chipemba died in 1890 or 1891.

MAKASA V MUKUUKU MWILWA. A son of Chitimukulu Chileshye,
he was passed over for appointment as Makasa IV by Chitapankwa who appointed his own son instead. However, Mukuuku
Mwilwa was given territory in Chilinda as solace. When Makasa IV died, Chitimukulu Sampa appointed Mukuuku as Makasa V
in about 1891. Nevertheless, he feared Sampa and built his
village on the Luchewe River in the north of Mpanda. He became active in trade with the Swahili, exchanging ivory and

slaves for guns and cloth.   His warriors were well armed.
In part because of his fear of Sampa, and in defiance of him,
Makasa V agreed to allow the White Fathers to set up Kayambi Mission (q.v.) on a hill near his village, Mipini.   He was
first approached in 1894, and in fact sent the missionaries
four freed slaves in mid-year.   At the beginning of 1895 Makasa interceded with Sampa for the missionaries.   In April he
invited the priests to choose a site, and the actual mission
was begun on July 23, 1895 by Rev. Joseph Dupont (q.v.).
While Makasa V never converted to Christianity, he had a deep
respect for Dupont, with whom he liked to have intellectual discussions.   At least one of his sons was a catechumen.

MAKASA, ROBERT SPEEDWELL.   Veteran Zambian nationalist
politician and diplomat, he was born on January 29, 1922, near
Chinsali.   His education began at Lubwa Mission and was eventually concluded on a scholarship to study public administration
at Oxford University.   A teacher and headmaster at Nkula,
Makasa became actively involved in politics in the late 1940's.
He became founder and chairman of the African National Congress branch at Chinsali in 1949.   Kenneth Kaunda served as
secretary, and the two spent most of their off-hours spreading
the ANC message.   His tactics regarding chiefs were widely
adopted in rural areas by UNIP in 1960.   He tried to create a
split between the chiefs and the Government by calling them
its creatures, while at the same time sending circulars to the
chiefs requesting that they lead their people and reject the
Government, perhaps even by joining the nationalist movement.
In 1956 Makasa quit teaching and became Northern Province
President of the ANC; two years later he claimed that there
were 165 branches in the Province.   He spent a year and a
half in jail for organizing a boycott against a merchant who
discriminated against Africans.   At the end of 1958 he led
the province's executive from ANC into ZANC.   During the
mass political arrests of March, 1959, Makasa was detained
at Solwezi.   When he was released he returned to politics, becoming President of UNIP's Luapula Province branch.   From
1961 to 1963 he was in Dar es Salaam, Tanzania as chairman
of the Pan-African Freedom Movement's refugee committee.
In 1964 he was elected to parliament from Chinsali.   In 1967
he became Minister of State for Foreign Affairs, and moved
the next year to Minister for the Northern Province.   His service since then has included diplomatic posts in Ethiopia, Tanzania, and Kenya.

MAKOLO (sing., Likolo).   An important form of social and political organization among the Lozi until their conquest by the
Makololo in the nineteenth century, it has now vanished from
the contemporary scene.   It seems to have begun under Mboo
(q.v.), the first Lozi King, who allowed some of his "brothers"
and "sisters" to create groups of men for military and labor
purposes.   These Makolo groups had leaders appointed for
them by the royals.   Thus territory could be distributed by

the King to the royals who had their own Makolo to aid them.
It is possible in the early days that these groups were actually
bands of followers, even relatives of the leader. The tradition may have come from the Lunda, or may have existed
among groups in the area before the Lozi arrived. At its
peak, the Makolo system included all Lozi. Everyone became
a member of his or her father's or guardian's Likolo at birth.
Unlike other African "regiment" systems that were primarily
military and based on age-groupings, the Makolo were kinship
and labor units.

Each Likolo was headed by an <u>induna</u> (councillor) at the
capital. Each Likolo had a site there where members could
reside while visiting or while trying to influence the decision-
makers through his induna. All Makolo had distinctive names
as well.

As leadership among the Lozi became more centralized in
the King, only he could create new Makolo and appoint their
leaders. He could also call upon them for public work or for
military duty. Some regular duties were assigned to certain
Makolo, such as providing salt to the capital. The system
was sometimes used to aid in the integration of conquered
peoples and land by making them subsections of existing Makolo. Thus the whole system was always being adapted to meet
the needs of the nation.

When the Lozi were overrun by the Makololo people around
1840, the Makolo system was disrupted. Although the Lozi
regained their kingdom in 1864, the Makolo system never regained its old importance. Occasionally the names of old Likolo would be used, notably during the 1885 civil war when Lubosi (Lewanika) is said to have led a certain Likolo against
one led by Mataa. As part of the attempt by Lewanika to restore a strong, centralized monarchy, he had tried to revive
the Makolo system. He even followed tradition by creating a
Likolo for his own reign, a practice abandoned by his two
predecessors. Nevertheless the revival was not really successful. It only alienated certain important indunas who would lose
a body of followers they had built up since the system's earlier
demise. Thus the project was abandoned and the system was
allowed to die, even though some indunas retained their titles
as Makolo heads a half century later.

MAKOLOLO (or KOLOLO). A Sotho-speaking people from the area
of the Orange Free State in South Africa who moved north and
had significant influence on the people of southern and western
Zambia for the three decades from the 1830's to the 1860's.
Their origin was in the same chaotic movement of peoples,
motivated by the attacks of the Zulu leader Chaka, that resulted in the Ndebele (q.v.) moving into Southern Rhodesia.
Like the Ndebele, the Makololo were warriors and herdsmen.
They were followers of Sebituane, a chief of the Fokeng, a
Sotho tribe, who fled north through what is now Botswana in
about 1823. Attracted by the cattle of the southern Zambian
peoples, especially the Tonga and Ila, they crossed the Zambezi

at Kazungula, upstream of the Victoria Falls, in the early
1830's. (Much of the story of the Makololo is told here under
the entries of their two major leaders: SEBITUANE and his
son SEKELETU.)

The major influence of the Makololo on Zambian history
stems from their victories over the Lozi, who they conquered
in about 1840 and ruled for almost twenty-five years. During
this time the Makololo controlled most of western Zambia, and
south across the Caprivi Strip into northeastern Botswana.
Their language is still the language of the Lozi today, and in
fact the word "Lozi" was a term they applied to the people
previously called Aluyana.

The only other group that caused the Makololo concern was
the Ndebele (q.v.), whom they greatly feared, but whom they
defeated in several battles. The other major problem to face
them was the fact that the Makololo capital was in a malaria-
ridden area near the Chobe River, and the fever gradually
decimated the tribe. Dr. Livingstone spent some time with
them in the early 1850's and noted the declining number of
able-bodied men. With their leader, Sekeletu, dying in 1863
and a succession dispute growing, the fever-weakened Makololo
were easy prey and were defeated at the hands of the Lozi in
August, 1864. The defeat was so total that a missionary who
had worked with them a few years earlier wrote in December
of that year that "there is not a vestige left of the tribe as
such." Yet thirty years earlier there were over thirty thousand Makololo.

MAKOSHI. The title of the "Queen Mother" or "Mother of the
King" among the Lozi. It is an office that is said to have begun when Mbuyu (q.v.) abdicated Lozi leadership to her son
Mboo. She thus became the first Makoshi. It is the duty of
the Makoshi to preside over the Anatambumu (q.v.).

MAKUMBA, CHIMFWEMBE MULENGA. Successor of his cousin
Sampa as the Chitimukulu of the Bemba, he reigned from 1898
until his death in 1911. There was some dispute over his
right to succession, but he received some physical support
from Chikwanda II and seized Sampa's wives near the beginning
of 1897, thus giving him the traditional right to the title. However his major opponent, Mwamba III, immediately attacked
them and took Makumba prisoner. After a series of bad
omens, Mwamba released Makumba, and conceded the title to
him, undoubtedly noting that Makumba's advanced age should
result in a short reign. Mwamba also found it easy to en-
croach into Makumba's territory without opposition. In 1903
Ponde (q.v.) was able to do much the same, as Makumba became increasingly senile. When he died in 1911, Makumba
was succeeded by Chikwanda.

MAKWAMBUYU. The most important group within the Lozi traditional court, they were full-blooded aristocrats who always sat
at the right-hand of the Litunga (King) in the meetings of the

Kuta. The Ngambela and Natamoyo both belonged to it. Its
numbers varied, as the King could create new titles or elevate
Indunas to higher ranks. The leaders of the Makolo (q. v.)
were chosen from this group as well, as it was also the duty
of members of the Makwambuyu to be liaisons with the public.
Despite their high-standing, however, they were not immune to
public punishment for crimes or insubordination, as King Lewanika demonstrated in February, 1897.

MAKWANGWA. Variant of Kwangwa (q. v.).

MALARIA. A major health problem in Zambia, it has become the
principal target for the country's health program. The malaria
parasite lives in and destroys red blood cells, causing chills,
high fever, and anemia. It is carried by the mosquito, a
creature that flourishes in Zambia's many swampy and low-
lying areas, however even the urban areas have experienced
outbreaks of it. Periodically it has caused devastation among
some tribes. The Makololo of Chief Sebituane were especially
hard hit by it when Dr. David Livingstone visited them in 1851,
a fact that contributed greatly to the loss of their political influence in southwestern Zambia in the following decade or so.

MALAWI. Known as Nyasaland until its independence on July 6,
1964, it is Zambia's immediate neighbor to the east. For the
ten years from 1953 to 1963 it was part of the Central African
Federation with the Rhodesias. Both countries are now independent, but relations between them are not as good as they
might be. This stems in part from the very conservative
foreign policy of Malawi's President, Dr. Hastings Kamuzu
Banda (q. v.).

MALUMA. A Tonga spiritualist who led his people in defiance of
attempts by the Native Commissioner to collect taxes in 1909
and 1910. He urged that his people overthrow the colonial regime and "drive all white people out of the country. " Maluma
actually led the Tonga in an unsuccessful attack, but British
troops arrested him and restored order. Taxes were then collected, albeit irregularly.

MALVERN, LORD see HUGGINS, GODFREY

MAMBARI. A term applied usually to the traders of mixed race
(Portuguese-African) who traveled from Angola to western and
southern Zambia to do business; however, it was sometimes
also applied to an African people, the Ovimbundu, who worked
closely with them. They usually traded cloth and guns for
slaves and ivory. Most of this trade occurred during the nineteenth century. Among their major trading partners were the
Lozi, Makololo, Lamba, Luvale, Kaonde, Tonga, Ila and Lunda.
Occasionally they would join in slave raids with Africans, such
as joining Mpepe (q. v.) of the Makololo in raids against the
Ila and Tonga. By 1912 the last Mambari slavers seem to
have disappeared from the country.

MAMBWE. One of the more significant ethnic and language groups
in Zambia. While there are about sixty-three thousand Mambwe
in the country, there are almost four times that number of
Mambwe-speakers. Most numerous of these are the Lungu
(q. v.), from whom the Mambwe are derived, plus the Iwa,
Tambo, and Namwanga.

The Mambwe are a farming people, but they also keep
cattle, a practice derived from their East African ancestors.
They have produced cotton for many years, being among the
first Zambian peoples to weave cloth from their own cotton.
Somewhat unique to them is the fact that they have traditionally used grass as a fertilizer, resulting in better agricultural
yields.

The Mambwe live in the extreme northeastern part of Zambia, near both Tanzania and the Bemba. Their origins seem
to be dual. The royal clan reputedly came from the area of
Zaire and might have been Lunda. Most of the Mambwe clans
(there are over sixty), however, are East African. They seem
to have split away from the neighboring Lungu sometime in the
early nineteenth century. Unlike most Zambians, the Mambwe
follow a patrilineal descent system and a patrilocal residence
pattern. When they lived in great fear of the Bemba, they
lived in large stockaded villages of two hundred or more huts,
but today a village may have as few as twenty to sixty huts.
The exterior walls of the huts are likely to contain very dis-
tinctively designed wall paintings.

The Paramount Chief of the Mambwe is found in the Nsokolo (q. v.) chieftainship, but before it existed there was a
Mambwe chief called Chindo, who appears to have been the
leader of the Mambwe from East Africa. Another Mambwe
group called Nkondo was led by a chief named Ntachimbwa ("I
take no prisoners") in the early 1800's, and lived in Bemba
country. Another southern Mambwe leader, Mpande II, was
killed by the Bemba early in the nineteenth century. A later
leader perhaps Mpande V, submitted to Ngoni force in the mid-
nineteenth century, and in fact joined with the Ngoni in defeating two of the paramount chiefs, Nsokolos VIII and IX.

Additionally the Mambwe came under the attack of various
Bemba leaders, so that they ultimately welcomed the installation of mission stations in their territory by the London Missionary Society in 1884 and 1887, and by the White Fathers in
1891. In 1890 Harry Johnston found two Mambwe chiefs,
Fwambo and Kela, who were willing to sign treaties. An administrative station followed in July, 1891, which the Mambwe
believed would help protect them against the Bemba. Over
two decades later some of the Mambwe had regrets over their
willingness to accept the intrusion of the Europeans, and in
1917 the Watch Tower Movement found many adherents among
the Mambwe.

MAMBWE MWELA (or OLD MAMBWE). A mission station, the
first set up by the White Fathers, that was established in July,
1891, by Father Lechaptois. It was near the Stevenson Road

(q. v.) in the eastern part of Mambwe country. The White Fathers would use this as a stepping stone into Bemba territory.
At times the mission became a sanctuary for Mambwe people
who feared Bemba attacks. In 1893 Sir Harry Johnston gave
the missionaries the right to acquire guns and ammunition to
help ward off attacks by Arab slave traders and Bemba raiders.
Later that year the White Fathers considered abandoning the
mission, but conditions eased, and Father Joseph Dupont (q. v.)
took over its leadership in May, 1895. When Dupont founded
Kayambi mission (q. v.) in July, however, Mambwe became unnecessary, and it closed in September. In August, 1896 the
missionaries formally abandoned it by selling it to the British
South Africa Company.

MAMILI (or MOWA MAMILI). A Lozi Ngambela (Prime Minister)
who replaced Njekwa in 1872, he was not especially favorable
toward the King, Sipopa. He finally organized a rebellion
against Sipopa and in 1876 had a force ready to attack him,
but Sipopa was assassinated before the battle could occur.
Mamili then successfully put forward the royal candidacy of a
teen-ager, Mwanawina. Very ambitious, Mamili soon pre-
empted numerous royal prerogatives and official protocol, an-
gering both the young King and the indunas. Finally they had
Mamili and his children and his elder brother executed in
about 1878.
    Another man named Mamili was the uncle of Sekeletu,
chief of the Makololo. When the latter died at Linyanti in
August, 1863, Mamili seized power and tried to establish his
son as successor. They were challenged by Mpololo (q. v.),
however, and were driven from Linyanti in October. They
fled to Lake Ngami, where Mamili was killed.

MAMOCHISANE. The daughter of the great Makololo chief, Sebituane, she was appointed by her father to be in charge of Nalolo, the southern capital of the Lozi who were under Sebituane's control. She was also his chosen successor, and when
he died in July, 1851 she became the tribal leader. Sebituane's
nephew Mpepe (q. v.) was her stand-in during certain ceremonies and also had ambition of his own. When he tried to
control her politically, Mamochisane tired of the stress of politics and decided to return to the role of a family woman. She
abdicated in favor of Sekeletu (q. v.), her younger half-brother.

MANDUMELETI. Lozi indunas who represented the Litunga (King)
among subject peoples outside Bulozi, such as among the Subiya and Nkoya. Their duty was to ensure a steady supply of
both laborers and tribute as needed in the Lozi homeland.

MANGE. A brother or probably a nephew of Mboo (q. v.), the
first Lozi King, he traveled east into the forest area outside
the valley and became leader of the Makwangwa people. According to tradition, he broke away because he was not included in the ruling elite. This area was later reconquered
by King Ngalama (q. v.) and restored to Lozi control.

MANKOYA. Both a place name in the Western Province of Zambia and a word used to designate the Nkoya (q. v.) people. In about 1970 the town and district called Mankoya were renamed Kaoma (q. v.). At that time the district, constituting the northeastern quarter of the Western Province, had a population of about fifty-seven thousand. The town (the district's administrative center) is located on the southern bank of the Luena River, in the eastern part of what was previously called Barotseland.

MANNING, COLONEL WILLIAM. Commander of the British Central Africa Rifles who left Blantyre on January 2, 1898 with a force of about 650 men in an attempt to subdue the Ngoni led by Mpezeni. The battle began on January 16 and lasted for several days. The results were defeat for the Ngoni, who had very few guns to use against the heavily armed British force, and the capture of Mpezeni (q. v.).

MANSA. The name of a town and district in the Luapula Province of Zambia. It is immediately east and north of the Congo (or Katanga) Pedicle that cuts into Zambia. In 1969 the district had a population of about eighty-one thousand people. The town of Mansa, the district's administrative center, is located about thirty miles east of the Luapula River and the Zaire border. Its population in 1969 was 5700 people. Until independence it was known as Fort Rosebery (q. v.).

MARAVI. Central African peoples who eventually settled, for the most part, in the territory which now bears a version of their name, Malawi. Some people derived from the Maravi live today in Zambia, where they are called the Chewa and the Nsenga (qq. v.).

MARSHALL, HUGH CHARLES. Long-time administrator for the British South Africa Company, he was sent by Harry Johnston (q. v.) to be the Collector of Revenue in 1891 at Chiromo in northeastern Zambia. He was assigned the duty to collect a variety of specific taxes from the Africans. Two years later he was appointed Magistrate and Collector for the Tanganyika District, north of Bemba country. He set up his administrative center at Abercorn near the village of Mbala, building an impregnable stockade which eventually became a sanctuary for many Africans fleeing Bemba raids. This post, he was told, would be well located for keeping a check on slave caravan routes to the Indian Ocean as well as for helping to defend white settlements near Lake Tanganyika from Bemba attack. (He was sent Sikh police to help him.) He was also instructed to try to establish good relations with the Bemba, as circumstances permitted. One important Bemba leader, Ponde (q. v.), spurned his friendly overtures.

In later years Marshall served as a higher level administrator for brief periods. From May until August, 1911, he was Acting Administrator of North-Eastern Rhodesia, and from

August 1920, until March, 1921, he was Acting Administrator
of Northern Rhodesia.

MASHASHA (or BAMESHASHA). One of Zambia's smaller ethnic
sub-groups, consisting of about nine thousand people. They
speak the language of the Nkoya (q. v.), and live in southwestern Zambia, east of the Lozi and west of the Ila.

MASHI. Among the smallest distinct sub-groups in Zambia, the
Mashi only number about nine thousand and live in the extreme
southwestern corner of the country. Tradition among the Lozi
says that a brother of their first King, Mboo, went to settle
there. His name was Ilishua, and he took his two sons with
him. The Mashi are Luyana-speaking people. Lozi officials
lived among them along the middle Kwando River in 1899,
forcing them to pay tribute.

MASHI RIVER. Also known as the Kwando, Linyanti or Chobe (q. v.).

MASHUKULUMBWE. Another name for the people usually called
the Ila (q. v.). Dr. David Livingstone spelled it Bashukulompo.
The word originated among their neighbors and conquerors,
the Lozi, and is a descriptive term referring to their charac-
teristic coiffure. The Ila do not like the word. Taxes were
imposed on them in 1906, and in July, 1907, the Collector
became convinced that an uprising was impending. Thus the
administrators, settlers, and even the missionaries prepared
for what was called the Mashukulumbwe Rebellion. Whether
or not a rebellion was in fact planned, the Ila never made a move.

MASTER PLAN. Related to the so-called "Cha Cha Cha campaign"
(q. v.) in 1961, the Master Plan was the response of UNIP and
Kaunda to the unsatisfactory Macleod Constitution. The burning of Identification Certificates (I. C. s or "passes") was the
first stage. The destruction of roads and bridges then occurred as the next stage. Stage three never was needed as
Colonial Secretary Maudling made adjustments in the election
formula that satisfied UNIP.

MATAA. At least three individuals with this name have made their
mark in Zambian history. One, Mubukwanu Mataa became secretary and later principal advisor to Lozi King Yeta III in the
1920's. His father had been appointed Ngambela late in 1919
and used the title Ngambela Mataa. Father and son were both
very close to the King, but in December, 1928, they were arrested for the ritual murder of two women. They were both
acquitted, but Yeta released them from their positions, perhaps because suspicion remained in the minds of many.
An earlier man named Mataa also became Ngambela and
played an important part in Lozi history. He was an ambitious
induna who was already seeking a higher post in the 1860's as
the Lozi were retaking their kingdom from the Makololo. He
was the son of Mwala, who had earlier betrayed the Lozi by
revealing a revolutionary plot to the Makololo.

With the overthrow of the young King Mwanawina in 1878 by several dissident Lozi groups, Mataa intrigued to get Musiwa, a son of Sipopa, on the throne. He was unsuccessful, however, and another group succeeded in getting Lubosi (later called Lewanika) as King. Mataa felt insecure, both because of his support of Musiwa and because his father's actions had resulted in the death of Lubosi's father Litia. Through duplicity he tried to win Lubosi's favor, but it was discovered by Lubosi by March, 1879. Nevertheless, for his aid in defeating Mwanawina, he was appointed Namuyamba by Lubosi.

Unsatisfied with this post (he aspired to be Ngambela), Mataa became very critical toward Lubosi and was the center of opposition to him. By early 1884 Lubosi knew Mataa would try something against him. As Mataa organized a coup, his chief ally was Numwa (q.v.), a bodyguard of the King. The actual uprising occurred in July, 1884, with Lubosi barely escaping with his life, as Mataa had united several groups of dissidents. Two months later Mataa became Ngambela, as his "candidate," Tatila Akufuna (q.v.), became King. Mataa intended to rule, with the king as his puppet. Other appointments went to Mataa's supporters; and he even welcomed Rev. F. Coillard (q.v.), who he had opposed in 1878, and offered him a mission site, hoping to add European sanction to his authority.

Mataa's downfall had two roots. First, there was a core of loyalists which would try to restore Lubosi as King. Second, Akufuna proved to be a very unpopular king, and even Mataa decided that he must be replaced. Mataa managed to defeat one loyalist force, but while he and Numwa were at Lukwakwa escorting their new king candidate, Sikufele, back to the valley, two large forces gathered by Lubosi and Silumbu (q.v.) prepared to attack them. Of the five principals just mentioned, only Lubosi survived the battle in early November, 1885. Lubosi now became known as King Lewanika.

MATABELE. Variant of Ndebele (q.v.).

MATAUKA. Born in 1842, the twin sister of Lubosi/Lewanika (King of the Lozi), she was appointed by him to be Mulena Mukwae (q.v.) at Nalolo, the Lozi second (and southern) capital. Fiercely loyal to her brother, she of course lost her position after the 1884 coup that led to a Lozi civil war. She was also very active in the counter-rebellion that restored her brother to the kingship, and thus regained her title near the end of 1885. She died in 1934.

MATEBELE. Variant of Ndebele (q.v.).

MATERO ECONOMIC REFORMS. Announced in a speech by President Kenneth Kaunda on August 11, 1969, at Matero, outside Lusaka, the reforms instituted new rules for the sharing of Zambia's copper wealth. First, the government would acquire a 51 percent share in the ownership of the mines. Payment,

it was later determined, would come out of the mines' own
dividends during roughly the next decade. Second, taxes in
the industry were recalculated in a manner that gave incentive
for expansion, while remaining at about the same level (73
percent of profits). Finally, it was declared that all mining
rights in Zambia were being appropriated by the Government.
The greatest practical effect of this was to give the Government more power over where new mining would begin (preferably less developed areas) and the power to grant mining licenses on condition that actual production would soon occur.

MATIPA. One of the most important of the Bisa (q.v.) chieftainships, its chief is always a member of the bena ng'ona or
Mushroom Clan. The chief rules a territory called Lubumbu,
which is a little to the northeast of Lake Bangweulu. The
first chief to hold the title of Matipa was named Muma, and
had succeeded Nkalamo as chief of Lubumbu about 1840. He
became known as Matipa I Muma, and ruled there until his
death in 1883.
     During the reign of Matipa I, Lubumbu was repeatedly at-
tacked or threatened by the Bemba, causing him to lead his
people periodically in flight to one or another island on the
lake. In the 1840's the Bisa fled to Nsumbu Island after attacks on their mainland capital by Mwamba I. All of Matipa's
children were killed by the Bemba. After Mwamba I died in
the late 1850's, Matipa returned to Lubumbu with the aid of
"magic" he received from Lungu leaders. Later a Lungu chief,
Mukupa Kaoma III asked for Matipa's aid to fight Mwamba II,
but the Bemba won the battle on the Lusenga River. In the
early 1870's Mwamba II attacked Matipa for his earlier support
of the Lungu. Matipa and his people fled the mainland, settling on Nsumbu Island after another Bisa chief turned him away
from Chilubi Island. Dr. David Livingstone visited him on
Nsumbu in 1873. Soon after, Matipa took over Chilubi Island
from its occupants where his people still lived when Matipa I
died in 1883.
     An early twentieth-century Matipa chief angered several
other African groups by supplying canoes to BSAC officials,
thus allowing them to reach the islands and tax them. The administrators had assisted him in gaining the contested chieftainship in 1902.

MATOKA, PETER WILFRED. An experienced administrator, he
was Minister of Development and Planning in 1975-76 and in
1977 became Minister of Economics and Technical Co-operation.
Although he was a civil servant without a very active record in
nationalist politics, he was appointed Minister of Information
and Posts at independence. In 1965 he was made Minister of
Health, and two years later Minister of Works (later called
Power, Transport and Works). He also served as Minister of
the Luapula Province and High Commissioner to London before
returning on June 1, 1971, to again become Minister of Health.
He also served as Minister of Local Government and Culture

(72-73) and of Local Government and Housing (73-75) before
receiving his current appointment.
     Born in the North-Western Province in 1930, Matoka was
educated at Munali Secondary School (q. v.), and at Ft.
Hare University College in South Africa (B. A., 1954). In 1964 he
was awarded a diploma in international relations at the American University in Washington. In the interim he had been a
civil servant.

MATRILINEAL DESCENT. A form of social and political organiza-
     tion, it is commonly found throughout most of Zambia, with a
     few exceptions in the extreme northeast and in the west. Zam-
     bia is somewhat unique in this custom, since most Africans
     practice patrilineal descent. Zambia is located directly within
     the so-called "matrilineal belt" that stretches across Africa.
          The matrilineal descent system follows the female line for
     the sake of inheritance and tracing blood lines. Property or
     titles may pass from brother to brother, but when the last
     brother is deceased they pass on to the sons of the sisters,
     not their own sons. Matrilineal societies may also be matri-
     local, meaning that men move to the village or area of their
     wife (as opposed to a virilocal society in which the woman
     moves to the area of her husband's family).

MATTAKO, J. ERNEST C. An early political activist, in 1930 he
     became a founder and vice-chairman of the Livingstone Native
     Welfare Association (q. v.). A court interpreter by profession,
     Mattako was transferred that same year to Ndola, and late in
     1930 he joined with a few others in forming a similar associa-
     tion there.

MAUDLING, REGINALD. Successor to Iain Macleod as British
     Colonial Secretary in October, 1961, it was his decision four
     months later that broke the constitutional stalemate. He an-
     nounced to the House of Commons on February 28, 1962, that
     he would agree to a slight modification in the Macleod Consti-
     tution (q. v.). The change would reduce the qualifying per-
     centage of votes in the "national" constituencies from $12\frac{1}{2}$ per-
     cent to 10 percent and remove the "or 400 votes" phrase.
     While this change seemingly made it all but impossible for
     anyone to win the seats, it was a constitutional plan that UNIP
     could accept. Thus the 1962 elections took place, and Kenneth
     Kaunda became Prime Minister.

MAXWELL, SIR JAMES CRAWFORD. Governor of Northern Rho-
     desia from 1927 to 1932. Educated as a doctor at the Univer-
     sity of Edinburgh, he served as a Medical Officer in Sierra
     Leone early in his colonial service, but later was Colonial
     Secretary in the Gold Coast where he became familiar with the
     administrative policy called Indirect Rule (q. v.). He intro-
     duced it in 1929 to all of Northern Rhodesia except the Barotse
     Province. He developed a generous and respectful approach to
     the Lozi King that pleased the latter. Maxwell did recommend

cautiously to the Lozi that certain changes in both administration and the courts would correct some obvious abuses.

Maxwell was very much opposed to any thought of amalgamation with Southern Rhodesia, a point on which he fully agreed with Lord Passfield (q. v.), the British Colonial Secretary. He did, however, encourage European immigration as long as it was carefully planned and land was only alienated in large enough units to be productive. When the worldwide Depression hit Northern Rhodesia in the early 1930's, Maxwell discouraged unemployed whites from staying in the territory. He feared they would drain the Treasury of funds that should be used on the Africans or even take lower jobs, thus leaving Africans unemployed. He felt that unskilled and semi-skilled whites should be given the same treatment as Africans by the Government, otherwise a color bar would be created.

Maxwell is also remembered for the fact that early work on the construction of the territorial capital at Lusaka began during his term as Governor.

MAYBIN, SIR JOHN ALEXANDER. Governor of Northern Rhodesia from 1938 to 1941. Born in Scotland and a graduate of the University of Edinburgh, he had served in Nigeria and other British territories before being assigned to Central Africa. He was in agreement with the Bledisloe Commission's Report which said that amalgamation of the Rhodesias and Nyasaland was not desirable at that time. He felt that native policies in the three territories would have to be standardized in a way agreeable to Africans as well before it could be considered. Southern Rhodesia's policies toward Africans were totally unacceptable, he felt, and job segregation especially must be rejected. He did see some economic advantages to amalgamation, but not at the expense of the Africans. He also saw no advantage to amalgamation with Nyasaland, as there were no real economic ties between the two territories.

Maybin also opposed the formation of an Inter-Territorial Council, which he saw as a waste of time and money. It also would create a body that would continue to push for amalgamation, he correctly predicted. While he did meet with leaders of the other territories to coordinate war efforts in 1940, he did not intend these meetings to have further political ramifications.

While he saw some advantages in increased European immigration, Maybin also feared it would result in more land being lost by Africans to whites. It would also result in the social disintegration of African peoples and their traditions. He felt that policy toward the Africans should be based on their traditional institutions, albeit adapted to modern life. To aid in administration, he saw to it that African clerks received improved training.

MAZABUKA. The most populated district in Zambia's Southern Province with over 160,000 people in 1969, Mazabuka bears the name of the town that is also its administrative center.

The town of Mazabuka lies along the line of rail south of the
Kafue River and serves the major European farming areas
nearby. Its population in 1969 was about 9400. The district
is one of the northernmost of the Southern Province, and part
of it is not much more than twenty-five miles from Lusaka.

MBALA (ABERCORN). One of the two northeasternmost districts
of the country, the Mbala district in the Northern Province includes most of the southern shore of Lake Tanganyika, as well
as about sixty miles of land border with Tanzania. The district had a population of ninety-four thousand people in 1969.
    The town of Mbala (known as Abercorn (q. v.) until after
Zambian independence) lies on a branch of the Great North
Road that continues to the railhead at Mpanda in Tanzania. In
1969 Mbala had a population of about fifty-two hundred people.

MBANGA. A Lozi ruler who succeeded his sister, Notulu (q. v.)
who had abdicated.

MBENI DANCE SOCIETY. While primarily a dancing society of
Bemba, its semi-secret nature and a similarity between the
cross on its uniforms and one that appeared on notices calling
for mine strikes in May, 1935, led mine and government officials to suspect that it was playing a role in the disturbances
that took place. No conclusive evidence was found, but some
observers feel that it did form a useful link between mines in
the absence of formal political organizations.

MBIKUSITA, GODWIN (also known as LEWANIKA, GODWIN MBI-
KUSITA). The word "ubiquitous" has been aptly used to describe this man, whose life and career tie together virtually
all of modern Zambian history. Born in 1907 at the court of
King Lewanika, he claimed to be the King's son and, presumably, this has since been accepted by the necessary authorities
as he spent the last eight and a half years of his life as the
Lozi King. At the Barotse National School he demonstrated
great intelligence and went on to both the University of South
Africa and the University of Wales (where he studied Social
Welfare). In 1935, after having worked as a Government clerk,
he was made Private Secretary to King Yeta III. In May,
1938, he went to London with the King for the British coronation, where they met the new King and also visited Paris. He
did not return home, however, as he was suspected of being
involved with Edward Kalue (q. v.) in a plot to overthrow Yeta.
    In 1941 he returned to Zambia, eventually becoming a
Senior African Welfare Officer for the Rhokana Corporation in
Nkana. A few years later he became the President of the
Kitwe African Society (q. v.). This led to his involvement in
the creation of the Federation of African Societies of Northern
Rhodesia (q. v.) in May, 1946. When that organization became
the Northern Rhodesian African Congress (q. v.) in 1948, he was
elected its president. His work at the lead of the country's
first true African nationalist organization did not satisfy some

activists, however, and he was replaced in 1951 by Harry
Nkumbula.

Meanwhile he had become active in labor unions as well.
Mbikusita lost to Lawrence Katilungu in a bid to head the African Mineworkers Union in 1947. In 1953 he became a leader
of the rival Mines African Staff Association (q.v.), composed
of salaried staff and supervising workers in the mines.

Mbikusita also returned to Barotseland. In about 1954 he
began the Barotse National Association (q.v.) designed initially
to show support for the Barotse National Government (although
another faction later reversed this). He also went to Switzer-
land where he took a course on Moral Re-Armament. He returned to Barotseland in 1956 and was nominated for the post
of Ngambela, but he was second in the balloting.

A supporter of the Central African Federation, he nevertheless stayed out of its politics until 1958 when he became
the first African member of the United Federal Party of Roy
Welensky. In November of that year he was elected with its
support to the Federal Assembly. He continued to support the
concept of "partnership" there, and even declared that apartheid
was an experiment, and as such he did not oppose it. He
eventually was made a junior minister in the Assembly. As a
Lozi "royal" and a member of the UFP he became part of a
curious proposal whereby Welensky would allow the breakup of
the Federation if Southern Rhodesia, the Copperbelt, and Barotseland (to supply labor for the Copperbelt) would be united
in a new Federation.

In 1967 Mbikusita was appointed to the Lozi House of
Chiefs, and the King then appointed him to the post of Natamoyo (q.v.). When the King died the next year, Mbikusita
was appointed his successor and installed on December 15,
1968. He died early in 1977.

MBOO (or MWANASILUNDU; MUYUNDA). The son of Mbuyu (q.v.)
and recognized as the founder of the present Luyi dynasty (now
called the Lozi). Preceding him, his mother was a noted
figurehead but not really an effective central leader. When
she abdicated to her eldest son, Mboo, he introduced such important institutions as indunas, the Makolo system, and the
payment of tribute. All of these were in a very elementary
stage, however, and the kingdom was not really very centralized.
Nor was it very extensive, for while he conquered a number of
groups within what is now the Kalambo District, he was stopped
in attempts to expand eastward along the Luena Flats, probably
by an Nkoya group. Essentially his territory was all within
the Kalabo region. In addition, several of his relatives, notably Mwanambinyi and Mange (qq.v.) broke away from his
rule.

Mboo's significance lies primarily in the fact that it is
from him that all claimants to the Lozi throne must demonstrate ancestry.

MBOWE. A small group of about thirteen thousand people who live

west of the Zambezi River and are considered to be part of
the Luyana sub-group of the Barotse language group.

MBUNDA. A distinct ethnic group of about sixty-seven thousand
people, they belong to the Lunda-Luvale linguistic sub-group.
They originated in Angola, but today live primarily in north-
western Zambia where, along with several other groups, they
are sometimes collectively referred to as Balovale. Today the
Mbunda are noted as excellent wood carvers, with their carved
masks especially in demand.
     The Mbunda probably arrived in Zambia in the late eigh-
teenth century, led by two chiefs, Mwene Ciengele (q. v.) and,
later, Mwene Kandala. The Mbunda were a highly decentralized people, relying more on local groups controlled by the
elders than on complex state systems. But each small group
had its Mwene or chief. They brought with them crops that
had been introduced by the Portuguese, notably cassava, millet,
and a small type of yam.
     The newcomers settled near the Lozi, in the vicinity of
Mongu and along the eastern forest. They revolutionized military tactics in the area, being expert with bows and arrows,
weapons unfamiliar to the Lozi, and they had a fighting axe of
special quality called the bukana (q. v.). The Lozi and Mbunda
combined to defeat both the Luvale and Nkoya in the area and
then other groups. Mwene Ciengele was given the status of a
Lozi prince and given a seat in the Kuta. The Lozi tried to
absorb them through the Makolo (q. v.) system, however, differences in their religious beliefs and political systems made
this impossible.
     The Mbunda became directly involved in Lozi politics
around 1830 when they participated in a succession dispute involving Silumelume (q. v.), who an Mbunda warrior killed.
Thirty years later, after the Makololo were evicted from Bulozi, Mbunda groups at Lukwakwa helped Sipopa overthrow and
kill Imasiku. They also sided with Musiwa, a competitor
of Lubosi, in 1880. When Lubosi discovered their involvement
in a scheme to protect Musiwa (see MATAA), Lubosi ordered
many Mbunda killed. Some crossed back into Angola to avoid
the attack, but those who remained and survived the murders
never forgave the King (Lubosi/Lewanika) and remained opponents of him.

MBUYU (or MBUYWAMWAMBWA). "The daughter of Mwambwa"
or "The daughter of God," she is the ancestress of the royal
line of the Lozi. She was an Aluyana princess who led her
people before they settled in Bulozi. She abdicated in favor of
her son, Mboo (q. v.), who became the first king in the new
Aluyana (later called the Lozi) dynasty. Mbuyu's divine origin
is insisted upon by the Lozi, who see this as an important
reason for retaining the specific ruling family.

MBUYWAMWAMBWA. Variant of Mbuyu (q. v.).

MBWELA. Some of the earliest Congolese migrants into West-
Central Africa, their descendants today are probably the people
known as Nkoya (q. v.). New groups followed in the sixteenth
and seventeenth centuries to either displace them or dominate
them. Among these were Lunda from the north led especially
by Kanongesha (q. v.). The Mbwela were also called the Lukolwe by the invaders. But the old name survived, as an
early twentieth-century missionary reports of the "Bembwela,"
and especially their leader, Kale (q. v.).

McKINNON, CHARLES. One of the first BSAC administrators to
get actively involved in conflicts with the Bemba, he was appointed Collector at Ikawa in the "Chambezi District" early in
1897. From the beginning McKinnon expressed interest in exploiting splits among Bemba leaders, notably those involving
the ambitious Bemba chief, Mwamba. He also requested that
the Company supply better military equipment, including a
Maxim gun, but the latter never came.

McKinnon's opposition to Mwamba was complicated by the
fact that the Bemba leader had the support of Arab slave traders. McKinnon sent his assistant, Robert Young (q. v.) to set
up a new boma at Mirongo (q. v.), near the Senga village of
Chief Chibale. The next month, September, 1897, the village
of Chibale (q. v.) was attacked by a force of Arabs and Bemba.
Young went to protect Chibale with a small force, but was soon
caught in the stockaded village. McKinnon arrived with reinforcements after five days to relieve the siege. The unit then
went on to destroy a number of Arab stockades and villages,
release captured slaves, and arrest Kapandansalu (q. v.), a
noted Arab slave trading chief.

McKinnon's opposition to Mwamba was finally mooted when
the Bemba leader died in October, 1898. The Collector was
disturbed by the presence of Rev. Joseph Dupont (q. v.) at the
village of Mwamba and wanted him to leave. He also ordered
Ponde, a claimant to the Mwamba title, to leave the village.
Early in 1899 McKinnon, Young, and several other BSAC administrators met at Kasama with some Company police and attacked Ponde's stockaded village. The Europeans were victorious, but Ponde escaped.

A decade later McKinnon was the Resident Magistrate in
Barotseland.

METAL MARKETING COMPANY OF ZAMBIA. A government-controlled organization, the formation of which was announced by
the Minister of Mines on October 30, 1968. Its purpose is to
supervise mineral marketing and pricing policy. The Zambian
Government holds 51 percent control, with the two major companies each having 24. 5 percent. The board chairman is appointed by the Government, and controls a majority of the
board of directors.

In 1973, the government formed MEMACO, the Metal Marketing Corporation (Zambia) Ltd. to reform the mining industry
under the Ministry of Mines and Industry.

MICHELLO, JOB E.   A nationalist politician of the 1950's and
1960's, he was primarily active in the African National Congress.   At the time of splits within the ANC in 1959, Michello
was the provincial secretary in the Southern Province.   He was
then selected by Harry Nkumbula to be the party's General Secretary.   In 1961, when Lawrence Katilungu died, Michello succeeded to his seat in the Legislative Council.   Elected to the
post in 1962, he became part of the UNIP-ANC coalition government, serving as Parliamentary Secretary for the Ministry
of Land and Natural Resources.
    In 1963 he broke with Nkumbula, however (he had opposed
the coalition and also disliked Nkumbula's handling of the campaign), and formed his own People's Democratic Congress
(q. v.), a conservative faction aided by both Roy Welensky and
the Congo's Moise Tshombe.   Michello and Nkumbula settled
their differences in December, 1963, but both groups failed in
the 1964 elections and the PDC folded.

MIDDLETON, GEORGE.   An Englishman who became very active
in Lozi affairs in the late nineteenth century, he first visited
there when he joined Rev. Coillard's missionary group as a lay
member in 1883.   He quit the mission in 1887 and went to
South Africa.   Three years later he returned to Sesheke as a
representative of a South African business firm.   He began a
campaign to convince the Lozi to repudiate the Ware Concession (q. v.), and to give a concession to himself rather than to
Frank Lochner, Rhodes' agent.   After the Lozi signed with
Lochner, Middleton arrived in the capital in September, 1890
and convinced King Lewanika that Coillard had deceived him
into selling his country to a private firm.   Middleton even
wrote a letter to Lord Salisbury for the King, in which Lewanika "repudiated" the deal with Lochner.   This was soothed
over, however, by the British High Commission in South Africa who assured Lewanika that he was under British protection.
In 1892 Middleton challenged the King to expel Coillard or he
himself would leave the country.   He still had hopes of gaining
advantages in Barotseland for his firm.   Instead, when Lewanika declined to dismiss the missionaries, Middleton was forced
to return to South Africa in April, 1892.

MILLET.   A cereal grain that has been one of the staples of the
Zambian diet.   There are indications that Early Iron Age Zambians used it as a food.   Other sources indicate that it was introduced by people coming from the former Portuguese territories of Angola and Mozambique about two centuries ago.
Regardless, it is not as popular today as in the past, with
maize supplanting it in the diet of many.   The chitemene (q. v.)
system of agriculture is one of the best ways of growing millet.

MILNER, AARON MICHAEL.   A Eurafrican born in Southern Rhodesia, he became a high-ranking officer in both UNIP and the
Government before being dismissed from the latter on August
2, 1977, under suspicion of corruption.

Born May 31, 1932, in Bulawayo, he was educated in
Southern Rhodesia but left school at sixteen to help support his
family. He worked as a tailor and later as a bookkeeper. In
1954 he began working in Northern Rhodesia, and gradually got
involved with political groups. He was elected Chairman of
the Euro-African Association, which he merged into UNIP in
July, 1960. In 1961 he was elected Deputy Secretary-General
of UNIP, a post he held for ten years, and also served on the
party's Central Committee. In 1964 he was elected to Parliament from Muchinga. He was placed in charge of the Civil
Service and served from 1964 to 1967 as Minister of State for
Cabinet Affairs and the Public Service. In the next six years
he served in a number of Cabinet posts including Minister of
State for Provincial and Local Government (1968-69 and 1971-
72), Minister of Power, Transport and Public Works (1969-70),
and Minister of Defense (Aug. -Dec. 1973) among others.
From 1970 to August, 1973 he was also Secretary General to
the Government. From December, 1973 until August 2, 1977
he served as Minister of Home Affairs.

MINE STRIKES, 1935 and 1940 see STRIKES OF 1935 and 1940

MINES AFRICAN STAFF ASSOCIATION (MASA). Created by the
copper companies in 1953, this was a union of African clerical
workers and foremen. It was designed to counter the influence
of the African Mineworkers Union. Its leader was Godwin
Mbikusita. The companies gave MASA the right to represent
Africans whom they had recently promoted to jobs previously
held by whites. In 1956 the animosity between the two unions
contributed to a series of "rolling strikes" that hindered production. In September, 1956 the Government declared a state
of emergency on the Copperbelt and made a number of arrests.
MASA changed its name to the United Mineworkers Union (q. v.)
in 1963.

MINES LOCAL STAFF ASSOCIATION (MLSA). When the United
Mineworkers Union (q. v.) had to be dissolved late in 1963, it
was changed to the Mines Local Staff Association. It now
claimed only to cover staff and supervisory employees in the
mines. In effect it reverted to the form of the Mines African
Staff Association (q. v.). It participated in the general Copperbelt strikes of September, 1966. As a result, some of its officials were arrested. In April, 1967 the MLSA merged with
the Zambia Mineworkers Union and the Mines Police Association to form the Mineworkers Union of Zambia.

MINEWORKERS' UNION OF ZAMBIA (MUZ). A union of about
44,000 workers that was formed in April, 1967 as a result of
the merger of the Zambia Mineworkers Union (q. v.), the
Mines Local Staff Association (q. v.), and the Mines Police
Association. Its main office is in Kitwe. The union consists
of branches at each mine which then send delegates to a conference. A seven-man executive and a supreme council are

elected by the conference. The council makes policy and reviews actions of the executive, endorsing or rejecting them.

MINING DEVELOPMENT CORPORATION OF ZAMBIA, LTD.
(MINDECO). A Government holding company that develops new
mining ventures. Based in Lusaka, its chairman is the Minister of Mines and Industry. It was set up after the Government
took fifty-one percent control of mining on January 1, 1970.
MINDECO thus holds the shares and options attached to new
prospecting licenses. Today it mainly is involved with the
Maamba Collieries, small mining developments, and new mining ventures not controlled by either Nchanga Consolidated
Copper Mines or Roan Consolidated Copper Mines.

MIRONGO BOMA. An administrative post set up in August, 1897
by Robert Young (q. v.), an Assistant Collector for the BSAC.
Its location was near the present site of Isoka. Its purpose
was to prevent raids by Arabs and Bembas on nearby villages,
and as such it was welcomed by the Africans. On the other
hand, the Bembas and the Arabs, each located about twenty
miles from the boma, threatened its inhabitants with death if
they did not leave. The situation culminated in a battle at the
village of a Senga chief named Chibale (q. v.) to whom Young
provided aid. Another official, Charles McKinnon (q. v.) succeeded finally in routing the Bembas and Arabs.

MITANDA (sing., Mutanda). Small garden villages, usually with
a maximum of twenty huts, where African families would live
amid their crops which they could then protect from any marauding or scavenging birds, rodents, or animals. The villages moved when people changed garden sites in the chitemene
(q. v.) cycle. Besides the practical effect, however, Africans
saw this way of life as a way to avoid contact with their traditional leaders, some of whom were now assisting BSAC officials in collecting taxes. Wishing to restore power to the
chiefs, the BSAC forbade both mitanda and the chitemene system in 1906. This forced the building of large new villages to
replace the many scattered mitanda. A great deal of social
and political unrest spread when the two institutions were
abolished, and even the chiefs called for the return of chitemene, which the Administration reinstated early in 1909.

MITI. The territory or icalo (q. v.) of the Bemba chieftainship
Nkolemfumu (q. v.).

MKANDA. One of the chieftainships of the Chewa (q. v.) people, it
was located partly in Zambia in the Chipata area, but part of
it was across the border in Malawi. The location gave its
chief special influence, located as it was along the trade route
between Tete in Mozambique and Zambian traders either in the
Luangwa Valley or in Kazembe's kingdom on the Luapula River.
Mkanda easily defeated some of the smaller and less-central-
ized peoples in the area. By the early part of the nineteenth

century, Mkanda was almost independent of Undi, the Chewa
paramount chief.   However Mkanda territory was being increasingly invaded by the Ngoni in the last third of the century,
and by 1880 the Ngoni leader, Mpezeni (q. v.) had killed the
Mkanda chief and taken over his kingdom.

MKETISO.   An institution within the Lozi system which required
subject peoples to send large numbers of young men and women
periodically to Bulozi to provide labor.   Indunas residing among
the subject peoples ensured the Lozi a continuing supply.

MLOZI.   A notorious Arab-African slave trader who was the main
dealer for Bemba slaves from 1883 to 1895.   His base was a
stockaded village about fifty miles east of Zambia's border,
near Karonga on Lake Malawi (formerly Lake Nyasa).   By
1887 he was clashing with both the British and the local Africans.   He made a truce with the British in 1889, but in December, 1895, a British force attacked and destroyed Mlozi's
village and he was hanged.

MOFFAT, SIR JOHN SMITH.   A Government official and political
figure in Zambia for over four decades.   Born in Nyasaland in
1905, he was a great-grandson of the famous missionary,
Robert Moffat.   Educated in South Africa and at Glasgow University, he joined the Colonial Service in Northern Rhodesia in
1927.   When the strike occurred at the Mufulira mine in 1935,
Moffat was the administrative officer in charge for the Secretary for Native Affairs.   While he attempted a peaceful settlement, the strike took place anyway, and he finally arrested
eight of its leaders.
   Ultimately Moffat rose to the position of Commissioner for
Native Development.   However, in February, 1951 he was appointed to a seat in the Legislative Council and to the Executive Council as well (as an Unofficial, q. v.).   In the Council
he cast one of four votes against the Federation, although his
position was that he actually approved of it, but didn't think it
should be forced upon the disapproving Africans.   The next
year he introduced "the Moffat Resolutions of 1954" (q. v.) in an
attempt to make the Federation work eventually in the interests
of the Africans.
   He finally resigned his seat in the Legislative Council and
was appointed in December, 1954 as European Member for
African Interests in the Federal House of Assembly.   He also
became chairman of its African Affairs Board which could delay bills it considered discriminatory against the Africans.
He was bitter, however, when the British Parliament approved
several important bills over the Board's reservations.   He
was knighted, however, in 1955.
   Disturbed with the action of the Federal Assembly on his
new version of the Moffat Resolutions, he resigned in 1958
and in February, 1959 he became a founder of the Central
Africa Party (q. v.) in hopes of fighting the Northern Rhodesia
elections with an organized policy.   His party won four seats,

and he himself was one of those elected.   When Garfield Todd
of Southern Rhodesia left the CAP, Moffat's Northern Rhodesian branch broke away and became the Northern Rhodesia
Liberal Party (q. v.).   In December, 1960 he attended the Federal Review Conference in London and stayed for the Constitutional Conference in January and February, 1961.   When the
United Federal Party quit the Government on February 22 as a
result of the so-called Macleod Constitution (q. v.), the Governor replaced the three UFP Ministers with three members of
the Liberal Party.   Moffat was appointed Minister of Land and
Natural Resources.   The Constitution was revised and presented finally in 1962.   Moffat supported it as the last chance
for Europeans to set up a true and effective partnership with
the Africans.   He saw the plan as a transitional one in which
he hoped the Liberal Party would be able to participate for
about five years while Africans were gaining some governing
experience.   While Kenneth Kaunda liked Moffat, he felt he
couldn't trust the sincerity of many other members of the Liberal Party.
    The Liberal Party was not successful in the 1962 elec-
tions, and in 1964 Moffat became a UNIP candidate for one of
the ten seats reserved for Europeans.   He lost to an NPP
candidate.   In December, 1967 he was appointed by President
Kaunda to serve on a three member Electoral Commission.

MOFFAT RESOLUTIONS OF 1954.   Presented by Sir John Moffat
    (q. v.) in July, 1954, they were passed by the Northern Rho-
    desia Legislative Council with only one opposing vote.   The
    four resolutions state that policies must be developed which
    will lead to fair legislative representation for everyone without
    provision for guarantees to racial groups.   The policies should
    attempt to alleviate fears that one or another race will domi-
    nate, by setting up a transitional period in which neither group
    will have an advantage but during which everyone's rights and
    interests will be protected.   Finally race and color must not
    be used to impede anyone's right to progress according to his
    own abilities and efforts.   Some saw Moffat's resolutions as
    only a wishful dream, while others, especially Africans, saw
    them as a way of delaying self-rule.   The 1959 Benson Consti-
    tution (q. v.) was based on these resolutions.

MOFWE LAGOON.   Located a little south of Lake Mweru, the area
    near the lagoon was the site of the capitals of each of the Ka-
    zembe kings until 1884 when Kazembe X built his capital about
    twenty miles south of the lagoon, where it remained.

MOIR, JOHN and FREDERICK.   Brothers who were founders of the
    African Lakes Company (q. v.).

MOKALAPA, WILLIE J.   The founder of the Ethiopian Church of
    Barotseland (q. v.), he was a Sotho evangelist who had worked
    for many years with Rev. François Coillard (q. v.) and his
    Paris Missionary Society in Barotseland before breaking with

him. Mokalapa had studied at the Lovedale Institute in South
Africa, where he heard of Ethiopian or separatist church movements, and he also became acquainted with the African Methodist Episcopal Church. In 1899 he and his colleagues expressed
their grievances against the Coillard mission, complaining about
low salaries and treatment as inferiors by the missionaries.
They requested a greater role in the mission's activities.
When this was refused he returned briefly to Basutoland and
South Africa where he became involved with Ethiopians and
joined the AME Church. Then he returned to the Lozi.

His first attempt to form an Ethiopian Church in Barotseland was aborted when Coillard intervened with King Lewanika
against his former aid. Later, however, Mokalapa succeeded
with the King by promising a school that would teach more
English and practical subjects. Africans completely controlled
the new Church, which was given a mission site in the Zambezi Valley and free labor to be used as needed. By 1904 the
new church was thriving and had a number of schools. Many
of its supporters had been attracted from the PMS Church.

Late in 1905, Mokalapa was sent to South Africa with
about £750 of Lewanika's money to buy wagons, carriages and
boats, but he was cheated out of the money by South African
merchants and did not return to Barotseland. The Church
quickly declined.

MOKAMBA. Believed by many Lozis to be one of their greatest
Ngambelas, he was himself the son of a great Ngambela,
Njekwa (q.v.). As a youth he was a companion of King Lewanika's oldest son, Litia (later King Yeta). When Frederick
Arnot (q.v.) opened a small school, Litia and Mokamba were
among its students. He fled into exile with the King in 1884,
and was one of the victorious warriors who restored Lewanika
the next year. He then was a student of Rev. Coillard, becoming both educated and sympathetic toward Christianity. He
later married a daughter of the King, and was soon given an
important indunaship.

In 1898 his name appeared on a list of those who might be
chosen to succeed a deceased Ngambela. Although only about
thirty-five at the time, he was chosen by Lewanika over several more mature candidates. The King felt that as a Christian
he had demonstrated an openness to new things. He would be
more receptive to modern technology and development. His
education would make him more realistic in dealing with the
BSAC, and also would make him a better representative in
dealings with Europeans. Indeed he was noted for being a
personable, tactful, and intelligent administrator. As Lewanika
grew older, Mokamba increasingly ran the affairs of the nation,
relying on the younger, educated Lozi for advice. After Lewanika's death, he served as Ngambela for his old friend King
Yeta (Litia) for several years. Mokamba died early in 1919,
having served for twenty years as Ngambela.

MONCKTON COMMISSION. Appointed by the British Conservative

Party Government to make recommendations for the Federal
Review Conference to be held in December, 1960, this twenty-
five member commission was chaired by Lord Walter Monckton,
chairman of one of Britain's largest banks. It visited the Central African Federation in February and March, 1960, and issued its report in October in the form of a 175 page "Report
of the Advisory Commission on the Review of the Constitution
of Rhodesia and Nyasaland. " The Commission consisted of
many Conservative Party politicians (the Labour Party refused
to be part of it) and at least three moderate to conservative
Africans, including Lawrence Katilungu (q. v.) of Northern Rhodesia. The Commission's hearings were boycotted by African
nationalists, in part because Prime Minister Macmillan had
indicated that the Commission was not to consider the possibility of secession by any of the territories.

Despite its conservative composition and Macmillan's statement, the Commission reached conclusions that were totally objectionable to the Federation's European population and its leader Roy Welensky. It concluded that only force could keep the
Federation together and that the right of secession should be
allowed; that the "color bar" prevented political development
and must be prohibited by legislation; that a Bill of Rights
should be instituted; that each of the territories should be allowed greater responsibilities; that Africans should be given at
least parity in the Federal Parliament and that more Africans
must be allowed to vote; and that England should provide more
economic aid to the Federation.

MONDO. The African signal drum, introduced to the Bemba in the
nineteenth century by the Lunda of Kazembe. It became a val-
uable aid in communication from village to village, especially
at the onset of sudden attacks.

MONGU. One of the districts in Zambia's Western Province (sometimes called the Mongu-Lealui District), as well as the name
of the urban center that is the capital of Barotseland. The
district is the largest one in the province and contained about
113,000 people in 1969.

The town of Mongu, located about 420 miles west of Lusaka, had a population of 10,700 in 1969, a figure that doubled
its population of six years earlier. Mongu became the administrative center of the Lozi after the British sent a Resident
Magistrate there. It was located about twenty miles southeast
of the old Lozi capital at Lealui. As Lozi leaders regularly
travelled to Mongu, it became the royal capital. The Lozi
royal village is still there, and the annual Kuomboka (q. v.)
ceremony still begins there.

MONGU-LEALUI AFRICAN WELFARE ASSOCIATION. Founded in
1939 by a small number of educated Africans working in Mongu,
its stated goals were "to promote co-operation and brotherly
feeling between Africans in Northern Rhodesia; to encourage the
spread of civilization by education, industrial and agricultural

development; to protect and further African interests generally."
The administration in Mongu recognized it formally in 1943.
One of its early goals was to persuade the Barotse National
Government to allow the institution of a Provincial Council like
the ones being started in the other provinces of Northern Rho-
desia. It did not succeed.

As membership grew in the 1940's to about a hundred it
consisted of many of the most educated Lozi, along with some
clerks and teachers from Nyasaland as well. In general it
was the professional, educated, employed, and frequently well-
traveled individual who joined. The membership did not really
want to depose Lozi ruling power; it just wanted to share some
of it. The members joined the royal house in opposing amalgamation with Southern Rhodesia in the late 1940's. In the
next decade many senior members of the organization were co-
opted into the Barotse National Government, at least in clerical and other minor administrative roles.

MONTEIRO, MAJOR JOSE. An officer in the Portuguese army
stationed in Mozambique, he was co-leader of an expedition
through Northern Rhodesia in 1831-32 with Antonio Gamitto
(q. v.).

MONZE. A town of about 4300 people (in 1969), it is located on the
east side of the line of rail in Zambia's Southern Province,
south of Mazabuka. It is named after a noted Tonga leader who
was the rainmaker at one of the principal rain shrines to which
many Tonga belonged. As such he had ritual and even some
political significance, but was not a "chief" as he has been
called by some. Monze's village was reached by many visitors
in the 1850's, including Mambari (q. v.) traders from the west,
Nsenga ivory traders from the east, and Dr. David Livingstone.
In the 1880's the Lozi, led by a rebel named Sikabenga, raided
Monze's cattle, but the Tonga called on the Matabele for assistance; Sikabenga was killed and other Lozi were routed. In
1902 Jesuit missionaries led by Father Joseph Moreau were allowed by the Tonga to set up a mission in Monze's area.

MOORE, SIR LEOPOLD FRANK. Perhaps the most interesting political figure in Northern Rhodesia in the first half of the
twentieth century, he was born in London and studied at night
school there to be a pharmacist ("chemist"). He went to work
for a Cape Town company in 1892, but opened up a pharmacy
in Mafeking the next year. He moved to Bulawayo in 1898,
but moved to a frontier-type post called "Old Drift" near the
Victoria Falls in 1904. As the bridge across the Zambezi was
completed in 1905, the town of Livingstone was established.
The next year Moore began his newspaper, the Livingstone
Mail, which he subsidized for many years from the profits of
his pharmacy. It soon became the voice of the settlers, and
Moore, its very opinionated editor, quickly plunged into most
political issues. He was very honest but full of prejudice, and
generally unrealistic in his political and economic expectations.

He was strongly opposed to rule by the BSAC, and felt that the few settlers could run all of Northern Rhodesia. Thus one of his goals was the formation of a self-governing Council. At the same time he was strongly opposed to the suggestions that amalgamation with Southern Rhodesia should occur. When an Advisory Council was formed in 1918, Moore was one of the five members elected. It was through his additional hard work that the BSAC was replaced by the British Government as rulers of Northern Rhodesia and that a Legislative Council was established.

Moore quickly became the leader of the "Unofficials" in the Legislative Council and soon began attacks on the British Government as well. He feared that the Colonial office would make the territory into a Native Reserve. Thus in the 1930's his position on amalgamation was reversed. He decided that a form of union between Southern Rhodesia, Northern Rhodesia, and Nyasaland might prove economically beneficial. One of the major factors in changing his mind was the decision to move the capital from Livingstone to a new town called Lusaka. He had vigorously fought the move but failed. Thus from 1933 on, Moore led the Unofficials in the fight for amalgamation. For one thing, he felt that settler votes would be more meaningful when united with Southern Rhodesia than they would be under continuing rule by the Colonial Office.

During the 1930's Moore's views moved a little more to the Left. He even called himself a Socialist and began to echo the anti-Imperialist arguments of the world's Leftists. He also became slightly more enlightened on native policy, even defending African interests on occasion, notably during the Copperbelt strike in 1935. While he felt whites were currently the most intelligent administrators and governors, this could change during the next century, as Africans were currently being kept down and unfairly prevented from advancing.

By 1937 Moore was arguing in London that an Executive Council should be formed, and that Unofficials should have equal representation with colonial officials. Africans should be allowed to build up parallel representative institutions and not be put on white councils, he felt. When elections were held in 1941, F. J. Sinclair, a member of Roy Welensky's Labour Party, won the Livingstone seat from Moore, who then left politics. He died four years later.

MORRIS, REV. COLIN. Born in England and educated as a minister, he spent the years 1956 to 1969 in Zambia before returning home. He became politically involved in Zambia on the left side of the European political spectrum and ultimately became a close advisor to Kenneth Kaunda. He still travels frequently to Zambia. He has also been President of the United Church of Zambia.

In 1957 Morris joined the Constitutional Party, and in 1960 became Vice-President of the Central Africa Party. When John Moffat created the Northern Rhodesia Liberal Party (q.v.) out of the CAP in October, 1960, Morris continued with

Moffat, again serving as his Vice-President. He also left his
pulpit at Chingola to devote his time to political affairs. He
was at the London talks (December, 1960 to February, 1961)
and played an important part in the constitutional negotiations.
Earlier in 1960 he co-authored a book with Kenneth Kaunda
called <u>Black Government</u>.
Morris was always an advocate of a multi-racial government. He felt that Moffat was the only European leader who
could gain support from both races. At the same time he
was trying to persuade Europeans that they must face reality
and work with the African leaders, especially Kaunda. In
1962 Morris split with Moffat and the Liberals over the question of cooperation with UNIP during the 1962 election campaign. Morris felt that a collaboration would be desirable.
Harry Franklin, a close friend of ANC's Nkumbula opposed
this and won Moffat to his view. On March 12 the party executive supported Franklin and Moffat, so Morris immediately
resigned.

MOSILIKATSE. Variant of Mzilikazi (q.v.).

MOSI-OA-TUNYA. The Lozi name for Victoria Falls (q.v.), it
means literally, "the smoke that thunders."

MOSI-OA-TUNYA NATIONAL PARK. One of the smallest of Zambia's national parks, it is limited essentially to the area
around Victoria Falls and is designed to facilitate the tourist
traffic.

MOWA MAMILI. Variant of Mamili (q.v.).

MOZAMBIQUE. Zambia's neighbor to the southeast, it was once
called Portuguese East Africa, and was controlled by the
Portuguese until it attained independence on June 26, 1975.

MP. Standard abbreviation for Member of Parliament, whether
elected or specially appointed.

MPANDA. The chiefdom belonging to the Bemba chief bearing the
title of Makasa (q.v.). It is located just to the north of the
Chambeshi River. It seems to have been conquered from the
Mambwe people in the early nineteenth century.

MPANDE. A major Mambwe chieftainship in the southern part of
Mambwe country (thus just north of the Bemba). The Bemba
killed Mpande II, who lived early in the nineteenth century.
Mpande V Chitongwa came under Ngoni influence in the 1860's
and became their ally. He even used them against Nsokolo,
the Mambwe paramount chief, who was killed by the Ngoni.
After the Ngoni were defeated at Chipekeni (q.v.) in about
1870, the Bemba expanded northward and killed Mpande V.
His successor fled to take refuge among the Namwanga, and
the Bemba made Mpande's people pay them tribute. Twenty

years later, in 1892, Mpande returned to settle near the White
Fathers' mission in Mambwe country.   About a decade later he
regained much of his territory from the Bemba.
See also IMPANDE SHELL.

MPANGO.   The Bemba term for what is known elsewhere as
lobola or bride-price.   This widely used practice involves payment in goods and services, made by a bridegroom and his
kin to the bride's kin.   Sometimes cash has been substituted
for the goods.   The concept has nothing to do with buying a
wife, but is a method of making a marriage legal and binding.
It constitutes a way of uniting the kinship groups.   In case of
a divorce, part of the mpango is sometimes returned.

MPEPE.   A nephew of Makololo chief Sebituane (q.v.), he became
a prominent leader of his people after his uncle's death.   Sebituane's initial successor was his own daughter, Mamochisane.
Mpepe substituted for her in certain ceremonies and acquired
a great deal of personal support as well.   Mpepe had been a
war leader for his uncle, and was noted for his successful
cattle raids.   He also assisted the Mambari (q.v.) in raids
against the Ila and Tonga peoples.   While befriending the Portuguese he received a small cannon from them.   When his cousin,
Sekeletu, became the Makololo chief, Mpepe took control of the
Makololo forces in Bulozi as a semi-independent ruler.   He
continued to conspire to become the chief of the entire nation,
if necessary by killing Sekeletu.   Instead the latter saw to it
that Mpepe was killed at the end of June, 1853.

MPEREMBE.   Son of the great Ngoni leader, Zwangendaba (q.v.),
Mperembe and his brother Mpezeni (q.v.) traveled south of
Lake Tanganyika into Bemba territory around 1850.   After defeating two Bemba leaders in the Chinsali area, Mpezeni took
his force considerably south.   Mperembe continued to raid
Bemba villages, but generally was not too successful.   Thus
he took his following to Chibungu in the southern part of Bemba
country, and near the Bisa.   From his village at Chibungu his
men raided in all directions, terrorizing the whole area.   They
destroyed the Bisa trade route to the kingdom of Kazembe, and
laid waste to numerous Bisa and Bemba villages.
        Around 1860 Mperembe took his following north to a new
settlement among the Lungu.   They also raided the Tabwa and
Mambwe peoples from their new location.   Meanwhile they
forced the Lungu to work and fight for them.   Mperembe's
Ngoni had several clashes with the Bemba in the 1860's, with
mixed results.   In one they routed Chief Makasa and set up
their own village (called Chipekeni) on the site of his village.
In about 1870 a large Bemba force consisting of over half a
dozen chiefs and their forces stormed Chipekeni.   Mperembe
led his remaining followers north to Namwanga country where
they stopped for about a year before they continued eastward
and settled permanently in what is now Malawi.

MPEZENI (or MPESENI).   Son of the great Ngoni leader, Zwangendaba (q. v.), Mpezeni and his brother Mperembe (q. v.) led
their people south of Lake Tanganyika into Zambia around
1850.   After their forces defeated a couple of Bemba groups,
Mpezeni led his forces further south, finally establishing the
main permanent Ngoni settlement in Zambia.
    En route to the southeastern part of the country, Mpezeni's
followers stopped briefly in the Muchinga Mountains before
crossing the Luangwa River into Nsenga country about 1860.
Increasingly they also encroached upon the northern Chewa
kingdom of Mkanda, which they totally overran by 1880, killing
Mkanda in the process.
    Mpezeni settled his people in a malaria-free area where
they could raise cattle (some of which they got in raids) in
addition to growing maize.   As Nguni people, Mpezeni's followers were organized into age-grade regiments that provided
them with organized warrior groups for military purposes.   In
addition, the Ngoni brought the Zulu short spear attack method
from southern Africa in their earlier migration.   Thus they
were very successful militarily, and also succeeded in integrating the vanquished peoples into their structure.   On the other
hand, the Ngoni adopted the language of the Nsenga.
    Ultimately Mpezeni was faced with the movement of Euro-
peans from the south and east who coveted his land, which they
believed contained gold.   In 1885 Mpezeni had given a large
mining concession to a German hunter and trader, Carl Wiese
(q. v.).   The German became a close advisor to the Chief.
Wiese made a large profit by selling his concession to a London group that became the North Charterland Company (q. v.),
which sent prospectors to the area in 1896.   Mpezeni tolerated
them, but had no intention of accepting British rule.   His son,
Nsingu, was his leading commander, and was eager to take on
the British in battle.   A force led by Colonel William Manning
(q. v.) entered Ngoniland from Nyasaland in January, 1898, on
the pretext of protecting Wiese and an official of the BSAC.
The large Ngoni force fought valiantly for several days, but
their spear techniques were no match for British artillery and
machine guns.   Nsingu was captured and shot, and Mpezeni
surrendered.   The British took Mpezeni's large herds of cattle.

MPIKA.   The name of both a district and its administrative center
in Zambia's Northern Province.   The district is the largest in
area and the southernmost of the province's districts, but its
population (about 58,000 people in 1969) makes it almost the
least populated as well.
    The town of Mpika is located on the western edge of the
Muchinga Mountains and is near the site of some productive
salt pans (see CHIBWA MARSH AND SALT PANS).   The town
grew from a BSAC administrative station that was established
there.   Mpika is conveniently located on both the Great North
Road, one of the country's best highways, and along the route
of the Tan-Zam or Great Uhuru Railway.

MPOLOLO. A Makololo leader in the nineteenth century, he was
the nephew of Chief Sebituane, and the man in charge of the
northern region of his people's territory. This was in Bulozi,
which he ruled from Naliele. When Chief Sekeletu, his cousin,
died, Mpololo led a force which overthrew Mamili who had
seized power. Much of Mpololo's support came from followers
who hoped he would serve as a regent for Sekeletu's son.
Once in power, Mpololo proved to be a cruel leader who
killed all his opponents. He also killed Litia, father of the
future Lozi King Lewanika, in 1863 when a Lozi plot to overthrow him was revealed by Mataa (q. v.). Finally in August,
1864, a Lozi uprising led by Njekwa (q. v.) massacred the
Makololo. Mpololo was wounded and committed suicide by
drowning.

MPOROKOSO (Chiefdom). One of the secondary chiefdoms
among the Bemba, it nevertheless has been important as
its chiefs are always sons of the royal bena ng'andu chiefs.
The bearer of the Mporokoso title who is of most historic interest is its originator, Mporokoso I Mulume wa nshimba. He
was given the territory called Maseba in about 1870 and expanded it considerably before his death in 1909. In the interim he used quarrels among other Africans (notably the Tabwa)
and the increased trade activity with East Africa to become one
of the most powerful Bemba chiefs at the beginning of the
twentieth century. It was during the 1870's that he traveled
northwest from Maseba to establish a new village at Kashinda
in Tabwa country. This location placed him in the middle of
a number of battles involving Africans and, on occasion, Swahili traders such as Abdullah ibn Suliman (q. v.). His relations
with the latter vacillated; sometimes they were in opposition,
and other times allied. Similarly Mporokoso was sometimes
wary of Europeans (when the first BSAC posts were set up in
1891), but very friendly to others, especially Poulett Weatherley (q. v.). In 1899 he refused to negotiate with Andrew Law,
the Collector at Abercorn, until a British force overwhelmed
his stockade.
     For an incident involving a later Chief Mporokoso, see
KALIMINWA.

MPOROKOSO (District and Town). Both a district in the Northern
Province of Zambia and the town which is its administrative
center. The district stretches from the border with Zaire and
the southwest corner of Lake Tanganyika southward for about
125 miles. It has two major parks and game reserves in the
north and is not densely populated. Its population in 1969 was
about sixty-eight thousand.

MPULUNGU. Located on the extreme southern end of Lake Tanganyika, this town is the terminus of a twenty-six mile tarred
road from Mbala. Barges leave from Mpulungu to connect
with the Tanzania railways at Kigoma. This was very important before the completion of the Tan-Zam Railway.

MSIRI. The leader of a group of Nyamwezi traders from Tanganyika, he and his followers (to be known as the Yeke, q.v.) settled in Katanga, west of the Lundu leader Kazembe. From this position they became raiders as well as traders, and dominated the area for several decades until Msiri was killed in 1891 by a member of an expedition sent by King Leopold of Belgium. His capital was a town called Bunkeya. From this location the Yeke, armed with guns, coerced the neighboring peoples to provide them with ivory, and even took over the copper mines. Msiri turned against his former friend, Kazembe, taking over some of his previous trade, and cutting off his links to the west with Mwata Yamvo and with Angola. Msiri also sent his men south into Zambia, where they raided such groups as the Aushi, the Unga, the Bisa, the Kaonde, and the Lamba.

An attempt by Alfred Sharpe, an agent for Rhodes, to get Msiri to sign a treaty with him late in 1890 was unsuccessful, perhaps the main reason that the Katanga copper mines are not part of Zambia today and the Congo Pedicle divides Zambia. On the other hand, when King Leopold's second expedition to the Yeke ended in an argument and Msiri's death, the Yeke meekly surrendered their territory to the Belgians.

MU-. A prefix in the Bantu languages (thus virtually all of Zambia) that when affixed to the name of a tribe or ethnic group indicates a single member of that group.

MUGANGA CHIPOYA see MWAMBA III MUBANGA CHIPOYA

MUBUKWANU. King of the Lozi when they were attacked by the Makololo in about 1840. The son of King Mulambwa (q.v.), he was the ruler of the southern part of the Lozi kingdom during his father's reign. When Mulambwa died there was a succession dispute between Mubukwanu and his brother, Silumelume (q.v.). The latter was the candidate of most of the northern indunas and of his father's Ngambela and Natamoyo. Silumelume was declared King, but supporters of Mubukwanu conspired to kill the new King, and an Mbunda warrior performed the deed. Thus a civil war broke out, as the North produced a new candidate. Shortly after Mubukwanu's warriors prevailed in the war, the Makololo invaded Bulozi. The two forces met in three battles, at Kataba near Sefula, at Nea near Nundu, and at Liondo. The Makololo won each battle. There seems to be uncertainty whether Mubukwanu died in battle or escaped to refuge at Lukwakwa where he is said to have died of poisoning. The period from the first invasion by the Makololo to the abandonment of Bulozi after the third battle was about 1840 to 1848.

MUCHINGA MOUNTAINS. Situated on the northwestern edge of the Luangwa River Valley in the eastern half of Zambia, these mountains jut upward to form an impressive escarpment. They are generally between four and six thousand feet above sea level, not much higher than the land to their west, but in some places almost three thousand feet higher than the river valley to the east.

MUDENDA, ELIJAH HAATUKALI KAIBA. Zambian Prime Minister from May, 1975 to July, 1977, he has been a member of the UNIP Central Committee since August, 1973. Mudenda was born June 6, 1927, at Macha near Choma, the son of a Tonga Chief. Like many UNIP leaders he was educated at Munali Secondary School. He attended Makerere College in Uganda and Fort Hare University in South Africa. He attended Cambridge University from 1952-54, where he received a B.S. in Agriculture. He spent the next eight years in the study and practice of agricultural methods before entering politics in 1962. After winning a seat in the Legislative Council in the 1962 elections he was appointed as Parliamentary Secretary for African Agriculture. When UNIP won the 1964 elections, Mudenda became Minister of Agriculture, a post he held from January, 1964 to November, 1967. He then served two years as Minister of Finance and four (until December, 1973) as Minister of Foreign Affairs. During the latter service he became a recognized leader on OAU conciliation committees and at the UN. He is noted as a skilled negotiator. In May, 1975 he was appointed Prime Minister. On July 20, 1977, he was replaced by Mainza Chona, seemingly receiving the blame for shortages in some important domestic goods such as sugar and cooking oil. He has served in Parliament since 1962, and continues on the UNIP Central Committee.

MUFULIRA. A Copperbelt city of over a hundred thousand people in 1969, its boundaries reach virtually to the Zaire border. It is one of the urban Districts of the Copperbelt Province and, of course, is the site of the important Mufulira mine (q. v.).

MUFULIRA MINE. One of Zambia's larger copper mines, production began in October, 1933, as it became one of the huge Rhodesian Selection Trust, Ltd. group. Today it is part of the Roan Consolidated Mines Ltd. group. In the intervening years its history has included several notable events. The strike of 1935 (q. v.) began there when taxes were raised. In September 1970 a huge cave-in resulted in the death of eighty-nine workers and a drastic curtailment of production. It was about four years before the mine could be returned to normal production levels. On the positive side, this mine is the second largest underground mine in the world. Also, a refinery was installed at Mufulira in 1952 to process the ore.

MUKABILO. Singular of Bakabilo (q. v.).

MUKULU see BENA MUKULU

MUKULUMPE. The father of Chiti and Nkole, the founders of the Bemba nation, he was a chief in an area of Zaire called "Luba"

or "Kola". According to one story he lived about 1670 on the
Lualaba River. Whether he was Luba or Lunda depends on
which legend you accept.   Regardless he was a powerful chief
(Mukulumpe means "the great one"), and had many wives.
One of them, Mumbi Mukasa, bore him three sons, Katongo,
Chiti, and Nkole, and a daughter, Chilufya Mulenga (qq.v.).
The sons defied him and built a large tower (says the Bemba
legend) which collapsed and killed many people.   The father
was furious, and blinded Katongo while banishing the other two.
Later he called them back from exile, but with the secret intention to trap and kill them.   They escaped his trap, but he
humiliated them by making them clean the royal courtyard.
Eventually all four children escaped and traveled eastward
into Zambia.
    The Bemba are not the only Zambian peoples to claim de-
scent from Mukulumpe, as several Bisa chieftainships also cite
a chief by that name as their ancestor.

MUKUNGULE. A Bisa chieftainship that was at one time presum-
    ably quite strong.   The territory was just west of the Muchinga
    escarpment and was called Mukumbi.   At one point prior to
    1800 Mukungule appears to have been the supreme Bisa chief
    to whom all Bisa were vassals.   By 1831, however, it is re-
    ported that all Bisa chiefs were independent of him.   The rea-
    son for his loss of power is unclear.   Late in the nineteenth
    century a Bemba leader, Chikwanda II, occupied some of the
    Mukungule's land, but the area had already been depleted by
    Ngoni raids.   For the Bemba, Mukumbi was an elephant-hunt-
    ing area.

MUKUPA KAOMA. The southern Lunga chieftainship, it appears
    to go back to the late eighteenth century when it occupied land
    to the east of its present boundaries.   The second chief in the
    line was Kaoma, who evidently lived around 1800.   He became
    involved in a conflict between a couple of Bemba leaders.
    When it was resolved Kaoma agreed with the Bemba on a com-
    mon border, evidently along the Luombe River.
        Kaoma's successor to the title, his brother, Chikoko,
    later got into a war with the Bemba chief, Mwamba I.   Chiko-
    ko was basically a weak leader, but he was drawn into a bor-
    der conflict with the Bemba and finally attacked across the river.
    A Bemba force repelled them and Chikoko was killed while his
    men recrossed the Luombe.
        In the 1860's Mwamba II attacked Mukupa Kaoma III Lubula
    over a wife of Mwamba who fled to Lubula's village.   He de-
    stroyed the village but the Lungu leader and the wife escaped.
    Lubula asked a Bisa leader, Matipa (q.v.) for aid, but the
    Bemba beat the combined Lungu-Bisa force in a battle on the
    Lusenga River.   Lubula fled to safety.   The chieftainship has
    continued to the current time.

MUKUPO, TITUS. A very active nationalist politician throughout the
    1950's, primarily in the African National Congress. Experienced

in journalism, in 1953 Mukupo aided Kenneth Kaunda and others
in the publication of the Congress News (q.v.).   In August,
1956, he was added to the ANC's National Executive Committee
with the title "Deputy Secretary." This was despite the fact
that earlier in the year he had briefly resigned from ANC over
Harry Nkumbula's "New Look" policy (q.v.); he rejoined before
the August party conference.
    In 1958 Mukupo was chosen to be the party's General Sec-
retary.   Always a man in favor of action, he began a serious
campaign to force white-owned cafés, hotels, cinemas, restau-
rants, and other similar facilities to "put partnership into
practice" by admitting Africans.   He found Nkumbula provided
minimal encouragement or support for such activities since he
had become a member of the Legislative Council.   In June,
1959, Mukupo and the party's General Treasurer urged Nkumbula to resign as ANC President.   On July 4 an informal party
meeting did likewise.   At the same time Mukupo was talking
to Paul Kalichini of the African National Independence Party
about a merger of the two parties.   On July 11 Nkumbula suspended Mukupo and seven other dissidents for their boycotts of
Indian shops without his permission.   Nkumbula also seized all
of Mukupo's files and guarded the offices.
    Now Mukupo openly proclaimed his opposition to the party
president, calling him an incompetent leader.   He also proposed that an attempt be made to unify several of the existing
political parties so as to reunite the nationalist movement.
The next two months were filled with political maneuvering.
Mukupo announced that the party's National Assembly would
meet on August 23.   His hope was to install Mainza Chona as
president.   The Assembly met for a week, and Nkumbula participated.   When it ended with Nkumbula still in charge, Mukupo called for it to reconvene the next day.   Nkumbula then
removed him from office, but Mukupo assembled almost half
the delegates who passed a resolution dismissing Nkumbula.
The latter then called for a General Party Conference on September 10.   The Mukupo-Chona group was outmaneuvered by
Nkumbula and the president was easily reelected.   The Mukupo-
Chona group met as a separate ANC faction and elected Chona
as President on September 13, 1959, with Mukupo as National
Secretary.   Finally the next month the new faction joined with
the recently organized United National Independence Party and
Chona was elected UNIP's president.   Due to family difficulties,
Mukupo did not run for party office and, in fact, never again
held office in a nationalist organization.

MUKUSHI see TEAK WOOD

MUKUUKA WA MALEKANO.   The first of the "modern" Bemba
    Chitimukulus, very little is known about his predecessors.
    His own dates are not certain either, although it appears that
    his reign began about the beginning of the final third of the
    eighteenth century.   His praise name, wa malekano, means
    "of the separation," and refers to the fact that he divided

Lubemba by establishing a separate chieftainship in the western part, Ituna. He appointed his brother, Chitunda, Chief of Ituna. This was one of the major developments during his reign, as it was the first known instance of such an act among the Bemba, a precedent that would be followed often in the future. Upon his death, Mukuuka was succeeded by his sister's son, Chiliamafwa (q. v.).

Another bearer of the name was Makasa V Mukuuka Mwilwa (q. v.).

MULAMBWA. Perhaps the longest reigning Litunga (King) of the Aluyana (later called Lozi), he is considered by the Lozi to be one of their best rulers. His reign appears to have lasted from about 1780 to about 1830. He was the son of Mwanawina (q. v.), himself a King, and succeeded his brother, Mwananyanda (q. v.), who was a weak ruler. He replaced the latter after a successful military challenge.

Mulambwa is remembered in part for his military achievements. Cattle raids among the Ila were recounted a century later to missionaries, and raids for slaves or booty are recorded in oral history. But Mulambwa's reputation is based on solidifying the nation and his creation of laws to ensure justice. His laws included punishment for thieves, compensation and care for relatives of men killed in war, and rules for tax collecting. Mulambwa refused to deal with the Mambari slave traders who entered Zambia from Angola.

Mulambwa succeeded in integrating into the state a large number of Mbunda immigrants led by Mwene Ciengele (q. v.) and Mwene Kandala. They helped him win several wars. On the other hand they could not stop the invading Makololo who arrived in Bulozi three years after Mulambwa's death. His long life contributed to a weakened state, as he was infirm and almost blind in his later years. Ultimately his death resulted in a civil war for succession between two of his sons, Silumelume and Mubukwanu (qq. v.).

MULASA. Tribute labor (in the Bemba language) owed to traditional leaders as part of the system of mutual obligations between ruler and ruled. In the period just preceding the First World War it became very uncommon, and the chiefs didn't enforce it (though it was presumably compulsory) even for those who periodically worked in Southern Rhodesia. The BSAC Administration even promised to enforce it by arresting anyone refusing a chief's request. In the mid-1920's, however, the traditional leaders began to demand it again. But by this time the Administration was increasingly reluctant to enforce it, maintaining that good leaders will not have difficulty with their people, and bad leaders don't deserve it. The chiefs also had added difficulty as more of their young men were increasingly attracted to work on the Copperbelt.

MULEMBA, HUMPHREY. A member of UNIP's Central Committee since 1973, he reached political prominence through his

work in unions. Born in September, 1932, at Lusaka, he was
educated at St. Canisius College at Chikuni. He then was employed as a miner at Nchanga but moved up to personnel work.
Joining the union, he rose to election as full-time secretary of
the General Workers' Union. In 1959 he was one of the ZANC
activists arrested during the "State of Emergency." On his
release he became active in UNIP. At one point he was UNIP's
Divisional Secretary for the North-Western Province. Later
he was UNIP's representative to Accra and London.

Mulemba was elected to Parliament in 1964 and was appointed Deputy Speaker that same year. From 1967 to 1969
he moved through three portfolios, as Minister of State for
Cabinet Affairs and the Public Service, Minister of the Luapula
Province, and of the Barotse Province. In 1969 Kaunda appointed him to UNIP's interim executive committee. He also
became Minister of Trade and Industry in 1969, but switched
to Mines and Mining Development where he served from 1970
until 1974. From 1973 to 1977 he served as Chairman of
UNIP's Economics and Finance Sub-Committee.

MULENA MUKWAE. An official position among the Lozi, it trans-
lates roughly as "princess chief." In Lozi custom, female
relatives of the King have always held special rank and a voice
in the government, but King Lewanika institutionalized this (and
solved a vexing problem) by appointing his sister to be the
ruler of the southern part of Bulozi, and giving her the title
Mulena Mukwae. Previously the rulers of the southern kingdom were always men, who then became contenders for a vacant northern throne. The result sometimes was a civil war.
Since women were not eligible to become the Litunga (King),
the Mulena Mukwae could not be a cause of dissension. As
the King's sister (or other close relative), she is usually a
strong supporter of him and a major consultant on important
questions. She is also expected to be the King's top critic
when she feels that he is being unjust.

MULENGA, ALICE LENSHINA see LENSHINA, ALICE MULENGA

MULENGA, CHILUFYA. The daughter of Mukulumpe (q.v.) and
his wife, Mumbi Makasa, she was the sister of Katongo, Chiti,
and Nkole. The latter two are considered the founders of the
Bemba nation. When Chiti and Nkole fled their father for the
second time, they realized that they had left behind their sister
and blind brother Katongo. They sent a half-brother, Kapasa,
to free them, which he did in a very clever fashion, but he
later made Chilufya Mulenga pregnant. Kapasa was disowned
by the family, now migrating eastward. When both Chiti and
Nkole eventually died, a son of Chilufya Mulenga, also named
Chilufya (q.v.) became their successor as leader of the Bemba
people.

MULIKITA, FWANYANGA MATALE. One of the best educated
members of the top echelon of both UNIP and the Government,

Mulikita was born at Sefula in Barotseland on November 24, 1928. A graduate of Munali Secondary School and Fort Hare University College in South Africa, he won scholarships to the United States. There he received a B.A. degree at Stanford University and an M.A. at Columbia University. He became a teacher and an author (A Point of No Return). In 1964 he began a three year appointment as Permanent Secretary of Education, and then completed a year (1967-68) as Zambia's first Permanent Representative at the United Nations. He was appointed to the National Assembly after the 1968 elections so he could be appointed to the Cabinet. In 1969 he briefly held the post as Minister of the Southern and Luapula Provinces, and from September, 1969, until June, 1971, he was Minister of Labour and Social Services. From 1971 to 1973 he was Minister of Power, Transport, and Works; and then served as Minister of Education until May, 1976. At that point he was made a member of the UNIP Central Committee.

MULONGWANJI. The National Council (Kuta) of the Lozi people, it has been the most important advisory body to the Lozi King (Litunga) and has been consulted traditionally on matters of national importance, especially war but also including a wide range of executive, legislative, and judicial decisions. The extent to which the King abided by its advice varied with the individual King. It is reported that Sipopa, for example, regularly ignored its advice and guidance. The membership of the Mulongwanji included indunas from several categories, including especially the Makwambuyu, the Likombwa, and the Linabi (qq. v.). At the discretion of the King, other individuals could be invited to attend for specific purposes. The National Council included within its ranks the individuals who made up four other Kutas: the Saa, the Sikalo, the Katengo, and the Situmbu sa Mulonga (qq. v.). Each had its specific roles and represented a different interest. In the mid-twentieth century, the British insisted that members of the younger and more educated non-royalists be added to the National Council to make it more representative and modern. This merely resulted in more conflict between the traditionalists and the non-traditionalists. See also BAROTSE NATIONAL COUNCIL.

MULUNGUSHI. Mulungushi Rock is a large, bare, black landmark north of the city of Kabwe. It was chosen by Alexander Grey Zulu, a Kabwe resident, as the site of the July, 1961 general conference of UNIP. It then became the annual meeting site for the party conference. It became famous as the result of Kenneth Kaunda's Mulungushi Declaration (q. v.) in 1968 which instituted major economic reforms including nationalization of many large firms.

Mulungushi Hall is a large conference complex built by the Zambian Government in 1970 at a cost of $10 million. It was built north of Lusaka for the Third World summit conference held that year.

MULUNGUSHI DECLARATION (or REFORMS). An announcement
made by President Kenneth Kaunda at Mulungushi on April
19, 1968, it instituted the first stage of the most dramatic
changes in Zambia's economic history. The reforms had a
number of distinct parts, the most prominent of which were:
     1) The Zambian Government, through its Industrial Develop-
ment Corporation (INDECO), q. v. , would become a 51 percent
partner in twenty-six of the major foreign-owned companies in
the country. Most of them were engaged in wholesale or retail trade, or in transportation. (The mining industry was
exempted from this nationalization until August, 1969, when
the Matero Reforms (q. v.) were announced.) The Government
agreed to reimburse the firms for the 51 percent share by
paying the owners out of company profits.
     2) Legislation would be introduced requiring all retail out-
lets outside the principal shopping areas of the ten major
cities to be owned by Zambian citizens (thus probably but not
exclusively Africans).
     3) New trading permits for areas outside the ten major
cities would not be issued to foreign companies or resident
non-citizens.
     4) Only companies that were at least 75 percent Zambian-
owned could be issued new road service and transport licenses.
     5) Government public works contracts of less than K100,000
($140,000) would only be granted to Zambian citizens.
     The reforms--along with subsequent changes over the next
several years--had two major purposes: the guarantee that
Zambian development would not be limited by people whose
primary concern was personal profit instead of the national interests; and that the peoples of Zambia would have the maximum opportunity to share in their country's growth, in keeping
with President Kaunda's philosophy of Zambian Humanism. It
was felt especially that non-citizen Asians had dominated wholesale, retail, and transport firms that could be handled by
Zambian citizens if given a chance. The transition period produced some hardships, as Asian shops in rural areas closed
for the lack of Zambians with both sufficient capital and experience to run the operation. Government loans helped to resolve the problem.

MUMBI MUKASA. The wife of Mukulumpe (q. v.) and the mother
of three sons, Katongo, Chiti, and Nkole, and a daughter,
Chilufya Mulenga (qq. v.). According to Bemba legend (Chiti
and Nkole are founders of the Bemba nation), Mumbi Makasa
was of divine origin. She is said to have come down from the
sky, to have been a member of the Crocodile Clan, and to
have had ears as large as an elephant.

MUMBUNA, MUFAYA. A former vice-president of the African
National Congress and a member of the National Assembly, he
became a founder of the United Party (q. v.) and its first president in May, 1966. The following year he relinquished the
leadership to Nalumino Mundia (q. v.). When the party was

banned, Mumbuna returned to activity in the ANC and was reelected to the Assembly in 1968. He was one of his party's
best-educated spokesmen.

MUMBWA. Administrative center of the Mumbwa District of the
Central Province of Zambia. The district is the western-most
of the province's districts, bordering the Western (formerly
Barotse) Province. In 1969 the district had about fifty-nine
thousand people. The town of Mumbwa is lightly populated.

MUNALI SECONDARY SCHOOL. The most important and best
known secondary school in the country (and for many years the
only one), it became the source of the Zambian educated elite
and thus also the breeding-ground of African politicians.
Eleven of the fourteen members of the March, 1964 Cabinet
attended the school, many of them at the same time. Thus it
provided a special unity for the early nationalist politicians as
well as for the subsequent Governments.
   Munali was founded in 1939 under the sponsorship of Governor Hubert Young as part of a plan for "native training."
It was developed by the Director of Native Education, Julian
Tyndale-Biscoe, despite the opposition of many of the territory's whites, including some on the Legislative Council who
felt that the African would have "book-learning ... but no desire to work." They might also become dissatisfied with their
position in life, it was charged.
   "Munali" is one of the names Africans gave Dr. David
Livingstone. Its exact meaning is in dispute. Some say it
means "the leader," others say "the red one" (referring to his
skin color), and others think it is a corruption of the Dutch
"mijnheer." The school was originally situated on high ground
southeast of Lusaka, near the home of the Governor. Its first
head was Frederick Hodgson. Planned as a junior secondary
school preparing its pupils for the English General Certificate
of Education, its first groups of pupils were limited to about
thirty in a class. Kenneth Kaunda spent two years there in
its early years.

MUNALULA, MBWANGWETA. Ngambela (Prime Minister) of Barotseland under King Yeta III from 1929 until his death in 1941.
He had been chief councillor (induna) of the Libonda Kuta in
Kalabo District. Generally he was a passive man, more likely to cooperate with the British than to resist them. Thus
when King Yeta was struck by paralysis early in 1939 but remained alive, the Provincial Commissioner, Gordon Read, appointed Munalula as Acting Paramount Chief. The Ngambela
was very accommodating to Read, and the Barotse National
Government was run, in effect, by the Commissioner. Munalula died in January, 1941, predeceasing King Yeta.

MUNDIA, NALUMINO. A political figure for two decades, his career includes leadership of three political parties, jailings by
several governments, and since 1976 the position of Cabinet
Minister for the North-Western Province.

Born at Kalabo in Barotseland in 1927, his education includes several years at the renowned Munali Secondary School.
In 1954 he completed a university degree in Commerce while
on a scholarship in India. He then studied Industrial Management at Stanford University. Returning to Northern Rhodesia
in 1957, he found the color bar working against him, and finally found employment in Southern Rhodesia. In October,
1959 he returned to Lusaka where he protested the Monckton
Commission with a public fast outside Government House. He
was soon chosen the Deputy-Treasurer of UNIP.

Mundia devoted much of 1960 and 1961 to organizing UNIP
in the western part of the country. At first he worked the
North-Western Province, but also spent time in his native Barotseland. There he formed the Barotse Anti-Secession Society (q. v.) in late 1960. In 1961 he was imprisoned a month
in Mongu for defying a deportation order (UNIP was still illegal in Barotseland).

In January, 1964 Mundia first ran for the legislature.
Victorious, he was given the Local Government portfolio by
Prime Minister Kenneth Kaunda. In September, preparing for
independence, Kaunda made him Minister of Commerce and Industry, a perfect position considering his education. However
he was removed from this position in January, 1966 on charges
of financial improprieties (conflict of interest). He was dismissed from UNIP and Parliament in March, 1967, but found
the one year old United Party to his liking and was elected its
president. The United Party (q. v.) was soon locking horns
with UNIP, especially on the Copperbelt. A clash between
their supporters in August, 1968 led to the banning of the UP
and the arrest of Mundia. United Party supporters quickly
switched to the African National Congress for the 1968 elections, and Mundia (although in jail) became a successful ANC
candidate for the National Assembly from the Western (Barotse)
Province. He helped maneuver an ANC sweep of the Western
Province seats. He remained under restriction in the Northern
Province until November, 1969, and thus was prevented from
taking his seat in the Assembly for nearly a year after the
election. Meanwhile in January, 1969 he had also been appointed the Deputy Leader of the ANC. Once in the Assembly
again he used this position to advantage, as he was a skilled
debater. In 1971, however, he was suspended from the Assembly for a three month period. He was allowed to return,
but remained a thorn in the side of UNIP leaders. In January,
1973 he was again detained without trial for several months
after the Government announced the plan for a one-party state.
Nevertheless, reconciliation occurred and three years later
Mundia was back in the Cabinet as Minister for the North-
Western Province.

MUNGULUBE. One of the major Bisa chieftainships, its chiefs belong to the bena ng'ona (q. v.) or Mushroom Clan. The chiefs
claim ancestry from someone called Mukulumpe (q. v.), thus
possibly having a connection with the Bemba, who have an

ancestor by the same name. The chieftainship was located on the upper part of the Luva River, about twenty-five miles south of the Chambeshi River. When the Ngoni came through the area in the mid-nineteenth century, Chief Mungulube fled to refuge among the Senga people. Eventually the chiefdom, also called Isunga, was occupied by the Bemba chief Nkula, who expanded southward into Isunga. Chief Mungulube was finally allowed to return to his territory in order to satisfy local ancestral spirits.

MUNTS. One of the most derogatory terms used by whites in reference to Africans. It derives from the word Muntu, the singular form of Bantu. It is not unlike the word "nigger."

MUNUNGA. One of the major Shila chiefs, his people live by Lake Mweru. The ancestors of Mununga are said to have migrated from Bemba country shortly before they were subdued by the Lunda of Chief Kazembe in the mid-eighteenth century.

MUNWA STREAM. The site of many rock engravings is located along this stream, about six miles south of Johnston Falls. Some of the designs and motifs, while engraved, are similar to some of the schematic paintings found elsewhere in Zambia. A typical motif shows several concentric circles with radiating lines filling the space between them. This is considered to be the work of Late Stone Age people.

MURANTSIANE SIKABENGA. Principal induna at Sesheke in the 1880's and a relative of Mataa who had led the rebellion against King Lubosi (Lewanika) in 1884. Murantsiane was himself associated with the rebellion at Sesheke. While destroying the rebellion elsewhere, Lewanika tried to temporarily quiet the situation at Sesheke by offering his sister, Matauka (q. v.) as a bride to Murantsiane. Before this was completed, however Lewanika was ready to purge Sesheke of the rebels and raided it in 1886. Murantsiane escaped eastward to Batoka. There he joined Tatila Akufuna (q. v.) and continued to foment opposition to Lewanika. The dissidents returned to Sesheke early in 1888 while the King was raiding the Ila and planned to invade the Bulozi valley. Lewanika returned and again attacked Sesheke and Murantsiane again fled to Batoka. He died there in August, 1888, during a Matabele raid.

MUSENGA. A twentieth-century Bemba leader, he was known as Mpepo III from 1925 to 1942. He then became Nkolemfuma VI for two years until he rose to Mwamba VI in 1944. He held that chieftainship until 1966 when he became the Chitimukulu. He died in 1969.

MUSHIDI. Variant of Msidi or Msiri (q. v.).

MUSHROOM CLAN see BENA NG'ONA

MUSUMBA. The village of a Bemba chief, it was usually very
large. As his capital it was well fortified, surrounded by
ditches and stockades.

MUSUNGU (or KAFULA MUSUNGU). An important twentieth-century
Bemba leader who served as Chitimukulu from 1946 until his
death in 1965. He was born into the royal family about 1890,
a son of Mandechanda and grandson of Nakasafya. His brother,
Bwembya, became Chitimukulu in 1969. Musungu was named
Chikwanda III in 1910 and became Nkula III in 1934. His succession to Chitimukulu followed a dispute over the rightful heir.
As Chitimukulu he was a thorn in the side of Roy Welensky, as
he fought the Federation, even traveling to England in an unsuccessful protest in 1952. He refused to ban the nationalist political parties in his areas, and in 1958 refused to meet with
Welensky when he toured Bemba country. The Government
then stripped him of some powers and downgraded him (at least
officially) to chief. He died in 1965.

MUTALE. A common name among Bemba leaders, the first notable bearer of it was Mwamba I Mutale (q. v.). In the twentieth century there have been Mutale Lwanga (who was Chikwanda
II before serving as Chitimukulu from 1913 to 1916), Mutale
Nshika (Mpepo IV from 1942 to 1945; Nkolemfumu VIII from
1945 to 1967; and then Mwamba VII), and Mutale (Chikwanda V
from 1946 to 1970 when he became Nkula V).

MUTOLO. The Bemba word for tribute, whether paid in services
or in kind, that was given to a chief by the people residing in
his chiefdom.

MUWAMBA, ERNEST ALEXANDER. A founder and chairman of the
Ndola Native Welfare Association (q. v.) in 1930, he was a
Tonga from Nyasaland who had worked his way up to head clerk
at the Ndola boma. His political activism ran in the family, as
he was closely related to Clements Kadalie, the founder of the
Industrial and Commercial Workers Union of South Africa. In
the early 1950's Muwamba was still active politically, a member of the Nyasaland Legislative Council.

MUWAMBA, I. CLEMENTS KATONGO. A Tonga from Nyasaland,
he was a founder and the chairman of the Lusaka Native Welfare Association in 1930. One of his first campaigns was
against the conditions under which Africans were forced to buy
meat, but the government would not intercede with the butchers.
In 1933 Muwamba tried to organize an association of welfare
associations and was chairman of a meeting at Kafue to which
several of the associations from other towns sent representatives.
Government opposition prevented such an association from developing further until 1946.

MUWEMBA. A word used to designate a single (one) member of
the Bemba tribe.

MUYUNDA.   Another name of Mboo (q. v.).

MWAANGA, VERNON JOHNSON.   Zambia's most experienced diplomat, he is currently out of government, working in the Lusaka
office of Lonrho Zambia Ltd. (q. v.), but he is serving on
UNIP's Central Committee.   Mwaanga was born on January 6,
1939 near Choma in the Southern Province.   His academic career was concluded in England at the Institute of Commonwealth
Studies, Oxford University, where he read political science and
international relations.
    The British began preparing him for a diplomatic career
before Zambia's independence, attaching him to their embassy
in Rome.   In October, 1964 he became Zambia's first diplomat, serving as Deputy High Commissioner in London.   In
1965 he became Ambassador to Moscow for one year.   Then
he returned to Zambia for two years as the President's Permanent Secretary; he was assigned to the delicate negotiations
with Rhodesia.   From 1968 to January, 1972 Mwaanga was
Zambia's Ambassador to the United Nations.   For two of these
years he was also on the Security Council, and he spent one
year as Vice-President of the General Assembly.   Several
other assignments at the UN were concurrent with these.
    In January, 1972 he was called back to Zambia where he
spent two years as Editor-in-Chief of the Times of Zambia.
From December, 1973 to May, 1975 he was Minister of Foreign Affairs.   He became a member of the UNIP Central Committee in 1975 also.   The next year he took a position with
Lonrho.

MWALULE.   An important location in Bemba history, it is the
principal burial site of the Chitimukulus.   It is located east of
the Chambeshi River, and consists of a thick grove of trees by
the Katonga stream.   The official guardian of the royal grave-
yard is called Shimwalule (q. v.).   The location was found by
the Bemba migrants after the death of their leader, Chiti.
Looking for a suitable gravesite they found the grove of majestic trees.   During the burial ceremonies Chiti's brother, Nkole,
choked to death accidentally and both leaders were buried there.

MWAMBA.   One of the senior chieftainships of the bena ng'andu,
the royal clan of the Bemba, its leaders rule the icalo (q. v.)
known as Ituna (q. v.).   It is just west of Lubemba, the icalo
of the Paramount Chief, Chitimukulu.   Because of the system
of promotion from one royal chieftainship to another, two
twentieth century Mwambas later became Chitimukulus, the
most recent being Musenga (q. v.).   During the nineteenth century, however, it was more likely for the two chieftainships to
be in competition.   For example Mwamba III Mubanga Chipoya
(q. v.) had more actual power than his contemporary, Chitimukulu Sampa.   He regularly extended his rule into areas traditionally dominated by Chitimukulu.   This trend had actually begun under Mwamba II Chileshye Kapalaula (q. v.), whose sons
were chiefs at Mporokoso and Munkonge, thus giving him

influence there as well. Mwamba's subordinates held lands
closer to the heart of the East African trade route and are
said to have channeled their ivory through him.
   The chieftainship at Ituna actually goes back to about 1800,
but the first of its chiefs to take the title Mwamba was Mutale,
the brother of Chitimukulu Chileshye. He received the title in
an unusual fashion. Another Bemba royal, Mutale Mukulu,
killed a Mambwe chief named Mwamba (the title still exists
among the Mambwe also) and called himself "Mwamba. " He
then went on a reign of terror and killed many people, including members of his own family. Chileshye's brother, Mutale,
stopped the terror by killing Mutale Mukulu. He then was rewarded with the title of Mwamba.

MWAMBA I MUTALE. The full brother of Chileshye Chepela (q. v.),
   one of the more notable of the Bemba Chitimukulus, he was
   awarded the title of Mwamba (q. v.) and the chieftainship of
   Ituna in about 1830. This came about as a result of Mutale
   killing Mutale Mukulu, a rampaging member of the royal clan
   who was terrorizing the country after killing a Mambwe chief
   named Mwamba. In addition to Ituna, Chileshye also gave his
   brother the right to reign over Miti, whose ruler, Nkolemfumu
   Chisanga had just died. Mutale thus built his village, named
   Kabwe, in the Miti portion of his lands. Mutale faced several
   threats to his land during his reign. One was when the Lungu
   chief of Mukupa Kaoma (q. v.) attacked Ituna across its western
   border. Both Mwamba I Mutale and the Chitimukulu sent
   soldiers, who routed the raiders and killed their chief, Chikoko.
   Mutale also had trouble with a Bisa chief, Matipa (q. v.), to the
   south over control of Lubumbu. Mutale was successful against
   him however, and Matipa fled to Nsumbu Island. In the late
   1850's Mwamba I Mutale and Chitimukulu Chileshye planned a
   campaign against the Iwa of Kafwimbi as punishment for the
   aid they gave the Ngoni. Mwamba did not reach the enemy,
   however, dying en route. He was succeeded by his eldest sister's eldest son.

MWAMBA II CHILESHYE KAPALAULA. Also known as Malama,
   he succeeded his uncle as Mwamba in the late 1850's, and held
   this important position until his death in early 1883 of smallpox. He was the elder brother of the great Chitimukulu Chitapankwa (q. v.), whose reign was almost coterminous with his
   own. The two succeeded in asserting Bemba hegemony throughout large parts of northeastern Zambia, distributing conquered
   lands to their sons and other close relatives. Before Chitapankwa became Chitimukulu, there had been two times when
   Mwamba II had been offered the post. Once he pointed to his
   elderly uncle, Bwembya, instead; the other time (when it was
   obvious that Bwembya had to be replaced) he said that he would
   prefer to keep his post and allow his younger brother (Chitapankwa) to be Chitimukulu. It has been conjectured that the
   increasingly lucrative East African trade passed near his borders, and that the lands of Chitimukulu were far from these

paths and the power that went with the trade and its wealth.
Shortly after becoming Mwamba, Chileshye moved to
strengthen his position. He sent a force to the southwest, under his son's leadership, where he defeated the Lungu. This
brought Mwamba into conflict with the Bisa, who were allied
with the Lungu. Thus Mwamba's men engaged two Bisa chiefs,
Matipa (q. v.) and Mukupa Kaoma (q. v.), both times emerging
victorious. Confrontations continued in this area for over a
decade.

During the 1870's Mwamba turned his attention to the north
and west of his home area (Ituna) in order to assure his influence along the East African trade route. One of his efforts involved aid to Kafwimbi (q. v.), a participant in a Tabwa succession dispute. The successful Kafwimbi then was forced to
reward Mwamba by giving him the area called Isenga in
southern Tabwa country. Even before adding this new territory, Mwamba had been involved with the East African trade,
notably through the Arab raider Tippu Tip (q. v.). He was
also active with Swahili traders, as ivory was sent to Mwamba
from peoples in the area under his control.

MWAMBA III MUBANGA CHIPOYA (or CHIPOYE). During his
reign as Mwamba, from 1883 to 1898, Mubanga Chipoya was
without question the dominant leader of the Bemba nation,
surpassing even the Chitimukulu, Sampa. Mubanga Chipoya
was a sister's son and also a son-in-law of Mwamba II, who
revived the title of Nkolemfumu (q. v.) for him around 1870
and gave him the territory called Miti as well as some Bisa
territory south of the Chambeshi River. He also added Mpuki,
a Bisa chiefdom further south, within a short time.

When Mwamba II died in 1883, Mubanga Chipoya (also
called Chisala) was a logical successor, although Sampa, soon
to become Chitimukulu, had his own candidate who was then
by-passed. The relationship between these two most powerful
Bemba leaders was further hampered by instructions by the
dying Chitimukulu, Chitapankwa, that the major Bemba chiefs
should not obey Sampa. Thus throughout his fifteen year reign
Mwamba III had a poor relationship with his "superior," who
in fact was now his inferior in both land and influence.

Despite a military defeat by the Swahilis in 1884, Mwamba
III maintained influence in Tabwa country to the northwest. He
then strengthened his control to the west and south, partly
through the appointment of chiefs at Miti and Mpuki. He also
established his son in territory to the south. Under the title
Luchembe, the son expanded into the territory belonging to
Chikwanda. Mwamba's appointees thus controlled large portions of northeastern Zambia west of the Muchinga Mountains
and the Luangwa River.

As the British entered Bemba country increasingly in the
1890's, Mwamba treated them with a cautious distrust rather
than open hostility. In mid-1896 he made a friendly overture
to the White Fathers, a Catholic missionary group. Rev.
Joseph Dupont was eager to respond to this. Meanwhile

Mwamba became a candidate to replace the deceased Sampa as
Chitimukulu. His principal opponent was Makumba (q. v.). In
the face of several bad omens, however, Mwamba conceded to
the elderly Makumba.
    In the first part of 1899 Mwamba was visited first by a
BSAC administrator, Robert Young (q. v.), and later by Rev.
Dupont. While neither made major progress with him, there
were indications that Dupont might eventually. Mwamba's
hopes of extending his area eastward at the expense of a weak
Chitimukulu were dashed when the BSAC was victorious during
a battle with Arabs at the Mirongo boma (q. v.). In fact a
minor confrontation between the BSAC and some of Mwamba's
men took place late in 1897 at Mwalule, with the Bemba re-
treating. The British continued to assure Chitimukulu Makumba of their support against Mwamba.
    In October, 1898, Rev. Dupont received word that he
should again visit Mwamba, which he did on October 11. The
chief was extremely ill, and obviously had not long to live.
Mwamba asked Dupont to build a camp nearby. If he died he
wanted Dupont to care for his people during the transition. It
was even implied that Dupont would succeed him, a promise
Mwamba could not actually make. Dupont eased his pain with
morphine, but the old chief, active and alert until the end,
died on October 23, 1898. In the succeeding months Dupont
(q. v.) had a dispute with the BSAC administrator, Charles
McKinnon, over his further responsibilities there.

MWANA LESA. Literally "the Son of God," it was a title adopted
by a "prophet" from Nyasaland, Tomo Nyirenda, who was a
noted preacher in eastern Zambia in the 1920's. While working at a mine near Mkushi in the mid-Twenties, he listened
to the Watch Tower doctrine preached by others from his country and, in early 1925, was baptized and began preaching in
the Mkushi District. He aroused enough enthusiasm that the
local Administrator jailed him, supposedly for not registering
as an alien. Released in April, 1925, he then declared himself to be "Mwana Lesa. "
    His doctrine was basically that of the Watch Tower, with
strong emphasis on preparing for the millenium. Great wealth
would be an ultimate reward for the baptized. Americans
would drive away the colonists, whose property would be divided among his followers. A strict code of living was to be
the order for all who awaited the Second Coming. He had
special promises for those who were baptized. They would not
die; they would see their forefathers; and the elderly would become young again. Moreover, those who would not immerse
properly during the baptism ceremonies were "witches" and
must be destroyed. A local Lala chief asked him to cleanse
his people of witchcraft. In May and June, 1925, sixteen Lala
were declared witches and killed, plus six other Africans in
another District. In Katanga 170 were killed. Many of the
victims were convinced that the test was legitimate and acqui-
esced to their own death. He was arrested in Northern Rho-

desia in September, 1925, received a trial, and was hanged.

MWANAKATWE, JOHN. One of Zambia's most respected government officials and administrators, he also bears the distinction of being the first Zambian to obtain a college degree. He
was born at Chinsali on November 1, 1926 into a Bemba family.
He attended Munali Secondary School (q.v.) before going to
Adam's College in South Africa. He obtained a teaching degree there in 1948 and a B.A. in 1950. He taught at several
schools, including Munali, before serving as the first African
Education Officer in Livingstone. He entered government service in June, 1961 as the Assistant Commissioner for Northern
Rhodesia in London, an extraordinary appointment at that time.
In 1962 he returned home to enter politics for the first time.
He became a UNIP candidate for one of the upper roll Legislative Council seats, and was successful. In the coalition government of 1962 he became Parliamentary Secretary for Labour
and Mines. He was unopposed in January, 1964 and was appointed Minister of Education, a post he held until 1967. One
month after independence he also passed his bar finals and received a law degree.
    Mwanakatwe served as Minister of Lands and Mines from
1967 to 1968, when he was unexpectedly defeated for re-election. He was appointed to a newly created post, Secretary
General to the Government. He then ran unopposed in a parliamentary by-election held in July, 1969. Reentering Parliament he became Minister of the Luapula Province for a year.
In 1970 he was made Minister of Finance. He held that post
until October, 1973. While remaining in Parliament since
then, he did not hold a Cabinet post until he returned as Minister of Finance in May, 1976. He was replaced in January, 1979.

MWANAMBINYI. Younger brother of Mboo (q.v.), the first King
of the Aluyana (Lozi). According to Lozi legend he outwitted
Mboo numerous times through his supernatural powers, thus
infuriating him. To escape Mboo's threats on his life, he
went south with his followers to the present Senanga District.
There his people (the Akwandi, q.v.) conquered the Ma-Subiya
and the Mbukushi and he set up a village at Imatonga near the
current town of Senanga.
    During the reign of a later King, Ngalama (q.v.), the
people of Mwanambinya were defeated and restored to the original kingdom. During the victory Ngalama captured the
Maoma royal and war drums (which Mwanambinyi had taken
from the Mbukushi); they have since become an important part
of Lozi installation rituals and ceremonies.

MWANANYANDA. An eighteenth-century Litunga (King) of the
Aluyana (later called Lozi), he succeeded his father, Mwanawina (q.v.). He was not a particularly good leader, as he is
referred to as "the unlamented" in tradition. When faced with
conflicts between the royal family and the indunas (as well as
challenges to his position as King), he resorted to suppression

and even executions as the "solution." The solution was not
permanent, however. He managed to defeat a major opponent,
Mwanamatia, the nation's southern ruler; but he was unsuccessful in meeting the challenge of his brother, Mulambwa (q. v.),
who succeeded him and became one of his people's greatest
leaders.

MWANAWINA I. An early nineteenth-century Aluyana (later called
Lozi) king, he succeeded Yubya (q. v.). Little of note is remembered of Mwanawina's reign, but Lozi tradition is that he
was a good leader. He was succeeded by his two sons; first
by Mwananyanda (q. v.), who was unpopular, and then by Mulambwa (q. v.).

MWANAWINA II. A young man who ruled as King of the Lozi from
1876 to 1878 before being deposed. He was the son of Sibeso,
a Lozi prince who had been killed by the Makololo while they
ruled Bulozi. When the Lozi King, Sipopo (q. v.), was overthrown in 1876, the seventeen-year-old Mwanawina (who had
been living in Sipopa's village) was offered the kingship by
Mamili (q. v.), a very ambitious Ngambela (Prime Minister).
The young man was very popular, and his nomination was acceptable to the major councillors. Mamili quickly demonstrated
that he would run the country and insisted on royal privileges.
Soon Mamili had alienated everyone, and he and members of
his family were executed. Now young Mwanawina was freer to
make his own decisions, but these too were not popular. The
new Ngambela he chose was unpopular with everyone; and his
appointments to other positions were heavily weighted toward
his maternal relations, who were from southern Bulozi, also
displeasing many. A plan to replace the old indunas with
young ones was also suspected. Thus the indunas took advantage of an army that had been organized for a raid on the Ila
in May, 1878, using it to depose Mwanawina, who fled to
Sesheke. He hoped to raise an army among the Ma Subiya.
Failing this he went to Batoka where he gathered a force. In
1879 he returned to Bulozi, but an army under the new king,
Lubosi (q. v.), was waiting for him. A fierce battle at the
Lumbe River in May, 1879 resulted in another defeat for
Mwanawina, who again fled to Batoka. He died in exile.

MWANAWINA III. The Litunga (King) of the Lozi from 1948 until
his death in 1968. The fourth son of King Lewanika, he was
born in about 1888 at Lealui. After being educated at Paris
Missionary Society schools, he attended Lovedale College in
South Africa, completing his education in 1913. He then
worked as secretary and interpreter for Lewanika. In 1916
he supported his father in promoting cooperation with the
British war effort, leading the Lozi soldiers in their march
to the east. He was twice honored by the British for his support during the two World Wars.
        Mwanawina was a principal advisor to his brother, King
Yeta III until 1937 when he was named Chief of the Mankoya

Kuta.   When King Imwika died in 1948 Mwanawina was selected
to succeed him by the Lozi leaders.   The major concern for
which he fought during his two decade reign was the continuation of the semi-autonomous status of his kingdom.   First he
opposed any amalgamation between Northern and Southern
Rhodesia; then he fought against the Federation; seeing the
rise of young nationalists he suggested separation from
Northern Rhodesia and special status within the Federation, or
perhaps status as a "Barotseland Protectorate" within Northern
Rhodesia.   As independence for Zambia approached he repeatedly sought British assurances that any Zambian Constitution
would ensure special status for Barotseland, although his preference was to secede from Zambia.   After independence he continued his struggle with UNIP for the continuation of the powers
of the Barotse National Government, the traditional ruling
class.   In all of this he was ultimately unsuccessful. He died
in November, 1968.

MWANDIBONENE.   One of the names surviving into fairly recent
times that was applied to some of the "little people" who once
inhabited many parts of Zambia.   While it may refer to pygmies, it more likely was applied to the Bushmen (q. v.).

MWANSABAMBA.   The Bisa chieftainship ruling Chinama, southeast of the Bangweulu swamps, it has become known as Kopa
(q. v.).   Its history goes back well into the eighteenth century.
There was a time in that century when Mwansabamba exercised control over other neighboring Bisa chiefs, including
those in Lubumbu, northeast of Lake Bangweulu.   This was no
longer the case by the end of the century.

MWASE.   Several Chewa (q. v.) chiefs named Mwase existed in the
Luangwa valley as early as the eighteenth century.   The name
was also that of an early Senga chief.   Finally, the Bemba
migration legend maintains that Chiti (q. v.) was involved in a
fatal battle with a chief called Mwase over Mwase's beautiful
wife.   It might be conjectured that Mwase was not a name at
all but a title which meant, loosely translated, "chief. "

MWATA YAMVO (or MWATA YAMVWA).   The western Lunda King
or Emperor, he was responsible, directly or indirectly, for
several of the chiefdoms and peoples currently inhabiting Zambia.   The title is said to mean "Lord of Wealth" and is still
used by Lunda leaders in southern Zaire today.   Mwata Yamvo's kingdom in Katanga began to expand in the eighteenth century or earlier, setting up new centers in distant areas.   They
continued to pay him tribute, and their trade enriched him.
One such new center was that of the eastern Lunda under Kazembe (q. v.) on the Luapula River.   West coast trade reached
Kazembe by way of Mwata Yamvo, and some east coast trade
reached the western Lunda through Kazembe.   Meanwhile other
traditions link western Zambians such as the Lozi, Nkoya, Luvale, and Ndembu with men who were sent out by Mwata Yamvo

to broaden his sphere of influence.   See also ISHINDE and
KANONGESHA.

MWAULUKA.   Ngambela (Prime Minister) of the Lozi from 1885
until his death in September, 1898.   He had supported Lewanika's attempt to regain power after the 1884 coup, even leading one of the regiments in a major battle near Lealui in November, 1885.   When Ngambela Silumbu (q. v.) died in the war,
King Lewanika chose Mwauluka, a strong traditionalist, as his
successor.   In this position he was a major advisor to Lewanika at the time of most of the major agreements signed with
Europeans, such as Lochner, Ware, and Lawley.   He was a
signatory to these concessions.   While Mwauluka was generally
a supporter of Lewanika, he saw the King's concern with British
"protection" as having potentially dangerous consequences for
the traditional Lozi governing structure, and he also saw missionaries as an eroding influence on the traditions of his
people.   He once even threatened to depose Lewanika if he
converted to Christianity.   With Mwauluka's death in 1898, the
traditionalists lost their strongest voice against change.

MWELA ROCKS.   An area of rocky outcrops and boulders near
Kasama, it is the site of Zambia's richest collection of animal
paintings.   The paintings produced probably by Late Stone Age
people, include a very realistic warthog, and a group of people
surrounding a large animal.   Some more recent paintings, both
realistic and schematic, can be found also at Mwela.

MWENE CIENGELE (or CHIEGELE).   A chief (Mwene) of the
Mbunda (q. v.) people in Angola, he led a band of followers into western Zambia in the early part of the nineteenth century.
They settled near Mongu, and the Lozi attempted to integrate
them into their system.   Ciengele was recognized as the senior
chief among the Mbunda in Bulozi (several other groups also
settled in the area), and was given the status of a Lozi prince.
This included a seat in the Lealui Kuta.   All this was under
King Mulambwa (q. v.).   When Mulambwa died there was a succession dispute between his sons Silumelume and Mubukwanu.
Mwene Ciengele took sides, secretly supporting the latter, and
arranged a special performance of his people's war dances for
Silumelume.   At a crucial moment, one of the Mbunda dancers
killed Silumelume with an arrow.

MWENYI.   A small group of about thirteen thousand Luyana-speaking people whose traditional homeland has been north of the
Lozi nation, along the Luanginga River in the far western part
of Zambia.

MWENZO.   The site of one of the early missions in Zambia, it
was located among the Namwanga people near the Tanzanian
border in northeastern Zambia.   The Livingstonia Mission of
the Free Church of Scotland opened the mission station there
in 1894-95.

MWENZO WELFARE ASSOCIATION. Perhaps the first true modern
protest (or political) organization formed in Zambia, it existed
as early as 1912 when Donald Siwale, David Kaunda (qq. v.)
and a number of other young Africans trained as teachers met
frequently to discuss problems arising from colonial rule.
The Association was formalized with a constitution in 1923
after Siwale contacted a friend, Levi Mumba, who had been
active in a similar Nyasaland Association. Mumba's constitution guided Siwale and Kaunda. It invited others to join, including "educated chiefs and Europeans." But its appeal was
primarily to the educated African in a professional-type position. While the organization was looked on suspiciously by the
Government, the District Commissioner, J. Moffat Thomson,
was convinced that it would be constructive rather than destruc-
tive. Indeed the organization at Mwenzo was primarily concerned with providing a forum for Africans to voice their views
on social and political questions. The high tax burden on Africans was one such issue, along with a related concern, that of
labor migration with its ramifications for family and village
life and agricultural productivity. The organization lasted five
years, folding in 1928 mostly because its principal leaders had
been transferred to other areas.

MWERU WANTIPA NATIONAL PARK. Located east of Lake Mweru
in the Mporokoso District of the Northern Province, it is not
far from the border with Zaire. The park is divided into a
Game Reserve and a hunting area. The total area involved is
about a thousand square miles. It includes the lake and surrounding swamp called Mweru Wantipa.

MWINILUNGA. One of the larger districts in Zambia's North-
Western Province, it had a population of about fifty-three thousand people in 1969. It is the extreme northwestern district,
jutting northward in such a way that its western border is with
Angola and its northern border is with Zaire.
     The district's administrative center is the town of Mwini-
lunga, which is located twenty-five miles south of a Zaire
border, along one of Zambia's better roads. A canning factory
was opened there in 1970, with pineapples being the first of
several fruits to be grown and processed.

MZILIKAZI (or MOSILIKATSE). The founder of the Ndebele nation,
he had been a military leader under Chaka, the great Zulu
king. He fled Chaka, however, and drifted through southern
Africa with his followers before ultimately settling in the
western part of what became known as Southern Rhodesia.
There had been numerous military conflicts with both Africans
and Europeans before the Ndebele (q. v.) settled down. As a
result they were much feared by their neighbors in southern
Zambia and in Bechuanaland (now Botswana). Many of the actions of the Makololo (q. v.) can be explained by the fear that
their leader, Sebituane, had for Mzilikazi. Sebituane's cordial
relations with Dr. Livingstone and George Westbeech were

efforts to provide a link of good will with Mzilikazi. The
Ndebele also made frequent raids into southern Zambia, where
the large cattle herds of the Tonga and Ila were the primary
temptation. Mzilikazi died in September, 1868, and was eventually succeeded by his son, Lobengula (q. v.).

- N -

NABULYATO, ROBINSON M. Speaker of the Zambian National Assembly since late 1968, he has been active in politics for thirty years. He was a teacher at the Kafue Training Institute in
the 1940's when in 1948 he was elected the first General Secretary of the Northern Rhodesia African Congress. A political
moderate, he also served in the Federal Parliament as one of
the nominated MP's. In 1959 he ran for the Legislative Council from the Southern Province against Harry Nkumbula, but
was defeated.

NACHIKUFU CAVE. The site of important archaeological findings
near Mpika. The major work was done there by J. Desmond
Clark (q. v.) in 1948. Three levels of Late Stone Age remains
were found, along with an Iron Age layer. There were
naturalistic rock paintings of animals and men found in the
cave.

NACHITALO HILL. A location in the southwestern part of Mkushi
District where naturalistic rock paintings were discovered in
1912 by J. E. Stephenson (q. v.). These were the first such
paintings reported in the country. Most of them are under an
overhang in a small cave near the top of the hill. The primary paintings are of antelopes, somewhat stylized, done in
purple pigment. Red schematic designs overlay the antelopes.

NAKAMBALA SUGAR ESTATES. A large plantation of 7645 acres
in central Zambia, it produces the vast majority of Zambia's
sugar. It even has its own refinery.

NAKAPAPULA. The site of a small rock shelter in the northern
part of Serenje District. There is a single purple antelope
very similar to those at Nachitalo Hill (q. v.) painted on the
wall. Superimposed on it is a large panel of red schematic
painting.

NALABUTU. An elderly and respected member of the Lozi National Council who fought for the choice of Lubosi (Lewanika)
as Lozi King over the other major candidate, Musiwa. As a
result of his successful struggle, Nalabutu had considerable
influence on Lubosi's policies, as the young King looked to
him for counsel. Nalabutu also led a group of traditionalists
that firmly opposed all white men, who they felt were there to
steal their land. They even opposed the missionaries, and resisted conversion. Perhaps Coillard's activities during the

Lochner Concession (q. v.) negotiations only confirmed their suspicion of all Europeans.

NALIELE. The site of the northernmost administrative center of the Makololo while they ruled the Lozi. Located on the eastern bank of the Zambezi, it was about fifteen miles south of Lealui. In that advantageous location, it was better situated than other Makololo centers to engage in trade with Portuguese in Angola. Among those who ruled from there were Mpepe (q. v.) and Mpololo (q. v.).

NALOLO. Located in the southern part of the Bulozi flood plain, it has been a second capital for the Lozi since the days of their Litunga (King) Ngombala (q. v.). He found it necessary to appoint a royal representative in the South because of the victorious expansion of the Lozi kingdom by the armies of his predecessor, Ngalama (q. v.). While it was a chieftaincy that was clearly secondary to the northern one, the "chief of the south" was the Litunga's equal in terms of ritual honor and prestige and was the second most powerful person in Bulozi. When a Litunga died, the ruler at Nalolo was always a prime candidate to succeed him. When he was not chosen, however, a civil war could break out, as it did on several occasions. The problem was ultimately resolved by Sipopa (q. v.) who appointed his sister as ruler at Nalolo. This reform of having a princess as chief has continued and has resolved the problem, as a woman can not become Litunga and her successor is not one of her children but a relative of the Litunga making the appointment.

NALUMANGO, NELSON. A pioneer in the struggle for African rights in Zambia, he was literally kicked into political consciousness in 1930 when a constable in Broken Hill beat and kicked him for standing on a sidewalk. In the winter of 1933 he and several other early nationalists like Godwin Mbikusita met in Kafue to try to organize an association of African Welfare Associations. He represented the association he had helped found in Livingstone. Nothing came of it then, but in May 1946 some of the same men, including Nalumango, met in Broken Hill and created the Federation of African Societies of Northern Rhodesia (q. v.). In 1948 he was appointed one of the first two African members of the Legislative Council. As such he was an opponent of any attempt at federation, insisting that Africans should have their views on the matter considered as well. In 1951 the African National Congress persuaded the African Representative Council to replace the two Africans on the Legislative Council (one being Nalumango) with two members of the ANC.

NAMIBIA. The name (based on the Namib Desert) chosen by African nationalists fighting to free the territory previously known in international circles as South West Africa (q. v.). Its Caprivi Strip (q. v.) borders southwestern Zambia, and some African freedom fighters have used Zambian soil for a base.

NAMUSO. The principal or northern chiefdom of the Lozi located
at Lealui (q. v.).   It is ruled by the paramount leader of the
Lozi, the Litunga.   Namuso is superior to the southern chiefdom of Lwambi (q. v.), which has its capital at Nalolo.

NAMWALA. One of the districts in Zambia's Southern Province,
the district had a population of thirty-seven thousand in 1969,
making it the country's fourth smallest.
    The town called Namwala is the district's administrative
center, and is situated on the south bank of the Kafue River,
about a hundred twenty-five miles west of Lusaka.

NAMWANGA. A small group (about 32,000) of Mambwe-speaking
people who live in the extreme northeastern corner of Zambia.
Their origins, along with their Lungu, Ila, and Mambwe neighbors, apparently are in East Africa.   However they are ruled
by a chiefly class of Congolese origin that arrived more recently.   The senior Namwanga chief is Chikanamulilo (q. v.).
At one point in 1877 he repelled a fierce Bemba attack, but
he was defeated by a Bemba raid in 1879.
    The Namwanga are primarily a pastoral people.   They
have had fame, however, as fine producers of iron products
as a result of smelting and smithing skills.   Their location
near the Bemba made them vulnerable to some of the more ag-
ressive Bemba leaders (as the above 1879 incident demonstrates), so the arrival of BSAC officials with treaties was met
favorably, both by Chief Mukoma, who signed with Harry Johnston in 1889, and Chief Chikanamulilo, who signed with Alfred
Sharpe in January, 1891.   It did not take long for them to regret this however, and in August, 1896 they started the first
popular demonstration in the Northern Province of African resentment to forced labor, at Ilendela village near the Ikawa
boma.   It was put down by a BSAC official, John Bell (q. v.),
who brought in police and finally burned down the village.   Perhaps it is not coincidence that twenty years later it was among
the Namwanga and their Mambwe-speaking neighbors that the
millenarian sect, the Watch Tower Movement, made its first
major gains in Northern Rhodesia.

NANZELA. A very small southern Zambian tribe living in the
western part of Ila territory, they are also sometimes called
the Lumbu or Balumbu.   Sometimes they are just included in
the designation "Tonga. "   One of their outstanding nineteenth-
century leaders was Sezongo I (q. v.).

NASORO see SULIMAN, NASORO BIN

NATAMOYO. One of the senior official titles in the Lozi traditional political system, the bearer of it is the only councillor to
the Litunga who must be a member of the royal family.   The
word itself means either "master" or "mother of life. "   The Natamoyo's special significance relates to judicial proceedings.
Both his person and his house constituted a sanctuary for an

accused individual. He could also overrule judgments of the
Kuta or the Litunga if he felt the penalties were unjust or too
severe. As the Lozi system modernized in the twentieth century, the bearer of the title of Natamoyo was considered to be
the Minister of Justice in the Barotse government.

NATIONAL ASSEMBLY see PARLIAMENT

NATIONAL COUNCIL OF UNIP. Along with the national officers
and the Central Committee, UNIP's National Council has been
an element of the party's organization since its inception in
1959. The structure was initially modelled after that of the
African National Congress, but Kenneth Kaunda reorganized it
prior to the 1962 elections. One thing he did was expand the
National Council, making it more representative of the party's
regional organization. The National Council has been retained
despite party reorganization in both 1967 and 1971. The 1971
party constitution provides that the National Council be composed of: members of the Central Committee, UNIP members
of Parliament, District Governors, two officials plus the regional secretary from each party region, six people elected by
the Zambia Congress of Trade Unions, two selected by the
Farmers Union, heads of Zambian Missions abroad, and executive officers of the national headquarters. A large and somewhat unwieldy body, it falls between the huge General Conference, and the smaller Central Committee in serving as a representative body. The National Council meets at least twice a
year and has the formal right to decide on party policy, which
is implemented by the Central Committee. The National Council also reviews decisions of the Central Committee and of
lower levels of the party, and decides what proposals shall be
included in the party program. It also has the power to amend
the party constitution.
      In practice, meetings of the National Council serve pri-
marily as a place for the party leader to announce new policy.
There is not usually much debate and the policies are adopted
unanimously. However the Council does provide a place where
regional officials can call the attention of national leaders to
matters of local concern. The Council's charge to review Central Committee decisions is also not very realistic, as the
Central Committee is clearly much more powerful. The agenda
of the Council is even controlled by the Central Committee and
its resolutions are drafted by a handful of men, some of whom
are members of the Central Committee.

NATIONAL DEVELOPMENT PLAN see FIRST NATIONAL DE-
VELOPMENT PLAN; SECOND NATIONAL DEVELOPMENT
PLAN

NATIONAL PROGRESS PARTY (NPP). The later name of the
Northern Rhodesia branch of the United Federal Party. The
change took place in late April, 1963. The leadership did not
change, however, as John Roberts (q. v.) continued to lead the

organization. A fundamental policy change did occur, however.
The party now recognized that the Federation would be dissolved and that European settlers would play a minority role
in the territory's future. Moreover, Roberts now recognized
that UNIP, not ANC, would be the ruling party. Therefore he
assured Kaunda of his future cooperation and assistance. This
assurance was notably forthcoming when Roberts understood
that Kaunda favored the existence of some reserved seats in
Parliament for Europeans in the Independence Constitution.
Representatives of the NPP participated in the London constitutional talks of May, 1964. With ten seats reserved for Europeans in the new constitution, the NPP contested each of the
seats in the 1964 elections, suggesting it could contribute more
as an experienced, loyal opposition than as members of the
ruling party. Nine of its ten candidates had served on the
Legislative Council, and its slogan was "experience counts."
All ten defeated the UNIP candidates, but the victory margin
was not large. Whereas UFP candidates in 1962 had captured
95 percent of the white vote, NPP candidates only received 63
percent. This did not prevent them from being very vocal in
Parliament. Since UNIP had no back benchers with parliamentary experience, NPP members presented the only true debate
in the first Parliament. This was in spite of the fact that the
Constitution only guaranteed these "reserved" seats for five
years. Primarily the NPP was active on economic questions,
especially those affecting European farmers. With the seats
no longer to be reserved, John Roberts announced on August
2, 1966 that the party would be disbanded, with each member
of Parliament deciding his own future. Thus in the December,
1968 elections for a new Parliament only one ex-NPP member
ran. Mr. Hugh Mitchley successfully contested a safe ANC
seat in the Southern Province as an independent candidate but
with the clear approval of the ANC. Also one of his former
NPP colleagues in Parliament, Mr. R. E. Farmer, was
elected as the ANC member for Pemba in a by-election in
1971.

NATIONAL PROVIDENT FUND (NPF) see   ZAMBIA NATIONAL
    PROVIDENT FUND

NATIONAL REPUBLICAN PARTY. A "party" that seemed to arise
    only for the sake of sponsoring two candidates for the two
    Federal Parliament seats for Northern Rhodesia's Africans.
    They won the election of April 27, 1962 with 25 and 22 votes.
    Called a front organization for the United Federal Party, it
    was combined in this campaign with a similar group, the Cen-
    tral African People's Union (q.v.) of Dixon Konkola, one of
    the two candidates.

NATIVE AUTHORITIES (or AUTHORITY). A term that developed
    from the British policy of Indirect Rule (q.v.). Under this
    policy, adopted in Northern Rhodesia in the late 1920's, chiefs
    and principal headmen were recognized as "Native Authorities"

and thus became British agents in a specific territorial unit.
They were permitted to make orders and rules for the regulation of their districts, but this was subject to a veto of a
white district commissioner (D. C.).   Also the D. C. could require a Native Authority to issue orders or enforce rules as
desired by the D. C.   Some judicial responsibility was also
given to the Native Authority.   In practice, however, D. C. 's
were not very willing to relinquish much authority to chiefs, so
Indirect Rule did not actually function much except perhaps in
Barotseland.   The major Native Authority ordinances were
passed in 1929 and 1936, with numerous amendments added in
subsequent years.   The importance of the system is that it
gave the British colonial rulers a basis for the control of African affairs in rural areas which would have been harder to
control otherwise.

NATIVE AUTHORITIES ORDINANCE, 1929.   The specific act of the
Northern Rhodesia Government that instituted the British policy
of Indirect Rule (q. v.) into the country in 1930.   In addition to
recognizing limited autonomy for each Native Authority (q. v.),
it continued to keep each chief and headman under the supervision of European administrators.   As a result of the ordinance, the chiefs developed their own staffs, each consisting
of a clerk, court assessors, and messengers.   It was hoped
by J. Moffat Thomson, the Secretary for Native Affairs, that
the ordinance would defuse potential native unrest by returning
to the chief some of the management of his peoples' affairs.
Under the previous law, the Administration of Natives Proclamation of 1916 (and amended in 1919), the chiefs and headmen
had become, said Thomson, "merely ... mouthpieces of the
government. "

NATIVE AUTHORITIES ORDINANCE, 1936.   A modification of the
Native Authorities Ordinance, 1929 (q. v.), it added native councils and councillors to the chiefs and headmen already included
as Native Authorities.   It thus allowed councils of Africans to
constitute the Native Authority in areas where traditionally
chiefs did not exist.   It also recognized the position of the
"chief in council" where such was the pattern more acceptable
to the Africans than an independent chief.   This Ordinance was
amended nine times in the next twenty-five years.

NATIVE AUTHORITIES ORDINANCE, 1960.   An ordinance that provided for the election of a deputy chief when the district commissioner determined that the existing chief is too aged, infirm, or otherwise incompetent to fulfill his administrative
duties.   This opened the way for Africans to interject party
politics (through the electoral process) into the traditional political system.   A notable example of this occurred among the
Yombe people in 1962.

NATIVE COMMISSIONER (N. C.).   Originally the term used by the
British South Africa Company to designate the head administrators

of the administrative districts they were setting up in North-
East Rhodesia around 1905. Sometimes the term "Collector"
was used instead, as a primary function of the men was to collect taxes from the Africans. After a few years, however, the
term "District Commissioner" (q. v.) replaced the two others.
Then the phrase "Native Commissioner" was used to refer to
assistants to the District Commissioner, each one of whom
was responsible to the D. C. for a portion of the district.

NATIVE COURTS ORDINANCE OF 1936. An act that gave to the
Governor of Northern Rhodesia the power to appoint African
courts and also to prescribe their procedures and powers.
However it gave the territory's regular (white) judiciary the
power to reverse, vary, quash, or re-try judgments from Native Courts. It repealed and replaced the Native Courts Ordinance of 1929 which had proven relatively ineffective in restor-
ing power to native courts because it ignored the existence of
native councils and other officials.

NATIVE RESERVES. A system instituted initially in the 1920's by
which Africans could be limited to certain sections of land
(reserves) in order to allow white settlers to move into territory traditionally belonging to the Africans. These were set
up primarily in areas that were specifically attracting European settlement. Reserves Commissions (q. v.) were appointed
in 1924, 1926, and 1927 to try to resolve the conflicts that
arose in those years.

NATIVE TREASURIES ORDINANCE, 1936. An ordinance that gave
the local Native Authority (q. v.) the power to collect the native
tax and spend money from this and other sources that were
designated later. It was intended to give African leaders a
greater stake in the success of local government activity. A
similar ordinance for Barotseland was passed in 1935. Considerable British supervision over the expenditure of the Barotse Treasury was provided by the 1935 ordinance.

NATIVE WELFARE ASSOCIATIONS see WELFARE ASSOCIATIONS

NCHANGA. A mining town adjacent to Chingola (q. v.), its "twin
town," it is situated farther north on the Copperbelt than all
cities except Chililabombwe. The town developed as a result
of the development of the Nchanga mine (q. v.).

NCHANGA CONSOLIDATED COPPER MINES LTD. (NCCM). Originally formed in 1937 with a capital of £5 million at the time
of the sinking of new shafts at the Nchanga mine, it was a
subsidiary of the Anglo-American Corporation of South Africa
Ltd. (q. v.). In the early 1970's, however, 51 percent of Anglo-
American's stock (held by another subsidiary, ZAMANGLO) was
to be transferred to a Zambian government corporation, ZIM-
CO. Thus the Nchanga company was amalgamated with Bancroft Mines Limited, Rhokana Corporation Limited, and Rhokana

Copper Refineries Limited. The amalgamated group was first called Bancroft Mines Limited, but it then changed its name to Nchanga Consolidated Copper Mines Limited. In effect, NCCM is the successor of the strong Anglo-American group in Zambia. ZIMCO owns 51 percent and 49 percent is owned by a new Anglo-American subsidiary, Zambia Copper Investments Limited. The main offices of NCCM are in Lusaka.

NCHANGA MINE. Located by the twin Copperbelt cities of Chingola-Nchanga, it is an enormous mine that is one of the largest (if not the largest) open pit copper mines in the world. Its ore was first discovered by two prospectors sent out by Edmund Davis (q. v.), named Frank Lewis and Orlando Baragwanath, around 1900. In October 1923 Raymond Brooks, a mining engineer working for Chester Beatty's Copper Ventures, reported that his crews had unearthed a large oxide ore-body at Nchanga. Brooks and an old copper prospector, William Collier (q. v.) continued drilling despite Beatty's financial difficulties and proved that commercial grade ore was available in quantity. Work ceased at Nchanga in 1931, the result of the world-wide depression, but new incline shafts were sunk in 1937. Nchanga Consolidated Copper Mines Ltd. (q. v.) was formed, and production began in 1939. In 1955 the mine began using enormous mechanical shovels in its open-pit process of mining and quickly became one of the world's largest producing copper mines. It is a unique site on the Copperbelt in that secondary minerals, such as azurite and malachite are found there to form "enriched ore." The mine is still the largest producer on the Copperbelt. Its parent company was formerly the Anglo-American Corporation, but now is a new company that is using the earlier name: the Nchanga Consolidated Copper Mines Ltd. (q. v.). Fifty-one percent of it is owned by the Zambian Government. The Nchanga mine was the prime target of a series of work stoppages in 1966 when wildcat strikes spread from Nchanga to all parts of the Copperbelt.

NDEBELE (or MATABELE; MATEBELE). One of the two major groups of Africans in Zimbabwe (Southern Rhodesia), they are originally an Nguni people from what is now the Natal region of South Africa. They were part of the Zulu nation led by Chaka (Shaka) when, in the 1820's, one of Chaka's generals named Mzilikazi fled westward with a large marauding band. The Ndebele, as they became known, were rejected or defeated by the indigenous peoples in several parts of southern Africa before the main band settled in Rhodesia. Mzilikazi died in 1868 but was succeeded by his son Lobengula (q. v.). The two men were responsible for numerous raids into southern Zambia, preferring to raid cattle herds when possible but they also took many slaves. Both the Makololo of Sebituane (q. v.) and the Lozi lived in fear of the Ndebele. The Lozi homeland was not really endangered, but some of their subject peoples in the area north and west of Victoria Falls were regularly threatened or attacked. It was King Lewanika's concern about the Ndebele that was a major factor in his seeking British protection through treaties. Only once, in 1891-92 was an Ndebele army sent toward the Lozi heartland, but it was recalled before conflict began. Lobengula died in 1894 and there was no successor. The British South Africa Company had signed "the Rudd Concession" in 1888 with Lobengula which gave them mineral rights in his territory. With no obvious successor to Lobengula, the Company took control of the area. See also NGABE.

NDEMBU. Numbering about fifty thousand people, the Ndembu live in northwestern Zambia near the Lunda and Luvale peoples to whom they are related. In fact, like the others, the Ndembu originated as a result of the expansion in the sixteenth or seventeenth century of the Kingdom of Mwata Yamvo (q. v.), the Lunda king in the Congo. They still sent him tribute as late as the nineteenth century. The Lunda intruders had settled among the Mbwela, but both factions took the name Ndembu. The Ndembu have been a very mobile people, always searching for better hunting or farming land. At one point, however, the mobility reflected a desire to avoid Angolan slave-traders. The Ndembu did not have a centralized chieftainship. The chiefdoms were autonomous, in fact the individual chiefs themselves had little real authority over their people except in matters of rituals. To some extent this reflected a failure of the Lunda invaders to really integrate the Mbwela into their value system. When the British instituted indirect rule (q. v.) among the Ndembu they created an administrative structure and a bureaucracy that previously had not really existed. Headmen became subchiefs with capitals, clerks, and messengers; also the British designated a senior chief.

NDOLA. Located near the southern end of the Copperbelt, Ndola is said to be the fastest-growing urban area on the Copperbelt. Its population in 1963 was eighty-six thousand, but jumped to 150,000 in 1969. A 1975 estimate is 225,000. Some of this growth is due to the reopening of its Bwana Mkubwa mine (q. v.) in late-1970. However it is also the capital of the Copperbelt Province and the distribution center for the Copperbelt region. Its international airport serves the whole region, and the oil pipeline from Dar es Salaam ends at Ndola. Numerous industries are located in Ndola, and both The Times of Zambia and the Zambia News are printed there. For tourists there is a fine zoo.

Ndola is an old center, as Africans used it as a market center and Arabs came for slaves there. In 1902 the BSAC had a boma located at Ndola. Around 1908 the line-of-rail reached the town. The Bwana Mkubwa mine is located within its boundaries and has been producing periodically for many years. Roan Consolidated Mines Ltd. (q. v.) has its regional headquarters there, and both copper and oil refineries are in Ndola. It is also the location of the Northern Technical College.

NDOLA MINE see BWANA MKUBWA MINE

NDOLA NATIVE WELFARE ASSOCIATION. One of the earliest
    welfare associations formed in Zambia, it was organized in
    1930 and was patterned after the one in Livingstone. An or-
    ganizer of the Livingstone association, J. Ernest Mattako, had
    been transferred to Ndola as a court interpreter and joined
    with two other civil servants, Ernest A. Muwamba and Elijah
    Herbert Chunga to set it up. The leaders proposed that all
    attempts at reform be approached in a moderate fashion to
    avoid restrictions by the Government. They then complained
    about health, housing, and food and water supplies. A new
    hospital for Africans was built by the Government at Ndola.

NEA. A battle site near N'undu a little north of the Kataba valley
    in southwestern Zambia. A Lozi leader, Mubukwanu, attempted
    to make a stand here against Sebituane's Makololo forces in
    about 1838. Although the Lozi forces were defeated, they did
    capture Sebituane's daughter, Mamochisane, who was later re-
    turned.

"NEW LOOK. " A term used by Harry Nkumbula and others in the
    ANC in 1956 when the nationalists began a policy of modera-
    tion. They rejected boycotts or anything else that might lead
    to violence. They even held a meeting with the European lead-
    ers of the Legislative Council at which they committed the
    Congress to gradual reform. Nkumbula promised to keep his
    followers under control and pledged an effort to improve race
    relations. In exchange the ANC wanted "respect" from Euro-
    peans and help and sympathy from liberal-minded Europeans.
    Kenneth Kaunda and other members of ANC were bitter in their
    opposition to the "New Look, " claiming that it would not gain
    anything. In September 1956, a strike by members of the
    African Mineworker's Union led to the Government declaring a
    State of Emergency on the Copperbelt. It detained forty-five
    leaders of the union. The Government's over-reaction to the
    strike led Nkumbula to drop his attempt at a "New Look, " as
    he claimed that the Government had rejected his hand of friend-
    ship.

NEWTON, (SIR) FRANCIS JAMES. Acting Administrator of North-
    Western Rhodesia from April to August, 1906.

NGABE (or NXABA). An Ndebele (q.v.) leader who invaded western
    Zambia in the 1840's, he was said by some to have been exiled
    by Mzilikazi (q.v.) and was seeking land for his large band of
    followers. Regardless of intent, the band sought a confronta-
    tion with Sebituane's Makololo (q.v.), who had just taken over
    Bulozi and were still pacifying the Upper Zambezi valley.
    Ngabe's followers got as far north as the Luvale of Kakenge
    (q.v.) and the Mbundu settlement at Nakalomo. At the latter
    they were supplied with guides who took them west towards the
    Makololo. Sebituane fled southward, and when Ngabe's force

followed they were left stranded by their guides. The Ndebele
were ambushed by the Makololo and most of them were killed.
Ngabe had not gone into battle and, upon hearing the news,
surrendered to the Lozi nearby on the island of Naloyela.
The Lozi, however, drowned Ngabe and the few remaining men,
but retained the women and children.

NGALAMA. The fourth Luyana king, he likely ruled sometime in
the seventeenth century. Some consider him to be the true
founder of what we call the Lozi (q. v.) State, rather than the
almost legendary Mboo (q. v.). Ngalama was a warrior who is
remembered as an expander of the kingdom. His warriors
conquered the breakaway states led by Mboo's relatives Mwanambinyi and Mange. These victories gave the Lozi control
over the Upper Zambezi flood plain (Bulozi, q. v.), and destroyed any possible rival.

NGAMBELA. A very important position among the Lozi traditionally, it is roughly equivalent to the title of Prime Minister or
Chief Minister. He is the principal councillor to the Litunga
(King) of the Lozi and is also head of the National Council.
It is the highest position to which a commoner can aspire and,
in fact, is held only by commoners because he is expected to
represent their interests against the royals. Thus a tension
has often existed (despite the fact that the Ngambela is chosen
and appointed by the King) as the Ngambelas have strongly opposed kings who they felt were ruling unjustly. In addition,
the Ngambela has the duty to serve as the intermediary between the King and the people. The word "Ngambela" means
spokesman or intermediary. Thus it is his duty to interpret
the desires of the one to the other. Some holders of the title
have had very strong influence on the actions of their Litunga.

NGOMBALA. According to some calculations, the sixth king of the
Luyana (later they were called Lozi), he lived probably in the
late seventeenth or early eighteenth century. Like a predecessor, Ngalama (q. v.), Ngombala was a militaristic leader who
was responsible for greatly expanding the area dominated by
the Luyana kings. His forces conquered the Subiya and Mbu-
kushu, and then moved further south overrunning most of the
southern border region of today's Zambia, including Sesheke
and the area near Victoria Falls. They even penetrated south
of the Zambezi to the land around Wankie. They traveled eastward along the northern side of the Zambezi through the land
of the Toka as far as the confluence of the Zambezi and Kafue
Rivers. The valley of the Chobe River (q. v.) on Zambia's
western border was also traveled by his forces, who overcame
the Mashi and Makoma peoples and some of the Mbunda. All
of these people were required to pay regular tribute to Ngombala and his successors, in the form of supplies from their
region, and also to supply the Luyana with labor when needed.
Indunas resided among the conquered peoples in order to insure payment. All of these military conquests were part of

Ngombala's plan to insure the homeland in the Zambezi flood
plain of sufficient quantities of supplies from the surrounding
forest areas.

Ngombala was also responsible for setting up the second
chieftaincy of his people, in the southern flood plain at what is
now Nalolo (q. v.). He first appointed his daughter, Notulu,
but after problems occurred, he replaced her as chief with his
son Mbanga.

NGONDE. A northern Malawi people to whom some of the north-
eastern Zambians (e. g. , Yombe, Lambya, and Fungwe) have
paid tribute in the past.

NGONI. The sixth-largest ethnic sub-group in Zambia, the Ngoni
number about 180,000, mostly Nyanja-speaking people living in
southeastern Zambia. There is a much larger body of them
residing in neighboring Malawi, however. Originally from
South Africa where they came from the same Nguni family of
peoples as the Zulu and Swazi, for example, they moved northward in a great migration that began about 1818 as they fled
from impending defeat at the hands of Chaka (or Shaka), the
Zulu leader. Their migration, led by their great leader Zwangendaba (q. v.), took them through parts of Mozambique and
Swaziland. In each territory they added to their numbers as
other Africans joined the migration. They crossed the Zambezi in 1835 and continued north through Zambia. They settled
for six years among the Senga in eastern Zambia before moving north to the southeastern shore of Lake Tanganyika.

After the death of Zwangendaba in 1845, a split occurred
among the Ngoni leaders and the story of the Ngoni then becomes that of leaders such as Mpezeni, Mperembe, (qq. v.)
and Mbelwa. Some of the Ngoni settled in Malawi, and others
settled at least temporarily near the Bemba and Bisa, becoming their competitors. Raids were common. Conflicts occurred between the Bemba and the Ngoni in the late 1860's.
Bemba guns, received in trade with the Arabs, held the Ngoni
warriors to a stalemate, neither gaining substantial advantages.
Ngoni fighters used the Zulu technique of stabbing with short
spears while protected by large oxhide shields. They had not
encountered bullets before and found themselves vulnerable.
Ultimately an Ngoni group under Mpezeni (q. v.) moved further
south and by 1880 had defeated the Chewa and Nsenga and occupied their territory near the present city of Chipata. There
they finally were defeated by a British force in 1898 led by
William Manning (q. v.). By that time the British South Africa
Company, working in part with a German, Karl Wiese (q. v.),
already claimed the area. Mpezeni surrendered, and the large
herds of Ngoni cattle (acquired mostly through raids) were con-
fiscated by the British.

The Ngoni people were traditionally a patrilineal society
with a warrior-state base. They have since settled down and
even adopted the matrilineal practices of the Chewa and Nsenga,
as well as their language, Nyanja. The traditional Ngoni

language is rarely used. Today they live by cultivation of maize and the herding of cattle. Ngoni chiefs have always had a degree of independence under a segmentary arrangement. The traditional age-regiment system common among the Nguni further to the south was maintained by the Ngoni as a method of providing links between the segmented chiefdoms. Also a reason for lack of real unity among the Ngoni was their practice of conquering other peoples and then tolerating their continuation under a kind of indirect rule. When Mpezeni was defeated in 1898, many subject people, not tightly controlled by the Ngoni, felt themselves free to break away. Under colonial rule the British appointed a paramount chief for the Ngoni. He was the administrative head of the area and was assisted by minor chiefs.

NGULU. Another name for Bulozi (q. v.).

NGWATO (or BAMANGWATO). The people of Chief Khama III (q. v.), inhabitants of part of Bechuanaland (the modern state of Botswana).

NGWEE. A word used by African nationalists as all or part of a rallying slogan in the period prior to independence (see KWACHA NGWEE). It is the root of a word meaning "brightness," but also can be an intensifying expletive. When the Zambian pound was replaced on January 1, 1968, by a new currency called the kwacha, it was decided that each kwacha could be subdivided into one hundred ngwee. Thus it is also a unit of Zambian currency.

NG'WENA. A Bantu word for crocodile, it was the name given by the leaders of the bena ng'andu (q. v.), or Crocodile Clan, to the site along the Kalungu River where they established their capital at the end of their long migration. This settlement was the beginning of the Bemba empire. The leaders chose the site when they discovered a dead crocodile on the riverbank and took it as a good omen.

NIAMKOLO (or NYAMUKOLO). The first actual mission station established by the London Missionary Society in Zambia, it was founded in 1885 near the southern shore of Lake Tanganyika in Mambwe country. It was evacuated in 1888 as another station had been opened recently, but was reoccupied in 1889.

NICOLL, JOHN LOWE. A representative of the African Lakes Company who obtained agreements with several Mambwe and Namwanga chiefs between 1891 and 1893. These agreements, in exchange for goods, gave the company rights to mining, game, taxes, and other privileges connected with the territory in northeastern Zambia. It is probable that the full legal and political implications of these documents were unknown to the African signatories.

NJEKWA. A Lozi commoner who organized and led the military
force that overthrew the Makololo (q. v.), who had controlled
the land of the Lozi for over two decades in the middle of the
nineteenth century. This overthrow was in 1864. It won him
so much popularity that Njekwa was offered the position of Litunga (King) despite his lack of royal blood. He declined it
and requested that Sipopa (q. v.), a member of the royal family in exile, take the post instead. Sipopa rewarded him with
the position of Ngambela (Prime Minister). The power and
popularity of Njekwa was so strong, compared especially to
some controversy over Sipopa's leadership, that the King felt
compelled to remove him. He thus "promoted" Njekwa by making him Prince Consort (Ishee Kwandu) to his daughter, Kaiko,
who ruled the southern Lozi chieftaincy at Nalolo (q. v.). This
marriage took place in 1871, but there were difficulties in the
marriage and in 1874 Njekwa had the marriage dissolved and
returned to the northern capital and asked for the King's mercy.
Soon thereafter Njekwa died, and many people suspected that
Sipopa was involved in the death somehow.

NKANA MINE. Perhaps named after a Lamba chief called Nkana,
it is located at Kitwe in the middle of the Copperbelt. It is
run by Rhokana Corporation Ltd. (q. v.), a part of the Nchanga
Consolidated Copper Mines Ltd. (q. v.). Copper was first produced there in November, 1931, and cobalt production began in
August, 1933. An electrolytic copper refinery began operation
in 1935. The important strikes (q. v.) of 1935 and 1940 both
occurred at Nkana, in addition to Mufulira and Nchanga.

NKANDABWE. A site in the Gwembe Valley by Lake Kariba that
produced coal from 1965 until 1969 when the deposit was exhausted and the mine closed. Fifty percent of the venture was
Government owned. While the coal was inferior in quality to
that imported from Wankie in Rhodesia, it provided an important supplement to Wankie imports, enabling the Zambian Government to resist the threat of extortion by the Rhodesian Government until an even better Zambian coalfield at Maamba
could begin production in 1968.

NKOLE. The younger brother of Chiti (q. v.), the man who led the
Bemba migration and who became the first great Bemba leader.
Nkole and his brothers were sons of Mukulumpe (q. v.) but they
fled from his rule. They left their Luba homeland in what is
Zaire today and crossed the Luapula River into Zambia. Chiti
was killed in a battle by another chief and Nkole carried away
the corpse to find a suitable burial place. A beautiful grove
of trees called Mwalule was found. Nkole sent a force to
avenge Chiti's death by murdering the other chief, Mwase.
During the burning of the bodies of Mwase and his wife (Chiti
had been involved in a love affair with her), the smoke from
the fire choked Nkole and he died. He was buried at Mwalule
near Chiti.

NKOLEMFUMU. One of the senior chieftainships among the Bemba,
it is held only by members of the bena ng'andu, or royal clan.
Holders of the title have sometimes given it up to succeed to
other chieftainships, notably Mwamba and Chitimukulu. The
territory (icalo, q.v.) of the Nkolemfumu is called Miti, and
is in the central part of Bemba country. Miti's western border is the Lukulu River.
    The title was derived from Nkole, a relative of Chiti and
Nkole (q.v.), the Bemba founders. He had settled in Miti instead of proceeding to the Kalungu River with most of the
other Bemba. Two other early Nkolemfumus were named
Mwalula and Chisanga. At the death of Chisanga around 1825,
there was no immediate successor. Mambwa I Mutale took
over Miti as well as his own Ituna. (At times in the past
parts of Ituna had also been ruled by Nkolemfumu.)
    The title of Nkolemfumu was revived around 1870 for Mu-
banga Chipoya, a son-in-law of Mwamba II. A warrior who
had successfully fought the Bisa, he now was to rule both Miti
and some Bisa territory. In 1873 he expanded into the Bisa
kingdom of Mpuki as well. In 1884 Mubanga Chipoya was promoted to Mwamba III. From 1884 to 1895 Mubanga continued
to rule Miti while also serving as Mwamba. In 1895 he was
replaced by Kanyanta (q.v.), himself to become a very prominent Bemba leader, eventually serving as Chitimukulu from
1925 to 1943. The chieftainship continues to the present day.

NKOLOMA, MATTHEW DELUXE. An active trade union leader,
in the 1950's he served as General Secretary of both the African Mineworkers Union and the Trade Union Congress. A
series of work stoppages in August 1956 led the Government to
declare a state of emergency in the Western Province. Nkoloma was one of forty-five labor leaders detained. He was
held in restriction for three years.

NKOMO, JOSHUA. A major African political leader in Southern
Rhodesia during the period of the Federation, twenty years
later he is competing against other Africans for the leadership
of his country while simultaneously fighting for African self-
rule for Zimbabwe against the white Government of Ian Smith.
During the 1950's and early 60's, however, Nkomo was the
principal African nationalist representative for his country,
working alongside Dr. H. K. Banda of Nyasaland (Malawi) and
Kenneth Kaunda. Their cooperation was never more in evidence than when they staged a walkout from the Federal Review
Conference of December, 1960. In early 1979 he was residing
in Zambia where many of his guerrilla forces were also based.

NKOYA (or MANKOYA). Descendants of the Mbwela, some of the
earliest Congolese migrants into west-central Zambia, the
Nkoya number somewhat less than fifty thousand today, living
east of the Lozi and west of Ila and Kaonde. The Nkoya came
under the strong influence of the Lozi, and in fact speak a
language that is a sub-group of the Barotse language group.

Some Nkoya traditions indicate that their ruling dynasty may
actually be related to the Lozi dynasty. Mboo (q.v.) is re-
puted to be a brother of Nkoya founders, Manenya and Isikena.
In the nineteenth century the Lozi exercised influence among
the Nkoya by situating among them Lozi indunas as representatives of the King of Barotseland. Related or not, the Nkoya
have resented their position as subject peoples to the Lozi.
When the Makololo (q.v.) overran the Lozi in the mid-nineteenth
century, they also conquered the Nkoya.

NKUBA. The principal chieftainship of the Shila (q.v.), a people
living in northeastern Zambia, south of Lake Mweru. Nkuba
IV was killed in about 1760 by Kazembe III of the Lunda, and
the Shila have continued to pay tribute to the Lunda since then.
Nkuba claims to be of Bemba origin, even to belong to the
Crocodile Clan of Chitimukulu. Once defeated by the Lunda,
however, Nkuba and his people have become "honorary Lunda."
The relationship between Kazembe and Nkuba bears some similarity to the British system of Indirect Rule.

NKUKA. A Bisa leader who was involved in lengthy litigation early
in the twentieth century over rights to the area near Mpika
called Kasenga. Nkuka claimed to bear the title of an old
Bisa chieftainship that had lost its Kasenga territory to a nineteenth century invasion by the Bemba Chief Chikwanda (q.v.).
The Nkuka and his followers had fled to the Luangwa Valley.
Other observers claimed that Nkuka was never a sovereign
chief but was always subordinate to Chikwanda. Nkuka took
the issue to the British administrators for a decision during
World War I, and in June, 1918, Hugh Marshall (q.v.) ruled
in favor of Chikwanda.

NKULA (or NKULA/CHEWE). One of the senior Bemba chieftainships, its chiefs have always been members of the royal clan,
the bena ng'andu (q.v.). The Nkula of the moment may later
succeed to other titles, including that of Chitimukulu. The
land (icalo, q.v.) of the Nkula is called Ichinga, which is
southeast of Chitimukulu's Lubemba. As chieftainships expand
or decline, additional land can be gained or lost. Nkula's
land expanded considerably during the rule of Nkula I Mutale
Sichansa (q.v.).
    The chieftainship has not always been known as Nkula.
Originally it was called Katongo (q.v.), as it was presumably
originated by Katongo, the brother of Chiti (the Bemba founder).
It has also been known as Chewe, named after a nephew of one
Katongo who had become Chitimukulu. Chewe was one of several possible successors to the position of Katongo, but defeated
his opponents, one of whom had dragged him from his hut.
After winning, Chewe added the name Nkula, derived from a
Bemba word meaning "to pull." Thus this man became known
as Katongo Chewe Nkula; also known as Kamponge. This man
seems to have died in the 1860's. He was unfortunate enough
to have the Ngoni (q.v.) attack his territory in the 1850's, and

had to temporarily flee his capital. On another occasion his
forces came into conflict with Chitimukulu Chileshye, and again
he was not successful. A subsequent Chitimukulu sent several
people, including Sampa (q. v.) to rule Ishinga temporarily.
Finally the appointment was made about 1870 of a man who became known as Nkula I Mutale Sichansa (q. v.). The leadership has been continuous since then, with the Nkula V now
ruling.

NKULA I MUTALE SICHANSA. One of the more active Bemba
leaders of the nineteenth century, he was a nephew of Chitimukulu Chitapankwa, and as a young man stole the royal
babenye (q. v.) from Bwembya (q. v.) to enable Chitapankwa to
become Chitimukulu. He was later rewarded, as Chitapankwa
appointed him to the Mwaba chieftainship. In about 1870 he
was moved up to the vacant chieftainship of Nkula (q. v.).
Chitapankwa gave him his daughter Mande as a wife as well.
The Chitimukulu wanted Mutale Sichansa to help fight off the
Ngoni from this new post. In this position, which he held until his death in September, 1896, he was actively engaged in
trade with the Arabs. His land, Ishinga, was close to the
great elephant herds, so ivory became a major item. The
famous Tippu Tip (q. v.) dealt with him, for example. The
French explorer Victor Giraud described Nkula's trade in detail.
      Mutale Sichansa was not content with his territory at
Ichinga. He also moved south into Isunga, the former chiefdom of Mungulube, and also in the 1870's he moved east into
Bisa chiefdoms. In 1884 he was also at war with Sampa (q. v.)
resisting his claims to the power and position of Chitimukulu
after Chitapankwa's death. Nkula also gained influence over
the Bisa territory formerly ruled by Chibesakunda (q. v.), and
put a son, Ndakala, in charge of it. After Nkula I's death in
1896, there was an attempt by Chikwanda (q. v.) II Mutale
Lwanga to take over his title and territory, but finally a son
of Chileshye (q. v.), Bwalya, was appointed as Nkula II (q. v.).

NKULA II BWALYA CHANGALA (also known as MUKWIKILE). A
son of Chitimukulu Chileshye, Bwalya (Mukwikile) had been appointed by Chitapankwa to succeed Mutale Sichansa as ruler
of Mwaba's country in the late 1860's. There were complaints
about his rule, however, so he was moved to Ichinga temporarily until he was given rule over Chingoli, the land of Chin-
kumba. When Nkula I Mutale Sichansa died in 1896 there was
a question over succession. A year or so previously Nkula I
had given Bwalya (Mukwikile) part of his land. But the BSAC
agent McKinnon supported Chikwanda II Mutale Lwanga for the
post of Nkula. He was never properly installed, however, and
Bwalya finally received the title of Nkula II. He held the post
until he died in 1934.

NKUMBULA, HARRY MWAANGA. Called by some the father of
Zambian nationalism, the son of a subchief among the Ila

people of southern Zambia was born in January, 1916, at
Maala in the Namwala District. During his education at Metho-
dist Mission schools he was inspired by George Padmore's
How Britain Rules Africa to stand against white supremacy.
He qualified as a teacher in 1934 at Kafue Training College
and taught at Namwala schools for several years. He joined
the United Missions in the Copperbelt teaching staff in 1942.
He was assigned to Mufulira where he became Secretary of the
Mufulira Welfare Association (q. v.). His vigorous political
activity there against the proposed amalgamation with Southern
Rhodesia led to his transfer to Kitwe. Here he became a co-
founder of the Kitwe African Society and remained active in
politics along with other nationalists like Godwin Mbikusita and
Dauti Yamba (qq. v.). Perhaps to remove him from politics
he was given a scholarship to Makerere College in Uganda.
In 1946 he received a government scholarship to England where
he earned a Diploma in Education and studied further at the
London School of Economics. While in England he met George
Padmore and became active in the Africa Committee with future African leaders such as Kwame Nkrumah, Jomo Kenyatta,
and H. K. Banda.

He left London in 1950 and worked briefly as a salesman
in East Africa before returning to Northern Rhodesia in July,
1951 to address the Northern Rhodesia African Congress. His
strong opposition to Federation led the membership to elect
him President of what he immediately renamed the African
National Congress.

Nkumbula began a vigorous campaign to oppose Federation
(he and Dr. Banda wrote a notable pamphlet against it in London in May, 1949), with primary emphasis on developing new
ANC branches, some as far away as South Africa. Provincial
officers were established and a national headquarters was set
up at Chilenje near Lusaka with one full-time employee. The
African National Congress (q. v.) was quickly growing in all but
the Eastern Province and the two westernmost provinces.
Nkumbula's militant campaign against the proposed Federation
included a public burning of a Government White Paper in
March, 1953. He also called a boycott campaign, which failed.
When the Federation began, Nkumbula's energy flagged and his
leadership seemed to drift. At the same time, younger party
members such as Kenneth Kaunda became very active. In January, 1955, however, Kaunda and Nkumbula were both jailed
for two months "at hard labour" for distributing prohibited literature (the ANC newspaper). In 1958 he burned another White
Paper, this containing new constitutional proposals. In February, 1958 Nkumbula and Kaunda proposed their own constitution
to the Governor, which called for universal adult suffrage.

A break in the ANC came in October, 1958 at a meeting
of the national executive. Nkumbula submitted his resignation
to the three hundred delegates, but he was reelected President
and the Kaunda-led opposition resigned to form ZANC. The
opposition felt that Nkumbula was not an effective head, had
mishandled party funds, and was not enough of a self-sacrificing

and committed leader. In addition his ultimate willingness to
"try" the new constitutional provisions had lost him the support of his more radical followers. Still he had much mass
support throughout the country.

In March, 1959, Nkumbula and the ANC did contest the
elections and he won a seat in the Legislative Council. But
other members were breaking away from the ANC also, and
with the eventual successes of the Kaunda-led UNIP in 1960,
the ANC was reduced to a shadow of its former strength. In
September, 1960, he was sentenced to a year in jail for dangerous driving, an incident that had resulted in one death. Out
on appeal, he attended the Federal Review Conference in London and the subsequent 1961 Constitutional Conference, during
both of which Kaunda was obviously leading the nationalist
side. In April, 1961 his appeals were denied and Nkumbula
was jailed until January, 1962. Meanwhile his seat in the
Legislative Council was declared vacant.

The year 1962 was devoted to preparing the ANC for the
December elections. The ANC was not nearly as well organized as the rival UNIP, and despite encouragement from
Roy Welensky's United Federal Party, the ANC only won seven
seats. This was enough, however, to make Nkumbula the
power-broker. He could join either the UFP or UNIP in a
coalition and put that group in power. Although he had an unofficial alliance with the UFP, Nkumbula chose to join Kaunda
in an African coalition. As a result he was named Minister
of African Education in the coalition cabinet. With a new constitution, however, the ANC was not as successful in the 1964
elections and at independence Nkumbula was leader of the Opposition Party in Parliament. His party had only ten seats to
UNIP's 55. The ANC had a resurgence in 1968. Combining
Nkumbula's traditional strength in southern Zambia with support from members of the banned United Party (q.v.), the
ANC won 23 seats to UNIP's 81. In 1972 he was fighting to
prevent the establishment of a one-party state in Zambia, but
when it occurred Nkumbula finally gave in. On June 27, 1973
he announced that he was joining UNIP. He said, "I cannot
sit idle or bury my head in the sand." In 1978 he failed in an
attempt to secure UNIP's nomination for President.

NKWETO. A Bemba chieftainship of the royal clan, the bena
ng'andu, it is somewhat remote from the current dominant line,
and as such is less important than others such as Mwamba,
Chitimukulu, and Nkula. Succession is more localized and its
chiefs do not succeed to the highest chieftainships, but there
is a special relationship and even succession pattern with the
Mumena chieftainships. The country ruled by Nkweto is called
Chilinda. It is in the eastern extreme of Bemba territory,
east of the Chambeshi River. During the mid-nineteenth century the area was invaded by the Ngoni (q.v.), and the Nkweto
fled. Makasa, another Bemba chief, tried to reassert Bemba
authority in Chilinda, but Makasa Kalulu was killed there by
the Ngoni around 1850 at the battle of Chisenga.

NOMBOTI (pl., Linomboti). A special official among the Lozi who lives in a village near the grave of a dead king.   It is his task to care for the grave, to care for the needs of the deceased leader, and to serve as the intermediary between the departed king and the people.   He is believed to have the power to communicate with the king, passing requests and special pleas to him when requested.

NORTH BANK POWER STATION   see   KARIBA DAMS AND HYDRO-ELECTRIC PROJECTS

NORTH CHARTERLAND EXPLORATION COMPANY.   A company organized in May, 1895 to exploit gold that was believed to exist in southeastern Zambia, especially in land occupied by the Ngoni under Chief Mpezeni.   The British South Africa Company owned 30 percent of the original shares.   The new company immediately sent out an expedition that was accompanied by Karl Wiese (q. v.), a German very friendly with Mpezeni. Wiese had owned concessions in the area since 1891 and had sold his rights in that territory to the North Charterland Exploration Company.   Despite his presence, prospectors soon had conflicts with the Ngoni.   Ultimately British-led troops with maxim guns were brought in to put down an Ngoni rebellion that began in December, 1897, and lasted two months. The village of Mpezeni (q. v.) was captured and the Chief fled. Now the North Charterland Company distributed the Ngoni land (still heavily populated) to European cattle-owners, a move that caused increased friction with the Africans.   The problem of relocating the Africans continued for four decades.

At the end of World War I, with new settlers arriving, the Company again requested that Africans (about 150,000) be moved from their lands in the Fort Jameson district so Europeans could purchase Company lands.   Despite both African and missionary protests, the Africans were removed from the best lands.   The Company owned ten thousand square miles in the area, but vigorously opposed a move in the 1920's and 1930's to create several thousand square miles of African Reserves in its territory.   It fought the British Colonial office in a strong lobbying campaign, but ultimately depleted its own resources in the process.   In 1936 it had to be reorganized with South African money.   The new board of directors continued to quarrel over lands for settlement, this time with the Northern Rhodesian Government.   This was resolved in 1941 after arbitration was instituted, and the Company received about £154,000 for 3,776,741 acres.   This land was opened to both African and European settlers.

NORTH-EASTERN RHODESIA.   A term used until 1911 to denote administratively the eastern portion of today's Zambia.   It was distinct from North-Western Rhodesia (q. v.), which was merely an inflated Barotseland.   The two parts were considered as different entities by the British South Africa Company early in the 1890's, as physical access to each was from vastly

separated points. The two were not formally divided administratively until 1899 when the line was drawn at the Kafue river.
In 1905 it was moved east a little to the narrow "waist" of the
country. In August, 1911, the two were again merged as a
single administrative unit, called Northern Rhodesia.

NORTH-EASTERN RHODESIA ORDER IN COUNCIL OF 1900   see
   ORDER IN COUNCIL OF 1900

NORTHERN COPPER COMPANY. One of the first European-owned
copper companies in Zambia, it operated mines along the Kafue River called the Sable Antelope and Silver King mines.   It
was owned by Edmund Davies (q. v.).

NORTHERN NEWS. Now existing as The Times of Zambia, this
paper was started in 1944 by Roy Welensky (q. v.) as a twice-
weekly.   It had a circulation of two thousand in 1951 when the
Argus news syndicate of South Africa bought it.   It was made
a daily in 1953.   Five years later its circulation had reached
eighteen thousand copies.   Throughout the 1950's and early
1960's it supported the Federation and, when necessary, argued
the cause of the settlers against the British Colonial Office.
It also supported Welensky's United Federal Party and all of
its projects.   When the UFP saw the need to cooperate with
African politicians, the paper supported the ANC along with
the UFP.   It promoted the continuation of white rule in
Southern Africa, but also supported Tshombe's secession of
Katanga from the Congo.   In 1962 it began to treat African nationalists, and especially Kaunda, in a more balanced fashion,
as it began to recognize the inevitability of Zambian independence.   In December, 1964, its ownership was purchased by
Lonrho (q. v.).   On May 18, 1965, Richard Hall (see his works
in the Bibliography) was appointed its editor.   He was a British
newspaperman who was a strong supporter of the Africans.   On
July 1, 1965, the paper was renamed The Times of Zambia
(q. v.).

NORTHERN PROVINCE.   Physically dominating the eastern half of
the map of Zambia, the Northern Province covers an area of
62,880 square miles.   It stretches almost from Lake Mweru
in the west to the upper stretches of the Luangwa River in the
east, and from the southern part of Lake Tanganyika to one
point only seventy-five miles from Zambia's southern border.
It has seven districts: Mporokoso, Kasama, Chinsali, Isoka,
Luwingu, Mbala, and Mpika.   They totaled 545,000 people in
1969, with Kasama, accounting for 20 percent, being the
largest.   Nevertheless the province's population had dropped
about 3. 4 percent since 1963.   The province is lightly populated, with a density of only ten people per square mile.   Part
of this is because the tsetse fly has been prevalent in some of
its regions, and also because its land is generally not very
fertile.   The traditional economy has never been much beyond
subsistence agriculture, supplemented by hunting and fishing.

The chitemene (q. v.) system of cultivation has been widely
practiced there.

Historically the Northern Province has been the scene of
many peoples crossing paths. Arab slave traders from the
northeast in Tanganyika have both fought and traded with the
Africans. Portuguese traders came up from the southeast.
The British South Africa Company made its first major inroads in the province, and missionaries also arrived in the
late nineteenth century. The Africans in the Northern Province
represent a very wide variety of ethnic divisions and subdivisions. While the Bemba dominated the province, other groups
well represented are the Bisa, Tabwa, Lungu, and Mambwe.
CiBemba is the lingua franca. With the land not the best for
agriculture, the people of the Northern Province have responded in large numbers to the need for mine workers. Thus
the Copperbelt has a large representation from the Northern
Province. Over 60 percent of the rural males of the province
leave their homes to find wage employment elsewhere. Some
deposits of manganese show potential as sources of future development in the province.

NORTHERN RHODESIA. The name officially attached to the country now called Zambia in 1911 when it was officially created
by the British South Africa Company through the convenient
merger of North-Eastern Rhodesia (q. v.) and North-Western
Rhodesia (q. v.). It remained the name until the territory became independent as the Republic of Zambia on October 24,
1964. Permission had been granted by the British Foreign
Office in 1897 for the BSAC to use the term "Northern Rhodesia" for its territories north of the Zambezi River.

NORTHERN RHODESIA AFRICAN CONGRESS. The first in a line
of African nationalist organizations that culminated in the
present ruling party, UNIP. The NRAC was founded in early
July, 1948. This occurred at a general conference of the Federation of African Societies of Northern Rhodesia (q. v.) when
the conference unanimously voted to change its name. It
elected Godwin Mbikusita as President, Robinson Nabulyato as
Secretary, and Mateyo Kakumbi as Treasurer. The stated
goals of the new organization included promoting the educational, political, economic, and social advancement of the Africans. The conference restated African opposition to rule by
Europeans and to either amalgamation or federation. It opposed having a European represent the Africans in the Legislative Council. It also demanded to be represented at the
forthcoming London constitutional conference. The NRAC was
generally a very moderate body, however, despite which it
received only negative responses from the Northern Rhodesia
Government. In August, 1951, its leadership was assumed by
Harry Nkumbula, who changed its name immediately to the
African National Congress (q. v.).

In 1937 there was another organization named the Northern
Rhodesia African Congress that consisted of a number of

successful farmers, teachers, and chiefs who were Plateau
Tonga and lived near Mazabuka. It was basically a local
group and its interests were mostly in the areas of agriculture
and land tenure. It was short-lived due to government disapproval. One of its leaders was George W. Kaluwa (q. v.).

NORTHERN RHODESIA COMMONWEALTH PARTY. A very minor
party, almost the personal organization of a very active, conservative politician, Guillaume Van Eeden (q. v.). He formed
it after he had been expelled from the Federal Party in 1955,
joining with some individuals who had been active in the Confederate Party (q. v.). The party campaigned on a segregationist platform for partition. In 1958 Van Eeden, who held
the Kafue seat from Northern Rhodesia in the Federal Parliament, joined forces with the Federal Dominion Party (q. v.).

NORTHERN RHODESIA LABOUR PARTY. A party that lasted
through most of the 1940's, the Labour Party was formed in
1941 by Roy Welensky (q. v.) and six other members of the
Legislative Council. Welensky became its president and moving force. He was a strong proponent of amalgamation with
Southern Rhodesia and, later, of Federation. The party policies reflected these thoughts. As a Labor-oriented party, it
was also against African competition for jobs, especially in
the mines and along the line of rail where its European supporters were employed. It also worked for increased power
for the Unofficials in the Legislative Council. Welensky, a
railway worker himself by experience, also worked hard for
closed shop agreements with employers. A 1948 visit to England disillusioned him with the British Labour Party, and he
disbanded his party to devote greater energies to the goal of
Federation.

NORTHERN RHODESIA LIBERAL PARTY. Formed in October,
1960, when Sir John Moffat took his successful Northern Rhodesian segment out of the otherwise floundering Central Africa
Party (q. v.) and renamed it the N. R. Liberal Party. Moffat,
Harry Franklin, and A. H. Gondwe had all won seats in the
Northern Rhodesia Legislative Council as CAP candidates in
1959. In February, 1961 they received ministerial posts on
the Executive Council when the United Federal Party withdrew
from the Government in protest over a new constitution for
Northern Rhodesia. The Liberal Party position (in essence,
the position of Moffat, its dominant figure) was that the Federation should be disbanded and a High Commission should be
set up for the three territories. Moffat felt that the Constitution should be considered by Europeans as a transitional one,
designed to allow Africans experience in leadership en route
to total self-government. During this period, probably only
five years, Moffat felt, Europeans would have one last chance
to prove to the Africans that true partnership was possible.
Then a new Constitution, presumably to allow for multi-racial
participation (a key to all Liberal Party thinking), could be

established to settle Northern Rhodesia's future. The party opposed the one man one vote concept, but did seek a wider franchise for Africans. The Liberal Party suffered from lack of membership and insufficient funds. In March, 1962, it had only fifteen registered branches and less than a hundred truly active members. Its policies were too liberal for most Europeans and too conservative for most Africans. Despite an electoral situation that seemed to aid any party that could get both European and African votes, the Liberal Party was trounced in the 1962 elections. In the upper roll (European) part of the election, its twelve candidates averaged about 125 votes each, 5 percent of the total cast; its lower roll total was much worse. Twenty-eight of its thirty candidates in the election lost their deposits. Only A. H. Gondwe made even a fair showing, but that wasn't good enough to win. The UFP had won 90 percent of the European vote. After the election Moffat disbanded the party.

NORTHERN RHODESIA ORDERS IN COUNCIL see ORDER IN COUNCIL OF ...

NORTHERN RHODESIA POLICE. Formed in 1912 by a merger of the North-Eastern Rhodesia Constabulary and the Barotse Native Police (q.v.), its membership at that point consisted of 27 British officers and 750 Africans. It was armed with rifles and a few machine guns, but no artillery and minimal motor transport. When World War I broke out, a detachment of Northern and Southern Rhodesia Police left the Victoria Falls Bridge and occupied the German post of Schuckmannsburg in the Caprivi Strip. Also a mobile column of N.R. Police rushed north to the Tanganyika border which was threatened by the German post at Bismarckburg, less than forty miles north of Abercorn. The Mobile Column was in time to assist in the defense of Abercorn and Fife late in 1914. In early 1915 a Mobile Column of the Northern Rhodesia Rifles (q.v.) provided needed reinforcement, notably at the battles around Saisi in mid-1915. In May, 1916, two columns of soldiers, including some forces of the N.R. Police, moved north into Tanganyika, occupying parts of German East Africa. The German leader there was Gen. P. E. von Lettow-Vorbeck (q.v.). He evaded a direct confrontation and ultimately moved his troops into Northern Rhodesia, capturing several northeastern towns before the N.R. Police and other military units could engage him in a battle late in 1918 just as the war was ending in Europe. In 1932 the Government of Northern Rhodesia separated the civil and military units of the Police, so that in 1933 the military unit became known as the Northern Rhodesia Regiment.

NORTHERN RHODESIA REFORMED TRADE UNION CONGRESS see REFORMED TRADE UNION CONGRESS

NORTHERN RHODESIA RIFLES. Growing out of a Rifle Association,

it was a totally European, volunteer, military unit in the
World War I effort. Its organizer was Major Boyd Alexander
Cuninghame, a Scotsman who bred cattle for market west of
Lusaka. His force numbered about three hundred officers and
men, about 135 of whom constituted a Mobile Column in March,
1915. This Column marched over 550 miles to reach the
northern border with German Tanganyika where most of their
clashes occurred. Eventually, however, they were limited to
border patrol and garrison duties. In 1916 the Mobile Column
disbanded and most of its members joined other military groups,
some in Southern Rhodesia, which were more actively engaged
in battles. Cuninghame died of typhoid fever in 1917 and no
strong leader emerged. By 1918 its membership was too low
to have it considered a dependable fighting unit.

NORTHERN RHODESIAN EURAFRICAN ASSOCIATION. An organization based in Ndola in the late 1950's, it was composed of
politically conscious members of the fairly small "colored" or
mixed race community of Zambia. In July, 1960, its Chairman, Aaron Milner (q. v.) led its members into a merger with
UNIP, although he had resisted earlier attempts because he
feared that its positions were too extreme.

NORTH-WESTERN PROVINCE. Bordering both Zaire and Angola
in the northwestern corner of the country, this lightly-settled
province had a population of only 231,000 in 1969. Its five
districts, Balovale, Kabompo, Mwinilunge, Solwezi, and Kasempa, had an average density of five people per square mile.
Kasempa had only two per square mile. The province is primarily settled by the Lunda, Kaonde, Luvale, Luchazi, Mbunda, and Ndembu peoples. Historically the people of the province have had more in common ethnically and commercially
with the people of Angola than with people in, for example,
Zambia's Northern Province. The province has some added
significance in that a number of important rivers begin in its
higher elevations (in some cases as much as 5000 feet above
sea level). These feed into the Zambezi and the Kafue Rivers.

NORTH-WESTERN RHODESIA. A term used until 1911 to denote
for administrative purposes the western portion of today's Zambia. As such it was distinct from North-Eastern Rhodesia
(q. v.). In 1899 its eastern boundary was placed along the
Kafue River, as it was meant to be essentially the territory
under Lozi domination or influence which had been acquired
from the Lozi by concessions. In fact it went much further
than Lozi influence. In 1905 the eastern boundary was moved
to a north-south line at the territory's narrow "waist." The
move effectively put all the good mining area under one jurisdiction. In August, 1911, however, the two halves were united
administratively as Northern Rhodesia.

NORTH-WESTERN RHODESIA FARMERS' ASSOCIATION. One of
the first politically active settlers' groups in Northern

Rhodesia, it began early in the twentieth century in the newly
established farming areas near the line-of-rail. By 1913 it
was urging the Administrator of Northern Rhodesia, L. A. Wallace, to establish a Legislative Council, with membership to
include the settlers.

THE NORTH-WESTERN RHODESIA ORDER IN COUNCIL OF 1899
see ORDER IN COUNCIL OF 1899

NORTH-WESTERN RHODESIA POLITICAL ASSOCIATION. Perhaps
the first significant formal political organization in Northern
Rhodesia, it grew out of the North-Western Rhodesia Farmers'
Association around 1920. It had less than a hundred active
members, mostly European farmers living in the western half
of the territory. It was led by Leopold Frank Moore (q. v.),
a pharmacist and editor in Livingstone. He fought first for
an Advisory Council and later for even greater self-government.
The farmers, notably those near the Kafue River, were also
eager to get amalgamation with Southern Rhodesia.

NOTULU. The daughter of King Ngombala and, according to Lozi
tradition, the first ruler of a second chieftaincy located in the
southern part of Bulozi. Accounts say that she requested to
go south and her father agreed, giving her royal drums and
indunas and making her the ruler there. She had a dispute
with her brother, Mbanga, who then killed her son. Later,
Notulu abdicated and Mbanga succeeded her as ruler of the
southern plain, the center of which is at Nalolo today.

NOYOO, HASTINGS NDANGWA. A Lozi political leader in the
1960's. Born in the Mongu District in 1928, Noyoo is a commoner but had ancestors on both sides of his family who had
served as Ngambela (q. v.). His education led to reception of
a medical certificate, and he worked in the Ministry of Health
in Mongu. He was a supporter of the ANC in the 1950's, even
resigning from government service to show his opposition to
the Federation. He later became active in UNIP. He was
elected in 1963 to the Katengo Kuta as a member of UNIP,
and was a leader of the elected members. At one point he
led a walk-out in protest against the Traditionalists who were
trying to retain their power in the Kuta (Council). Noyoo and
his supporters took a middle ground on the issue of Barotseland independence or inclusion in Zambia. They wanted inclusion in Zambia but with special status for Barotseland. This
position conflicted with UNIP's. In mid-1964 he was suspended
for six months from UNIP for this stand. Meanwhile he was
appointed assistant Ngambela (q. v.) in March, 1964, and
Ngambela (Prime Minister) in December, 1964 by the Council.
After independence Noyoo as Ngambela expressed again the
will of the Council to be independent of Zambia, though associated in a loose federation with it. The Government of Zambia did not accept this and passed the Local Government Bill
(q. v.) to reduce the power of the Lozi leaders. Noyoo now

turned to electoral politics again, and became active in the
United Party. When it was banned he joined the ANC and ran
for Parliament in 1968. He was one of eight Lozi ANC candidates who were successful.

NSAMA. The dominant chieftainship among the Tabwa, it was
founded by members of the bazimba (Leopard) clan who settled
in Itabwa southwest of Lake Tanganyika late in the eighteenth
century (see TABWA). A major controversy over succession
to the chieftainship involved a man named Kafwimbi (q. v.),
who ultimately became Nsama V.

NSENGA. The fifth largest ethnic group in Zambia, numbering
about 190,000, the Nsenga live in southeastern Zambia, and are
especially strong in the Petauke District. Nyanja-speaking,
the Nsenga seem to have originated in the Congo centuries ago,
and are probably of Luba background. They seem to be an
offshoot of the Chewa (q. v.), and thus were part of the group
known as Maravi who inhabited the area now part of Malawi
(a variant form of Maravi). However there is another theory
that they may have closer ties, because of similar social patterns, with the Bisa and Lala, who are also of Luba origin.
The Nsenga are a matrilineal people like the Lala and Bisa.
     In the eighteenth and nineteenth centuries the Nsenga were
actively engaged in trading ivory with the Europeans. They
also grew cotton and wove it into cloth. In the 1860's and
1870's the Ngoni of Chief Mpezeni (q. v.) invaded Nsenga territory and dominated it, both by raiding and by requiring the
payment of tribute. The Ngoni intermarried with the Nsenga
and also adopted their language. Portuguese influence was also strong in the area, but in the three years after 1887 an
Nsenga chief, Mburuma, mounted a guerrilla war against the
Portuguese and even gathered a force of two thousand warriors
to lay siege to Zumbo (q. v.) in 1888. Nsenga chiefs traditionally had firm political and judicial authority based on their
rights in their lineage. Each chiefdom was based on a single
clan, and all Nsenga chiefs were considered about equal.
British colonial officials, however, appointed a senior chief.

NSHIMA. The staple diet of many Zambians, it is a dish made of
mealiemeal (cornmeal) mixed with water.

NSOKOLO. The paramount chief of the Mambwe (q. v.), whose
territory is north of the Bemba in northeastern Zambia. The
chieftainship was weakened somewhat in the mid-nineteenth
century as its location put it in the path of both the Ngoni
(q. v.)--two holders of the title were killed by Ngoni in the
1860's--and the Bemba. Chitapankwa, a Bemba Chitimukulu,
defeated Nsokolo at one point, taking away both slaves and
cattle from the Mambwe leader. Other Bemba raids continued,
so the Mambwe eagerly accepted the protection promised by
BSAC agents. However in the early 1920's the reigning Nsokolo was vigorous in protesting tax increases and penalties to

the Secretary for Native Affairs.   The tax was then reduced in 1925.

NUMWA.   A Lozi warrior and a senior induna who eventually became a leader of the rebellion against Lubosi (q. v.), the Lozi
King.   Actually Numwa is a military praise name and his real
name was Muyunda.   A son of Muwela, his home area was in
Nanga.   At the time when Lubosi was one of two candidates
for King, Numwa supported him.   In fact, it was a force led
by Numwa that later forced its way to the hideout of Musiwa,
Lubosi's opponents, and delivered him to Lubosi to be killed.
In 1884, however, Numwa supported Mataa (q. v.) who led a
successful rebellion that deposed Lubosi.   Numwa had been
one of Lubosi's bodyguards, but turned against him when the
King had one of Numwa's close relatives murdered.   In addition, he opposed the royal decree compelling indunas to cultivate their own lands.   Thus Numwa joined forces with Mataa
and ultimately helped to install Tatila Akafuna (q. v.) as King.
However Lubosi and his followers fought back, and in 1885 a
major battle between the opposing forces was won by Lubosi.
Both Mataa and Numwa were killed in the battle.

NYAMBE.   The Lozi name for the God who, they claim, begat the
first Lozi King with his wife-daughter, Mbuyu.   Any misfor-
tunes or disasters that beset the Lozi have been attributed to
the anger of Nyambe.   Therefore the reigning monarch, as
Nyambe's direct descendant, is the only one capable of inter-
ceding with Nyambe on behalf of the whole nation.

NYAMPENJI.   A chieftainess involved in the Vakakaye riots (q. v.).

NYAMUKOLO.   Variant of Niamkolo (q. v.).

NYAMUNYERENDA, HELEN.   The mother of Zambia's first president, Kenneth Kaunda and wife of David Kaunda (q. v.).   She
was born around 1885 at Chisanya village near Ekwendeni in
Ngoni territory (now part of Malawi).   Her father, Mugagana
Nyirenda was a Phoka.   In 1893 her parents left the Ngoni
and moved to Karonga.   In 1900 she went to Overtoun Institution to study to be a teacher.   David Kaunda, also an Overtoun
product, married Helen in 1904.   Their first child, Katie, was
born in 1907, and five years later Robert was born, both in
Chinsali.   The family lived in Nkula from 1913 to 1915.   Kenneth was the eighth child, and was born at Lubwe near Chinsali
in 1924.   She became a widow in 1932 and raised the children
by herself.

NYAMWEZI see YEKE

NYANJA.   The dominant language in Zambia's Eastern Province,
it is also one of the official languages of the country.   The
people speaking it are primarily Chewa, Nsenga, Ngoni, Kunda,
and Chikunda.   Together they constitute about 16 percent of the

country. The Asians in the Eastern Province also speak Nyanja, as do most whites who live there.   It is taught in the
schools of the province as well.

NYASALAND.   Known as Malawi (q. v.) since independence on July
6, 1964, it is the country immediately east of Zambia.   It
was called the Nyasaland Protectorate by the British from
1891 to 1893 and again from 1907 until independence.   From
1893 until 1907 it was called the British Central Africa Protectorate.   Between 1953 and 1963 it was a partner with
Northern and Southern Rhodesia in the Federation of Rhodesia
and Nyasaland (the Central African Federation).

NYENGO.   A site in the northwestern part of Bulozi (q. v.) to
which many Luyana (Lozi) refugees fled after being defeated
by the Makololo.   Another group fled to Lukwakwa (q. v.).
The Nyengo group chose Imbua (q. v.), a younger brother of
Mubukwanu, as their king.   While most of the royal family
went to Nyengo, the site was not a permanent attraction.
Some of the refugees returned to the valley, where the Makololo eventually executed them.   Others moved on to Lukwakwa,
including Imbua himself who went there in 1864, attracted by
the iron ore deposits.   By the time the Makololo were overthrown, Nyengo had ceased to exist as a separate chieftaincy.

NYERERE, JULIUS.   The first President of Tanganyika (and later,
Tanzania), he has been a close personal friend and constant
inspiration for Kenneth Kaunda.   When Zambia became independent in October, 1964, Nyerere was the only foreign Head
of State present.   In 1963 consultations between Kaunda and
Nyerere led to what has become a symbol of their cooperation,
the Tan-Zam Railway.   Kaunda's organization of UNIP and his
"Zambian Humanism" have both been influenced by similar patterns in Tanzania.   In the late 1970's the two men are working closely in an attempt to bring about African majority rule
in Zimbabwe (Rhodesia).

NYIKA NATIONAL PARK.   A small national park along the Malawi
border in northeastern Zambia.   It has rest houses for the
convenience of overnight guests.

NYIRENDA, ISAAC RANKIN.   A civil servant from Nyasaland working in Livingstone in the 1920's, he and Edward Franklin Tembo became founders of the Livingstone Native Welfare Association (q. v.) in 1930.   He presided at its inaugural meeting.
Nyirenda and Tembo first suggested the formation of a "Northern
Rhodesia Native Welfare Association" to the Government in 1929.
Early in 1930 the Secretary for Native Affairs, James Moffat
Thomson, encouraged them (although requiring that it be
limited to Livingstone), even helping the two prepare a constitution for what the Government thought would only be a harm-
less social club.   Instead, it soon became a pattern for territory-wide political organizations.

NYIRENDA, TOMO. A messianic prophet in the mid-1920's who
called himself Mwana Lesa (q. v.).

NYIRENDA, WESLEY PILLSBURY. One of Zambia's more prominent politicians in the last fifteen years, Nyirenda has been
Chairman of UNIP's Subcommittee on Appointments and Discipline since 1973. Born January 23, 1924, near Lundazi in
the Eastern Province, he was educated at the Lubwa Mission
School and in South Africa. In 1948 he won a medical school
scholarship for Witwatersrand University, but family obligations in Zambia forced him to decline it. As a teacher (and
later headmaster) he supported his brothers while also studying for a B.A. part-time. He earned this in 1953 and then
studied at the University of London, receiving a B.Sc. (Economics) in 1955. Returning to his country he became a principal at Ndola but also became active in the ANC, where he
was not pleased with the leadership of Harry Nkumbula (q. v.).
He did accept the appointment in 1958 as President of the
ANC in the Western Province, but resigned after only a few
days. He eventually joined UNIP. In 1962 he successfully
ran for Parliament. In January, 1964 he was appointed its
Deputy Speaker, then becoming Speaker at independence. He
continued as the National Assembly's Speaker until 1968. In
December, 1968 he was named Minister of Education, a title
he held until December, 1973. He has been on UNIP's Central Committee for many years, and has held his current
party position since 1973.

- O -

OLD MAMBWE (or MAMBWE MWELA). Among the first mission
stations in Northern Rhodesia, and the first to be started by
the White Fathers (q. v.), the Old Mambwe mission was set up
in July, 1891. It was located southeast of Lake Tanganyika,
not far from what is today the Tanzanian border, near the
Stevenson Road (q. v.). At one time the British South
Africa Company also had a trading post there. Father Van
Oost (q. v.) was its first Superior, but upon his death he was
succeeded by Rev. (later Bishop) Joseph Dupont (q. v.). As
early as October 15, 1893, the White Fathers decided to abandon the site because the slave caravans through the area hindered their mission work. The subsequent successes, especially Dupont's, with the Bemba kept the White Fathers at Old
Mambwe for two more years until they opened a new mission
at Kayambi.

"ONE MAN/ONE VOTE. " The popular phrase used by many African nationalists by which they called for the implementation of
universal adult suffrage. This was especially used in territories like Northern Rhodesia where the existence of European
settlers moved the Colonial officials to start less democratic
systems of weighted votes or separate voting rolls. The cry

was heard prominently in Northern Rhodesia in 1957 and 1958 after the Tredgold Report (q. v.) appeared.

ORDER IN COUNCIL OF 1899. Promulgated by the British Crown in November, 1899, this decree provided that administration and justice in the area known as Barotseland and North-Western Rhodesia should be carried on by the British South Africa Company under the control of the British High Commissioner for South Africa. The eastern border of this territory was to be the Kafue River. Lozi King Lewanika had not been told by the Company that this would remove his sovereign rights over his land. In so far as administration was concerned, it also superseded the Lawley Concession of 1898 (q. v.) which Lewanika signed with the Company. As a result of pressure from the Company (BSAC) in 1905, the eastern boundary was pushed eastward to the narrow waist of Zambia. This placed all of the line-of-rail and the Copperbelt under the rules of the 1900 Order in Council even though these territories had never been formally under the jurisdiction of Lozi Kings.

ORDER IN COUNCIL OF 1900. The British administrative order that formally placed the area known as North-Eastern Rhodesia under the administrative jurisdiction of the British South Africa Company. It required the appointment of an Administrator whose duties included controlling the development of communications, exercising authority over any Europeans in the area, and maintaining law and order through a police force and Native Commissioners. It also created a High Court to dispense justice under English law (except in civil cases between Africans).

ORDER IN COUNCIL OF 1911. An order by the British Crown that amalgamated North-Eastern and North-Western Rhodesia into Northern Rhodesia, something that the British South Africa Company had been encouraging for a long time. No approval by Africans was needed for it to take effect. Certain provisions were included to safeguard some previously attained rights of the Lozi people. However the Lozi did object to the clause that the Company could sell land outside the reserve area to Europeans. Otherwise it bore great resemblance to the Order in Council of 1900 (q. v.). It provided for an Administrator for the whole territory to be appointed by the Company with the approval of the British Secretary. A High Court was also set up, but no Council.

ORDER IN COUNCIL OF 1924. There were actually two separate Orders in Council promulgated at this time. The Northern Rhodesia Order in Council, 1924, provided that the territory would be removed from the jurisdiction of the British South Africa Company and placed under the direct administration of the British Government. There would be a Governor and an Executive Council nominated by the Crown. Article 41 was a provision recognizing Barotseland's special status. The

Northern Rhodesia (Legislative Council) Order in Council, 1924, provided for the territory's first legislature, to consist of nine officials and five unofficial elected members. Ordinances were to respect native laws and customs where they did not conflict with the Crown's prerogatives, and no laws were allowed that would discriminate on racial bases, except those concerning arms, ammunition, and liquor.

ORDER IN COUNCIL OF 1953 see FEDERATION (CONSTITUTION) ORDER IN COUNCIL

ORDER IN COUNCIL OF 1953 (BAROTSELAND). At the time of the creation of the Central African Federation, the British Government promulgated a separate Order in Council. The Lozi King and Council (Kuta) had made this a prerequisite for their acceptance of the Federation. It merely stated that Barotseland is a Protectorate within Northern Rhodesia and re-stated the rights guaranteed to Lozi traditional authorities by the 1924 Order in Council.

ORDER IN COUNCIL OF JANUARY 3, 1964. The British administrative order that formally conferred self-rule upon Northern Rhodesia. By this order, only defense, public order and the police, and foreign affairs remained in the Governor's control until the date of final independence.

ORMSBY-GORE, WILLIAM G. A. (LORD HARLECH). Member of the British Parliament who headed a commission called by his name that was sent to Africa in 1925 to investigate the desirability of establishing closer association among the British East and Central African territories. It limited its hearings in Northern Rhodesia to the southernmost city, Livingstone, however, and does not seem to have consulted Africans. It did learn that the governments of Northern Rhodesia and Nyasaland preferred a southern economic association to a northeastern one. The Ormsby-Gore commission thus recommended improving the infrastructure between East and Central Africa before considering a broad federation. Ormsby-Gore (later Lord Harlech) served as undersecretary of state for the Colonies from 1922 to 1924 and from 1924 to 1929. As Colonial Secretary from 1936 to 1938 he refused to encourage those who wished to amalgamate Northern Rhodesia and Southern Rhodesia. He specifically expressed concern that no concessions be granted to the settlers that would endanger the interests or security of native Africans. From May 24, 1941, to May 13, 1944, he served as British High Commissioner for South Africa.

- P -

PAN-AFRICAN FREEDOM MOVEMENT FOR EAST, CENTRAL (AND SOUTHERN) AFRICA (PAFMECA or PAFMECSA). The Pan-African Freedom Movement for East and Central Africa was

formed at Mwanza in Tanganyika in 1958. It was a loose
grouping of political parties in the area of its title that was
designed to encourage the success of the independence movements. Julius Nyerere and Tom Mboya were its prominent
leaders. Kenneth Kaunda was active from the beginning. At
Addis Ababa in February, 1962, Kaunda was elected President
of PAFMECA and the group decided to concentrate political
and financial aid on Zambia. That same year it added
"Southern" to its title when both South Africa's ANC and PAC
joined. When the Organization of African Unity was formed in
May, 1963, PAFMECSA became a redundant organization and
ceased operation.

"PAPER ZAMBIANS. " A derisive term used by black Zambians to
refer to many of the Asians and Europeans during the early
years of independence. It was felt that many of the minority
peoples wished to take advantage of the economy without becoming citizens or investing in long term projects.

PARAMOUNT CHIEFS. A term used commonly in areas under
British colonial rule to designate the single overall leader of
a people, one superior to all other chiefs or headmen. It also served the purpose of denying the use of other royal terms
such as King, which would have implied a prestigious sovereign
ruler. When Robert Codrington (q. v.) became Administrator
of North-Western Rhodesia in 1907 he specifically ordered that
"paramount chief" be used to describe the Lozi leader, Lewanika, and that terms such as King and Prince should be discon-
tinued.

PARAMOUNTCY, DOCTRINE OF. A British colonial policy enun-
ciated originally by the Duke of Devonshire in 1923 regarding
East Africa and extended to Northern Rhodesia and Nyasaland
by Lord Passfield (q. v.) in 1930. The policy stated that African interests shall be paramount when they come into conflict
with the interests of immigrant peoples. Whereas Devonshire
had only meant Asians when he said immigrant peoples, Passfield applied it also to Europeans, thus stirring up a hornet's
nest in Central Africa. As a result of settler protests, a
Joint Select Committee of Parliament issued a report slightly
modifying the doctrine in late 1931. Three years later the
new Governor, Sir Hubert Young, modified it almost out of
existence.

PARASTATAL. A term used to describe the many agencies that
operate, in effect, as governmental subsidiaries. Most of
them are economic by nature. Among the best examples are
the Zambia Industrial and Mining Corporation, the State Finance and Development Corporation, and the Mining and Development Corporation (qq. v.). Other parastatal bodies include
the Zambia Youth Service, the Agricultural Rural Marketing
Board, the Bank of Zambia, Zambia Railways, and Zambia
Airways. As of the early 1970's there were already about

seventy state-owned companies and statutory bodies in Zambia's parastatal sector.

PARIS MISSIONARY SOCIETY (PMS) (Also PARIS EVANGELICAL MISSION SOCIETY (PEMS) or SOCIETE DES MISSIONS EVAN-GELIQUES). A French Protestant (Huguenot) society devoted to the mission field, it began its work in southern Africa in 1835 among the Sotho, where it was very successful. Its pioneer missionary to Zambia was François Coillard (q.v.) who first attempted to cross the Zambezi in July, 1878. He proceeded only to Sesheke where he waited for a response from the Lozi King Lubosi. The favorable reply suggested that Coillard return after the capital, Lealui, was completed. Rev. Coillard returned to Europe for funds and supplies for a Barotseland mission station. He returned to the Zambezi in 1884 and contacted the Lozi leaders. The sudden outbreak of a war among the Lozi prevented Coillard's party from arriving until early 1885 when he was warmly welcomed to Lealui. A mission site was given them twenty miles away at Sefula. In 1887 the PMS missionaries set up a school, the first of a number of schools, mission stations and dispensaries that they instituted throughout North-Western Rhodesia. The Coillards were joined by Adolphe and Louis Jalla (q.v.) and their wives, among other noted PMS missionaries. Many of them played important parts in Lozi history, both through their schools and as trusted advisors to Lozi Kings, especially Lewanika.

PARLIAMENT. The Parliament of Zambia consists of the unicameral National Assembly. It must meet at least once a year, and normally will be elected every five years, unless dissolved earlier. It has the power of legislation and the sole power to amend the Constitution. The Prime Minister must be a member of Parliament and is appointed by the President and serves as his spokesman. Under the Second Republic constitution, there are 136 members: 125 are elected, 10 are chosen by the President, and a Speaker is elected by the members. The House of Chiefs (q.v.) is a purely advisory body. Under the 1964 (Independence) constitution, the President was also identified as part of Parliament.

PARTNERSHIP. A term used mostly in the 1950's, before and during the existence of the Central African Federation, to indicate the principle that the interests of neither the Africans nor the Europeans in Central Africa should be subordinate to the other, and that each group should recognize the rights of the other to a permanent home there. This was, at least, the definition given to it by Colonial Secretary James Griffiths (q.v.) at the Second Victoria Falls Conference, in 1951. The word was first used in the context of Central African race relations in 1935 by Sir Stewart Gore-Browne (q.v.). It was also used by the Northern Rhodesia Secretary for Native Affairs, Rowland S. Hudson (q.v.) before the African Representative Council in 1948. In his context, he encouraged "genuine partnership" between the races in the form of "whole-hearted cooperation" for the sake of the best interests of everyone. Nevertheless it was the Griffith definition which was significant, because it indicated clearly a move by the British away from the previously dominant doctrine of "paramountcy" (q. v.) put forth in 1930. The problem with the term partnership was that it allowed too many different interpretations. Africans quickly realized that Europeans saw themselves as senior "partners," who would have to tutor their junior "partners" for a long time before granting them a semblance of equality. This was supported when a man of the stature of Godfrey Huggins was quoted as saying, in effect, that a racial partnership would be similar to that between a man and his horse: they work together, but do not eat or sleep together. Nevertheless the British and the Government of Northern Rhodesia worked from 1951 to 1953, trying to find a definition of partnership that the Africans would find acceptable. This was presumably to be used as a justification for the impending Central African Federation, which the British saw as an experiment in racial partnership. Some "moderate" Africans accepted the Federation for a while as being just that, a hoped-for solution to problems of racial disharmony. Kenneth Kaunda, however, doubting the true resolve of the Europeans, saw it as the "partnership of the slave and the free. " The fact that African education was grossly neglected, compared to European education, was proof of this, the Africans felt. Ultimately, by the early 1960's few European politicians still pretended to favor partnership, especially as the Federation was obviously doomed by the success of African nationalism in both Nyasaland and Northern Rhodesia.

PASS. An identification certificate that Africans in Northern Rhodesia were required to carry as a result of a 1927 ordinance. Special travel permits were also required. Africans were required to show it to authorities upon request. It was designed to place limits on freedom of movement. A special pass was needed to move at night outside your residential area. European authorities saw it as a way to maintain order. Africans protested it as a restriction on human rights.

PASSFIELD, LORD (SIDNEY WEBB). English social reformer and economic historian, he served as Secretary of State for the Colonies (1929-1931) and Dominions (1929-1930) as part of a Labour Party Cabinet. As Colonial Secretary in 1930 he issued a White Paper, called "Memorandum on Native Policy in East Africa, " the so-called Passfield Memorandum. In this controversial document he extended the doctrine of "paramountcy" (q. v.) to Northern Rhodesia and Nyasaland. The policy, which stated that African interests must be considered paramount over those of immigrant peoples, was proclaimed by the Duke of Devonshire in 1923 for East Africa. The settlers in Northern Rhodesia reacted bitterly to this policy and from then on fought for amalgamation with Southern Rhodesia. Previously

Europeans in Northern Rhodesia had preferred a status separate from their southern neighbor. During his time in office,
Passfield also encouraged more education for Africans as a
step toward Africanization in employment.

PASSIVE RESISTANCE CAMPAIGN. A special project of UNIP
from June until November, 1961. Led by Kenneth Kaunda (who
had always considered Mahatma Gandhi as an inspiration), it
was in protest against British changes in the previously accepted Macleod plan as a result of right wing pressures. Kaunda
pledged non-violence during the campaign, but there were a
number of disturbances and attacks from July through October.

PEOPLE'S DEMOCRATIC CONGRESS (PDC) (or PEOPLE'S DEMO-
CRATIC PARTY). A party formed on August 5, 1963, by Job
Michello (q.v.) when he split with Harry Nkumbula of the African National Congress (ANC) in anticipation of the 1964 pre-
independence election. The party had a conservative approach
to politics and received encouragement and support from conservatives like Roy Welensky (q.v.) and the Congo's Moise
Tshombe. One of the main battles with the ANC during the
remainder of 1963 was over the question of which faction would
receive the large financial support reportedly offered by
Tshombe. While some money surfaced, evidently neither
group ever got the rumored £100,000. Actually the main reason for the PDC-ANC split was that Michello and his followers
were unhappy over Nkumbula's leadership. As a result of the
split, both pushed the British to hold the election in May instead of January, 1964, supposedly to allow adequate time for
voter registration. In fact both were struggling desperately
for financial and voter support and to put together slates.
Attempts at merging the groups failed until late December,
just before nomination day for the candidates. Even with later
adjustments, there were four constituencies where ANC and
PDC candidates were both entered against UNIP. After the
merger (a last resort for the floundering factions), the ANC
identity survived and the PDC folded.

PEREIRA, GONÇALO CAETANO. The head of a family of Goan
adventurers who led an expedition from Portuguese East Africa into northeastern Zambia in 1796. This had been instigated
in 1793 when a group of Bisa with ivory for sale visited him
in Tete and said that the Lunda leader, Kazembe, wanted to be
friends. Pereira and his son Manuel went to Kazembe in 1796
along with some Bisa and returned in 1798 with two ambassadors from Kazembe, announcing that the Lunda wanted to organize ivory trade with the Portuguese at Tete, and even invited the Europeans to set up a trading post near his territory.
Francisco de Lacerda (q.v.) had different plans and took both
Pereiras with him as guides as they attempted to travel through
Kazembe's country. The mission ended in failure, and only
the knowledge of the Pereiras brought many of the travellers
safely back to Tete. The Pereira family continued to dominate

trade in the area immediately southeast of Zambia well into
the middle of the nineteenth century.

PERPETUAL KINSHIP.   An extension of the practice of positional
    succession (q.v.) that is found mainly among the Lunda but
    also among the Bemba to some degree.   It is a practice that
    linked titled positions rather than the individuals.   For ex-
    ample, two brothers may be chiefs of A and B, two neighbor-
    ing segments of a nation.   If the original chief of A had been
    the father of the original chief of B, however, and had given
    his son the position of leadership, the two current holders
    must maintain the father-son relationship.   The entire kingdom
    would thus consist of many positions that were all linked in a
    series of specific familial or kin relationships that had nothing
    to do with actual blood ties.   Non-related ethnic groups could
    even be integrated into the system by appointing their leaders
    to traditional titles, thus making them part of the familial net-
    work.   Thus, for example, the Ndembu (q.v.) became linked
    with the Lunda.

PETAUKE.   The southernmost of the three districts of the Eastern
    Province of Zambia.   It shares a border of over a hundred
    miles with Mozambique.   The 1969 census revealed a popula-
    tion of 125,000 in the district, and a density of seventeen
    people per square mile.
        The city named Petauke is about twenty-five miles north
    of the Mozambique border and about eighty-five miles southwest
    of Chipata, along the Great East Road (q.v.).

PIGEON-HOLES see HATCH SYSTEM

PIM, SIR ALAN.   Britain's foremost expert on colonial finance,
    and senior author, with S. Milligan, of the 1938 publication
    Report of the Commission Appointed to Enquire into the Finan-
    cial and Economic Position of Northern Rhodesia.   It is still
    recognized as the best general study of Zambia's economic his-
    tory between the First and Second World Wars.   In the early
    1930's Pim made similar studies of Basutoland, Swaziland,
    and Bechuanaland.   Much of the Pim-Milligan Commission's
    investigation took place in 1937.   The Commission was ap-
    pointed to see how the Government might reduce spending in
    Northern Rhodesia.   Instead Pim recommended an increase,
    especially noting the backward condition of many social ser-
    vices.   Increased investment would be needed in health ser-
    vices, roads, urban housing, schools, agricultural development,
    and secondary industries.   The Second World War soon began,
    however, and few results were seen for quite a while.   Pim
    also specifically noted that the mineral royalties still being
    accrued by the British South Africa Company instead of the
    Government would have been sufficient for most of the needed
    expansion.   The Commission also made recommendations on
    modernizing the traditional Government of Barotseland.   Some
    of the savings could assist in the financing of development in
    the region.

PINTO, FATHER FRANCISCO JOAO.   The chaplain for the expedition led by de Lacerda (q. v.) that left Tete in 1798 with a goal
   of reaching the Atlantic.   They reached Kazembe's capital on
   the Luapula River but before seeing Kazembe, de Lacerda died.
   Father Pinto took command and was finally granted an audience.
   No trade agreements (or even passage rights) were made, however, and after internal quarrels among the Portuguese, Father
   Pinto and the remnants of the group turned back on July 26,
   1799.   The return to Tete was beset with confrontations with
   the Africans, especially the Bisa.   His diary records the value
   of the expertise of his guide, Gonçalo Pereira (q. v.).

PINTO, SERPA.   A Portuguese army officer who made a transcon-
   tinental trip from Angola to Mozambique in the 1880's as Portugal was trying to lay claim to the entire band across the continent.   Pinto traveled through Barotseland where he met the
   young King Lewanika (then Lubosi).   Pinto would have arranged
   the sale of arms and ammunition that Lewanika wanted.   The
   deal fell through when the Lozi Ngambela and Kuta objected
   and forced the King to expel Pinto.   Later, in 1889, Pinto was
   a leader of Portuguese forces in Nyasaland as both the British
   and Portuguese tried to solidify their East African land holdings.

PLATEAU TONGA.   One branch of the larger grouping called
   Tonga (q. v.), this group of people lives in southern Zambia on
   the Batoka Plateau, north of Lake Kariba (q. v.).   The Tonga
   are related linguistically and perhaps ethnically to some of
   their neighbors, notably the Ila, Lenje, Toka, Sala, Soli, and
   Leya.   The Tonga seem to have been among the earliest of
   the present inhabitants of Zambia.   The Plateau Tonga seem
   to live a life relatively unchanged for over five hundred years.
   One source suggests that they may have migrated there from
   the South, across the Zambezi.   It is a society without chiefs
   or much oral history.   Rainmakers at the rain shrines do have
   some ritual importance and thus some "political" influence.
   Thus some of them were appointed "Government chiefs" when
   the British tried to impose Indirect Rule (q. v.).   The system
   of age mates (basimusela) provided some group unity, as it
   does in other cattle-raising societies.   In addition to cattle
   raising, the Plateau Tonga also practice some chitimene agriculture, maize and groundnuts being common crops in 1855.
   The Plateau Tonga also were active in trade, making tools and
   weapons from iron for export to other African groups.   As the
   nineteenth century progressed, the Plateau Tonga were occasionally hit by cattle raids.   The Lozi and Makololo were their
   chief attackers, but the Ndebele also raided them.   The Plateau Tonga have also been active in modern politics.   They
   have provided Harry Nkumbula (from Ila country) and his African National Congress a consistent support in elections, as
   has the Southern Province in general.   As early as 1937 a
   group of Tonga chiefs, farmers and teachers formed a Northern
   Rhodesian African National Congress to protest local problems.
   It soon folded as a result of Government pressure.

PLYMOUTH BRETHREN.   A community of Christians, originally
most of whom were British, and who were opposed to organized religion.   They disagreed with numerous practices of the
Anglican church, and felt that the sacraments were just as
valid in the hands of laymen.   They also actively preached the
Bible.   One of their early meetings was in Plymouth, England
in 1830.   They soon decided to spread the Gospel through missionary activity in foreign lands.   Their first African missionary was Frederick Arnot (q. v.) who spent eighteen months
among the Lozi (1882-1884) before moving on to Angola where
he established a string of mission stations.   He then went to
Katanga for several years, living with the autocratic leader,
Msiri.   Other members of the order followed to Central and
Southern Africa, including some who established a mission station on the western shores of Lake Mweru, from which again
they proselytized in Northern Rhodesia in the 1890's.   One of
the missionaries, Dan Crawford, interceded between the Lunda
leader, Kazembe, and the British to prevent bloodshed.   At
the same time, some of the Brethren in Angola began to work
in North-Western Rhodesia.

POMBEIROS.   Half-caste traders who were so-named by the Portuguese.   They played an important role as middlemen between
the Portuguese and the Africans, carrying products and cultural communication in both directions.   The word means traveling agents (Portuguese: "pombo" means "road").   The term
"Pombeiros" is sometimes applied specifically to Amaro José
and P. J. Baptista (q. v.).

PONDE.   An important Bemba leader for forty years, ultimately
holding the post of Chitimukulu from 1916 until his death in
1923.   The nephew of both Chitapankwa and Mwamba II (who
was also Ponde's father-in-law) as the son of one of their
sisters, Ponde was given authority over the Lungu of Chief
Tafuna (q. v.) in about 1880.   This was the country in the
northwest extreme of Bemba-controlled territory, between Isoka and the Luombe River, and the Bemba had just conquered
it.   It was generally in the sphere of influence of Mwamba II.
Ponde became noted as a military leader, especially for laying
long siege to a place he was trying to conquer.   In the 1890's
he, as also many other Bemba leaders, was busily engaged in
trading ivory and slaves to Arab and East Coast traders for
firearms and cloth.   It was undoubtedly some of Ponde's raids
that were reported by early London Missionary Society missionaries who wrote about the fierce Bemba.   Yet some of
Ponde's villages were themselves attacked in 1893 by Sampa
when LMS missionaries arrived in the area.   Ponde did not
accept the LMS then.   In December, 1895, Ponde's forces
killed Chief Chitimbwa IV, captured his village, and carted off
the spoils.   It is said that one event involving Ponde was responsible for the Bemba ultimately becoming subject to the
British.   When the Mwamba died in 1898 (see DUPONT,
FATHER JOSEPH), Ponde was determined to succeed to that

title. He informed some of the representatives of the British
South Africa Company of this fact. Two of them, Charles
McKinnon and Robert Young, opposed Ponde's claim, partly
because they feared his strong personality and militancy. He
had challenged and rebuffed a number of European officials.
A force led by McKinnon moved him away from Mwamba's
village peacefully in late 1898. But by March, 1899 he was
again determined to win and built a fortified village on a rocky
hill near Kasama. Again the British approached and, after
several brief battles, they stormed his village and captured it.
Ponde and some followers escaped, but he surrendered a
month later. He became active again about five years later,
however, taking over the southern part of Lubemba from the
aged Makumba (q. v.). He finally became Chitimukulu in 1916,
serving until he died seven years later.

PORTUGAL. As a colonial power with territories adjacent to Zambia in both the West (Angola) and the East (Mozambique), Portugal's involvement with the Zambian territory goes back several centuries and has continued until the two countries became
independent in 1975. Although two Portuguese explorers passed
through the southeastern corner of Zambia as early as 1564,
the real beginning of exploration came over two hundred years
later. Men like de Lacerda, Baptista and José, Monteiro and
Gamitto, Silva Porto, and Serpa Pinto (qq. v.) traversed Zambian land for a variety of political, economic, and adventurous
reasons from 1798 to 1878. During the scramble for Africa
following the Berlin Conference of 1884-85, Portugal made a
determined effort to secure rights to an entire band of territory from Angola on the Atlantic Ocean to Mozambique on the
Indian Ocean. This came into direct conflict with the British
"Cape to Cairo" dream. Ultimately Portugal lost in their bid
for Zambian territory. As late as 1905 a decision in international arbitration by King Victor Emmanuel of Italy was needed
to settle the boundary dispute between Portugal and Britain
over the Angola-Barotseland border. Few problems arose with
Portugal then until Zambian independence in 1964. Many of the
Angolan and Mozambiquan nationalist forces had offices or even
bases in Zambia. Despite the fact that ports in Portuguese
Africa were crucial to Zambia's copper exports (not to mention
a variety of imports, such as petroleum), the Zambian Government canceled all trade agreements with Portugal in December,
1964.

POSITIONAL SUCCESSION. A practice common among the Lunda
but also to some extent among the Bemba. A successor to a
traditional post receives not only the title, authority, rights
and duties of his predecessor, but also takes on all of his social and political relationships to the point where he virtually
"becomes" the person he succeeded. An extension of this is
the concept of perpetual kinship (q. v.).

PRAIN, SIR RONALD. One of the most important financiers and

industrialists in Zambia's history, he was born in Chile in
1907 but educated in England. In 1936 he became Director of
the Anglo-Metal Company, three years later became Director
of Rhodesian Selection Trust, and in 1943 became Managing
Director of Roan Antelope Copper Mines Ltd. and Mufulira
Copper Mines Ltd. By 1950 he was Chairman of all three
copper organizations, in addition to many other important di-
rectorships. An economic and political realist, he consistently led the way to reform of the racist economic patterns. In
1953 he announced that the Rhodesian Selection Trust would
break the industrial color bar before the Africans took things
in their hands and broke it themselves. He thus led the way,
gradually to be sure, in opening up more mining jobs to Africans, despite the complaints of European workers and unions.
In the 1950's Prain invested large amounts of money in development plans in the Northern and Luapula Provinces. He has
also helped finance programs to improve African education.
In the early 1960's he stressed the importance of Africans
and Europeans learning to work together, utilizing each other's
skills in a balance that would be mutually profitable and just
to all. Nevertheless his cautious, gradualist approach did not
win favor with many African nationalists.

PRESBYTERIAN CHURCH. The main Presbyterian missionaries to
    enter Zambia came as the Free Church of Scotland (q. v.).
    One of their early converts and evangelists was David Kaunda,
    father of Zambia's first President. In 1924 the church was
    renamed the Church of Central Africa, Presbyterian. It
    later became part of the United Church of Zambia (q. v.).

PRESERVATION OF PUBLIC SECURITY ORDINANCE. A law pro-
    mulgated in 1959 by the Government which feared that the na-
    tionalist political groups might instigate disruptions. It gave
    the Governor extensive emergency powers when he deemed
    them necessary. He would have the power, for example, to
    arrest and detain people without trial. The Ordinance was
    bitterly opposed by many. It was first used on May 11, 1960,
    following the attack on Mrs. Lillian Burton (q. v.). The Gov-
    ernor banned UNIP in the Western Province and declared its
    branches unlawful. He also restricted five UNIP leaders, in-
    cluding Kenneth Kaunda, Simon Kapwepwe and M. K. Sipalo,
    from entering the Western Province. As a result of further
    disturbances in August, 1961, several of the Ordinance's regu-
    lations were also applied to the Luapula and Northern Prov-
    inces. Also, in both provinces the branches of UNIP were
    declared unlawful under the Societies Ordinance (q. v.).

PRESIDENT. The office of President was a new one for Zambia,
    initiated by the 1964 (Independence) Constitution. It specifi-
    cally named Kenneth Kaunda as the country's first President.
    After completion of Kaunda's first term of office (tied to Par-
    liamentary elections, thus a maximum of five years), the
    President was to be elected by universal suffrage. The

President was to choose his own Vice President from the members of the National Assembly. The Vice President is the President's chief assistant and Leader of Government Business in the National Assembly. The President is also Head of State, Head of Government, Commander-in-Chief of the Defense Forces, and Chairman of the Cabinet. The Cabinet Ministers are solely responsible to him, appointed by him and dismissed by him. He is also free to appoint five extra members to the National Assembly (ten in the 1973 Constitution) to provide added expertise where needed. The 1964 Constitution specifically defined the Parliament as the President and the National Assembly. The two are elected on a joint ballot, with the Presidential candidates receiving the votes cast for any National Assembly candidates explicitly paired with him (supported by him) on the ballot plus any votes for unopposed candidates. When Parliament is dissolved or completes its term, new elections bring forth a new Assembly and President. Only bills that have been passed by Parliament and receive presidential approval become law. The President may declare a state of emergency but the Parliament has five days if in session (twenty-one if not) to extend or revoke the presidential decree. The 1973 Constitution establishes a one-party state. A Prime Minister replaces the Vice President but is otherwise similar. The President's term of office is not limited; he is the head of the United National Independence Party, the Central Committee of which has more powers than the Cabinet has. The new Constitution makes it very difficult to remove an incumbent President. He can be rejected only if the General Conference of UNIP fails to approve him as their candidate or if a majority of the electorate fails to vote for him even though he is the only candidate. Neither is likely under normal conditions.

PRIME MINISTER. Prior to Zambian independence, the parliamentary form of government provided for a Prime Minister to be head of government. In 1964, the year of independence, Kenneth Kaunda was in that position. Under the Independence Constitution, however, the post was dropped, as the President sat in Parliament. The 1973 Constitution, however, reinstated the office of Prime Minister. He is to serve as head of government administration and to be the main spokesman on government matters. He is appointed by the President, subject to approval by Parliament, and serves at the pleasure of both. He is also an ex-officio member of the UNIP Central Committee.

PRIMITIVE METHODIST MISSIONARY SOCIETY. A group that was at odds with the orthodox branch of Wesleyanism, they sent a few missionaries to southern Africa in the late 1880's. They were led by Rev. Arthur Baldwin (q. v.). They were prevented from entering Bulozi by the Lozi themselves until 1891 when Rev. F. Coillard interceded for them. They spent two years in Bulozi before King Lewanika decided to allow them to move

into the territory of the Lumbu and the Ila. This was part of
Lewanika's attempt to assure the Ila that he would be a peaceful overlord.

PROTECTORATE. While Great Britain preferred to describe
Northern Rhodesia as a protectorate, implying a request for
protection and assistance from the indigenous people, in fact
it was treated more like a conquered colony. Only the Lozi
had made any kind of overtures to England that could have
been construed as requests for protection, and the Lozi certainly did not get what they requested.

PROVINCIAL COMMISSIONER. Under the British system of Indirect Rule (q. v.), there was a provincial commissioner as
administrative supervisor for each province. Responsible to
them were district commissioners, each of whom was superior
to the local chiefs, for whom they were also the main source
of administrative communication. The provincial commissioners
were responsible to the Governor of Northern Rhodesia. The
provincial commissioner also served as an appeals judge from
District Courts.

PROVINCIAL COUNCILS. Instituted by action of the Legislative
Council and the Northern Rhodesia Government in 1943, the
Regional Councils (to be renamed Provincial Councils in 1945)
were designed by the Government to serve as forums for African feelings and grievances. They were purely advisory, without administrative or statutory functions. In effect they were
an extension of the Urban Advisory Councils (q. v.). They
were to give the Africans a feeling of involvement, no matter
how illusory, in their government, thereby to stave off the
growth of nationalist organizations. Some better educated
Africans did indeed try to work through the Councils for
awhile until, frustrated by their ineffectiveness, they became
active in the Congress movement. When the Provincial (Regional) Councils were first formed, they heavily represented
the traditional leaders and rural interests (unless a major urban area happened to be in the region). If there was no urban area to send representatives, local African Associations
could choose delegates. But the majority on each of these
councils was still rural and traditional. Each province had at
least one such council, and up to as many as three for the
larger provinces. Barotseland had none, however, as the
Government of Northern Rhodesia felt that the Lozi Kuta could
serve the same purpose. The Provincial Commissioner usually
presided at the meetings of the Provincial Councils. When
the territory-wide African Representative Council (q. v.) was
formed in 1946, delegates to it were selected from each of the
Provincial Councils as well as from the Urban Advisory Councils.

PUTA, ROBINSON. A nationalist political figure in the 1950's who
was also active in the trade union movement. Contrary to

Lawrence Katilungu (q.v.), he felt that the unions should work closely with the African National Congress for mutual benefit. At one point in the mid-50's, he was both the Vice President of the Northern Rhodesia African Trade Union Congress (ATUC) and Deputy President of the African National Congress. He lost both positions in 1956. Later he became the head of the Zambia Railways Board. In the early 1970's, he was active in the United Progressive Party (q.v.) which was quickly banned.

- Q -

QUELIMANE. A port city on the Indian Ocean in Mozambique, north of the mouth of the Zambezi River. It was not unusual for ivory traders from the area of Zambia, especially the Bisa, to bring their ivory here.

- R -

RAILWAY AFRICAN WORKERS TRADE UNION (RAWU). Formed in the early 1950's, it remained for some time as one of the two strongest unions in Northern Rhodesia. Its president in its formative years was Dixon Konkola (q.v.).

RAIN SHRINE. A ritual institution found especially among both the Plateau Tonga and the Valley Tonga. Their small villages had few normal interconnections except for a rain shrine that often served a half dozen or more villages. In a region of relatively low and variable annual rainfall, these shrines had great importance. Sometimes they were at the graves of important men, or perhaps were locations founded by respected local rainmakers. A variety of rituals to the rain gods were performed. In recent years some of the priests at these shrines have added a political function, helping to settle differences and even aiding in the establishment of military alliances. The British, looking for chiefs (among these chief-less societies) in order to institute Indirect Rule (q.v.), sometimes chose rain-priests. One founder of a successful rain cult who also became a strong political figure was Monze (q.v.).

RAWLINS COMMISSION. A Commission appointed by the Northern Rhodesia Government in 1957 to consider possible reforms in the Barotse Native Government. The conservative membership (both Lozi and European) led many to predict, accurately, that few changes would be recommended. The Commission satisfied none of Mwanawina's opponents, some of whom joined UNIP in despair. The Commission seemed designed to justify the status quo.

REFORMED TRADE UNION CONGRESS (RTUC). Disagreements among the leadership of the Trade Union Congress in 1960 over the political activities of its president, Lawrence Katilungu (q. v.)--who was simultaneously Acting President of the African National Congress and a member of the Monckton Commission--caused the creation of the RTUC. The new leaders were Jonathan Chivunga, Albert Kalyati, and Mathew Mwendapole. It was composed mostly of smaller unions that Katilungu dismissed during the controversy. While it had little money and a small number of workers enrolled, the RTUC included some active members of UNIP, some with connections in international unionism. Nevertheless it was independent of UNIP and rejected overt politicization (the disagreement with Katilungu) and presented an alternative to the TUC. After Katilungu lost an important union post in December, 1960, the TUC and RTUC reunited in February, 1961, as the United Trade Union Congress (q. v.). Chivunga was elected its President.

REGIONAL COUNCILS. Early name of Provincial Councils (q. v.).

RENNIE, SIR GILBERT. Governor of Northern Rhodesia from 1948 to 1954, when he was appointed the first High Commissioner in London from the Central African Federation. He had been active in the Colonial Government for decades. In 1930, for example, he was Provincial Commissioner in Barotseland. As Governor he was a strong supporter of racial partnership, assuring the Africans that the British Government retained ultimate responsibility for them. Rennie stated that partnership could work when based on honest intention and good will. However, as a supporter of men like Sir Godfrey Huggins and Sir Roy Welensky who were pursuing a plan for Federation, Rennie described Kenneth Kaunda as an agitator. As Governor he also opposed the promotion of Africans in the mines to more skilled positions. As Federation approached, Rennie, a former colonial official in Barotseland, visited there several times to persuade the King and his Kuta that the Federation was not only desirable for them but would even enhance the status of the Kingdom.

REPUBLIC OF ZAMBIA. The official name of the country, formerly Northern Rhodesia, when it became independent on October 24, 1964. When a new Constitution went into effect in 1973, some people began referring to the changed status as the Second Zambian Republic. This in no way changes the official name, however.

RESERVES COMMISSIONS. Three commissions appointed in 1924, 1926, and 1927, to work out certain land problems in the East Luangwa District, the Railway Belt, and the Tanganyika District, respectively. The commission for East Luangwa sought to solve the overcrowding problem there. The Railway Belt Commission tried to settle fears of competition between European and African farmers. The Commission for Tanganyika, chaired by J. Moffat Thomson (q. v.), hoped to provide more

land for European coffee planters by shifting Africans to reserves and getting the British South Africa Company to give up
parts of its Tanganyika Estate. The 1927 commission received
strong opposition from chiefs when they were told that the land
would be divided into African and European areas. The chiefs
wanted no more Europeans.

RHODES, CECIL JOHN. South African financier and politician
whose ambitions and actions opened up the land north of the
Limpopo River to British control and to exploitation by his
company, the British South Africa Company, not to mention
giving the Rhodesias his name. Born in England on July 5,
1853, he left school at the age of sixteen to go to South Africa
for his health. The early 1870's saw diamond fever hit South
Africa, and Rhodes made a youthful fortune with his half ownership of the Kimberley Mine. He later added the largest
mine, De Beers Mine, to his increasing holdings, which now
earned him an income of a half million pounds a year. He
made several trips back to England in the 1870's, earning a
degree from Oxford University in the process. Perhaps the
period from 1888 to 1891 was his busiest. In 1888 he sent
his partner, Charles D. Rudd to make a deal with Lobengula,
the powerful Matabele leader. The "Rudd Concession," although of questionable validity, gave Rhodes rights in much of
the territory between the Limpopo and Zambezi Rivers. He
then persuaded the British in 1889 to grant a charter to the
British South Africa Company (q. v.), which quickly began func-
tioning to help fulfill the "Cape-to-Cairo" dream. Rhodes
hired agents like Sir Harry Johnston and Alfred Sharpe (qq. v.)
to pursue treaty agreements with Africans in the eastern half
of today's Zambia and in Malawi. He also had Frank Lochner (q. v.), one of his agents, negotiate and sign a treaty and
concession with Lozi King Lewanika in 1890. Ultimately it
gave the Company control of land far beyond that under Lozi
control. He also became South Africa's Prime Minister in
1890, a post he held until 1897 when he resigned. He died
in the Cape Province of South Africa on March 26, 1902.

RHODES-LIVINGSTONE INSTITUTE. Established in 1937 under the
guiding hand of William V. Brelsford (q. v.), it has been renamed the Institute of Social Research since Independence. In
Lusaka since 1952, it was first founded in Livingstone in association with the Rhodes-Livingstone Museum (now the National Museum of Zambia). The Institute's purpose was to encourage research in the Rhodesias and Nyasaland in the social
sciences. Its regular publications have been the source of
much new knowledge about that area. Sometimes the Government has explicitly commissioned studies, although it is not
controlled by the Government of Zambia. Its headquarters
house a library. Membership is solicited and grants privileges.

RHODESIA. The word was introduced in 1895 in tribute to Cecil
J. Rhodes (q. v.). The British Government approved its use

in 1897. Later the word was used during the period of the
Central African Federation to refer to both Northern and
Southern Rhodesia together. After Northern Rhodesia quit the
Federation and became Zambia, Southern Rhodesia adopted the
name for itself, dropping the "Southern" prefix. Since it declared its independence from Great Britain in 1965, Rhodesia
and Zambia broke many of their old commercial and communication links. This split was accentuated as many nationalists
from Rhodesia (Zimbabwe) have offices and bases in Zambia.

RHODESIA ANGLO-AMERICAN CORPORATION, LTD. The Rhodesian branch of the Anglo-American Corporation of South
Africa, it was set up in 1928. By 1930 it was running major
copper mines at Nkana and Nchanga, as well as the small and
older Bwana Mkubwa mine (q. v.). The Rhokana mine soon followed, and copper production at its Bancroft mine began in
1957. After independence in 1964 the corporation changed its
name to Anglo-American Corporation of Zambia, Ltd. It is
now called the Nchanga Consolidated Copper Mines, Ltd. (q. v.), a
corporate name actually instituted in 1937.

RHODESIA COPPER COMPANY. A consolidated grouping of a number of mining companies owned by Sir Edmund Davis (q. v.).

RHODESIA REFORM PARTY. A minor party during the last
couple of years of the Central African Federation, it had a
very conservative orientation. It appears to have been started
by John Gaunt (q. v.) as early as October, 1960, as an offshoot of his earlier Northern Rhodesia Association. It gained
greater respectability in January and February, 1962, when
Ian Smith and other right wing dissidents from the United Federal Party joined with Gaunt. It claimed a middle ground between the UFP and the Dominion Party. It opposed forced integration and the Build-a-Nation campaign (q. v.). By mid-
March, 1962, Winston Field was putting together his Rhodesian
Front, however, and the Rhodesia Reform Party dissipated as
most of its membership joined with Field and Ian Smith.

RHODESIAN FRONT. Formed in March, 1962, as a merger of
the Federal Dominion Party and several other small groups, it
was the political party in Southern Rhodesia, led by Winston
Field and Ian Smith, that defeated the United Federal Party in
the December, 1962 elections. It has continued to dominate the
political scene in Rhodesia (Zimbabwe) into the late 1970's
under Smith.

RHODESIAN MAN. Same as Broken Hill man (q. v.).

RHODESIAN NATIVE LABOUR BUREAU. An organization formed
in Southern Rhodesia in 1906 under authorization by the British
South Africa Company to seek laborers in Northern Rhodesia
to work south of the Zambezi River. It was formed after the
report of a committee in 1905 looked into the problem of labor

shortage in Southern Rhodesia. One of its duties, in addition
to recruitment, was to assist the workers in surviving the
transportation from the recruitment stations to the job sites.
It provided clothing, blankets, food, and medicine. It also
arranged to defer some salary so the worker would have some
money waiting for him with the North-Eastern or North-Western
Rhodesia Administration.

RHODESIAN RAILWAYS. Begun as a part of Cecil Rhodes' "Cape
to Cairo" dream, the core of this system went from South
Africa through the eastern edge of Botswana and north through
Southern Rhodesia. In 1905 the line from Cape Town crossed
the Zambezi River at Victoria Falls and progressed through
Lusaka to Kabwe. Four years later it was extended to the
Congo border and in 1910 went into the Congo. Another line
cut eastward from Southern Rhodesia to Mozambique and the
ports of Beira and Lourenço Marques. From 1929 to 1949 it
was totally owned by the British and Portuguese Governments
(with the Portuguese controlling only the Mozambique portions).
In 1953 its ownership was turned over to the Federation of
Rhodesia and Nyasaland. When the Federation broke up in
1963, the Governments of Rhodesia and Zambia shared equally
the responsibility for both the assets and liabilities of the Railways. Since 70 percent of the facilities were in Rhodesia, a
problem arose when Rhodesia declared its independence in 1965
but this new status was not recognized by Zambia. Seven
months of bargaining ended in June, 1967, with an agreement
on many of the issues. The Zambia Railways Act of 1967
created Zambia Railways (q. v.) as an independent national system. The Rhodesian Railways system had been crucial to the
export of Zambia's copper, although the recently opened Tan-
Zam Railway (q. v.) has provided an alternative through friendly territory politically. The name Rhodesian Railways sur-
vives in the part of the system south of the Zambezi River.

RHODESIAN REPUBLICAN PARTY. A minor, white extremist
party led by men such as Colin Cunningham (q. v.) and Dr. G.
A. Smith, it contested both sets of 1962 elections and then
seemingly disappeared. It ran nine candidates in the April 27
Federal elections. All of them lost. It ran five candidates
in late October. The two upper roll candidates totaled sixty-
five votes, two-tenths of one percent of the valid votes cast.

RHODESIAN SELECTION TRUST LTD. (RST). A major international mining company that was set up in Northern Rhodesia in
1928 after the American Metal Company Limited of New York
(now the American Metal Climax) acquired a major interest in
Roan Antelope Copper Mines Limited. Subsidiaries were
formed to handle new mines, as well as the concentrators,
smelters, and refineries on the Copperbelt that became part
of the RST Ltd. system. Its facilities were located especially
at Mufulira, Chibuluma, Chambishi, Luanshya, and Ndola.
On December 16, 1964, the name was changed to Roan Selection Trust, Ltd. (q. v.).

RHODESIAN TEAK see TEAK WOOD

RHOKANA CORPORATION LTD. Part of the Anglo-American mining group (now the Nchanga Consolidated Copper Mines Ltd.),
the company's production of copper and cobalt comes from its
Nkana mine (q.v.) at the city of Kitwe on the Copperbelt.
Copper was first produced at Nkana in November, 1931, and
an electrolytic refinery began in 1935. In August, 1933,
Nkana also began producing cobalt. Over the decades it has
continued to be among the top several mining operations in
Zambia.

RIDLEY REPORT. Published in June, 1959, it was actually titled
Report of an Inquiry into All the Circumstances Which Gave
Rise to the Making of the Safeguard of Elections and Public
Safety Regulations, 1959. It was the result of a Government-
appointed Race Relations Committee, chaired by Mr. N. C. A.
Ridley. On one side it seemed to recognize that discrimination was occurring that should gradually be abolished. On the
other hand, however, it reported at great length on the anti-
government actions of the Zambia African National Congress
(ZANC). By suggesting that ZANC was prone to promoting violence it suggested that government actions to suppress ZANC
were justified. Its evidence against ZANC was weak, however.

ROAN ANTELOPE MINE. Located at what is now the mining center and city of Luanshya, the Roan Antelope mine was first
discovered in 1902 by two prospectors, William Collier and
Jock Donohue, working for the Rhodesia Copper Company.
Early rights were forgotten, however, and new companies began prospecting the area in 1923. The Rhodesian Selection
Trust (RST) came into being in 1928 and controlled the mine,
which began production in 1931. The mining disturbances of
1935 hit the mine in late May of that year and six miners
were killed. Over the four decades since it has continued to
be one of the top producing copper mines in Zambia.

ROAN CONSOLIDATED MINES LTD. (RCM Ltd.). Fifty-one percent state owned, this huge copper mining company is the contemporary continuation of the original Rhodesian Selection
Trust, Ltd. (RST) that was founded in 1928. It changed its
name to Roan Selection Trust on December 16, 1964. RCM
Ltd. was created after the Zambian Government took over control of 51 percent of the shares of RST Ltd. through the Mining and Industrial Development Corporation (q.v.), on January
1, 1970. In February, 1975, the Government also took over
management and sales of the company. Since the 1920's, RST
was one of the two huge mining companies that dominated the
economy of the country. Much of its stock was owned by
Americans, especially American Metal Climax, Inc. In 1965
it was producing 45 percent of Zambia's copper, to the Anglo-
American Corporation's 51 percent. Its principal producing
mines have been the Roan Antelope mine at Luanshya, which

began production in 1931, and the Mufulira mine (1933).   Its
other major mines are at Chibuluma (April, 1956) and Chambishi (1965).

ROAN SELECTION TRUST LTD. (RST Ltd.).   The new name of
Rhodesian Selection Trust, Ltd. (q. v.) as of December 16,
1964.   After the Zambian Government nationalized the mining
industry in 1970, RST Ltd. was reincorporated in the United
States as RST International, Inc.   This company acquired
20 percent of the stock in Roan Consolidated Mines Ltd.
(q. v.), the corporation now controlling the former holdings of
RST Ltd.

ROBERT WILLIAMS AND COMPANY.   A Katanga-based firm that
recruited laborers for the Union Miniere du Haut-Katanga mining company in Katanga.   It was very successful in both the
Northern and Luapula Provinces of Northern Rhodesia in the
early decades of the twentieth century.

ROBERTS, JOHN.   One of the most active of the European politicians in Northern Rhodesia during the Federation period.   Born
in England in 1919, he came to Northern Rhodesia with his
parents in 1928.   After serving in World War II, he learned
farming techniques in England and South Africa before acquiring his own farm in the Broken Hill district of Northern Rhodesia in 1949.   It became a successful tobacco, maize, and
cattle farm.   A member of the Federal party, in 1954 he was
elected to the Legislative Council to take the Broken Hill seat
vacated by his friend, Sir Roy Welensky.   He was soon elected
Federal Party leader in the Council and became Minister of
Health, Lands, and Local Government.   While he worked for
measures to improve housing for Africans, he also demanded
greater control over African trade unions and the recruitment
of more locally-born white policemen.   He also fought for an
upgrading of authority for elected European members of the
Council.   In May, 1956, he demanded in vain that he be named
Chief Minister.   He was reelected to the Council in March,
1959 and was appointed Minister of Labour and Mines in the
Executive Council.   During the next several years of constitutional politics he attempted to get more power for the elected
European members, supporting the position that eventually a
mature and responsible African leadership would emerge, but
Europeans should stay in control now.   When a contrary constitutional decision was announced by England in February, 1961,
he and his other United Federal Party Ministers resigned in
protest.   (The Federal Party had become the United Federal
Party in November, 1958, and Roberts remained the leader of
its Northern Rhodesian branch.)   In June, 1962, recognizing
the inevitability of constitutional change, Roberts represented
the UFP in talks with Harry Nkumbula of the ANC concerning
an electoral alliance.   The anti-UNIP alliance that developed
was successful in the October, 1962, elections, but ANC joined
UNIP in a parliamentary coalition instead.   In April, 1963,

Roberts changed the name of his party to the National Progress
Party.   He also started talks with Kenneth Kaunda about possible cooperation with UNIP in guaranteeing some European seats
in a new Zambian parliament.   He pledged to help Zambia by
providing a constructive opposition, advising the Government
with the experience and economic knowledge his party could
provide.   Under Roberts' leadership the party won all ten European seats in the 1964 elections.   The NPP itself was dissolved in 1966.

ROBOSI.   Variant spelling of Lubosi (q. v.).

ROCK ART.   There is a considerable amount of rock painting in
    Zambia, as well as some rock engraving.   Among the better
    engraving sites are Chifubwa stream, Nyambwezu Falls, Mun-
    wa stream, and Ayrshire Farm (qq. v.).   The painting exists
    mostly in the northeastern quadrant of Zambia, with just a few
    examples in the northwest and southern parts.   Some of the
    painting seems to be by Late Stone Age peoples, perhaps simi-
    lar to the Bushmen, although it doesn't really resemble the
    so-called "Bushmen art" of Southern Africa.   If anything,
    there are strong similarities to East African painting.   Most
    of these early works are naturalistic depictions of animals of
    red or purple pigment, but sometimes black.   Any figures of
    human hunters are far more stylized than the animals.   Among
    the best locations of these paintings are Nachitalo Hill, Mwela
    rocks, and Rocklands Farm (qq. v.).   A second style of paint-
    ing, more abstract and schematic, is also found in Zambia.
    It is dated later, probably by Iron Age people, and in some
    cases produced in the last couple of centuries.   Grid patterns
    and a white, greasy pigment are found frequently in this newer
    work, along with yellow and red pigments.   Among the better
    sites where these works are to be found are Zawi Hill (where
    the other style is also found), Nsalu, and Rukuzye (qq. v.).

ROCKLANDS FARM.   A site seven miles south of Chipata (Fort
    Jameson) on the road to Chadiza where there is an excellent
    example of African rock art.   On a tall hill there is a large
    painting of an eland.   Outlined in red, the five-foot drawing
    contains color shading elsewhere also.   It is a naturalistic
    drawing on granite and is similar to some such art found else-
    where in East Africa.

ROLLING STRIKES.   A term developed in 1956 to describe the
    situation on the Copperbelt where as soon as one strike was
    ended another began somewhere else.

ROMAN CATHOLIC.   The Christian Church with the largest mem-
    bership in Zambia, approximately 900,000.   Its history in
    Zambia began in 1879 when Jesuit missionaries crossed the
    Zambezi near Victoria Falls.   Several efforts to establish mis-
    sion stations failed until the Jesuits succeeded in 1902 among
    the Tonga.   Meanwhile the White Fathers (q. v.) came into

Bemba territory from the North in 1891 and were far more successful. Other missionary orders came later. Lusaka became an Archdiocese in May, 1959. Kasama followed a few years later. There are also six dioceses. In 1969 and 1973 Africans were named archbishops at Lusaka and Kasama.

ROTSE (or ROZI). Both are variants of Lozi (q. v.). The Rotse spelling was prevalent among the missionaries, travelers, and early administrators, thus the words "Barotseland" and "Barotse. "

RUKUZYE. Site of a dam north of Chipata, the rock surfaces of the hills provided many "canvases" for traditional rock painting. For the most part they are red grid patterns, although a serpent's outline also appears.

RUSSELL COMMISSION. A commission of enquiry, chaired by Sir William A. Russell, that was appointed to investigate the 1935 disturbances on Northern Rhodesia's copperbelt. The report of the commission, issued the same year, concluded in part that the Watch Tower Movement was an important cause of the disturbances and that any poor treatment of the African miners by their European bosses was only a secondary factor. It said that the primary cause, however, was the inadequate manner in which a tax increase was announced to the miners. The Commission seems to have overlooked the long-standing grievances.

RUSTICATION. A policy practiced by the Government of the Central African Federation by which they kept African nationalist leaders jailed or otherwise under detention in places far from their actual home area for the reason of easier security.

- S -

SAA KUTA. A traditional council of the Lozi and a sub-group within the larger Mulongwanji (q. v.). Its membership consisted of Makwambuya, Likombwa, and Linabi (qq. v.). These traditional leaders met to discuss national problems and pending policy matters, with their recommendations passed on to the Sikalo Kuta (q. v.). In the twentieth century the revived Katengo Kuta (q. v.) would often bring its suggestions to the Saa Kuta for further consideration. Under British colonial rule, in the mid-twentieth century, the Saa and Sikalo were merged for administrative purpose and became known as the Saa Sikalo, and more commonly as the Barotse Native Government.

SAKWE. Located near Chadiza in the Eastern Province, it is the site of an unusual piece of schematic rock art by Late Stone Age Zambians. Horizontal and vertical stripes produce a checkered grid.

SALA. A small group of about fourteen thousand Tonga-speaking
people living immediately west of Lusaka. An early Sala language has become extinct as a result of Ila and Tonga domination.

SALISBURY. The capital of Rhodesia and, during the Federation,
of the Federation of Rhodesias and Nyasaland itself. In earlier years, before the Copperbelt was fully developed, it was
an attractive magnet for Zambians who desired paid jobs
(which the hut tax (q.v.) virtually required). It was named
after Lord Salisbury (q.v.).

SALISBURY, LORD. The Third Marquess of Salisbury and British
statesman in the late Victorian age. From June, 1886, until
1892 he was Britain's Prime Minister and Foreign Secretary.
His granting of the Charter to Cecil Rhodes for the British
South Africa Company in 1889 was a crucial milestone in the
colonial history of Zambia. He was also responsible for
numerous other acts which opened up East, Central, and
Southern Africa to direct English involvement.

SAMFYA. An archaeological site on the western shore of Lake
Bangweulu, where "grinding grooves" are found on the flat
rock surfaces. Of uncertain purpose, and possibly stemming
from the Late Stone Age, the grooves are each about fifteen
to eighteen inches long, four inches wide, and two to three
inches deep. Similar grooves have been found in West Africa.
Early Iron Age pottery has been found at Samfya that has been
radiocarbon-dated at about A.D. 400.

SAMPA MULENGA KAPALAKASHA. The Chitimukulu (paramount
chief of the Bemba) from 1884 to 1896, he was the Bemba
leader most hostile to the spread of the British South Africa
Company administration. A younger brother of Chitimukulu III
Chitapankwa, he generally appears to have been hard to get
along with, and very egotistical. On several occasions he
had arguments with his older brothers, one being Chitapankwa
(q.v.) himself, over areas of land they had given him. He
blinded his brother-in-law in one fight over land. But he also
had a following equipped with guns which he supposedly got by
raiding caravans. When Mwamba II Chileshye died in 1883,
Chitapankwa wanted to appoint Sampa to that chiefdom, but he
refused, preferring to wait for Chitapankwa himself to die so
he could become Chitimukulu. This angered the older brother,
but he did indeed become ill and died in October, 1883, and
Sampa became paramount chief, the Chitimukulu in 1884.
Many people opposed Sampa, including other Bemba chiefs.
This was awkward because at that time, while the Chitimukulu
was the senior and paramount chief, the Mwamba, Mubanga
Chipoya was the strongest. Suspicion and hostility existed between the two leaders throughout their reigns. Battles between
their forces occurred on a number of occasions, if not head to
head, at least in each other's sphere of influence. It is said

that once Sampa even attacked Mwamba's village, but he was
beaten back. Sampa did add to his influence by winning over
a few of Mwamba's vassals, one being Ponde (q. v.), his
nephew and later himself Chitimukulu. In general, however,
Sampa's control was limited to the core chiefdom of Lubemba,
and he did not really dominate other Bemba chiefdoms.

One thing that added to Sampa's power was his dealing
with Arab traders. They had advised him not to have any
dealings with the Europeans because their presence could doom
the lucrative slave trade. While he was more concerned about
the White Fathers (q. v.) and the BSAC administrators, his
most devastating run-in was with a German administrator,
Hermann von Wissman (q. v.) in mid-1893. On one of his regular raids, Sampa took his men north into Tanganyika a little.
While attacking a Lungu village, his large slave-raiding force
confronted Wissman's sixty soldiers, a cannon, and a Maxim
gun. Despite being warned by Wissman, Sampa let the battle
proceed and his men were routed. The news spread that
Sampa's forces had been humiliated, and Sampa returned in
shame.

One of the neighboring Bemba chiefdoms with which Sampa
had a recurring argument was Makasa's. His problems were
with three successive ones, Makasa III, IV, and V. At one
point he hoped to have one of his own sons named Makasa V,
but this did not work out as there were senior candidates available. Ironically it was Makasa V Mukwuka's fear of Sampa
that led him to make favorable contacts with European missionaries. Sampa had four of his warriors attempt to assassi-
nate Bishop Dupont, but they did not succeed. Later (in December, 1895) he invited Makasa and the White Fathers to his
capital "to talk about some important affairs. " They refused,
unsure as to whether they were being lured into a trap. In
March, 1896, he tried again, asking that the priest might help
him stop the increasing influence of BSAC administrators in his
area. Again he was turned down. Indeed it seems from his
other actions that Sampa may have been in earnest this time,
but this man who had killed so many was not trusted by either
his fellow chiefs or the Europeans. He died in mid-May, 1896,
presumably of something he caught while leading a raid five
months earlier across the Sangwe River into Nyakyusa country.

SANDYS, DUNCAN. British Secretary of State for Commonwealth
Relations and Colonial Affairs from 1960 to late 1964. He also served as R. A. Butler's replacement as Minister responsible for Central Africa. In 1962 a visit by Sandys to the Central African Federation stirred up excitement when his meeting
with the King of Barotseland resulted in a request to him that
the Lozi be allowed to secede from Northern Rhodesia. In
May, 1963 he contacted the Lozi King and invited him to a
meeting with Kaunda and Sandys in London. Sandys was also
the official responsible for the abortive Federal Review Conference of December, 1960. He had frequent meetings with
many Zambian leaders during the period when the Federation
was dissolving and Zambia was becoming independent.

SARDANIS, ANDREW SOTIRIS. Zambian businessman who was one
of the most important European participants in government in
the early years of the Republic of Zambia. Born March 13,
1931, on Cyprus, he emigrated to Zambia in 1950. He then
held a variety of business and management positions. In June,
1965, he became Chairman and Managing Director of the Industrial Development Corporation, a post he held until April, 1970.
He served as Managing Director of the Zambian Industrial and
Mining Corporation (ZIMCO) and its subsidiaries INDECO and
MINDECO from April, 1970 until December, 1970. Meanwhile
in 1968 he was Permanent Secretary of the Ministry of Commerce, Industry and Trade, and in 1969 and 1970 he was Permanent Secretary in the Ministry of State Participation. He
resigned from government at the end of 1970 and worked briefly for a subsidiary of Lonrho in 1971 before entering private
business in Lusaka. In the December 10, 1962 by-elections
for the Legislative Council, Sardanis had been an unsuccessful
candidate for UNIP.

SAVIMBI, JONAS. Angolan nationalist leader and President of the
National Union for the Total Liberation of Angola (UNITA).
His residence permit was not renewed in 1967 by the Zambian
government because raids, reportedly by his men based in
Zambia, had disrupted rail lines on which Zambian trade traversed Angola. The Portuguese found it necessary to delay
this traffic, thus stimulating Zambia's action.

SCHUCKMANNSBURG. A World War I site in the Caprivi Strip
(q. v.). The Germans (controlling Caprivi) had established a
fort at Schuckmannsburg, three miles across the Zambezi River from Sesheke (q. v.). To secure the Zambezi border, a
detachment of BSAC Police and a force from the Northern Rhodesia Police captured the fort on September 21, 1914, without
a shot being fired. Control was left in the hands of the N. R.
Police.

SCOTT, (DR.) ALEXANDER. Owner of the Central African Post
and a leader of a Progressive Party briefly in the early 1950's.
Considered to be liberal for the time, he was nevertheless
elected to the Federal Parliament and helped to found the
multi-racial Constitution Party (q. v.).

SEBANZI HILL. An important archaeological site on the Kafue
Flats in south-central Zambia. The area has been continuous-
ly occupied by the Tonga since about A. D. 1100. The people
there then were farmers and fishermen who had large herds
of cattle and goats. They were Early Iron Age people. Pottery from the twelfth century is similar to local Tonga pottery
of the nineteenth and twentieth century. Evidence indicates
that cotton cloth was manufactured in Zambia also in the
twelfth century or so.

SEBITUANE (or SEBITWANE; SIBITWANE). The leader of the

Makololo (or Kololo), he was one of the more remarkable of
the numerous outstanding African leaders of the nineteenth century.   Sebituane was born about 1800 of Sotho parents, and became a chief of a Sotho clan, the Fokeng at about the age of
twenty.   He became chief because his older brother was killed
by a lion.   Living in the area of the present Orange Free
State near Lesotho, they fled the region when the ripple effect
of the wars of Chaka the Zulu caused disruptions throughout
south-central Africa.   Marching northward in about 1823, they
were defeated by a former Zulu general who was now fleeing
Chaka, Mzilikazi, leader of the Ndebele (Matabele).   But Sebituane and his followers veered westward into the land of the
Tswana peoples and further north through parts of the Kalahari
Desert and the Okavango and Chobe swamps.   In the 1830's the
Makololo crossed the Zambezi River at Kazungula (the eastern
tip of the Caprivi Strip).   Fearing the Ndebele of Mzilikazi
who were now to their south, the Makololo fled north into
Tonga and Ila country, pursuing the cattle of those two groups.
Sebituane tricked many Tonga leaders into a council meeting
and had them massacred.   He had less luck with the Ila who
recaptured their cattle at night.   He settled for a while at Ka-
poli near Kalomo, but withdrew to Sachitema when an army of
Ndebele retaliated for an attack by Makololo on their cattle.
There Sebituane's men won in about 1840, but hearing of another approach by the Ndebele, he fled with his large following
to the west where he subdued the Lozi who were in a civil
war over the royal succession (see SILUMELUME).   In the
next ten years he was to conquer much of the Zambezi Flood
Plain that was home to the Lozi, including the southern part
at Sesheke and further south to Linyanti in the Caprivi Strip.
His only stern competition in this area of southwestern Zambia
came from the Ndebele.   Results of several battles were the
same, Sebituane's warriors bested the Ndebele.   In addition to
his battles against the Ndebele and Lozi, his warriors continued
to dominate the Ila, the Nanzela (q.v.), and most of the other
southern tribes.   Meanwhile Sebituane was also dealing with
both Arab and European traders.   The Arabs were especially
eager to acquire Lozi men in the slave trade, and Sebituane
could provide them.   He also acquired guns in trade with the
Mambari traders to the west and Silva Porto (q.v.), the Portuguese slave trader.   It is interesting that he saw the need to
integrate Lozi leaders into his highly centralized political and
military organization, perhaps to insure their loyalty.   Thus
Sipopa (q.v.), a future Lozi King, spent a number of years at
Sesheke with the Makololo.   Sebituane also welcomed Dr.
David Livingstone, in 1851, just two weeks before the African
died.   He hoped that the European could provide him with more
magic to ward off the Ndebele spears.   But Sebituane would not
need it, as he died of pneumonia from an infection in an old
spear wound.   It is interesting to note that the neighboring Ila
people say that the previous story found in Livingstone's writings is not correct.   They claim that Sebituane insisted on
riding the Doctor's horse.   The horse was in a gallop and

made a sudden swerve, throwing the chief. His death occurred
on July 7, 1851. He was ultimately succeeded by a son, Sekeletu (q. v.).

SECOND NATIONAL DEVELOPMENT PLAN (SNDP). First outlined by President Kaunda at the Mulungushi Conference of
UNIP in May, 1971, its specifics were presented in January,
1972. This plan was designed to cover the period 1972 through
1976, and was a follow-up to the FNDP. Both plans were hindered by the closing off of trade with Rhodesia and by fluctu-
ating world copper prices, mostly moving downward. The initial projection was for a 6.8 percent annual growth rate during
the SNDP. On the discouraging side, an increase of sixty-
seven thousand workers annually was projected, while only
twenty thousand new jobs would be provided each year. Educational facilities would be improved, according to the plan,
so that every child would be guaranteed a minimum of a fourth
grade education, and 80 percent would finish primary school.
The greatest emphasis in the plan, however, was on agricultural development. It was hoped that rural areas could be developed and that all economic and quality-of-life differences
between rural and urban areas could be erased. A plan was
formulated to create special Intensive Development Zones.
These areas would be chosen for good soil and access to transport. Ideally such plans would help reduce food imports by
utilizing sites with high production-growth potential. Finally,
the plan called for the expansion and diversification of industry
and mining. A 15 percent increase in manufacturing was targeted.

SECOND ZAMBIAN REPUBLIC. The title given the Zambian Government since the establishment of a one-party participatory
democracy that was created on December 13, 1972. Technically, however, the new Constitution was not formally written,
adopted by Parliament and signed by Kaunda until August, 1973.

SECRETARY GENERAL OF UNIP. Under the original constitution
of UNIP there was no president. The highest position was
Secretary General, and was filled by Kenneth Kaunda in 1969.
Under the condition of a one-party participatory democracy instituted by the 1973 Zambian Constitution Act that set up the
Second Zambian Republic (q. v.), UNIP has a President who is
also President of Zambia. The position of Secretary General
is both a party post and a governmental one. He serves under
an appointment by the President. He must have been a member
of the party's Central Committee and his appointment is subject
to the approval of the National Committee. His duties are to
be all party duties assigned to him by the President. He is,
according to Zambia's Constitution, responsible for the administration of UNIP. He is also an ex officio member of the Cabinet. Perhaps of ultimately greater importance, however, he is
to replace the President of Zambia in his absence, illness or
death, for a period up to three months. The post was held
since 1973 by A. Grey Zulu (q. v.), until he was replaced by
Mainza Chona (q. v.) in June, 1978.

SEERS REPORT.   Officially titled The Economic Survey Mission
   on the Economic Development of Zambia: Report of the
   UN/ECA/FAO Mission and published in 1964, it was to set
   guidelines for Zambia's First National Development Plan (q. v.).
   Some of its recommendations were designed to ensure an economically feasible form for the goals of the politicians.

SEFULA.   The first mission station in Barotseland of Rev. Coillard (q. v.) of the Paris Mission Society.   It was located about
   twenty miles south of Lealui, a site suggested by King Lewanika.   Founded in October, 1886, the station had its first school
   opened in March, 1887, with the King's permission.   On October 28, 1892, Coillard moved his headquarters to a new station at the Lozi capital, Lealui.

SEJAMANJA.   The site of Late Stone Age rock paintings near
   Chadiza in the Eastern Province.   Reptiles are depicted in sil-
   houette with red pigment.

SEKELETU (or SIKELETU).   A son of Sebituane (q. v.), and a
   King of the Makololo (or Kololo).   Sebituane died on July 7,
   1851.   His daughter, Mamochisane, was his chosen successor.
   She quickly found that ruling a kingdom conflicted with her preferred family-oriented life style and abdicated in favor of her
   younger, half-brother Sekeletu.   The fact that he was only
   about eighteen, added to the fact that his mother was a captive
   woman, not a Sotho, made his succession questionable for
   some Makololo.   Unfortunately also, he did not have the natural leadership abilities of his father.   He alienated many of
   his own people, in addition to the conquered Lozi whom his
   father had managed to placate.   He was a bitter man, obsessed
   with witchcraft, especially after he acquired leprosy, which
   forced him into seclusion.   Yet he continued his father's pattern of cattle-raiding against the neighbors, especially the Ila.
   He also used Dr. Livingstone's return visit in 1853 to open up
   direct trade with the Atlantic Coast areas of Angola, bypassing
   Mambari middlemen.   He hoped to persuade Livingstone to set
   up a mission among his people, thinking that it might dissuade
   the feared Ndebele from attacking.   Sekeletu also had trouble
   among his own followers, an attempt by Mpepe (q. v.) to kill
   him ended with the reverse occurring.   Sekeletu's brutal reign
   united many of his opponents, including, some say, his elder
   half-sister Mamochisane.   His execution of everyone he even
   suspected of a plot against him finally brought the kingdom to
   the edge of chaos.   Subject people were claiming their independence.   He died (strangled, says one Sala elder) in August,
   1863.

SELBORNE, LORD.   Governor of the Transvaal and High Commissioner for South Africa from 1905 to 1910.   He toured the Rhodesias in 1906, reporting favorably on the BSAC administration
   of the territory, even north of the Zambezi River.   He was
   also the recipient of petitions from Lewanika, King of the Lozi,

who pleaded with him as representative of England to require
the BSAC to fulfill its end of the concessions agreements and
to retract its hut tax. In October, 1906, the King traveled to
Bulawayo to meet with Selborne personally on these matters,
but the High Commissioner found little merit in the Lozi arguments.

SELF-RULE. The penultimate step in the progress of Zambia
toward independence, self-rule was attained as the result of
the Order in Council of January 3, 1964 (q. v.).

SENA. An administrative center set up by the Portuguese some
time in the sixteenth or early seventeenth century. It was
founded on the south bank of the lower Zambezi River, at its
confluence with the Shire River, about half-way between Tete
and the Indian Ocean. Around 1700 the Portuguese became interested in the area north and west of Sena, including today's
Malawi and Zambia. Dr. Francisco de Lacerda (q. v.) became
governor at Sena in 1797 before he started on his trip to meet
Kazembe, the Lunda King.

SENANGA. One of the rural districts of the Western Province in
contemporary Zambia. It is itself divided into two separate
parliamentary constituencies. The district has a border with
Angola, but also stretches east to the Zambezi River. The
town of Senanga is on the Zambezi itself and was the site of
the conquest of the Subiya by an early Lozi leader, Mwanambinyi. The district had a population of 91,602 in 1969.

SENGA. A Tumbuka-speaking people, numbering about forty-five
thousand, who live along Zambia's eastern border. Derived
from the Luba of the Katanga area from whence they came
two or three hundred years ago, they may at one time have
been part of the Bisa (q. v.). Another possibility is that they
are originally Tumbuka (q. v.) but came under the influence of
later Bisa immigrants. Culturally they are close to the Tumbuka, for example they have similar clan names and speak the
language. On the other hand, they wove cloth from their own
cotton like the Bisa. They bartered this cloth along with tobacco and basketwork in trade. The Bemba, to whom the
Senga were sometimes subject, traded especially for the tobacco. The homeland of the Senga in the Luangwa Valley also
became the site of Arab traders involved in the slave trade,
notably Kapandansalu (q. v.) and Koma Koma. Kapandansalu
and some neighboring Arabs allied with the Bemba in 1897 to
attack twice the village of a Senga chief, Chibale (q. v.). The
Senga won both battles but only with the aid of Robert Young
(q. v.) and a force of BSAC police from Nyasaland. This
spurred on the establishment of a Company boma at Mirongo,
near Chibale's village.
    The Senga have a traditional senior chief, called Kambom-
bo, but he has little political authority. He was usually the
most important trader, however, and thus accumulated much

material wealth. Chiefly titles are hereditary. Unlike most Zambian peoples, the Senga use a patrilineal descent system.

SERENJE. The eastern-most district of the Central Province of Zambia, it had a population of 52,981 in 1969. The district shares its entire western border with the Shaba (Katanga) Province of Zaire. The town of Serenje is close to the middle of the district.

SESHEKE. Both a district and a town in modern Zambia, it is especially of interest as a nineteenth century community often visited by Europeans and fought over by Africans. Today it is a district in the Western (formerly Barotse) Province. It extends north a long distance from its border with the Caprivi Strip (q. v.). Its population in 1969 was forty-nine thousand, a 14.6 percent increase since 1963. The town itself, on the north bank of the Zambezi River near where it turns eastward from its southern course, is not very large. The area has been traditionally the home of the Subiya people (q. v.), who came under Lozi political control early in the eighteenth century. With the invasion of southern Barotseland by the Makololo under Sebituane (q. v.), however, the new rulers controlled it. The Makololo used both Sesheke and Linyanti as major political centers, in part to keep the Ndebele from penetrating the upper Zambezi Valley. By the mid-1860's both Sebituane and his successor Sekeletu were dead and the Makololo were considerably weakened. The Lozi began again to assert themselves in the area around Sesheke, firmly integrating it into Barotseland in 1886 when Lewanika (q. v.) appointed Kabuka as senior induna there. Meanwhile many Europeans passed through Sesheke. Dr. Livingstone entered the town in 1851, using his medical skills to befriend Sebituane. The trader, George Westbeech (q. v.), had a house there, and Rev. Coillard waited there for permission to visit the Lozi capital at Lealui. Ten years earlier the Lozi King Sipopa had made Sesheke the temporary capital of the Lozi, perhaps because the area was not the most secure part of the Kingdom and needed his personal authority there.

SEZONGO. A nineteenth-century leader of the Lumbu people (see NANZELA), he established himself as chief at Nakalomwe in southern Zambia. His leadership of the Lumbu (Nanzela) made him wealthy in ivory, slaves, cattle, and impande shells. His raids against the Ila, Tonga, Nkoya, and Barotse made him feared and added both to his wealth and (through slaves) the size of his following. At one point he massacred about three hundred Matabele who were fleeing Sebituane (q. v.). Eventually the latter attacked Sezongo, and despite the desertion of a large force led by his younger brother Shambala, Sezongo and his men fought a lengthy battle against the mighty Makololo before he was killed.

SHABA see KATANGA

SHAIWILA. A Lala chief in the 1920's who supported the millenarian church of Mwana Lesa (q. v.) run by Tomo Nyirenda. The
enthusiasm of his people for the movement was considered dis-
ruptive by the British, who brought him to trial and sentenced
both the chief and Nyirenda to hang.

SHANGOMBO. An important border town in the Senanga district of
the Western Province. It is on the eastern side of the Kwando
River, immediately across the river from Angola. It is located on a north-south border road.

SHARPE, ALFRED. A big game hunter in Central Africa who was
hired by Harry Johnston, the British consul in Mozambique, to
acquire mineral concessions from African chiefs for Cecil
Rhodes. He left in 1890 as a temporary vice consul and
headed north of the Zambezi. He was very unsuccessful
among the Ngoni and most of the other peoples. He did get a
mineral concession from the Lunda leader, Kazembe, who
wanted British protection, but his land did not extend into Katanga, which was under another Lunda chief, Msiri. Thus
Rhodes could not claim Katanga. Sharpe also received a mineral concession from the Tabwa chief, Nsama, who Sharpe
foolishly declared to be "King of the Bemba People. " Thus
Rhodes and the BSAC claimed that they had rights to minerals
on all Bemba land. Nevertheless these concessions were the
basis for some of the British claims when settling the borders
with Belgium and Germany in the 1890's.

SHILA. A Bemba-speaking people, about thirty thousand in number, who are primarily fishermen. Sometime before the
eighteenth century they moved into the Luapula river valley
and along the shores of Lake Mweru. They pushed out the
pre-Bantu occupants, the Bwile in doing this. They claim
that their principal chieftainship, Nkuba, is of Bemba origin
and migrated from the east after quarreling with Chitimukulu.
The Lunda defeated the Shila several times in the eighteenth
century, with several different Nkubas as victims. Nkuba IV
was killed by the forces of Kazembe III around 1760, and since
then the Shila have paid tribute to the Lunda while remaining
on the land.

SHIMWALULE. One of the most important leadership positions
among the Bemba, the Shimwalule is the hereditary undertaker
or burial priest. He guards the main royal burial grove, Mwalule, which is situated east of the Chambeshi River, thus in
the easternmost part of Bemba country. In fact, the original
Shimwalule was not Bemba but a Bisa headman named Kabotwe,
and his matrilineal descendants have succeeded to the position
and title. In addition he has a certain amount of secular authority as both a village headman and authority over some
neighboring headmen. It has also been customary that no
Shimwalule bury more than one Chitimukulu (q. v.). If a
second one dies, the Shimwalule must be replaced before the

burial occurs. This custom was broken by Chimbwi Shinta in
the 1890's.

SHINDANO, HANOC CHIMPUNGWE. An aggressive and successful
leader of the Watch Tower Movement (q. v.), notably in the
Northern Province of Northern Rhodesia. A Mambwe born in
Tanganyika, he went to Southern Rhodesia as a herder in 1905.
Later he worked in the mines and learned about the Watch
Tower from his fellow miners. Six of them, including Shindano, were deported for their religious activities in October,
1917. Shindano, who had been a student of Donald Siwale
(q. v.), returned to the Abercorn area to preach. His leadership and preaching were both very successful. He preached
disobedience to all civil authority, African as well as European,
and told his followers not to work for either Europeans or the
chiefs, all of whom were "devils. " He was first arrested by
the Government in September, 1918, but was acquitted. He
later spent several periods in jail in the next decade. Some
writers indicate that, unlike other Watch Tower leaders, he
was power hungry and greedy for material gain. Collections
were evidently pocketed for his own enrichment. Nevertheless
he was an outstanding preacher who promised the African millenium was coming and the Europeans would be pushed out of
the country. Shindano's main church was at Tukamulozya in
the Abercorn District. Although still active in the Movement
in the mid-1930's, his influence had become minimal.

SHINDE. Variant of Ishinde (q. v.).

SIBITWANE. Variant of Sebituane (q. v.).

SICABA ("NATIONAL") PARTY. A party founded in Barotseland in
June, 1962, to contest the Legislative Council seats from Barotseland in the 1962 elections. Its organizers were traditionalists who opposed UNIP and who wanted Barotseland to secede
from Northern Rhodesia. A victory, its leaders felt, would
convince Great Britain that this should be allowed. The Barotse King and the Kuta favored the party, but did not specifically endorse it. On the other hand, during the campaign
three Land Rovers and a public relations man plus miscellaneous equipment was supplied by Welensky's United Federal Party.
Nevertheless, UNIP's strong campaign and the Sicaba Party's
failure to get many traditionalists registered to vote produced
an overwhelming UNIP victory. The two Sicaba candidates,
Francis Suu and Griffiths Mukande received 65 and 42 votes
respectively, while the UNIP victors won 1057 and 688 votes.
After the election, several major Sicaba leaders, including
Francis Suu, resigned, announcing the futility of opposing
UNIP, and their regret and surprise concerning the UFP help.
They announced that they would dissolve the party. However
Ngombala Lubita became its president as the executive board
reorganized the party. Lubita attempted to work out an alli-
ance in 1963 with the ANC, but this failed and the party dis-
solved the same year.

SIKALO KUTA. A traditional council of the Lozi and a sub-group
within the larger Mulongwanji (q. v.). It consisted of the most
important and senior members of the Mulongwanji plus the
Ngambela and the Natamoyo. It was the group most likely to
closely represent the interests of the King and his Ngambela
(Prime Minister). In addition, because of the importance of
its members, its advice was given more weight by the King
than that of the Saa Kuta (q. v.), a larger group with which it
interacted on governmental matters. All members of the Sikalo were also members of the Saa Kuta. Under British colonial rule in the mid-twentieth century, the Saa and Sikalo
were merged for administrative purposes and became known as
the Saa Sikalo, and more commonly as the Barotse Native Government.

SIKALUMBI, WITTINGTON K. An important nationalist politician
in the 1950's. A member of the ANC, he helped Kenneth Kaunda work on the "Congress News, " a political newspaper.
He also organized a somewhat successful campaign against the
hatch system (q. v.) in 1954. By 1958 he had quit the ANC
and briefly joined the Constitution Party. However in October,
1958, he was at the inaugural meeting of the Zambian African
National Congress and was named Deputy Secretary of the
Party. In 1959 he was arrested by the Government in its
sweep of ZANC leaders and rusticated at Namwala. This did
not prevent him for writing letters abroad for international
support.

SIKHS. Soldiers and policemen from India (specifically, adherents
of the Sikh religion, from East Punjab) who served with the
British South Africa Company in the early days of BSAC rule
in Central Africa. The British trusted them and recruited
them for military duty because they had remained loyal to the
British during the Indian Mutiny of 1857-58. Among the British
victories in which they participated were those over Ponde and
Mporokoso.

SIKOLOLO. The language of the Makololo people (q. v.) who invaded southwestern Zambia during the nineteenth century. The
language is basically Sotho, as that is also the ethnic deriva-
tion of the Makololo (or Kololo). It became so widespread
among the Lozi (the people affected most by the invasion) that
missionaries such as Rev. Coillard setting up mission schools
between 1880 and 1900 among the Lozi taught in Sotho and Sikololo, not Siluyana, the language of the Lozi royal court. The
language is still the common language of the Lozi today, although minor changes have occurred, and it is now more commonly called either Silozi or just Lozi.

SILALO. A significant administrative unit of the Lozi, also used
by the British for their own administrative purposes. Each
silalo consisted of a number of silalanda (itself a unit consisting of several villages under an influential headman). The

silalo was under the authority of an induna (q. v.), a councillor. The induna was appointed by the King to supervise the silalo for him with the aid of a local kuta (council) of headmen and silalanda heads. The induna did not have to be from that area and might be given an area of land that went with the title Silalo Induna. Each silalo also had a representative at the national Kuta. This whole administrative structure made it easier to incorporate conquered people and territories into the Lozi political system. This system was disrupted by the invasion of the Makololo (q. v.), but was revived in the late nineteenth century by King Lewanika. The British misconstrued the nature of the silalo, failing to realize its administrative role and its part in the national structure. However they decided to use the silalo as a convenient subdivision for taxation and similar purposes. The silalo and silalo induna have remained as parts of the Barotseland Native Government structure.

SILOZI.   Also just called Lozi, it is the language of most of the Lozi people today (although Siluyana was the royal language in the past). Actually the language is basically Sikololo (q. v.) with the added influence of other minor local languages. It is spoken by many people who are either Lozi or who are members of closely allied or neighboring peoples.

SILUMBU.   One of the main champions of Lubosi (Lewanika) in his attempt to claim the Lozi throne in the 1870's. Thus Silumbu, who had been the Namuyamba, was appointed Prime Minister (Ngambela) by Lubosi. One knowledgeable witness, Rev. Coillard, called Silumbu "the most influential man of the tribe and the real ruler. " When a successful rebellion occurred among factions that lost the throne to Lubosi, Silumbu led a large army in July, 1885, to reconquer the Bulozi valley and reclaim the throne for Lubosi from Tatila Akufuna (q. v.). During the civil war, Silumbu died, but his King was restored to the throne as Lewanika and saw that Silumbu had an almost royal funeral.

SILUMELUME.   A son of the Lozi King Mulambwa, who died in 1830, Silumelume competed with his brother Mubukwanu. The former had his support among northern Lozi, whereas the latter's support was in the southern part of the Kingdom. Actually Silumelume was chosen King by the National Council and declared to be so by both his father's Ngambela, Muswa, and the Natamoyo. Realizing his insecurity so long as his brother lived, Silumelume decided to plan an attack upon him. In this he counted on the loyalty of a force of Mbunda warriors, but a counter-plot was arranged by a supporter of Mubukwanu. He persuaded the Mbunda to support him secretly, so at a ceremonial Mbunda war dance in front of Silumelume and his Council, one of the Mbunda assassinated him with an arrow. The Kingdom remained in a very divided condition even then, and thus was very vulnerable when the Makololo (q. v.) soon invaded.

SILUYANA. The official court language today in Bulozi (Barotseland). While it is spoken by the ruling dynasty, it is uncertain
whether it was introduced by them when they first invaded the
area (see ALUYANA) or whether it was spoken by the invaded
peoples. It is one of a number of similar languages now
grouped under the term Luyana.

SILVA PORTO, ANTONIO FRANCISCO FERREIRA. A Portuguese
ivory and slave trader, based in Angola, who had actively
traded with the Lozi in 1848 and with the Makololo in 1853.
In 1854 he sent agents from his base at Bihe in Ovimbundu
country through the land of the Lozi, Ila, Lamba, and Bisa
until they reached Portuguese territory at Tete on the lower
Zambezi. He was the first white man to enter Barotseland.

SIMBO HILL. A site of rock paintings, it is located seventeen
miles west of the Petauke administrative center. It contains
red pigmented drawings of reptiles, perhaps from the Late
Stone Age of Zambian history. There are also some more recent drawings in a greasy white paint that are crude human
figures and perhaps hoes or axes. There is some local tradition indicating that these could have been done in the nineteenth
century.

SINKALA, PETER. A colleague of Donald Siwale (q. v.) and David
Kaunda at Mwenzo. He died from Spanish influenza in 1918.

SIOMA NGWEZI NATIONAL PARK. Located in the extreme southwestern corner of Zambia, bordering both Angola and Namibia/
South West Africa (at the Caprivi Strip), this park includes the
scenic Sioma Falls.

SIPALO, MUNUKAYUMBWA. Perhaps one of the most vigorous of
the young nationalists in the ANC, ZANC, and UNIP during the
1950's and 60's, he was certainly the most active in Pan-
African affairs and one of the best orators. Born in December,
1929, in Barotseland, he received his basic education there,
ultimately studying Economics at New Delhi University. In India he edited a magazine about Africa, was elected President
of the African Student's Association in Asia, and attended the
Bandung Conference. He did not finish the degree but returned
to Central Africa via Egypt where he worked closely with Nas-
ser for two months in 1956. Back in Northern Rhodesia he
joined the ANC and became private secretary to Harry Nkumbula, its President, and a member of ANC's executive body.
An aggressive and dynamic leader filled with ideas to make
ANC more active, he soon became an attractive alternative to
some who opposed Nkumbula's more conservative brand of leadership. In September, 1957 he was removed from ANC's executive on the urging of Nkumbula, and in early 1958 was expelled from the party. His year in the party had shaken up
the members, however, and made the party much more active,
for example in beer hall boycotts.

He worked on the Copperbelt for most of 1958 before helping to form ZANC in October. As Secretary he was second
only to Kaunda. His vigorous travel throughout the country
and stimulating oratory made him an excellent party organizer.
It was also the Government's reason for detaining him at
Feira in March, 1959, for several months and then charging
him with treason. He was sentenced to a year at hard labor,
and shared a cell in Salisbury with Kaunda. When released in
January, 1960, he and Kaunda joined UNIP. Again Sipalo became Secretary-General to Kaunda's President. He then went
in April to a series of Afro-Asian meetings in Ghana and
Guinea, addressing huge crowds. In December he joined the
UNIP delegation in London at the Federal Review Conference
(q.v.) and later returned for the Northern Rhodesia Constitutional Conference. He was chosen Secretary of the All African People's Conference in Cairo shortly after that. However,
at UNIP's Mulungushi Conference of 1961 he was replaced as
Secretary because of alleged alcoholic abuses. In 1962 he
served as UNIP's representative in Ghana. In December,
1962, he suffered serious burns from a petrol-bomb attack,
but was back in politics within two years. In September,
1964 Kaunda named him Minister of Health in the Independence
Cabinet, but he was replaced the next January. He returned
to the Cabinet in May, 1966 as Minister of Labour and Social
Development, and continued in the Labour post until August,
1967. Sipalo was one of the UNIP leaders from Barotseland
who was defeated by a Bemba-Tonga coalition when running for
re-election to the party's Central Committee in August. He
resigned from the party but was persuaded by Kaunda to retract this. He returned to the Cabinet when Kaunda appointed
Sipalo as Minister of Agriculture on September 8, 1967. However Sipalo's farewell to Zambian politics occurred in December, 1968 when he lost his seat in Parliament when the banned
United Party (q.v.) helped the ANC unseat three UNIP Cabinet
members from Barotseland in the general elections.

SIPOPA (or SEPOPA; LUTANGU SIPOPA). King (Litunga) of the
Lozi from 1864 to 1876, he was the son of the Lozi King, Mu-
bambwa (q.v.). He was known as Lutangu in his youth. Captured by the Makololo King Sebituane (q.v.), he lived with the
invaders for many years as an "adopted" son. With Sebituane
dead and his brutal son Sekeletu ruling in 1859, Sipopa fled the
Makololo and went to a northern Lozi stronghold, Lukwakwa.
The next year he helped to overthrow and kill Imasiku (q.v.),
the unpopular leader there and was eventually made king there.
He became quite close to a Lozi nobleman, Njekwa (q.v.), who
was mainly responsible for the military victory over the Makololo. Njekwa invited Sipopa to take over as Lozi King in
the restored kingdom in 1864. Njekwa was then made his
Ngambela or Prime Minister. Immediately Sipopa had opponents. Some felt he had been influenced too much by the
Makololo. Other opposition emerged as a result of his own
political ineptness. He even became jealous of Njekwa and

replaced him, losing the support of a large faction of traditionalists in the process. (This despite the fact that only Njekwa's popularity kept a force from deposing Sipopa in 1869.)
Sipopa turned out to be despotic and cruel, ignoring the National Council for a coterie of private supporters. In July,
1874, he moved his capital south to Sesheke, an area made
secure in 1866 by his conquest of the local Toka and Subiya
peoples. He had a close relationship there with the trader,
George Westbeech, who sold him guns. A revolt was brewing,
however, and as he fled his capital, a gunshot wound by an
assassin serving as his bodyguard proved to be fatal. However
Sipopa is remembered favorably for making one major and lasting reform. The Lozi had been split on several occasions by
having two semi-independent leaders, one in the north and one
in the south. Sipopa appointed his sister to be the southern
leader (at Nalolo). When she died in 1871 he appointed his
daughter. By having a female ruling at Nalolo and dependent
on appointment by the male ruling at Lealui, no rival claimant
to the throne was created yet the dual capitals remained. This
remains the pattern today.

SITUMBU SA MULONGA. An inner council within the Lozi Mulongwanji (q.v.), its membership varied according to the choice of
the King. It would usually include the Ngambela, the Natamoyo
and the head of the Likombwa, of course, but otherwise was
comprised of the most trusted and wisest indunas plus whichever
outsiders the King chose to add. It was a private council that
could be called to the palace on a moment's notice if necessary,
and thus was usually limited to individuals living at or near the
capital. It was especially important for emergency decisions
when there was no time to call the full Mulongwanji together.

SITUPA. Zambian word for the identity certificate or pass (q.v.)
required of Africans by the Northern Rhodesian government.

SIWALE, DONALD R. A Northern Rhodesia government clerk and
teacher for many years, he was also an early nationalist. In
1923 he received a copy of the constitution of the North Nyasa
Native Association from a former classmate at Livingstonia.
Inspired by this, Siwale, David Kaunda (father of Zambia's
President) and several others organized the Mwenzo Welfare
Association. It was to be a forum for African social and political views. In 1924 they protested heavy taxes on rural Africans. When Siwale was transferred, his organization folded.
(Actually Siwale and his friends had been organized informally
almost twenty years previous, as they had been trained as
teachers at Livingstonia in 1904 and continued to meet periodically.) In the early 1950's the elderly Siwale, now retired,
was still active politically. In 1950 as a member of the
Northern Provincial Council and again in 1952 as a member of
the African Representative Council, Siwale spoke out against
white domination and the proposed Federation, arguing instead
that Africans should be granted at least equal representation
with Europeans in the Legislative and Executive Councils.

SIYUBO, SILUMELUME. Ngambela (Prime Minister) to the Lozi
King Mwanawina for about a year in the early 1960's. A
strong traditionalist, he accompanied the King to London in
1963 to plead for a Barotse right to secede from Northern
Rhodesia. He clung to this hope even though the King eventually indicated a willingness to concede to UNIP. Elected councillors tried to persuade the Barotse National Council to replace Siyubo with an elected Prime Minister. After a near-
violent demonstration against him in Lealui, he resigned on
October 18, 1963.

SJAMBOKS. Whips made of thongs that were carried and used by
Europeans in the early days of exploring and settling Northern
Rhodesia. European farmers in more recent times were also
known to use them on recalcitrant Africans. They were feared
weapons of torture.

SKINNER, JAMES JOHN. A Lusaka lawyer who became an active
worker for UNIP and later became Zambia's Attorney-General
and Chief Justice. Born in Dublin, Ireland, on July 24, 1923,
he was called to the Irish Bar in 1946 and to the Northern
Rhodesia Bar in 1951. Considered radical by some Europeans,
he supported the African nationalists in their campaigns, joining UNIP in 1960. In 1962 he was the legal advisor to UNIP
as well as one of its principal campaign advisors. He wrote
the Election Workers Handbook in 1962, a twenty-two page
manual that was sent to all UNIP officials at all levels to
guide them through the intricacies of election procedure. He
himself was an unsuccessful UNIP candidate for the Luangwa
National seat in 1962, but he was elected to Parliament in
1964. He was appointed Attorney-General of Zambia in September, 1964, a position he held until January, 1969. He
was simultaneously Minister of Justice from September 24,
1964 until January 22, 1965 and Minister of Legal Affairs
from September 8, 1967 until January 4, 1969. In March,
1969, Skinner was appointed the Chief Justice of Zambia. A
controversy over a decision by Justice Ifor Evans (q. v.) led to
Skinner's resignation in September, 1969. He has been Chief
Justice of Malawi since 1970.

SLAVE TRADE. Slavery among Africans in Zambia has existed
for centuries. History abounds in tales of a strong chief and
his people slaughtering their enemy, except for the young
people who are put into slavery. The outside slave trade began primarily in the early nineteenth century. The Portuguese
had been using slaves at the gold mines near Zumbo for two
hundred years already, but near the end of the eighteenth century the Portuguese at Mozambique had begun to provide slaves
for Indian Ocean island sugar plantations of the French. Soon
there was also a new demand for slaves in Brazil. At first
most of the slaves came from the area of the lower Zambezi
River, especially the Chewa. The Portuguese attempted to
open up slave trade with Kazembe, the Lunda leader who had

for years been sending slaves west to Mwata Yamvo. At the
same time the Portuguese in Angola were buying slaves from
Lamba, Luvale, and Lunda chiefs in northwest Zambia. The
early nineteenth century also saw Arab traders from Zambia
coming in search of slaves and other "commodities," mostly
from the northeastern quadrant of Zambia. By the 1870's and
1880's this trade was heavily in the hands of the Bemba, who
were active in slave raids. In the West, the Lozi dominated
their neighbors for the sake of the slave trade. Portuguese
themselves raided villages in southeastern Zambia in the mid
and late nineteenth century as the demand for slaves was
strong, even though technically the trade was now illegal. A
Portuguese-speaking African from Tete named Kanyemba was a
ferocious slave hunter throughout southern Zambia in the 1870's
and 1880's. Ivory trade and slave trade were interrelated as
the slaves were often used as ivory porters. Ultimately one
of the major factors in stopping the slave trade was the coming of the British, as missionaries and BSAC officials worked
to eliminate the trade and served as protection for its victims.

SMITH, IAN. Prime Minister of Southern Rhodesia and leader of
the Rhodesian Front since April, 1964. A longtime Rhodesian
politician, he initiated his country's unilateral declaration of
independence in November, 1965. He has been the principal
adversary of President Kaunda in matters involving Zambian-
Rhodesian relations. Guerrilla forces in Zambia have been attempting to bring down Smith's Government, a factor in Smith's
animosity toward Zambia.

"SMOKE THAT THUNDERS." The oft-quoted English translation of
Mosi-oa-tunya, the African name for Victoria Falls (q.v.).

SOCCER. The favorite spectator sport in Zambia, its season lasts
eight months. Also called football in Zambia (and many countries other than the United States), it is the national sport.

SOCIETE DES MISSIONS EVANGELIQUES. The French name of the
Paris Missionary Society (q.v.).

SOCIETIES ORDINANCE. A law passed by the Northern Rhodesia
Legislative Council in November, 1957, it was aimed at controlling nationalist political organizations. It required them to
register their branches and to supply the Government with detailed information about their organization, officers, and activities. Both ZANC and UNIP were especially harassed by the
application of the Ordinance.

SOKO, AXON JASPER (or ACKSON JOSEPH). One of the early
ZANC and UNIP activists, he served in numerous government
positions from 1967 to 1977 when in April, 1977, he was dismissed from the Cabinet, accused of engaging in the activities
of a banned political party, the United Progressive Party.
Born June 10, 1930, at Chipata, he eventually became an

accountant-bookkeeper. He served as Regional Secretary at
Ndola of both ZANC and UNIP from 1959 to 1964, although he
was restricted to Luwinga in 1959 because of his party activity.
In 1964 he was elected an M. P. from Lundazi. In 1967 he
was appointed Minister of State for Finance, but later that
year he was switched to Minister for the Eastern Province.
At one year intervals he held the same position for the
Northern, Central, and Copperbelt Provinces. In 1971 he became Minister of State for Technical and Vocational Training.
He joined the Cabinet on April 19, 1971 as Minister of Trade
and Industry. In 1973 he became Minister of Mines and Industry, holding this position until he was dismissed in April, 1977.

SOKOTA, PASKALE. A Bemba teacher who was an early member
of the ANC and a member of the Legislative Council. He was
headmaster of the Kitwe African School from 1941 to 1951.
However in 1949 he became a member of the Western Province
African Provincial Council and of the African Representative
Council. An active member of the ANC, he and Dauti Yamba
were placed on the Legislative Council with ANC support, replacing two relatively non-political men who were in the two
"African" seats. In 1954 he was re-elected for another term.
He was an African representative at the Lancaster House Conference (q.v.) in London in 1952 and, as at the Victoria Falls
Conference of 1951 (q.v.), he opposed the idea of federation.
In August, 1956 he was replaced on the ANC National Executive Committee. His replacement was the younger and more
militant Simon Kapwepwe. In 1959 he ran unsuccessfully for
the Legislative Council as Independent. In May of that year he
was one of the founders of the African National Freedom Movement (q.v.).

SOLI. One of the groups of Tonga-speaking peoples of south-central Zambia, near Lusaka. There are about forty thousand
Soli today. They traded with the Portuguese in the eighteenth
century at Zumbo and Feira, both a little east of them. Nineteenth-century reports indicate that the Soli were adept at iron-
smelting and smithing. With but one exception, the Soli chiefdoms were founded by members of the nyendwa clan. The system of matrilineal descent is followed among the Soli. Generally speaking, it has been a people without many truly notable
traditional leaders.

SOLWEZI. One of the districts in Zambia's North-Western Province, as well as a town about twenty miles south of the Zaire
border. In 1969 the Solwezi district had about fifty-three thousand people. The town itself is not particularly large, but two
major roads service it. In 1969 residents of the area as well
as its traditional leaders showed their displeasure with the
UNIP Government for its failure to provide any development
for the region by failing to vote "yes" in a national referendum.

SORGHUM. One of the better cash crops of Zambia, its production is greatest in central and northern Zambia, although it is also grown among the Bemba and Lozi, for example. It is sometimes called "kaffir corn." Production of sorghum is most common in villages using chitimene (q.v.) agriculture. One reason for its popularity is that it can be used for malt in breweries. Sorghum seeds have been found in several Early Iron Age sites in Zambia.

SOTHO. One of the larger ethnic subdivisions of the Bantu people of southern Africa. Most of the people in both Lesotho and Botswana are Sotho, as are some Africans in South Africa. Rev. Coillard had worked among the Sotho before coming to Barotseland, and brought with him some Sotho evangelists. The Makololo who invaded the Lozi were also Sotho. An interesting separatist church movement was set up by a Masotho, Willie Mokalapa (q.v.).

SOUTH WEST AFRICA (NAMIBIA). Zambia's neighbor along a stretch of border in southwestern Zambia. This piece of Namibian land is known specifically as the Caprivi Strip (q.v.).

SOUTHERN PROVINCE. Located along a major part of the border with Rhodesia/Zimbabwe, this province lies generally north and west of the area of the Zambezi River that is dominated by Victoria Falls and Lake Kariba. The province had about a half million people in 1969, up 7.1 percent since 1963. It consists of six districts (listed here in descending order by population): Mazabuka, Choma, Kalomo, Gwembe, Livingstone, and Namwala. Among the principal groups inhabiting the area are the Tonga, Toka, Ila, Leya, and Subiya. The Southern Province had regularly supported the ANC during election periods, primarily because its leader, Harry Nkumbula, is from the province and had numerous contacts in the area, notably among the traditional leaders.

SOUTHERN RHODESIA. One of Zambia's principal neighbors to the South and a source of conflict because of its white-ruled government. It has used the name Rhodesia since the time when Northern Rhodesia changed to Zambia. Africans attempting to restore the territory to majority rule prefer to use the term Zimbabwe, after an old and successful civilization that existed there.

SOUTHERN RHODESIA NATIVE LABOUR BUREAU. The principal recruiting agency that persuaded Zambians to work in Southern Rhodesia, it was active from 1903 to 1933. In the latter year the Depression drastically reduced the need for foreign laborers. When demand increased again, there was such a large supply of ready workers that formal recruitment became unnecessary.

STANLEY, SIR HERBERT JAMES. A South African who was appointed by the British as the first Governor of Northern

Rhodesia. He served from April 1, 1924, until he retired in 1927. One of his most popular actions took place on October 22, 1925 when he announced at Kasama that the head tax had been reduced from 10s. to 7s. 6d. However, he also stated that problem tribes would have their tax increased as a punishment. From April 6, 1931, to January 6, 1935, Stanley served as High Commissioner for the United Kingdom in South Africa.

STEPHENSON, J. E. ("CHIRUPULA"). One of the more colorful of the early BSAC administrators, he came to Northern Rhodesia in 1899 to work for the company. He served for many years as a Native Commissioner, setting up bomas in many areas of North-East Rhodesia. In 1905 he set up the boma at Ndola on what became the Copperbelt. He freely admitted later that the Company had no treaty and no rights there. His administration was very paternalistic, feeling that the race factor automatically made all Africans like children who did not know what was good or bad for them. He eventually settled down at Mkushi with several African wives. In 1937 he published an autobiography, Chirupula's Tale.

STEVENSON ROAD. An important communication link early in the period of colonization of Central Africa, it was built by the African Lakes Company beginning in 1881. It extended from the northern tip of Lake Nyasa (Malawi) to the southern end of Lake Tanganyika roughly along the present Zambia-Tanzania border. Its purpose was to support "legitimate" (non-slave) trade. It was paid for by James Stevenson, a merchant from Glasgow, Scotland and a member of the board of the Church of Scotland Mission. His £15,000 would also provide a way of linking early mission stations near the two lakes. The route soon attracted other mission groups, such as the White Fathers at Mambwe. Meanwhile the African Lakes Company built two trading posts on the road in the early 1890's, calling them Fife (q.v.) and Abercorn (q.v.). A telephone wire existed along the road by World War I, and the Germans were always cutting it.

STIRLING, COLONEL DAVID. A moderate to liberal European politician who founded the Capricorn Africa Society (q.v.) in 1949 and who was also a founder of the multiracial Constitution Party (q.v.) in 1957.

STORRS, SIR RONALD. Governor of Northern Rhodesia from 1932 to 1934. A fine writer with a sharp intellect, he was very popular, but the Central African climate affected his health and he was transferred without having any real time to affect policy.

STRIKES OF 1935 AND 1940. Perhaps the most notable labor unrest in Zambia occurred during the Copperbelt strikes of 1935 and 1940. Although economic and social in origin, they demonstrated a rising political consciousness among the Africans.

They were motivated by several things. First, the very low wage
rates and inferior food and housing conditions (especially when
compared to European miners in the same mines). Second,
Africans resented the color bar that reserved all advanced jobs
for Europeans. Third, the Africans disliked the insulting and
even brutal behavior of Europeans against Africans both in the
mines and outside them. Almost nothing was achieved by the
1935 strike, which did not last long. The 1940 strike was
more vigorous and ended after a week or more only when
seventeen strikers were killed and sixty-five injured during an
attack by the miners on a compound office.

STUBBS, FRANK N. African National Congress candidate for the
Luapula National seat in the 1962 election. A conservative to
moderate European, he won the seat in the December 10 by-
election after campaigning vigorously on the platform that he
would quit ANC rather than join in a governing coalition with
the "radical" UNIP. When he won, however, it was discovered
that Stubbs and C. E. Cousins, also of the ANC, were the
only Europeans elected by either UNIP or ANC. As the Constitution required that two of the Ministers must be Europeans,
without Stubbs an ANC-UNIP coalition could not take office.
Stubbs came under much pressure to renege on his campaign
pledge to allow an all-African coalition to come to power.
Harry Nkumbulu of the ANC used the two Europeans to bargain
for ministerial parity with UNIP. Stubbs finally announced that
he would return to his constituents to discuss the situation.
On December 15 he returned to Lusaka and announced that he
would join the Government to "serve the interests of the country." He became Minister for Transport and Works, a post
he held until UNIP decisively won the 1964 elections.

SUBIYA (or SUBIA). One of the numerous ethnic subdivisions of
southwestern Zambia, the Subiya in Zambia number perhaps
twenty-three thousand today. Their homeland is generally that
area squeezed between the Chobe and Zambezi Rivers, mostly
south of the Zambezi. Thus most Subiya actually live in the
Caprivi Strip (q. v.) of Namibia. While one group of Subiya
speak Tonga, most of them are Lozi-speaking, as a result of
their numerous contacts with the Lozi. Historians feel that
the Subiya were pushed south out of the Zambezi flood plain
when the Lozi (then the Luyi) began moving south. This was
in the seventeenth century when Mwanambinya (q. v.) conquered
them and set up a capital near today's Senanga. However it
was the sixth Lozi king, Ngombala (q. v.), who brought them
firmly under Lozi rule in the early eighteenth century. Lozi
indunas were placed in the area to live and thereby represent
the Lozi King. Tribute was paid in grain, fish, meat, skins,
ivory, or honey. An attempted revolt by both the Subiya and
the Toka in 1865-66 was ruthlessly suppressed by Sipopa, the
Lozi King. Later he attempted to win their support by restor-
ing some of their land and giving them lower governmental
positions.

SU'ID IBN HABIB. One of the more active Arab traders in
Northern Rhodesia in the mid-nineteenth century. Livingstone
wrote in 1868 that he possessed 5250 pounds of ivory and
10,500 pounds of copper at that time and was plotting how to
transport all of this when his brother, Salem bin Habib, was
killed by Africans. Smith and Dale claim that the same man
was active in the slave trade in Ila territory and also urged
Sekeletu (q.v.) of the Makololo to attack a neighboring people.

SULIMAN, ABDULLAH IBN (BIN). A prominent Arab trader who
lived in northern Zambia in the late nineteenth and early
twentieth century. He was originally sent there by Kumba
Kumba (q.v.), leading a squad of elephant hunters. Abdullah
and his men assisted Nsama VI Chimutwe in regaining his capital from his rivals. A couple of years later, in 1884, Tippu
Tip (q.v.) sent Abdullah again to aid Chimutwe, this time
against Mporokoso (q.v.). A large force of Bemba, including
the Mwamba himself, aided Mporokoso, but the Bemba eventually were repelled. Abdullah was given much land for his
reward, and his heirs still live in the village he built on
Kaputa stream. Chimutwe had an argument in 1891 with Abdullah over a woman and also interfered with his caravans.
Abdullah allied himself with the Bemba and Chimutwe was
killed at his capital by the combined force. The new Nsama
had Abdullah's backing. Abdullah died at his village in 1916.

SULIMAN, NASORO BIN. An Arab trader from Muscat and a fol-
lower of Mlozi (q.v.). Upon the latter's defeat in 1895, Suliman and his followers set up camp near the Bemba leader,
Mporokoso. A British attempt to visit the Bemba leader in
April, 1899, was repulsed by Suliman and his followers.
Eventually the Arabs fled to Abdullah bin Suliman (q.v.) who
turned over Nasoro to the British in June, 1899.

SUMBU NATIONAL PARK. One of the nicer tourist attractions of
Zambia, the Sumbu National Park is a game reserve near
Zambia's northern border, adjacent to the southwest portion
of Lake Tanganyika. Kasaba Bay on the Lake provides excellent fishing, notably for Nile perch, tiger fish and giant cat-
fish. It only has three camps (two on the water), but elephants are numerous in the park.

SUPREME ACTION COUNCIL. Set up by the African National Congress in February, 1952 at its Conference, this Council was
planned as a special nine-member leadership group of the
ANC. Its main duty was to fight the development of a Federation with whatever means that were necessary. Work stoppages were to be a principal weapon, thus five of the nine
seats were filled by members of the Trade Union Congress.
Kenneth Kaunda was a member of the Council.

SUU, FRANCIS L. A Lozi politician who was active in the Sicaba
Party of Barotseland in 1962. Born in 1892, he had been an

administrative secretary to King Yeta III. He was not part of
the subsequent administration, but had returned to the royal
court in the 1950's. In April, 1962, he was a member of the
Barotse delegation at constitutional discussions in London. In
June he helped organize the Sicaba Party (q. v.) and became
one of its two candidates in the October, 1962 Legislative Council elections. He was overwhelmingly defeated by Arthur Wina,
receiving only sixty-five votes. The next month he announced
his retirement from politics and his intention to dissolve the
Party.

SWAHILI. A term with both ethnic and linguistic connotations,
Swahili is a language widespread in East Africa and well-known
in parts of Central Africa. It is a hybrid of Arabic and Bantu
languages. When the term refers to people, however it refers
to Arabs who live near the coast. ('Sawahil" is the plural
form of "sahil, " which in Arabic means "the coast. ") To
other Arabs, these coast-dwelling Arabs were inferior, even
though they had established fine coastal trading cities. Later,
in the nineteenth century, many traders on the coast sent their
Swahili representatives into Central Africa to bring out the
caravans of ivory and slaves, especially. In this way they got
into northern and eastern Zambia, trading (or fighting) notably
with the Bemba people, but also with Kazembe and the Lunda
in 1831. Several of the Swahili established fine military repu-
tations as a result of their victories, especially over Bemba
forces (see ABDULLAH IBN SULIMAN). In the late nineteenth
century they also were confronted by British attempts to halt
the slave trade.

SWAKA. A small tribe in eastern Zambia, it is an offshoot of the
Lala (q. v.). They constitute about one percent of Zambia's
population.

                              - T -

TABWA. A matrilineal people who straddle the Zambia-Zaire
border in northeastern Zambia, they number close to fifty
thousand. They speak the Bemba language today, and in other
ways resemble them, being the northern neighbors of the
Bemba, living between Lake Mweru and Lake Tanganyika. The
early Tabwa wore cotton clothing, not the clothing of many
other peoples. It was from the Tabwa that the Bemba acquired
the thumb piano (q. v.). The Tabwa first came south to their
present lands in the late eighteenth century, as chiefs from
the leopard clan led the migration. The Lunda emperor, Kazembe III obtained tribute from them around that same time.
The most important Tabwa chieftainship, that of Nsama, was
founded in Itabwa (the land of the Tabwa) near the end of the
eighteenth century by a man named Nsama who was a member
of the chiefly Zimba (leopard) clan. The main group of
bazimba was under his rule. A later off-shoot of this group

was the Mulilo chieftainship. The strongest Tabwa leader was
Nsama III, Chipili Chipioka. He soundly defeated Arab traders
in 1841-42 and a coalition of Arabs and Kazembe VII two decades later. In 1867, however, a caravan led by Tippu Tip
(q. v.) defeated him, and foreign traders dominated Itabwa from
then on. The line of Nsama chiefs continued, however. In
the next ten to fifteen years, some groups of Bemba took advantage of the weakened Tabwa and took some of their territory, notably that area called Isenga. In the mid-1930's the
Tabwa put a claim for Isenga to the Colonial Government, but
the British did not give it serious attention. In 1889 Harry
Johnston received a signed "treaty" for the BSAC from the
Mulilo chieftainship of the Tabwa, and Alfred Sharpe likewise
signed a "treaty" with Nsama a year or two later.

TAFUNA. The title given to Paramount Chief of the Lungu people
of northern Zambia, near the southeastern corner of Lake
Tanganyika. Other Lungu chiefs were secondary to him. The
royal capital was at Isoko with the exception of a brief period
under Tafuna III. In 1870 Tafuna IV Kakunga returned the
capital to Isoko but he fled north to Kasanga around 1883 when
the Bemba of Chitapankwa ravaged the area, notably killing
Zombe, another Lunga leader. No Tafuna returned to Isoko
for many years, and the Bemba under Ponde ruled the area.
The Tafuna in 1930 urged the Northern Rhodesian government
to remove the Bemba who were still occupying Lungu land,
but he was turned down. Another encounter with the Europeans
occurred in 1891 when the Tafuna was exiled and imprisoned
when he refused to supply workers to the London Missionary
Society and the African Lakes Corporation.

TALKING-DRUM. An important aid to communication in much of
Africa, this percussion instrument is capable of variable pitch
within a wide range, and thus can send messages in much
more than just a code pattern. The Lunda of Kazembe had
mastered the technique of making and using the instrument.
The Bemba seem to have learned (or relearned) about it from
the Lunda.

TAMBO. A very small tribe that resides in the extreme north-
eastern part of Zambia, its numbers probably do not exceed
fifteen thousand. They are part of the Mambwe-speaking language group. Living on the upper Luangwa River, they grew
cotton in the nineteenth century and wove their own cloth.
Their tradition indicates that they are related to the Bisa,
breaking away when the population grew too large. They then
moved eastward into the unoccupied territory they now occupy.
While retaining their Bisa totem names, they have become patrilineal, cattle-keeping people like their new neighbors. Some
conflicts occurred in the nineteenth century with Iwa chiefs.

TANGANYIKA DISTRICT. One of the more important administrative
subdivisions of North-Eastern Rhodesia under the British South

Africa Company jurisdiction, being the location of such groups
as the Bemba, Lungu, Mambwe, and Tabwe. The slave trade
and ivory trade were both very active in the area, and inter-
tribal fighting was also common. In addition this was the district into which some of the early missionary groups came.
While Abercorn was the principal administrative center, there
were also other bomas at Sumbu, Katwe, and Mporokoso. At
the turn of the century there were about a hundred policemen
stationed in the district.

TANGANYIKA ESTATE. A 4310-square mile territory that had
    been acquired by the British South Africa Company from the
    African Lakes Corporation. It was in extreme northeastern
    Zambia, mostly in the Abercorn area but extending into the
    Isoko area. The Reserves Commission of 1927 persuaded the
    BSAC to give up parts of it to allow more Europeans to ac-
    quire the land for coffee plantations. Despite African protests,
    the Crown Lands and Native Reserves (Tanganyika District)
    Order-in-Council, 1929, created both native reserves and
    crown lands in the area. The attempt to bring in more Euro-
    peans was very unsuccessful.

TAN-ZAM RAILWAY. As early as May, 1963, Kenneth Kaunda
    had discussed with British leaders the need for a railway link-
    ing Zambia with the Indian Ocean at Dar Es Salaam, Tangan-
    yika in order to reduce Zambia's dependence on hostile lead-
    ers in white-ruled countries around them. This became even
    more crucial after Rhodesia's unilateral declaration of inde-
    pendence in November, 1965. After being turned down by
    England, the U.S., the World Bank, and the U.N., Kaunda
    was offered an interest free loan from the People's Republic
    of China. First payment on the thirty year loan would not be-
    gin until 1983.
        Actual construction was done by almost twenty thousand
    Chinese. Work began in 1970 and was completed in early
    1976, although emergency shipments of wheat arrived in Zam-
    bia via the railway in 1975. The railway, which extends all
    the way to Zambia's Copperbelt, became a crucial commercial
    lifeline after the Benguela railroad through Angola was closed
    due to civil war there. The Tan-Zam railway is also called
    the Great Uhuru (Freedom) Railway.

TANZANIA. The African country bordering Zambia at its extreme
    northeastern borders. It was created by the uniting of two
    independent states, Tanganyika and Zanzibar in 1964. Its im-
    portance to Zambia rests in part on the fact that it has repre-
    sented Zambia's most stable outlet to the ocean, now more so
    than ever due to the Tan-Zam Railway (q.v.). Also Julius
    Nyerere, its president, has been a close friend and advisor to
    Kenneth Kaunda of Zambia.

TEAK WOOD. An export product of Zambia, it is important
    enough that the industry was nationalized by the Mulungushi

Declaration of 1968. The teak forests are found especially in southern Barotseland where they are commercially exploited. The product is variously known as Rhodesian teak, Zambesi redwood, or Mukushi. Its scientific name is <u>Baikiaea pJ</u><u>lurijuga</u>. At first used only for plank supports in the mines, its beauty has made it popular for furniture, railway sleeping cars, and parquet floors. In 1967 the forests produced over two million cubic feet of "teak."

TEMBA, FRANKLIN. One of the founders and the first Chairman in 1932 of the Abercorn Native Welfare Association. Within a few years he had switched to the Kasama Native Welfare Association, where by 1937 he was Secretary of the Association. His activities in these associations in the 1930's made him an early advocate of African autonomy. (Sources are unclear as to whether this is the same man as the Edward Franklin Tembo who was a co-founder of the Livingstone Native Welfare Association in 1930.)

TEMBE. The word for the stockaded villages belonging to the Arab slave-traders. They were found primarily in the Luangwa valley of northeastern Zambia in the late nineteenth century.

TEMPLE, REV. MERFYN M. A Methodist minister in Lusaka and author of several books on the church in Zambia, notably <u>African Angelus</u> and <u>Rain on the Earth</u>. He had been active in various liberal, multi-racial groups, including the Constitution Party (q. v.) of which he was Chairman. As UNIP began to rise in the early 1960's, Rev. Temple became an active campaigner for European support of UNIP. In 1964 he was appointed the first director of the Zambia Youth Service (q. v.).

TETE. Located on the lower Zambezi between its confluences with the Luangwa River and the Shire River, it has been an important trade center for many centuries. It is southeast of the modern Cabora Bassa Dam. Arab traders passed through Tete in the twelfth or thirteenth centuries on their way to Ingombe Ilede (q. v.). Portuguese traders and officials were based there in the seventeenth century. Early in the next century gold was discovered in the vicinity, attracting more people. Meanwhile Bisa were traveling south to Tete with their ivory, as were the Lunda of Kazembe. Later, slaves were brought in trade from the north. At the same time, Portuguese explorers like Lacerda began their trips to Zambia from Tete, as did Monteiro and Gamitto. Silva Porto ended his Zambian trip there. Today it is part of Mozambique.

THIRD NON-ALIGNED SUMMIT CONFERENCE. A prestigious meeting of representatives of states that was held in Lusaka, Zambia in late 1970. The speeches and debates in Mulungushi Hall concentrated on southern African issues. The largest Third World summit conference up to that time, it condemned the white-ruled countries of southern Africa and urged that drastic action be taken against them.

THOMAS, J. H. British Secretary of State for Dominion affairs
    from June 1930 until November 1935. In 1931 he refused a
    request by the Southern Rhodesian Government (with support
    by some elected members of the Northern Rhodesian Legisla-
    tive Council) that a conference be held to consider amalgama-
    tion of the two territories. He stated that Northern Rhodesia
    still needed time to develop as a separate entity.

THOMSON, JAMES MOFFAT. Secretary for Native Affairs in
    Northern Rhodesia in the late 1920's and 1930's. His first
    job in Central Africa had been as a shop assistant for the
    African Lakes Corporation. He later worked for fourteen years
    for the British South Africa Company. In 1910 he discovered
    the Nkana mine. He took over as Secretary for Native Affairs
    in 1928. A strong backer of indirect rule (q. v.) he supported
    the Native Authority Ordinance of 1929 which returned much
    authority to traditional leaders. On the other hand he opposed
    certain nationalistic or progressive movements that did not use
    the traditional system. He opposed the Watch Tower Move-
    ment (q. v.), for example, and although he had spoken favor-
    ably of the formation of a Mwenzo Welfare Association when he
    was head administrator of the Tanganyika District in 1923, he
    opposed the formation of a United African Welfare Association
    in the early 1930's. In 1927 he also served as Chairman for
    the Reserves Commission of the Tanganyika District, the job
    of which was to provide more land to European coffee plant-
    ers by getting the BSAC to relinquish part of its Tanganyika
    Estate and by resettling local Africans in Reserves.

THOMSON, JOSEPH. A noted East African explorer who in late
    1890 was sent by Cecil Rhodes into the heart of Zambia to ob-
    tain concessions from the Africans in exchange for protection
    against the Ngoni and Chikunda raiders. His success in get-
    ting "treaties" with leaders among the Lamba, Bisa, Lenje,
    Lala, and Aushi, combined with similar success by Alfred
    Sharpe (q. v.), allowed Rhodes and his Commissioner for Cen-
    tral Africa, Harry Johnston, to establish what would soon be
    called North-Eastern Rhodesia. Thomson became very ill on
    the trip, and his porters had smallpox, making a visit to the
    Yeke king impossible. Thomson was also unsuccessful in get-
    ting a treaty with Mpezeni (q. v.). Despite the fact that the
    signatures Thomson got were on documents otherwise not valid
    today, Rhodes was able to use them to claim large parts of
    Central Zambia, including the Copperbelt. Especially impor-
    tant were the "agreements" with the Lamba leader, whose area
    did not include the Copperbelt. This did not prevent the
    British South Africa Company from claiming it, however.

THUMB PIANO. While this interesting African musical instrument is
    found among the Bemba (who seem to have gotten it from their
    northern neighbors, the Tabwa), it also appears that what may
    have been iron keys from thumb pianos have been found in iron age
    villages of central and southern Zambia which date from the 5th,
    6th, and 7th centuries. See also KALIF PIANO OF KALIMBA.

THE TIMES OF ZAMBIA. Taken over by UNIP in 1975, presumably because of criticism of the government, this daily newspaper is Zambia's largest, with a circulation of about 65,000.
Even when it was owned by the multi-national corporation,
Lonrho, it got much of its information from government agencies, notably the Zambia Information Services (q.v.). An
English language paper, it is now published in Lusaka.
Founded in 1944 as The Northern News (q.v.) its news was
aimed toward a European readership until 1963. As a twice-
weekly it was under the ownership of Roy Welensky (q.v.),
and later the Argus newspaper chain of South Africa. Under
the ownership of Lonrho, however, it became The Times of
Zambia on July 1, 1965. Six weeks earlier it acquired Richard
Hall as Editor. His several books on Zambia are among the
best now available. Under his editorship it became a moderate if slightly pro-government paper, with some coverage of
international news supplementing a national and local emphasis.
It was published in Ndola. Under Dunston Kamana, editor in
the early 1970's, however, the Times became critical of some
UNIP politicians and of government inefficiency. Early in 1972
he was replaced by the intervention of the Government, which
appointed its own editor, Vernon Mwaanga (q.v.). UNIP took
it over in 1975.

TIPPU TIP (or TIPPOO TIB). Perhaps the best known of Arab
traders, this native of Zanzibar (where he died of malaria in
1905) was actually named Hamed ibn Muhammed el Murjebi.
Both Tippu Tip and Pembamoto were names by which Africans
knew him. His first trip to Central Africa was evidently in
1863-64 when he traveled on a mission seeking to trade for
ivory. In 1866 he returned and visited the Bemba chief,
Mwamba, and also the powerful old Tabwa chief Nsama. Seeing Nsama's huge storehouses of ivory and copper, Tippu Tip
decided that he must have them. His Arab fighters used guns
against the spears and bows of the Tabwa, and Nsama was finally defeated in 1867. A thousand slaves, thirty tons of ivory,
and ten tons of copper were taken, according to the biography
that appeared in 1906 based on his records. In this victory he
had aid from Lungu warriors who had reason to hate Nsama.
His use of guns revolutionized warfare among Africans, as they
saw how easily the mighty Nsama was beaten. After this victory Tippu Tip returned to the coast via Bemba territory (where
he had left his half brother, Kumba-Kumba). With his success,
Tippu Tip returned to trade in 1869-70, visiting Tabwa country
as well as several of the Bemba chiefs, notably Mwamba and
Chitimukulu. He then set up a permanent trade depot at
Nsama's village, headed by Kumba-Kumba (q.v.). Also with
the help of Tippu Tip, Kakunga, a Lunga royal, was able to
defeat his opposition and became Tafuna IV at Isoko. Moving
west with his caravan, Tippu Tip helped a Lunda leader, Lukwesa, regain his throne as Kazembe, again through armed
force. He then moved into Katanga. Later in his life, King
Leopold II of Belgium made him provisional governor of the

Upper Congo. Tippu Tip also accompanied Henry Stanley on
the expedition to rescue Emin Pasha. In his old age he retired to Zanzibar.

TOBACCO. An increasingly popular crop in Zambia, especially
since World War II. By the mid-1970's Zambia was averaging
over 6000 metric tons per year, with Virginia tobacco the most
popular. While Virginia flue-cured tobacco is produced mainly
in central and southern Zambia, the Burley tobacco is produced in the Eastern Province, and small plots of Turkish tobacco is grown in scattered parts of northeastern Zambia. It
has been a good cash crop, with its sales second only to
maize. Tobacco was first imported in the early nineteenth
century, but several decades later the Gwembe Tonga and
Senga were exporting it already. Around 1914 Europeans were
growing tobacco on large farms near Fort Jameson for export.
It became Northern Rhodesia's main export in 1926-27, but its
market slowly collapsed until after World War II.

TODD, REGINALD STEPHEN GARFIELD. Prime Minister of
Southern Rhodesia from 1953 to 1958, and simultaneously
President of the United Rhodesia Party. Born in New Zealand
in 1908, he was a missionary in Southern Rhodesia from 1934
until he became Prime Minister in 1953. He was first elected
to Parliament in 1946. In 1959 he helped form the Central
Africa Party (q. v.), a party active in Northern as well as
Southern Rhodesia briefly during the middle part of the Fede-
ration's decade of existence. Todd's moderately liberal view
of race relations and political rights for Africans found sympa-
thy among some Northern Rhodesian liberals such as Sir John
Moffat (q. v.). The same views caused his removal from the
Prime Minister's seat under pressure of his own party, the
United Rhodesia Party, which deemed him to be too radical.

TOKA. A small group of about twenty-two thousand who live in
extreme southern Zambia, north of Victoria Falls and then
east along the Zambezi River. The Batoka are sometimes
called southern Tonga. They are part of the Tonga-speaking
language group. Like the Tonga they are a decentralized
people, not ruled by any one dominant leader. Thus they
were very susceptible to raids by strong nineteenth century
groups, such as the Kalolo under Sebituane and Sekeletu, the
Lozi, notably under Lewanika, and the Matabele under Mzilikazi. On the other hand, groups of Toka helped to overthrow
Lubosi (Lewanika) for a brief period, almost tricked Sebituane
into an ambush, and themselves raided the Gwembe (Valley)
Tonga in the 1850's. The Toka were cattle herders (although
the rinderpest was disastrous to them in 1895) and thus were
the object of the greed of their stronger neighbors. They
were also known to grow some grain, and were eager traders.
The tribe was weakened severely by the smallpox epidemic of
1892-93. In the 1890's the Toka began to migrate south of
Zambia, especially to work in the mines. The 1900 "Lewanika

Concession" to the British South Africa Company allowed the
BSAC to provide Europeans with land grants in Toka territory,
further evidence that the Lozi considered the Toka to be their
vassals.

TOMBOSHALO. A Lungu leader around the beginning of the twentieth century who refused to accept the authority of Chief Kaliminwa, a Bemba chief. Tomboshalo had been a slave of the
Ngoni for a time in his youth, and when freed lived at the
London Missionary Society mission at Nyamukolo. His father's
land was now being administered by Chief Kaliminwa. Encouraged by James Hemans (q.v.), a missionary, he led a
band armed with spears and bows and publicly defied the
Chief's authority. Headmen of several neighboring villages
joined in the defiance. The Native Commissioner intervened
and finally got Tomboshalo to recognize Kaliminwa's authority
over his village. But the next year, in May, 1904, Tomboshalo again protested the Bemba rule by conquest. A few
weeks in prison persuaded him to accept the alien rule.

TONGA. Both a linguistic and an ethnic term. The Tonga-speaking
family of Bantu peoples include the Lenje, Soli, Ila, Toka,
Leya, Sala, Tonga, Gowa and others. They comprise almost
20 percent of the population of Zambia. Ethnically, the Tonga
are a people numbering over half a million, probably the
largest ethnic sub-group in Zambia. They are subdivided into
two groups according to geographic habitat, the Plateau Tonga
(q.v.) and the Valley or Gwembe Tonga (q.v.). The Tonga
live in southern Zambia, generally along the western half of
the Zambezi River border with Rhodesia and north from the
Zambezi almost to the Kafue River. The earliest known Tonga
settlement in Zambia is on top of Sebanzi Hill (q.v.) on the
edge of the Kafue flats. Occupation there dates back to 1100
A.D. The people there were farmers and fishermen, but also
herded some cattle and goats and hunted local antelope. Evidence from pottery shows that today's Tonga are their direct
descendents. Living in small, decentralized villages and with
no complex political organization, the Tonga people developed
no real tribal or ethnic consciousness. When the British came
they even had to appoint chiefs, sometimes choosing the local
rainmaker. (See Plateau Tonga for much more information ap-
plicable to most Tonga.)

TOTELA. One of the minor tribes of southwestern Zambia, with
a little over thirty thousand members, they were under Lozi
domination at least since the reign of Ngombala, the sixth Lozi
king, in the mid-eighteenth century. They occasionally intermarried with the Lozi, who were known to loan out cattle to
the Totela because of their good pasture area south of the
Lumbe River. A noted traveler, Emil Holub, described the
Totela as being excellent ironworkers, second in southern
Africa only to the Zulus. Their ironwork was an important
trade item for them.

TOWN BEMBA. A dialect of ciBemba, the language of the Bemba people. It is spoken throughout the Copperbelt and the Central and Northern provinces as a common language for many people of diverse ethnic origins.

TRADE UNION CONGRESS (TUC). Founded by Lawrence Katilungu in 1950, it was a federation of many of the newly-formed African trade unions. The African Mineworkers Union, of which Katilungu was also president was the most prominent of the member unions. In 1955 he was replaced as the President of TUC by Dixon Konkola. In 1960 Katilungu's participation on the Monckton Commission (q.v.) and as acting president of the African National Congress caused a bitter controversy within the TUC and many unions formed a new Reformed Trade Union Congress (q.v.). When he was replaced as leader of the African Mineworkers Union in December, 1960, it took only two more months for the TUC and RTUC to reunite as the United Trade Union Congress (q.v.).

TRADE UNIONS AND TRADE DISPUTES ORDINANCE. An important law designed to create stable industrial relations, it was passed in December, 1964 and went into effect early the next year. It stopped trade unions from receiving outside assistance, especially financial aid, and it established the Zambia Congress of Trade Unions (q.v.) to which all unions were encouraged to affiliate. The law gave considerable power to the Registrar of Trade Unions, to the Minister of Labour, and to the ZCTU. The law required secret ballots in union elections and required a minimum of one hundred members for a trade union in order to prevent the proliferation of minor unions.

TRANSITIONAL DEVELOPMENT PLAN (TDP). Inaugurated in January, 1965, this plan, following the pattern of the Emergency Development Plan of 1964, emphasized educational expansion. It carried on the primary and secondary education projects of the earlier plan and established a goal of universal primary education. Its budget of £35 million also added projects for developing a university and teacher-training colleges, along with adult education. The TDP ended in July, 1966, when the First National Development Plan (q.v.) was begun.

TRYPANOSOMIASIS. Commonly known as sleeping sickness, this disease affects both animals and man in a wide band that stretches across Africa on both sides of the Equator. Much of Zambia experiences it. Spread by the tsetse fly, it can be deadly, thus many infested areas are sparsely inhabited and under-cultivated. In Zambia, attempts by the Government to inoculate the cattle of Africans met serious resistance, spurred on in the 1950's by the ANC which warned that inoculations would harm the cattle. One notable resistance incident occurred in 1958 at Choma. In 1977 a scientific team led by Drs. Hiroyuki Hirumi and John Doyle grew the infective form of the parasite in a test tube. It is hoped that the studies made possible by this feat will result in a truly effective vaccine.

TSETSE FLY. The principal transmitter of trypanosomiasis (q. v.).

TSHOMBE, MOISE. Leader of the Conakat Party based in the Katanga province of the Congo (now Zaire) in the early 1960's.
He led a secessionist movement attempting to withdraw Katanga
from the Congo. Although this uprising was finally quelled
with the aid of United Nations troops, later in the 1960's
Tshombe served as Prime Minister of the Congo. As a conservative politician supported in part by the financial backing
of mining interests, he also became involved in Zambian politics. Roy Welensky (q. v.) evidently attempted to set up alliances and aid agreements between Tshombe and leaders of
Zambia's ANC such as Lawrence Katilungu and Harry Nkumbula. Dixon Konkola's Central African People's Union was
another possible connection for Tshombe. Although some
money from Katanga sources evidently reached these party
leaders, Kaunda himself made two trips to visit Tshombe,
once as President of PAFMECSA in which he reportedly urged
Tshombe to commit himself to Pan-African goals. He also
urged Tshombe to discontinue his support of the more conservative Zambian politicians.

TUMBUKA. Both a linguistic group and a distinct ethnic group.
Tumbuka-speaking people include the Senga and the Yombe, as
well as the Tumbuka themselves. As a distinct group, the
Tumbuka number about eighty thousand people, according to
one estimate, most of them living near the eastern border of
Zambia, near the Senga and the Ngoni. The Tumbuka seem
to be related to the Senga, but the Ngoni were invaders who
settled in Tumbuka territory in about 1855, led by sons of the
Ngoni leader, Zwangendaba (q. v.). Mbelwa was elected Ngoni
chief there. The Tumbuka are some of the earlier inhabitants
of Zambia. They are linked with the Yombe in the myth of
Vinkakanimba (q. v.). They lived in villages or small scattered
hamlets, without centralized chiefdoms. The corporate descent
group was the main unit of social organization, and the society
was matrilineal. After 1855 came years of domination by the
Ngoni, and many traditions and customs were lost. Since the
coming of colonialism, however, a Tumbuka-consciousness has
reemerged. Nevertheless, in early 1909 the Tumbuka were
very receptive to the preaching of Kamwana, the noted preacher of the Watch Tower Movement.

TWA. Both numerically and physically small, the Twa are an
ethnic group related to either the Bushmen or Pygmies or both.
The Twa are found in the Kafue Flats and in the Lukanga
swamps of the Kafue River, where they fish. While some
speak the language of neighboring tribes, others have a language of their own.

TWIN RIVERS KOPJE. A site about eighteen miles southwest of
Lusaka that has produced artifacts from the Zambian Middle
Stone Age. Radiocarbon-dating of the objects found there

point to a date around 21,000 B.C. They are mostly crude
stone tools.

- U -

UNDI. The principal chieftainship of the Chewa people of southeastern Zambia, it has been called perhaps the oldest of surviving chiefly dynasties in the country. Some Luba traveled
to what is now southern Malawi before the fourteenth century.
In the sixteenth century the first Undi split from the group
and moved west, where Portuguese reported an Undi capital
at Mano in 1614. Undi's empire, including fellow Phiri clans-
men who remained in Malawi, went under the name Maravi
(the basis for the modern national name). It was from the
Undi kingdom that the Portuguese often traveled deep into Zambia. The Undi sold ivory to the Portuguese, probably accounting for the expansion of the Undi territory. Around 1760 gold
was discovered near Undi's capital, and before the end of the
century it was also found in two of his vassal states. Failing
to capitalize on this luck by mining it themselves, the Chewa
allowed the Portuguese and slaves to do the work in return for
tribute. Portuguese brought in settlers and armed hunters,
and the Undi saw his power over the area greatly reduced.
     In 1958 the reigning Undi, the Chewa Paramount Chief,
went to London with Harry Nkumbula for talks at the Colonial
Office. The same man attended the Federal Review Conference
in 1960 and followed Kenneth Kaunda and Joshua Nkomo in their
famous "walk-out. "

UNGA. A small tribe that split from the Bemba in the mid-
eighteenth century as the Bemba passed round the northern end
of Lake Bangweulu. The Unga settled in the Bangweulu swamps
where fishing became their way of life. They traded some of
their catch for iron and other products, as well as produced
otter skins for export. Although their swamp life made them
less vulnerable than other peoples, they were subjected to a
series of raids by the Yeke (q.v.) in the second half of the
nineteenth century. The Unga were somewhat more successful
resisting the invasion of European administrators, especially
tax collectors, as they were notorious tax defaulters, almost
defying the British to enter the swamp with force. The Bemba-
speaking Unga number about twenty-three thousand today.

UNILATERAL DECLARATION OF INDEPENDENCE. The statement
of the Government of Rhodesia (Southern Rhodesia), dated November 11, 1965, in which it affirmed its sovereignty, free
from that of Great Britain. While this act was not legitimized
by any other country, it had an effect on Zambia's relations
with its southern neighbor. Its long term effects included dis-
ruption of trade through Rhodesia, and especially fuel and other
shortages which hampered the fulfillment of Zambia's First
National Development Plan (q.v.).

UNION MINIERE DU HAUT-KATANGA. The major mining company
which was formed October 28, 1906, to take over the Katanga
mines from Tanganyika Concessions Ltd. It remained the
principal owner of Katanga mines for over half a century. As
such as it was the employer of many Zambians.

UNITED AFRICAN CONGRESS. In about May, 1959, the President
of the Rhodesian African Railway Workers Union, Dixon Konkola (q. v.) and a small group of followers organized the
United African Congress, promising a non-violent campaign
for self-government. In June of the same year the UAC
joined with the like-minded new group, the African National
Freedom Movement to create the United National Freedom
Party (q. v.).

UNITED CENTRAL AFRICA ASSOCIATION. The predecessor of
the Federal Party and thus also of the United Federal Party,
it had been created in the 1940's to campaign for a federation
of Northern Rhodesia, Southern Rhodesia and Nyasaland.
When the British accepted the idea and the first federal elections were called for in 1953, the Association became the
Federal Party in order to be able to compete in them.

UNITED CHURCH OF ZAMBIA. After Roman Catholicism, this
is the largest Christian Church in Zambia. Although organized
in 1958, it actually grew out of church unity movements over
the previous three decades. The Union Church on the Copperbelt created in the 1920's was perhaps the beginning. Presbyterian groups united as the Church of Central Africa in Rhodesia, and the Paris Evangelical Mission became the Church
of Barotseland. In 1958 all of these came together along with
the Methodists, the London Missionary Society, and the Church
of Scotland to create the United Church of Central Africa in
Rhodesia. This name was changed in 1965 to the United
Church of Zambia. Its synod headquarters are in Lusaka.

UNITED FEDERAL PARTY (UFP). A Federal level party that in
1958 had the greatest amount of support in the territorial legislatures in all three parts of the Central African Federation.
In addition it ruled in the Federal Parliament. It was created
by a merger of the Federal Party (q. v.) and the United Rhodesia Party (basically a Southern Rhodesian party). While negotiations for the merger began early in 1957, the actual union
did not occur until March, 1958. While Roy Welensky (q. v.)
was spokesman for the party at the federal level, within
Northern Rhodesia his protégé, John Roberts (q. v.), was the
man in charge. In June, 1962, seeing that despite the party's
efforts the Federation was doomed, Roberts and the UFP arranged an alliance with the ANC for the October, 1962, elections in Northern Rhodesia. In addition it organized "front"
groups of Africans, such as the National Republican Party
(q. v.) and the Central African People's Union (q. v.). In preparation for the election, the UFP had begun to recruit African

membership. In November, 1961, Welensky also started the
unsuccessful Build-a-Nation (BAN) Campaign (q. v.). The actual 1962 campaign did not change many minds. To most
Africans, the UFP was the party of white supremacy and the
unjust Federation; to Europeans, it represented responsible,
"civilized" government and personal security. The election
resulted in a stalemate. The UFP won all but one of the
fourteen upper-roll seats, with 21,558 valid votes. But in the
lower-roll races it won nothing, receiving only 183 valid votes.
It did, however, win two African seats in the National constituencies. Thus it had fifteen seats in the thirty-four seat Legislative Council. ANC won only five seats, but if it combined
with UFP, a "conservative" coalition could control the LC.
After a period of indecision, however, Nkumbula of the ANC
decided to form a coalition with Kaunda's 14 UNIP legislators
instead. Six months later, in April, 1963, John Roberts
changed the name of the Northern Rhodesian branch of the
UFP to the National Progress Party (q. v.).

UNITED MINEWORKERS' UNION (UMU). The new name of the
Mines African Staff Association in 1963 when it attempted to
claim that it represented all mine employees. The African
Mineworkers' Union (AMU) bitterly contested that claim. Before the year was finished the UMU was dissolved and reorganized as the Mines Local Staff Association. During its
existence it was closely associated with UNIP, which opposed
the ANC connections of the AMU.

UNITED MISSIONS IN THE COPPERBELT (UMCB). An agency
formed in 1936 by the Methodist Missionary Society, the London Missionary Society, the Church of Scotland Mission, and
the Anglican Church's Universities Mission to Central Africa.
Concerned with areas such as education and welfare, it was
responsible for the administration of all the schools for Africans in the Copperbelt. By 1948 its teachers included such
future African political figures as Kenneth Kaunda, Simon Kapwepwe, and John M. Sokoni.

UNITED NATIONAL FREEDOM PARTY. A small, short-lived party,
but nevertheless an important parental predecessor of the United
National Independence Party. It was born in June, 1959, when
two other small parties, the African National Freedom Movement
and the United African Congress, merged. Dixon Konkola became
its president-general, while Solomon Kalula and Barry Banda became its vice-president general and secretary-general. The
leaders publicly stated that their true leader was the imprisoned
Kenneth Kaunda, as most of the members were from the recently-
banned Zambia African National Congress. The leaders opposed
both Harry Nkumbula (of the ANC) and the Federation. They
called for immediate self-government. The party merged with the
African National Independence Party to form the United National
Independence Party (UNIP). Three different respected sources
claim variously that the merger occurred "on August 1," "in

September," and "in October."   All agree that the year was 1959.

UNITED NATIONAL INDEPENDENCE PARTY (UNIP).   The ruling
party of Zambia since 1962, it is now the basis for the one-
party participatory democracy established in Zambia in 1972
as its Second Republic.   When the Zambia African National
Congress (q.v.) was banned in March, 1959, and most of its
major leaders were detained in rural provinces by the Government, the ANC was temporarily left as the only significant
African party in Zambia.   In September, however, another split
occurred in the ANC and one of the dissidents, Mainza Chona
(q.v.) joined UNIP in October, 1959 and became its President.
Actually he joined a party that was in the process of emerging
from the amalgamation in September of two minor, new groups,
the African National Independence Party (q.v.) and the United
National Freedom Party (q.v.).   These two groups had been
formed by men who wished to keep ZANC's spirit alive until
Kaunda could return from prison to head their party.
     The policy of UNIP at this point was to strive for the
disintegration of the Federation by legal, non-violent action,
and to boycott the Monckton Commission (q.v.) that was to
make recommendations to the Federal Review Conference.
UNIP found its strength limited to areas of Bemba influence,
mostly the northeastern quadrant of the country and the Copperbelt mining towns.   As ZANC leaders emerged from their
government restrictions in late-1959, they joined UNIP, thus
providing some organization in other provinces.   Kenneth Kaunda
was released from prison on January 9, 1960, and on January
31 he was elected President of UNIP at a party conference,
with Chona becoming Deputy President.   The party's immediate
concern was to organize and expand its membership.   It was
successful at both.   Although it was banned on the Copperbelt
in May (the ban was lifted in November), and despite widespread opposition by both chiefs and the Government, UNIP
claimed over three hundred thousand members by the end of
1960.   In December, 1960 it had representatives in London
at the Federal Review Conference (q.v.).   Its actions there
and at the subsequent talks on the Northern Rhodesian constitution led almost directly to Great Britain's decision to disband
the Central African Federation.   Although the next stages in
the direction toward Northern Rhodesian autonomy and eventual
Zambian independence saw numerous conflicts between England
and the leaders of UNIP, especially over the makeup of interim
legislatures and electoral processes, in fact the crucial battle
had been won by UNIP by early 1961.   Most of 1961 and 1962
were spent in improving UNIP's organization and, eventually,
preparing for the October, 1962 Legislative Council elections.
UNIP sought support from members of the labor union movement, and financial aid and acceptance from other successful
African countries.   Leaders from Ghana, Liberia, and Tanganyika were all helpful in providing both approval and economic
assistance.
     At first UNIP's organizational structure was similar to

that of the ANC. It had a President and other national officers
at the top, along with a permanent executive, the Central Committee, which Kaunda took care to keep balanced among the
various ethnic and language groups. There were also eight
provincial divisions, each of which had considerable freedom
because of inadequate communication and controls from the
center. Kaunda reformed this late in 1961, changing the eight
provincial sections into twenty-four regional organizations,
each with a full-time organizing secretary appointed by and responsible to the Central Committee. In addition, the Youth
and Women's Brigades were integrated more closely into the
party. Finally the party's National Council (the chief policy-
making organ, which was called into session by the Central
Committee) was expanded and made more national in membership. It now also included the twenty-four regional secretaries.
All this organization was crucial, as the 1962 elections were
vigorously fought.

To win control of the Legislative Council, UNIP would need
European support as well. The complicated election formula
required a mixture of support to win the National Constituencies
that would provide some party with a majority in the Council.
UNIP had several hundred white members in 1962, with Sir
Stewart Gore-Browne, James Skinner, and Merfyn Temple
(q. q. v.) the most notable. Skinner provided excellent help by
publishing a brochure to aid UNIP members through the maze
of election rules and procedures. UNIP was also the only
party to stage a major drive to register new voters, even
forming registration schools to aid voters through the Government's literacy tests.

In the crucial 1962 elections, UNIP won twelve lower roll
seats (with 78. 2 percent of the vote) but only one upper roll
seat (19. 75 percent of the vote), plus the National seat reserved for Asians. Thus it had fourteen of the thirty-four
seats in the Legislative Council. After considerable delibera-
tion, the ANC brought its five seats into a coalition with UNIP
and the two prepared a ruling Cabinet. In the Cabinet they
divided evenly the six Ministerial positions, with UNIP leaders
Kenneth Kaunda, Simon Kapwepwe, and Reuben Kamanga holding
its three. Four Parliamentary Secretaries and the Chief Whip
were also UNIP men. It was this core that led Northern Rhodesia and UNIP through the final steps leading to independence.
Prior to that, however, elections were again held, in January,
1964. This time the Parliamentary elections were based on
universal adult suffrage. UNIP's two main competitors in 1962
were now much weaker. The UFP had dissolved and its successor, the National Progress Party, only competed for the
ten seats reserved for Europeans. It beat UNIP candidates in
each case. The ANC had been torn by splits. As a result,
UNIP won fifty-five of the regular seats to ANC's ten. UNIP
won twenty-four of those without even a contest. In the forty-
one contested seats, UNIP received 69. 6 percent of the votes.
Thus at independence UNIP had a 55-20 majority in Parliament.

The next important year for the Party was 1967. A new

party constitution had been passed by the party's National Council at a meeting in June, 1966 (and formally adopted at the
general conference in August, 1967). A major change in the
party structure was that Central Committee posts would be
contested on an individual basis, rather than on a carefully
balanced "team" ticket. As a result there was a bitter party
election at the 1967 General Conference in which tribal divisions within UNIP surfaced, as coalitions of different ethnic
groups campaigned along tribal lines. This caused considerable
grief within the party, some of it still not healed in 1979. As
a result of the elections, Simon Kapwepwe became UNIP's national Vice-President, defeating the incumbent, Reuben Kamanga.
The new national Secretary and Treasurer were Mainza Chona
and Elijah Mudenda, respectively. The tribal based victory of
ciBemba-speakers and their allies forced President Kaunda to
proceed with numerous changes in the Cabinet in order to satisfy the losing groups.

General elections were again to be held in December, 1968.
As the ruling party, UNIP could run on its successful record.
Its only active opposition was the ANC. Another group, the
United Party (q.v.) was banned on August 14, 1968 as a result
of some violence that occurred. UNIP had hopes of expanding
even further its convincing Parliamentary majority. This did
not occur, however, as the newly-expanded Parliament contained
after the election 81 UNIP seats to 23 for the ANC, plus an
additional Independent. The ANC had won heavily in both the
Southern Province and (with help from former United Party
members) in the Barotse Province. This was despite the fact
that ANC had a terribly weak financial situation during the campaign. After the election, the intraparty rivalry in UNIP surfaced again. In August, 1969, a meeting of the party's National Council was abruptly closed by the President because of
a motion to oust Kapwepwe as Vice-President. He later resigned but was persuaded by Kaunda to stay until the party's
next elections. At the same time Kaunda dissolved the Central
Committee and took over party power as its Secretary-General.
He then appointed three Ministers of State to aid him in party
administration, finance, and publicity.

Kaunda then appointed the Chuula Commission (q.v.) to
draft a new party constitution. The results were highly controversial, however, and its key proposals concerning the Central Committee were rejected. Finally a General Conference
at Mulungushi in May, 1971, approved a new party constitution
and endorsed the list of new Central Committee members submitted to it by the National Council. Soon, however, a new
political party, the United Progressive Party (q.v.) was formed
(in August, 1971), and its leaders were former leaders of UNIP,
notably Simon Kapwepwe and Justin Chimba, both ciBemba
speakers. The existence of the UPP was a further sign that
sectionalism was still a major problem for UNIP. Under the
1971 constitution, the Central Committee remains the party's
major administrative body, but has less power than it had
under the 1967 constitution. Kaunda's position of Secretary-

General was made stronger, however.   Also the outgoing Central Committee presents an official slate for its replacements to the National Council and, ultimately, the General Conference. The slate is kept balanced according to provinces, with a little added weight to the more populated provinces.   Although the General Conference wields ultimate power over important matters (changing the constitution, and voting on the membership of the Central Committee), in fact the Central Committee retains the greatest influence, because of its smaller size and thus flexibility and availability.

With the coming of the Second Zambian Republic and its creation of a one-party state, the role of UNIP became even more important to Zambia.   New constitutions for both the country and the party were promulgated in 1973.   However the main party bodies, the Central Committee, the National Council, and the General Conference, were essentially unchanged.   Since the country's new constitution makes UNIP the sole legal party, the party's constitution becomes virtually a direct instrument of the Government.   The Secretary-General of UNIP (Alexander Grey Zulu succeeded President Kaunda) is to replace the President of the country in his absence, illness, or death.   He is appointed by and responsible to the President.   Meanwhile the President of the party and of the country are to be the same person.   Once he has been selected as UNIP President by the party's General Conference, he is automatically the only candidate for election as Zambia's President.   The people can only vote yes or no for this candidate. A national majority of no votes would require the party to act again on its choice for UNIP President.   In elections held in December, 1973, Kaunda was reelected President, although only 39 percent of the electorate voted.   Areas that used to vote ANC cast many "no" votes against Kaunda.   In 1977 there were further signs that opposition parties are not dead, as a Cabinet Minister was dismissed for his activites with the banned UPP.   In 1978 Kaunda was reelected President of both UNIP and Zambia.

UNITED PARTY.   Reportedly founded in March, 1966, it held its inaugural general conference in Lusaka May 29 and 30, 1966. Its leaders were both members of Parliament: Mufaya Mumbuna, former Vice-President of the ANC, was elected President, and Dickson Chikulo of UNIP was made treasurer.   After registration as a party, it was officially recognized by the Speaker in the National Assembly on July 20, 1966.   To counteract that, UNIP and ANC joined in amending the constitution to require any MP to resign from Parliament if he changed his party after his election.   Thus the seats were contested in a by-election and UNIP won them both.   Meanwhile two UNIP Cabinet Ministers, both Lozi-speaking, had been replaced in the Cabinet in January, 1966, because of alleged corruption. They were Nalumino Mundia (q.v.) and Mubiana Nalilungwe (q.v.).   In March, 1967, Mundia was dismissed from both the Party and Parliament and became involved with the United Party.   He was quickly elected its President.   The UP gained

strength, especially in Barotseland. The Government had taken
action against South Africa by refusing to allow Wenela (q.v.)
to recruit labor in Zambia. This hit hardest the Lozi, who
were heavily recruited, many of whom were currently living in
a government compound on the Copperbelt. The UP organized
heavily on the Copperbelt, drawing from those who were previously UNIP supporters. The ruling party did not idly accept
this, however, and the UP accused it of confiscating party
literature, refusing permission for meetings in Barotseland,
and refusing to recognize the election of a chief who supposedly
was a UP supporter. UP officials were arrested on weak
grounds (and acquitted), UP supporters were beaten by gangs
of UNIP youths, and the party was generally harassed by lower
level UNIP officials. When an incident occurred in mid-August,
1968, resulting in the death of two UNIP officials at the hands
of some UP members, the party was banned on August 14,
1968 and Mundia was detained. Shortly many UP supporters
joined ANC, which was preparing for the December, 1968 general elections. A loose alliance formed, with Mundia and
other former UP members running for most of the Barotseland
seats in Parliament. The ANC won 8 of the 11 Barotseland
seats, defeating three of the four Lozi Cabinet ministers in the
process. Most of the victory was due to UP organization.
Mundia won his seat and became an ANC leader in Parliament.

UNITED PEOPLE'S PARTY. Formed October 1, 1972 by a number
of former members of the United Progressive Party, some of
them recently freed from detention. Its goal was to fight the
plan for a one-party state. The leaders announced that Kapwepwe would head it when freed from detention. On October
19, 1972, it was banned and its leaders arrested.

UNITED PROGRESSIVE PARTY (UPP). Only a legal party for about
six months, it had greater importance for contemporary Zambia,
because its existence was one of the primary causes of the
creation of a one-party system in Zambia. At the beginning of
August, 1971, there were reports in Zambia that a new party
had been formed on the Copperbelt, primarily by dissident members of UNIP. Four Bemba Members of Parliament were disciplined by President Kaunda for their connections with the
United Progressive Party. Simon Kapwepwe (q.v.), a former
Vice-President, resigned from his Cabinet position on August 21,
1971 and announced that he was the actual leader of the UPP.
He said that the party's goal was to "stamp out all forms of
capitalism, tribalism, and sectionalism." UNIP supporters
reacted negatively, demanding a one-party state and harassing
and intimidating UPP supporters. Over a hundred UPP supporters were detained. Of its leaders, only Kapwepwe remained
free. In by-elections held December 21, 1971, Kapwepwe won
back his seat in Parliament. Growing unemployment due to an
economic recession accounted for part of his success and his
party's following. On February 4, 1972, the UPP was banned
and Kapwepwe and many more followers were detained without

trial. In March, 1972, some members of the UPP formed the
Democratic People's Party (q. v.).   In April, 1977 two government ministers, Mr. Axon Soko (q. v.) and Mr.
Zongani Banda,
were dismissed from the Government "for engaging in activities of a banned opposition party, " the UPP.

UNITED TRADE UNION CONGRESS (UTUC).   Formed in early 1961
by a merger of the rival Trade Union Congress and Reformed
Trade Union Congress, its leadership consisted mostly of the
old RTUC leaders, with Jonathan Chivunga as President.   The
leadership was strongly pro-UNIP.   It was weakened considerably in July, 1962, when the African Mineworkers Union withdrew from it.   Its leadership became split by factionalism and
UNIP finally stepped in to call for new elections.   The Zambian Government paid £5,614 in 1965 to wipe out its debt so
that a newly formed Zambia Congress of Trade Unions (q. v.)
could begin fresh.

UNOFFICIALS. A term used to describe those members of a
colonial legislative body who did not hold their seat because of
their membership in the official colonial administration.   It
was a particularly important step for a territory when the number of Unofficials in the territory's Executive Council outnumbered the Officials.   In Northern Rhodesia during the 1930's
most of the Unofficials were Europeans who urged amalgamation with Southern Rhodesia.   For many years, the leader of
the Unofficials was Sir Stewart Gore-Browne (q. v.), but he
was replaced in 1946 by Sir Roy Welensky (q. v.).

UNIVERSITIES' MISSION TO CENTRAL AFRICA.   Founded under
the inspiration of Dr. David Livingstone, this Anglican body
sent its first expedition toward Zambia in 1860.   Led by Bishop Charles Mackenzie and leaving from a mission station
south of Lake Malawi, the expedition never fulfilled its goal.
The Bishop and others died of malaria en route, and the
travelers also were met by hostile slave traders.   The UMCA
was successful in establishing itself in Northern Rhodesia in
1907.   The UMCA was also the first mission body to ordain
an African priest in Central Africa.

UNIVERSITY OF ZAMBIA.   Founded in 1965, the University opened
its doors to its first students in March, 1966.   In 1969 it already had about a thousand full-time students and now is over
half-way to its goal of enrolling five thousand students.   It is
located in Lusaka, and graduated its first class in 1969.   Its
first engineers graduated in 1971 and its medical school produced its first graduates in 1972.   In 1973 the University
opened its schools of agriculture and of mines.   In August,
1971 the school had an incident occur which resulted in it
being temporarily closed.   The incident involved student protests and demonstrations at the French Embassy because
France sold its Mirage jets to South Africa.   Police stopped
the demonstrations, but ten students wrote an open letter to

President Kaunda, criticizing his handling of the whole situation. The students were permanently expelled and two white
teachers were deported. Another incident occurred in February, 1976, resulting in a closing of the University until the
end of May. There had been student demonstrations which the
Government claimed were instigated by foreign lecturers trying
to arouse opposition to the Government's policies. Three foreign lecturers were detained and then deported. One Zambian
lecturer and seventeen students were kept under further detention.

UPPER ROLL. Part of a system of qualified franchise by which
    eligible voters are divided into two voting categories, an upper
    roll and a lower roll. The 1962 Constitution for Northern
    Rhodesia provided for this kind of arrangement. Placement on
    the upper roll was determined by meeting any of a large num-
    ber of special qualifications which were based primarily on edu-
    cation, income, property, or status in your community. In
    fact, the upper roll consisted mostly of Europeans while the
    lower roll consisted almost exclusively of Africans. Once
    membership on the two rolls was determined, the election
    machinery required candidates to receive proportions of votes
    from each roll in order to win certain "National" seats. Also
    each roll voted independently for other seats.

URBAN ADVISORY COUNCILS. The first such councils were es-
    tablished on the Copperbelt by the Government of Northern
    Rhodesia in 1938. They could only meet four times a year,
    but were designed to alert the Government to opinion trends
    among the Africans as well as to advise it on matters of Afri-
    can welfare and other problems and difficulties that faced the
    African population outside the mine compounds. The African
    members of the councils were appointed by the District Com-
    missioner. Generally speaking, these councils had little in-
    fluence and accomplished less. The members failed to repre-
    sent their fellow workers adequately. In both Lusaka and
    Broken Hill the appointees remained the same for five years.
    Yet the Government saw these councils as a step toward poli-
    tical evolution and a way of airing grievances. Despite the
    Government feelings on the matter, national political conscious-
    ness in the late 1940's was not channeled through these coun-
    cils and was much farther advanced. Nevertheless, in 1942-
    43, the Government arranged to expand these councils to towns
    outside the Copperbelt and to add Provincial Councils to the
    structure. After World War II some of the members were to
    be elected, which brought them closer to the level of African
    opinion. They were still only advisory, however, and their
    only real link with the European-controlled local Government
    was the District Commissioner.

USHI (or AUSHI). A group of people who claim descent from the
    Luba and who live in the area north and east of the upper
    Luapula River and west of Lake Bangweulu. They were under

the influence of Kazembe's Lunda for much of the nineteenth
century. Many died during a smallpox epidemic in 1883. One
population estimate projects that there are about 125,000 Ushi
in Zambia.

UYOMBE. A small chiefdom in a corner of the Isoka District in
Zambia's Northern Province. It is a mountainous area occupied by the Yombe (q.v.), a Tumbuka-speaking people. The
area covers about 625 square miles and includes forests, several rivers, and good agricultural land.

- V -

VAKAKAYE RIOTS. A series of disturbances in the North-Western
Province of Northern Rhodesia in 1956 in the form of anti-
administration protests. Several hundred people participated,
urged on by Nyampenji, a chieftainess who had had difficulties
with the colonial administration when it withdrew recognition of
her in 1946. She resented her lack of control over the new
Luvale Native Authority. Her followers in the protests denounced the controls by the modern authorities, along with opposition to increased taxes.

VALLEY TONGA. Another term for the Gwembe Tonga (q.v.).

VanEEDEN, GUILLAUME FRANCOIS MARAIS. A leader in several
European parties in Central Africa, he was born in Fort
Jameson, Northern Rhodesia. He was elected to its Legisla-
tive Council in 1948, but resigned to run successfully in 1953
for the Federal Parliament, taking the Kafue seat. In 1955 he
left the United Federal Party and helped form and lead the
Northern Rhodesia Commonwealth Party. But in 1958 he helped
form the Federal Dominion Party, working with Winston Field.
On March 6, 1961, however, he resigned from the Dominion
Party and announced that he would support the efforts of the
United Federal Party. By 1963 he was working with John
Roberts in the National Progress Party, the heir of the UFP.

VAN OOST, FATHER. One of the early White Fathers' missionaries and the Superior at the Old Mambwe mission, preceding
Father Dupont (q.v.). Dealing mainly with the Bemba chiefs,
his first meeting was with Chilangwa in August, 1892. In
January, 1894 a visit to a Bemba headman named Chitika led
him (and his companion, Father Depaillat) to a series of meetings with an important chief, Makasa V, a son of Chitimukulu.
The meetings occurred over a fifteen month period and were
cordial on both sides, despite the priest's opposition to Makasa's part in the slave trade. Attempts by Makasa to set
up a visit to Sampa miscarried. He did invite the priests to
choose a site for a new mission near him. On that trip, Fr.
van Oost died of the blackwater fever on April 20, 1895.

VICE-PRESIDENT. A position in the Zambian Government under
the Independence Constitution, but eliminated in the Constitution
of the Second Republic. The Vice-President assisted the President and was assigned certain responsibility for subjects which
were part of the President's portfolio. In the executive reorganization completed in April, 1969, Finance and Development
Divisions became part of the Office of Vice-President (as had
been Cultural Services and the Judicial Department). The
Vice-President also carried out some presidential functions on
behalf of the President. He had the assistance of a Minister
of State. The Vice-President was Leader of Government Business in the National Assembly, serving as the leader of debate.
He also was eligible to succeed the President in office should
the President be removed, resign, or die in office. All three
men who served as Vice-President had been important founders
or organizers of UNIP, Reuben Kamanga, Simon Kapwepwe,
and Mainza Chona.

VICTORIA FALLS. Named for England's Queen Victoria by David
Livingstone in November, 1855, they are known by the Africans
as "Mosi-oa-Tunya," or "The Smoke that Thunders" when translated from the Lozi language. A majestic tourist attraction
near the town of Livingstone, in Zambia, the Falls are on the
Zambezi River and are thus shared by Zambia and Rhodesia
(Zimbabwe). A footbridge built over the Knife Edge in 1969
makes viewing from the Zambian side much better than before.
The Falls are fairly new in the course of history, as geological evidence points out that thirty thousand years ago the Falls
were about five miles downstream until the present gorges
were formed. At 304 feet high they are twice as high as
Niagara Falls, and at 1,860 yards wide they are one and a
half times the width of Niagara Falls. The first railway and
road bridge across the gorge just below the Falls was built
in 1905 and is 219 yards long. In recent years, the hotels
near Victoria Falls have been the sites of a number of conferences important to Central and Southern Africa. For several
of them, see the following entries.

VICTORIA FALLS CONFERENCE (FEBRUARY, 1949). Sometimes
called "the first Victoria Falls conference," it was an informal
meeting of leading White politicians from Northern and Southern
Rhodesia and Nyasaland, led by Roy Welensky and Godfrey Huggins (qq.v.). Its goal was to investigate the possibility of a
federation in Central Africa. The idea of "amalgamation" was
abandoned and replaced by the proposal for a "federation" in
which control of native affairs would be retained by the territorial governments. The delegates clearly felt that African
participation in the political life of the federal state would be
decades away. The British Government refused to extend official recognition to the conference.

VICTORIA FALLS CONFERENCE (SEPTEMBER, 1951). The so-
called "second Victoria Falls Conference," it was called by

the British Government and the three Central African territorial governments.   An agreement was reached to form a Central African Federation, and the basic ideas were used later in
drafting a more detailed plan for federation.   Although the
African Councils were represented at this meeting, the African
representatives from Northern Rhodesia and Nyasaland refused
to accept the agreement.   The term "partnership" (q. v.) was
introduced to the conference by the British Colonial Secretary,
James Griffiths (q. v.).

VICTORIA FALLS CONFERENCE (June, 1963).   A meeting of the
leaders of all three Central African Governments, both African
and European, primarily to decide finally on the date for the
end of the Central African Federation.   It was agreed that this
would be December 31, 1963.

VINKAKANIMBA.   According to Yombe tradition, he was an elephant hunter from Uganda who followed the herds south and entered the territory now called Uyombe.   He became the first
chief of Uyombe, with his capitol at Zuzu.   With him in his
travel were five men who became the founders of most of the
Tumbuka chiefdom's royal clans.   He died after eventually being defeated in a battle with the Chief of Kambombo.   His son
Mughanga succeeded him.

VOICE OF UNIP.   The official publication of the United National
Independence Party, it was started in 1960 by the chief pub-
licist of UNIP, Sikota Wina (q. v.).   His writing was often a
little more inflammatory than the words of his party leaders,
but it was a much read source of nationalist information, especially prior to independence.

VORSTER, JOHANNES BALTHAZAR.   Prime Minister of South
Africa from September, 1966 until September, 1978.   In 1967 he
made a blunt attack on Zambia, warning it not to try violence on
South Africa or "we will hit you so hard that you will never forget
it."   Kaunda's reply that Zambia could defend itself and that
Vorster was seeking a fight when Zambia had threatened no
one, led to a Vorster reply that South Africa desired peaceful
relations with Zambia.   In mid-1968 there was a series of
letters and other contacts between Vorster and President
Kaunda in which relations between their countries were frankly
discussed.   They both showed concern that the Rhodesia question be settled without major fighting.   Further evidence of
mutual concern over the Rhodesia/Zimbabwe question has been
demonstrated by attempts of the two leaders in the mid-1970's
to persuade the opposing forces to begin reasonable negotiations.
Notable in this regard was their agreement in December, 1974,
called the Lusaka Agreement, on the subject of Rhodesian constitutional talks.   According to the agreement, neither side
would lay down preconditions for the talks.

- W -

WADDINGTON, SIR E. J. Governor of Northern Rhodesia from
     1941 to 1948. His first major problem occurred in 1942 when
     the (European) Mine Workers Union led by Frank Maybank, a
     socialist, threatened production on the Copperbelt by talking
     about disruptive activities unless the Government responded to
     a wide range of grievances. Waddington ultimately called in
     the Southern Rhodesia Armored Car Regiment which arrested
     Maybank and his top assistants. In 1942 Waddington set up a
     War Committee within the Executive Council that included Un-
     officials of the Council. This led him to agree in 1944 to the
     establishment of an Unofficial majority in the Legislative Coun-
     cil. It took effect the next year. Finally, during the war
     years Waddington was active in the Inter-Territorial Conference
     (q. v.) with the Governors of Nyasaland and Southern Rhodesia.
     When the subject of amalgamation of the territories was re-
     peatedly raised, he opposed it. He favored instead a council
     form of inter-territorial cooperation on common interests.
     His position won, and at the end of 1944 he announced the
     creation of the Central African Council (q. v.).

WALLACE, SIR LAWRENCE AUBREY. An important administrator
     for the British South Africa Company, he was Administrator of
     North-Eastern Rhodesia from April, 1907, to January, 1909.
     At that time he became Administrator of North-Western Rho-
     desia, a position he held until the two units were combined and
     he was made Administrator for all of Northern Rhodesia. He
     served in that capacity from August, 1911, to March, 1921.
     Born in Natal, South Africa, he had worked as a civil engineer
     and surveyor. He also built railways in Argentina before com-
     ing to Central Africa. He was a conciliatory person, and will-
     ing to compromise in favor of the settlers (at the expense of
     Africans), notably on job reservations. He did oppose exces-
     sive criminal punishment, however. In 1913 he suggested to
     the Directors of the BSAC that an Advisory Council would be
     useful. It was instituted, after considerable debate, in 1918.

WALUBITA, MUHELI. Ngambela (Prime Minister) of Barotseland
     from 1948 to 1956. He succeeded S. K. Wina (q. v.) in that
     position although the King, Mwanawina, wanted to appoint
     Akabeswa Imasiku, a relative by marriage. Resident Commis-
     sioner Glennie prevailed, however, and Walubita was appointed.
     Walubita was born in 1897 at Kazungula. His father was Chief
     Councillor (Liashimba) at Sesheke. He was educated both there
     and in Barotseland at PMS schools. He received administra-
     tive experiences as clerk at the Mwandi Kuta and as secretary
     to the chief at Sesheke. When his father died, Walubita suc-
     ceeded him as Chief Councillor at Sesheke in 1938. In 1945
     King Imwiko appointed him educational induna of Barotseland,
     and in 1947 he switched to induna for agricultural developments.
     In 1948 he became Ngambela. In the mid-1950's a dispute
     arose over whether or not the Barotseland National Government

was too much a close-knit, family group, and not open enough
to the modernizing element among the Lozi. Walubita opposed
the conservative King on this question. When the King again
indicated that he wanted his in-law, Akabeswa Imasiku, as
Ngambela, Walubita resigned early in 1956.

WARE, HARRY. A hunter and trader who arrived in Africa
     around 1880, making a number of journeys north to the Zam-
     bezi River. Advertising in European papers, he became a
     guide for British sportsmen wishing to hunt in South-Central
     Africa, promising also to show them Victoria Falls. In June,
     1889, he arrived in the Lozi capital, Lealui, seeking a mining
     concession from Lewanika (q.v.) to prospect and dig for gold
     and other minerals in certain distant parts of the Lozi empire.
     Working on behalf of a South African mining syndicate, he re-
     ceived a mineral concession to the Batoka territory, from the
     Machili River to the borders of the Ila land for a period of
     twenty years. It was an area larger than Ireland. Ware, on
     his part, promised to pay Lewanika two hundred pounds an-
     nually plus a 4 percent royalty on the mineral output. Ulti-
     mately Ware sold the concession in October, 1889 to two
     speculators who, several weeks later, sold it to Rhodes'
     newly formed British South Africa Company. Ware had won
     over the Lozi leaders in part through gifts of Martini-Henry
     guns, ammunition, blankets and clothes. Rev. Coillard (q.v.)
     had urged Lewanika that a concession to Ware might lead to
     the British protection that Lewanika wanted. At the same time,
     Coillard secretly hoped that it would bring "civilization" to the
     area. Instead it brought the BSAC, with its Royal Charter to
     promulgate laws, maintain a police force, and acquire new
     concessions (see LOCHNER CONCESSION).

WARE CONCESSION OF 1889 see WARE, HARRY

WATCH TOWER BIBLE AND TRACT SOCIETY. Also known as the
     Watch Tower Movement, and (since 1931) Jehovah's Witnesses.
     The governing body and legal agency for the international reli-
     gious sect, now called Jehovah's Witnesses, that was founded
     in 1884 by Pastor Charles Taze Russell in the United States.
     It claims 57,000 active members in Zambia and about one
     hundred thousand adherents. Zambia has a higher proportion
     of Witnesses than any other country in the world. Its Zambian
     base is in Kitwe. The Movement's teachings have regularly
     caused difficulties for governments worldwide, and Zambia has
     been no exception. The Witnesses teach that the Devil is in
     the world, but he will soon be defeated and Christ will reign
     for a glorious millenium. To avoid destruction in this battle
     of Armageddon, Witnesses must stop identifying themselves
     with the current world of politics and commerce and must re-
     fuse any allegiance to earthly "satanic" powers. Thus they
     refuse to salute national flags, sing national anthems, vote in
     elections, or be drafted into military service. They believe
     all current human governments will be destroyed, including

current administrations. The Witnesses entered Zambia in
1917 when African witnesses who joined the movement in South
Africa (where it arrived in 1907) and Southern Rhodesia returned North of the Zambezi. Specifically a group of six were
deported from Southern Rhodesia and preached their message
as they returned to their homes, mostly in the northeastern
corner of Northern Rhodesia. The influence of a preacher
from Nyasaland, Elliot Kamwana, also spread westward. By
the end of 1918 there were thousands of Africans newly converted, mostly among the Iwa, Bemba, Mambwe, and Namwanga peoples. The work of Hanoc Shindano (q.v.) was a
particular source of concern for the Administration. Since
all authorities were affected by the teachings, however, tribal
leaders, missionaries and employers joined the Colonial Administration in opposing what some saw as a revolt and modern writers see as the beginnings of African nationalism.
Noteworthy is the teaching by some Witnesses that the millenium would rid the country of settler injustices and white op-
pression. Arrests of preachers were made. One incident involved a District Commissioner, Charles Draper (q.v.). Another involved a preacher, Jeremiah Gondwe (q.v.).

The Copperbelt disturbances of 1935 were also seen by the
Witnesses as the beginning of Armageddon. After the violence
and killings of that strike, Fred Kabombo, the Watch Tower
leader on the Copperbelt, was extremely successful in making
conversions. After 1935, however, the Watch Tower Movement became less controversial, as the Government allowed
leaders from the South African witness movement to enter
Northern Rhodesia and impose more order upon the preachers.
A European, Llewellyn V. Philips, came to Lusaka in 1935
for this purpose.

The Movement has continued to be active in Africa since
independence, much to the consternation of leaders like Dr.
Banda in Malawi and Kaunda in Zambia. Like the former
Colonial officials, many African leaders see it as potentially
subversive. The refusal to acknowledge patriotic symbols or
to demonstrate support by voting seems traitorous to some,
although it is consistent with the long-standing theology of the
Witnesses. Kaunda denounced Watch Tower members, who refused to register to vote, during a rally in 1966. A clash
with UNIP members occurred in the Luapula Province in 1969.
As a result forty-five of the sect's Kingdom Halls and 469 of
its homes were destroyed there. Some of the Witnesses fled
into the Congo. Similar problems in Malawi heightened when
on October 23, 1967, the government banned the Witnesses as
an unlawful society. Attacks and persecution began. Thousands fled into Mozambique and Zambia as the reign of terror
became worse in 1972. Obviously this only caused more difficulties in Zambia. The UNIP Government encouraged them to
return to Malawi, but as a result of renewed violence in
Malawi, over three thousand returned to Zambia late in 1975.

WE.   A term used occasionally to designate the Valley Tonga (q.v.).

WEATHERLEY, POULETT. A European sportsman and hunter who
lived for several years (especially 1895-1898) near the Bemba
chiefs Mporokoso and Ponde in the area between Lakes Mweru
and Tanganyika. His informative communications, notably with
Sir Harry Johnston (q. v.) of the BSAC, were insightful and
helpful in shaping policy. He also had the respect of Mporokoso, who agreed to sign a peace settlement in December,
1896, if Weatherley was the European contact. The BSAC refused. Some of his reports were published in the British
Central Africa Gazette.

WEBB, SIDNEY. Later Lord Passfield (q. v.).

WELENSKY, SIR ROY (ROLAND). Major European politician for
a quarter of a century from the late 1930's, and notably Prime
Minister of the Federation of the Rhodesias and Nyasaland from
1956 to 1963. Born January 20, 1907 in Salisbury, Southern
Rhodesia to Lithuanian immigrant parents, Welensky received
minimal education and worked in stores and on the railway as
a teenager. A large man, he was heavyweight boxing champion
of Rhodesia from 1926 to 1928. A railway engine driver, he
moved to Broken Hill in Northern Rhodesia during the 1930's
and became active in trade unions as well. He was elected
to the N. R. Legislative Council in 1938 and formed the N. R.
Labour Party (q. v.) in 1941. He consistently opposed African
competition for "European jobs." A forceful leader, in 1946
he was chosen chairman of the Unofficials (q. v.) in the Legislative Council. He campaigned vigorously for amalgamation
(q. v.) of the two Rhodesias, working closely with Godfrey Huggins of Southern Rhodesia. From the time of the Victoria
Falls Conference of 1949 (q. v.), however, Welensky worked
for federation instead. When the Federation was achieved in
1953 he became its Minister of Communications and Posts.
In 1955 he became Deputy Prime Minister until he was made
Prime Minister in 1956. It was clear from the beginning of
the Federation that Welensky, a firm white supremacist, was
being groomed to succeed Huggins. Meanwhile in 1953 Welensky had helped form the Federal Party (q. v.) to contest the
first elections of the Federation. Welensky and Huggins pledged
themselves to the concept of "partnership" among "civilized
peoples," clearly meaning to exclude almost all Africans by
this last term. Their victory and the retirement of Huggins
in 1956 led to Welensky replacing Huggins as both Prime
Minister of the Federation and as leader of the Federal Party.
In March, 1958, the formal merging of the Federal Party with
the United Rhodesia Party resulted in a new group, the United
Federal Party (q. v.). As Federal Prime Minister, Welensky
fought immediately for complete independence from British control through dominion status. He also opposed any liberaliza-
tion of the Northern Rhodesian Constitution which could lead
to greater African representation. He counted on the Federal
Review Conference (q. v.) of 1960 to result in greater independence for the Federation and constantly lobbied for that in

London. Instead the abortive conference resulted eventually in greater independence for both Nyasaland and Northern Rhodesia. At the end of 1963, despite all of his efforts in the interim, Welensky's Federation folded. His book, Welensky's 4000 Days, published in 1964, tells his story. In 1964 Sir Roy also decided to try a parliamentary comeback, but was decisively defeated by the Rhodesian Front candidate. Since then he has lived in Salisbury, Rhodesia, occasionally commenting on political issues, increasingly sounding like a moderate within the very conservative European community there. In 1977 he spoke out in favor of turning over the Rhodesian Government to the Africans.

WELFARE ASSOCIATIONS. A social phenomenon primarily of the 1930's and 40's in Northern Rhodesia, the Welfare Associations were attempts within the towns to provide brotherhood and support from Africans to Africans. They provided also an outlet for grievances against both the Europeans and the traditionalists. As such they were early examples of African political consciousness and even nationalism. The first one in Northern Rhodesia was the Mwenzo Welfare Association (q.v.). Inspired by an association in Nyasaland, the organization in Mwenzo was started by Donald Siwale and David Kaunda (father of Zambia's President) among others. It did not last long, but in 1930 an association began in Livingstone. In the next decade or so, important welfare associations began in Ndola, Broken Hill, Lusaka, and Mazabuka, as well as in Choma, Luanshya, Abercorn, Kasama, and Fort Jameson. Eventually on May 18, 1946, the associations united in a Federation of African Societies of Northern Rhodesia (q.v.). In 1948 it became the Northern Rhodesia African Congress (q.v.), the first truly nationalist body among Africans in Northern Rhodesia.

WEMBA. Variant of Bemba (q.v.).

WENELA see WITWATERSRAND NATIVE LABOUR ASSOCIATION

WESTBEECH, GEORGE. An Englishman who spent twenty-six years in southern Africa, much of it living among the Barotse as a trader. Arriving in Natal in 1862, he soon traveled to Matabeleland where he established a business relationship with George A. Phillips that lasted over twenty years. Westbeech would dominate trade in Barotseland, while Phillips controlled the trade in Matabeleland. They gained the confidence of old King Mzilikazi and his successor, Lobengula. They accompanied the latter on a long trip in 1868 and in 1870 attended his coronation. This friendship allowed them to prevent Lobengula from raiding the Lozi, which fact raised Westbeech's influence among the Lozi. Meanwhile Westbeech gained the personal respect of the Lozi Kings Sipopa and Lewanika, thus allowing him extensive trade and hunting privileges. In turn he eased the way for travel to Barotseland by many Europeans, both hunters and missionaries. Revs. Arnot and Coillard both owed him a great deal for smoothing the way with Lewanika, for example. Westbeech opened up and improved wagon routes, and established a trading community at Pandamatenga, south of the Zambezi. The upper Zambezi River became his personal highway, as he exported large quantities of ivory, and brought in items for trade. The closeness of his personal friendship with Lozi leaders as well as other Africans can not be over-stated. Their respect for his integrity and manly virtues made his success attainable. His fluency in African languages also helped. He was considered to be a headman by Lozi leaders, and became a member of the Barotse council of state. In 1875 he married the daughter of a Transvaal farmer. West-beech died of liver disease July 17, 1888, in the Transvaal. His diary contains many interesting insights for the historian of this period.

WEST LUNGA NATIONAL PARK. A game reserve in the North Western Province of Zambia, lying between the West Lunga and Kabompo Rivers, northward from their point of intersec-tion.

WESTERN PROVINCE. One of the eight major administrative sub-divisions of Zambia, in the 1969 census it had 417,000 people. It has five administrative districts: Sesheke, Senanga, Mongu-Lealui, Kalabo, and Kaoma (formerly Mankoya). It is bordered on the west by Angola and on the south by the Caprivi Strip (q. v.). This description only fits the term "Western Province" since 1969, in which year President Kaunda decreed that the area hitherto called Barotseland or Barotse Province would now be a fully integrated part of Zambia to be called the Western Province. Prior to 1969 the "Western Province" was north-east of Barotseland, and has since been renamed the Copper-belt Province. At an even earlier date in Zambian history, the term Western Province included basically the areas today encompassed by both the Copperbelt and the North-Western Provinces.

WHITE FATHERS. A Roman Catholic order founded in 1848 by Cardinal Lavigerie to do mission work in Algeria. Its missionaries came southward from their mission fields in Uganda and Tanganyika to establish a mission at Mambwe Mwela on the Stevenson Road in July, 1891. They also established a mission station at Kayambi on July 23, 1895. By 1918 the order was active in most of the Northern Province of Zambia. Their primary work was among the Bemba. Much of the important early work is in the stories of Father van Oost and Father Joseph Dupont (q. v.).

WHITEHEAD, SIR EDGAR.   Important political leader in Southern
Rhodesia during the last part of the Federation period.   In
1957 he was appointed the first representative of the Federation in Washington.   In February, 1958, he was recalled to
Africa to be the leader of the United Federal Party and thus
Prime Minister.   In the European community he was originally
considered to be a "moderate" between the party's extremes--
although later he would become more conservative.   As Prime
Minister of Southern Rhodesia he distrusted Africans who demanded political advancement, preferring a paternalistic approach, regardless of African desires.   He fought to retain
the Federation, opposing Britain's efforts, but his party lost
the crucial election in December, 1962, to Winston Field's
Rhodesian Front Party.

WIESE, KARL.   A German-born trader who began living in Central
Africa in and near Ngoni territory in 1885.   His claims in
June, 1891, that he had a number of concessions from chiefs
in the area, including one for exclusive timber, railway and
mineral rights from Mpezeni (q. v.) forced Harry Johnston
(q. v.) to grant certificates of claim to the BSAC or risk Wiese
claiming the territory for Germany.   Thus the area was placed
under BSAC administrative control.   Nevertheless Cecil Rhodes
bought out Wiese, who continued to live near the Ngoni capital
of Chief Mpezeni, over whom he had some influence.   Military
action against Europeans by the Ngoni in December, 1897, led
to Wiese appealing to the North Charterland Exploration Company (q. v.) for military assistance, as a number of Europeans
were surrounded by the Ngoni.   In January, 1898, two forces
of British-led troops put down the "Ngoni rebellion" (q. v.) and
freed Wiese.   In the process the Ngoni and Mpezeni were subjugated.

WILLIAMS, ROBERT.   A friend of Cecil Rhodes and founder of the
Zambezi Exploring Company (q. v.) in 1891.   He acquired large
concessions of land in Northern Rhodesia.   Later, in 1899, he
received land in Katanga from King Leopold of Belgium.   An
employee, George Grey, began in 1899 a serious prospecting
search that led to discovery of Katanga's great copper deposits.
In 1912 Williams negotiated a concession with the Portuguese
to build the Benguela Railway (not completed until 1931).   He
was also head of an important mine labor recruiting firm,
Robert Williams and Company (q. v.).

WINA, ARTHUR NUTULUTI LUBINDA.   Zambia's first minister of
Finance, serving in that post from 1964 until 1967.   This
elder brother of Sikota Wina (q. v.) is the son of a noted Lozi
Ngambela, Shemakono Wina (q. v.).   While a student at Makerere College in Uganda he first used the word "Zambia" to
mean Northern Rhodesia.   It was in a poem published in 1953.
While studying in California at UCLA in 1959 he was named
UNIP's representative in the United States, his first position
in active politics.   With his appointment he immediately be-

came interested in the question of party organization and the
methods of attaining grass-roots support from less-educated
Zambians. Upon his return to Zambia he became involved
with UNIP, soon becoming its treasurer. In the 1962 elections, Wina, a strong opponent of the secession of Barotseland
from Zambia, defeated Francis Suu of the traditionalist Sicaba
Party (q.v.) by 1057 votes to 65. In the ANC-UNIP cabinet
of December, 1962, Wina became Parliamentary Secretary in
the Ministry of Finance. He was reelected to Parliament in
1964, and became Zambia's first Minister of Finance. In the
party's Central Committee elections of August, 1967 he was
defeated by Elijah Mudenda, and lost his Finance position. He
accepted the post of Minister of Education, which he held from
September 8, 1967 until he lost in the December, 1968 general
elections. His attempt to return to Parliament was turned
back by Lozi voters of the banned United Party (q.v.) voting
for ANC candidates. He retired into private business, but in
1971 he was appointed Chairman of the Zambia State Insurance
Company.

WINA, SHEMAKONO KALONGA. Ngambela (Prime Minister) of
Barotseland from 1941 to 1948, and the father of two important
Zambian cabinet officials, Arthur and Sikota Wina (q.v.). Born
in 1878, he was the son of an induna at the Lozi capital,
Lealui. After his education in PMS schools, he married one
of Lewanika's daughters in 1905. He became an induna at
Sesheke until 1922 when his father died and he succeeded him
as Induna Wina Lioma at Lealui. In 1936 he joined Daniel
Akafuna as his chief councillor at the Balovale Kuta. The
British Government disbanded that kuta in 1941, detaching the
Balovale District (q.v.) from Barotseland. His cooperation
with the British, notably his support of the war effort and his
long-time personal friendship with the King, Yeta, combined
with his natural leadership ability to make him an obvious
choice as Ngambela. He was also made Acting Paramount
Chief. He remained as Ngambela under King Imwiko, but was
dismissed by King Mwanawina in 1948. The two had clashed
when Wina supported Mwene Mutondo in an earlier dispute with
Mwanawina. The King saw fit to spread a number of accusations against Wina and then announced to the Resident Commissioner that Wina should not remain as Ngambela. He thus retired.

WINA, SIKOTA. An active nationalist and both an important member of UNIP and a member of the Zambian Government until
he retired from politics in 1976. The younger (and more
"radical") brother of Arthur Wina (q.v.) and son of a former
Lozi Prime Minister, Shemakona Wina, he was born August
31, 1931, at Mongu. Enrolled in 1953 at Fort Hare College
in South Africa, he was expelled in 1955 for planning a protest
strike as Secretary of the Student Representative Council. He
returned to Lusaka and became an editor for the Northern
Rhodesia Government Information Department. He resigned

in January 1957 when he was hired as editor of the Nchanga
Drum, but in December he switched to an independent magazine for Africans, African Life. He had a chance here to
voice some of his nationalistic ideas, and here his talent for
political journalism began to really show.   It also resulted in
his arrest as a possible subversive in 1959, and he was rusticated (q.v.) at Luwingo in the Northern Province. His confinement lasted from March until November, 1959. Upon his
release he immediately joined with UNIP and became Director-
General of its International and Publicity Bureau.   (In October,
1958, he had been elected to ZANC's Central Committee, a
fact kept secret as he was still an active journalist.) In 1960
and 1961 he was a member of UNIP's delegation at constitutional conferences in London.   He was also a member of its
executive committee.

In 1962, Wina's strong rhetoric got him into trouble with
party leaders.   In a speech he proposed demoralizing the
white man by declaring Roy Welensky a Prohibited Immigrant
when UNIP takes power.   Kaunda chastized him for racial re-
marks and forced Wina to resign as UNIP's Director of Elections.   Two months later, however, he was back organizing
UNIP's Committee of Thirty (q.v.), a body designed to map
out the party's policies and campaign strategy.   He successfully ran for the Legislative Council in 1962, and was named
Chief Whip in the first African Government.   Three weeks
later, however, he was also made Parliamentary Secretary
for Local Government and Social Welfare (serving under
Kaunda).   He remained Government's Chief Whip until 1971.

Reelected to Parliament in 1964 he became Minister of
Health briefly in 1964 before becoming Minister of Local
Government on January 22, 1965.   He held that position until
January 4, 1969 when he became Minister of Information,
Broadcasting, and Tourism.   From December, 1973, until his
retirement in January, 1976, he was Minister of Broadcasting.
From August, 1973, until January, 1976 he was also a member
of UNIP's Central Committee and Chairman of its Election,
Publicity and Strategy Committee.   Upon retiring from politics
he has become Executive Chairman of the Zambian Publishing
Company, of which he had first become Chairman in March,
1969.

WISSMANN, HERMANN VON. The Imperial Commissioner for
German East Africa near the end of the nineteenth century.
In an attempt to deter the slave trade in the area between
Lakes Malawi and Tanganyika, he intercepted a large slave-
raiding force led by the important Bemba leader, Sampa (q.v.)
in mid 1893.   The Bemba force was just inside German territory and heading south when it approached the stockaded village
of a Lungu headman, Nondo.   Inside were Wissmann, sixty
trained soldiers, a cannon, and a Maxim gun.   The Bemba approached late on July 6 and fired a few shots, gradually moving a large force (the Germans estimated five thousand) within
striking range of the stockade.   The next morning Wissmann

talked with Sampa's emissary who suggested that the Germans should quickly leave and be spared. Wissmann replied that Sampa would risk much by waging battle against Europeans. A few shots were fired from the stockade. Wissmann threw a grenade. The Germans brought out their Maxim gun, and riddled the Bemba front lines, and the Bemba fled in disarray. Sampa was humiliated by the rout, and the story quickly spread to other Bemba leaders, as Sampa was Chitimukulu (the pre-eminent Bemba chief). While the Bemba remained hostile to the European invaders, a respect for the European military capacity made the Bemba easier to deal with as well.

WITWATERSRAND NATIVE LABOUR ASSOCIATION (WENELA). Although labor had flowed from Zambia to Johannesburg for decades, the flow was intensified in 1940 when agents of the Jo'burg-based Wenela began recruiting in Barotseland for the South African mines. As many as five to six thousand men traveled annually from Barotseland to South Africa, where they earned about £5 a month. Wenela paid the Litunga (King) of Barotseland an annual fee for each worker recruited. In 1964 this fee was doubled to 24 shillings per head, an increase of about £5000 a year, on the request of the Lozi Litunga. In 1966, however, the Zambian Minister of Labour, also a Lozi, prohibited all further recruitment by Wenela in Barotseland. This was a serious blow, depriving the area of its greatest single source of cash income. President Kaunda defended it by saying that all ties helpful to the continuation of racism in South Africa must be severed. The Lozi became a fertile recruiting ground for the new United Party (q.v.).

WORTHINGTON, FRANK VIGERS. Acting Administrator of North-Western Rhodesia for a very brief time, from April to July, 1904. A BSAC official, he and Colonel Colin Harding (q.v.) were signatories of the concession by King Lewanika on October 17, 1900. He later served as the Secretary for Native Affairs.

WOWO. The royal clan of the Yombe (q.v.) people of northeastern Zambia. This traditional ruling clan is subdivided into six branches. The founder of one of the two primary lineages of the clan was Vinkakanimba (q.v.), who came from Uganda and entered Zambia from the East after crossing Lake Nyasa (Malawi). This was perhaps near the end of the eighteenth century.

- Y -

YAMBA, DAUTI. A teacher and a nationalist politician in the 1940's and 1950's. Yamba had visited South Africa and had come back with the idea of forming an African Congress. Meanwhile he became headmaster of the Luanshya African School from 1941 to 1946, when he was appointed Education

Councillor to the Lunda Native Authority. In May, 1946, however, his interest in nationalist politics led him to be a major organizer of the Federation of African Societies (q.v.), a group that would become the Northern Rhodesia African Congress only two years later. Yamba had been secretary of the Luanshya Welfare Association, and was elected president of the new Federation. He did not become a top officer of the NRAC. In 1951 he was chosen by the African Representative Council to fill one of the two African seats on the Legislative Council of Northern Rhodesia. When it voted in 1953 on the formation of the Central African Federation, Yamba was one of only four to vote against it. In 1953 Yamba was chosen (through indirect election) as one of the two African representatives from Northern Rhodesia to the Federal Parliament. There he was ridiculed by Prime Minister Huggins when Yamba spoke out during a debate, arguing that "partnership" could be made meaningful only if true equality for all races in all public places would be enforced by Federal legislation. His efforts as an MP proved futile, but he served until March, 1962. In the Northern Rhodesia General Election of 1962, he ran as a member of ANC for a Northern Province seat in the Legislative Council but only received 87 votes out of almost four thousand cast. Prior to that, in 1959 he had been active as a founding organizer of the African National Freedom Movement (q.v.).

YAO.   The Yao are not a people of Zambia, living east of Lake Malawi. They are important for their interactions with Zambian peoples however. As the leading traders of east central Africa, the Yao were middlemen in the trade between the Indian Ocean ports and the Bisa (and thus also Kazembe's Lunda) of Zambia. Ivory was an important commodity in this trade. Ngoni men also regularly married Yao women.

YEKE.   The name given to a large group of traders from Nyamwezi in Tanganyika who settled in Katanga in the nineteenth century. Attracted by reports by Arab travelers of the Katanga copper mines, a group from Nyamwezi were encouraged by the Lunda leader, Kazembe (q.v.), to settle in Katanga, and they became known as the Yeke. Quickly building up a substantial trade as well as a reputation for raiding, the Yeke and their chief Msiri became respected. In fact their trade hurt that of their benefactor, Kazembe. In addition to sporadic raids on the Ushi, Bisa, and Unga, Msiri exacted tribute from the Lamba and the Kaonde. In the 1880's he even attacked the Lunda. Once the Yeke even occupied the Lunda capital and Kazembe could only repel them by getting help from a Bemba force in 1893. The Yeke supported a Lunda rebel claimant of the Kazembe chieftainship. The Yeke were not only traders and raiders, but they mined copper and became excellent wire drawers. They built large natural-draught furnaces that improved the recovery of copper from ore. By developing the technology to an art they learned to draw copper wire until it was less than 0.5 mm. thick and could be rolled on a core of wood fiber to form a fine bracelet. In 1891 two expeditions from Belgium's King Leopold reached Msiri. Someone in the second group became violently angry and shot Msiri. The dead chief's followers showed no resistance, so Leopold was able to claim and control the entire Yeke kingdom.

YETA I. One of the earliest of Lozi kings, according to some lists he succeeded the founder of the Lozi state, Mboo (q.v.). He has been referred to as the consolidator of the kingdom, during whose reign (perhaps late seventeenth or early eighteenth century) the kingship in Kalabo was recognized by both the Lozi and their neighbors. He is still remembered in Lozi praise songs. Among his other accomplishments was the creation of a Lozi bureaucracy through the institution of indunas (q.v.).

YETA III. The son of the Lozi King, Lewanika, he was known as Litia until he became King (Litunga) on March 13, 1916 as Yeta III. Forty-two years old at the time, Yeta had gone through excellent training. He was among the first Lozi to attend a mission school and served as chief of Sesheke from 1891 to 1916. Upon becoming King (he insisted to the British that he was not just a Chief), he brought a number of educated, young Lozi of royal blood into the highest councils. They were very well informed about the position of their kingdom and fought the BSAC. Yeta pointed out, for example, that mineral rights were conceded to it only if it properly administered the country; but since the BSAC had almost totally ignored its part of the bargain, such as providing adequate health care, education, and transport services, any mineral concessions granted earlier were void as a result of default. Appeals and petitions were sent to London in 1917, 1921, and 1923, for example. Yeta argued that the BSAC had reneged on its pledge to contribute a share of the hut tax to the Lozi treasury. When the British Crown rule replaced the Company rule in 1924, Yeta was partly satisfied and he and his advisers, though not totally satisfied, accepted a financial package worked out by Governor Herbert Stanley. A highlight of his reign for Yeta was his visit to London for the coronation of George VI in 1938. A low point was the controversy over the Balovale District (q.v.) that same year. He was struck by paralysis and left speechless in early 1939, and remained that way before reluctantly resigning in 1945. He died the next year.

YOMBE. One of the smaller ethnic subdivisions of Zambia, the Yombe are only about ten thousand in number. Living in Zambia's easternmost territory, the Yombe are Tumbuka-speaking peoples. Their ruling clan is the Wowo (q.v.). The Yombe cultivate maize, beans, and millet. Their territory, called Uyombe (q.v.), was inhabited by Bisa until the coming of Vinkakanimba (q.v.).

YOUNG, SIR HERBERT. Colonial Governor of Northern Rhodesia

from 1934 to 1938. His philosophy concerning the area included the following positions. He did not want to see South Africa's policies adopted there, and he did not think that Southern Rhodesia should be absorbed into South Africa. But he also felt that the interests of the European minority should not be subordinated to those of the African majority. He also tried unsuccessfully to convince the British Colonial Secretary, William Ormsby-Gore, that the mineral claims of the BSAC to the Copperbelt were extremely weak, and that the Territory could use the income to improve social services and public works.

YOUNG, ROBERT. An official with the BSAC for about two decades until his retirement at Chinsali in 1916. At first only assistant collector, "Bobo" Young made an important contribution to Zambia's history by writing a history of the Bemba based on his conversations with the Bemba. Included was a chronological list of Bemba leaders. In 1897 he was assigned to build an outpost at Mirongo, where he set up his residence. On August 14, 1904, Young set up a new post at Chinsali, where he became a Commissioner for the BSAC. There he gained the respect of David Kaunda, father of Zambia's President. In his two decades of work, he dealt with most of the Bemba chiefs of the day.

YUBYA. The seventh king of the Lozi, he was noted for his extravagant standard of living. His flaunting of wealth and monopoly of tribute stirred resentment among his indunas. As a result he introduced a system whereby the indunas could take a portion of his tribute for themselves. He probably ruled in the early to mid-eighteenth century.

- Z -

ZAIRE PEDICLE. Same as Congo Pedicle (q.v.).

ZAIRE REPUBLIC. Zambia's neighbor on the north, known as the Belgian Congo until independence, and as the Congo until its president, Mobutu Sese Seko, changed its name on October 27, 1971. The intrusion of the copper-rich Congo Pedicle (q.v.) into the heart of Zambia's midsection at the Copperbelt gives the two countries much in common. The Benguela Railway (q.v.) has the potential also of being mutually beneficial. On the other hand, a civil war in Shaba (formerly Katanga) in 1977 overlapped into Zambia, causing temporary concern as planes from the Zaire Air Force attacked a village across the border in Zambia. The same war flared again in 1978.

ZAMANGLO. The Anglo-American Corporation of Zambia Ltd. See ANGLO-AMERICAN CORPORATION OF SOUTH AFRICA, LTD.

ZAMBESIA.   The term used in the nineteenth century to refer to
the territory north of the Limpopo River and south of the
Congo Free State and west of Lake Nyasa (Malawi) but east of
Angola.   The Zambezi (or Zambesi) River intersected the area,
thus leading many to refer to northern Zambesia and southern
Zambesia.

ZAMBEZI EXPLORING COMPANY.   A subsidiary of the British
South Africa Company it was founded in 1891 by Robert
Williams (q.v.), a friend of Cecil Rhodes.   Convinced of the
location of a large supply of minerals, he obtained a conces-
sion for two thousand square miles near the source of the
Kafue River.

ZAMBEZI PLAIN.   The area along both sides of the upper Zambezi River, it is something called Bulozi (q.v.) by the Lozi,
who consider it to be the heart of their country.   It is about
a hundred miles long and between ten and thirty miles wide.

ZAMBEZI REDWOOD   see   TEAK WOOD

ZAMBEZI RIVER (or ZAMBESI).   Flowing a length of 2200 miles,
the Zambezi is one of Africa's greatest rivers.   It starts at
Kalene Hill in the northernmost tip of Zambia's North-Western
Province, from where it moves south through the Western
Province (see ZAMBEZI PLAIN).   It then heads east, forming
the Rhodesia-Zambia border.   It tumbles over Victoria Falls
and then enters Lake Kariba.   The Kariba Dam slows it down
and sends a controlled flow in a northeasterly direction.
Passing Feira, Zambia, it leaves the country and continues
east and then southeast through Mozambique, past the towns
of Tete and Sena on its way to the Indian Ocean south of Quelimane.   Early on its trip it picks up a major tributary, the
Kabompo River.   In the middle of its journey, past the Kariba
Dam, the Kafue River adds its flow, followed by that of the
Luangwa River just as the Zambezi is leaving Zambia.   People
in Europe did not fully appreciate the significance of this river
until the reports of Dr. David Livingstone (q.v.) informed the
world.

"ZAMBIA."   The word itself first became prominent on October 24,
1958, when Kenneth Kaunda and his followers named their new
party the "Zambia African National Congress."   But the question of the exact origin of the word is in doubt.   It was obviously derived from the Zambezi River, which flows through
much of the country and from the word Zambezia (q.v.).   In
1953 Arthur Wina (q.v.) had used the word to mean his country in a poem he wrote while attending Makerere College in
Uganda.   Stories differ as to whether the word was suggested
at the first ZANC meeting by Kapwepwe, Kaunda, or Sikalumbi.
Regardless, the group preferred it to the other suggestions,
Muchinga (after the Mountains in Zambia) or Zambesia.

ZAMBIA. The name of an English language, monthly magazine
published in Lusaka by the Zambia Information Services.

ZAMBIA AFRICAN NATIONAL CONGRESS. Founded on October
24, 1958, it was created by some of the younger, more militant members of the African National Congress (q.v.). A
split had been brewing in the ANC for some time over a
variety of issues, but especially acts of conciliation (ZANC
members called it "weakness") by the leadership, notably
Harry Nkumbula (q.v.). Perhaps the immediate cause was
Nkumbula's apparent willingness to participate in the 1959
Legislative Council elections. The leaders of ZANC, the
quickly adopted acronym, pledged to boycott the elections and
the so-called "Benson Constitution" because of its poor provisions for African electoral participation. The founding of
this party brought the name "Zambia" to public use for the
first time. The leadership of ZANC was given to Kenneth
Kaunda as President, Munukayumbwa Sipalo as General Secretary, and Simon Kapwepwe as Treasurer. Their deputies were
Paul Kalichini, W. K. Sikalumbi, and Reuben Kamanga, respectively. Sikota Wina, A. Grey Zulu, and Lewis Changufu
were added to the executive committee. All these officers
were officially elected at a general conference in Broken Hill
on November 8, 1958. The immediate goals of ZANC were to
establish an effective African boycott of the 1959 election, and
to replace ANC as the territory's major nationalist party. It
made quick strides toward the latter goal, as ZANC leaders,
many of them from the Luapula and Northern provinces of the
country, brought thousands of former ANC members from those
regions into the new party. On the other hand, its success in
the South and West was never what the leaders desired. No
split was in evidence in the South as late as February, 1959.
ANC also managed to continue to have some support in all
parts of the country, even in some ZANC strongholds. Nevertheless, ZANC's campaign to boycott the elections (primarily
by not registering) began to succeed enough by January, 1959
that the Government was concerned. Likewise, registration of
ZANC branches under the Societies Ordinance (q.v.) were confused because a number of ANC branches had converted totally
to ZANC branches, often without informing the Government.
Throughout February the Government became very anxious about
ZANC. Some public meetings were held despite police bans,
and the rhetoric of some ZANC leaders sounded extreme to
some Europeans, despite Kaunda's constant pledge of non-violence. The need to declare a State of Emergency in Nyasaland
on March 2 probably was the final motivation for the Government to act. On March 11, 1959, ZANC was banned and most
of its leaders were quickly arrested and rusticated to distant
provinces.
      Governor Benson even compared ZANC's leaders with the
Chicago "organization of killers" in the 1930's, Murder Incorporated. Although the results of the March 20 election showed
that 85 percent of registered Africans voted, the registration

was only about 25 percent of what was anticipated.   By the
time most ZANC leaders were free in early 1960, a new organization, the United National Independence Party (UNIP) had
been created as a successor to ZANC and only awaited the
release of its true leaders.

ZAMBIA AFRICAN NATIONAL DEMOCRATIC UNION.   A minor
party that never attained much following or prominence.   Its
formation was announced in May, 1969.   Its leaders had previously been involved with both ANC and the United Party, of
which it was considered to be a small splinter.

ZAMBIA AIR FORCE.   One of the two branches of the Zambia
Defence Force, in 1975 it had about eight hundred members
and eighteen combat aircraft.   Italian air force personnel have
been training Zambian pilots, and some trainer aircraft have
been purchased from Yugoslavia.   The air force is not considered to be a strong point of the Defence Force.

ZAMBIA AIRWAYS.   A parastatal body formed in 1967 by the Zambian Government with the assistance of Alitalia Airlines.   It
became the national airline, replacing the Federation's Central
African Airways, the assets of which were distributed among
Zambia, Malawi, and Rhodesia at the end of 1967.   It has service to Europe as well as to a number of African countries.

ZAMBIA ARMY.   One of the two segments of the Zambia Defence
Force, in 1975 it consisted of about five thousand members.
Its principal role is to guard the country's frontiers, patrolling
against hostile infiltration.   Nevertheless it was placed on war
alert by President Kaunda in 1977 when the threat of invasion
arose.   The army has three infantry battalions, one reconnais-
sance squadron, one battery of 105 mm. howitzers, one engineer company, a signals platoon and supporting services.
Many of its officers were British-trained, some of them having attended Sandhurst.

ZAMBIA BROADCASTING SERVICES.   The government-controlled
ZBS was founded January 1, 1966.   It manages both television
services and sound broadcasting (radio).   The services operate
in English on both radio and television plus seven Zambian
languages on the radio.   The General Service radio network is
only in English and includes B.B.C. programs in addition to
locally produced educational and entertainment programs.   The
Home Service network broadcasts in eight languages, and its
biggest difficulty is shifting times so that no language gets
more air time.   Television Zambia has stations in Lusaka,
Kitwe, and Kabwe.   It has been used in schools since 1963.

ZAMBIA CONGRESS OF TRADE UNIONS (ZCTU).   Established
early in 1965 by a parliamentary act, the Trade Unions and
Trade Disputes Ordinance (q. v.), which was passed in December, 1964.   Its purpose was to have a new trade union congress

to which all trade unions would affiliate. It has come close to reaching that goal. In 1975 it had sixteen affiliated unions, with a membership of about 142,000 members. Its President is Newstead Lewis Zimba (q.v.). Only the forty thousand members of the Zambian African Mining Union constitute a notable bloc outside the ZCTU. When it was instituted, it was to replace the old United Trade Union Congress (q.v.) which had fragmented and was deep in debt. In order to solve this problem, the 1964 Ordinance not only passed important rules for unions, but also defined the powers of the ZCTU. After affiliation with it, for example, all trade unions were required to pay it a part of their collected dues, and its approval was required for certain decisions such as a strike ballot, strikes, amalgamation, or dissolution. Not only did the Minister of Labour appoint the first officers of the ZCTU, but the Ordinance gave him the authority to dissolve it without challenge. One limitation on the ZCTU was that it could not intervene directly in a specific employer-employee dispute. This provision caused considerable ferment among unionists later.

ZAMBIA DAILY MAIL. A Government-owned daily publication with articles in both English and African languages, it is published in Lusaka. It originated in 1960 as a weekly, the African Mail (assisted financially by the London Observer). In 1962 it became the Central African Mail (q.v.), and fought for independence and against the Federation. The Government of Zambia bought the paper in early 1965, changing its name to the Zambian Mail when the Observer stopped its financial support. The Government instructed its editors that it should explain and support government policies while also reflecting public opinion. It was only published twice weekly for several years. Primarily appealing to the educated, urban reader, its international news is nevertheless somewhat limited. It concentrates on covering all parts of Zambia. Its daily circulation in 1975 was 32,000.

ZAMBIA DEFENCE FORCE. It has two primary parts, the Zambia Army (q.v.) and Zambia Air Force (q.v.).

ZAMBIA EXPATRIATE MINERS' ASSOCIATION (ZEMA). Formed after independence by a merger of the Mines Workers Society and the Mines Officials and Salaried Staff Association. Attempts to get it to merge with the African union, the Zambia Mineworkers' Union (q.v.), proved futile. Doubts and fears on both sides hindered such a merger. Early in 1969 the Minister of Labour announced that he no longer recognized ZEMA. Since expatriates only came on fixed-period contracts, no important effects of this ruling have been noticeable.

ZAMBIA INDUSTRIAL AND MINING CORPORATION (ZIMCO). Founded as a parastatal organization in 1969, its duty is to oversee the Government's interests in mining, industrial, and commercial enterprises. It holds 51 percent shares in the

Industrial Development Corporation (q.v.), the Mining Development Corporation (q.v.), the Financial Development Corporation (q.v.), the National Import and Export Corporation, and a half dozen other parastatal bodies over which it spreads like an umbrella. The chairman of the board is President Kaunda. Financially it has been among the world's largest organizations. In 1975 it had 87,000 employees and owned assets of about one and a half billion kwacha.

ZAMBIA INFORMATION SERVICES (ZIS). An office of the Ministry of Information and Broadcasting, its press section is the official distributor of governmental news both inside and outside the country. The ZIS also makes films and recordings about current events, publishes several semimonthly magazines, some in English and others in local languages, and serves some diplomatic goals.

ZAMBIA MINEWORKERS' UNION (ZMU). The new name of the African Mineworkers' Union (q.v.) as of January, 1965. In April, 1976, the AMU merged with the Mines Police Association and the Mines Local Staff Association to form the Mineworkers' Union of Zambia (q.v.). During the brief existence of the ZMU, it had one notable impact on the country. In 1966 it was behind a huge strike that crippled the industry for a time.

ZAMBIA NATIONAL PROVIDENT FUND. Established in 1966 and beginning operations in October, 1966, it is a retirement and permanent disability program, providing these benefits for employees who are Zambian citizens. Similar to the American Social Security System, for example, it requires monthly contributions from both employer and employee. Aside from cases of permanent disability, one must be forty-five years old and fully retired in order to begin to collect one's benefits.

ZAMBIA POLICE FORCE (ZPF). Transformed from the old Northern Rhodesia Police Force, the ZPF was established by the Independence Constitution as one of the national public (civil) services. The Commissioner of Police is appointed by the President. The ZPF has its primary headquarters in Lusaka, and has a national membership of about seven thousand. It includes a mobile force, a light aircraft unit, and a helicopter corps. In addition to its normal police functions across the country, it has the duty of patrolling Zambia's borders. In this capacity it is now assisted by the Zambian Army, especially along the Rhodesian border.

ZAMBIA RAILWAYS. Founded as a parastatal body in 1967 as a result of the Zambia Railways Act of 1967. It developed out of the dissolution of Rhodesian Railways (q.v.) when the Central African Federation broke up, and especially when Rhodesia unilaterally declared its independence in 1965. Negotiations with Rhodesia resulted in a division of the rolling stock. In

addition to the line of rail from Victoria Falls to the Zaire
border through the Copperbelt, the Railways now controls the
Zambian portion of the Tan-Zam Railway (q.v.) finished by the
Chinese workers in 1976. In general Zambia Railways today
operates at a loss and will continue to require financial support from the Government.

ZAMBIA YOUTH SERVICE (ZYS). A parastatal body formed in
1964 with the goal of tackling the problem of unemployed youth
drifting aimlessly through the urban areas. Rev. Merfyn Temple was appointed its first director. Anyone aged sixteen to
twenty-five who did not complete or go beyond secondary school
could join the ZYS. Its camps were designed to provide training to fill the nation's future needs. Boys were trained in
areas such as the trades, or in modern agricultural practices.
Girls received training in home economics or in running village
cooperatives. For a number of years it was considered to be
very successful, and even received international financial support. This is despite the fact that during the 1969 judiciary
crisis, members of the ZYS stormed and ransacked the High
Court building. In 1971 it was abolished as not really accom-
plishing its original goals, and replaced by the Zambia National
Service. Most of the members of the ZNS were recruited from
the UNIP Youth Brigade.

ZAMBIAN HUMANISM. The guiding philosophy of Zambian life, it
has been introduced by numerous writings, speeches, and programs of President Kenneth Kaunda. It places stress on the
inherent worth of individual human beings, but only as long as
that individual himself emphasizes societal values such as cooperation. When individuals place too much emphasis on personal gain and possessions or become class conscious, they
violate Humanism's basic values. Thus capitalism can be cor-
rupting as it emphasizes possessions, but communism is also
bad because it deemphasizes the importance of the individual.
The values found in traditional African socialistic societies are
closer to Kaunda's concept of Humanism. Concern for one's
fellow human beings is an important aspect of Kaunda's philosophy, which finds roots in his strongly Christian upbringing and
convictions. Society should be man-centered, not possession-
centered, and one should always be willing to share with others,
help others, and cooperate with others. Government policies
and programs have been designed to further these same points,
and Humanism is taught in all the schools and included in the
media.

ZAMBIAN POUND. The principal unit of currency used in Zambia
until January, 1968, when it was replaced by the kwacha, (q.v.).

ZAMBIANIZATION. A primary goal set down by President Kaunda
just after independence, it is the process by which non-citizen
Europeans and Asians are replaced by Zambian citizens in employment of all kinds, industry, business, civil service, the

defense force, the judiciary, and the professions. Zambian
citizens of European and Asian origin are not excluded from
this term, but the implication is that Africans will be increasingly placed in middle and upper level positions, replacing non-
citizens as quickly as possible. Unfortunately at the time of
independence there was a scarcity of qualified Africans to fill
most of the positions. Educational and training programs instituted during the 1960's have helped to speed the process
considerably. A strike by white miners in 1965 resulted in
greater guarantees of job security and benefits for those Europeans who were still needed. In 1968 President Kaunda outlined a four point program for Zambianization of the skilled
labor force by 1980. It included training programs to upgrade
existing skills, recruiting foreigners to train Zambian replacements, redefining jobs so less skilled people could fill them,
and maximum utilization of Zambian manpower. 1968 legislation limited foreign-owned businesses to certain complex activities and to major urban areas. There was an awkward period
during which many businesses changed hands to meet this law.
1972 legislation placed further limits on the activities non-
Zambian businesses could engage in. In November, 1971, a
Zambianization Commission was set up to speed up the process
of hiring and promotion and to check on the need for expatriates. Consciousness of the process of Zambianization is widespread, however, and many of the major industries (notably
mining) are making major efforts to recruit and train qualified
Zambians.

ZAWI HILL. A site about seventeen miles north of Chipata where
two groups of early Zambian rock art are found. The more
faded and probably older group is naturalistic and depicts an
eland and a large bird, perhaps an ostrich, both in red pigment. The other painting, a few feet away on the large vertical rock face near the top of the hill, is an example of
schematic art.

ZIMBA, NEWSTEAD LEWIS. President of the Zambia Congress of
Trade Unions (q. v.) since 1972. He is controversial and outspoken, but has the strong following of most of its over
140,000 members. A teacher by profession, he was made a
headmaster in Ndola in 1967. In 1971 he became full-time
president of the National Union of Teachers, a member of the
ZCTU. He has been a member of UNIP since 1960 and has
always been a political activist.

ZIMBA CLAN see BAZIMBA

ZOMBE. A strong Lungu leader in the last half of the nineteenth
century, he was a grandson of Tafuna I, but not himself holder
of the Tafuna chieftainship. His stockaded village was along
the Lucheche River, southeast of the southern end of Lake
Tanganyika, and northeast of Isoko. Both David Livingstone
and Joseph Thomson visited his village. Zombe was involved

in several clashes with the Bemba, and at first miraculously
was successful. In 1872 he withstood a three month siege by
Chitapankwa and, with reinforcements from other Lungu leaders,
routed the Bemba leader and his Swahili allies. Many of the
Bemba guns were left behind as they fled. By 1880 Zombe
was so powerful that he evicted Tafuna IV Kakungu from Isoko.
Kakungu went to the Bemba and especially Chitapankwa for aid.
The latter recruited forces from Bemba chiefs Makasa and
Nkula and possibly from the Mambwe chief Kela. Early in the
1880's this huge force moved on Zombe's large village and,
using a decoy with great success, crushed Zombe, killing him
and destroying the village. In 1893 the administrative center
Abercorn was founded near the site.

ZUKAS, SIMON BER. A European immigrant who later became a
civil engineer, he was a political activist and close friend of
early African trade unionists and nationalists. The Government
deported him in 1952. Immigrating to the Copperbelt from
Lithuania as a youth in the 1930's with his parents, Zukas became a sergeant in the King's African Rifles. He began to
question colonialism when he had to put down an African riot
in Buganda, and later questioned the morality of the color bar
while a student at the University of Cape Town. In the late
1940's his "radical" and even "Communist" ideas made him
active in groups such as the Anti-Federation Action Committee
in Ndola where he published The Freedom Newsletter with co-
editors Reuben Kamanga, Justin Chimba, and Mungoni Liso
(q. q. v.). In 1951 they all joined the ANC. On March 1, 1952,
it was announced that he was being deported to England for his
"Communist" activities. Nevertheless he continued to keep in
touch with the nationalists both through correspondence and when
some of them, such as Harry Nkumbula, traveled to London.
After self-government under Kenneth Kaunda was granted in
1964, Zukas was given a hero's welcome back to Zambia by
his earlier political companions.

ZULU, ALEXANDER GREY. One of the more prominent of the
Zambian nationalists in the 1950's and 1960's, he has since
held a number of governmental and political posts. Born
February 3, 1924 at Chipata, he was educated at the noted
Munali Secondary School in Northern Rhodesia. In the early
1950's he became interested in the cooperative movement and
in 1953 became an accountant of the Kabwe Cooperative Marketing Union. By 1962 he had become its first African manager. Meanwhile he had become active in ZANC with Kaunda
and Kapwepwe, joining its first executive committee in November, 1958. In March, 1958 they were all jailed. By 1962 he
was involved full-time in politics and active in UNIP. In the
Legislative Council election that year he won his Copperbelt
seat by an overwhelming twelve thousand votes. At that time
"Grey" Zulu was one of UNIP's five National Trustees. Joining the new Government first as Parliamentary Secretary for
Local Government and Social Welfare, a few weeks later (in

January 1963) he moved to the Ministry of Native Affairs. With the coming of self-government in 1964, however, he was named Minister of Commerce and Industry and, in September, 1964, the Minister of Transport and Works. On January 22, 1965, he was named Minister of Mines and Co-operatives, which on January 1, 1967, became the Ministry of Lands and Mines. In September, 1967, he became Minister of Home Affairs until January 8, 1970, when he became Minister of Defense, a crucial post considering the guerilla action in neighboring Rhodesia. In 1973 he left that post to become Secretary-General of UNIP. He was replaced in that position in June, 1978, when he was made Chairman of UNIP's Defense and Security Committee.

ZUMBO. A Portuguese outpost on the north bank of the Zambezi River and the east bank of the Luangwa River at their confluence. It is located across the Luangwa from Feira, Zambia. Portuguese traders operated from there as early at 1700. By 1752 they bought ivory and copper from Zambian peoples. By the beginning of the nineteenth century there was trading there by Lamba, Ambo and even Toka from the Victoria Falls. Items received in return included Goan and Indian cloth, and beads. In 1804 Zumbo was destroyed by a neighboring chief, and the Portuguese abandoned it in 1836. In 1862 they reopened it for trade, mainly to expand the ivory trade, but slaves also passed through en route to Brazil. Since the Portuguese government didn't have much control at Zumbo, it left the traders free to form their own armies. Trade with Bemba, Bisa, and Nsenga was reported, with guns one item returned in trade for ivory. In 1888 the Nsenga chief Mburuma laid siege to Zumbo, but the Portuguese strengthened their armed forces there and appointed a governor in 1890. During the entire two centuries, Zumbo had a major role in Portuguese trade for gold, primarily from the people south of the Zambezi River.

ZWANGENDABA. An Nguni clan military leader who fled the power of his overlord, Chaka the Zulu after a battle on the Mhlatuze River in Natal in 1818. Fleeing northward with his people through Swaziland and Mozambique he collected a large following on his flight that lasted almost three decades. The Ngoni, as they were to be called, crossed the Zambezi River in 1835. They spent six years among the Senga, added recruits and then by-passed Bemba country, ending up near the southern part of Lake Tanganyika at Ufipa in Tanganyika. The Ngoni (q.v.) were nomadic herdsmen as well as excellent warriors who terrorized the farmers en route. Zwangendaba died at Ufipa in 1848 and the Ngoni moved south again into Zambia and Malawi under such leaders as Mpezeni, Mperembe, and Mbelwa (q.q.v.).

BIBLIOGRAPHY

BIBLIOGRAPHY: TABLE OF CONTENTS

INTRODUCTION

The literature concerning Zambia/Northern Rhodesia is very abundant, as the length of this bibliography will certify. While no bibliography can be complete on its topic, this one is considerably longer than any other seen by this writer. Fortunately it appears that at least one major bibliography should be available shortly. It is William Rau's A Bibliography of Pre-Independence Zambia: The Social Sciences. Good bibliographies dealing with specific aspects of Zambian life are found in L. H. Gann's The Birth of a Plural Society; J. A. Barnes' Politics in a Changing Society; Andrew Roberts' A History of Zambia; Richard Hall's Zambia, 1890-1964; and Area Handbook for Zambia, second edition, prepared by the Foreign Area Studies of the American University, Washington, D. C. Other bibliographies are mentioned in the appropriate section below.

Wading through this bibliography can be tedious for the average reader who would just like a few good suggestions for further reading. With this in mind, the following works are suggested.

The easiest introduction to the people of Zambia is found in four of the essays in Seven Tribes of British Central Africa, edited by Elizabeth Colson and Max Gluckman. Also good is W. V. Brelsford's The Tribes of Zambia. Specifically, however, one should turn to any of the works by Gluckman (on the Barotse), Colson (on the Plateau Tonga), Audrey Richards (Bemba), J. A. Barnes (Ngoni), I. G. Cunnison (Eastern Lunda), or Victor Turner (Ndemba), just to mention a few of the anthropologists noted for their work in Zambia.

The numerous archaeological studies by J. D. Clark, D. W. Phillipson, and Brian Fagan will cover the period up to 1900 as well as most readers will wish. A. J. Wills' Introduction to the History of Central Africa places the development of Zambia in its broader context. A new History of Zambia by A. D. Roberts is excellent, although the author has chosen not to elaborate upon periods of Zambia's history covered in detail by good standard works that are still readily available.

Barotseland is almost an entity in itself within Zambia. It has been described well by Mutumba Mainga in Bulozi Under the Luyana Kings and its appropriate sequel (although not so intended and prior-published), Gerald Caplan's The Elites of Barotseland, 1878-1969. Missionary work in this part of Western Zambia is covered in many volumes, but most notably in François Coillard's On the Threshold of Central Africa.

An important history of another Zambian group, the Bemba, is Andrew Roberts' A History of the Bemba. A man who traversed the land of both the Bemba and the Barotse plus many more peoples was the famous missionary, Dr. David Livingstone. His own writings are contained in numerous volumes, but George Seaver's David Livingstone: His Life and Letters is one of the more notable biographies.

The Colonial Era is described in Lewis Gann's A History of Northern Rhodesia: Early Days to 1953. The Period of the Central African Federation is described in Patrick Keatley's The Politics of Partnership and, in a contrasting view, Sir Roy Welensky's 4000 Days.

Nationalist movements are covered well by Robert Rotberg's The Rise of Nationalism in Central Africa: The Making of Malawi and Zambia, 1873-1964. Rotberg's numerous articles, especially in the magazine Africa Report, are also noteworthy. Henry Meebelo's Reaction to Colonialism covers nationalism in Northern Zambia from 1893 to 1939. David Mulford's Zambia: The Politics of Independence, 1957-1964 is the standard work on that period, and Politics in Zambia, edited by William Tordoff, was published in 1975 as an attempt to provide a sequel to it. It is one of the two best studies of contemporary Zambia. The other is Jan Pettman's Zambia: Security and Conflict.

The outstanding figure in Zambia today is Kenneth Kaunda. His speeches and writings have been published in numerous volumes, but his autobiography, Zambia Shall Be Free, is a classic of its kind. His friend, Fergus Macpherson, wrote Kenneth Kaunda of Zambia, a good but uncritical biography. Several books by Richard Hall, including a biography of Kaunda, can also be recommended.

Hall's The High Price of Principles, along with the Pettman book already noted, deal well with Zambia's foreign affairs problems. Foreign policy is covered also by Timothy Shaw in several recent articles. The broader context of Central and Southern Africa conflict is described by Kenneth Grundy in Confrontation and Accommodation in Southern Africa. Likewise recommended is Southern Africa in Perspective, edited by Christian Potholm and Richard Dale, and South Africa in Africa by Sam C. Nolutshungu.

Perhaps the one outstanding book on Zambian economics has yet to be written, but Constraints on the Economic Development of Zambia, edited by C. Elliott, is a good place to start reading on the subject. The mining industry is treated in numerous volumes, notably Economic Independence and Zambian Copper, edited by M. Bostock and C. Harvey, and Richard Sklar's Corporate Power in an African State. Alistair Young's Industrial Diversification in Zambia investigates another aspect of Zambia's economy.

For those readers who prefer journal and newspaper reading, one must certainly recommend the numerous articles cited below in Africa Report, the Journal of African History, and the Journal of Modern African Studies. Two lively daily newspapers are the semi-official Times of Zambia, and the tabloid Zambia News.

1. GENERAL

General Information and Guides

Brelsford, W. V. (ed.). Handbook to the Federation of Rhodesia and Nyasaland. London: Cassell and Co., Ltd., 1960.

British Information Services. Zambia. London: Central Office of Information, July 1966.

Brown, A. Samler, and G. Gordon Brown. The South and East African Year Book and Guide. London: Sampson, Low, Marston and Co., 1925.

Clements, Frank. Getting to Know Southern Rhodesia, Zambia and Malawi. New York: Coward-McCann, Inc., 1964.

Davies, D. H. (ed.). Zambia in Maps. London: University of London Press, 1971.

Dickie, John, and Alan Rake. Who's Who in Africa: The Political, Military and Social Leaders of Africa. London: African Development, 1973.

Dresang, Eliza T. The Land and People of Zambia. Philadelphia: Lippincott, 1975.

Faber, Mike. Zambia--The Moulding of a Nation. London: Africa Bureau, 1968.

Fagan, B. M. (ed.). The Victoria Falls: A Handbook to the Victoria Falls, the Batoka Gorge and Part of the Upper Zambesi River. Northern Rhodesia: Commission for the Preservation of Natural and Historical Monuments and Relics, 1964 (2nd ed.).

Gordon-Brown, A. (ed.). The Year Book and Guide to Southern Africa, 1950. London: Sampson, Low, Marston and Co., 1950.

Gregor, Gordon. "Tourism in Zambia," Horizon, Vol. 9 (September 1967).

Hailey, Lord W. An African Survey: A Study of Problems Arising in African South of the Sahara. London: Oxford University Press, 1938 and revised in 1956.

Hall, R. Zambia. London: Pall Mall Press, 1965.

Handbook to the Federation of Rhodesia and Nyasaland. Salisbury: Government Printer, 1960.

Hanna, A. J. The Story of the Rhodesias and Nyasaland. London: Faber and Faber, 1960.

Illustrated Handbook of North-Eastern Rhodesia. Fort Jameson: Administration Press, 1906.

James, Selwyn. South of the Congo. New York: Random House, 1943.

Mlenga, Kelvin G. Who Is Who in Zambia. Lusaka: Zambia Information Service, 1968.

Norton, John (ed.). Guide to Southern Africa. London: Robert Hale, 1969.

The Occasional Papers of the Rhodes-Livingstone Museum, Nos. 1-16. Atlantic Highlands, N.J.: Humanities Press, 1975.

Ogrizek, Dore, (ed.). South and Central Africa. New York: McGraw-Hill Book Co., 1954.

Pirie, George. "North-Eastern Rhodesia: Its People and Products," Journal of the African Society, Vol. 5 and 6 (1905 and 1906).

Pitch, Anthony. Inside Zambia--and Out. Cape Town: Howard Timmins, 1967.

Segal, Aaron. "Zambia," published in The Traveler's Africa, Allen, Philip M., and Aaron Segal (eds.). New York: Hopkinson and Blake, 1973.

Tanser, G. H. British Central African Territories: Southern Rhodesia, Northern Rhodesia and Nyasaland. Cape Town: Juta, 1952.

Universities' Mission to Central Africa Pub. Board. Beyond the Waters That Thunder: A Book About Northern Rhodesia. Westminster: 1932.

Where to Stay in Zambia. Lusaka: Zambia National Tourist Bureau, 1967.

Wilson, Tim (ed.). A Brief Guide to Northern Rhodesia. Lusaka: Government Printer, 1960.

Wood, Anthony St. John. Northern Rhodesia: The Human Background. London: Pall Mall, 1961.

Woods, Jonah. A Guide Book to the Victoria Falls. Bulawayo: Stuart Manning, 1960.

Zambia Information Services. Zambia Today: A Handbook to the Republic of Zambia. Lusaka: Government Printer, 1964.

Demographic Statistics

Bettison, D. G. Numerical Data on African Dwellers in Lusaka, Northern Rhodesia. Livingstone: Rhodes-Livingstone Institute, 1960.

Jackman, Mary Elizabeth. Recent Population Movements in Zambia. Lusaka: University of Zambia Institute for African Studies, 1973.

Kay, George. Maps of the Distribution and Density of African Population in Zambia. Lusaka: University of Zambia, Institute for Social Research, 1967.

_____. A Social Geography of Zambia: A Survey of Population Patterns in a Developing Country. London: University of London Press, 1967.

Kuczynski, R. R. Demographic Survey of the British Colonial Empire, Part II. London: Oxford University Press, 1949.

Travel and Description

Bent, Newell Jr. Jungle Giants. Norwood, Mass.: Plimpton Press, 1936.

Berghegge, F. "Account of a Journey in Central Africa," Rhodesiana No. 3, 1958.

Bigland, Eileen. The Lake of the Royal Crocodiles. New York: Macmillan, 1939.

_____. Pattern in Black and White. London: Lindsay Drummond, 1940.

Butt, G. E. My Travels in North-West Rhodesia. London: E. Dalton, 1909.

Cambell, J. S. "I Knew Lewanika," Northern Rhodesia Journal, Vol. 1, No. 1 (1950).

Chapman, James. Travels in the Interior of South Africa (2 volumes). London: Bell and Daldy, 1868.

Colville, Olivia. One Thousand Miles in a Manchilla: Travel

and Sport in Nyasaland, Angoniland and Rhodesia.   London:
Walter Scott, 1911.

Cullen, Lucy Pope.   Beyond the Smoke That Thunders.   New
York: Oxford University Press, 1940.

Curzon, Marquess.   Tales of Travel.   London: Hodder and
Stoughton, 1923.

Dann, H. C.   Romance of the Posts of Rhodesia and Nyasaland.
London: F. Godden, Ltd. , 1940.

Davidson, H. Frances.   South and South Central Africa.   Elgin:
Brethren Publishing House, 1915.

Debenham, Frank.   The Way to Ilala.   London: Longmans, Green,
1955.

Decle, Lionel.   Three Years in Savage Africa.   New York: M. F.
Mansfield, 1898.

Duffy, Kevin.   Black Elephant Hunter.   London: Peter Davies,
1960.

Gibbons, Alfred St. Hill.   Africa from South to North Through
Marotseland.   London: John Lane, 1904.

_____.   Exploration and Hunting in Central Africa 1895-1896.
London: Methuen & Co. , 1898.

_____.   "Journey in Marotse and Mashikolumbwe Countries,"
Geographical Journal, Vol. 9, No. 2 (February 1897).

Giraud, Victor.   Les Lacs de l'Afrique Equatoriale.   Paris: 1890.

Glave, E. J.   "Glave in the Heart of Africa," Century Magazine,
No. 30 (1896): pp. 589-606, 765-781, 918-933.

Gouldsbury, C.   An African Year.   London: Edward Arnold, 1912.

Gouldsbury, C. , and H. Sheane.   The Great Plateau of Northern
Rhodesia: Being Some Impressions of the Tanganyika Plateau.
London: Edward Arnold, 1911.

Goy, Madame M. K.   Alone in Africa, or Seven Years on the
Zambesi.   London: James Nisbet & Co. , 1901.

Harding, Colonel C.   In Remotest Barotseland.   London: Hurst
and Blackett, 1905.

Hazard, C. J.   "Recollections of North-Western Rhodesia in the
Early 1900's," Northern Rhodesia Journal, Vol. 3 (1959).

Holub, Emil. "Journey Through Central East Africa," Proceedings
of the Royal Geographical Society, ii (1880).

_____. Seven Years in South Africa (2 vols). London: Sampoon
Low, 1881.

_____. Von der Capstadt ins Land der Maschukulmbe, Reisen
im Sudlichen Afrika in den Jahren 1883-1887, 2 vols. Wien:
Alfred Holder, 1890.

Hubbard, Mary G. African Gamble. New York: G. P. Putnam's
Sons, 1937.

Hubbard, Wynant Davis. Ibama. Greenwich, Conn.: New York
Graphic Society, 1962.

King, Ralph W., and John P. DeSmidt. The Rhodesias and
Nyasaland: A Pictorial Tour of Central Africa. Capetown:
Timmins, n.d.

Letcher, Owen. Big Game Hunting in North-Eastern Rhodesia.
London: John Long, 1911.

Long, Basil. Sir Drummond Chaplin. London: Oxford University
Press, 1941.

Mackintosh, C. W. The New Zambesi Trail: A Record of Two
Journeys to Northern Western Rhodesia: 1903-1920. London:
Marshall Bros., 1922.

Mansfield, Charlotte. Via Rhodesia: A Journey through Southern
Africa. London: Stanley Paul, 1913.

Marcosson, Isaac F. An African Adventure. New York: John
Lane Co., 1921.

Oswell, W. Edward. Wm. Cotton Oswell: Hunter and Explorer,
2 vols. London: Heinemann, 1900.

Payne, Faith Naegeli. "Zambia's Kasaba Bay," Africa Report,
Vol. 2, No. 6 (June 1966): pp. 51-52.

Pretorius, P. J. Jungle Man: The Autobiography of .... New
York: E. P. Dutton, 1948.

Read, Grantly Dick. No Time for Fear. New York: Harper &
Brothers, circ. 1955.

Schulz, A., and A. Hammar. The New Africa, Journey up the
Chobe, etc. London: William Heinemann, 1897.

Scott, E. D. Some Letters from South Africa, 1894-1932. London: Sharratt & Hughes, 1903.

Selous, F. C. A Hunter's Wanderings in Africa. London: R. Bentley, 1881.

_____. Travel and Adventure in South-East Africa. London: Rowland Ward, 1893.

Sharpe, Alfred. "Travels in the Northern Province and Katanga," The Northern Rhodesia Journal, Vol. 3 (1957): p. 4.

Statham, J. C. B. With My Wife Across Africa by Canoe and Caravan. London: Simpkin, Marshall, Hamilton, Kent, 1924.

Tabler, W. C. The Far Interior. Cape Town: Balkema, 1955.

Thwaits, D. C. "Trekking from Kalomo to Mongu in 1906," The Northern Rhodesia Journal, Vol. 3, No. 4, (1957).

"Undiscovered Zambia," Africa Report, Vol. 17, No. 1 (January 1972): p. 30.

Wadia, Ardaser Sorabjee N. The Romance of Rhodesia Being Impressions of a Sight-Seeing Tour to Southern and Northern Rhodesia. London: J. M. Dent & Sons, 1947.

Waugh, Evelyn. Tourist in Africa. Boston: Little, Brown and Company, 1960.

Bibliographies

Derricourt, R. M. Supplementary Bibliography of the Archaeology of Zambia, 1967-1973. Lusaka: Government Printer, 1975.

Jones, Ruth. Bibliography for South-East Central Africa and Madagascar. London: International African Institute, 1961.

Phillipson, D. W. (compiler). An Annotated Bibliography of the Archaeology of Zambia. Lusaka: Government Printer, 1968.

Rau, William. A Bibliography of Pre-Independence Zambia: The Social Sciences. Boston: G. K. Hall and Co., 1978.

Rhodesia and Nyasaland. A Select Bibliography of Recent Publications Concerning the Federation of Rhodesia and Nyasaland. Salisbury: Federal Information Dept., 1960.

Rotberg, Robert I. "Then and Now in Central Africa," Africa Report, Vol. 13, No. 5 (May 1968): pp. 22-24.

2. CULTURAL

Archaeology

Chaplin, J. G. "A Preliminary Account of Iron Age Burials with Gold from the Gwembe Valley, Northern Rhodesia," Proceedings of the First Federal Science Congress, 1960, Salisbury.

Clark, Desmond J. "Digging Up History," Northern Rhodesia Journal, Vol. 3, No. 5 (1958).

_____. Kalambo Falls Prehistoric Site, Vol. I. Cambridge: Cambridge University Press, 1969.

_____. Kalambo Falls Prehistoric Site, Vol. II. Cambridge: Cambridge University Press, 1974.

_____. The Stone Age Cultures of Northern Rhodesia. Cape Town: South African Archaeological Society, 1950.

Fagan, B. M. Iron Age Cultures in Zambia, Vol. I. London: Chatto and Windus, 1966.

_____. Iron Age Cultures in Zambia, Vol. II. London: Chatto and Windus, 1967.

_____. "Iron Age in Zambia," Current Anthropology, (1966).

_____. "The Iron Age Sequence in the Southern Province of Northern Rhodesia," Journal of African History, Vol. 4, No. 2 (1963): pp. 157-178.

_____, and D. W. Phillipson. "Sebanzi: The Iron Age Sequence at Lochinvar and the Tonga," Journal of the Royal Anthropological Institute, No. 95, Part 2 (1965).

Gabel, Creighton. Stone Age Hunters of the Kafue: The Gwisho A Site. Brookline: Boston University Press, 1965.

Mills, E. A. C., and N. T. Filmer. "Chondwe Iron Age Site, Ndola, Zambia," Azania, Vol. 7, (1972): pp. 129-147.

Phillipson, D. W. "The Early Iron Age Site at Kapwirimbwe, Lusaka," Azania, Vol. 3 (1968): pp. 87-105.

_____. "The Early Iron Age in Zambia--Regional Variants and Some Tentative Conclusions," The Journal of African History, Vol. 9, No. 2, (1968): pp. 191-211.

_____. "An Early Iron Age Site on the Lubusi River, Kaoma District, Zambia," Zambia Museum Journal, Vol. 2 (1971): pp. 51-57.

_____. "Early Iron Age Sites on the Zambian Copperbelt," Azania, Vol. 7 (1972): pp. 93-128.

_____. "Excavations at Twickenham Road, Lusaka," Azania, Vol. 5 (1970): pp. 77-118.

_____. "Iron Age History and Archaeology in Zambia," Journal of African History, Vol. 15, No. 1 (1974): pp. 1-25.

_____. "Notes on the Later Prehistoric Radiocarbon Chronology of Eastern and Southern Africa," Journal of African History, Vol. 11 (1970): pp. 1-15.

Sampson, C. Garth. The Stone Age Archaeology of Southern Africa. New York: Academic Press, 1974.

Vogel, J. O. Kumadzulo: An Early Iron Age Village Site in Southern Zambia. Lusaka: Zambia Museum Papers, Part III, 1971.

Fine Arts

Brelsford, W. V. African Dances. Lusaka: Government Printer, 1948.

_____. African Dances of Northern Rhodesia. Livingstone: Rhodes-Livingstone Museum, 1948.

_____. "Notes on Some Northern Rhodesian Bowstands," Man, No. 40 (1940): pp. 39-40.

_____. "Some Reflections on Bemba Geometric Decorative Art," Bantu Studies, No. 12 (March 1937).

Chaplin, J. H. "Some Aspects of Folk Art in Northern Rhodesia," Man, No. 63 (May 1963).

Clark, J. D., and B. M. Fagan. "Charcoals, Sands, and Channel-decorated Pottery from Northern Rhodesia," American Anthropologist, Vol. 67, No. 2 (April 1965): pp. 354-371.

Cooper, C. "Village Crafts in Barotseland," The Rhodes-Livingstone Journal, Human Problems in British Central Africa, No. 11 (1951).

Goodall, Elizabeth (et al.). Prehistoric Rock Art of the Federation of Rhodesia and Nyasaland. Salisbury: National Publications Trust, Rhodesia and Nyasaland, 1959.

Jones, A. M. African Music in Northern Rhodesia and some other places. Lusaka: Government Printer, 1949.

_____, and L. Kombe. The Icila Dance, Old Style. Roodepoort: Longmans, Green, 1952.

Summers, R., (ed.). Prehistoric Rock Art of the Federation of Rhodesia and Nyasaland. London: Chatto and Windus, 1959.

Linguistics

Barnes, B. H., and C. M. Doke. "The Pronunciation of the Bemba Language," Bantu Studies, No. 3 (1927).

Epstein, A. L. "Linguistic Innovation and Culture on the Copperbelt, Northern Rhodesia," Southwestern Journal of Anthropology, Vol. 15, No. 3 (1959).

Fortune, G. "A Note on the Languages of Barotseland," Conference of the History of the Central African Peoples, Lusaka: Rhodes-Livingstone Institute, 1963.

Jacottet, E. Etudes sur les langues du Haut-Zambeze: Textes originaux. Paris: Ernest Leroux, 1896.

Kashoki, Mubanga E. A Phonemic Analysis of Bemba. Manchester: University of Zambia Institute for Social Research, 1968.

Ohannessian, Sirarpi, and Mubanga E. Kashoki. Language in Zambia. London: International African Institute, 1977.

Sambeck, J. van. A Bemba Grammar. London: Longmans, Green & Co., 1955.

Sims, G. W. An Elementary Grammar of Cibemba. Basutoland: Morija Printing Works, 1959.

Literature

Chalinga, G. B. M. Maloko mwa Makande (Old Luyana Proverbs), Northern Rhodesia Publications Bureau, 1960.

Masiye, Andreya. Before Dawn. Lusaka: National Education Company of Zambia, Ltd., 1971.

Mulaisho, Dominic. Tongue of the Dumb. London: Heinemann, 1971.

Shaw, Mabel. A Treasure of Darkness: An Idyll of African Child Life. London: Longmans, Green & Co., 1936.

Torrend, J. Specimens of Bantu Folklore from Northern Rhodesia. London: Kegan Paul, Trench, Trubner, 1921.

3. ECONOMIC

Agriculture

Allan, W. The African Husbandman. Edinburgh: Oliver and
Boyd, 1965.

Dixon-Fyle, Mac. "Agricultural Improvement and Political Protest
on the Tonga Plateau, Northern Rhodesia," Journal of African
History, Vol. 18, No. 4 (1977).

Dodge, Doris J. Agricultural Policy and Performance in Zambia.
Berkeley: University of California Institute of International
Studies, 1977.

Donkin, J. "Marketing Organizations of Zambia," Monthly Agricultural Bulletin, Lusaka (August 1967).

Fraser, Robert H. "Land Settlement in the Eastern Province of
Northern Rhodesia," Rhodes-Livingstone Journal, No. 3 (1945).

Hellen, J. A. Rural Economic Development in Zambia, 1890-1964.
Munich: Weltforum-Verlag, 1968.

Hobson, R. H. Rubber: A Footnote to Northern Rhodesian History.
Livingstone: Rhodes-Livingstone Museum Occasional Papers
13, 1960.

Kay, George. "Agricultural Progress in Zambia's Eastern Province," Journal of Administration Overseas, Vol. 5, No. 2
(April 1966).

_____. Changing Patterns of Settlement and Land Use in the
Eastern Province of Northern Rhodesia. Hull, 1964.

_____. "A Regional Framework for Rural Development in
Zambia," African Affairs, Vol. 67, No. 266 (January 1968):
pp. 29-43.

Levin, Nora. "Cooperation Brings a Grassroots Revolution,"
Africa Report, Vol. 17, No. 4 (April 1972): pp. 15-18.

Lombard, C. Stephen. "Agriculture in Zambia Since Independence,"
East Africa (Nairobi), Vol. 8, No. 3 (March 1971): pp. 17-19.

_____. "Farming Co-operatives in the Development of Zambian
Agriculture," Journal of Modern African Studies, Vol. 10,
No. 2 (July 1972).

_____. The Growth of Co-operatives in Zambia, 1914-1971.
Lusaka: University of Zambia Institute for African Studies,
1971.

Makings, S. M. Agricultural Change in Northern Rhodesia and Zambia, 1945-1965. Stanford: Stanford University Press, 1966.

Peter, David U. Land Usage in Barotseland. Lusaka: Rhodes-Livingstone Institute Communication No. 19, 1960.

Quick, Stephen A. "Bureaucracy and Rural Socialism in Zambia," Journal of Modern African Studies, Vol. 15, No. 3 (1977).

Ranger, T. O. The Agricultural History of Zambia. Lusaka: Neczam, 1971.

Scudder, Thayer. Gathering Among African Woodland Savannah Cultivators: The Gwembe Tonga. Lusaka: University of Zambia Institute for African Studies, 1971.

Trapnell, C. G. "Ecological Results of Woodland Burning Experiments in Northern Rhodesia," Journal of Ecology, No. 47 (1959): pp. 129-168.

_____. The Soils, Vegetation and Agriculture of North-Eastern Rhodesia. Lusaka: Government Printer, 1943.

_____, and J. N. Clothier. The Soils, Vegetation and Agricultural Systems of North-Western Rhodesia. Lusaka: Government Printer, 1937 and second edition, 1957.

Van Horn, Laurel. "The Agricultural History of Barotseland, 1840-1964," in Palmer, Robin, and Neil Parsons, (eds.), The Roots of Rural Poverty in Central and Southern Africa. Berkeley: University of California Press, 1977.

Zambia Commercial Farmers' Bureau. Zambian Farming Today. New York: International Publications Service, 1969.

Commerce and Business

Barclays Bank D. C. O. Zambia: An Economic Survey. Lusaka: Government Printer, 1968.

Beveridge, Andrew. Converts to Capitalism: The Emergence of African Entrepreneurs in Lusaka, Zambia. Unpublished Ph.D. Dissertation, Yale University, 1973.

Goodman, S. H. "Investment Policy in Zambia," in Fortman, B. de G. (ed.), After Mulungushi: The Economics of Zambian Humanism. Nairobi: East African Publishing House, 1969.

Harvey, Charles. "The Control of Credit in Zambia," Journal of Modern African Studies, Vol. 11, No. 3 (September 1973): pp. 383-392.

Resources and Opportunities in the Rhodesias and Nyasaland: A
Guide to Commerce and Industry in the Territories. Nairobi:
Guides and Handbooks of Africa Publishing Co., 1963.

United States, Department of Commerce. "Establishing a Business
in Zambia," Overseas Business Report, (December 1967).

_____. "New Zambian Economic Program Involves Takeover of
Some Firms, Limit on Repatriation of Profits," International
Commerce, (April 29, 1968).

Woodruff, H. W. The Federation of Rhodesia and Nyasaland
(Southern Rhodesia, Northern Rhodesia, and Nyasaland):
Economic and Commercial Conditions. London: HMSO, 1955.

"Zambia: Exploiters and Exploited," Africa: An International
Business, Economic and Political Monthly, No. 48 (August
1975): p. 29.

Development

Baldwin, R. E. Economic Development and Export Growth: A
Study of Northern Rhodesia, 1920-1960. Berkeley and Los
Angeles: University of California Press, 1966.

Barber, William J. The Economy of British Central Africa: A
Case Study of Economic Development in a Dualistic Society.
Stanford: Stanford University Press, 1961.

_____. "Federation and the Distribution of Economic Benefits,"
in Leys, C., and C. Pratt (eds.), A New Deal in Central
Africa. London: Heinemann, 1960.

Bates, Robert H. Rural Responses to Industrialization: A Study
of Village Zambia. New Haven: Yale Press, 1976.

Clements, Frank. Kariba: The Struggle with the River God.
New York: Putnam's, 1960.

Elliott, C. (ed.). Constraints on the Economic Development of
Zambia. Nairobi: Oxford University Press, 1971.

Fortman, B. de G. (ed.). After Mulungushi: The Economics of
Humanism. Nairobi: East African Publishing House, 1969.

Gappert, Gary. Capital Expenditure and Transitional Planning in
Zambia. Syracuse: Syracuse University Program of East
African Studies, 1966.

Gregory, Sir Theodore. Ernest Oppenheimer and the Economic
Development of Southern Africa. Cape Town and New York:
Oxford University Press, 1962.

Hancock, W. K. Survey of British Commonwealth Affairs, Vol. 2, Part 1. Problems of Economic Policy, 1918-39. London: Oxford University Press, 1942.

Howatch, David. Shadow of the Dam. London: Collins; New York: Macmillan, 1961.

Jolly, R. "How Successful Was the First National Development Plan?" in Six Years After (supplement to the Zambian Mail, November 1969).

_____. "The Seers Report in Retrospect," African Social Research, No. 11 (June 1971).

Kaunda, K. D. Economic Revolution in Zambia. Lusaka: Government Printer, 1968.

_____. Zambia: Towards Economic Independence. Address to the National Council of UNIP at Mulungushi, April 19, 1968. Lusaka: Government Printer, 1968.

_____. "Zambia's Economic Reforms," African Affairs, Vol. 67, No. 269 (October 1968).

Muntemba, Maud. "Thwarted Development: A Case Study of Economic Change in the Kabwe Rural District of Zambia, 1902-1970," in Palmer, R., and N. Parsons (eds.), The Roots of Rural Poverty in Central and Southern Africa. Berkeley: University of California Press, 1977.

Myers, Robert J. "Rural Manpower in Planning in Zambia," International Labour Review, CII, No. 1 (July 1970): pp. 15-28.

Report of the Commission Appointed to Enquire into the Financial and Economic Position of Northern Rhodesia (Pim-Milligan Report), Col. No. 145. London: HMSO, 1938.

Rothchild, D. "Rural-Urban Inequities and Resource Allocation in Zambia," Journal of Commonwealth Political Studies, Vol. 10, No. 3 (1972).

St. Jorre, John de. "Zambia's Economy: Progress and Perils," Africa Report, Vol. 12, No. 9 (December 1967): pp. 36-39.

Scarritt, James R. "European Adjustment to Economic Reforms and Political Consolidation in Zambia," Issue, Vol. 3, No. 22 (Summer 1973): pp. 18-22.

Scudder, Thayer. "The Kariba Case: Man-made Lakes and Resource Development in Africa," Bulletin of the Atomic Scientists, (December 1965).

Seers, Dudley. "The Use of a Modified Input-Output System for an Economic Program in Zambia," Institute of Development Studies Communications, No. 50, University of Sussex, 1970.

Shaw, Timothy M. Dependence and Underdevelopment: The Development and Foreign Policies of Zambia. Athens, Ohio: Ohio University Center for International Studies, 1976.

Siddle, D. J. "Rural Development in Zambia: A Spatial Analysis," Journal of Modern African Studies, Vol. 8, No. 2 (July 1970): pp. 271-284.

Simonis, Heide, and Udo Ernest Simonis (eds.). Socio-Economic Development in Dual Economies: The Example of Zambia. Munich: Weltforum Verlag, 1971.

Thomas, P. A. "Zambian Economic Reforms," Canadian Journal of African Studies, Vol. 2, No. 1 (Spring 1968).

Thompson, C. H., and H. W. Woodruff. Economic Development in Rhodesia and Nyasaland. London: Dennis Dobson Limited, 1954.

United Nations, Economic Commission for Africa. Report of the Economic Survey Mission on the Development of Zambia. Ndola: Falcon Press, 1964.

Zambia, Republic of. Second National Development Plan. Lusaka: Ministry of Development Planning and National Guidance, 1971.

Industry: Mining

Bancroft, J. A. Mining in Northern Rhodesia. London: British South Africa Company, 1961.

Bostock, M., and C. Harvey (eds.). Economic Independence and Zambia Copper: A Case Study of Foreign Investment. New York: Praeger, 1972.

Bradley, Kenneth. Copper Venture: The Discovery and Development of Roan Antelope and Mufulira. London: Mufilira Copper Mines, 1952.

Copperbelt of Zambia Mining Industry Year Book 1966. Kitwe: Copper Industry Service Bureau, 1967.

Faber, M. L. O., and J. G. Potter. Towards Economic Independence: Papers on the Nationalisation of the Copper Industry in Zambia. London: Cambridge University Press, 1966.

Gann, L. H. "The Northern Rhodesian Copper Industry and the World of Copper, 1923-52," Rhodes-Livingstone Journal, Vol. 18, (1955): pp. 1-18.

Prain, Sir Ronald. Copper: The Anatomy of an Industry. London: Mining Journal Books, 1975.

Sklar, Richard L. Corporate Power in an African State: The Political Impact of Multinational Mining Companies in Zambia. Berkeley: University of California Press, 1975.

Stamp, Maxwell and Associates (commissioned by). A History of the Mineral Rights of Northern Rhodesia. London: 1961.

Industry: Other

Brelsford, W. V. Fishermen of the Bangweolu Swamps. Rhodes-Livingstone Institute Papers, No. 12, 1946.

Clausen, Lars. "On Attitudes Towards Industrial Conflict in Zambian Industry," African Social Research, No. 2 (December 1966).

Davis, J. M. (ed.). Modern Industry and the African. London: Macmillan and Co., 1933.

Scudder, Thayer. "Fishermen of the Zambezi," Rhodes-Livingstone Journal, No. 27 (1960).

Seidman, Ann. "The Distorted Growth of Import-Substitution Industry: The Zambian Case," The Journal of Modern African Studies, Vol. 12, No. 4 (December 1974): pp. 601-31.

_____. The Need for an Industrial Strategy in Zambia. Lusaka: University of Zambia, Dec. 1973.

Young, Alistair. Industrial Diversification in Zambia. New York: Praeger, 1973.

_____. "Patterns of Development in Zambian Manufacturing Industry Since Independence," Eastern African Economic Review, Vol. 1, No. 2 (December 1969).

Labor

Angi, C., and T. Coombe. "Training Programs and Employment Opportunities for Primary School Leavers in Zambia," Manpower and Unemployment Research in Africa. Lusaka: November, 1969.

Bates, R. H. "Input Structures, Output Functions and Systems Capacity: A Study of the Mineworkers' Union of Zambia," Journal of Politics, No. 32 (1970): pp. 898-928.

_____. Unions, Parties, and Political Development: A Study of Mine-Workers in Zambia. New Haven: Yale University

Press, 1971.

Berg, E. J., and J. Butler. "Trade Unions," in Coleman, J. S. and C. G. Rosberg (eds.), Political Parties and National Integration in Tropical Africa. Berkeley and Los Angeles: University of California Press, 1964.

Berger, Elena L. Labor, Race and Colonial Rule: The Copperbelt from 1924 to Independence. Oxford: Clarendon Press, 1974.

Bettison, David G. "Factors in the Determination of Wage Rates in Central Africa," The Rhodes-Livingstone Journal, No. 28, December 1960.

Heisler, Helmut. "The African Workforce of Zambia," Civilizations, Vol. 21, No. 4 (1971): pp. 425-434.

Jolly, R. "The Skilled Manpower Constraint," in Elliott, C. (ed.), Constraints on the Economic Development of Zambia. Nairobi: Oxford University Press, 1971.

Moore, R. J. B. These African Copper Mines: A Study of the Industrial Revolution in Northern Rhodesia, with Principal Reference to the Copper Mining Industry. London: Livingstone Press, 1948.

Ohadike, Patrick O. Development of and Factors in the Employment of African Migrants in the Copper Mines of Zambia, 1940-1966. Manchester: University of Zambia Institute for Social Research, 1969.

Perrings, Charles. "Consciousness Conflict, and Proletarianization: An Assessment of the 1935 Mineworkers' Strike on the Northern Rhodesian Copperbelt," Journal of Southern African Studies, Vol. 4, No. 1 (1978).

Philpott, R. "The Mulobezi-Mongu Labor Route," Rhodes-Livingstone Institute Journal, No. 3, June 1945.

Prain, R. L. "The Stabilization of Labor in the Rhodesian Copperbelt," African Affairs, Vol. 121 (October 1956).

Read, Margaret. "Migrant Labor and Its Effect on Tribal Life," International Labour Review, Vol. 45 (July 1942).

Rhodesian Selection Trust Group of Companies. The African Mine Worker on the Copperbelt of Northern Rhodesia. Salisbury: 1960.

Sanderson, F. E. "The Development of Labor Migration from Nyasaland, 1891-1914," Journal of African History, Vol. 2, No. 2 (1961): pp. 259-271.

Spearpoint, F. "The African Native and the Rhodesian Copper

Mines," Journal of the Royal African Society, Vol. 36 (July 1937).

Van Velsen, Jaap. "Labor Migration as a Positive Factor in the Continuity of Tonga Tribal Society," Economic Development Cultural Change, Vol. 8 (1960).

Transportation and Communications

Bailey, Martin. Freedom Railway: China and the Tanzania-Zambia Link. London: Rex Collings, 1976.

Craig, J. "Zambia-Botswana Road Link: Some Border Problems," Zambia and the World. Lusaka: University of Zambia, 1970.

Fraenkel, Peter. Wayaleshi. London: Weidenfeld and Nicolson, 1959.

Haefele, E. T., and E. G. Steinberg. Government Controls on Transport: An African Case. Washington, D.C.: Brookings Institution, 1965.

Hall, Richard, and Hugh Peyman. The Great Uhuru Railway: China's Showpiece in Africa. London: Victor Gollancz, 1976.

Mutukwa, Kasuka S. Politics of the Tanzania-Zambia Railway Project. Washington: University Press of America, 1977.

_____. "Tanzania-Zambia Railway: Imperial Dream Becomes Pan-African Reality," Africa Report, Vol. 17, No. 1 (January 1972): pp. 10-15.

Segal, Aaron. "The Tanganyika-Zambia Railway Project," Africa Report, Vol. 9, No. 10 (November 1964): pp. 9-10.

Yu, George T. "Working on the Railroad: China and the Tanzania-Zambia Railway," Asian Survey, Vol. 11, No. 11 (November 1971): pp. 1101-1117.

4. HISTORIC

General

Bradley, Kenneth G. The Story of Northern Rhodesia. London: Longmans and Green, 1940; rev., 1946.

Cambridge History of the British Empire, Vol. III. The Empire-- Commonwealth 1870-1919. Vol. VIII. South Africa, Rhodesia and the Protectorates. Cambridge: University Press, 1936.

Clay, G. C. R. History of the Mankoya District. Lusaka:

Rhodes-Livingstone Institute Communication, No. 4, 1965.

Gann, L. H. A History of Northern Rhodesia: Early Days to
   1953. London: Chatto and Windus, 1964.

Griffiths, James. Livingstone's Africa Yesterday and Today.
   London: Epworth Press, 1958.

Needham, D. E. Iron Age to Independence: A History of Central
   Africa. New York: Longman Inc., 1975.

Phillipson, D. W. The Prehistory of Eastern Zambia. Nairobi:
   British Institute in Eastern Africa, 1976.

Ranger, T. O. Aspects of Central African History. London:
   Heinemann, 1968.

Roberts, Andrew. A History of Zambia. New York: Africana
   Publishing Co., 1976.

Rotberg, R. I. A Political History of Tropical Africa. New
   York: Harcourt, Brace and World, 1965.

Stokes, E., and Richard Brown (eds.). The Zambesian Past:
   Studies in Central African History. Manchester: University
   Press, 1966.

Theal, G. M. Records of South-Eastern Africa, Vols. I-IX.
   Cape Town: The Government of Cape Colony, 1898.

Walker, E. A. A History of Southern Africa. London: Longmans,
   Inc., 1957.

Wills, A. J. An Introduction to the History of Central Africa.
   London: Oxford University Press, 1964; and third edition,
   1973.

Pre-Colonial: The Barotse

Clay, G. C. R. "Barotseland in the 19th Century Between 1801
   and 1864," Proceedings of the Conference on the History of
   the Central African Peoples. Lusaka: Rhodes-Livingstone
   Institute, 1963.

Mainga, Mutumba. Bulozi Under the Luyana Kings. London:
   Longmans, Inc., 1973.

_____. "The Lozi Kingdom," in Fagan, B. (ed.), A Short His-
   tory of Zambia. Nairobi: Oxford University Press, 1966.

_____. "New Light on the Origin of the Lozi," Proceedings of
   the Conference on the Central African Peoples. Lusaka:
   Rhodes-Livingstone Institute, 1963.

_____. "The Origin of the Lozi: Some Oral Traditions," in Stokes and Brown (eds.), The Zambesian Past. Manchester: Manchester University Press, 1966.

Mupatu, Y. W. Bulozi Sapili (Barotseland in the Past). Cape Town: Oxford University Press, 1959.

_____. Mulambwa Santulu U Amuhela Bo Mweve (King Mulambwa Welcomes the Mbunda Chiefs). London: Macmillan, 1958.

Muuka, L. S. "The Colonization of Barotseland in the 17th Century," in Stokes and Brown (eds.), The Zambesian Past. Manchester University Press, 1966.

_____. "The Colonization of Barotseland in the 17th Century," Proceedings of the Conference on the History of the Central African Peoples. Lusaka: Rhodes-Livingstone Institute, 1963.

Nalilungwe, Mubuana. Makolo Ki Ba (The Coming of the Kololo). Cape Town: 1958.

Sakubita, M. M. Za Luna Li Lu Siile (Our Vanishing Past). London: 1958.

Smith, E. W. "Sebitwane and the Makololo," African Studies, Vol. 15, No. 2 (1956).

Pre-Colonial: Contact with Arab Traders

Baxter, T. W. "Slave Raiders in North-Eastern Rhodesia," The Northern Rhodesia Journal, Vol. 1, No. 1 (1950).

Brode, Heinrich. Tippoo Tib: The Story of His Career in Central Africa. London: Edward Arnold, 1907.

Cunnison, I. "Kazembe and the Arabs," in Stokes and Brown, (eds.), The Zambesian Past. Manchester: Manchester University Press, 1965.

Farrant, Leda. Tippu Tip and the East African Slave Trade. New York: St. Martin's Press, 1975.

Miracle, Marvin P. "Ivory Trade and the Migration of the Northern Rhodesian Senga," Cahiers d'Etudes Africaines, Vol. 3, No. 3 (1963): pp. 424-434.

_____. "Plateau Tonga Entrepreneurs in Historical Interregional Trade," Rhodes-Livingstone Journal, No. 26 (December 1959).

Roberts, Andrew Dunlap (ed.). "The History of Abdullah ibn Suliman," African Social Research, No. 4 (1967).

Swann, A. J. Fighting the Slave Hunters in Central Africa. London: Seeley, 1910.

Tippu, Tip. "Maisha ya Hamed bin Muhammed," Supplement to the Journal of the East African Swahili Committee, Vol. 28, No. 2 (1958), Vol. 29, No. 1 (1959).

Pre-Colonial: Other Groups and General

Alimen, H. The Prehistory of Africa. London: Hutchinson, 1957.

Alpers, E. A. "North of the Zambezi," in Oliver, Roland (ed.), The Middle Age of African History. London: Oxford University Press, 1967.

Brelsford, W. V. The Succession of Bemba Chiefs: A Guide for District Officers. Lusaka: Government Printer, 1944.

Chibanza, S. J. "Kaonde History," Central Bantu Historical Texts I. Lusaka: 1961.

Clark, J. Desmond. "A Note on the Pre-Bantu Inhabitants of Northern Rhodesia and Nyasaland," Northern Rhodesia Journal, Vol. 1, No. 2 (1950-1952).

_____. The Prehistory of Southern Africa. Harmondsworth: Pelican Book, 1959.

_____. The Stone Age Cultures of Northern Rhodesia. Cape Town: South African Archaeological Society, 1950.

Cunnison, I. G. History on the Luapula. Rhodes-Livingstone Institute Papers, No. 21, 1951.

Fagan, Brian M. "Early Farmers and Traders North of the Zambezi," in Oliver, Roland (ed.), The Middle Age of African History. London: Oxford University Press, 1967.

_____. "Pre-European Ironworking in Central Africa with Special Reference to Northern Rhodesia," Journal of African History, Vol. 2, No. 2 (1961): pp. 199-210.

_____, ed. A Short History of Zambia from the Earliest Times until A.D. 1900. Nairobi: Oxford University Press, 1966.

_____. Southern Africa. London: Thames and Hudson, 1965.

Hall, R. N. Prehistoric Rhodesia. London: T. F. Unwin, 1909.

Hanna, A. J. The Beginnings of Nyasaland and North-Eastern Rhodesia, 1859-1895. Oxford: Clarendon Press, 1956.

Langworthy, H. W. Zambia Before 1890: Aspects of Pre-Colonial History. London: Longman, 1972.

Marwick, M. G. "History and Tradition in East Central Africa Through the Eyes of the North Rhodesian Cewa," Journal of African History, Vol. 4, No. 3 (1963): pp. 375-390.

Miracle, Marvin P. "Aboriginal Trade Among the Senga and Nsenga of Northern Rhodesia," Ethnology, Vol. 1, No. 2 (1962): pp. 212-222.

Munday, J. T. "Kankomba," Central Bantu Historical Texts I. Lusaka, 1961.

Mushindo, Paul. The Life of a Zambian Evangelist: The Reminiscences of Rev. Paul B. Mushindo. Lusaka: University of Zambia, Institute for African Studies, 1973.

Oliver, Roland A. (ed.). The Middle Age of African History. London: Oxford University Press, 1967.

Omer-Cooper, J. D. The Zulu Aftermath. London: Longman, 1966.

Poole, Edward Humphrey Lane. The Native Tribes of the East Luangwa Province of Northern Rhodesia. Livingstone: Government Printer, 1934.

_____. The Native Tribes of the Eastern Province of Northern Rhodesia: Notes on Their Migration and History. Lusaka: Government Printer, 1938.

Read, Margaret. "The Moral Code of the Ngoni and Their Former Military State," Africa, Vol. 11, 1938.

Roberts, Andrew Dunlop. "Chronology of the Bemba (North-Eastern Zambia)," Journal of African History, Vol. 11, No. 2 (1970): pp. 221-240.

_____. A History of the Bemba. Madison: University of Wisconsin Press, 1973.

_____. "The History of the Bemba," in Oliver, Roland (ed.), The Middle Age of African History. London: Oxford University Press, 1967.

_____. "Migrations from the Congo (A.D. 1500 to 1850)," in Fagan, B. (ed.), A Short History of Zambia. Nairobi: Oxford University Press, 1966.

_____. "The Nineteenth Century in Zambia," in Ranger, T. O. (ed.), Aspects of Central African History. London: Heinemann, 1968.

Smith, Alison. "The Southern Sector of the Interior, 1840-1884,"
in Oliver, Roland, and Mathew Gervase (eds.), History of
East Africa, Vol. I. Oxford: Clarendon Press, 1963.

Thomas, F. M. "Historical Notes on the Bisa Tribe, Northern
Rhodesia," Rhodes-Livingstone Communication, No. 8,
Lusaka, 1962.

Vansina, Jan. "Long Distance Trade Routes in Central Africa,"
Journal of African History, Vol. 3, No. 3 (1962): pp. 375-
390.

_____. "South of the Congo," in Oliver, Roland (ed.), The
Dawn of African History. London: Oxford University Press,
1961.

White, C. M. N. "The Balovale Peoples and Their Historical
Background," Rhodes-Livingstone Journal, No. 8 (1948): pp.
26-41.

_____. "The History of the Lunda-Lubale Peoples," Rhodes-
Livingstone Journal, No. 8, 1949.

Contact with Europeans: Dr. Livingstone

Adams, Henry Gardiner. The Life and Adventures of Dr. Livingstone in the Interior of South Africa. London: James Blackwood, 1879. Previously published as Dr. Livingston: His
Life and Adventures in the Interior of South Africa. London:
Houlston and Wright, 1857.

Anderson, W. H. On the Trail of Livingstone. California:
Pacific Press Publishing Ass., 1919.

Blaikie, William Garden. The Personal Life of David Livingstone.
New York: Harper and Brothers, 1881.

Campbell, R. J. Livingstone. New York: Dodd, Mead, 1930.

Chamberlain, D. Some Letters from Livingstone. London: Oxford
University Press, 1940.

Chambliss, J. E. The Life and Labors of David Livingstone.
Philadelphia: Hubbard Brothers, 1875.

Coupland, Reginald. Livingstone's Last Journey. London: Collins,
1945.

Finger, Charles J. David Livingstone: Explorer and Prophet.
Garden City, New York: Doubleday, Page and Co., 1927.

Gelfand, R. Livingstone the Doctor: His Life and Travels.
Oxford: Blackwell, 1957.

Hughes, Thomas. David Livingstone. London: MacMillan and
    Co. , 1897.

Hunt, B. L. "Lewanika Visits Livingstone," Letter in Northern
    Rhodesia Journal, Vol. 5, No. 5 (1964).

Livingstone, David. The Last Journals of David Livingstone in
    Central Africa, Vol. 1, (ed.) H. Waller. London: John
    Murray, 1874.

_____. Missionary Travels and Researches in South Africa.
    London: John Murray, 1857.

_____. The Zambezi Expedition of David Livingstone, 1858-
    1863, Vol. 1. The Journals, Vol. 2. The Journals Con-
    tinued, with Letters and Despatches Therefrom. (ed.) J.
    P. R. Wallis, Oppenheimer Series. London: Chatto and
    Windus, 1956.

_____, and Charles Livingstone. Narrative of an Expedition
    to the Zambesi and Its Tributaries; And of the Discovery
    of the Lakes Shirwa and Nyassa, 1858-1864. New York:
    Harper & Bros. , 1866.

Macnair, J. Livingstone the Liberator. London: Collins, 1940.

_____, ed. Livingstone's Travels. London: J. M. Dent and
    Sons, 1954.

Miller, Basil. David Livingstone: Explorer-Missionary. Grand
    Rapids, Mich. : Zondervan Publishing House, 1941.

Pachai, Prof. B. , ed. Livingstone: Man of Africa. New York:
    Longman, Inc. , 1973.

Polack, W. G. David Livingstone. St. Louis, Mo. : Concordia
    Publishing House, 1929.

Roberts, John S. The Life and Explorations of David Livingstone.
    Boston: B. B. Russell, 1875.

Schapera, I. , ed. David Livingstone, Family Letters, 1841-1856,
    2 vols. London: Chatto and Windus, 1959.

_____. Livingstone's Africa Journals, 2 vols. London: Chatto
    and Windus, 1963.

_____. Livingstone's Missionary Correspondence, 1841-1856.
    London: Chatto and Windus, 1961.

_____. Livingstone's Private Journals: 1851-1853. London:
    Chatto and Windus, 1960.

Seaver, G. David Livingstone: His Life and Letters. New York:
    Harper & Bros., 1957.

Waller, H. (ed.). Last Journals of David Livingstone. London:
    John Murray, 1874.

Wallis, J. P. R. The Zambezi Expedition of David Livingstone,
    2 vols. London: Chatto and Windus, 1956.

Contact with Europeans: Cecil Rhodes

Baxter, T. W. "The Barotse Concessions" Part I, Northern
    Rhodesia Journal, No. 3 (June 1951): pp. 39-49. Part II,
    Northern Rhodesia Journal, No. 4 (December 1951): pp. 38-45.

Caplan, Gerald L. "Barotseland's Scramble for Protection,"
    Journal of African History, Vol. 10, No. 2 (1969): pp. 277-
    294.

Gross, Felix. Rhodes of Africa. London: Cassell, 1956; New
    York: Praeger, 1957.

Hole, H. M. The Making of Rhodesia. London: Macmillan, 1926.

McDonald, J. G. Rhodes: A Life. London: Phillip Allan, 1927.

Millin, Sarah Gertrude. Rhodes. London: Chatto and Windus,
    1952 (rev. ed.).

Mitchell, Lewis. Life of Rhodes. London: Arnold, 1910.

_____. The Life and Times of the Right Honorable Cecil John
    Rhodes 1853-1902, 2 vols. New York: Kennerly, 1910.

Piomer, William. Cecil Rhodes. New York: D. Appleton and
    Co., 1933.

Radziwell, Princess Catherine. Cecil Rhodes: Man and Empire-
    Maker. New York: Funk and Wagnalls, 1918.

Williams, Basil. Cecil Rhodes. New York: Henry Holt & Co.,
    1921.

Woodhouse, C. M., and John G. Lockhart. Cecil Rhodes. Lon-
    don: Hodder and Stoughton, 1963.

Contact with Europeans: Others

Baxter, T. William. "The Concessions of Northern Rhodesia,"
    Occasional Papers of the National Archives of Rhodesia and
    Nyasaland, No. 1 (June 1963).

Bertrand, Alice E.   Alfred Bertrand, Explorer and Captain of
Cavalry.   London: R. T. S. , 1926.

Birmingham, David.   "Central Africa and the Atlantic Slave Trade,"
in Oliver, Roland (ed.), The Middle Age of African History.
London: Oxford University Press, 1967.

Bradley, K.   "Statesmen: Coryndon and Lewanika in North Western
Rhodesia," African Observer, Vol. 5, No. 5 (September 1936).

Brelsford, W. V.   Generation of Men: The European Pioneers of
Northern Rhodesia.   Lusaka: Stuart Manning, 1965.

Burton, Richard F. , translator.   The Lands of Cazembe: Lacerda's
Journey to Cazembe in 1798.   London: John Murray for the
Royal Geographical Society, 1873.

Cairns, H. A. C.   Prelude to Imperialism: British Reactions to
Central African Society, 1840-1890.   London: Routledge and
Kegan Paul, 1965.

Campbell, Dugald.   In the Heart of Bantuland: A Record of Twenty-
Nine Years' Pioneering in Central Africa Among the Bantu Peoples.   London: Seeley Service & Co. , 1922.

Clay, Gervas.   Your Friend Lewanika, Litunga of Barotseland,
1842-1916.   London: Chatto and Windus, 1968.

Coupland, Sir R.   The Exploitation of East Africa, 1856-1890,
The Slave Trade and The Scramble.   London: Faber and
Faber, 1939.

Cunnison, I.   "Kazembe and the Portuguese," Journal of African
History, Vol. 2, No. 1 (1961): pp. 61-76.

Fisher, W.   Singleton and Julyan Hoyte.   Africa Looks Ahead:
The Life Stories of Walter and Anna Fisher of Central Africa.
London: Pickering & Inglis, Ltd. , 1948.

Gamitto, A. C. P.   King Kazambe and the Marave, Cheva, Bisa,
Bemba, Lunda, and Other Peoples of Southern Africa Being
the Diary of the Portuguese Expedition to that Potentate in the
Years 1831 and 1832.   Lisbon: 1960. (2 vols. translated by
Ian Cunnison).

Gann, Lewis.   "The End of the Slave Trade in British Central
Africa, 1889-1912," Rhodes-Livingstone Journal, No. 16 (1954):
pp. 27-51.

Hall, Richard.   "Portuguese Expeditions in Zambia," in Fagan,
B. M. , A Short History of Zambia.   Nairobi: Oxford University Press, 1966.

Harding, Colonel Colin. Far Bugles. London: Simpkin Marshall, 1933.

Harrington, H. T. "The Taming of North-Eastern Rhodesia," The Northern Rhodesia Journal, Vol. 2, No. 3 (1954).

Hawthorne, John. Dan Crawford: The Gatherer of the People. London: Pickering & Inglis, n. d.

Hole, H. M. The Passing of the Black Kings. London: P. Allen, 1932.

Holmberg, A. African Tribes and European Agencies: Colonialism and Humanitarianism in British South and East Africa, 1870-1895. Goteberg: Akademiforlaget, 1966.

Holub, Emil. Emil Holub's Travels North of the Zambezi. (Translated by Christa Johns; edited by Ladislav Holy). Manchester: Manchester University Press, 1975.

Hudson, R. "Memories of Abandoned Bomas. No. 4 Nalolo," Northern Rhodesia Journal, Vol. 2 (1953).

Jalla, Adolphe and Emma. Pionniers parm les Ma-Rotse. Florence: Imprimerie Claudienne, 1903.

Johnston, Sir Harry. British Central Africa. London: Methuen and Co. , 1896.

Johnston, James. Reality versus Romance in South-Central Africa. London: Hodder and Stoughton, 1893.

Langham, R. W. M. "Thornton and Rumsey of Mbesuma Ranch," The Northern Rhodesia Journal, Vol. 4, No. 4 (1960).

Lawley, Arthur. "From Bulawayo to the Victoria Falls: A Mission to King Lewanika," Blackwood's Magazine (December 1898).

Luck, R. A. Visit to Lewanika, King of the Barotse. London: Simpkin Marshall, 1902.

MacQueen, James. "Journeys of Silva Porto with the Arabs from Benguela to Ibo and Mozambique through Africa, 1852-1854," Journals of the Royal Geographic Society, Vol. 30 (1860).

Mathers, E. P. Zambesia: England's El Dorado in Africa. London: King, Sell & Railton, 1892.

Oliver, R. A. Sir Harry Johnston and the Scramble for Africa. London: Chatto and Windus, 1957.

Pedroso, Gamitto A. C. King Kazembe and the Marawe, Cheva,

Bisa, Bemba, Lunda and Other Peoples of Southern Africa, 2 vols. Lisbon: Junta de Investigacoes do Ultramar, 1960.

Poole, Edward Humphrey Lane. "An Early Portuguese Settlement in Northern Rhodesia," Journal of the African Society, Vol. 30 (1931).

Rukavina, Kathaleen Stevens. Jungle Pathfinder: The Biography of Chirupula Stephenson. London: Hutchinson, 1952.

Serpa Pinto, A. de. How I Crossed Africa from the Atlantic to the Indian Ocean, 2 vols. London: Sampson, Lowe, Marston, Searle, and Rivington, 1881.

Stirke, D. E. C. Barotseland: Eight Years among the Barotse. London: John Ball Sons & Danielson, Ltd., 1922.

Tabler, Edward C., ed. Trade and Travel in Early Barotseland: The Diaries of George Westbeech, 1885-1888, and Captain Norman MacLeod, 1875-1876. London: Chatto and Windus; Berkeley: University of California Press, 1963.

_____. The Zambezi Papers of Richard Thornton, I. 1858-1860, II. 1860-1863, Robins Series No. 4. London: Chatto and Windus, 1963.

Venning, J. H. "Early Days in Balovale," Northern Rhodesia Journal, Vol. 2 (1955).

Wallis, J. P. R., ed. The Barotseland Journal of James Stevenson-Hamilton: 1898-1899. London: Chatto and Windus, 1953.

Colonial and Company Rule

Akafuna, Ishee Kwandu Sikota. "Lewanika in England, 1902," Northern Rhodesia Journal, Vol. 2, No. 2 (1953).

Bate, H. Maclear. Report on the Rhodesias. London: Andrew Melrose, 1953.

Brelsford, W. V. The Story of the Northern Rhodesia Regiment. Lusaka: Government Printer, 1954.

Chandos, Viscount (Oliver Lyttelton). The Memoirs of.... London: Bodley Head, 1962.

Crawford, D. Thinking Black: Twenty-Two Years Without a Break in the Long Grass of Central Africa. London: Morgan and Scott, 1912.

Dann, H. C. Romance of the Posts of Rhodesia and Nyasaland. London: F. Godden, Ltd., 1940.

Evans, I. L. The British in Tropical Africa. Cambridge: Cambridge University Press, 1958.

Gann, L. H. The Birth of a Plural Society: The Development of Northern Rhodesia Under the British South Africa Company. Lusaka: Manchester University Press for Rhodes-Livingstone Institute, 1958.

_____. A History of Northern Rhodesia: Early Days to 1953. London: Chatto and Windus, 1964.

Glennie, A. F. B. "The Administration Officer Today: Barotseland," Corona, Vol. 2, No. 3 (March 1959).

Hailey, Lord. Native Administration in British African Territories, Part II, Central Africa. London: H. M. S. O. , 1950.

Hall, Richard. Zambia 1890-1964: The Colonial Period. London: Longman, 1976.

Harding, C. Frontier Patrols: A History of the British South Africa Police and Other Rhodesian Forces. London: G. Bell & Sons, 1937.

Indakwa, John. Expansion of British Rule in the Interior of Central Africa. Washington: University Press of America, 1977.

Jones, N. S. Carey. "Native Treasuries in Northern Rhodesia," Rhodes-Livingstone Journal, Vol. 2 (1944).

Keatley, Patrick. "The Guilty Partner," Africa South in Exile, Vol. 6, No. 1 (October-December, 1961): pp. 45-55.

_____. "Monckton and Cleopatra," Africa South in Exile, Vol. 5, No. 2 (January-March 1961): pp. 63-71.

Kirkman, W. Unscrambling an Empire--A Critique of British Colonial Policy, 1956-1966. London: Chatto and Windus, 1966.

Mason, P. The Birth of a Dilemma: The Conquest and Settlement of Rhodesia. London: Oxford University Press, 1958.

Mbikusita, Lewanika (Godwin). The Paramount Chief Yeta III's Visit to England. Lusaka: 1937.

Memorandum on Native Policy in Northern Rhodesia (Gardiner-Brown Report). Lusaka: 1950.

Perham, Margery, ed. Ten Africans. London: Faber and Faber, 1936.

Pim, Alan. "Anthropological Problems of Indirect Rule in Northern Rhodesia," Man, Vol. 38 (1938).

Pollock, Norman H., Jr. Nyasaland and Northern Rhodesia: Corridor to the North. Pittsburgh, Pa.: Duquesne University Press, 1971.

Report on Native Taxation. Lusaka: Government Printer, 1938.

Report on the Administration of North-Eastern Rhodesia, 1900-1903. Fort Jameson: Administration Press.

Roberts, Andrew Dunlop. "The Political History of 20th-Century Zambia," in Ranger, T. O. (ed.), Aspects of Central African History. London: Heinemann, 1968.

Rotberg, R. I. "The Missionary Factor in the Occupation of Trans-Zambezia," The Northern Rhodesia Journal, Vol. 5, No. 4 (1964).

_____. Gore-Browne and the Politics of Multiracial Zambia. Berkeley: University of California Press, 1978.

Slinn, Peter. "Commercial Concessions and Politics During the Colonial Period: The Role of the British South Africa Company in Northern Rhodesia, 1890-1964," African Affairs, No. 70 (1971): pp. 365-384.

Stokes, George. "Memories of Abandoned Bomas, No. 12: Old Fife (Period 1900-1919)," The Northern Rhodesia Journal, Vol. 3, No. 4 (1957).

Summers, Roger, and L. H. Gann. "Robert Edward Codrington, 1869-1908," The Northern Rhodesia Journal, Vol. 3 (1956).

Wallace, L. A. "Beginning of Native Administration in Northern Rhodesia," Journal of the African Society, Vol. 21 (1922).

Williams, R. How I Became a Governor. London: John Murray, 1913.

Nationalist Politics: Kaunda

Hall, R. Kaunda--Founder of Zambia. London: Longmans, 1964.

Hatch, John. Two African Statesmen, Kaunda of Zambia, Nyerere of Tanzania. Chicago: Henry Regnery Co., 1976.

Kaunda, Kenneth. Africa's Freedom. London: Allen and Unwin, 1964.

_____. Dominion Status for Central Africa. London: UCD and MUF, 1957.

_____. "Rider and Horse in Northern Rhodesia," Africa South, Vol. 3, No. 4 (July-September, 1959): pp. 52-56.

_____. Zambia Shall Be Free: An Autobiography. London:

Heinemann, 1962; New York: Praeger, 1963.

_____, and C. Morris. Black Government. Lusaka: United Society for Christian Literature, 1960.

Macpherson, Fergus. Kenneth Kaunda of Zambia. London: Oxford University Press, 1974.

Melady, T. Kenneth Kaunda of Zambia: Selections from His Writings. New York: Praeger, 1964.

Mpashi, S. Betty Kaunda. London: Longmans, 1969.

Munger, Edwin. President Kenneth Kaunda of Zambia: An Extraordinary Human Being Facing Extraordinary Problems. American Universities Field Staff Reports, Central and Southern Africa Series, Vol. 14, No. 2 (1970). Hanover, New Hampshire: AUFS, 1970.

Sokoni, J., and M. Temple. Kaunda of Zambia. London: Nelson, 1964.

Nationalist Politics: Religion and Nationalism

Assimeng, J. M. "Sectarian Allegiance and Political Authority: The Watch Tower Society in Zambia," Journal of Modern African Studies, Vol. 8, No. 1 (1970).

Barnes, J. A. "African Separatist Churches," The Rhodes-Livingstone Journal, No. 9 (1950).

Fernandez, J. W. "The Lumpa Uprising: Why?" Africa Report, Vol. 9, No. 10 (November 1964): pp. 30-32.

Heward, Christine. "The Rise of Alice Lenshina," New Society, Vol. 4 (August 13, 1964).

Ranger, T. O. "The 'Ethiopian' Episode in Barotseland, 1900-1905," The Rhodes-Livingstone Journal, No. 37 (1965).

Roberts, Andrew Dunlop. The Lumpa Church of Alice Lenshina. New York: Oxford University Press, 1972.

_____. "The Lumpa Church of Alice Lenshina," in Rotberg, R. I., and A. A. Mazrui (eds.), Protest and Power in Black Africa. New York: Oxford University Press, 1970.

Rotberg, R. I. "The Lenshina Movement of Northern Rhodesia," Rhodes-Livingstone Journal, No. 29 (1963).

Shepperson, G. "The Politics of African Church Separatist Movements in British Central Africa, 1892-1916," Africa, Vol. 24, No. 3 (1954).

Nationalist Politics: Other

Billing, M. G. "Tribal Rule and Modern Politics in Northern Rhodesia," African Affairs, Vol. 58, No. 231 (April 1969).

Chona, Mainza. "Northern Rhodesia's Time for Changes," Africa South in Exile, Vol. 5, No. 2 (January-March 1961): pp. 72-76.

Davidson, A. B. "African Resistance and Rebellion Against the Imposition of Colonial Rule," in Ranger, T. O. (ed.), Emerging Themes of African History: Proceedings of the International Congress of African Historians, Dar es Salaam, 1965. Nairobi: East African Publishing House, 1968.

Davis, J. A., and J. K. Baker (eds.). Southern Africa in Transition. London: Pall Mall Press, 1966.

Dixon-Fyle, Mac. "Agricultural Improvement and Political Protest on the Tonga Plateau, Northern Rhodesia," Journal of African History, Vol. 18, No. 4 (1977).

Epstein, A. L. Politics in an Urban African Community. Lusaka: Manchester University Press for Rhodes-Livingstone Institute, 1958.

Henderson, Ian. "The Origins of Nationalism in East and Central Africa: The Zambian Case," Journal of African History, Vol. 11, No. 4 (1970): pp. 591-603.

Hodgkin, T. African Political Parties. Harmondsworth: Penguin, 1961.

_____. Nationalism in Colonial Africa. London: Frederick Muller, 1956.

Hooker, J. R. "Welfare Associations and Other Instruments of Accommodation in the Rhodesias Between the World Wars," Comparative Studies in Society and History, Vol. 9, No. 1 (1966).

Meebelo, H. Reaction to Colonialism: A Prelude to the Politics of Independence in Northern Zambia, 1893-1939. Manchester: Manchester University Press, 1971.

Mulford, D. C. The Northern Rhodesia General Election 1962. London: Oxford University Press, 1964.

_____. "Northern Rhodesia--Some Observations on the 1964 Elections," Africa Report, Vol. 9, No. 2 (February 1964): pp. 13-17.

_____. Zambia: The Politics of Independence, 1957-1964.

London: Oxford University Press, 1967.

Ranger, T. O. "Connections Between 'Primary Resistance' Movements and Modern Mass Nationalism in East and Central
Africa," Part I, Journal of African History, Vol. 9, No. 3
(1968).

_____. "Nationality and Nationalism: The Case of Barotseland,"
Journal of the Historical Society of Nigeria, Vol. 4, No. 2
(June 1968).

Rotberg, R. I. "Inconclusive Election in Northern Rhodesia,"
Africa Report, Vol. 7, No. 11 (December 1962): pp. 3-6.

_____. The Rise of Nationalism in Central Africa: The Making
of Malawi and Zambia, 1873-1964. Cambridge, Mass.: Har-
vard University Press, 1965.

_____, and A. A. Mazrui, eds. Protest and Power in Black
Africa. New York: Oxford University Press, 1970.

Sikalumbi, W. K. Before UNIP. Lusaka: National Educational
Company of Zambia, Ltd., n.d.

The Federation

An Account of the Disturbances in Northern Rhodesia. Lusaka:
Government Printer, July to October 1961.

Allighan, Garry. The Welensky Story. London: Macdonald, 1962.

Alport, Lord. The Sudden Assignment: Being a Record of Service
in Central Africa During the Last Controversial Years of the
Federation of Rhodesia and Nyasaland 1961-1963. London:
Hodder & Stoughton, 1965.

Banda, H. K., and Harry Nkumbula. Federation in Central Africa.
London: 1951.

Barber, W. J. "Federation and the Distribution of Economic Benefits," in Leys, C., and C. Pratt (eds.), A New Deal in Central Africa. London: Heinemann, 1960.

Barton, Frank. "Portrait of a Failure: Sir Roy Welensky," Africa
South, Vol. 3, No. 4 (July-September 1959): pp. 64-69.

_____. "Rhodesian Liberals in Dilemma, the Roads to Union,"
Africa South, Vol. 3, No. 2 (January-March 1959): pp. 61-64.

Baxter, G. H., and P. W. Jodgens. "The Constitutional Status
of the Federation of Rhodesia and Nyasaland," International
Affairs, October, 1957.

Bibliography   380

Black, Colin. Rhodesia and Nyasaland. New York: Macmillan, 1961.

Broomfield, Gerald W. 1960--Last Chance in the Federation. London: Universities' Mission to Central Africa, 1960.

Castle, Barbara. "Labour and Central Africa," Africa South, Vol. 3, No. 4 (July-September 1959): pp. 84-92.

Charlton, Leslie. Spark in the Stubble: Colin Morris of Zambia. London: Epworth, 1969.

Clegg, E. Race and Politics: Partnership in the Federation of Rhodesia and Nyasaland. London: Oxford University Press, 1960.

Creighton, T. R. M. The Anatomy of Partnership: Southern Rhodesia and the Central African Federation. London: Faber and Faber, 1960.

_____. "The Future of the Federation," Africa South in Exile, Vol. 5, No. 3 (April-June 1961): pp. 62-67.

Dunn, Cyril. Central African Witness. London: Victor Gollancz, Ltd., 1959.

The Federation of Rhodesia and Nyasaland. London: Barclays Bank, 1959.

Franck, T. M. Race and Nationalism: The Struggle for Power in Rhodesia-Nyasaland. London: Allen & Unwin, 1960.

Franklin, H. Unholy Wedlock: The Failure of the Central African Federation. London: George Allen & Unwin, 1963.

Gale, W. D. Deserve to Be Great: The Story of Rhodesia and Nyasaland. Bulawayo: Stuart Manning, 1960.

Gibbs, Henry. Africa on a Tightrope. London: Jarrolds, circ. 1954.

Gibbs, Peter. Avalanche in Central Africa. London: Arthur Barker, 1961.

Gribble, Howard. The Price of Copper. London: Universities' Mission to Central Africa, n.d. (ca. 1962).

Gussman, Boris. Out in the Mid-Day Sun. London: Allen & Unwin, Ltd., 1962.

Jones, Arthur Creech. "Central Africa (II), the Challenge of Federation," Africa South, Vol. 2, No. 1 (October-December 1957): pp. 73-83.

Keatley, P. The Politics of Partnership: The Federation of
Rhodesia and Nyasaland. London: Penguin African Library,
1963.

Kirkwood, Kenneth. "British Central Africa: Politics Under
Federation," Annals of American Academy of Political Science,
March 1955.

Leys, Colin, and Cranford Pratt. A New Deal in Central Africa.
New York: Frederick A. Praeger, 1961.

Mason, P. Year of Decision: Rhodesia and Nyasaland in 1960.
London: Oxford University Press, 1960.

McWilliams, M. D. "The Central African Liberals," Africa
South, Vol. 3, No. 1 (October-December 1958): pp. 83-86.

Mittelbeeler, Emmet V. "After Federation: Some Predictions,"
Africa Report, Vol. 8, No. 4 (April 1963): pp. 11-13.

Morris, Colin. The Hour After Midnight: A Missionary's Experiences of the Racial and Political Struggle in Northern Rhodesia.
London: Longmans, 1961.

_____. A Humanist in Africa: Letters to Colin M. Morris
From Kenneth D. Kaunda, President of Zambia. Nashville,
Tenn.: Abingdon Press, 1966.

Mtepuka, Elias M. "Central African Federation (I), the Attack,"
Africa South, Vol. 1, No. 4 (July-September 1957): pp. 73-81.

Phillips, C. E. Lucas. The Vision Splendid: The Future of a
Central African Federation. London: Heinemann, 1960.

Reed, John. "The Salisbury Talks," Africa South in Exile, Vol. 5,
No. 3 (April-June 1961): pp. 56-61.

Report of the Advisory Commission on the Review of the Constitution of Rhodesia and Nyasaland (Monckton Commission), Cmmd.
1148. London: HMSO, 1960.

Rotberg, R. I. "The Federation Movement in British East and
Central Africa, 1889-1953," Journal of Commonwealth Political
Studies, Vol. 2 (1964).

_____. "White Rule and the Federation of British Central
Africa," Southern Africa in Transition. New York: Praeger,
1966.

Sanger, Clyde. Central African Emergency. London: Heinemann,
1960.

_____. "A Long Time Dying: Central African Federation,"

Africa South in Exile, Vol. 6, No. 1 (October-December 1961): pp. 39-44.

Spiro, H. J. "The Rhodesias and Nyasaland," in Carter, Gwendolen M. (ed.), *Five African States: Responses to Diversity*. London: Pall Mall Series, 1964.

Stonehouse, John. "A Central African Report," *Africa South*, Vol. 4, No. 1 (October-December 1959): pp. 81-86.

Taylor, Don. *Rainbow on the Zambesi*. London: Museum Press, 1953.

_____. *The Rhodesian: The Life of Sir Roy Welensky*. London: Museum Press, 1955.

Welensky, Sir Roy. *Welensky's 4000 Days: The Life and Death of the Federation of Rhodesia and Nyasaland*. London: Collins, 1964.

Werbner, R. P. "Federal Administration, Rank and Civil Strife Among the Bemba Royals and Nobles," *Africa*, Vol. 37, No. 1 (1967).

Williams, S. *Central Africa: The Economies of Inequality*. London: Fabian Commonwealth Bureau, 1960.

Since Independence

Brown, R. "Zambia and Rhodesia: A Study in Contrast," *Current History*, No. 48 (1965).

Cross, Sholto. "Politics and Criticism in Zambia," *Journal of Southern African Studies*, Vol. 1, No. 1 (1974): pp. 109-115.

Garrison, Lloyd. "Africa's Good Guy Under Pressure," *The New York Times Magazine*, August 7, 1966.

Gregor, Gordon. "President Kaunda--Champion of the Common Man," *Horizon*, No. 9 (January 12, 1968).

Hall, Richard. "Zambia and Rhodesia: Links and Fetters," *Africa Report*, Vol. 11, No. 1 (January 1966): pp. 8-12.

_____. "Zambia's Search for Political Stability," *World Today*, Vol. 25, No. 11 (November 1969).

Heron, Alastair. "Zambia: Key Point in Africa," *World Today*, Vol. 21, No. 2 (February 1965).

Hunter, Guy. "Unification of Zambia's Two Economics," *Optima*, No. 16 (June 1966).

Jennings, Peggy, and Paul Changuion, Jr. "On Voluntary Service in Zambia," Horizon, No. 9 (March 1967).

Kaunda, K. D. Address to Parliament on the Opening of the Third Session of the Second National Assembly, January 8, 1971. Lusaka: Government Printer, 1971.

_____. Africa in the Sixties: The Decade of Decision and Definition. Lusaka: Zambia News Agency, 1969.

_____. Economic Revolution in Zambia. Lusaka: Government Printer, 1968.

_____. I Wish to Inform the Nation. Lusaka: Government Printer, 1969.

_____. A Path for the Future. May 8, 1971.

_____. Take Up the Challenge. Lusaka: Government Printer, 1970.

_____. Towards Complete Independence. Lusaka: Government Printer, 1969.

_____. Zambia: Independence and Beyond. The Speeches of Kenneth Kaunda, ed. Legum, C. London: Nelson, 1966.

_____. Zambia: Towards Economic Independence, Address to the National Council of UNIP at Mulungushi, April 19, 1968. Lusaka: Government Printer, 1968.

_____. Zambia's Guidelines for the Next Decade. Lusaka: Government Printer, 1968.

Keith, Grace. The Fading Colour Bar. London: Robert Hale, 1966.

Leech, John. "Zambia Seeks a Route to Fuller Independence," Issue, Vol. 2, No. 4 (Winter 1972): pp. 6-11.

Legum, C., ed. Zambia: Independence and Beyond. The Speeches of Kenneth Kaunda. London: Nelson, 1966.

Martin, A. Minding Their Own Business: Zambia's Struggle Against Western Control. London: Hutchinson, 1972.

Ostrander, F. T. "Zambia in the Aftermath of Rhodesian UDI: Logistical and Economic Problems," African Forum, Vol. 2, No. 3 (Winter 1967).

Rotberg, R. I. "Tribalism and Politics in Zambia," Africa Report, Vol. 12, No. 9 (December 1967): pp. 29-35.

_____. "What Future for Barotseland?" Africa Report, Vol. 8, No. 7 (July 1963): pp. 21-23.

Sklar, R. L. "Zambia's Response to the Rhodesian UDI," in Tordoff, W. (ed.), Politics in Zambia. Berkeley: University of California Press, 1974.

Sutcliffe, R. B. "Crisis on the Copperbelt," The World Today, Vol. 22, No. 12 (December 1966).

_____. "Zambia and the Strains of UDI," The World Today, Vol. 23, No. 12 (December 1967).

Welch, Claude E., Jr. "Zambia and Lesotho--The Transfer of Power," Africa Report, Vol. 9, No. 6, (June 1964): pp. 10-11.

Zambia, 1964-1974: A Decade of Achievement. Lusaka: Zambia Information Services, 1974.

Zambia: Six Years After. Lusaka: Zambia Information Services, 1970.

5. POLITICAL

Constitution, Law and Government: Law and Justice

Bradley, Kenneth. Native Courts and Authorities in Northern Rhodesia. London: Longmans, Green, 1948.

Epstein, A. L. The Administration of Justice and the Urban African. London: Colonial Research Studies, No. 7, 1953.

_____. Juridical Techniques and the Judicial Process. Rhodes-Livingstone Papers, No. 23, 1954.

_____. "The Role of the African Courts in Urban Communities of the Copperbelt in Northern Rhodesia," Rhodes-Livingstone Journal, No. 13 (1953).

_____. "Some Aspects of the Conflict of Law and Urban Courts in Northern Rhodesia," Rhodes-Livingstone Journal, No. 12, 1951.

Laws of Zambia, 1964. Lusaka: Government Printer, 1965.

"The Legal Organization of a New State--Zambia," Review of Contemporary Law, No. 12 (Spring 1965).

Roberts, Andrew Dunlop. "Zambia: White Judges Under Attack," The Round Table, No. 236 (October 1969): pp. 423-426.

White, C. M. N. "The Changing Scope of Urban Native Courts in Northern Rhodesia," Journal of African Law, Vol. 8, No. 1 (Spring 1964).

Constitution, Law and Government: Administration

Dresang, D. L. "Ethnic Politics, Representative Bureaucracy, and Development Administration: The Zambian Case," American Political Science Review, Vol. 77, No. 4 (December 1974): pp. 1605-1617.

Glennie, A. F. B. "The Administration Officer Today: Barotseland," Corona, Vol. 2, No. 3 (March 1959).

Greenfield, C. C. "Manpower Planning in Zambia," Journal of Administration Overseas, Vol. 7, No. 4 (October 1968).

Harvey, C. R. M. "The Fiscal System," in Elliott, C. (ed.), Constraints on the Economic Development of Zambia. Nairobi: Oxford University Press, 1971.

Heisler, Helmuth. "Continuity and Change in Zambian Administration," Journal of Local Administration Overseas, Vol. 4, No. 3 (July 1965).

Hudson, W. J. S. "Local Government Reorganization in Isoka District," Journal of Local Administration Overseas, Vol. 4, No. 1 (January 1965).

Martin, Robert. "The Ombudsman in Zambia," Journal of Modern African Studies, Vol. 15, No. 2 (1977): pp. 239-259.

Ohadike, Patrick O. "Counting Heads in Africa: The Experience of Zambia, 1963 and 1969," Journal of Administration Overseas, Vol. 9, No. 4 (October 1970).

Schaffer, Bernard, ed. Administrative Training and Development: A Comparative Study of East Africa, Zambia, Pakistan, and India. New York: Praeger, 1974.

Taylor, P. L. "Local Government Training in Zambia," Journal of Local Administration Overseas, Vol. 5, No. 1 (January 1966).

Tordoff, William. "The Administration of Development in Zambia," in Collected Seminar Papers on Bureaucratic Change in New States, I. C. S., No. 9 (October 1969 - March 1970).

_____. "Provincial and District Government in Zambia," Journal of Administration Overseas, Vol. 8, No. 3 and 4 (July and October 1968).

_____. "Provincial and Local Government in Zambia," Journal of Administrative Overseas, Vol. 9, No. 1 (January 1970).

Wood, G. "Administrative Training in Zambia," in Schaffer, B. (ed.), Administrative Training and Development. New York: Praeger, 1974.

Constitution, Law and Government: Other

Apthorpe, Raymond, ed. From Tribal Rule to Modern Government. Lusaka: Rhodes-Livingstone Institute, 1959.

Baxter, G. H., and P. W. Jodgens. "The Constitutional Status of the Federation of Rhodesia and Nyasaland," International Affairs (October 1957).

Caplan, G. L. "Barotseland: The Secessionist Challenge to Zambia," Journal of Modern African Studies, Vol. 6, No. 3 (October 1968): pp. 343-360.

_____. The Elites of Barotseland, 1878-1969: A Political History of Zambia's Western Province. Berkeley and Los Angeles: University of California Press, 1970.

Clay, Gervas. "African Urban Advisory Councils in the Northern Rhodesia Copperbelt," Journal of African Administration, Vol. 1 (1949).

Davidson, J. W. The Northern Rhodesian Legislative Council. London: Faber & Faber, 1948.

Gregor, Gordon. "Sea Cadets of Land-Locked Zambia," Horizon, No. 9 (October 1967).

Gupta, Anirudha. "The Zambian National Assembly: Study of an African Legislature," Parliamentary Affairs, Vol. 19, No. 1 (Winter 1965-1966).

Heath, F. M. N. "The Growth of African Councils on the Copperbelt of Northern Rhodesia," Journal of African Administration, Vol. 5 (1953).

Molteno, R. V. "National Security and Institutional Stability," (forthcoming).

_____. The Zambian Community and Its Government. Lusaka: Neczam, 1974.

Peaslee, Amos J. "Constitution of Zambia," Constitution of Nations, I, Africa. The Hague: Martinus Nijhoff, 1965.

Silverman, Philip. Local Elites and the Image of a Nation: The

Incorporation of Barotseland within Zambia. Unpublished Ph. D. thesis, Cornell University, 1968.

Tordoff, William, and Robert Molteno. "Parliament," in Tordoff, W. (ed.), Politics in Zambia. Berkeley: University of California Press, 1974.

Humanism

Graham, Stuart. "Zambia's Humanism: Credo for Survival," The New Africa, Vol. 7, No. 2.

Kandeke, Timothy K., ed. A Systematic Introduction to Zambian Humanism. Lusaka: forthcoming.

Kaunda, Kenneth. A Guide to the Implementation of Humanism. Lusaka: Government Printer, 1967.

_____. Humanism in Zambia. Lusaka: Government Printer, April 1967.

_____. Humanism in Zambia and a Guide to Its Implementation. Lusaka: Government Printer, 1968.

_____. A Humanist in Africa: Letters to Colin Morris from Kenneth Kaunda, President of Zambia. London: Longmans, 1966.

_____. "Ideology and Humanism," Pan-Africa Journal, Vol. 1, No. 1 (Winter 1968).

_____. Ten Thoughts on Humanism. Kitwe: Veritas Corporation, 1970.

Lacy, Creighton. "Christian Humanism in Zambia," Christian Century, No. 89 (February 16, 1972): pp. 191-195.

Meebelo, Henry S. "The Concept of Man-Centeredness in Zambian Humanism," The African Review, Vol. 3, No. 4 (1973).

_____. Main Currents of Zambian Humanist Thought. New York: Oxford University Press, 1973.

Molteno, Robert. "Zambian Humanism: The Way Ahead," The African Review, Vol. 3, No. 4 (1973).

Soremekun, F. "The Challenge of Nation-Building: Neo-Humanism and Politics in Zambia, 1967-1969," Genève-Afrique, Vol. 9, No. 1 (1970): pp. 3-41.

_____. "Kenneth Kaunda's Cosmic Humanism," Genève-Afrique, Vol. 9, No. 2 (1970): pp. 3-30.

Bibliography   388

_____. "Zambia's Cultural Revolution," East Africa Journal
(Nairobi), Vol. 7, No. 5 (May 1970): pp. 26-34.

Zambia, Republic of. "Humanism and Our Foreign Policy," in
Humanism Radio Commentaries Numbers 1-42. Lusaka:
Ministry of Development Planning and National Guidance, 1972.

Zulu, J. B. Zambian Humanism. Lusaka: Neczam, 1970.

Politics and Political Parties

Billing, M. G. "Tribal Rule and Modern Politics in Northern
Rhodesia," African Affairs, Vol. 58, No. 231 (April 1969).

Chaput, Michael, ed. Patterns of Elite Formation and Distribution in Kenya, Senegal, Tanzania, and Zambia. Syracuse:
Syracuse University, Programme of East African Studies,
1968.

Gertzel, Cherry, et al. "Zambia's Final Experience of Inter-
Party Elections: The By-Elections of December, 1971,"
Kronick van Afrika (Leiden), Vol. 12, No. 2 (1972): pp. 57-
77.

Hall, Richard. "Zambia's Search for Political Stability," World
Today, Vol. 25, No. 11 (November 1969): pp. 488-495.

Harries-Jones, Peter. Freedom and Labour: Mobilization and
Political Control on the Zambian Copperbelt. New York:
Schocken Books, 1975.

Molteno, R. V. "Zambia and the One-Party State," East Africa
Journal, Vol. 9, No. 2 (February 1972).

Mtshali, B. Vulindlela. "South Africa and Zambia's 1968 Election," Kronick van Afrika, No. 2 (1970).

"Party Merger in Zambia," Afriscope (Lagos), Vol. 3, No. 9
(September 1973): pp. 19-22.

Pettman, Jan. "Zambia's Second Republic--the Establishment of a
One-Party State," The Journal of Modern African Studies,
Vol. 12, No. 2 (June 1974): pp. 231-244.

Rasmussen, Thomas. "Political Competition and One-Party Dominance in Zambia," Journal of Modern African Studies, Vol. 7,
No. 3 (October 1969): pp. 407-424.

Scarritt, J. R. "Adoption of Political Styles by African Politicians
in the Rhodesias," Midwest Journal of Political Science, Vol.
10, No. 1 (February 1966).

_____. "Elite Values, Ideology and Power in Post-Independence
Zambia," African Studies Review, Vol. 14, No. 1 (April 1971):
pp. 31-54.

_____. "Political Values and the Political Process in Zambia,"
Bulletin, No. 1, Institute for Social Research, University of
Zambia, 1966.

_____. "The Zambian Election--Triumph or Tragedy?" Africa
Today, Vol. 16, No. 1 (February-March 1969).

Scott, Ian, and R. V. Molteno. "The Zambian General Elections,"
Africa Report, Vol. 14, No. 1 (January 1969): pp. 42-47.

Segal, Ronald. Political Africa: A Who's Who of Personalities
and Parties. New York: Praeger, 1961.

Tordoff, William. "Political Crisis in Zambia," Africa Quarterly,
Vol. 10, No. 3 (October-December 1970).

_____, and Ian Scott. "Political Parties: Structures and
Policies," in Tordoff, W. (ed.), Politics in Zambia.
Berkeley: University of California Press, 1974.

Young, R. A. "The 1968 General Elections," in Davies, D. H.
(ed.), Zambia in Maps. London: University of London Press,
1971.

Zambia, Republic of. The Constitution of the United National
Independence Party. Lusaka: Government Printer, 1973.

_____. Report of the National Commission on the Establishment
of a One-Party Participatory Democracy in Zambia. Lusaka:
Government Printer, 1972.

_____. UNIP National Policies for the Next Decade, 1974-1984.
Lusaka: Zambia Information Service, 1974.

Race Relations

Berger, Elena L. Labor, Race and Colonial Rule: The Copperbelt
from 1924 to Independence. Oxford: Clarendon Press, 1974.

Burawoy, Michael. The Colour of Class on the Copper Mines.
Lusaka: University of Zambia Institute for African Studies, 1972.

Clegg, E. Race and Politics: Partnership in the Federation of
Rhodesia and Nyasaland. London: Oxford University Press,
1960.

Dotson, F. and L. O. The Indian Minority of Zambia, Rhodesia
and Malawi. New Haven: Yale University Press, 1968.

Franck, T. M. Race and Nationalism: The Struggle for Power in Rhodesia-Nyasaland. London: Allen & Unwin, 1960.

Gray, J. R. The Two Nations: Aspects of the Development of Race Relations in the Rhodesias and Nyasaland. London: Oxford University Press, 1960.

Rotberg, Robert I. "Race, Relations and Politics in Colonial Zambia: The Elwell Incident," Race, Vol. 7, No. 1 (July 1965).

Foreign Affairs

Anglin, D. G. "Confrontation in Southern Africa: Zambia and Portugal," International Journal, Vol. 25 (1970).

_____. "The Politics of Transit Routes in Land-Locked Southern Africa," in Cervenka, Z. (ed.), Land-Locked Countries of Africa. Uppsala: Scandinavian Institute of African Studies, 1973.

_____. "Reorientation of Zambia's External Relations-Disengagement from Southern Africa and Integration with East Africa: A Transaction Analysis," in Shaw, T. M., and K. A. Heard (eds.), Cooperation and Conflict in Southern Africa: Papers on a Regional Subsystem. London: Longman and Dalhousie University Press, 1975.

_____. "Zambia and Southern African 'Detente'," International Journal, Vol. 30, No. 3 (Summer 1975): pp. 471-503.

_____. "Zambia and the Recognition of Biafra," African Review, Vol. 1, No. 2 (1971).

_____. "Zambia and the Southern African Liberation Movements," in Shaw, T. M. and K. A. Heard, (eds.), Politics of Africa: Development and Dependence. London: Longman and Dalhousie University Press, 1975.

_____. "Zambian Versus Malawian Approaches to Political Change in Southern Africa" in D. S. Chanaiwa (ed.), Profiles of Self-Determination. Northridge: California State University Foundation, 1976.

Ballance, F. Zambia and the East African Community. Syracuse: Syracuse University Program of Eastern African Studies, 1971.

Bone, Marion. "The Foreign Policy of Zambia," in Barston, Ronald P. (ed.), The Other Powers: Studies in the Foreign Policies of Small States. New York: Barnes & Noble, 1973 (pp. 121-53).

Caplan, G. L. "Zambia, Barotseland and the Liberation of Southern Africa," Africa Today, Vol. 15, No. 4 (1969): pp. 13-17.

Delius, Anthony. "Africa's Guerrillas Extend Their Fight," The Reporter, No. 37 (October 5, 1967).

Grundy, Kenneth W. Confrontation and Accommodation in Southern Africa: The Limits of Independence. Berkeley: University of California Press, 1973.

________. "Host Countries and the Southern African Liberation Struggle," Africa Quarterly, Vol. 10, No. 1 (April-June 1970).

Hall, R. The High Price of Principles: Kaunda and the White South. London: Hodder & Stoughton, 1969.

Hill, C. R. "The Botswana-Zambia Boundary Question: A Note of Warning," The Round Table, No. 252 (October 1973): pp. 535-541.

Levin, Nora. "Cooperation Brings a Grassroots Revolution," Africa Report, Vol. 17, No. 4 (April 1972): pp. 15-18.

Martin, Anthony. Minding Their Own Business: Zambia's Struggle Against Western Control. London: Hutchinson, 1972.

McKay, V. P. "The Propaganda Battle for Zambia," Africa Today, Vol. 18, No. 2 (April 1971): pp. 18-26.

Molteno, R. V. Africa and South Africa--The Implications of South Africa's "Outward-Looking" Policy. London: Africa Bureau, 1971.

________. "South Africa's Forward Policy in Africa," Round Table, No. 243 (July 1971).

Mtshali, B. Vulindlela. "Zambia and the White South," in Cervenka, Zdenek (ed.), Land-Locked Countries of South Africa. Uppsala: Scandinavian Institute of African Studies, 1973.

________. "Zambia's Foreign Policy," Current History, Vol. 58, No. 343 (March 1970).

________. "Zambia's Foreign Policy Problems," African Social Research, No. 11 (June 1971): pp. 50-54.

Mujaya, M. S. Zambia's Foreign Policy: A Study. Dar es Salaam: University of Dar es Salaam Political Science Paper No. 7, 1970.

Mwaanga, Vernon. "U. S. -African Relations: The View from Zambia," Africa Report, Vol. 19, No. 5 (September-October 1974): pp. 37-39.

________. "Zambia's Foreign Policy: To Play a Full Part in the Affairs of the Human Family," Enterprise, No. 3 (1974): pp. 56-59.

_____. "Zambia's Policy Toward Southern Africa," in Potholm, C. P., and R. Dale (eds.), Southern Africa in Perspective: Essays in Regional Politics. New York: Free Press, 1972.

Nolutshungu, Sam C. South Africa in Africa: A Study of Ideology and Foreign Policy. New York: Africana Publishing Co., 1975.

Oudes, Bruce. "Kaunda's Diplomatic Offensive," Africa Report, Vol. 20, No. 3 (May-June 1975): pp. 41-45.

Pettmann, Jan. Zambia: Security and Conflict. New York: St. Martin's Press, 1974.

Shamuyarira, Nathan M. "The Lusaka Manifesto," East Africa Journal, (November 1969).

Shaw, T. M. Dependence and Underdevelopment: The Development and Foreign Policies of Zambia. Athens, Ohio: Ohio University Centre for International Studies, 1976.

_____. "The Foreign Policy of Zambia," The Journal of Modern African Studies, Vol. 14, No. 1 (March 1976): pp. 79-105.

_____. "The Foreign Policy of Zambia: An Events Analysis of a New State," Canadian Political Science Association. Edmonton: 1975.

_____. "The Foreign Policy System of Zambia," African Studies Review, Vol. 19, No. 1 (April 1976): pp. 31-66.

_____. "Regional Cooperation and Conflict in Africa," International Journal, Vol. 30, No. 4 (Autumn 1975): pp. 671-688.

_____. "Southern Africa: Cooperation and Conflict in an International Sub-System," The Journal of Modern African Studies, Vol. 12, No. 4 (December 1974): pp. 633-655.

University of Zambia, Faculty of Humanities and Social Studies. Zambia and the World: Essays on Problems Relating to Zambia's Foreign Policy. Lusaka: 1970.

6. SCIENTIFIC

Geography

Bond, G. "The Origin of the Victoria Falls," in Fagan, B. M. (ed.), The Victoria Falls: A Handbook to the Victoria Falls, the Batoka Gorges and Part of the Upper Zambezi Valley. Livingstone Commission for the Preservation of Natural and Historical Monuments and Relics, Northern Rhodesia, 1964.

Bradshaw, Benjamin F. "Notes on the Chobe River, South Central Africa," Proceedings of the Royal Geographical Society, Vol. III, 1881.

MacDonald, John F. Zambesi River. London: Macmillan & Co., 1955.

Geology

Cahen, L., and J. Lepersonne. "Equivalence entre le système du Kalahari du Congo Belge et les Kalahari beds d'Afrique australe," Mem. Soc. Belge Geol., Vol. 8, (1952).

Dixey, F. "The Geology of the Upper Zambezi Valley," in Clark, J. Desmond, The Stone Age Cultures of Northern Rhodesia. Cape Town: The South African Archaeological Society, 1950.

Gair, H. S. The Karroo System and Coal Resources of the Gwembe District, North-East Section. Lusaka: Government Printer, 1959.

Garlick, W. G. "Geomorphology," The Geology of the Northern Rhodesian Copperbelt (ed. F. Mendelsohn). London: Macdonald, 1961, pp. 11-16.

_____. "The Sygnetic Theory," The Geology of the Northern Rhodesian Copperbelt (ed. F. Mendelsohn). London: Macdonald, 1961, pp. 146-165.

Hitchon, Brian. The Geology of the Kariba Area. Lusaka: Geological Survey Department, Report No. 3, 1958.

Mendelsohn, F., ed. The Geology of the Northern Rhodesian Copperbelt. London: Macdonald, 1961.

Pelletier, R. A. Mineral Resources of South-Central Africa. Cape Town: Oxford University Press, 1964.

Phillips, K. A. The Geology and Metalliferous Deposits of the Luiri Hill Area (Mumbwa District): Explanation of Degree Sheet 1527, N.W. Quarter. Lusaka: Northern Rhodesia, Department of Geological Survey, Report No. 4, 1958.

Reeve, W. H. The Geology and Mineral Resources of Northern Rhodesia, Vol. 1. Lusaka: Government Printer, 1963.

Taverner-Smith, R. The Karroo System and Coal Resources of the Gwembe District, South-West Section. Lusaka: Government Printer, 1960.

Bibliography   394

Medicine

Doell, E. W. Hospital in the Bush. London: Christopher Johnson, 1957.

Gelfand, M. Northern Rhodesia in the Days of the Charter: A Medical and Social Study, 1878-1924. Oxford: Basil Blackwell, 1961.

Griffith, P. G. "Leprosy in Northern Rhodesia," Science and Medicine in Central Africa. London: Pergamon Press, 1965.

Leeson, Joyce. "Traditional Medicines: Still Plenty to Offer," Africa Report, Vol. 15, No. 7 (October 1970): pp. 24-25.

Phillips, C. M. "Problems of Blindness in Northern Rhodesia," Science and Medicine in Central Africa. London: Pergamon Press, 1965.

Pollock, Norman H., Jr. The Struggle Against Sleeping Sickness in Nyasaland and Northern Rhodesia, 1900-1922. Athens, Ohio: Center for International Studies, Ohio University, 1969.

Turner, V. W. Lunda Medicine and the Treatment of Disease. Rhodes-Livingstone Museum Occasional Papers, No. 15, 1964.

_____. "A Ndembu Doctor in Practice," Magic, Faith and Healing. Glencoe: The Free Press, 1964.

Natural Science and Zoology

Ansell, W. F. H. The Mammals of Northern Rhodesia. Lusaka: Government Printer, 1960.

Fairweather, W. G. Northern Rhodesia: Meterological Report and Statistical Survey. London: Waterlow and Sons, 1925.

Fanshawe, D. B. Fifty Common Trees of Northern Rhodesia. Lusaka: Government Printer, 1962.

Horscroft, F. D. M. "Vegetation," in Mendelsohn, F. (ed.), The Geology of the Northern Rhodesian Copperbelt. London: Macdonald, 1961.

Jackson, P. B. N. Fishes of Northern Rhodesia. Lusaka: Government Printer, 1961.

Lagus, Charles. Operation Noah. London: William Kimber, 1960.

Trapnell, C. G., and I. Langdale-Brown. "The Natural Vegetation of East Africa," in Russell, E. W. (ed.), The Natural Resources of East Africa. Nairobi: East African Literature Bureau, 1962.

_____, J. D. Martin, and W. Allan. Vegetation-Soil Map of
Northern Rhodesia. Lusaka: Government Printer, 1947.

7. SOCIAL

Anthropology and Ethnology: The Barotse

Bertrand, Alfred. The Kingdom of the Barotsi, Upper Zambesia.
London: T. Fisher Unwin, 1898.

Burles, R. S. "The Katengo Council Elections," The Journal of
African Administration, Vol. 4, 1952.

Caplan, G. L. The Elites of Barotseland, 1878-1969: A Political
History of Zambia's Western Province. Berkeley and Los
Angeles: University of California Press, 1970.

Gibbons, A. St. "Marotseland and the Tribes of the Upper Zambesi," Proceedings of the Royal Colonial Institute, No. 29,
1897-1898.

Glennie, A. F. B. "The Barotse System of Government," The
Journal of African Administration, Vol. 4, No. 1 (January
1952).

Gluckman, Max. Administrative Organization of the Barotse Native
Authorities, with a Plan for Reforming Them. Rhodes-Livingstone Institute Communication, No. 1 (1943).

_____. "African Land Tenure," Rhodes-Livingstone Journal,
Vol. 3 (June 1945).

_____. Economy of the Central Barotse Plain. Rhodes-Living-
stone Institute Papers, No. 7 (1941).

_____. Essays on Lozi Land and Royal Property. Northern
Rhodesia: Rhodes-Livingstone Papers, No. 10 (1943).

_____. The Ideas of Barotse Jurisprudence. Atlantic Highlands,
N.J.: Humanities Press, 1965.

_____. The Judicial Process Among the Barotse of Northern
Rhodesia. Glencoe: Free Press, 1955.

_____. "The Lozi of Barotseland in North-Western Rhodesia,"
in Colson, E., and M. Gluckman (eds.), Seven Tribes of
British Central Africa. Manchester: Manchester University
Press, 1951.

_____. "Technical Vocabulary of Barotse Jurisprudence,"
American Anthropologist, October 1959.

Hudson, R. S., and H. K. Prescot. "The Election of a 'Ngambela' in Barotseland," Man, Vol. 24, No. 103 (1924).

Jalla, Adolphe. Lewanika, Roi des Ba-Rotsi. Geneva: 1902.

_____. Litaba za Sicaba sa Malozi. Capetown: Oxford University Press, 1921; rev. in 1959.

_____. The Story of the Barotse Nation. Lusaka: Lusaka Publications Bureau, 1961.

Jones, Stanley. "Mankoya in 1925 to 1927," Northern Rhodesia Journal, Vol. 4, No. 2 (1959).

Jordan, E. K. "Mongu in 1908," Northern Rhodesia Journal, Vol. 4, No. 2 (1959).

Mackintosh, C. W. Lewanika Paramount Chief of the Barotse. London: Lutterworth Press, 1942.

_____. Yeta III Paramount Chief of the Barotse (Northern Rhodesia): A Sketch of His Life. London: Pickering & Inglis, 1937.

Palmer, R. H. Lewanika's Country. Canada: Privately Printed, 1955.

Report of the Committee Appointed to Inquire into the Constitution of the Barotse Native Government Together with the Comments Thereon of the National Council (Rawlins Committee), Lusaka: 1957.

Sikota. "Notes--Lewanika in England, 1902," Northern Rhodesia Journal, Vol. 2 (1953).

Stokes, Eric. "Barotseland: The Survival of an African State," in Stokes, E., and Brown (eds.), The Zambesian Past. Manchester: Manchester University Press, 1966.

Turner, V. W. The Lozi Peoples of North-Western Rhodesia. London: International African Institute, 1952.

Watt, Nigel. "Lewanika's Visit to Edinburgh," Northern Rhodesia Journal, Vol. 2, No. 1 (1953).

Anthropology and Ethnology: The Bemba

Brelsford, W. V. Aspects of Bemba Chieftainship. Rhodes-Livingstone, Communication No. 2, 1944.

_____. "The Bemba Trident," NADA (Salisbury), No. 13 (1935): pp. 18-21.

_____. "Notes on Some Northern Rhodesian Bowstands," Man,
No. 40 (1940): pp. 39-40.

Gluckman, M. "Succession and Civil War Among the Bemba: An
Exercise in Anthropological Theory," Rhodes-Livingstone
Journal, No. 16, 1954.

Jordan, E. Knowles. "Chinsali in 1920-1922," The Northern
Rhodesia Journal, Vol. 5, No. 6 (1964).

Labrecque, E. "Le tribu des Babemba: I. Les origines des
Babemba," Anthropos, No. 28 (1933).

Makungo, I. F. "Description of Some Traditional Bemba Customs,"
Bulletin, No. 1 (1966).

Mpashi, S. A. Abapatili Bafika Ku Babemba. Lusaka: Oxford
University Press, 1966.

Richards, A. I. "The Bemba of North-Eastern Rhodesia," Seven
Tribes of British Central Africa. London: Oxford University
Press, 1951.

_____. "Bow-Stand or Trident?" Man, No. 35 (1935): pp.
30-32.

_____. Chisungu, A Girl's Initiation Ceremony Among the
Bemba of Northern Rhodesia. New York: Grove Press, 1956.

_____. Hunger and Work in a Savage Tribe. Glencoe: Free
Press, 1948.

_____. Land, Labour and Diet in Northern Rhodesia: An
Economic Study of the Bemba Tribe. London: Oxford University Press, 1939.

_____. "The Life of Bwembya, a Native of Northern Rhodesia,"
in Perham, M., (ed.), Ten Africans. London: Faber &
Faber, 1936.

_____. "A Modern Movement of Witchfinders," Africa, Vol. 8,
No. 3 (October 1935).

_____. "The Political System of the Bemba Tribe--North-
Eastern Rhodesia," in Fortes, M. and E. E. Evans-Pritchard,
(eds.), African Political Systems. London: Oxford University
Press, 1940.

_____. "Tribal Government in Transition: The Bemba of
North-Eastern Rhodesia," Supplement to the Journal of the
Royal African Society, Vol. 34 (1935).

Whiteley, Wilfred. "Bemba and Related People of Northern

Rhodesia," Ethnographic Survey of Africa, East Central Africa, Part II. London: International African Institute, 1951.

Anthropology and Ethnology: Other Groups (Specific)

Apthorpe, Raymond. "Northern Rhodesia: Clanship, Chieftainship, and Nsenga Political Adaptation," From Tribal Rule to Modern Government. Lusaka: Rhodes-Livingstone Institute, 1959.

_____. "Problems of African Political History: The Nsenga of Northern Rhodesia," Rhodes-Livingstone Journal, Vol. 28 (1960): pp. 47-67.

Barnes, J. A. "The Fort Jameson Ngoni," in Colson, Elizabeth, and Max Gluckman (eds.), Seven Tribes of British Central Africa. London: Oxford University Press, 1951.

_____. "History in a Changing Society," Rhodes-Livingstone Institute Journal, Vol. 11 (1951).

_____. Politics in a Changing Society. London: Oxford University Press, 1954.

Bond, G. C. "Kinship and Conflict in a Yombe Village," Africa, Vol. 52, No. 4 (October 1972).

_____. The Politics of Change in a Zambian Community. Chicago: The University of Chicago Press, 1976.

Chiwale, J. C. Royal Praises and Praise-names of the Lunda-Kazembe of Northern Rhodesia: Their Meaning and Historical Background, Central Bantu Historical Texts No. 3, Rhodes-Livingstone Institute Communication, No. 25 (1962).

Clark, J. Desmond. "The Bushmen Hunters of the Barotse Forests," Northern Rhodesia Journal, Vol. 1, No. 3 (1950).

Colson, Elizabeth. "Ancestral Spirits and Social Structure among the Plateau Tonga," International Archives of Ethnography, Vol. 47 (1954): pp. 21-68.

_____. "Every Day Life Among the Cattle-Keeping Plateau Tonga," Rhodes-Livingstone Museum Papers, N.S., No. 9 (1953).

_____. Marriage and the Family Among the Plateau Tonga of Northern Rhodesia. Manchester: Manchester University Press, 1958.

_____. "Marriage and the Family Among the Plateau Tonga of Northern Rhodesia," Rhodes-Livingstone Journal, No. 1, (1958).

_____. "The Plateau Tonga of Northern Rhodesia," in Colson, Elizabeth, and Max Gluckman, (eds.), Seven Tribes of British Central Africa. London: Oxford University Press, 1951.

Cunnison, I. "Headmanship and the Ritual of Luapula Villages," Africa, No. 26 (1956): pp. 2-16.

_____, ed. and trans. Historical Traditions of the Eastern Lunda, by Mwata Kazembe XIV. Rhodes-Livingstone Institute, No. 23, 1962.

_____. Kinship and Local Organization on the Luapula: A Preliminary Account of Some Aspects of Luapula Organization. Rhodes-Livingstone Institute, 1950.

_____. The Luapula Peoples of Northern Rhodesia. Manchester: Manchester University Press, 1959.

_____. "Perpetual Kinship: A Political Institution of the Luapula People," Rhodes-Livingstone Journal, No. 20 (1956).

Doke, Clement M. The Lambas of Northern Rhodesia: A Study of Their Customs and Beliefs. London: Harrap, 1931.

Gluckman, Max. "Zambesi River Kingdom," Libertas, Vol. 5 (July 1945).

Ikacana, N. S. Litaba za Makwangwa (Traditions of the Kwangwa). Northern Rhodesia Publications Bureau, 1964.

Jalla, Louis. Sur les Rives du Zambeze: Notes ethnographiques. Paris: Société des missions évangéliques, 1928.

Jaspan, M. A. "The Ila-Tonga Peoples of North-Western Rhodesia," Ethnographic Survey of Africa, West Central Africa, Part 4. London: International African Institute, 1953.

Kay, George. Chief Kalaba's Village. Manchester: Manchester University Press, 1964.

Kazembe XIV. "Historical Traditions of the Eastern Lunda," Central Bantu Historical Texts--II. Lusaka: 1962. Translated by Ian Cunnison.

Krige, E. J., and J. D. The Realm of a Rain-Queen: A Study of the Pattern of Lovedu Society. London: Oxford University Press, 1943.

Marwick, M. G. "History and Tradition in East Central Africa Through the Eyes of the Northern Rhodesian Cewa," Journal of African History, Vol. 4, No. 3 (1963): pp. 375-390.

_____. Sorcery in Its Social Setting: A Study of the Northern

Rhodesian Cewa. Manchester: Manchester University Press, 1965.

McCulloch, M. The Lunda, Luena and Related Tribes of North Western Rhodesia and Adjoining Territories. London: International African Institute, 1951.

Richardson, E. M. Aushi Village Structure in the Fort Rosebery District of Northern Rhodesia. (Rhodes-Livingstone Communication, No. 13). Lusaka: Rhodes-Livingstone Institute, 1959.

Slaski, J. "Peoples of the Lower Luapula Valley," Ethnographic Survey of Africa, East Central Africa, Part II. London: International African Institute, 1951.

Smith, E. W., and A. M. Dale. The Ila-Speaking People of Northern Rhodesia, 2 vols. New York: Macmillan, 1920.

Stefaniszyn, Bronislaw. Social and Ritual Life of the Ambo of Northern Rhodesia. London: Oxford University Press, 1964.

Tuden, Arthur. "Ila Slavery," Rhodes-Livingstone Journal, No. 24 (December 1958).

Turner, Victor W. The Forest of Symbols: Aspects of Ndembu Ritual. New York: Cornell University Press, 1967.

_____. "A Lunda Love-Story and Its Consequences," Rhodes-Livingstone Journal, No. 19 (1955): pp. 1-26.

_____. Lunda Rites and Ceremonies. Livingstone: Rhodes-Livingstone Museum, 1953.

_____. "A Ndembu Doctor in Practice," Magic, Faith and Healing. Glencoe: The Free Press, 1964.

_____. Revelation and Divination in Ndembu Ritual. Ithaca, New York: Cornell University Press, 1975.

_____. Schism and Continuity in an African (Ndembu) Society. Manchester: Manchester University Press, 1957.

_____. "Symbols in Ndembu Ritual," Closed Systems and Open Minds. Chicago: Aldine, 1964.

Van Velsen, Jaap. "Labour Migration as a Positive Factor in the Continuity of Tonga Tribal Society," Economic Development and Cultural Change, Vol. 8 (1960).

Watson, W. Tribal Cohesion in a Money Economy: A Study of the Mambwe People of Northern Rhodesia. Lusaka: Manchester University Press for Rhodes-Livingstone Institute, 1958.

White, C. M. N. Elements in Luvale Beliefs and Rituals. Rhodes-
   Livingstone Institute Paper, No. 32 (1961).

_____. "Luvale Political Organization and the Luvale Lineage,"
   Tribal Rule to Modern Government. Lusaka: Rhodes-Livingstone Institute, 1959.

_____. The Material Culture of the Lunda-Luvale Peoples.
   Rhodes-Livingstone Museum Occasional Papers, No. 3 (1948).

_____. An Outline of Luvale Social and Political Organization.
   (Rhodes-Livingstone Papers, No. 30). Manchester: Manchester
   University Press for the Rhodes-Livingstone Institute, 1960.

Winterbottom, J. M. "Outline Histories of Two Northern Rhodesian
   Tribes," Rhodes-Livingstone Journal, No. 9 (1950).

Anthropology and Ethnology: Groups (General)

Brelsford, W. V. The Tribes of Northern Rhodesia. Lusaka:
   Government Printer, 1956.

_____. The Tribes of Zambia. (2nd ed.) Lusaka: Govern-
   ment Printer, 1965.

Colson, E., and Max Gluckman, eds. Seven Tribes of British
   Central Africa. Lusaka: Manchester University Press for
   Rhodes-Livingstone Institute, 1951.

Coxhead, J. C. The Native Tribes of Northern Rhodesia. Royal
   Anthropological Institute, Occasional Papers, No. 5. London:
   (1914).

Fortes, M., and E. E. Evans-Pritchard, eds. African Political
   Systems. London: Oxford University Press, 1940.

Thomson, J. Moffat. Memorandum on the Native Tribes and Tribal
   Areas of Northern Rhodesia. Lusaka: Government Printer,
   1934.

Vansina, Jan. Kingdoms of the Savanna. Madison: University of
   Wisconsin, 1966.

White, C. M. N. "The Ethnohistory of the Upper Zambesi,"
   African Studies, Vol. 21, No. 1 (1962): pp. 10-27.

Anthropology and Ethnology: Miscellaneous

Gluckman, Max. "Anthropological Problems Arising Out of the
   African Industrial Revolution," in Southall, A. W. (ed.),

Social Change in Modern Africa. London: Oxford University Press, 1961.

_____. Custom and Conflict in Africa. Oxford: Basil Blackwell, 1955.

_____. Order and Rebellion in Tribal Africa. London: Cohen & West, 1963.

_____. Politics, Law and Ritual in Tribal Society: Some Problems in Social Anthropology. Oxford: Oxford University Press, 1965.

Marks, Stuart A. Large Mammals and a Brave People: Subsistence Hunters in Zambia. Seattle: University of Washington Press, 1976.

Mitchell, J. Clyde (with M. Gluckman and J. A. Barnes). "The Village Headman in British Central Africa," Africa, Vol. 19, No. 2 (April 1949).

Richards, Audrey I. "Motherright among the Central Bantu," Essays Presented to C. G. Seligman, (eds., E. E. Evans-Pritchard, R. Fitch, B. Malinowski, and I. Schapera). London: Keegan Paul, 1933.

_____. "The Village Census in the Study of Culture Contacts," Methods of Study of Culture Contacts in Africa, International Institute of African Languages and Cultures, Memorandum XV. New York: Oxford University Press, 1958.

Shaw, Mabel. Dawn in Africa: Stories of Girl Life. London: Edinburgh House, 1932.

Turner, Victor W. The Drums of Affliction. London: Oxford University Press, 1968.

White, C. M. N. Witchcraft, Divination and Magic. Lusaka: Northern Rhodesia Government, 1947.

Education

Ahmed, Mushtag. "Functional Literacy Experimental Pilot Project in Zambia: Reasons for Drop-Out," Indian Journal of Adult Education, Vol. 33, No. 8 (August 1972): pp. 3-5.

Angi, C., and T. Coombe. "Primary Schools Leavers and Youth Programmes in Zambia," Education in Eastern Africa, No. 1 (1970).

Bullington, Robert Adrian. "African Education in Northern Rhodesia," Science Education, No. 47 (October 1964).

Careccio, J. "Mathematical Heritage of Zambia," Arithmetic
Teachers, Vol. 17, No. 5 (May 1970): pp. 391-395.

Coombe, Trevor. "The Origins of Secondary Education in Zambia,
Part II: Anatomy of a Decision, 1934-1936," African Social
Research (formerly Rhodes-Livingstone Journal), No. 4 (De-
cember 1967).

_____. "The Origins of Secondary Education in Zambia, Part
III: Anatomy of a Decision, 1937-1939," African Social Research, No. 5 (June 1968).

Etheredge, D. A. "The Role of Education in Economic Development: The Example of Zambia," Journal of Administration
Overseas, Vol. 6, No. 4 (October 1967).

Fox, Frederic. 14 Africans vs. One American. New York:
Macmillan, 1962.

Jones, Thomas Jesse. Education in East Africa. New York:
Phelps-Stokes Fund, circ. 1924.

Kuntz, Marthe. "Education indigene sur le Haut-Zambesi," Le
Monde Non Chrétien, Primiere série, No. 3 (1932).

Macdonald, Roderick. "Reflections on Education in Central
Africa," Africa Report, Vol. 8, No. 4 (April 1963): p. 10.

Molteno, R. V. "Our University and Our Community," Jewel of
Africa, Vol. 2, No. 3 and 4 (1970).

Mortimer, M. "History of the Barotse National School: 1907 to
1957," The Northern Rhodesia Journal, Vol. 3, No. 4 (1957).

Mwanakatwe, J. M. The Growth of Education in Zambia Since
Independence. Lusaka: Oxford University Press, 1968.

_____. "The Progress of Education in Zambia Since Indepen-
dence," Optima, No. 17 (December 1967).

Roan Antelope Copper Mines, Ltd. Notes on African Education.
March 3, 1959.

Robertson, James S. "Education in Zambia," in Rose, B. (ed.),
Education in Southern Africa. London: Collier Macmillan,
1970.

Shaw, Mabel. God's Candlelights: An Educational Venture in
Northern Rhodesia. London: Livingstone Press, 1941.

Wincott, N. E. "Education and the Development of Urban Society
in Zambia," in Pachai, B. (ed.), Malawi Past and Present.
University of Manchester, 1967.

Religion and Missions: François Coillard

Addison, James Thayer. <u>François Coillard</u>. Hartford, Conn.:
   1924.

Coillard, François. <u>A Lealuyi: Lettres récentes de Coillard</u>.
   Paris: 1892.

————————. <u>La Mission au Zambeze</u>. Paris: 1880.

————————. <u>On the Threshold of Central Africa</u>. London: Hodder
   and Stoughton, 1897.

————————. <u>Sur le Haut-Zambeze voyages et travaux de mission</u>.
   Paris: Berger-Levrault, 1898.

————————. <u>The Valley of the Upper Zambezi</u> (two letters).
   London: 1898.

————————. <u>Zambesia: Work among the Barotse</u>. Glasgow: 1894.

Dieterlen, H. <u>François Coillard</u>. Paris: Société des Missions
   Evangéliques, 1921.

Favre, Edward. <u>François Coillard 1834-1904</u>, 3 vols. Paris:
   Société des Missions Evangéliques, 1908.

Mackintosh, C. W. <u>Coillard of the Zambezi</u>. London: T. Fisher
   and Unwin, 1907.

Shillito, Edward. <u>François Coillard, a Wayfaring Man</u>. London:
   SCM, 1923.

Religion and Missions: Frederick S. Arnot

Arnot, F. S. <u>From Natal to the Upper Zambezi: First Year
   among the Barotse</u>. Glasgow: The Publishing Office, 1883.

————————. <u>Garenganze, or Seven Years Pioneer Mission Work in
   Central Africa</u>. London: J. E. Hawkins, 1889.

————————. <u>Garanganze West and East</u>. Glasgow: Pickering and
   Inglis, 1902.

————————. <u>Missionary Travels in Central Africa</u>. Bath: Office
   of "Echoes of Service," 1914.

Baker, Ernest. <u>The Life and Explorations of F. S. Arnot</u>. London: Seeley, Service and Co., 1921.

Ellis, J. J. <u>Fred Stanley Arnot: Missionary, Explorer, Bene-
   factor</u>. London: Pickering and Inglis, 192?

Religion and Missions: Other Missionaries and General Religion

Baeta, C. G., ed. Christianity in Tropical Africa: Studies Presented and Discussed at the Seventh International African Seminar, University of Ghana, April, 1965. London: Oxford University Press, 1968.

Baldwin, A. A Missionary Outpost in Central Africa (The Story of the Baila Mission). London: W. A. Hammond, 1914.

_____. Rev. Henry Buckenham, Pioneer Missionary. London: Joseph Johnson, 1920.

Bloom, A. G. The History of the Universities' Mission to Central Africa, Vol. III, 1933-1957. London: Universities' Mission to Central Africa, 1962.

Bolink, P. Towards Church Unity in Zambia: A Study of Missionary Cooperation and Church-Union Efforts in Central Africa. Sneek: T. Wever-Franeker, 1967.

Chapman, William. A Pathfinder in South Central Africa: A Story of Pioneer Missionary Work and Adventure. London: W. A. Hammond, 1909.

Colson, Elizabeth. "Converts and Tradition: The Impact of Christianity on Valley Tonga Religion," Southwestern Journal of Anthropology, Vol. 26, No. 2 (Summer 1970): pp. 143-156.

Garvey, Brian. "Bemba Chiefs and Catholic Missions, 1898-1935," Journal of African History, Vol. 18, No. 3 (1977): pp. 411-426.

Groves, C. P. The Planting of Christianity in Africa, 4 vols. London: Lutterworth Press, 1948-1958.

Grubb, Norman R. C. T. Studd, Athlete and Pioneer. Grand Rapids, Mich.: Zondervan, 1937.

Hooker, J. R. "Witnesses and Watchtower in the Rhodesias and Nyasaland," Journal of African History, Vol. 6, No. 1 (1965): pp. 91-106.

Howell, A. E. Bishop Dupont: King of the Brigands. Franklin, Pa.: News-Herald Printing Co., 1949.

Jacottet, E. Contes et traditions du Haut-Zambeze. Paris: E. Lechevalier, 1895.

Johnson, Walton. Worship and Freedom: A Black American Church in Zambia. London: International African Institute, 1977.

Kerswell, Kate L. Romance and Reality of Missionary Life in Northern Rhodesia. London: W. A. Hammond, 1913.

MacConnachie, J. An Artisan Missionary on the Zambesi: Being the Life Story of William Thomson Waddell. Edinburgh: Oliphant, Anderson & Ferrier, 1910.

Mackintosh, C. W. Some Pioneer Missions of Northern Rhodesia and Nyasaland. Livingstone: Rhodes-Livingstone Museum, 1950.

Macqueen, James. News from Barotseland, 1898-1916. Magazine of the Paris Evangelical Missionary Society.

Merle, Davis, J., et al. Modern Industry and the African: An Enquiry into the Effect of the Copper Mines of Central Africa Upon Native Society and the Work of Christian Missions. London: Macmillan, 1933.

Mills, Dora S. Is It Worth While? London: Universities' Mission to Central Africa, 1912.

Morrill, Leslie, and Madge Haines. Livingstone: Trail Blazer for God. Pacific Press Publishing Association, 1959.

Morris, Colin. The Hour After Midnight: A Missionary's Experiences of the Racial and Political Struggle in Northern Rhodesia. London: Longmans, 1961.

Mushindo, Paul. The Life of a Zambian Evangelist: The Reminiscences of Rev. Paul B. Mushindo. Lusaka: University of Zambia, Institute for African Studies, 1973.

Rotberg, R. I. Christian Missions and the Creation of Northern Rhodesia, 1880-1924. Princeton: Princeton University Press, 1965.

_____. "The Missionary Factor in the Occupation of Trans-Zambezia," The Northern Rhodesia Journal, Vol. 5, No. 4 (1964).

Shepperson, G. "Church and Sect in Central Africa," The Rhodes-Livingstone Journal, No. 33 (1963).

_____. "The Politics of African Church Separatist Movements in British Central Africa, 1892-1916," Africa, Vol. 24, No. 3 (1954).

Smith, Edwin William. The Blessed Missionaries. Cape Town: Oxford University Press, 1950.

_____. Great Lion of Bechuanaland: The Life and Times of Roger Price, Missionary. London: Independent Press, 1957.

_____. The Way of the White Fields in Rhodesia. London: World Dominion Press, 1928.

Smith, Julia A. Sunshine and Shade in Central Africa. London: Edwin Dalton, 1908.

Stevenson, W. C. Year of Doom, 1975: The Story of Jehovah's Witnesses. London: Hutchinson, 1967.

Stone, W. Vernon. "The Livingstone Mission to the Bemba," The Bulletin of the Society for African Church History, Vol. 2, No. 4 (1968).

Tanguy, Francois. Imilandu Ya Babemba. Lusaka: Oxford University Press, 1966.

_____. "Kayambi: The First White Fathers' Mission in Northern Rhodesia" (Trans. Clifford Green), The Northern Rhodesia Journal, Vol. 2, No. 4 (1954).

Taylor, Rev. H. J. Cape Town to Kafue. London: W. A. Hammond, Holborn Hall, 1915.

_____, and Dorothea Lehmann. Christians of the Copperbelt: The Growth of the Church in Northern Rhodesia. London: SCM Press, 1961.

Temple, Merfyn M. African Angelus. London: Cargate Press, 1950.

_____. Rain on the Earth: Scenes of the Church in Northern Rhodesia. London: Cargate Press, 1956.

Wilson, George Herbert. The History of the Universities' Mission to Central Africa. Westminster: U. M. C. A., 1936.

See also citations under Part 4, HISTORIC: National Politics-- Religion and Nationalism; Contact with Europeans: Dr. Livingstone.

Sociology: Urbanization

Epstein, A. L. "The Network and Urban Social Organization," Rhodes-Livingstone Journal, No. 29 (1961).

Gluckman, Max. "From Tribe to Town," Nation (Sydney, Australia), (September 24, 1960).

Heisler, Helmut. "Creation of a Stabilized Urban Society; A Turning Point in the Development of Northern Rhodesia/Zambia," African Affairs (London), Vol. 70, No. 274 (April 1971): pp. 125-145.

Bibliography   408

_____. Urbanization and the Government of Migration. New
York: St. Martin's Press, 1974.

Mitchell, J. Clyde. African Urbanization in Ndola and Luanshya.
Rhodes-Livingstone Communication No. 6, Lusaka (1954).

_____. "Occupational Prestige and Social Status among Urban
Africans in Northern Rhodesia," in Van den Berghe, P. L.
(ed.), Africa, San Francisco: Chandler Publishing Co., 1965.

_____. "Power and Prestige among Africans in Northern
Rhodesia: An Experiment," Proceedings and Transactions of
the Rhodesian Scientific Association, No. 45, 1957.

_____, ed. Social Networks in Urban Situations: Analyses
of Personal Relationships in Central African Towns. Manchester: Social Research Institute, University of Zambia, 1969.

_____, and A. L. Epstein. "Occupational Prestige and Social
Status among Urban Africans in Northern Rhodesia," Africa,
Vol. 29, No. 1 (January 1959).

Mlenga, Kelvin. "Rural-Urban Migration--A Perennial Problem,"
Horizon, Vol. 9 (December 1967).

Ohadike, Patrick O. "The Nature and Extent of Urbanization in
Zambia," Journal of African and Asian Studies, Vol. 4, No. 2
(April 1969): pp. 107-121.

Parkin, David, ed. Town and Country in Central and Eastern
Africa. Lusaka: International African Institute, 1976.

Powdermaker, H. Copper Town. New York: Harper and Row,
1962.

Read, Margaret. "Migrant Labour and Its Effect on Tribal Life,"
International Labour Review, Vol. 45 (July 1942).

Simmance, Alan J. F. Urbanization in Zambia. New York: Ford
Foundation, 1972.

Wilson, Godfrey. An Essay on the Economics of Detribalization
in Northern Rhodesia, Part I. Rhodes-Livingstone Papers,
No. 5 (1941) and Part II, Paper No. 6 (1942).

Sociology: Marriage

Barnes, J. A. Marriage in a Changing Society. Rhodes-Livingstone Papers, Rhodes-Livingstone Institute, No. 20 (1951).

_____. "Measures of Divorce Frequency in Simple Societies,"
Journal of the Royal Anthropological Institute, No. 79 (1949).

Epstein, A. L. "Divorce, Law and Stability of Marriage among
the Lunda of Kazembe," Rhodes-Livingstone Journal, No. 14
(1954).

Gluckman, Max. "Kinship and Marriage among the Lozi of
Northern Rhodesia and the Zulu in Natal," in Radcliffe-Brown,
A. R., and C. D. Forde (eds.), African Systems of Kinship
and Marriage. London: Oxford University Press, 1950.

Mitchell, J. Clyde. "Aspects of African Marriage on the Copperbelt of Northern Rhodesia," Rhodes-Livingstone Journal, No.
22 (September 1957).

Ohadike, Patrick O. "Aspects of Domesticity and Family Relationship: A Survey Study of the Family-Household in Zambia,"
Journal of Asian and African Studies, Vol. 6, Nos. 3-4 (July
and October 1971).

Phillips, Arthur, ed. "Marriage Laws in Africa," Survey of
African Marriage and Social Change. London: Oxford University Press, 1953.

Richards, Audrey I. Bemba Marriage and Present Economic Conditions, Rhodes-Livingstone Papers No. 4 (1940).

_____. "Variations in Family Structure among the Central
Bantu," in Radcliffe-Brown, A. R., and C. D. Forde (eds.),
African Systems of Kinship and Marriage. London: Oxford
University Press, 1950.

Sociology: Other

Barnes, J. A. "The Material Culture of the Fort Jameson Ngoni,"
Occasional Papers No. 1. Livingstone: Rhodes-Livingstone
Museum.

_____. "The Perception of History in a Plural Society: A
Study of an Ngoni Group in Northern Rhodesia," Human Relations, No. 4 (1951): pp. 295-303.

_____. "Some Aspects of Political Development Among the
Fort Jameson Ngoni," African Studies, Vol. 7, Nos. 2-3
(June-September, 1948).

Bates, Robert H. A Study of Village Zambia. New Haven: Yale
University Press, 1976.

Colson, E. Social Consequences of Resettlement. Atlantic Highlands, N.J.: Humanities Press, 1971.

Dahlschen, Edith. Children in Zambia. Lusaka: National Educational Company of Zambia, Ltd., 1972.

Hall, Barbara, ed. Tell Me, Josephine. New York: Simon & Schuster, 1964.

Hicks, R. E. "Similarities and Differences in Occupational Prestige Ratings; A Comparative Study of Two Cultural Groups in Zambia," African Social Research No. 3.

Kapferer, Bruce. Co-Operation Leadership and Village Structure. Manchester: University of Zambia Institute for Social Research, 1967.

Kay, G. Social Aspects of Village Regrouping in Zambia. Hull: University of Hull, 1967.

Long, N. Social Change and the Individual: A Study of the Social and Religious Responses to Innovation in a Zambian Rural Community. Manchester: Manchester University Press, 1968.

Mitchell, J. Clyde. The Kalela Dance. Manchester: Manchester University Press, 1956.

Mlenga, Kelvin. "The Role of Youth in Zambia's Changing Society," Horizon, No. 10 (January 1968).

Powdermaker, Hortense. "Communication and Social Change Based on a Field Study in Northern Rhodesia," Transactions of the New York Academy of Sciences, Series II, Vol. 17, No. 5 (March, 1955).

_____. "Social Change Through Imagery and Values of Teen-Age Africans in Northern Rhodesia," American Anthropologist, Vol. 58, No. 5 (1956).

Ritchie, J. F. The African as Suckling and as Adult. Rhodes-Livingstone Papers No. 9, 1943.

University of Zambia, Institute for Social Research, E. L. Deregowska (comp.). Some Aspects of Social Change in Africa South of the Sahara, 1959-1966. Lusaka: Institute for Social Research, 1966.

Wilson, Godfrey and Monica. Analysis of Social Change, Based on Observations in Central Africa (first published 1945). Cambridge, England: Cambridge University Press, 1954.